# THE LONG MARCH

Simone Lucie-Ernestine-Marie-Bertrand de Beauvoir was born in 1908. She is known primarily for her treatise *Le Deuxième Sexe*, 2 vol (*The Second Sex*) a scholarly and passionate plea for the abolition of what she called the myth of the "eternal feminine." This seminal work became a classic of feminist literature. Schooled in private institutions, de Beauvoir attended the Sorbonne, where, in 1929, she passed her *agrégation* in philosophy and met Jean-Paul Sartre, beginning a lifelong association with him. Her novels expound the major Existential themes, demonstrating her conception of the writer's commitment to the times. In addition to treating feminist issues, de Beauvoir was concerned with the subject of ageing, which she addressed in *Une Mort très douce* (1964; *A Very Easy Death*). She died in 1986.

*Also by Simone de Beauvoir*

Adieux: A Farewell to Sartre
All Men are Mortal
All Said and Done
America Day by Day
The Blood of Others
Brigitte Bardot and the Lolita Syndrome
The Coming of Age
Djamila Boupacha
Force of Circumstance
Letters to Sartre
The Mandarins
Memoirs of a Dutiful Daughter
Old Age
The Prime of Life
The Second Sex
She Came to Stay
A Very Easy Death
When Things of the Spirit Come First: Five Early Tales
Must we Burn de Sade?
The Woman Destroyed
Beloved Chicago Man (Phoenix Press)

# THE LONG MARCH

## An Account of Modern China

Simone de Beauvoir

*Translated by Austryn Wainhouse*

PHOENIX
PRESS

5 UPPER SAINT MARTIN'S LANE
LONDON
WC2H 9EA

A PHOENIX PRESS PAPERBACK

Originally published under the title *La Longue Marche*
by Librairie Gallimard in 1957
First published in Great Britain
by André Deutsch and Weidenfeld & Nicolson in 1958
This paperback edition published in 2001
by Phoenix Press,
a division of The Orion Publishing Group Ltd,
Orion House, 5 Upper St Martin's Lane,
London WC2H 9EA



A CIP catalogue record for this book
is available from the British Library.

Acknowledgement is made to the following for their kind permission to quote passages from their publications: Methuen & Co Ltd, *The Good Earth* and *My Several Worlds* by Pearl Buck; A & C Black Ltd, *The Invasion of China by the Western World* by E.R. Hughes; SCM Press Ltd, *Humanity and Labour in China* by Adelaide Mary Anderson

Printed and bound in Great Britain by
Clays Ltd, St Ives plc

ISBN 1 84212 399 8

# CONTENTS

# PRELIMINARIES

*September 1955*

In the plane flying east over the Gobi Desert there were two Czechs, three Russians, a Hungarian woman with her little girl, a South African, two French people. The first five were technicians, the sixth a technician's wife, all regaining posts they had been assigned to; the last three were on their way to China as guests of the government. At Bandung Chou En-lai had made an invitation good not only for the Conference nations but extended to include every country in the world: "Come and see." Not a little surprised at it and at our own selves, we were taking advantage of the offer. The South African was fair-haired, easygoing, casual; he was wearing a checked shirt and in his hand he held a carved and handsomely decorated primitive hatchet; he had just put in several months wandering from the Cape to Paris, London, Helsinki, Warsaw; at the Moscow airport there had been the drone of loud-speakers, but when he picked out the word *Peking* he rubbed his eyes: "Wake me up," he had said to a neighbor, "I must be dreaming." For my part, groggy from no real sleep and the thirty-six hours of flight punctuated by a series of silly little naps and red caviar breakfasts, I had the feeling not so much of traveling somewhere as of going to a ceremony. At Irkutsk, on the border between the USSR and Mongolia, the Russians had celebrated the imminent crossing of the line: it had been rounds of vodka, and we had touched glasses with Spanish and Portuguese passengers from another plane. We had landed at Ulan Bator, in the midst of a prairie that smelled of aniseed and warm grass; I had recognized figures, horses, the steppes I had once seen in *Storm Over Asia.* And now my nose to the porthole glass, gazing down at this colorless and naked desert beneath this misty sky, I was coming around to convincing myself that, pretty soon, I would be arriving in Peking; what, I wondered, just what am I going to see?

Ancient China did not interest me much. For me, China was this patient epic that starts in the dark days of *Man's Fate* and ends on the First of October, 1949, in an apotheosis on the Tien An Men; China, for me, was this stirring and reasonable revolution which had not only delivered peasants and workers from exploitation, but had rid an entire land of the foreigner.

The heroic age was over now; the problem at present was to industrialize a country where out of six hundred million inhabitants more than five hundred million till the soil and seventy-five million gain their livelihood from handicraft.

To me it seemed a great opportunity to be able to see—to see in the flesh—the beginnings of such a transformation. It was occurring, I knew, in a very unusual social and economic context. China depends in great measure upon the USSR, without which she would be unable to create a heavy industry; however, China is profoundly unlike the other People's Democracies. Although directed by the Communist Party, her revolution is only halfway accomplished. Capitalism, private property, profit, inheritance still remain. They are scheduled to disappear by stages, without violence. I was sure ahead of time that China would not resemble any of the countries which are solidly anchored in capitalism; I also suspected that China would differ from those where socialism has already triumphed. What, exactly, would she look like? I knew she was poor; but had I been well advised to bring along a supply of soap, tooth paste, ink, writing paper, stocking up as though for a polar expedition? China had airplanes—many of them? Could I hope, for instance, to get to see something of Tibet? What I had been given to understand by reports I had read, people I had talked to, was that life in the China of today is exceptionally pleasant; travelers who had found Moscow austere had extolled the loveliness of Peking, the charm of Canton; French, Czechs, Argentines, they had all remembered their China with sighs of nostalgia. Plenty of fond dreams are authorized by the idea of a country where the government pays the people's way through school, where generals and statesmen are scholars and poets. In Paris I had seen the Peking Opera: I now imagined glittering traditions blending with the innovations of an effervescent present. "This land, both completely new and infinitely old"—the slogan engendered other seductive syntheses; I anticipated China, at once orderly and fantastic, where poverty had the mildness of abundance, a China which, despite the severity of the tasks to be performed, enjoys a freedom unknown in other Eastern places. In China, red is the color of happiness: my vision was of rose. The land I was about to become acquainted with looked as unreal to me as the Shangri-La of *Lost Horizon*, as Cabet's Icaria: here each contrary chimed harmoniously with every other.

Six weeks later I crossed the Gobi again, in the opposite direction. It lay golden under a bright sun; snow-capped mountains glistened off in the distance. China had changed. Black, gray, rose, these were not suitable any more, no symbolic color would do: China had become a reality. The seeming richness of images translates their radical poverty: the true China had infinitely exceeded the concepts and the words with which I had tried to visualize and foregauge it. China was no longer an idea; it had assumed flesh and bone. It is that incarnation I am going to tell about.

When you travel by air, appearances are abrupt. All of a sudden the fog has vanished, the earth has come alive: down below me, there is China, China extends as far as the eye can see, flat, sliced into thin slivers, mauve, dark green, cocoa; here and there, lonely as an island, a puddled-clay village takes shape, its houses make one compact block, rectangular, its darkness lightened by a spattering of small courtyards. The multicolored pattern of the ground contrasts with the vast monochrome surface of the Siberian kolkhozes; plainly, these Chinese fields are not collectivized, each ribbon is a private plot. It takes me a while to realize why this landscape strikes me as so desolate: it is because there is not one tree in sight; upon the village, not a shadow; from aloft, this fertile plain looks as bare as wasteland.

"The Great Wall," somebody says. I can just distinguish it. The plane banks, sinks, wheels around a lake; I see a tall pagoda leaning against the sky, then a golden-roofed kiosk: buildings which are such conventional symbols of China that I feel a little bit taken aback. Peking is pointed out to me, over there; but I see no city over there, only gray trees. We land; the South African leaps for the door, I a step behind him; the air hostess stops us; an official comes aboard to examine our papers. First surprise: it is not Icaria, this is a real country, in certain respects similar to all others. Second surprise: "Communist" China, I had thought; but "Communist"—the concept embraces so much and is so abstract that it had hidden the most elementary geographical factors from me; stepping out of the plane, I stare at yellow-skinned, black-haired men in light cottons who are busy about the airport, and I realize I am in Asia. While delegates, dressed in the strict suit with the small-collared jacket adopted by the Kuomintang's adherents back in 1911, advise us that "the Chinese people have been impatiently awaiting our arrival," I inhale deep breaths of the pungent vegetal odors the ground exudes; the warm moist air, the raging red of banked flower beds dazes me; I did not expect China to give me this impression of sultry exoticism which I had formerly known in Guatemala, in Africa, and which I had ever since associated with slavery, with oppression.

Sitting at one end of a long table in a large room hung with portraits of Lenin, Stalin, Bulganin, Khrushchev, while waiting for our baggage we drink lemonade, which is, after green tea, the second national drink of the Chinese. Then, accompanied by a young interpreter, Mr. Tsai, we climb into a car. The road is yellow; on both sides are growing plants of which I recognize only corn; stripped to the waist, some men in blue trousers are digging, hoeing; others are drinking tea in open wooden sheds; shouldering the traditional bamboo pole from which hang buckets, baskets, bales, still others are walking at a smart pace: in their broad straw hats, they so exactly resemble the classical images of the Chinese coolie that I would readily take them for actors who have just come on stage to notify us that now we are in China. We are indeed in China, and these old stereotyped figures belong right enough to the present. The People's Republic was not born of the sea foam one fine morning, it has a past, that past lives on in it. Wheelbarrows, carts pushed by men and drawn by mules, bicycles, a few trucks: different periods of time stack up in layers, and I am smothering in their midst. I am a very long way from Paris, somewhere in the Far East—but where? The women wear their hair cut short or, if long, in two plaits, one falling on either side of the face; like the men they have on blue trousers and matching jackets or white blouses. We reach an intersection: under a clump of trees are parked some tricycle-taxis, known here as push bikes or pedicabs: the drivers loll about upon their vehicles, talking, gesturing, snoozing like Italian coachmen. "Soon we'll have cars, the pedicabs will disappear," says the interpreter. We pass construction projects, buildings going up, new houses. We go through a gate in a high gray wall, we find ourselves in narrow streets lined by low houses, also gray, and showing us nothing but blind fronts; there is beaten earth underfoot. Here are tiny shops, stalls whose windows are covered with bright red Chinese characters; red standards adorned with black characters serve as price-markers: it is all very nice, but this feels like an overgrown village we are entering; can it actually be the capital of China? Tsai seems to have been reading my thoughts: "Soon," says he, making a sweeping gesture, "this quarter will be razed; it's called for in the plans." "Ah yes," I say to myself, recovering my bearings: this disdain for the picturesque, this confidence in the future assure me that I am in one of the progressive countries. We emerge into a broad avenue, down its center run trolley tracks, grass borders its edges; this is the main artery of Peking. The traffic consists of a stream of bicycles, as many as in a Dutch street; an occasional automobile; I see a bus, chrome letters spell "Skoda" on the hood. On cylindrical pedestals, striped in black and white and sometimes surrounded by a ring of massed flowers, policemen conduct traffic through a megaphone; their tunics and trousers are a yellow orange, their gaiters, gauntlet gloves, and helmets white. The car is driving very slowly. To our left Tsai indicates a wall painted an ocher red: the wall of the Forbidden City. A red-and-gold pavilion embedded in this wall protrudes forward to the sidewalk's edge: this was once a gate to the Imperial Palace. It is now the entrance to the seat of the new government. The wall thickens until it becomes a terrace, here is another pavilion dominating another passageway: we are passing in front of Tien An Men. These monuments also disconcert me; I know that their vermilion colonnades, their horned roofs covered with gilt tile are authentically Chinese; and yet they do not seem to me to be an integral part of the city.

Like the pagoda and the temple I glimpsed from the plane, these appear to be symbolic signs which announce Peking to me but do not give it to me.

Peking is not to be given me this evening; we are at the hotel. From the window of my room I gaze a while down at the avenue upon which night has fallen. Street lights show brick constructions, neither ugly nor attractive nor anything else. To the left of the esplanade, shirtless boys are playing basketball; on the other side of the road there is a brilliantly illuminated stadium where several hundred spectators are watching a game of basketball on an outdoor court. When they have demolished the little gray streets, will all of Peking look like this boulevard? Where ought one to stand in order to get a clear view of China? Between the past whose fallacious appearance Tsai had rejected with a fine gesture and the future as yet invisible, the present does not seem like very safe or certain ground. At any rate, I have already understood that this country is not a political entity nor an idea to be analyzed: it has its climate, its flora, its customs; the question is of trying to decipher not statistics but a living reality.

The Old China Hands chuckle at those they call "the travelers," who go and explore China unequipped with any comprehensive knowledge of China's past and none at all of her language. The anti-Communists apply themselves to discrediting eyewitness accounts which, in their virtual unanimity, are favorable to the regime. Fano, who does not know Chinese, recounts* how at Hong Kong friends of his split their sides when one of these visitors conceded that he had indeed only talked with the Chinese through the intermediary of an interpreter; lest we continue to abuse ourselves, Fano explains that no Chinese would under any circumstances, even in privacy, have dared to open up sincerely with a foreigner. Guillain† finds that, in present conditions, no meaningful observations can be fetched home by any observer, unless he be Guillain; having paid his own way there and back, he further insinuates

* In *Le Figaro*, 1956.

† Robert Guillain, *Le Monde's* special correspondent and expert on China. It is to his long and important series of articles that appeared in the winter of 1954–1955, first in the pages of *Le Monde*, later in book form (*600 millions de chinois sous le drapeau rouge*, Paris, 1956), that the author refers here and subsequently. (Translator's note)

that spending six weeks at a government's expense is tantamount to winding up in its hire—which is to set a rather low price on his own honesty and on the honesty of others. Had I been hostile to China beforehand I would have declined China's invitation; but in accepting it, I contracted no engagement; China takes her chances, and I have at no moment felt myself under any obligation to her except to be fair. As for the lack of a thorough background and the particularly serious drawback of my ignorance of Chinese, these are handicaps which I am by no means prone to underestimate; they did most certainly limit my experience; I deny that they robbed it of all value. If anti-Communists reject it a priori, they do so in the name of a curious thesis: that which one sees with one's own eyes, they hold, is necessarily sheer mirage. So it was that Martinet* who did not attend the Vienna Congress could declare that Sartre, owing to the very fact that he was present at it, had been unable to understand a word of what went on there; and Guillain spots a piece of Machiavellian cunning in Chou En-lai's "Come and see." For these initiates the world is mystery, conjuration, conspiracy, everything happens in smoke-filled back rooms; the naive spectator, dazzled by superficial appearances, is blinded to the underlying truths. More alert, more adroit, whenever they want to know whether the sun is shining, our clairvoyants look not out of the window but into their crystal ball. Guillain admits that the authorities are not very well able to fake a whole country over thousands of miles and for an entire year—although struggling with might and main, he was often reduced to believing his eyes: he saw properly dressed peasants, highways, factories, a hygiene, an order, achievements which amazed him; but in his fortuneteller's instrument he discovered famines, forced-labor camps. I confess not to have had any such talisman in my traveling kit. On the other hand, I am perfectly willing to admit that mere eyesight is not enough to bring out everything an object may contain; nevertheless, I have very often found that eyes are not useless and that objects when looked at disclose something. To walk down a street is an immediate, irrecusable experience for which no hypothesis about a city, however ingenious, can be a substitute or

* Gilles Martinet, member of the editorial committee of *France-Observateur*, a Paris weekly review of political affairs. (Translator's note)

as instructive. With its avidity for the arcane low-down the inside-track-on-China elite is too apt to forget that appearances also have their reality. Every fact requires to be interpreted, of course; but why need seeing prevent one from finding out and formulating opinions and criticisms? Let me give full details of the conditions under which the elements of this account were established.

As always but even more so in the China of today than anywhere else, the center around which the traveler's days gravitate and the city takes shape is the hotel where he stays. I stayed at the Peking Hotel, on the big avenue opposite the part of town where the legations used to be, and close to Tien An Men. The Peking Hotel is a ten-story structure which is separated from the sidewalk by an esplanade; it is made up of two buildings: the newer is also the more sumptuous, but when I arrived its front was still half hidden by scaffoldings. My room, located in the old wing, was immense: all to myself I had two brass double beds, covered with a bright pink silk embroidered with winged genii.* I had a mirrored wardrobe, a desk complete with everything needed for writing, a vanity table, a couch, armchairs, a low coffee table, two night tables, a radio; on the bedside rug were a pair of bedroom slippers, cigarettes and fruits were placed every day on another table. There was soap in the bathroom, and I felt ashamed of my precautionary purchases all the more so because, downstairs in the lounge—poorly lit, austerely furnished with round tables and leather easy chairs—was a counter where one could buy toilet articles, writing paper, parlor games, fruits, inexpensive cookies, and in their superb red "Peking-Moscow" boxes, Russian chocolate which is not inexpensive; the salesgirl does her figuring on an abacus. Near the entry is an information bureau where obtaining information is difficult, since only Chinese is spoken there. To one side the lounge opens into a spacious room with a gleaming floor and a grand piano at which, every morning, a little Chinese girl applies herself to practicing a Bach fugue. The other side leads to the lounge of the new building, three times the size of the old and luxuriously decorated: gilt columns, porcelain jars, carpets,

* Called *apsaras*. They are of Buddhistic origin and figure very widely in decorative motifs.

polychrome ceiling. A shop features prints, periodicals in English, Chinese books in English translations. Further on there is a post office, a beauty salon, a billiard room, another for gambling. A banquet hall capable of accommodating a thousand persons takes up most of the ground floor; almost every evening sounds would reach me in my room of a dinner, of a dance, of a meeting.

My meals are taken in a dining room belonging to the old building; the decorator has made fullest use of local color; two rows of painted columns support the ceiling; reproductions of prints—clouds, lakes, and mountains—adorn the walls. There could hardly be a more cosmopolitan place than this dining room. Under Pekingese lanterns with their weird genii, delegates from every nation on earth dine side by side on the offerings of an international cuisine and drink Chinese lemonade or beer. Pakistani and Hindu women swathed in gorgeous saris, little Burmese dancers in their vests of brocaded silk, Japanese in kimonos or Western business suits: all Asia is there, Africa, Australia, Europe, and America at its elbow. There are Soviet engineers with their robust wives and their blond youngsters; here a delegation of Italian women, a group of Germans, an English lawyer; there the Yugoslav ambassador and his family. French, English, Spanish, Portuguese, you hear every language spoken; and round one of the tables you see the silent, swift gesticulations of a party of Czech deaf-mutes.

The menu is in English and the service amazingly quick; young women in white jackets, a bow of ribbon in their short hair, bring on everything and remove the last crumb all inside less than twenty-five minutes. Tsai told me that when traveling abroad with his friends they were exasperated by the amount of time meals absorbed. My room is also done in the twinkling of an eye: I go down for a cup of tea, return to find everything in order. One morning, noticing in the hallway that I'd gone out without my bag, I retraced my steps and discovered a foursome in the midst of sweeping, dusting, tidying. But the number does not provide the whole explanation; I have observed that, without being in any apparent haste, the Chinese work in a remarkably efficient manner.

The enlarged Peking Hotel is today the Times Square crossroads of the cosmopolitan activity that goes on at a great rate from April to December and reaches its pitch toward the start of October; not long ago, existing only as the old wing, it was one of the centers of Occidental life. Built by the French, it later belonged to the Japanese: the bald old elevator man kept imperturbably at his post throughout these several avatars. Flanked by a wide roof garden, the tenth-floor salons were the headquarters of an Anglo-French Club where the white elite used to dance and drink their boredom away; and, when drunk, another of their distractions was to go down and urinate on the corner policeman—who, though in uniform, a patched and very dirty uniform, was only a Chinaman underneath it all. In those days, the main avenue was half its present width: on the other side extended a polo field, bordering on the diplomatic section that was surrounded by a wall studded with machine-gun nests. As for the esplanade, a Frenchman named Casseville in about 1934 used these terms to describe it: "At the foot of this palatial establishment, heaps of ungodly rubbish litter vague banks of flowers; filthy beggars swarming amidst an army of coolies, whose rickshaws are lined up as though for a review, spit, pluck at their lice, and howl their lamentations."

The esplanade is a parking lot today. Taxis do not exist in Peking, neither do private automobiles; all these cars belong to departments of the government. There are Russian Pobiedas, Czech Skodas, some British cars—China buys cars from England—and a fleet of sleek American cars, a bequest of Chiang Kai-shek's administration. The chauffeurs are at it early in the morning: equipped with red, long-handled feather dusters, they whisk every speck of dust from the gleaming cars, inside and out.

Two or three times a day we go off for a drive in one of them. Tsai accompanies us. He is thirty, wears glasses, has a youthful and engaging look, but he is very reserved. At nine every morning, at two o'clock every afternoon he rings up from the lobby: "I'm ready." He takes us to see temples, palaces, parks, or else craft cooperatives, universities, hospitals, depending on a program mapped out somewhere up above. We are free by five. But if it is to be theater in the evening, one must dine at six thirty: curtains rise at half past seven in China. By eleven the streets are deserted. Peking is asleep.

The disadvantages of this sort of organizing are obvious. But I wish right away to state that, notwithstanding the allegations of the Fanos and the Guillains, in China an interpreter is not a detective. Guillain neglected to point out that it had been proposed to him that he bring along an interpreter of his own. If Tsai accompanies me, it is because, without him, I am deaf, dumb, lost: he is a necessity to me. But he is not under instructions to erect fences around me or to sieve the remarks made by people I meet. Never once was my freedom of movement hindered. I took walks by myself, as many and whenever I wanted. In Peking we frequently went out, unescorted, with L——, a French newspaperman who speaks Chinese. When, in Shanghai, we expressed the wish to meet some French who happen to be notoriously hostile to the regime, our desire was immediately satisfied. Only our ignorance of the language made it impossible to have contacts between ourselves and the man in the street. L——, who has been living in Peking for a long time, while out gathering material for a story stops in whatever villages he pleases, talks freely with the peasants; in all of this the authorities find nothing to object to. A Sinologist who left Peking in 1953, who spent a few days there again in 1955, told me he had sensed no awkwardness when chatting with the shopkeepers whose customer he had formerly been. However Guillain may choose to interpret the fact, we talked at length, alone, with Chinese who know English or French. When our visits were prepared in advance, this was not concealed from us; each time we were to be shown some new development or achievement of exceptional importance, we were told so; we made impromptu entries into houses. In Shanghai and Canton, among other places, without our having asked, we were shown through overcrowded and poor sections the equivalents of which are passed over in delicate silence by the Baedekers to bourgeois countries. No, they did not hide China behind their backs, they had not daubed hundreds of villages with stage paint or draped camouflage nets over thousands of miles of countryside; they had us see China.

Concerning the method they adopted, I learned to put up in patience with certain of its defects. There were some fifteen hundred of us delegates roaming the length and breadth of China and almost all of us stayed a good while in Peking too; to us all, which is normal, they showed the same vestiges of the past, the same new achievements: to prevent us from trouping all at once into factories or theaters, those in charge must have had to work out a system as complicated as the ones that regulate the movements of railway trains: it would have been too much to insist that a logical order be observed in the "program." It included a few pretty exhausting items. I remember how irritated I was over a trip to the Kwanting Reservoir. From eight a.m. till noon the train rolled through tunnels: this was a newly constructed line, inaugurated in July 1955, and the Chinese are proud of it for the good reason that it tunnels through mountains seventy-five times; they are also proud of the reservoir and dam which controls the once dreaded rising of the Hwai River. But while munching sandwiches in a hut with a delegation of Danes I thought about the four hours of darkness and soot ahead of me and asked myself just why they had sent me all the way out here. I could have got along very nicely with photographs and magazine articles. Later on I understood their stubborn desire to show me public works, hospitals, factories, laboratories which, when I saw them, did not seem at all extraordinary to me: what is extraordinary is that these things exist in China today. Westerners and Japanese had outvied each other repeating that, thrown on her own, China was capable of nothing beyond growing kaoliang: every tunnel blasted, every machine manufactured is a lofty reply to that challenge. The Chinese do not have the familiarity with the products of their labor which in Europe makes us take electric power plants as much for granted as we do highways; over and above its practical use, a telephone, like a railroad, represents a victory won against the past, a stride ahead toward a new future. They want the visitor to bear witness to this conquest: that is why he must ascertain it, verify it in person and on the spot; if he just relies on photographs, takes the word of reports, once home again doubting interlocutors may suspect him of having been the dupe of propaganda; he must therefore to be able to say: I saw these things with my own eyes.

The majority of the accomplishments I was shown were in fact interesting; my one big objection is to the explanations that were given me. When it was a monument we were going to see a guide would be waiting for us at the door and during the tour would recite a few facts and figures. For no matter what factory, school, village anywhere from Peking to Canton, the ritual would never vary one iota. You enter a large room whose walls are covered with red banners bearing gold inscriptions: these are tokens of satisfaction conferred by the government, or messages of friendship, or various kinds of commemorative diplomas. You sit down on a sofa protected by garnet-red slip covers before a low table loaded with cigarettes and cups which an attendant keeps at all times brimful of green tea. If it is not a room it may be a shed or a hangar, the seats may be benches, but the red banners are always tacked on the walls and the tea keeps flowing like a waterfall. Some person of rank, a cadre,* sets forth the situation. Next, you inspect the premises. After that, it is back to the seats for more tea drinking and the question period; the cadre earnestly solicits suggestions and criticisms we are generally altogether incapable of formulating.

In view of the number of delegates, we are all, I admit, treated to the same prefabricated discourse, each of us having the opportunity to ask individual questions afterward. What one regrets is the optimist bias manifest in the answers. That prison warden who candidly and simply acknowledged the numerous failures "re-education" has met with was an exception. I ask the Vice-President of the Women's Association how the principle of the equality of the two sexes is being received in the villages, of the younger generation's independence with regard to the elder. Listening to her, one would believe the Marriage Act had solved every problem for good and all. In the nurseries, in the schools, the children are not punished; well, if one of them persists in misbehaving, then what do you do? The case, I am told, does not arise. A lazy student? There are none. Between factory directors and workers, never any conflicts. I am back in Icaria again: in full-blown unreality.

When, even after explanations, a question that interests us remains obscure, there is a means for elucidating it. "A lecture will be arranged for you," says Tsai. Inquiring after information on illiteracy, on the national budget, we betook ourselves to the Department of Cultural Relations whose headquarters occupy a large

* A "cadre" is of course a person in a position of responsibility, a leader, but in a general sense: while having specific technical qualifications—as, for example, an engineer—his preparation has also included ideological training; he may be a Party member; he is at any rate an "activist"; his role is that of an exemplary citizen. (Translator's note)

mansion in the area where the foreign legations used to be. Seated facing a panel upon which painted flowers and birds symbolize peace, we listened to the statements of a specialist: he had pulled papers out of his brief case, read them to us, we had asked him a few questions. The information thus obtained was more authoritative and coherent than the sketchy notes which went with the program; but, skirting all the difficulties, what the expert told us was still just as two-dimensional.

During the first days the daily routine and its inadequacies were especially trying in that, so far, I had not even had the compensation of discovering Peking. Peking was eluding me. From the hotel's top-floor terrace, from the artificial hills rising behind the Palace I saw neither streets nor roofs: nothing but a large park; the gray-green foliage of trees hid everything. At street level my glances got no further than walls. The day after my arrival I had visited "the new Peking," beyond the old city limits; then, inside a great walled enclosure, the Imperial Palace; going to the theater that evening we had driven quite a while—between walls the whole way. Where, I wondered, where do the people live in this city? Where are their houses? Where is the real Peking? The car had stopped: to the right was the illuminated front of a playhouse, to the left, stalls where gay mortuary crowns made of multicolored paper flowers were being sold. Was I still in Peking? Or in a suburb? On the days that followed I rambled through commercial streets, but without knowing just where they lay; Peking remained bits of this and that for me: I needed to do considerable exploring, on foot, but the program left me hardly any spare time, and then when I found myself with a little, it rained, hard and steadily.

On the first Sunday we were free in the morning, but that wretched rain did not let up; the avenue was practically deserted. The traffic policeman's fine tangerine-colored uniform was hidden under a slicker, the pedicab men were disappearing under yellow rubber rain-capes, the few pedestrians were lost under those wide umbrellas of red oiled paper that smells of fish glue. Two young men went by, barefoot, carrying their fragile canvas shoes. I was restless; idle, stuck in a phantom capital city, I felt as if I had no grip at all on this seamless China polished smooth by official optimism. Up until now we had had virtually no personal contacts with the Chinese. Tsai spoke good French; but his customary work is in connection with an athletic association, he was shy in this new role and said as little as he could get away with. A "cultural relations" functionary had drunk some cups of jasmine tea with us: we had done no more than discussed itineraries. An initial dinner with some writers had been hardly very fruitful: they knew nothing about us, we knew nothing about them; the main topic of conversation had been Chinese cooking. Were things going to change for the better? When? While wondering, I turned on the radio: I picked up Hong Kong, Tokyo, Moscow, got first a Chinese opera, then some American jazz; that dreary morning I heard Yves Montand sing Prévert's *Feuilles mortes*. That was when I made an important discovery. The previous day the Writers' Association had sent me an assortment of things in English translation: books, pamphlets, magazines. Owing to the policy whereby China is bidding for prestige in Asia, a good many Chinese texts are translated into English, and certain reviews are directly published in that language, for English is spoken in India, Pakistan, Burma, Japan, and even in Indonesia. Every day I found a little bulletin on my table, the *New Day Release*, which gives a brief summary of the press of the previous day, and above all follows the comings and goings of delegations: there was little to be got out of it. But in leafing through the bulky literature put at my disposal I realized that it could be a great help to me. *China Pictorial* runs to naive propaganda. *China Reconstructs* is more substantial despite its deliberately enthusiastic tone. *People's China* contains, either verbatim or in condensed—but faithfully abridged—form, numerous official documents: I quickly noticed that these texts, emanating straight from the Government or directly inspired by it, were of a very different character from the briefings and statements that are meted out to foreign delegations. Among other things I read Li Fu-chuan's "Report on the Five-Year Plan"; the obstacles to be overcome, the mistakes that had been made, the lags and gaps and deficiencies were stressed with an outspokenness and a sharpness the equal of which one is not apt to encounter in any other country.* The speeches,

* These self-criticisms are so incisive, so uncompromising that, in manufacturing their indictments of the People's Republic, the anti-Communist experts operating in Hong Kong, in America, in Paris need simply lift out

directors' reports, articles in *The People's Daily* strike the same note: no, all the products of Chinese factories are not of highest quality, not every student becomes a first-rate engineer at the end of four years; the "feudal" mentality hangs on in many rural districts; the building of socialism is not child's play; the inert weight of the past is formidable, the future involves risks. China becomes real again.

Edited by Mao-Tun, the present Minister of Culture, *Chinese Literature* is a quarterly review devoted to modern and to past Chinese writing; it also publishes articles and chronicles on cultural problems of the moment. Many contemporary works have been translated in full. Carefully observing the principles of socialist realism, novels, tales, stories struck me if not as works of art, at least as interesting documentary performances. In them, the conflicts and contradictions of the period are not glossed over or ignored; quite the contrary, they comprise the central theme. Here too I found portraits of a life-size and living China. Later on, I was often to consider the places I visited as individual illustrations of broader truths I had learned in books.

Why then, you may say, there was no point in my going all the way to Peking. That is not so. Books only acquired their impact and the truth in them its decisiveness due to the living examples they complemented and rounded out, also due to the context in which I read them. The novels of Ting-ling and of Chou Li-po would not have significantly instructed me about the land reforms if I had not seen Chinese countryside, villages, and peasants. Moreover, the initial situation I have been describing was soon modified. We were granted leisure, and the sun began to shine: from then on we went for walks in the Peking streets, daily and alone. The Pekingese are discreet, they mind their own affairs. If in the quarters far removed from the center of town people now and then glanced at us with a bit of curiosity, they certainly did not gawk; but quickly, almost at once, politely looked away. Once or twice little children fell in step behind us: grownups stopped them. I think we were often taken for Russians. At any rate, the Chinese

---

fragments from declarations published by the Chinese Government. They tear them from their context and construct catastrophic prophecies on these fake premises: and thus they achieve their effect.

know that the foreigners they see in their streets nowadays are "good" foreigners, friends of the Chinese people. The interest they sometimes took in us was always kindly.

Usually, to go home, we would get into pedicabs; not being sure we could properly pronounce our address, we carried an album with us, on its cover was a photograph of the hotel. At the start, unable to ask the two drivers how much the fare came to, we guessed at one yuan, I handed it to them; they shook their heads: a yuan was too much. Then I placed some little notes in my palm and invited both to choose; the drivers paused a moment, calculated, and took part of the money. This exactness gave me a high opinion—which all subsequent experience confirmed—of the honesty of the Pekingese.

And we also made some acquaintances. Conversation had increased and become more interesting: I shall speak further on of my various encounters. For the time being I wish only to indicate through what agencies I got into touch with China.

There was Tsai. He gradually warmed up. It began one morning by his telling us about himself while we were on a visit to the Polytechnical Institute. Before the war it had been one of the major Peking universities and he had done his final studies there. Coming from the region of Shanghai the son of average peasants, he had successfully passed two examinations, one admitting him to the university in his province, the other to this one in Peking, and he had chosen the latter. When he had finished school he had been attached as an interpreter to an athletic group. He had spent ten days in Paris with his team the year before. That was all he told us that day; but a little later, as we were coming out of a nursery located in the middle of Pei Hai Park, he declared point-blank: "When I have children I'll put them there." "Are you married?" I asked and he soberly replied that he was. After a moment he drew a photograph from his pocket: "That's my wife." She was then completing medical studies near Nanking, they only saw one another at vacation times, but once she received her degree, she would get a post in Peking. Tsai afterward gave me a quantity of details about his budget and way of living; his remarks, his reactions helped me get a picture of the young Chinese city dweller of today.

In the course of a trip from Mukden to Canton we were accompanied by a novelist, Madame Cheng; she is my own age, spent fifteen years of her youth in France, and has French literature at her finger tips. Before going to bed, we talked together in the Pullman car for a long while and became very attached. For me she represents a typical example both of the Chinese intellectual and of the Chinese woman of her generation. Keenly intelligent, exceedingly cultivated, and a remarkable observer, she furnished me with all sorts of precious information on all sorts of subjects Never a word of nonsense or propaganda from her lips; she is so firmly convinced of the benefits conferred by the regime and of its necessity that she has no need to tell fibs to herself or anyone else; independent, spontaneous, fond of laughing and fonder yet of talking, she knows nothing of self-censorship: witty, tranquil, her frankness in great measure made up for the inflexibility of most of the cadres I had dealings with.

L——, the journalist I have already mentioned, has a good knowledge of China and a simultaneously sympathetic and critical attitude toward it; he showed us various aspects of Peking and supplied us with interesting information. And it almost goes without saying that we spent considerable time chatting with Rewi Alley. He is one of the most picturesque figures in Peking; in America he would be called a character: every traveler will tell you about him, and so shall I. "That man knows everything about China—more than any Chinese does," an Argentine friend had said to me in Helsinki. "Get to meet him." As soon as I arrived I undertook to do so, asking after his whereabouts, I was told he lived in the Peking Hotel also. "There he is now"—walking across the esplanade was a stout personage, his hair was white and thick, his legs—for he was wearing shorts, which are not by any means common in Peking—were sturdy and muscular. At closer range, one notices his hardy countryman's color, his generous nose, but, above all, the bright blue of his eyes, and his smile. He is a New Zealander, and I did not find his English easy but he had a willingness to be understood, and was. He has been installed in China for thirty years. After having fought in France with the British Army during the First World War, he came to Shanghai where, toward 1927, he was named Inspector of Public Health.

This experience convinced him that the only salvation for the Chinese was to win their economic independence. In 1938, to counter the Japanese blockade, he thought up the scheme of decentralizing Chinese industry by setting up production co-operatives in the interior of the country. Several years before, a missionary by the name of Baillie—an eccentric who thought that a Christian's foremost duty was to feed the starving among his fellow men—had founded a kind of technical school for young Shanghai apprentices. So futile did his own efforts seem to him, what with the scale of Chinese poverty and the general corruption, that he committed suicide in 1935. But the students he had trained took to Rewi Alley's idea. In July 1938 he was made Head Technical Advisor of the CIC—Chinese Industrial Co-operatives, the movement known as Gung Ho—which at that point possessed neither technique nor personnel. By October 1940 Gung Ho, with 2,300 workshops scattered through sixteen provinces, had stretched as far as Mongolia and 300,000 persons were actively participating in it. Alley organized many additional centers in the guerrilla-controlled zones, extending them as far down as Kansu. He particularly concerned himself with the one he had created in Sandan, a remote village in the Northwest, and he managed to put a Tibetan Living Buddha at the head of a textile co-operative. The Chungking Government took a dim view of this movement which was actively establishing a new type, a popular type, of economy. But owing to prevailing circumstances—the war, the guerrillas—Chungking was kept at bay and Gung Ho preserved its independence. Following the Liberation, New Zealand selected Alley to be a delegate to the committee that was to prepare the Pacific Peace Conference, and he settled in Peking. His room is full of old books, prints, treasures, for he is almost as interested in China's past as he is involved in her present. He has made English adaptations of numerous ancient poems, and related his Chinese experience in two books: *Yo Banfa!* and *The People Have Strength.*

At the University of Peking I came to know a couple who had lived a long time in Paris and who speak French admirably: Lo Ta-Kang and his wife. She is a professor of French; he is connected with the French section of "Literary Research" which assesses and classifies works of foreign literature according to Marxist specification and perspective. They receive a quantity of French reviews, *Les Temps Modernes* among them, and are familiar not only with all the important works which appear in France, but also with the latest and best dictionaries. Lo Ta-Kang translates French texts into Chinese and has accomplished the nice feat of rendering old Chinese tales and poems into an excellent French. With the Los conversation was easy, a delight, and extremely rewarding to me.

Guided tours and unconducted promenades, lectures and discussions, various meetings, interviews, supplementing and shedding mutual light on each other, finally provided me with a considerable mass of material. I did not consider it sufficient; back again in Paris I consulted specialists and a good number of books. Desiring to hear "the other side of the argument" I went meticulously through the literature aimed against People's China:* and I can assert that, apart from ill-willed and malevolent commentaries, I found scarcely anything in it by way of information that had not been given to me by the Chinese themselves. From the standpoint of method this concordance struck me as entirely satisfactory. One of the major objections that is likely to be leveled against this book is that it will be out of date tomorrow. That is very true. But the history being made in China is so exciting that each of its different phases merits recording.

The period I should like to try to give an account of is defining itself essentially as a period of transition. What is going on is the passing from a democratic to a socialist revolution. In China this transformation is taking place in a unique fashion, adapted to the unique situation of the country.

Up until 1949 China was second only to Indonesia as the poorest nation on earth. In 1939 the average annual income per person figured in American dollars was 554 in the United States, 283 in France, 34 in India, 29 in China. A UN report dating from 1949 shows a similar relationship in the figures pertaining to the amount of power consumed per day and per individual: in the United

* It all comes from one source: Hong Kong. The Chinese living in that enclave receive all the newspapers and magazines printed on the mainland, can easily tune in on Radio Peking; news and gossip filters across the border. Hong Kong is the headquarters for translating, scissoring, deforming, or forging the texts that are then exported for use by Formosa, America, and David Rousset.

States, 37.6 HP; in China, 0.5 HP. For every thousand square miles, the United States had 80 miles of railroad track; China had 3. The number of motor vehicles in the United States was 250 per thousand inhabitants; 0.2 in China, which produced a bare 3 per cent of the world's electricity. In the year 1948-1949 the average Frenchman's food consumption was in bulk five times that of the average Chinese, whose diet was extremely low in protein content. The average life expectancy stood at 64 years in the United States, 62 in Great Britain. In China it was 25.

"We're not performing miracles," all the Chinese leaders say. During the five years they have spent reorganizing the country, electricity, locomotives, trucks, machines have not sprung up magically out of nowhere. The first glaring truth that assaults the visitor's eye is how terribly poor China still is today. At the gates of Peking they are going at building tooth and nail: apartment houses, schools, hospitals, offices—and not a crane, not a pneumatic hammer, not a dump truck—not one single machine. There are a few carts with solid rubber tires on the wheels, which, it seems, represent a great advance over the old carts whose wheels were rimmed with iron; they can take a one-ton load or so, but most of the construction material is brought to the site on human backs, on the ends of balanced bamboo poles. Ground is leveled by masons pulling on ropes fastened to cylindrical stone rollers; stone disks, tamps, managed by ropes passing through holes drilled in the center, are hauled into the air and let fall by gangs of five or six men. It is with these four-thousand-year-old techniques that they are building the new Peking. That is also how they are building dams, railways, the tremendous bridge spanning the Yangtze at Hankow. Several days after getting to Peking I met the South African in the street; he no longer had his hatchet with him, but the expression on his face was more limply astonished than ever: "Why, my God, everything's missing around here!" said he. "I never thought they were as hard up as all that."

Potentially, though, China is rich: she possesses abundant as-yet-unexploited natural resources. Eighty-five per cent of her land surface is uncultivated, including the fertile Sinkiang with three times the area of France; the Chinese subsoil contains great deposits of coal, oil, iron. But vast virgin tracts cannot be cleared with hoes and spades, pickaxes are not enough for extracting minerals. The day when tractors make large-scale agriculture feasible, when railroads make ore fields accessible, when China has the necessary equipment and power, then immense possibilities will open up for her; for the time being, her wealth is in a deepfreeze. Thanks to Soviet aid, to the installations with which the Japanese endowed Manchuria, to economic planning, and to the last five years' effort, she has started the process that is to lead toward prosperity; the factories of the Northeast mean the beginning of industrialization; but until the machines have been manufactured, the electric power stations built in sufficient number, Chinese heavy industry will remain in the immediate sense unproductive: at the present stage, no profits are accruing from the capital being invested in it by the state.

Among China's resources must be counted her population: it represents a very considerable labor force. In spite of the dearth of machinery, new constructions are going up with extraordinary speed in outlying Peking. Whole streets are penned in by those curious dummy edifices of bamboo scaffolding and safety nets. The number of workmen offsets the insufficiency of equipment. The laborer's pace of activity is not at all frantic, rather on the side of nonchalance; but an entire crowd is involved on a project. As a matter of fact, there is a glut of manpower today and China is suffering from semiunemployment. To avoid leaving people idle the administrations and the state enterprises hire more hands than are needed—which, as I said, was apparent at the Peking Hotel. Many of the workers in the factories potter about at odd jobs or even do nothing at all. In the private shops and lofts work is shared out among the various members of the family while one person could do most or all of it: buyers never stand in line, it is the sellers who do the waiting. In short, there is an excess of population, unproductive but which must be fed. When the system that is being put together gets properly under way and finally hits its stride, the balance will be struck. Harvests obtained, due to tractors, fertilizers, and new methods, will feed better and better an ever greater number of peasants and workers; exports will facilitate new investments, the rhythm of industrial output will accelerate; the economy will develop along the snowball pattern; between the end of the Third and the Sixth Five-Year Plans, China will have made such progress that, by the close of this century, she will find herself on a par with the most advanced powers—at least that is what her leaders anticipate.

But the great and burning problem at the present moment is to get through the first stage. It will be fifteen years before the important technical transformations shall have come about, and during this interval China must find the means to feed her population—which is growing every year—and to nourish that ravenous fledgling, her infant heavy industry. If she fails, the snowball could come to a sudden stop. Heavy industry would be at a standstill, natural resources would remain untapped, and the population would die of hunger—the pit is bottomless.

Chinese political and economic strategy in every domain is dominated by this imperative: close the gap. That is to say, this tour de force has got to be accomplished: China must pull herself up by the bootstraps out of misery to opulence. Every other country that has attempted a socialist reconstruction has also had to take its departure from a situation of economic deficiency; and, despite it, some have launched out into enterprises which have proved ill-advised and costly. China, on the contrary, has realized that the entire undertaking calls first of all for an extreme prudence; in her actual emergency situation, a crisis, a depression might bring on general collapse. To start with, the essential thing is to see to it that no ground is lost, that the situation does not worsen; care must be taken that nothing is wasted, that all the eggs are not put in one basket. "Let's use yesterday as a steppingstone to tomorrow"—the slogan's application extends beyond the realm of culture, it expresses an over-all general necessity. An overnight scrapping of the country's old economic and social structure would be the surest way not to transform but to wreck it. Therefore the advance is cautious, one slow tier of bricks at a time; the foundation remains the past; when there is no avoiding it, that past is consolidated; wherever possible, it is harnessed, but it is never chucked out disdainfully—the day the goal is attained the past will have died its own quiet death. Even while conserving it the object being aimed at is its final disappearance. Whence it is that the Chinese reality and all that is happening today in China has the temporal dimension I mentioned above: New China is in every sense transition.

As a consequence—of which I had had an inkling the very same day I arrived there—in China it is not possible to take a position instantly. It is shifting, too fleeting. The abstract philosophical definition here turns up as the most concrete of all truths: the present is nothing but evolution, a becoming. The pleasures of contemplating the scene are denied to the tourist; he is obliged to remember that the reality of whatever sight he sees is simultaneously that of a survival from the past and that of something in the throes of being born; and he knows that to come to conclusions about it as it is in its present shape, to pinpoint and immobilize it would be to denature it; between China's static past history and today's rigorous planning there is not enough room to insert a knife blade, no room either for dreams. And that also is why I was quick to realize that, in the usual sense of the word, a report on China would not do at all. The reporter explores a stable present whose various elements are there to serve as reciprocal keys; by way of contingent facts, each with its meaning but overshadowed by its implications, he strives to get beyond the individual trees to an over-all picture of the woods. In China, nothing is contingent, the trees are all saplings or seedlings, the meaning of a thing takes its definition, not from its relationship to every other thing, but from the future it has in common with everything else. The forest is on its way; that is why it is futile to set about describing this country—it demands to be explained.

# 1. THE DISCOVERY OF PEKING

How old is Peking? Two centuries or twenty? Several villages one after another occupied the site or an approximate one. The town of Yu-chou was conquered in 936 A.D. by the Khitan invaders. Upon its ruins rose a city, Yenkin, which the emperors made their southern capital. Totally wrecked in 1212 by Genghis Khan, rebuilt in 1267 by Kublai Khan who appointed it as his capital, under the name of Cambaluc, it evoked the admiration of Marco Polo and of the Franciscan Odoric. However it was once again rebuilt in the fifteenth century by the Emperor Yung Lo. It was he who raised the high black wall protected by fortified gates which encloses the most ancient part of Peking. Adjacent communities sprang up outside the ramparts, and they were compassed by a second wall, concentric to the first. When the Manchus seized power in the seventeenth century the Chinese, expelled from the central city, were resettled in the between-walls zone. Demolished once again in 1679, this time by an earthquake that took a toll of four hundred thousand lives in and about the city, and which was followed the next year by a fire that razed the Imperial Palace, Peking rearose from its ashes in the course of the eighteenth century. And so the city we see today is hardly two hundred years old; but it is laid out along the lines of a plan dating back to much earlier times.

In the elaboration of that plan no part was left to chance: there is no city more artificial than Peking. Human beings built the hills which to the north protect The Forbidden City, the emperor's residence; surrounded by walls, accessible to none but a privileged few, it occupied the geometrical center of the capital. Peking had the shape of a rectangle then; it still has and today, as in former times, it is subdivided into rectangular blocks, or *fangs*, oriented toward the four cardinal points. The height of the houses was regulated by imperial prescription; a maximum of two stories prevented them from rising above the Palace buildings. Strict laws also governed the color of the roofs; only the emperor had gilded tiles, blue tiles were for the Temples of Heaven, green for other temples and official structures; common folk had the right to a gray that blended well with soil and walls. The site was chosen arbitrarily by an imperial decision that ignored the disadvantage of founding a city where there is no river. But between 1280 and 1283 Kublai had a canal built—bordered today by little gray willows—that put Peking in touch with the rich midlands lying between the Yellow River and the Yangtze. Owing to its administrative role and the importance of the waterways serving it, Peking was, like Rome, one of the very few cities to reach a million inhabitants a long while before the industrial age. Today it numbers three million.

I said that Peking hides itself. Impossible to get the kind of panoramic, synthetic view one can have of Paris from atop Notre Dame, or of New York from the Empire State Building. On the other hand, as one looks about one's gaze is arrested by no monuments of the sort which elsewhere have the significance of focal and rallying points. The Dagoba can be seen from afar, but its misplaced Tibetan whiteness jars with the rest of the city. Tien An Men, recently become its emblem, is only visible from near by. And the Imperial Palace, the capital's political and geometrical center, is screened from view by walls. The Kremlin too has for centuries loomed up like a kind of Forbidden City in the middle of Moscow; but at least the onion-shaped spires of its churches are within everyone's sight. No presence affirms itself in the heart of Peking; rather, a vast absence yawns there.

All of which to a European is very odd. The cities of Europe accreted around the great buildings—the churches, town halls—that in the public imagination still incarnate them; around these nerve centers lay the squares and market places toward which the streets converged, channeling the tide of citizens who would gather there at appointed times. The center of Peking is the opposite of a pole of attraction. In former days the population did not have the right to approach the Palace; instead of ordering itself around that core, Peking was thrust back from the red walls, the Chinese themselves driven out of the inner *enceinte* whose battlements took on a negative and hostile quality.

The quadrille pattern defining Peking excluded any notion of convergence; it emphatically indicates how the city was born not from the needs of a population but from the decree of a prince. Numerical considerations alone influenced the partition of space that here functioned simply as a container, like a box, and had no qualitative dimensions. And the traveler is amazed to find that, similar to the historyless agglomerations of America, South Africa, and Australia, this infinitely old city presents the appearance of so much real estate mechanically sliced up into lots.

For despite its age Peking has no history either; the history of Paris is the history of the Parisian people; and the Pekingese people never existed as a totality. In France and Italy, in England and Flanders the inhabitants of cities knit themselves together by covenants and, uniting their voices, claimed rights: they succeeded in holding certain powers collectively and in governing themselves; to the townsmen those towers and steeples and belfries reflected the image of their community's underlying oneness. Having no bourgeois townsmen, Peking never erected itself into a township possessing a town's municipality, organization, and autonomy; assisted by the mandarins, the Emperor reigned over a horde of scattered individuals whose solidarity stopped beyond the family threshold and who in the streets entertained none but external business relations with each other; like the population, the various sections of Peking are simply juxtaposed; no organic unity binds the city into a piece.

In Christian lands religion strengthened communal ties. The Church being at once hierarchical and universal, the cathedral both dominated the parishes and was open to everybody; each quarter of town had its priest and its ordinary ceremonies, the entire city had a single bishop and festivals that brought all the inhabitants together. It thus had not one but two hearths around which in a complex manner its temporal and spiritual existences revolved. No universal Church ever existed in China; only the Emperor had the right to sacrifice to the Lord on High whose soaring temple lay beyond the sphere of the common people; for them, excluded from the official worship, prohibited from entering the sacred precincts, the land had no religious center. The minor temples in the various quarters were flanked by market places and constituted secondary centers, but they were scattered, unconnected by any shared ties; each belonged and was meaningful to a fraction of the population, none to its entirety.

The Son of Heaven was not, like the Roman Emperor, the delegate of his people; nor did he consider himself its father: the people were men, he was Man, and between him and the others the distinction was absolute. His subjects could not recognize themselves in him and the city was never the incarnation of his person. Inversely it was not in the interest of the inhabitants that the emperors built and rebuilt Peking, but for the sake of affirming their own grandeur. It has sometimes been asked why, instead of using stone, they used wood that often had to be brought from great distances at great expense, since trees are rare in China. The choice in any case proves that they were more concerned with display than with producing something durable; they did not build for eternity and felt no respect for the works of their predecessors. Peking has often been leveled, whether by fire or quake, or deliberately by a new conqueror; starting from scratch, the rebuilding would end up with an identical Peking every time: its past being obliterated wholesale and repeatedly, no mark imparted by the centuries ever lasted long. Peking never shifted a bit to this side or that, never changed: there are thus no superimposed layers to dig down into, no traces of a vital heritage to unearth; Peking was just begun again and again. It dates back beyond Rome; and yet paradoxically its avenues—especially at nightfall when the neon signs go on—make me think of certain of the more crowded, bigger thoroughfares in Brooklyn or Chicago; as there, the width of the streets here further dwarfs the two-story or three-story houses arranged in regular blocks; wooden and pisé construction has a provisional, makeshift character and ages fast—that is why a two-thousand-year-old city, like one that has yet to have its centennial, looks simultaneously callow and wizened.

Thus, spatially as well as temporally, Peking has nothing beyond the unity imposed by repetition. One finds the same hutungs* everywhere. In the Tartar City† they have poetic names: the Street of the Singing Magpie, Street of the Ten Thousand Lights, Street of the Shady Bower. In the Chinese City they are more prosaically titled: Street of the Jades, Street of the Silks. They are all narrow rectilinear thoroughfares of gray unpaved beaten earth, lined by gray walls, surmounted by gray tile roofs. As in Arab towns, one sees no façades: temples, villas, houses are all concealed behind walls. Trees grow in inner courts but rarely along the street itself whose monotony is hardly alleviated by the little stone lions and ceramic dragons that guard an occasional doorway. From the ground rises a tart, somewhat fermented earthen smell by which I could recognize Peking blindfold. Save for an infrequent bicycle, no vehicle goes down the street, where small children play undisturbed. Sometimes you hear the hand bell of a noodle vendor or grocer: he transports his merchandise in baskets slung at both ends of the shoulder pole, or perhaps in some sort of little cart. At once intimate and accessible, to me these streets seem private roads open to everybody: that is one of the secrets of their charm. Another is their very monotony. I understand why at first it constantly seemed to me that the *real* Peking was *elsewhere*: the street you are in the act of following is never oriented toward anything or anywhere, it does not belong as a part to any organized whole, you do not sense the presence of an over-all Peking all around it. But after you have done a good deal of walking you come to have an altogether different feeling, an extraordinary and pleasant feeling of ubiquity. Each lane looks as if it were the prototype, as if it were the idea and the truth of all the others: being here or there is being everywhere. The stroller sees the same gray, silent alleyway unendingly reborn around him; he moves along and with each

* Residential streets.

† The ring immediately circling the Forbidden City.

step the scenery recreates itself, identically. I do not know just why this indefinite repetition of a single form is somehow enchanting, but it is—perhaps it gives one the illusion of draining this form dry of all the pith and sense it contains, while all those contents are restored as the myth of depthlessness goes on coining itself, mile after mile.

I visited several Pekingese interiors;* nothing on the outside distinguishes the most luxurious residence from a hovel, although the door to the first is often painted a handsome oxblood red and the door to the second is gray: but during the daytime, the doors being open, there is no color to be seen. Neither can you get a glimpse of the inside of the house, for one's view is interrupted by an ordinarily white brick screen, the *chao p'ing;* once upon a time its purpose was to protect the dwelling against evil spirits, it now protects it from inquisitive passers-by. One enters the doorway, makes several sharp turns to reach the inner courtyard around which the rooms of the house are distributed. This arrangement has its disadvantages in bad weather, for the rooms do not intercommunicate, one must re-enter the court to get from one to the other; but it affords each family a patch of earth and sky all to itself. In the middle of the patio there is often a fountain providing drinkable water. The humblest of these dwelling units had four rooms: a kitchen and three very sparsely furnished bedrooms; seated at a table, a young man was reading; outside, children were playing, an old woman was keeping an eye on them from a distance. The family included a married couple, a grandmother, and five youngsters. It was cramped quarters for eight, but the household was neat and clean. In the elaborate villas—in, for example, the one given over to the Writers' Association—there is a series of courts arranged, as one comes in from the street, one behind the other, several steps often lead up to the buildings; at any rate, courts and buildings are never on the same level and where there are two or more courts, the level of each will rise as one moves in toward the last of them. Thresholds have high wooden sills—hence the Chinese opera convention whereby the actor raises his foot several inches to indicate entering or leaving a house. The prettiest

* Several of these visits were improvised; it was upon my suggestion that Tsai requested this or that housewife to allow me to enter her house.

of the houses I saw—those belonging to Lao-She and Ting-ling—contained a single court. The buildings are all constructed according to the ancient traditional design. The roof ties sit directly on wooden posts, not on the walls which function simply as protection, and this is why the interior partitions can be so light: frail crisscrossing laths, the interstices filled with old newspapers in poorer houses, in elegant ones faced with rice paper. Luxury asserts itself above all in terms of flowers planted in the courtyards—some of which are veritable gardens of chrysanthemums—and in terms of furnishings.

Today as in the past the population of Peking is by and large made up of civil servants, tradesmen, and artisans. Peking's shopping streets are therefore of considerable importance. I was unprepared for their colorfulness and gaiety, Western propaganda so firmly attaching the idea of an iron or bamboo curtain to that of austerity. Indeed, at first glance you see nothing to indicate that you are in a country actively heading toward socialism; rather, it seems as if one had taken a jump in the other direction and were walking in the semifeudal world of yesterday's China. Running the length of avenues and little streets are multitudes of small shops, some protected by windows decorated with red characters, others, doorless and windowless, opening straight onto the sidewalk; hand-made pottery, clothing, shoes, furniture, coffins, wickerware objects, musical instruments are manufactured in many of them. Large red-and-black signs designate their specialty. Neon signs glow at night. Chinese characters are always decorative: illuminated in green or red, winking capriciously on and off across shopfronts or up and down, you would call this a swarm of fairyland butterflies.

Right by the hotel there is a wide street bordered with little willows under which pedicabs wait. The stores here cater to a foreign clientele; they have display windows, are on the modern and fashionable side: brocades, photographs of works of art, genuine and imitation antiques, silk jackets lined with fleece or mink—lots of pretty things, lots of ugly ones too. At the sign of a vast fedora there are fur caps for sale, and those square tuques in quilted velvet the Uzbeks wear. A Hindu shop proposes saris and silk neckties with painted genii and dragons. A taxidermist offers stuffed animals. There are several oddly timeworn clothing shops whose signs represent ladies in turn-of-the-century, floor-length gowns, men buttoned up in Edwardian suits; the display windows feature dresses in a vaguely Occidental style, strong where comes to color but of uncertain cut—these, it seems, are for the Russian women customers—and over a little to one side are men's shirts in white silk modeled after what is popular with Russian men. Two huge bookstores, both run by the state, face each other on opposite sides of the street. One carries Chinese books; it is full of buyers and browsers. The other has an international stock: American books, French, German, Russian, English, all in the original, and American translations of Russian novels, Russian translations of American works. At the end of the street, opposite where they are putting up a big state store, a portrait of Mao Tse-tung announces the entrance to a market, a maze of covered, right-angled passageways where everything on earth is sold: knickknacks, phonograph records, pots and pans, sewing materials, hats, tobacco, vinegar-preserved fruits, cakes and rolls stuffed with strained red peas, velvet flowers and butterflies, paper articles, porcelain, carved jade and lacquerware, earthenware, basketry, and jewelry—here, too, there are hideous objects and delightful ones. In one alley a line of stalls bulging with secondhand books: much foreign literature, narratives from the pens of missionaries, dictionaries, and a bin of used "egg books,"* containing more pictures than text and which are spread by the million through the rural areas.

The street terminates at an intersection: from within an elevated glass cage at one corner a policeman directs traffic. Other commercial avenues lead off every which way. Sometimes a wooden arcade marks the entrance to an open-air market. There is the jade and jewelry market; the flower market is farther on: all the courtyards are gardens whose flower beds spill out into the street and continue right and left along the walls; the emphasis is upon potted chrysanthemums and potted green plants but you also find birds and red feather dusters with handles as long as broomsticks.

Perhaps the prettiest of all are the shops where tea is sold—three walls covered with painted wooden drawers, and the carefully

* In China eggs are the prototype of the cheap staple.

labeled chests, boxes arrayed in rows behind the counter, all this reminds one of old-fashioned pharmacies—they have every kind of tea on hand, black, green, aromatic, and even those compressed tea bricks the Tibetans prefer. There are two kinds of true pharmacies: modern ones, similar to ours; others, selling traditional remedies, display curious powders and pills, and those strange ginseng roots, as weirdly gnarled as mandrake root, which are reputed to cure numerous illnesses and which cost their weight in gold.

Inside and at the foot of the rampart bounding the "Tartar City" quarters on the south there is a permanent flea market. Here is where one picks up American surplus, cheap clothing, old hardware; people eat at tables set up between stalls.

To get out into the "Chinese City" you go by way of a fortified gate, Kien Men: above a tunnel bored through the rampart, which at this point widens into a terrace, rises a bastion in bare brick sheathed with glazed tiles; the roof of soft green contrasts with the structure's military fierceness. You then arrive in the southern districts where the Pekingese settled after the Manchus pushed them beyond the city's walls. Later, racial discrimination died down but a kind of economic segregation remained in force. Only merchants able to pay for costly patents were authorized to establish themselves in the neighborhood of the Forbidden City; the others stayed where they were, in the Chinese City. It was here, in this in-between ring, one used to find the localities dedicated to amusements and debauchery: theaters, public baths, renowned restaurants which still exist, and opium dens and brothels which exist no more. Hereabouts, until 1911, there were even houses of male prostitution legally tolerated and frequented by the Manchu nobility. As for the brothels, they numbered 377 in 1920, contained 3,130 girls divided into four classes according to their youth and beauty; they were bought while still very young from needy families, or they were simply kidnaped. In houses of the first and second order their age ranged from sixteen to eighteen; upon the doors to their cells appeared their names on copper or wooden plaques, or embroidered on strips of silk; in return for gratuities, newspapers publicized them openly, printing their photograph, name, and phone number as if advertising a brand of laundry soap. Recounting their adventures, tourists of the period were cheerfully wont to extol the charm and gracious manners of those to whom they referred as "The Singsong Girls."

Today there are no more prostitutes, no more smell of opium in these streets, only opera airs coming over radios, red-and-black shop signs swaying above shops. In the middle of this section of perpendicularly laid-out streets runs a broad avenue with trolley tracks. The houses are three or four stories high; their fronts are embellished by wooden sculpture, enlivened by lacquerwork; the ground-floor bazaars open wide onto the street, at night they are shut by barricades—they are chock-full of merchandise. Umbrellas, yellow oilcloth, overcoats, furs, sheepskins hang from the ceiling; heaps of cotton goods, silks, varicolored blankets are piled on the counters; on the walls you see colored pictures representing Marx, Lenin, scenes from the operas. The most attractive façades belong to the public baths and the theaters. Restaurants and teahouses hide in nooks; on the other hand, a lot of eating is done out-of-doors. There are roofless restaurants everywhere throughout the whole city: a couple of wooden tables, always pushed up against a wall, and a stove on wheels. At eight in the morning, while the Paris office employee is dunking a *croissant* in his *café au lait*, the Pekingese clerk is sitting on a bench, usually opposite the wall, and his breakfast consists of vermicelli soup and little rolls more braised than baked. At any time of day you will see cooks drawing and braiding hanks and skeins of spaghetti the way candy sellers at carnivals used to pull taffy; then they cut it up in lengths and put handfuls of it in little pots, sometimes they stuff macaroni with red-pea purée or finely ground meat. Others make pancakes, boil vegetables, or roast sweet potatoes under coals. The aromas rising from these stoves and combining with the acid smell of earth produces an odor unlike anything we have in our Mediterranean lands; the Chinese do not use olive oil, their cooking smells of soybean oil, pepper, pimento—a spicy smell, subtle and sharp.

Itinerant kitchens, peddlers, strawberry vendors, a myriad of single-item retailers and handicraftsmen: these streets evoke medieval times but have one most unmedieval quality: they are aseptically spick and span. The travel agencies' slogan which in the West defines the picturesque section of a city, "narrow and evil-smelling little streets," does not apply here. These streets, without any disagreeable odor, are beyond all comparison with the rattrap vennels of Naples, Lisbon, or Barcelona; you see no fluttering old newpapers or leaking garbage cans as in Chicago alleyways; you see no down-and-out old men such as straggle about the Bowery in New York. All the children are properly, carefully dressed. The least scratch or scrape is painted with mercurochrome or covered with a bandage. All over the world experience would seem to show that the fatal implications of poverty are filth, lack of sanitation, and epidemics. Every one of Peking's visitors, be he the most unfriendly of them all, is astonished at the way in which men have given the lie to this immemorial tradition.

However Peking used once to provide a thundering confirmation of it; the city was famous for its dirt and dilapidation. From an old guidebook I take the following: "I walked down streets, or rather canyons, gouged twenty feet deep by wagon wheels; looking up, the ancient gutters, smashed or dangling in space, seemed like giant stairs leading to the narrow path bordering the house-fronts on each side of the precipice. . . . I walked up to my thighs through a fetid drift of secular impurities." That from the Comte de Beauvoir, writing in the year 1867.

This from another Frenchmen, Marcel Monnier, who wrote in 1895:

> Extraordinary place, this city: a cloaca of stenches, filth, and decrepitude. Vermin, rags, running sores, a grievous neglect and decay. Buildings tottering to ruin, tattered crowds against a grandiose décor . . . The city, a good third of which is garden or wasteland, has more the look of a forest, of an immense park surrounded by crenelated walls, with, here and there, an occasional clearing, or a village.

Things hadn't changed forty years later. Casseville, a great admirer of the old Manchu order, a fervent adept of the elite morality, said in 1934: "For the traveler, the word *hutung* designates tiny streets strewn with virtual pitfalls, where a rickshaw outing means aches and pains, ungodly smells, ordures, half-naked beggars, and entirely naked children."

Filth, offal, beggars were still there in 1949. *The Pit of the Bearded Dragon*, a film based on a play by Lao-She, presents,

I am told, an accurate image of what Peking used to be like. The main characters live in mud kennels grouped about a court whose door opens onto an alleyway; the latter is almost entirely taken up by one of those "smashed or dangling" gutters; a narrow ledge on either side overlooks semistagnant water in which household garbage and every variety of carrion rot; it is bridged every now and then by a plank. When it rains the ditch overflows, muck invades the courtyard, penetrates into where people are living; the walls crack or melt, threaten to or do collapse; a week later the inhabitants are still wallowing in a mire. The little incident that serves as a pretext for the film has happened more than once: crossing the ditch one stormy day, a little girl slips on a rotten plank, falls into the stew underneath and drowns. I myself have seen the exact spot whose metamorphosis is described in the second part of the story; and I was able to understand what a victory a paved street, decent houses on solid foundations, telephone poles, the absence of odors and waste can represent. In the past one went long distances to fetch polluted water; today pure water runs from a tap placed at every intersection in Peking. No more open sewers, no more flies, no more rats; where there used to be swamps they have built parks.

Obviously, the more radical measure would have been to make a clean sweep: dynamite the old Peking and reconstruct a new one. But while it might have wanted to, the government lacked the means. Tsai was a good bit ahead of time with the broad gesture of his that cleared away a whole quarter. China is still too poor to blow its past to smithereens; she must make use of it. What is unusual in her approach is that, peacefully, skillfully, she is obtaining service from a very weary old horse. Peking has hardly changed in the last five years, and yet it has been transformed.

It is this at once energetic and cautious policy which explains the quasi-medieval aspect of the city. Had the authorities undertaken to expropriate merchants and artisans with one stroke of the pen, they would have created a terrible mess and gravely imperiled the country's economy. Adhering to a thesis in whose behalf he had argued for years, Mao Tse-tung declared in July of 1949: "To bear up under imperialist pressure and to emerge from her inferior economic situation, China must utilize every element of urban and rural capitalism which, for the national economy, constitutes an asset and not a danger." He won the cooperation of the merchants and artisans by conceding them the private ownership of their funds. The Chinese economy is made up of three kinds of enterprises: state enterprises, joint state and private enterprises in which capital shares are equally or unequally divided between the state and individuals, and private enterprises. In September 1955, the number of businessmen still operating on a private basis stood at seven million, and the state stores—of which there are not many as yet—fixed their prices to match those of small business in order not to ruin it. The great majority of the artisans were still independent at that time. They number between fifteen and twenty million, furnish one fifth of the country's industrial product, 15 per cent of its income. From 60 to 80 per cent of the articles used by the peasants are manufactured by artisans.

However, the traveler who is charmed by the picturesque but outmoded quaintness of the Chinese City or the flower markets would be wrong to suppose that nothing has changed since yesterday. The government at once took control of the market by creating purchasing and selling agencies for basic products—coal, furs, building materials. In 1953, for reasons I shall come back to, it established a monopoly on grains and vegetable oils for home consumption, in September 1954, on cotton; by law it alone can buy and sell these products. In numerous branches of light industry the government is either the producer or the producers' principal or unique customer. It is only for the distribution of commodities that—together with the state stores and jointly run and owned firms—it utilizes private retailers.*

The latters' situation has been transformed profoundly. Under

* Li Fu-chuan's "Report on the Five-Year Plan" specifies: "Private wholesalers are authorized to continue to sell certain products in which the State organisms do not deal and for which the State constitutes only part of the market . . . Retailers make up the overwhelming majority of private tradesmen. Most of them are vendors, little shopkeepers, peddlers who operate alone, without employing help. To these must be added the artisans who sell their own products . . . After the winter of 1953 the volume of private retailing business diminished rather too suddenly. Readjustments have since been made . . . The State has temporarily halted the upswing in its retail sales . . . The cooperatives have also reduced their retailing trade efforts, concentrating instead upon wholesaling."

the Kuomintang, small businessmen were the regular victims of organized gangs and corrupt officials; they above all suffered from staggering inflations that brought economic crises in their wake; in Shanghai, during the Chiang regime's final years, the shopkeepers, obliged to dispose of their goods in exchange for an utterly valueless issue of paper money, saw their shops literally pillaged. Threatened by ruin, for the most part their only hope of survival lay in borrowing, and usurious rates of interest hastened them toward bankruptcy. The elimination of gangsterism and corruption, the suppression of usury, and particularly the stabilization of currency guaranteed them all an inestimable blessing: security. In case of difficulty, the state lends them money in return for an extremely modest rate of interest. Both buying and selling prices have remained stable.

The other side of the coin is that the merchant has lost the liberty to speculate and the possibility to cheat. The "Five-Anti's" campaign aimed against the exactions of private capitalism has produced its effects from the bottom to the top of the ladder; buy a package of cigarettes or tea and with your purchase the salesman must give you a receipt. The prices of important commodities are fixed by official regulation. As for luxury articles, if one shopkeeper charges exorbitant prices, the others criticize him severely; and the case is rare, for the imperative of a fair price has been taken to heart: every traveler has remarked—in Peking, at least—the scrupulous honesty of the shopkeepers; those who knew the old China are all the more struck by what was not formerly a Chinese virtue.

But they have done more than set business in order: capitalism survives on a tentative basis; socialism is under way. New state stores are being created. And, above all, the state is investing ever-increasing amounts of capital in private enterprises so as to transform them into joint enterprises. The definitive stage is being approached at which the small owners will become employees of the government.

With regard to the artisans, they are encouraged to form cooperatives. These in September 1955, for the whole of China grouped only 1,130,000 members, but the movement has been picking up speed: in January of 1956 all the artisans of Peking belonged to co-operatives. The advantages of this collectivization are many. From the outset it brings about an increase in productivity and a hike in the profits of those involved; effectively permitting a general reduction of costs and a more rational and efficient distribution of labor, it creates the leeway needed for plowing capital back into the enterprise. Its long-range objective is the fulfillment of the socialist revolution: the concept of collective ownership gradually replaces that of private property, which advances the workers' attitudes toward the socialist outlook.

In Peking I visited several handicraft co-operatives; one of them was a factory specializing in cloisonné enamelware. A great many vases, pots, cups, bowls, ash trays are hand-wrought by this old technique which was imported from Arabia in the fourteenth century. The enterprise occupied four or five rooms spaced around a courtyard. In the first room, craftsmen hammer sheet copper, fashioning it into the shape of the vase or bowl; next the process is continued in another room where workers, holding the piece in fine pliers, snip, burr, bend, and glue thin slivers of copper, applying them to the form in this or that manner, depending on the pattern to be reproduced; the result is a curious object decorated in relief, copper on copper. The overlay is permanently fixed by annealing: the vase goes into a kiln, is heated red, then left to cool—one worker handles this part of the job whereas in other shops six or seven are involved in it. When cool, the vase is turned over to painters who cover it with thick layers of bright colors: upon a yellow or green background appear flowers, birds, a landscape. The object is kilned once, twice again; it becomes as smooth as porcelain. If it is a vase or a jar the neck and base are ringed with bands of copper.

Here, the advantages gained by organizing the work are plain. Each step in the manufacture requiring a longer or shorter period of time, a private owner will have difficulty co-ordinating the various operations undertaken by his workers; there will be a particularly great loss of time during heatings and coolings. On the other hand, joining forces allows an efficient sharing of the work so as to avoid idle moments and bottlenecks. The result of co-operation: much higher profits for everyone than if he proceeded on his own.

Artisans working at home can be co-operatively grouped. For example, women need not leave the house to make embroideries for tablecloths, napkins, etc. A central organism takes care of purchasing and distributing the linen cloth and supplies of silk thread in the hues called for by the model to be copied; the organism also selects the patterns, inspects the pieces, supervises any necessary corrections, and sees to the laundering of the finished work; it also has charge of relations with the clientele—receiving orders, filling them. The housekeepers of Peking who earn a supplementary income from needlework have no worries about getting rid of their merchandise, waste no time looking for models or buying the necessary materials. Here too the advantages of collectivization are self-evident.

One thing surprised me at first: the unproductive character of the objects manufactured: enamelware, embroidered napkins. But, as I have pointed out, there is an overabundance of labor in China at present; for centuries popular art—handmade objects in lacquer, jade, silk, porcelain, hand-woven cloth, and the like—has fed a very sizable number of Pekingese; in order that they not suffer unemployment the regime has decided to encourage de-luxe handicraft; the state helps find outlets and places orders. A new form of production, the co-operative creating articles of no primary use and by means of old and sometimes ancient techniques—this is a paradox which is not out of keeping with the general physiognomy of Peking where socialism forges ahead behind the outward appearances of an ageless Oriental bazaar.

The ingenious policy consisting in squeezing every last drop out of everything carried over from the past has often aroused the mirth if not the indignation of ill-disposed observers. One detail among others elicits the gleeful sarcasm of the anti-Communists: the survival of pedicabs. It seeems that certain French liberals visiting Peking have, for their part, refused to climb into them, estimating the use of such contraptions an insult to the human dignity of the Chinese. Tsai probably feared a similiar reaction from us when he declared that they would soon be replaced. Certainly the Chinese count on shortly reaching the stage where other means of conveyance will be substituted for this; but they also consider that there is no degradation in performing a task that is useful to society. The attitude the government has adopted on this point concurs with the one set forth in 1927 by Mao Tse-tung in the province of Honan: the peasants, having just grouped themselves in powerful unions, wanted to outlaw the use of the palanquin; Communist leaders replied that, if they did, they would only worsen the plight of the carriers and suggested instead that palanquins continue and carrying rates be raised. Likewise, when Peking was liberated, certain Chinese and Occidental bourgeois trembled lest they be compelled to dismiss their servants; but no, they were enjoined to keep them in their pay and to triple it. Had pedicabs been done away with, an entire category of workers would have been thrown out of work; they are, moreover, rendered necessary by the shortage of buses and streetcars, by the nonexistence of taxis. No hesitation: they were retained.

Retained, yes, but the lot of the drivers has changed since yesteryear. In her reporting for *Paris-Presse*, Madame F. Rais declares that they were happier in the good old Kuomintang days when they could caress the dream of being "splashed" with capitalist gold. Better acquainted than this imaginative journalist with the ins and outs of their trade, the pedicab men know very well that barring holdup or murder their chances for appropriating the contents of their clients' billfolds stood squarely at zero, and they were splashed with a sight more mud than gold. They were exploited by the contractors who rented them their vehicles and in exchange took a whopping percentage of their receipts: if at day's end they brought back an insufficient sum, it was to receive a beating from the boss. Often too, once delivered to his destination, the client would prefer to give the operator a thrashing rather than his money: the Westerners and Kuomintang officials knew that the corner policeman would automatically take their side. Today, the pedicab men do not by any means constitute the most favored segment of the population; their pants, which they wear rolled up to the knees, may often be patched; but they are not reduced to habitual idleness, as Madame Rais would have it, nor despised, as Madame Berlioux believes, nor filthy and in rags and tatters as commiseratingly depicted by Madame Gosset.* The vehicles are rented to the men, either by the state or by government-supervised companies, for a set and very reasonable fee; some own their vehicles; whichever the case, they keep all of what they earn. Pedicab fares being moderate, the population makes wide use of them: Sunday earnings normally come to five or six yuan. Everything considered, the operator makes just about what a workman gets; that is to say, he can provide a decent livelihood for a wife and two or three children. The operators belong to insurance associations which help them in the event of ill-health; evening courses have been organized for them, and at present most can read and write. They do not overexert themselves keeping their vehicles in trim; however, I did see one whose seats were upholstered in sky blue against which were flying white doves of peace.

The watchword of thriftiness guiding this transitional period has been heeded everywhere save in one area: in the parks, on the main avenues, and above all in the vast suburb called "New Peking" they have put up apartment houses whose magnificence takes one aback. Toward 1925 Chinese architects evolved a style termed "national" and which strives to conciliate the requirements of modern life with tradition: it was in this spirit the University of Peking and the central Public Library were designed. When in 1949 large-scale building began, the desire was to keep the new edifices in harmony with the old city: the national style was agreed upon. Thus the enormous hotel still going up on the edge of the city is composed of typically "Chinese" pavilions. The green tiled roofs have a wide overhang, tip upward like prows at the corners. The interior reproduces certain ancient palace elements and themes inspired by Buddhist temples. I also saw handsome green-roofed houses on the edge of Pei Hai Lake: these are offices and dormitories intended for civil employees. In 1950 complaints were leveled at the architects, the expenses incurred by this

* Mesdames Rais and Berlioux have contributed articles on China to the French press; with her husband, Pierre Gosset, Madame Renée Gosset produced a coverage for the magazine *Réalités*. (Translator's note)

mode of construction were too high. The roof of the Peking police headquarters cost so much that, to keep within the estimate, one story had to be trimmed off the number anticipated in the plans; the Mayor of Peking expressed keen disapproval and the Government asked that the national style be abandoned. Certain architects complied. However in 1953 the Learned Society of Chinese Architects was founded and began to publish a review in which the principles of ancient architecture were championed. An old professor, Liang Ssu-Cheng, explained that modern materials, steel and reinforced concrete, are less appropriate for massive walls in the Western tradition than for structures following the Chinese concept of the "skeletal framework"—actually the principle of the skyscraper, in which the walls simply fill in the gaps left by the framework, is the same one that has always governed the design of Chinese houses.

Building therefore went on in the old way. But in 1955 this obstinacy was definitely condemned. Among the economy measures Li Fu-chuan recommends in the "Report on the Five-Year Plan," it is urgently stressed that the "so-called national style" must go.

> The last few years have seen enormous waste and extravagance in the construction of nonproductive buildings . . . In 1954, 24 per cent of the capital earmarked for construction was poured into nonproductive investments. This unreasonable figure must be modified. There has been inexcusable waste due for example to blind, irresponsible adherence to the national style. Instead of holding to the principle of "suitability, thrift, and elegance where possible," large and unnecessary sums have been squandered on sumptuous façades, in employing refined and costly materials. In the thirty-eight edifices raised in the Peking area by various Government departments, 5,400,000 yuan has been thrown away on great high-pitched roofs after the style of the Imperial Palace . . . Excessive ornamentation not only costs money, but reduces the amount of utilizable space.

A traditional roof of glazed tile comes four times dearer than an ordinary roof and, what with its cant and high crest, can take up the space an entire story might otherwise occupy. In a certain sanitarium the kitchen and even the laundry are thus covered. A cartoon that appeared about the end of April 1955 in *The*

*People's Daily* shows the old Dowager Empress—famed for having diverted a share of the Navy's budget into reconstructing the Summer Palace—tapping on the shoulder of a stout bespectacled architect who is holding a T square and blueprints; she is pointing to a pavilion surmounted by an imposing series of roofs. "Why," runs the caption, "you're even better at this than I am—when I was fixing up the Summer Palace, it never occurred to me to put such a magnificent roof over a kitchen."

It seems as though, in the elation of victory, the Chinese architects were in too great a hurry to apply Lenin's dictum: "Nothing is too beautiful for the people." Lenin once said that the day will come when public urinals are cast in solid gold—how far into the future he was looking! For the moment making sure that everybody has enough to eat is still a problem in China; another one, tougher yet, is to get everybody housed. The press, the radio, even the cinema are now joined in a campaign against "the big roofs" which have become synonyms of every extravagance. The plans for thirteen new buildings projected for construction in Peking have been revised in this direction, and while lopping off a sizable chunk of the building's estimated cost, these amendments have also increased their utilizable space.

Certain aesthetes, enamored of old China, miss the flies, the ragged people: "No more beggars! Why, this isn't Peking anymore," one connoisseur exclaimed to me, reproach in his tone. Brawls, altercations between the natives used also to be appreciated: they gave its local color to Peking, the way Flanders derives its from cockfighting. Guillain deplores the fact the present regime has deprived him of these pleasures; he finds things dull in Chinese streets these days. True, you no longer hear any screaming or shouting when two bicycles or pedicabs collide; those involved exchange smiles. This general good humor is, in my view, one of the charms of the city. I noticed it as soon as I arrived. I had come there from France; not long before then I had been in Spain. In both those countries the faces of people who have spent the whole day working are, by evening, pinched, tense, morose;* along the road in from

* A jovial expression used also to be a rare sight in China, if one may take Pearl Buck's word for it. The following lines are from *The Good Earth* (New

the airfield not only those people who were returning to the city after a day's work but those who were tilling the soil or carrying burdens looked cheerful, all of them. That first impression was subsequently confirmed. In Peking, like it or not, there is a happiness in the air.

There are fewer people in the streets than I had imagined there would be, but—except at night—they are always animated. What is most striking about the tranquil and gay crowd at one's side is its homogeneity. Men are not all of the same station in China, but Peking offers a perfect image of a classless society. Impossible to tell an intellectual from a worker, a charwoman from a capitalists wife. This is in part owing to the notorious uniformity of dress that so grieves Monsieur Guillain; but the first to poke fun at it are the Chinese themselves: an often reproduced cartoon figures a family whose members are holding hands: "Grandfather, Grandmother, Papa, Mom, me, and my little sister," and everyone is wearing the selfsame classical outfit of blue cotton. Women are today urged to get into skirts and sweaters, or into dresses that follow the ancient traditional pattern; textile factories turn out cotton material in flower prints.* Nothing doing. The fact is that

York, 1931): "Their faces in repose were twisted as though in anger, only it was not anger. It was the years of straining at loads too heavy for them which had lifted their upper lips to bare their teeth in a seeming snarl, and this labor had set deep wrinkles in the flesh about their eyes and mouths. They themselves had no idea of what manner of men they were. One of them once, seeing himself in a mirror that passed on a van of household goods, had cried out, 'There is an ugly fellow!' And when others laughed at him loudly he smiled painfully, never knowing at what they laughed . . ."

* In the review *New Perspectives,* Madame Chang Ch'in-Ch'iu, Vice-Minister for Textile Industries, wrote about July of 1955, "once the New China was established, and a climate of austerity and hard work came to exert its influence upon every level of society, a constantly growing number of men and women adopted uniform dress. However, inasmuch as the population's standard of living is steadily on the rise, there is no reason at all why the women and children of New China should not show a renewed interest in ornament and variety. Everyone has a sense of beauty, and a reasonable degree of elegance in dress does not by any means indicate a decadent mentality . . . Above all else, there ought to be a wider difference in the clothing worn by men and women."

During May of 1956 a great fashion show was put on in Peking's large state department store: 400 different models were shown, dresses and ensembles in both the Western style and the traditional Chinese style.

It would seem that uniformity of dress has been current in North China for in Peking blue trousers and jackets seem to be as ineluctable as black hair: these two colors go so well together, blend so happily with the lights and shadows of the city that there are moments when you would think you were walking through a scene from Cézanne. But this crowd's unity stems from a deeper source: nobody is arrogant here, nobody is grabby, nobody feels himself above or below anybody else; people have a dignified air but no trace of haughtiness, they seem at once reserved and open. One must be laboring under a curious delusion to be able to take them for an army of ants.* Homogeneity does not signify sameness. As a matter of fact, I know of no place where uniformity reigns so thoroughly and to such disastrous effect as in the better districts and drawing rooms of Paris, where the individual indefatigably manifests his class and is devoured by it. Here, the cleavage between social categories is not apparent: those one stands among are a multitude of individuals, infinitely unalike. Through their features, through their structure, Chinese faces are exceedingly varied; and as their expressions conform to no ritual of class each of them evokes a unique self and tells a story all its own.

Natural, relaxed, smiling, and diverse, the Pekingese crowd is well-behaved. In it, complain Western visitors and especially the French, one never meets with lovers walking hand in hand. If perchance one notices an arm familiarly around a shoulder, these are always two comrades of the same sex. Boys and girls do not touch one another with ten-foot poles; a kiss in public would be marked down as an obscenity. This stiffness cannot be laid at the door of the regime: rather, it is Confucianism which over the centuries has built up an intricate system of taboos between men and women. In return, the order, the decency reigning in the city are innovations. Not one drunkard. Wine flows like water in Chinese novels and operas; Taoist philosophy, friendly to every sort of ecstasy, encouraged inebriation; a host of poets have celebrated

---

a long time. Pearl Buck tells us that when, newly married, she left the South and went to the North, the monotony of the people's clothes there saddened her. "It was impossible to distinguish between the rich and the poor, for a rich lady wore her satin coat underneath the dull cotton one and was no better to look at than any farm woman." (*My Several Worlds*, New York, 1956.)

* Robert Guillain's expression. (Translator's note)

it; but it is very rarely that a Chinese gets "high" on anything today.

The streets of Peking are not mysterious: the "mystery" of a city implies the misery and the dereliction of a part of the population, the existence of lower depths and an underworld. Here, each person has a place of his own, each thing is where it properly belongs. This general rightness does not exclude a rather picturesque quiet. The past is so weighty, the future so imperiously prefigured that the present always seems a little bit out of kilter—either a step behind or a step ahead of itself. One of Peking's charms, for instance, is its children: exuberant, merry, they are everywhere. Their healthiness, their cared-for look show that they are being raised according to the most up-to-date rules of hygiene. The littlest toddlers are bundled up in bright red or orange coats of quilted cotton or silk; on their heads they wear funny little hats which remind one of a jockey's cap. When they are bigger, the boys wear flowery outfits whose long trousers are ingenuously slit in front and behind. Even when trouping along in orderly fashion under the supervision of a young woman with her hair in braids, the little Chinese, with their visored caps and their rainbow-colored clothes, always give me the impression of youngsters heading for a costume party. Only the red-scarfed Pioneers match up to the idea one has of how Pioneers are supposed to look. The children who spend the day in nurseries or kindergartens are very sensibly rounded up in the morning and taken there, and brought back home in the afternoon: they are transported to and fro in pedicabs fitted out like little trucks—miniature school buses which seem to belong less to an official organization than to an amusement park. In every facet and corner of Peking you notice it: between end and means, between the object and its purpose, between institutions and men there is a kind of play, as if things were not adjusted to a snug fit. At ten in the morning the functionaries line up in front of the administration buildings for a session of calisthenics. Nothing more reasonable than the principle of compulsory physical education. All the same it always struck me as mildly incongruous to see an array of blue-clad officeworkers, their faces no longer those of high-school lads, conscientiously loosening up and deep-knee-bending to the count of an instructor on the sidewalks of Peking. In this case it is the men who seem in arrears of the idea. Sometimes it is the other way around, with the people ahead of the technique. Most everyone in Peking knows how to read by now; the demand for newspapers outstripping the number that can be printed, copies are fastened up on panels at main intersections. Pedestrians pause to scrutinize them at length.

Some larger billboards display posters: advertisements for Chinese or foreign films, or pictures illustrating the latest slogans—"Let's Free Formosa"; "Economize on Food"; "On With the Five-Year Plan: Do Your Part." As Pierre Gascar has noted, the faces portrayed are oddly pink, the eyes hardly at all slanted. A housewife wearing a surgeon's gauze mask and brandishing a fly swatter is shown on one poster; but there are not many of these posters left now; the sanitation campaign has been won; the gauze masks, once so commonplace, have practically disappeared; they are no longer worn save by policemen and a few street cleaners on days when a wind blows up dust.

I never tired of walking in Peking; there was always something to see. In the beaten-earth streets I saw old women pitpatting along on tiny feet in pointed slippers; their swollen ankles seemed frightfully deformed. At midday people eat inside the shops or on the threshold; bowl in one hand, chopsticks in the other, they squat in a position which looks uncomfortable to me but which they can imperturbably hold for hours. From time to time one comes upon a gleaming tray of bright felt slip covers intended to protect the seats of bicycles; bicycles are numerous in Peking and their owners go in strongly for trappings. For lack of livestock raising, almost no draft animals exist: there are a few Mongol ponies that draw rubber-tired carts; but the carriage I saw—it was extraordinarily ancient, nearly collapsing under the weight of six passengers and innumerable packages and bundles—seemed to have careened out of another world. For virtually all transportation it is either men or pedicabs: the latter serve as moving vans, ambulances, delivery wagons. One morning I saw more than a hundred of them go by laden with great, vividly colored paper ornaments: somewhere they were holding a ceremony in honor of an important Japanese Communist who had died in China.

I notice that there are extremely few animals in the streets: as germ carriers, dogs and cats have been got rid of. Their maintenance, furthermore, is costly and the Chinese are not so fond of pets as to sacrifice a share of their daily bread.* Tsai had been shocked in Paris to see elegant women towed around by dogs. In olden times the emperors and mandarins made much of cricket fights; there are shops where you can still buy crickets, and school children like to keep them in their desks.

While enjoying the sights in the streets I gathered details on the daily existence of the Pekingese. Although identically dressed in blue cotton, they do not all have the same standard of living. First, there is among them an inequality of inherited wealth and present earnings; second, there is a wage scale, of which I will say more later on.

In order to compute what a Chinese earns and spends it is necessary to start by defining the value of the yuan, the monetary unit now. Formerly, they used the tael, which was not a coin but a weight—a little over an ounce of silver—so that merchants carried little scales for doing their calculations. After the Opium War (1839-1842) Mexican, American, and other silver coins were allowed free circulation; a silver yuan of similar appearance was struck in 1933. When in 1934 the United States nationalized silver, she bought it, offering a high price, everywhere throughout the world: Chinese bankers sold whole cargoes of yuan to the Americans, and a disastrous inflation resulted. In 1935 the Kuomintang introduced the gold standard, but inflation persisted; everyone wanted to swap Chinese coins for American paper dollars. However, back in 1928, a national currency had been minted in the Red Zone, and as the years went by the value of these yuan steadily rose while the Kuomintang notes steadily fell. Kuomintang money ceased to be legal tender in 1949 and the use of foreign currencies was abolished: the value of the new Chinese yuan held its own.

March of 1955 saw a monetary readjustment. When I first looked at the menu at the Peking Hotel I was surprised to see dishes listed

* In Shanghai in 1949 Cartier Bresson made some amusing photographs of Chinese walking about with bird cages. You do not see them any more.

at figures ranging from 0.5 to 1 yuan, for in the articles I had read about China food prices running into tens of thousands of yuan had been cited. The answer is that one new yuan is worth 10,000 old yuan. Whereas the revaluations of the Kuomintang in 1935, 1948, 1949 had been designed to profit the state and had been immediately followed by further inflations, the object of this readjustment was merely to simplify financial figuring, it being easier to count in terms of a unit of 1 instead of in terms of units of 10,000. This reform has precipitated no economic upheavals. In banks the yuan's present rate of exchange is one to 150 francs.* This I find a rather arbitrary equivalent. But we can better decide by making a few concrete comparisons between salaries and the cost of living.

Per month, a worker earns from 40 to 80 yuan: 40 if he is unskilled, 80 if qualified. As an interpreter Tsai makes 70 yuan, which is the salary earned by many civil servants and employees. A university professor makes in the neighborhood of 140 yuan. Certain famous actors and stage directors receive 240 yuan. The profits earned by shopkeepers, industrialists, writers, etc. are (so far )not subject to limitation.

Modest quarters for a family rent at 8 or 10 yuan a month. For food one must count on spending a monthly 5 to 10 yuan per person; this figure presupposes a very simple diet: vermicelli, rice, vegetables, a very, very small amount of meat or fish which is mixed with cereals. A dozen eggs costs 0.5 yan, a chicken one yuan or, in some regions, as little as half that. Eight yuan is the price for a cotton suit: one usually needs two suits a year. A quilted cotton-stuffed blanket costs about 20 yuan. A pair of canvas shoes, 10 yuan; leather shoes are much harder to obtain at 39 to 45 yuan—all leather goods are expensive, and so are woolens. For a woolen suit one must pay 80 yuan. Fountain pens are cheap: 7 yuan. A book costs 1.20. An excellent seat at the theater: one yuan; admission to a movie: 0.25. A good meal at a restaurant: one yuan. For a bicycle: 150 yuan.

Here is Tsai's budget. He is lodged rent-free at the athletic

* In 1955 the legal rate of exchange was 350 French francs to the American dollar, the unofficial rate approximately 390. (Translator's note)

association headquarters to which he is attached. Monthly salary: 70 yuan. Dining-room board: 15 yuan. (This figure is appreciably higher than the one for food indicated above. The figure of 5-10 yuan per person holds true where cooking is done for several individuals by the mistress of the household; Tsai pays for service and for all domestic work as well as for a particularly rich and copious fare since the table at which he eats is set for athletes.) On Sunday he goes to a restaurant: 5 more yuan per month. He allows 2 yuan for transportation, 2 for the cinema, 6 for clothing, mending, laundry. (He has two cotton suits, a third one of wool, sweaters, leather shoes.) He thus spends 30 yuan a month, put 40 in a savings bank. His wife, a student who has a part-time office job, has a similar budget. Between the two of them they save about 1,000 yuan a year. With this money they will be able to set up and furnish their household. Tsai has several fountain pens, a wrist watch, a camera.

We asked to visit a family of average means and were taken to see a household where both husband and wife are secondary school teachers. They have three children and own the house they live in: a rather large, modestly furnished one. If it did not belong to them they would pay a 20-yuan monthly rent for it. They spend 50 yuan for food: 40 for rice and flour, 10 for vegetables and meat. They wear cotton clothing, seldom go out in the evening unless it be to an occasional movie, rarely attend the theater; they invite relatives every week but not many friends. They are unable to afford trips away from Peking during vacation periods.

People who have the means can enjoy a certain luxury in their food; but measures have been taken against wastefulness and hoarding. Commodities of prime necessity are rationed. Anti-Communist observers point to this as proof that the standard of living of the Chinese has sunk; they discern a regression, identify it as the consequence of the sacrifices required by the development of heavy industry—the exporting of cereals, necessary for the purchase of machinery, is said to be bringing starvation to the people. This is false. Since 1952 China has exported an annual 1,722,300 tons of grain and soybeans, soy representing over half of the total figure. Which means that each citizen's yearly cereal ration has been trimmed by less than 3½ pounds: the quantity is negligible: The Chinese consume an average of 365 catties* of grainstuff per year per person; in 1954 the figure went as high as 560 catties, notwithstanding the regular growth in population. The real reason for the rationing is that people's purchasing power and hence the demand for goods have soared. Hundreds of thousands of men and women who were dying of hunger yesterday are eating properly today; they used to live in rags, half-naked, every one of them buys cotton clothing now. The increase of production has yet to catch up with the increase of demand. And that is why it has been necessary to regulate the distribution of commodities. Commerce in basic food products was nationalized in 1953, in cotton in 1954. Farmers sell their surplus grain to the state which distributes it through the agency of retail stores; during a preliminary trial period the amounts customarily spent on such-and-such a commodity in a given region are analyzed, statistics assembled, a rationing system consequently worked out; the consumer's needs are not defined a priori by any over-all theory but in accordance with practice. As a result, according to a formula cited to us, "You can buy no more than you can eat." The question is not one of restricting consumption but rather of regulating its increase in such a way that it nowhere imperils the plan of production. In August 1955 the Government drew up a scaled rationing system for the urban populations; nine categories were charted, the factors being the age of the consumer and the nature of his work; those employed in heavy labor are alotted 48.5 pounds of flour products per month, children 36; in the South, the basic foodstuff is rice and the quantity apportioned slightly lower. Restaurants and bakeries receive supplies according to a plan approved by local authorities. Concerning cotton, everyone has the right to sixteen yards of it per year. Only the wealthy can consider these measures restrictive; they amply cover the normal needs of moderately well-to-do and poor people. Over and above the specific reasons for these measures, they echo the standing orders to economize and waste nothing.

By and large the richer Chinese lead a life that is just about as simple as that led by the poorer. To begin with they would not dare put on a parade of wealth which might give rise to severe

* One catty equals 1⅓ lbs.

criticism; and many have a native disdain for display. And then again there are very few privileges which money can buy today. Automobiles are vehicles for use only in connection with work. Night clubs and brothels have gone. Frequent evenings at the theater, restaurants, choice food and silken garments at home, buying paintings, furnitures, antiques—that is about as far as you can go with luxurious living. Moreover, the inequalities inherent in capitalism are destined to disappear rapidly; and if there are people with upper-bracket incomes, the wage scale is matched by an effort scale: they who contribute most are best paid: the most exacting demands are made upon their time, their energies, they simply have no opportunity to lead the life of the gods. According to the plans, it will be several years before the standard of living of the Chinese marks a significant advance, the urgent task at hand being to push heavy industry ahead; the austerity that prevails will not be over with tomorrow morning; to be sure, it is less enticing than abundance but one breathes better in this atmosphere of "uniformity" than in countries where glaring contrasts turn poverty into a scandal.

Ramparts, some gateways, some bastions—of its distant past that is about all Peking discloses to the sight-seer. The two outstanding monuments—the Palace where dwelt the Master of the world below, the Temple in which he worshiped the Lord above—were carefully located at a distance from the city: the former is surrounded by walls, the latter is outside the walls. To enter the Palace grounds one passes through the famous Tien An Men Gate. When I caught my first glimpse of it coming from the airport, I saw a speaker's platform; there were high grandstands set up in front of the wall—where, Tsai told us, we would be sitting on the First of October—facing the immense square that the Chinese consider their Red Square, Tien An Men today gazes at Peking and belongs to it. On maps of China, Peking is designated by the sketched outline of Tien An Men. The allegorical emblem of the People's Republic is Tien An Men with five stars shining down upon it, sheafs of wheat circling it, and a cogwheel below. But it was only with the Liberation that Tien An Men assumed this meaning: previously, instead of partaking of the city, it held the city at bay:

it was the key bastion of a bristling fortress; the gilded pavilion contained soldiers whose task was to guard the tunnel which pierces the thick wall and gives access to the Palace. Between the wall and the great square is a canal spanned by marble bridges with sculptured balustrades. In front of the bridges rise *hua piao*, marble pillars upon which dragons and clouds are sculptured; the devices at their peaks show bird wings and clouds. The familiar silhouette of these pillars decorates the red background of cigarette packs.

On the other side of the vaulted tunnel you find yourself in the outer courtyard of the Imperial Palace—it is thus the Chinese refer to it today, denying it that fine title, "The Forbidden City," which used to inspire dreamy thoughts in Western visitors. The Chinese are right; if the idea of a forbidden city intrigues, beckons, it is because of a contradiction in terms: a city into which the population is not admitted has obviously usurped the title of a city.* It was nothing but their pride that enabled the old emperors to suppose that their presence in the place they inhabited raised it to the rank of a city; as a matter of fact, their city was never anything beyond a palace. To it they gave yet another gorgeous name: The Violet-Purple City. Here too disappointment awaits the over-credulous traveler. The enclosing walls and the inside walls are of a somewhat drab red bordering on the color of brick. Actually, the "violet-purple" epithet designated not a visible hue but a symbolic one. Violet purple is emblematic of the North Star where lies that supreme celestial palace whereof the imperial residence claimed to be the terrestrial counterpart: the absolute center of this world as the polar star is the pivot round which turns the world above.

Its scheme was dictated by antique traditions. All the emperor's palaces of ancient China were rectangular closes oriented upon the meridian axis: along it buildings and courtyards were arranged in succession so that when the Son of Heaven gave his audiences his countenance always faced the south. The great ceremonial halls and official buildings were constructed around the vast court of the southern part, these courts being used for receptions and festivals. To the north the innumerable pavilions lodging the

* Mecca, Lhasa have also been forbidden cities; but forbidden only to foreigners. For Moslems and Buddhists they constituted great religious and urban centers.

Imperial Family were distributed in a more capricious manner. When he decided to install himself in the heart of Cambaluc, Emperor Kublai had his architects copy this immutable model. When in their turn the Mings made Peking their capital, Yung Lo had the palace entirely rebuilt. Burned in 1641 at the moment the dynasty fell, restored by the Manchu emperors, its present *enceinte* measures about 3,300 feet from north to south, about 2,580 from east to west; the wall stands about 23 feet high. A canal surrounds the outer rampart at whose four corners are fortified salients.

Within the walls courtyards and marble terraces supporting gilt-roofed pavilions extend one after the other for more than half a mile; the main buildings trace the central axis; on either side lesser buildings are disposed asymmetrically. At the far end are "The Palace of Cloudless Heaven" given over to the Emperor and "The Palace of Earthly Peace" where the Empress lived. The terraces, for which the marble was brought from the Burmese frontiers on the backs of elephants, are surrounded by gleaming white sculptured balustrades, influenced probably by Hindu art. The buildings are purely Chinese. They are similar to clay models of ancient houses found in tombs dating back several thousand years. Their most remarkable feature is their roofs, characterized—as in the imitations everybody is familiar with—by their steep pitch, their jutting edges, their upturned corners; they are covered with half-cylindrical tiles whose golden glaze glows more than shines. Processions of fabulous animals extend downward along the angles, or hips, of the roofs—owls and dragons symbolizing imperial virtues—at the edges of the gutters other fantastic creatures are there to drink the waters from heaven and prevent floods.

These entrance halls and porches are built upon the same principle as the common houses from which the inspiration for them was drawn and which, I mentioned earlier, is exactly the same as that of the skyscraper: the walls support nothing, they are simply brick or mud filling between uprights which, whether distinct from or sheathed by the partitions, alone support the framework of the roof whose concave lines offset the stiffness of the horizontal beams and vertical members. The whole of this armature is visible and heightened by polychrome decoration; in the remote past, the paint was first intended as protection against weather, rot, parasites; vermilion was already being employed for this purpose by 1000 B.C. Ever since, the purpose of bright painting has been, above all, to create pleasing effects and to point up the frankness of the construction. "We take as much pleasure in contemplating the structural lines of a building, the initial expression of its idea, as, in painting, we enjoy seeing the rhythmic adumbration of color. That is why we do not conceal the wooden framework of partitions and why beams and rafters remain deliberately exposed, inside as well as out," wrote the essayist and novelist, Lin Yutang.

I concede that one may have a taste for the rudimentary and at the same time refined elegance of this architecture and for the harmonies that can be achieved through the use of mineral colors. For my part, though, a stucco-and-wood palace will never be as handsome as a house of stone. Stone resists the ravages of time while reacting to it. Its history does not by-pass it but becomes a part of it, stays part of it. These other materials crumble, their colors shine but they do not take on any patina; new or old they always seem to belong to a certain undefined period. The Imperial Palace does not have a restored look, nor has it an ancient one: this hesitation makes it appear not eternal but precarious and like an imitation of itself.

It affects me more strongly if instead of the buildings I turn my attention to the spaces they delimit: courtyards, terraces, stairways. As in certain modern private houses and developments an ambivalence between the ideas of outside and inside is reflected here; this porch was only meant to be a thoroughfare, that court was a ballroom where people stood for hours on end. One must not, therefore, consider this parvis, these tiered gardens as mere devices for setting edifices in perspective; they constitute architectural objects in themselves; their proportions, their dimensions, symmetry subtly played against asymmetry, the solemn quality of the stairways, the balustrades' gracefulness compel admiration. Here, I feel, is where the imperial architects won their outstanding success: in imparting this movement to space, where, with stately, gradual rhythms, pauses and ascents are ordered with the sure mastery that also prescribes oblique promenades in the maze of lateral alleys and sequestered walks.

All the same, this beauty strikes me as chill, and I know why. There is nothing accidental about the impermanence of the materials; it is simultaneously the cause, the effect, the expression of a troubling fact: the traces left upon this palace by the past are so few that, paradoxically, I would hesitate to call it a historical monument; it was, like Peking, begun anew by each dynasty: it preserves the mark of none of them. Versailles—that is Louis XIV; and the Escorial is Philip II; whatever else they may be—stirring, detestable, awe-inspiring—the ghosts haunting the castles of Europe are distinctive. Here, nothing conjures up Kublai, Yung Lo, or Ch'ien Lung. One has the feeling this inner city never really belonged to them, that they never belonged to it—in all likelihood because they never belonged to themselves. Between the encroachments of their private debauches and the sacred character of their public office, they were too hemmed in to affirm their personalities; those who may have possessed such a thing frittered it away in this enclave, estranged from their mandate and seeking oblivion in pleasure; that is why the hot-blooded barbarian conquerors found Peking so boring. The only shade lingering still in the phoenix-and-dragon-adorned apartments is that of "the Old Buddha," the Empress Tzu Hsi, and she scarcely fires one's imagination. This palace, in which not one dated memory is inscribed, strikes me as the unalterable seat of an unalterable institution and not the dwelling place of men who were one time alive.

Nor does the guide escorting me recount a single tale or legend: he shows me symbols which, without the minutest variation, I shall find in all the buildings I am to visit in China. The most famous of them all is the dragon; in this land where the river is master, it incarnated the spirits of the waters. Dragons used to be imagined as slumbering in the depths of wells, lakes, streams, seas; thunder would wake them, then they would spring aloft toward the sun; their breath would create clouds which they would mount, and the pressure of their bodies would turn the clouds into rain; capable of producing either floods or drought, theirs was the supreme power and that is why their image was likened to the Emperor's. Paintings and marble bas-reliefs represent them wafted upon waves or riding clouds. Upon the terraces, between the walls of brass and the braziers where incense was burned, one sees cranes and tortoises, symbols of longevity. The tortoise was the schematic equivalent of the universe for the Chinese. They imagined the sky as a hemisphere, the earth as flat and square: the tortoise's convex shell, its flat ventral plate reminded them of the celestial dome covering the terrestrial platter. A pair of marble or brass lions often guards stairways or bridges; they resemble dogs, wear a bell around the neck; the male is playing with a sort of brocaded ball, between her paws the female holds one of her young. None of these sculptures presents anything of great artistic interest. The most elegant details are the marble tapestries inlaid in the ramp which divides the stairways, the "pathway of the spirit"; the bearers of the imperial palanquin mounted and descended the steps to right and left: and, floating above the inclined plane finely sculptured with dragons and clouds, the Emperor was like unto those spirits which soar to the mountaintops without ever touching the earth.

The entire palace is symbolic. The macrocosm-microcosm analogy is one of the essential themes in ancient Chinese thought. I have never been able to overcome a feeling of keen distaste in reading the Taoist tracts which compare the human organism to the universe. Gazing at The Stream of Golden Waters, duplicate of The Celestial Stream—that is, our Milky Way—I feel the same irritation. Built according to the laws of geomancy, the Violet-Purple City was alleged to enclose heaven and earth—for, living apart from everybody else, the Son of Heaven was not to be excluded from anywhere—it suggests that the world is an intact, sealed whole, that the inventory of its contents is complete, and that the entire business can be reproduced in a pocket-sized model; it reduces the world to the ludicrous dimensions of somebody's private life; it negates the world. In the entire Imperial Palace there is not a single spot from which one can get a glimpse of Peking. The sultans of the Alhambra exploited their people: but glancing from their window, they used at least to look down with affectionate pride at the city and the rich Vega sprawled out at their feet; and, framed between two alabaster colonnettes, the hills of Granada were guests in the palace. The imperial retreat afforded the Son of Heaven not a point of view upon the world but a rampart protecting his august person from outside contagions. It was edified in order to realize an absolute divorce.

The barriers have tumbled. The Forbidden City has become a public place; now everyone strolls freely through its courtyards, sips tea under its porches; Young Pioneers in red neckerchiefs visit the exhibits mounted in its hallways; certain buildings have been turned into palaces of culture, into libraries; in another part of it the government has its seat. Beneath this new life invading it the original meaning of the palace remains unimpaired; I seldom succeeded in forgetting it. But there was one time when, wandering at random, with nothing of old history or myths in my head, I fell in love with some abandoned secondary courtyards gone to weeds or else planted with little dark trees, infinitely deserted and solitary. In one corner dandelions would be growing; the reddish wall capped by gilt tiles and running along an ill-paved court made me think of farms I have seen in Burgundy. Bucolic, divested of all purpose, this too frequently restored palace speaks in the moving language of ruins.

"This monument bears witness to the Chinese people's splendid capacity for work," said the guide whose job is to explain the Temple of Heaven to visitors. But he said it without great conviction. Surely, workers and laborers were men of the people; but like Peking, like the Imperial Palace, this temple was decreed by imperial edict, it did not emanate from the will of the people; the common folk of Peking never shared in the worship celebrated there in honor of the supreme divinity: the Lord on High. Heaven was conceived of in two manners: in its impersonal and cosmic aspect, it was one with the firmament. But it was also allowed the attributes of a Providence: it governed the destiny of mankind, punished and rewarded men's deeds. When envisaged thus a personal character was often ascribed to it and Heaven then received the name of Lord on High or Supreme Ruler; these terms stressed his mightiness as a universal overlord while the word "Heaven" denoted his essence. As Heaven, everybody could adore and pray to him; but only the Emperor had the right to sacrifice to the Lord on High during official ceremonies. The sacrificial mound, as bare and as round as Heaven itself, was always situated in the southern outskirts of the capital. The rites began after midnight and ended before dawn upon dates fixed by the calendar. The ritual scarcely changed in the course of the four thousand years it lasted; the Emperor made offerings to Heaven, asked that the harvest be good and the Empire made to prosper. In early times the ceremony was performed in silence; all that could be heard were the requests and prayers of those officiating. In the year 111 A.D. the best beloved of the Emperor Wu, a musician, induced him to have the gestures and chants accompanied by music; tradition from then on included music. When the Ming dynasty established itself in Peking one of the first tasks the Emperor Yung Lo took upon himself was to erect in the southern suburb the open-air altar and the temples required by the official cult which was subsequently celebrated there every year at the winter solstice until 1916. Under the last of the Manchus the ceremony was enacted in this way: the Emperor sets out from the palace in his official elephant-drawn chariot; accompanied by a train of some two thousand persons including the highest dignitaries of the Empire, the princes, musicians, and retainers, he goes toward the Temple of Heaven. The procession follows the street leading south, passes through the Cheng-yang Gate which is opened for no one but His Majesty, and, two miles further, arrives at the Tien-tan. The Emperor repairs first to the Chai-Kung, or Palace of Abstinence, where by a solitary meditation he prepares himself for the fulfillment of his duties. The ceremony begins when all the officiating priests have taken their respective places. The animals are killed and when the odor of the burnt flesh rises into the air and bears the sacrifice to the gods, the Emperor performs the rite, scrupulously adhering to the indications given him by the masters of ceremony. Worship of the Heaven takes place at midnight. The numerous poles (the thousands of torches and lanterns) surrounding the great altar, the fire shedding a bright light on the marble terraces as well as the rich costumes of the celebrants give an impressive character to this ceremony.* The Emperor knelt upon the second terrace of the open-air altar, at the foot of the steps leading up to the higher terrace, and facing north: he would assume the posture of an

* Cf. S. W. Williams, *The Middle Kingdom* (London, 1883).

inferior so as to acknowledge himself the subject of Heaven. On the uppermost terrace was placed a tablet consecrated to the Supreme Ruler and symbolizing his presence; around and below it other tablets were disposed, these being consecrated to the Emperor's ancestors, to the sun, the moon, the stars, to all those who dwell in heaven. Prayers of thanksgiving were addressed to the celestial divinity for the blessings received from on high in the course of the year just ended. Before the Heaven's tablet was laid a scepter of green jade, emblem of omnipotence. After the holocaust and the libations an officer would read out an invocation, the text of which was then cast, along with pieces of silk and other offerings, into the braziers filled with burning coals. Meanwhile musicians were playing and mimes dancing at the foot of the altars. Inasmuch as these rites occurred on a late December night, the spectators, despite their high lined boots and thick fur wraps, would shiver in the bitter cold.

When in 1912 Yüan Shih-k'ai seized power, he too offered the imperial sacrifice but had a new ritual elaborated and a hymnary of Taoist inspiration devised. He died August 30, 1916, and the sacrifice was not celebrated the following winter. Thus ended the national cult of the Supreme Being on High.

Today, soldiers camp in the millenary cypress groves surrounding the terrace upon which rise the edifices with roofs of green and blue tiles. On the terrace itself—a wide flagged concourse some hundred yards in length—others are having close-order drill: in khaki shorts, they march and about-face to the military music coming from an amplifier. Located on a triple terrace of marble similar to those of the Imperial Palace is the "Hall of Prayer for the Year": a wooden temple, round and sky blue: its circular form is almost unique in China. One gains access to it by any one of eight flights of stairs, each of twenty-seven steps—nine per terrace level. A railing of seventy-two balusters surrounds each terrace. The triple roof is supported inside by three rows of cylindrical columns: three is the symbolical number for *yang*, and heaven is *yang* in contradistinction to the earth which is *yin*. The structure is ninety-nine feet high. Struck by lightning and burned down in 1889, it was reconstructed in an expensive hardwood imported from America. The fact that Chinese monuments indicate no definite age happens to work in this temple's favor: it does not look any older or any newer than the Imperial Palace. I like its perfect proportions, the green-and-blue harmony of its walls and especially the luminous blue of roofs whose shape reminds one of a half-opened parasol dominated by a golden globe.

At the other end of the terrace that bisects the Imperial Way there is another temple, round and blue also, but smaller than the first and covered with just one roof. In this "Hall of Prayer" the Emperor prayed for good harvests; in this sanctuary he meditated preparatory to betaking himself to the Altar of Heaven where he made the sacrifice.

This altar is surrounded by a double red wall crested with dark blue tile. The outer *enceinte* is in the form of a square, like the earth; while the inner, like the sky, is round. It is composed of three circular terraces whereof the lowest is 210 feet in diameter, the next 150 feet, the top one 90 feet. The upper terrace is paved by nine concentric rings of circular slabs, the inmost ring containing nine, the next eighteen, and so on to the last one of eighty-one stones.

I do not know whether the architects who designed this unit had studied the laws of acoustics or whether the mysteries of geomancy are accountable for these lesser prodigies: upon the Imperial Way there is a particular spot where sounds give back a triple echo; another spot where, if you pronounce a few words, your voice returns amplified and vibrant as if coming over a microphone; speak in a whisper as you stand facing a certain point of the circular enclosure and a listener placed diametrically opposite you, a long distance away, will distinctly hear every syllable. These games are played by all the visitors. They are numerous: many Chinese but foreigners also, some of whom are Russians; they are easy to recognize, the men by their Panama hats and the women by their strong figures and exuberantly gay dresses.

The parks surrounding the Imperial Palace—except on the south side where the Red Square extends—play an integral role in Peking life. Created by the emperors, they are carefully kept up today; the pathways are paved, the trees trimmed, the ponds dredged and the fish in them lovingly looked after. Many are the Pekingese who pay the penny fee at the entranceway and go for walks under the age-old arbors. You will see some practicing the ancient Chinese gymnastics in the morning, others rowing out on the lakes or, in wintertime, skating on the ice. They gather in teahouses for green tea with which they chew sunflower or melon seeds; they read the daily papers fastened up on panels; and dance on Saturday night. Nursery children and Pioneer Scouts play on the lawns.

The "Coal Hill"—or, as the Chinese call it, "The Mount of the Numberless Years"—rises, lying on its axis, behind the Palace. Covered with arbors and ancient cypresses, its girth is four thousand yards. At its summit are five wall-less summerhouses: twin rows of columns sustain green and blue roofs. The uppergmost of these kiosks is square, the others are polygonal. They were built between 1522 and 1566, and as best I know this is one of the only spots in Peking with which a precisely dated event is associated: in 1644, defeated by a powerful warlord, Li the Bold, the last of the Ming emperors committed suicide in the "Imperial Storeroom for Hats and Belts," and a faithful eunuch followed him in death. The story has it that toward five in the morning on that fateful day the Palace bell, as usual, tolled the hour of the imperial audience: but nobody appeared. Wherewith the Emperor removed his ceremonial attire, put on a short tunic brocaded with dragons and a purple-and-yellow coat; his left foot was unshod. He ascended the Coal Hill and on the lining of his coat he wrote: "Feeble and of little virtue, I have given offense to Heaven: rebels have seized my capital thanks to the treachery of my ministers. I die, and it is with shame I present myself thus before my ancestors. I take off my imperial hat, my sparse hair falls over my face; may the rebels dismember my body. But may they work no ill against my people." Thereupon he hanged himself.

Li was driven out by the Manchus. Upon a neighboring hill—the "Green Hill" Kublai had raised and planted with rare trees—the first Manchu emperor built the "White Pagoda," or Dagoba, the tallest monument in Peking, the only landmark that can be seen from afar. It is a kind of great tower, made of brick covered with a dazzlingly white plaster; it tapers as it rises and its slender neck is banded by a wide copper collar from which bells are suspended. A sculptured Buddha seems to be guarding an entrance. In one outlying district of Peking, in the middle of a market place, there is another of these stupas, and many more, only on a smaller scale, in the surrounding country. They are imitations of a Tibetan structure the principle of which, legend says, Buddha himself taught to his disciples: having folded his garments into squares, he piled them one upon the other, starting with the biggest square, ending with the smallest; on the top of this pyramid he deposited, inverted, his wooden beggar's bowl and upon that planted his walking staff. Originally, the stupa was in fact a hemispherical dome set upon a terrace and surmounted by a parasol; foundations and crown have acquired a greater and greater importance while the hemisphere has taken on height, lengthening into a cylinder. The Emperor, in order to humiliate the Chinese, chose the most conspicuous site for this exotic edifice and used it as a watchtower from which to keep an eye on his newly conquered subjects. In building the Dagoba he at the same time commemorated the visit of a Tibetan monk and gave friendship guarantees to Tibet, upon which he had designs.

Surrounding the hill dominated by the Dagoba is Lake Pei Hai, "The Sea of the North"; it was also called "The Pond of the Great Secretion" through analogy with a famous lake which had once lain at the edge of the palace of the Emperor Wu* and whose waters, it was said, were "the saliva of Yin and Yang, collected to form a lake." On Lake Pei Hai there are flat-bottomed scows accommodating a dozen persons; boatmen propel them with sculls. I boarded one to go to the other end of the park and see "The Wall of the Genii," its most interesting monument. Just inside the outer portals of temples, as inside the doorways of private houses, there is always a chao p'ing screen which one must walk around to reach the interior. This particular temple was burned during the repression that ensued after the Boxer Rebellion but the screen remained standing. This rectangular wall—the largest, highest, and finest of its kind in Peking—is adorned with painted and glazed terra-cotta bas-reliefs; it is also called "The Wall of the Nine Dragons" since, on both surfaces, nine dragons—in blue, green, yellow, eggplant purple—are gamboling upon the waves, playing with a large ball, the "pearl" which as a symbol was imported from India. The pearl is thought by some to represent the sun

* Of the Han dynasty.

whose hibernation the dragon ends by snatching it from the bosom of the waters; others hold it to be an image of the moon. From the standpoint of their material these ceramics make one think of bathroom decorations; but they have an authentic beauty nevertheless. The dragons' supple bodies swirl and thrash so violently that no part of the frieze seems in repose; the artist has succeeded in rendering their very movement in the sculpture.

Along the lake front runs "The Floating Gallery": a covered walk lined with intricately interwoven wooden railings. There are many similar galleries, and also kiosks and pavilions, in almost every Chinese park. I have pointed out that Chinese architects make plastic use of space; landscape architects like to wed structures with their natural settings. Particularly appealing were the round openings cut in the side of the arborway, apertures through which one sees a framed portion of landscape as though peeking through an enormous spyglass; when one steps back, the reflection in the lake is like that of the arch of a bridge over water; thus doubled, the landscape turns into one of those artificial spectacles the Chinese love to compose out of sky and trees.

Nature and art blend in the rockwork adorning all Chinese gardens; these are stones, to be sure, but they seem to have been fashioned by a sculptor attempting to imitate nature, their role is comparable to the one our statues play; their placement is carefully planned, they are usually mounted on pedestals. Long chapters are given over to rockwork in the *Yuan Yeh*, a treatise on gardening published at the time of the Mings. The more tortuous, the more baroque, the more the rockwork is a maze of bumps and cavities, the better the specimen. Much appreciated were those found in lakes in the South and especially those of Tai-Lu, weirdly wrought by the action of the water. The painter Mi Fei who lived in the twelfth century would bow before one of these marvels and salute it as "my brother," such was his admiration for it.

It is for similar reasons the Chinese are fond of the strangely shaped, extravagantly colored fish bred from the honest and homely carp, the chi yü, eaten everywhere from the north to the south of China. Ordinarily gray, it sometimes has a handsome orange tint: it was perhaps this anomaly that led a Chekiang mandarin of the Sung era to include the carp in his "Animal Emancipation Pond" and later, in the twelfth century, a Sung emperor to put them into the ornamental lakes of his Hangchow palace. Whereupon two varieties developed: one white, the other spotted; this oddity was found amusing; beginning in the sixteenth century, private individuals set to breeding their own chi yü, and instead of aristocratic ponds the fish had to be content with more modest glazed earthenware basins; they became smaller in narrower confines, their shape changed, new varieties appeared; like the rock gardens, these finned monsters in which nature seemed to imitate human extravagances inspired numerous poems; treatises were written on the art of raising them and provoking mutations: between 1848 and 1925 methodical breeding produced a further ten varieties. The Chinese of today remain faithful to this tradition. Twenty-seven new varieties are emerging. There are now seven thousand fish in Pei Hai Park whereas thirty-five years ago the figure had slipped down to a hundred. In great wooden or glazed earthenware basins—preferable, it seems, to glass aquariums—swim samples of the *phoenix* goldfish, marbled gray and reddish brown, the *lion's head, red-head, frog's head, dragon's eye, pearl-scale,* with globular eyes, fantastic shapes, glittering and strange colors: bronze, violet, black, purple, and gold. They may live as long as twenty years. The keeper in charge of them comes from a family that has been raising fish for five centuries. The sanitation measures taken by the regime have left him with a tough problem on his hands: the fish used to be fed a diet of water fleas which formerly swarmed in gutters; they have vanished. Substitutes were tried: the fish pined away. There has been no way out: water fleas are raised especially for them.

I must confess that these gardens arouse little enthusiasm in me. They are not, like English gardens, bits of living nature; nor works of art having their own laws and harmonies, like Italian gardens or French parks; nor again voluptuous open-air bowers, like the gardens of the Generalife in Granada; nor finally quiet retreats, like the garden of a rural vicar. These are would-be microcosms. According to Taoism, with which ancient Chinese thought is saturated, the two essential elements of this world are the streams and mountains respectively representing the arteries of the earth and its bone structure; and the gardens are arranged in keeping with this doctrine. Hills are created artificially; artificial lakes are dug and given the names of seas. Nor are these mountains and seas directly copied from real models; the source for the gardens is the painted landscape—and, in their pictures, the artists would strive to express a Taoist view of the world. The kiosks and pavilions afford multiple perspectives upon this bite-sized world, but from no one angle must the eye be able to take in everything at a single glance: for a panoramic view would reveal too apparently its finitude; only a concerted disorder can suggest a feeling of infinity. That, I say, was the opinion of Chinese landscape architects; it is not mine. For I sense no feeling of infinity here; on the contrary, the gulf is too great between the word and the object it designates, the one makes a mockery of the other: the word "sea" does not make a pond grow in size, but makes it dwindle. By dint of pretending to be other than it is, the garden dissipates itself into symbols, loses its reality, and one ends up seeing nothing in it at all.

The Chinese however did love nature and its untamed aspects which the West did not begin to admire until the eighteenth century; in solitary mountains, beside remote lakes sages have always sought refuge from the conformism of society; poets and painters celebrated places that were unmarked by man. But whereas the Taoist hermit sincerely wished to forget his fellow creatures and himself in the embrace of the cosmos, the owner of a piece of real estate who had experts build him a park strove to conciliate a liking for the infinite with the advantages of his position; instead of giving himself up to nature he undertook to make it his property; he mistakenly enclosed nonhuman grandeur within domestic confines where rockery was the substitute for mountains; he calculated thus to assure himself the ecstasies of contemplation without taking leave of his easy circumstances or his civilized ego.

To tell the truth, I was hardly seduced by what I was able to glimpse in Peking of old Chinese civilization; and I honestly wondered how the young China is going to be able to adhere to her past to any great extent. The parks with their ponds and verdure are annexed to the present-day world and the Pekingese are perfectly willing—and right—to enjoy them. But the chill, the aloofness I sensed in the Palace and the Temple of Heaven, despite their evident beauty, probably reflect a comparable quality I notice in the Chinese themselves. They restore their old edifices, they maintain and visit them conscientiously, they put them to practical use; but how can their hearts be touched by them? Even though the architectural style of these monuments has a popular origin, they express nothing of the Chinese people, simply the ambition of the emperors, their sovereign isolation, and the oppression with which they taxed their subjects.

The environs of Peking are not lacking in charm. Westward the plain gives way to wooded heights concealing many an ancient building. From time to time, behind a hedge, on the edge of a field, one makes out a little forlorn stupa overgrown with moss. Here and there old pagodas subside into ruins. On hilltops, in valleys weeds have invaded old and more or less dilapidated temples. Triumphal arches of a sort, called pai lou, commemorate the famous among the deceased, or just the rich; constructed either of wood or stone, they have three or five openings, the columns are sculptured, the lintels decorated by friezes, and they are coped by glazed tile.

It is out here, at the foot of the western hills, that Emperor K'ang-hsi built a park which he called "The Paradise of Undying Springtime"; his successor, Yung Chêng, had another palace raised near by; and Ch'ien Lung, the great builder, completed their work by uniting the two residences and by constructing further buildings. He asked Western missionaries and accomplished painters to decorate their walls. In 1860 the Chinese, revolting against "the unequal treaties," tortured French and English truce representatives in the Summer Palace enclosure; by way of reprisal, English soldiers burned it to the ground. Tzu Hsi decided to rebuild it: this was the project upon which she spent money earmarked for the Chinese Navy, thereby contributing to its defeat in the Sino-Japanese War of 1894.

I derived little pleasure from visiting this Trianon which "the Old Buddha" had made her favorite residence. It of course features man-made hills and an artificial lake in imitation of the famous "Lake of the West" at Hangchow; there is even, in the middle of it, an artificial island whose foundation is of marble and which is connected to land by a marble footbridge of seventeen arches; this bridge's lines are delightful, so also are those of the graceful camel-back bridge whose single arch spans the canal. Facing opposite the island, a two-story pavilion raised upon a marble substructure in the form of a junk pokes out beyond the water's edge: it is exceedingly ugly. Covered galleries circle the lake. On the flanks of hills are pagodas and summerhouses. The one monument belonging to the style of the period—having been built of stone and brick, it escaped burning—is the Temple of the Thousand Buddhas, on the brow of the highest hill. Its style is Sino-Hindu. Beneath the glazed-tile roof all four of the yellow brick walls are studded with little niches: their glazed interiors are green, each one houses a little Buddha about eight inches high of yellow china.

The Empress' apartments lack the least charm; they are crammed with dreadful curios: screens covered with brocaded bird feathers, hulking porcelain vases, fussily intricate lacquerware, overelaborate knickknacks. I notice, encrusted in the backs of certain chairs, stones whose marbled veins suggest scenes of cloud-wrapped mountains: this natural stone imitating an artificial imitation of nature used to be particularly pleasing to the Chinese. In one of the courtyards there is an open-air theater where companies of eunuchs put on plays: I have no desire to dally in these latitudes; this ponderous aristocratic gloom routs me.

Fortunately, it is Sunday. Lustily singing scouts are climbing the hills; families are picnicking under the arbors or are lunching at tables in the outdoor restaurants on the shores of the lake; some lads are playing guitars; lots of people are out on the water in big squarish boats, the decks sheltered by an awning; others have gone rowing. In the middle of the lake I see a little boat: in it a young woman is lying down peacefully asleep while two little youngsters are frisking about and playing with the oars. Our boatmen cups his hands. "Hey!" he calls. "Look out for those kids!" The woman rubs her eyes, she smiles, picks up the oars; shows the children how they work: all three have a radiant look. Is there anything more depressing than a Paris public garden of a Sunday? Yowlings, nagging, tears, grumpiness; children and parents lug their discontent out for an airing and back. In Peking leisure hours truly have the air of a holiday: these people all seem to have a talent for happiness. Seeing them lays the ghost of the old imperial civilization whose pleasures called for castration, bound feet, child slaves. A Chinese one day said to Robert Payne that the worst perversions had been encouraged by the Japanese, the manchus, and also, he added, "by the fondness we have for everything that is complicated."* The "age of complication" seems, thank heaven, to have passed; there is also a Chinese tradition of simplicity and it is with it that these people on a Sunday outing, content with sunshine and greenness, a little music, food and friendship, join hands.

L—— and T——, two French people, took me to the southern district to see that sort of permanent carnival known as The Bridge of Heaven, Tien Ch'iao. Before the Liberation you elbowed your way through a throng of prostitutes, thieves, and beggars; the peddlers paid protection to gangsters. There is a scene in *The Pit of the Bearded Dragon* showing one of these racketeers tearing through the terrified crowd with the arrogance of an Al Capone except that he is not doing sixty in a sedan with bulletproof windows but perhaps twenty in a pedicab and his strong-arm boys escort him on bicycles. In 1949 these big characters were rounded up and put on public trial right in Tien Ch'iao itself.

No more thieves, no more prostitutes, no more vagrant scoundrels; people go for family walks there. Tumblers, jugglers, storytellers attract curious passers-by, the enormous pots of food, the teeming crowds remind one of the Djelma el Fna Square in Marrakech and of medieval fairs. But there too the Middle Ages have been tidied up. No trash on the ground, no stench, neither grinding poverty nor riot in the little dirt streets which meet at right angles; standing behind their trays, merchants sell old shoes, bits of hardware, cakes of soap, shoelaces. The open-air restaurants are rudimentary: one long table, benches, a counter covered with things to eat, a stove; however, the wooden table is well scrubbed, the pots look scoured, they serve appetizing dishes, pleasant in appearance and aroma. The people who come and go without uproar or jostling glance at us in a friendly way. "New shoes!" exclaims a youngster; "Oh, look! Russians!"

* *Journey to Red China.* I quote from memory.

We enter one booth where a girl is doing something with coins and a whirling umbrella; then she juggles some plates in the air. In another there are three musicians sitting on a stage playing on Chinese violins a traditional tune with an insistent rhythm; standing in front of them are two women, each wielding in one hand a slender baton to beat time, in the other holding two pieces of bamboo which they use somewhat like castanets; the first narrates, the second personifies the characters in the story.

There are also numerous theaters at Tien Ch'iao. We take seats in one of them; it is a kind of shed, there are rows of very narrow benches with backs upon which are strips of wood for setting the cups of tea that a little boy keeps filling throughout the performance; it used to be this way in all Chinese theaters before they were westernized. A classical opera is being staged. The lack of means induces a respect for ancient tradition one no longer finds in the elegant theaters: here the changing of props, shifting of furniture—indicating a change of scene—goes before the eyes of the spectators; whenever a character changes costume the other actors form a screen in front of him to shield him from the audience; the curtain never goes up or down, there are no wings. All the roles are filled by boys of fifteen or sixteen, extremely inexperienced and not very good when it comes to assuming a deep voice or keeping a beard from falling off. I was more able here than anywhere else to sense how much of a popular sport Chinese opera is: in the workers' quarters, in the villages, in the family circle itself, it is a game that can be played without expert actors and at a minimum of expense. I should however add that, even on this barren stage, the costumes were amazingly lavish and the style of the actors, the measure, the rhythm of their speech and gesture and that of the music, faultless.

Admission price to all these booths and sheds amounts to a fraction of a cent and the public comes from very modest walks of life; few women, almost none; they are equally rare in the restaurants; some stroll with their husbands and children in the alleyways, cast passing glances at goods displayed for sale but seldom stop. In Peking the woman is still essentially a housewife and she stays at home.

It seems that The Bridge of Heaven such as it is today is

destined to disappear. In its place a cultural park—like Moscow's Gorki Park—will be built. A large theater has already gone up on the edge of the avenue bordering Tien Ch'iao. It is a pity. At nightfall neon butterflies were twinkling on the façades of the little theaters, oil lamps shining above the stalls while saber-play flashed and laughing voices blended round the storytellers; unexpected encounters with light and sound, strolling crowds: the picturesque sat enthroned. For my part I hope that the Pekingese, so judicious and reasonable, will grant it these several *fangs* and that their diversions won't become too stringently organized.

The Chinese intellectuals we met and also our French friends often invited us out to restaurants. Whether plain or luxurious, these eating places were always composed of private dining rooms or isolated booths. No decoration: the accessories indicating in Paris or San Francisco that such-and-such a restaurant is Chinese are unnecessary in Peking. There was usually no scarcity of clients. Chinese like eating out. They take the whole family to the restaurant or go there in groups. Someone orders a bowl of vermicelli, two others vegetables with a little meat or fish, a fourth some soup; each person serves himself from the main dishes and gets a complete meal for a small share of the bill.

At table the Chinese, like the French, readily discuss food; it is also a convenient topic when strangers find themselves side by side and the conversation lags. I was thus amply informed about Chinese cooking. In Peking, the basic foodstuff is wheat; it is consumed in the form of steam-cooked rolls, ravioli, fritters, flaky pastry, and especially, vermicelli, the Chinese having invented the pastes Marco Polo took back with him to Italy. South China feeds basically on rice. The variety of culinary styles based on these elements is considerable. Szechwan appreciates red pepper, other provinces prefer pimento, vinegar, or spices; the Cantonese sweeten almost all their dishes. But whatever regional differences there may be, all of China is firmly united in this: everything that can possibly be eaten, is eaten. Livestock raising and dairy farming being virtually nonexistent, the Chinese have never been able to develop a taste for dairy products and meat—indeed, they have a distaste for them, finding that, owing to their diets, Westerners have a peculiar odor.* But save for raw oysters all their own country's flora and fauna strike them as eligible to be eaten. The Cantonese are among those having a reputation for consuming dogs, cats, rats, snakes. And in time of famine the peasants used to try to appease their hunger by swallowing a certain kind of earth, most erroneously termed "earth of mercy." "Oh, yes," the poet Ai Ts'ing told me one evening at table, "we eat everything: everything on four legs except the table; and except for our friends and relations, everything on two." Lin Yutang also wrote: "We eat everything on earth that is edible; crabs by way of preference, the bark of trees when we must." Therein lies the key to Chinese cooking: a people hounded by starvation learned to put everything the human stomach can digest into the pot and upon the plate; a people condemned to the monotony of millet, vermicelli, or rice has contrived to give subtle flavors to these thin broths. Starting from there the wealthy Chinese interested in refinements have elaborated an entire art.

What characterizes Chinese gastronomy, whose diversity is extreme, is that no matter what it is the ingredient's origin is cunningly disguised; what you eat is neither animal nor vegetable but seems to be a pure product of human industry. The meat is boned and chopped up into tiny morsels; all food is ready for consumption, you never have to battle against it with knife and fork. The Chinese are proud of their culinary tradition; it is one of the aspects of their past they are most eager to perpetuate.

* Pearl Buck relates (in *My Several Worlds*) that she felt much the same way: back again in America, she had trouble getting accustomed to the smell of her compatriots.

# 2. THE PEASANTS

The history of China is that of her peasantry. Although bordered east and south by the ocean, China, unlike the lands around the Mediterranean Basin, never developed a great maritime civilization. Her economy has been a continental country's: for four thousand years virtually the only resource she has exploited has been her soil. Between 2000 and 1500 B.C. agrarian populations settled in the great fertile alluvial plain watered by the Yellow River. They cleared the land, cultivated it, defended it against the nomadic hunters on its edge; in the course of the centuries they cleared and colonized the immense expanse of territory swinging from Manchuria to Kwangtung, which the Emperor Shih Huang Ti was the first to unify a hundred years before Christ. This area divides itself into three distinct regions. North of the Yangtze stretch alluvial plains and loess plateaus where the climate is that of the steppes; wheat, millet, kaoliang, soybean are grown here, and here are found small numbers of draft animals: horses and mules. South of the river the climate is subtropical; the soil produces tea and cotton; mulberry trees are cultivated; apart from a few water buffalo there are no draft animals. Szechwan to the west is a rich basin where the reddish soil is farmed in terraces; shut in by mountains, the region's only link with the rest of China is the Yangtze. The mountains have been bare of trees since ancient times and for centuries the peasants tore up whatever bush or scrub growth was able to take root: the forest resources of the country are practically nil. The settled farmers left livestock raising to the nomads who had been driven into the highlands: China proper has no pasture lands. The Occidental traveler who flies over it in an airplane or who crosses it by train is amazed to discover neither prairies nor wooded country: nothing but kaoliang, rice, and countless little backyard vegetable plots.

The fields are intensively exploited by methods similar to those used in market gardening, and their individual area is not much greater than a tennis court. Only a small fraction—about 17 per cent—of the country is presently arable. In fact, except in Szechwan, only the plains and valleys are cultivated; the peasants have crowded into them and they have become artificially overpopulated. The average density of population is 934 per square mile of arable land, and climbs to over 3,000 in southern China. In past centuries the inhabitants were less numerous but the territory was not completely settled; concentration in these lands has always been excessive and that is why, despite the fertility of his fields, the Chinese peasant has never known anything but an extremely low standard of living. Another reason for his eternal impoverishment has been the inevitable and periodic recurrence of natural catastrophes: floods and droughts. There being no trees to hold it, the loess of the hill country and peneplains is swept down by rains, chokes rivers, raises their beds; midway along their course, silt deposits will be so deep that rivers will rise to a height of from ten to thirty-three feet above the adjoining plain; further downstream, mud forms veritable dams and perforce floods result. In rainy years the countryside is submerged; and then there are whole years without a drop of rain. The centuries have been a tale of successive famines in which the peasants perished by the million.

The economic unbalance due to overpopulation and to the chronic short supply of food explains why very early in China men began to entertain thoughts of regulating agriculture and of land reform. In her early history the country was a feudal society;* barons owned the land and extorted heavy taxes and tributes in kind or *corvée* from the peasants, leaving them scarcely the where-

* Later there was born the idea of an ancient empire which had preceded the feudalism—this Golden Age is purely mythical.

withal to struggle through from one day to the next: it was impossible for them to provide against emergency by storing grain from year to year. Feudalism could work, and did work, in other countries where the conditions of production were stable; in China the fearful misery to which natural disasters reduced the peasants brought about the ruin of kingdoms. The early princes who, not content to wage war over the length and breadth of the land, also nourished political ambitions, realized that some economic organization was indispensable, China not having that margin of prosperity which would permit a systemless cultivation of her resources. And so it was that about 350 B.C. the sovereign of the kingdom of T'sin—what is now Shensi—doled out land to the farmers, subjecting them to a tax proportional to the area of their grants. When Shih Huang Ti had achieved the revolution that laid feudalism low and unified the Empire, he extended this reform to embrace all of China. Many were his successors who carried on the program of replacing laissez faire with a planned economy.

Unhappily, this planning was itself short-range. The emperors were after quick profits. They made no attempt to guarantee the peasant class the kind of security and prosperity which are conducive to stabilization and increase of production; the emperors' concerns were purely monetary; the idea was to deprive real-estate owners of the profits yielded by agriculture, and to monopolize it themselves. Moreover the ruler was unable effectively to enforce his laws throughout an empire as vast as this; the very men who were delegated the task of seeing to their execution were those who had the most to gain from violating them, since imperial officers were also property owners. For two thousand years the land was the prize fought over in the insoluble conflict between government and propertied bureaucrats: the situation of the peasants remained at all times tragically precarious.

In the reign of Shih Huang Ti they received lands, but famines soon drove them to sell their holdings and then themselves and their families too as slaves. Two centuries after the land reform "one saw the fields of the rich standing in rows of a hundred and a thousand, whilst unto the poor was lacking earth enough to plant a needle." The usurper Wang Mang in 9 A.D. again meted out plots to the poor, allotting some twelve acres per family of eight; he declared the state sole proprietor; officials were instructed to regulate the market, fix prices, store unsold produce, grant loans at 3 per cent monthly interest. The tax was based upon tithes attaching to the yield. But the reform was not wrought for the improvement of the peasants' lot: it was a device aimed against the new feudality and to profit the government. After having crippled nobility and commerce, the state monopolies bore down on the farmers who were left helpless in the face of droughts and floods; so terrible was the ensuing famine that men became cannibals. They rose en masse and "The Red Eyebrows" brought Wang Mang's reign to an end.

Ownership of the land theoretically remained with the state; every adult peasant was accorded seven and one-half to fifteen acres upon a life-tenure basis, and outright possession of four acres transmissible to his heirs. At his death the concession was reabsorbed into the communal holdings. Wang had been careful to forbid all purchase and sale of terrain as well as of slaves. But the officials arrogated to themselves the privilege of acquiring lands and of handing them on to their descendants; crushed by taxation and debt, starving, law or no law, the peasants sold their fields anew, becoming serfs to all intents and purposes; and once again the land reverted into latifundia, the gigantic estates: in the middle of the eighth century 5 per cent of the population owned it all. A writer of the Sung period, Su Hsün, said in the eleventh century:

> The soil has ceased to belong to those who till it, and they who have the owning thereof toil not in the fields. Of their yield the landlord takes one half; for every ten farmers there numbers but one proprietor and thus it is that, daily laying his share aside, he fattens in prosperity whilst the others, exhausting theirs in order to keep every day alive, sink into poverty and hunger. And there is naught they can do.

Wang An-shih endeavored to modify the situation. But he too seems to have aimed only at swelling the state's revenues without worrying about the fate of agriculture. He left the latifundia alone; he merely altered the system of collecting taxes: the farmer now paid them in produce instead of in labor; and Wang revised the old assessment system. He created a state loan scheme, but the rate of interest was 20 per cent, and since, in order to enrich the treasury, the peasants were pressured into going into debt, their misery only became greater.

The Chins and then the Mongols carved themselves vast dependencies by expropriating any number of Chinese; in compensation they too lent money to the population, but these were onerous loans, in actuality constituting a new form of extortion. Under the Mings the latifundia extended their grip. After the Manchus took power they restored a part of the domains of the imperial house to the state, confiscated the great holdings, and yet another time these were parceled out to the peasants; a farmer who had for several generations been cultivating a plot of ground was declared its owner. The land was cut up into hardly practicable bits but the peasants' circumstances temporarily improved.

The Manchus thrown out, a victorious bourgeoisie had in its turn to confront the agrarian problem; but being for the most part made up of property owners it was not willing to contemplate a reform. Starting in 1927 the Kuomintang meticulously quashed every peasant movement. Not only did Chiang Kai-shek allow rélatively extensive domains to develop at the expense of the small owners, but he put the rural districts under the legal jurisdiction of the great landlords and to them turned over the job of levying and collecting taxes. A new feudal class emerged. These gentlemen were not of the stature of the Hindu zamindars, the majority of them were very small landowners with holdings usually not exceeding a hundred mus,* that is to say, some sixteen or seventeen acres which, in a country like France, is considered less than a medium-sized holding.† But the Kuomintang's "moderately well-off" peasant possessed no more than six to twelve mus, the poor peasant less than an acre, and there existed a vast agrarian proletariat lacking "earth enough to plant a needle." "Rich" was the word designating the peasant who owned over a dozen mus—above two acres—and cultivated some part of it himself. But as for the gentry, they never put hand to spade or plow; and some were absentee landlords. They rented their holdings to sharecroppers for 50 to 60 per cent of the yield; in bad years—which were not occasional but frequent—the peasants were obliged to go to the big proprietors

* A mu equals one-sixth of an acre.

† But a French holding often includes some woodland, pasture land, fallow ground. Every square inch of a Chinese holding is cultivated to the hilt.

and borrow the grain necessary for their sustenance and sowing; the interest rates were exhorbitant; the farmer staggered under rent and debt, was sometimes forced to surrender as much as 90 per cent of his harvest. When the crop was good, the farmer's benefit was slight; the deficiency of the market in foodstuffs—due in part to the constant disorganization of transport—and the instability of currency worked, in time of plenty, a swift collapse of selling prices—which was not, however, paralleled by any decrease in the prices paid by the consumer. The prisoner of a vicious, infernal circle, no matter what happened, the small peasant was doomed to misery. His fields, his life itself were at the mercy of the landed proprietor who, doubling as tax collector, enjoyed virtually unlimited authority. The meanness of his condition rendered this local despot's tyranny all the harsher. With his penny grubber's avarice he was wont to try to pick the bone clean, that often led to "blood crimes" in which big landowners did not directly dirty their hands. Tradition had once given Chinese landowner-bureaucrats the power of life and death over their tenants. The Yüan code prescribed one hundred and seven blows of a staff for the proprietor who beat a farmer to death; Ming legislation repealed this law. The Manchus re-established it and in theory all murder was outlawed under the Kuomintang; in practice local tyrants did just about what they pleased, the peasants' situation being one of practical impotence.

This economic system was buttressed by a social structure and a body of religious belief calculated to be of mutual support to one another. Like all agrarian societies, this one was founded on the patriarchal family. The inhabitants of a village belonged to a single clan reputed to descend from a common ancestor; the clan was divided into family units; but these were indivisible, each being attached to a plot of ground that each collectively owned and worked. Each family had a self-contained economy, producing everything it needed; occasionally families would help one another, lend a hand in bringing in the harvest; but between one family and the next, between village and village there was virtually no intercourse. The system was autarkical. What was peculiar to China was that institutions reinforced the cohesion of the producer group in such a way that the individual was absolutely subjugated to it. Religion sanctified this organization; all agrarian societies have honored gods of the hearth but Confucianism refined this worship into a minute and inflexible system whose intention was to preserve the feudal structure of the family. It was, as with peasants the world over, accompanied by animistic beliefs. These found expression in the practice of divination and magic, in taboos, in customs which impregnated every least detail of the peasant's everyday life. When his woes became unendurable he would sometimes revolt, and then he would turn his superstitious faith against the established order; but these outbreaks of violence could not affect the society's economic bases. The system maintained itself intact, unalterable, for centuries; the religion emanating from it consolidated it by imposing upon the peasants an unconditional respect for long-standing traditions.

These not only blocked social progress, they daily contributed to aggravate the poverty of the peasants in binding them by irrational and often fatal rules. For example, geomancy forbade digging a well to the east of a village, installing a gate in the southern wall, running irrigation channels in a straight line. Custom called for absurdly expensive ceremonies. Mourning clothes of white hempen material are useless in the fields. Marriage ceremonies entailed such an outlay that a Honan proverb observed: "Take a wife and you throw away a chance to buy an ox." Most serious of all, the peasants' "magic" mentality made them indifferent to the most elementary dictates of hygiene. Many an observer has been dumfounded by the filth of Chinese villages. "Under the trees, the villages are overcrowded," writes Pearl Buck, "the flies swarm, garbage rots in the sun. The children there are dirty and bedraggled."* "It being the primary fertilizer used on the farm, human excrements are preserved in half-exposed pits behind the house," reports Ksiou Tong-Fei.† "Along the southern bank of the river the road is bordered by these pits. The government has asked the peasants to discontinue their use, but nothing has been done." Instead of outdoor pits, tubs were often placed inside the house, right in the middle of the room where the family lived. At Phenix,‡ a village in the South situated on the river of the same name, the

* From *My Several Worlds.*

† These passages are from a thesis published in 1938 in France.

‡ Cf. the study of the American sociologist D. H. Kulp, *Country Life in South China. The Sociology of Familism. Vol. I: Phenix Village, Kwangtung, China* (New York, 1925), from which the quotations following are drawn.

sanitary conditions were abominable. "Even in the better houses one can find piles of rotted refuse, pools of stagnant water, uncovered buckets of night soil, geese covering the courts and walks with their excreta; . . . The odor of animal manure pervades the courts and the surrounding rooms in such homes. . . .

"From the courts of each great house are built drains to carry off the rain water as it falls from the inner roofs. But they are practically useless. They are constructed according to the demands of necromancy; they are run in crooked and zig-zag courses. They cannot be cleaned and so soon choke up and keep the drainage in the courts. Around all the houses, particularly in the old and more congested part of the village, there are piles of refuse in the streets and alleys. These are attacked by the wandering pigs and rooted into the mud and water of adjacent pools. During the rainy season these places breed flies and seldom dry up. . . .

"Some of the finer and better houses have their private wells. But even though these are capped with stone, they are not lined to prevent the seepage into them of befouled surface drainage. Some of the village women draw their water from Phenix River just where others may be washing clothes or the toilet buckets." The frequent floods would bring on all kinds of diseases: mosquitoes spread malaria, microorganisms carried in the water brought on dysentery and grave liver infections. In Phenix the walls of the houses were damp and their inhabitants suffered from rheumatism. "Yet one can readily detect the yellow lines in the rooms of village houses and on the walls of the exteriors that indicate the high water marks of floods. . . . Any close observer is sure to notice the yellow mud that tints the beautiful blackwood carved furniture." In addition, there were lepers and numerous cases of tuberculosis due to malnutrition. The crops were ravaged one year by floods and the next by drought, and as a result half the villagers lived under the constant threat of starvation: of Phenix' 650 inhabitants 18 per cent could be classified as well to do, 31 per cent as belonging to a middle category, 51 per cent as poor. "The 'poor' live from hand to mouth, at the mercy of nature and the goodwill of their kin. They depend largely upon the aid granted them by the village leaders from the income of the public property . . ." Kulp concluded that the village was living below the subsistence level: "Over half of the familist groups are thus compelled to carry on incessantly the relentless struggle for existence and succeed mainly by virtue of the ideals and organization of the familist system that really bears them along on a tide of mutual aid." He further reports that children were betrothed between the ages of eight and ten, married between sixteen and eighteen. Little girls were left more or less to die of hunger; many of them were sold as slaves. Widows were prohibited from remarrying. Poverty was worsened by the enormous waste necessitated by wedding and other religious ceremonies. And despite it all the peasants had a quite remarkably high level of intelligence; they had an innately developed artistic sense. A more rational organization, Kulp notes, would suffice to see a considerable betterment in living conditions. This final observation is interesting; it helps one to understand how the new regime, even before inaugurating improved agricultural techniques, was able to increase production and boost the standard of living of the peasants: it has organized them.

Lenin pointed out that in the Eastern countries, where large property has not a capitalist but feudal character, the peasants' struggle, directed against a retrograde stage of society, must be considered progressive. One of his most important and most novel theses was the implicit alliance of the revolutionary proletariat with the poor peasants. Mao Tse-tung realized that in the case of China one had to go further yet; Mao's line of thinking, namely that the Chinese peasantry must become the principal force and bulwark of the revolution, won out in 1927 against the opposition of Ch'ên Tu-hsiu. Agrarian reform was simultaneously the first objective aimed at by the Chinese Communists and the instrument they employed to guarantee their victory. In the liberated regions, the Red Army won over the peasants by distributing land to them. The reform was interrupted in 1935 in order to incite the big proprietors to join the front of resistance against the Japanese: the Communists confined themselves to reducing "the rent" and bailing farmers out of debt. Confiscation was resumed in 1946, and in 1947 a National Agrarian Conference elaborated the bill that was enacted as law on June 28, 1950. Landowners who exploited their holdings exclusively through rent-paying intermediaries were expropriated; the land and chattels belonging to temples, monasteries, churches, missionary schools were requisitioned.

Rich peasants were allowed to keep that much of the soil they themselves had personally worked; the rest was removed from their possession. The fields of the middle-class peasant were not touched. Confiscated land was apportioned to poor peasant and landless agricultural laborer families at the rate of three mus per person, including women and young children. They also received shares of the farming implements, beasts of burden, furniture, buildings which had formerly belonged to the landowners.

This reform was carried out with a minimum of violence; only those owners who had a "blood debt" to pay were executed* or sentenced to life imprisonment. Beyond that group no one has been radically despoiled: landowners not convicted of any crime were able to remain in the village and received a share equivalent in size to that of a poor peasant.† On the other hand, the reform was not aimed at establishing absolute equality among all the peasants: its main concern was with productivity. Rich and middle-class peasants retained bigger plots than those turned over to the poor. In order to insure the social stability vital to production, the reform was carried out on a definitive basis: families which have since then grown or dwindled have not had their individual lots augmented or diminished.

The reform was completed by August of 1952: 115,000,000 acres were distributed; about 300,000,000 peasants—that is, 77 per cent of the total farming population—benefited from it. The law affected everyone but national minority groups.

One of the most interesting things about the reform is the use the leaders made of it as a means for awakening class consciousness in the peasants. The Communist militants were under instructions not to take into their own hands the matter of eliminating the landowners but to persuade the peasants to do it for themselves. The object was to give them a sense of their own strength. Why? In order that they cease fearing a return of the old regime; in order that the old regime's grip upon their outlook and attitudes be broken. For, as it turned out, that was precisely it: they were still afraid. Inured to passive resignation—all the while hating their masters they also respected them—their dread, bent inward, took

* The number was about 5,000.

† Some served sentences of 3 to 5 years and then took possession of their shares.

the form of guilt feelings; they feared the wrath of heaven: after the land reform there were certain peasants who went on secretly paying rent to their one-time landlord.

In her novel *The Sun Shines Over the Sangkan River*, Ting-ling has brought this aspect of the problem into focus:

> Yumin* knew the people hoped to get land but were unwilling to take any initiative. They still had their doubts. Unless the old powers were overthrown, they were afraid to show enthusiasm. There were several racketeers in the village, and to suppress them thoroughly would not be easy. That spring they had chosen a comparatively weak opponent to try: Landlord Hou, a bed-ridden old man. The cadres felt nobody ought to be afraid of him, but to their surprise only a few enthusiasts got worked up and shook their fists. Members of the peasants' association in the crowd shouted: "Speak up! Just one word!" Then people shook their fists and shouted with them, but at the same time looked furtively to where Schemer Chien† was squatting at the back. Hou was fined a hundred piculs of grain, payable in terms of seven acres of his land which was divided among some score of families. Some people were pleased, others were afraid after the land was taken and dared not even walk past Landlord Hou's gate, while Tenant Hou‡ secretly returned the land thus received . . . Schemer Chien was an army dependent and presumably should not be tried, or even if he deserved trial, he could not possibly be held guilty enough for a death sentence—such, very naturally, was Yumin's view based on long experience. That spring the higher authorities had corrected a wrong trend in land reform. A number of landlords whom the people wanted to execute had been sent to the county court. After being imprisoned for two months they were sent back for retrial with the explanation that the policy was to be lenient, because the previous year it had been implemented too radically. The people were still afraid there might be a change in the political situation. They felt that if a man were tried it must be for his life, lest he take vengeance in the future. Accordingly people like Schemer Chien, under existing conditions, presented quite a problem.§

An important landowner, Li, has fled from the village; the peasants go to his house to demand the property deeds from his

* One of the peasant cadres.

† A local tyrant.

‡ A poor relative of the landlord.

§ *The Sun Shines over the Sangkan River*, Foreign Languages Press, Peking, 1954, pp. 167-168.

wife. But mixed fear and respect halt them; and they come away empty-handed:

> The few tenants stood in the empty courtyard exchanging glances, not knowing what to say. The bamboo curtain of the north room rattled and Mrs. Li came out. She was wearing a blue cotton jacket and trousers, her hair was uncombed, hanging limply. Red rims round her eyes, caused by crying, were conspicuous on her plump white face. In her arms she was carrying a red lacquered box. One of the tenants called out: "Mrs. Li!"
>
> She hurried down the steps to kneel by the side of a porcelain tub holding an evergreen shrub, tears streaming down her face. "Masters," she said, sobbing, "please be kind to us and have pity on a poor woman and children. This is my husband's . . . please take it, it's a hundred and thirty-six mu and a half of land altogether and one house. You all know that quite well, good friends and neighbors. My husband's no good, the children and I can't depend on him. Now we're counting on you who've all been our friends for so many years. We're feudalistic landlords and ought to have our land divided. I've nothing to say against that. Only please, masters, remember I'm only a woman, and have pity on the children. I'll kowtow to you! . . ." Then she kowtowed to them all repeatedly and took up the box again, her face streaming with tears. Lanying also knelt at her side, while the two younger children standing among the crowd started howling.
>
> All the tenants who had entered so boldly seemed struck dumb at the sight of the woman kneeling before them. They thought how she had been born into a rich family and never known hardship, and they began to remember her little acts of charity, until some of them pitied her present plight. No one moved to take the box. They forgot what they had come for . . .*

The cadres gradually manage to bolster the peasants' courage. Schemer Chien is finally arrested and made to face his accusers.

> Then three or four militiamen took Schemer Chien up to the platform. He was wearing a lined gown of gray silk and white trousers, his hands tied behind him. His head was slightly lowered, and his small beady eyes were screwed up, searching the crowd. Those reptilian eyes of his which used to strike fear into people's hearts still cast a blight and quelled many of those present. His pointed mustaches made him look more sinister. Nobody said a word . . .
>
> For thousands of years the local despots had had power. They had

* *Ibid.*, pp. 163-164.

oppressed generation after generation of peasants, and the peasants had bowed their necks under their yoke. Now abruptly they were confronted with this power standing before them with bound hands, and they felt bewildered, at a loss. Some who were particularly intimidated by his malevolent look recalled the days when they could only submit, and now, exposed to this blast, wavered again. So for the time being they were silent.

All this time Schemer Chien, standing on the stage gnawing his lips, was glancing around, wanting to quell these yokels, unwilling to admit defeat. For a moment he really had the mastery. He and his many years of power had become so firmly established in the village it was difficult for anyone to dislodge him. The peasants hated him, and had just been cursing him; but now that he stood before them they held their breath and faltered. It was like the pause before two gamecocks start fighting, each estimating the other's strength. The longer the silence lasted, the greater Chien's power became, until it looked as if he were going to win.

At this point a man suddenly leaped out from the crowd. He had thick eyebrows and sparkling eyes. Rushing up to Schemer Chien he cursed him: "You murderer! You trampled our village under your feet! You killed people from behind the scenes for money. Today we're going to settle all old scores, and do a thorough job of it. Do you hear that? Do you still want to frighten people? It's no use! There's no place for you to stand on this stage! Kneel down! Kneel to all the villagers!" He pushed Chien hard, while the crowd echoed: "Kneel down! Kneel down!" The militiamen forced him to kneel down properly.

Then the rage of the masses flared up, they tasted power and stirred indignantly. A child's voice was heard: "Put on the hat! Make him wear the hat!"

Young Kuo jumped forward and asked: "Who'll put it on? Whoever'll put it on, come up here!"

While the crowd was shouting, "Make him wear the hat! Put on the hat!" a boy of thirteen or fourteen jumped up, lifted the hat and set it on Schemer Chien's head, at the same time spitting at him and cursing: "Here you are, Chien!" Then he jumped down amid laughter.

By now Chien had lowered his head completely, his malevolent eyes could no longer sweep their faces. The tall paper hat made him look like a clown. Bent basely from the waist, screwing up his eyes, he had lost all his power, had become the people's prisoner, a criminal against the masses.*

* *Ibid.*, pp. 285, 286-287.

From there on the peasants' anger mounts. Chien is insulted, beaten, and owes his life solely to the intervention of the militia. His lands are confiscated but he himself is given leave to take refuge with his son, a Red Army soldier.

Such episodes did actually occur in all the villages of China; the anti-Communists interpret the public trials as due to the provocations of the cadres, against the true will of the peasants. Ting-ling's novel indicates that while this will was in fact paralyzed by the deadening weight and appalling memories of the past, it did nevertheless exist, deep-seated, passionate, despairing; and that the role of the cadres was to aid the peasants in realizing their desires by freeing them from fear and hypnosis.

A similar situation appears in Chou Li-po's novel, *The Hurricane.** Cadres are sent to a village to expedite the reform; they call a meeting, everyone comes to it, old and young alike. One of the activists, Liu Sheng, gets up on a table and says:

"We want to rise up together and stand on our own feet. Down with the potbellies! We poor men must take the power into our own hands and arm ourselves." He carried his speech a little further and then concluded it with a question:

"Do you agree to tackle the potbellies here?"

"Yes" came from a dozen voices.

"I agree." This was from an old old man with a white beard. He turned around and grinned at Li Chen-chiang, who was standing behind him.

"Who are the potbellies of this village?" asked Liu.

A prolonged silence ensued .

"Why don't you speak up?" Liu turned to the old man with the white beard, the one who had said, "I agree," and said: "You tell us, uncle."

"I haven't been here very long—I came to this village only after the Japanese surrender in 1945." Li Chen-chiang, who was standing behind him, muttered something over his shoulder, and White Goatee continued: "I hear there are no big landlords in this village, and I believe it's true."

"Then why did you just say now that you agreed we should tackle the potbellies?"

* Ting-ling received a Stalin Prize in 1951, so also did Chou Li-po.

"There aren't any here," explained White Goatee, "but there are plenty in other villages. We can attack them."

"Comrade, can I say something?" put in another old man in a black felt hat. "From time immemorial man has bent to the law as grass bends under the wind. Whatever the government says goes. Our land-reform workers here represent our government. When they say they'll fight the potbellies to help us poor folks come up on top, of course we're pleased." He turned to the audience and asked: "Do you agree, folks?"

Cries of approval came from every side, the voices of old men and children intermingling. There was a burst of applause too.

"Comrades, you've heard with your own ears we all welcome you," went on the old man in the black hat. "It's nearly midnight now, and time the meeting broke up. Please don't be offended if I go home now to sleep . . ."*

Disappointed, Liu realizes that the reform is not going to be easy to accomplish. He queries the poor peasants, gets to know who the local tyrants are and what they are like, and little by little persuades the villagers to expose their grievances in public. Finally, the biggest of the landowners, Han, who bedeviled the peasants and collaborated with the Japanese, is put under arrest.

By the time Han was standing beside the "people's tribunal," murmured comments ran through the crowd.

"This time, he'll be put in jail."

"Look! His hands are tied."

"Is he going to die—or live? What do you say?"

"That depends on what his crimes are."

Some people were not particularly enthusiastic about the struggle, not because they were Han's relatives or sworn brothers, but because they owned land themselves and had had dealings with the Japanese. They were afraid that after Han had been dealt with it would be their turn. Others thought that Han's son, who was with the Kuomintang army, might one day stage a comeback and take reprisals. Still others thought Han deserved a trial, but did not intend to speak against him themselves. After all, exposed rafters are the first to rot. They decided to wait and see which way the wind blew. These three kinds of people kept silent.

Some of Han's agents were there, imagining people didn't know

* Chou Li-po, *The Hurricane* (Peking, 1955), pp. 19-20.

who they were. They acted like the keenest of the keen, shouting louder than anyone else.

Han stood beside the table, hanging his head. He was paler than last time. A number of children had swarmed round him to look curiously at the rope round his waist. One of the bolder children asked him to his face, "Mr. Han, why haven't you brought your big stick today?"*

The second meeting begins. Han attempts his defense.

"I'm a bad egg," started Han, "a man with a feudal mentality. My mother died when I was a little boy. My father remarried and my stepmother beat me every day."

"Stop this nonsense!" someone cursed.

"Don't let him drivel."†

But Han goes on, reciting his unhappy past, his mistakes.

Somebody said: "He's owned up to all his faults, he's sure to reform." Somebody else echoed: "He's all right except for his land holdings. And now he's given them up." There was a movement toward the door, and though no one had left yet, there was a relaxed feeling.‡

However, Kuo, presiding over the meeting, brings up the services Han rendered to the Japanese. An aged peasant comes forward: "Old Tien took off his tattered straw hat and looked with hatred and fear at his oppressor. He was trembling with rage, and sweat was breaking out on his wrinkled sunburned forehead." His story is damning; having given him permission to build a house on a piece of land, Han, the first year, had requisitioned and given to the Japanese all the wood Tien had brought from the forest. Two years later, the house completed, Han seized it and turned it into a stable. He wished to take Tien's pretty sixteen-year-old daughter for his wife; she refused; he had three men seize her.

"The four of you dragged her to the backyard and tied her to the tobacco rack with a straw rope. When she screamed, you rammed a handkerchief into her mouth. Then you yanked off her clothes and whipped her naked body with a willow switch. Her blood was coursing down her body, and then . . . and then . . ." Old Tien could not go on

* *Ibid.*, p. 99.
† *Ibid.*, p. 100.
‡ *Ibid.*, p. 101.

—he cried aloud. The crowd surged nearer. People shouted: "Beat him! Beat him!" A brick came flying from somewhere and landed close to Han. His face turned pale, and he stood there trembling, knee knocking against knee.

"Strip him first!" shouted somebody.

"Kill him!" added somebody else.

A man came up and slapped Han across the face. Blood gushed from his nose.

"Good! A good blow! Give him another!" shouted somebody else.

However, the sight of blood melted the hearts of many, especially women, and silence fell. Who had dealt the blow? Han looked up, saw it was Li Chen-chiang,* and understood. He bent his head lower to let the blood flow in big drops so that everybody could see . . . Old Tien had stepped back a little in surprise, but Kuo urged him:

"Go on, Old Tien."

"I've nothing more to say," he answered . . . and withdrew behind the table.†

Li Chen-chiang casts feigned insults at Han and proposes that he be fined and his property confiscated. Hsia, the cadre, detects the maneuver. Li Chen-chiang's behavior is drawn from that of a character in *The Romance of the Three Kingdoms:* a general has another general, secretly his ally, cruelly beaten before sending him back to the enemy in order to deceive it. But Hsia's efforts to keep the meeting going seem to be in vain. Timid, fearful, easily duped, the peasants do however finally pick up courage. Once again they bring Han to trial. And this time they give evidence; it is damning. Han is convicted of seventeen murders; for his own and his son's pleasures he has taken forty-three women by force. He has reduced his farmers to famine, refused to pay laborers in his employ, handed people he did not like over to the Japanese who deported them. The Japanese gone, he worked with the Kuomintang army and fought against the Reds. He is sentenced to death, led out beyond the village compound after having been given a thorough beating by the peasants, and shot.

In these matters the policy prescribed and followed by the regime is very significant. Long experience in the liberated zones taught the government that one must not blindly count upon

* One of Han's creatures.

† *The Hurricane*, pp. 103-104.

spontaneity from the peasant masses; they are too backward to dare to act of their own accord in their own interests. The leaders nevertheless wished to have the Chinese people consider the Revolution theirs; they must not passively receive its benefits but conquer them. Land was not given to the peasants; they were ingeniously helped to take it. This joint action, teaming cadres with the masses, is one of the most unusual features of the Chinese Revolution; from the outset it has been achieved in a remarkable manner and this is one of the facts accounting for the support given—despite certain hesitations and difficulties—by the countryside to a regime it is aware of having in large measure installed.*

So far, every land reform since the days of Shih Huang Ti has been followed by the reconstitution of the latifundia. And once again, predict the anti-Communists, the pendulum, having swung one way, will soon swing the other. But for the emperors land reform was little more than an expedient for replenishing their treasure chests; moreover, even had they wanted to, they lacked the means to make a reform endure: private property persisting, reconcentration had sooner or later to recur. To insure that the reform be permanent it would have been necessary to go beyond it and abolish private ownership, which is not a reformist but a revolutionary measure. Today, however, we see land reform as

* In Eastern Europe, too, the peasants hesitated over taking the holdings that were offered to them during the land reform effected in 1945. The phenomenon was particularly widespread in Hungary. "What was uppermost in the minds of the Hungarian peasants, terrorized by so many atrocities, rapes, assassinations, victims of so many requisitions, plunderings, what weighed upon them in 1945 was naked fear . . . The Communism about which they had been told such dreadful stories terrified them now. And so, when the first Communist militants appeared in the villages to incite the peasants to formulate demands upon the great domains in the vicinity, the initial reaction was of mistrust. Once before the 'masters' had fled, in 1919, and later returned with policemen in tow. The policemen might well be gone now too; but mightn't they return?" (François Fejtö, *Histoire des démocraties populaires.*) The order for the reform having been issued by the Soviet High Command, a Postulation Committee was formed in each village; but those Committees were in anything but a hurry to claim the lands abandoned by the "masters" who had moved out as the Red Army had moved in. Actually, the peasants' initiative went no further than an often meek and always reluctant "postulation," the result being that the reform took place in an atmosphere very unlike the one in China. Nowhere in Europe did the peasants proceed of their own accord to the expropriation of "owners."

the initial step in nothing short of a thoroughgoing change: socialist revolution. The Communists have never viewed the redistribution of land as an end in itself but as the first stage in a movement that is to end in collectivization. The existence of a working class, the industrialization of China, a technological revolution substituting the tractor for the hoe will enable them to attain this objective in a few years' time; private property will then be abolished and the road leading back to the past definitely blocked. For the Communists there has been no problem save that of tactics, a problem essentially of time: how to reach the goal as quickly and as efficiently as possible. Ought collectivization to be accompanied by, and hence wait for, the mechanizing of agriculture or should it precede it? The second course was unhesitatingly adopted—and this for two reasons.

Mechanization will take another ten or fifteen years. Now, there is an element of truth in the anti-Communists' prophesies; the survival of private property and, more particularly, of the conditions under which the reform has been accomplished can warrant the fear that rural wealth may in time gravitate again into the hands of a few. Certain ancient inequalities have been maintained and they have given rise to fresh ones: whereas soil allotments are fixed, fluctuations occur within the framework of the family whose status must necessarily be affected in consequence. Thus, the peasant whose wife has given birth to three or four children since 1949 is poorer now than then. The peasant whose sons are of a young age has more trouble farming his land than the man helped by grown sons. One must reckon on illnesses, disabilities, differences in capacity for work and zeal. Poor peasants now and again sell their land; the holdings of middle-class and upper-class peasants increase. New poor appear, new members of the middle class, of the rich. The well-to-do hire the labor of the neediest. It is essential to prevent a return to exploitation and to capitalism.

Likewise, acre for acre, more must be produced, cultivation of the virgin territories being impossible at present. The peasants have become proprietors, finding themselves delivered from the enormous burden of rent and debt; but the breaking up of the land into small plots, the scarcity of equipment and livestock forbids a more intensified farming. And indeed, prior to the Liberation, according to well-informed observers, the Chinese agricultural methods were wringing everything that could be got from the soil, methods and conditions then being what they were: intensification is not possible unless these methods and conditions are changed. But the peasants shall be able to improve their equipment only by pooling their resources, they will not rationalize the cultivation of the soil except through collective endeavor and planning: they must move beyond the stage where each man works only for himself.

Each of the two lines of reasoning thus leads to the same conclusion: in order both to forestall the resurrection of rural capitalism and to enrich peasants and state alike, collectivization must be achieved without delay. Of the two designated objectives, the leaders began by giving priority to the second. Notwithstanding propaganda slogans which attribute "enthusiasm for the building of socialism" to every last citizen, the government knows full well that their individual welfare is still the prime concern and motive for action among the peasants today. They are not therefore exhorted to dedicate their energies to the interest of the state. It will be explained to them that co-operatives alone can rescue them from poverty. In 1943 Mao Tse-tung had already declared, "The one way in which the peasants can overthrow their poverty is by progressively collectivizing; and according to Lenin the one way to collectivization is via co-operatives."

Starting in 1947 experiments began with mutual-aid teams and collectives in Manchuria, in North China—Shantung and northern Kiangsu. In 1949 the Central Committee, in the course of its Second Plenary Session, decided that collectivization of agriculture was necessary. Article 34 of the Common Program* stipulates:

> In all regions where land reform has been altogether completed, the Popular Government should proceed to the central task of organizing the peasants and all the manpower available for agriculture in order to develop agricultural production and allied activities. Observing the principle of free consent and mutual interest, it must furthermore encourage and gradually lead the peasants into organizing various forms of mutual aid in work and of co-operation in production.

* This Program served as a provisional Constitution between the years 1949 and 1954.

The mutual-aid team is the first step in collectivization. "We have concentrated our main attentions upon setting up mutual-aid teams," said Kao Kang in his 1950 survey of the first year of the Common Program's application in Manchuria. The Chinese peasants have always practiced mutual aid to a greater or less degree: as long ago as 300 B.C. Mencius recommended founding mutual-aid groups. In case of an urgent job, the farmer lent a hand to his neighbor who at some other time received help in return; but this sort of temporary and casual co-operation gave rise ,to differences which led to quarrels. Shortly after the land reform had taken place most of the peasants recognized the advantage in giving it a more stable form. They constituted mutual-aid units whose principle is, without disturbing private property, to *collectivize work*, which allows planning. For example, in a village of twenty-three families there was a total of three privately owned water buffaloes and three water wheels for irrigation. Certain families numbered more able-bodied men than were needed to cultivate the family plots, other families were short-handed. When the rice seedlings are thinned, the whole job must be completed in the space of a day or two: now, a single man can thin no more than two mus in a day. The peasants realized that if they pooled their labor the village's thirty-five able-bodied adult men could easily and without loss to anybody cultivate the total 190 mus they owned. At first they teamed up for the period covered by the heavier tasks, and in 1950 harvested 315 catties of rice per mu as against the 240 of preceeding years. They then decided, in 1951, to create two permanent mutual-aid brigades, one incorporating fourteen families, the other eight. The women scheduled their work to fit in with the men's, a plan was drawn up. A rating system was devised, allowing points for the amount of work done, each point corresponding to a share of the profits. The 1951 production rose to 380 catties per mu. In return for payment to their owners, the buffaloes and water wheels were employed by the community.

In an important appraisal of these initial experiments, Wang Kuang-wei, a member of the regional government of Manchuria, relates:

In 1947, a large mutual-aid unit involving twenty-five families was organized upon an obligatory participation basis in the village of Yingcheng. Then, upon orders from superior authorities, smaller voluntary participation units were constituted.* In 1949, due to proper leadership and excellent planning, the mutual-aid teams augmented the village's agricultural output. However, numerous controversies arose concerning salaries, the apportioning of tasks, weeding, fertilizers, the collective working schedule, questions relating to harvesting and sowing, transfers, there were differences among the cadres, the progressive elements, and the peasant masses. After much discussion, the system of a working standard based upon the quality and size of the fields was introduced, as was the system of production norms, likewise fixed according to the quality and size of the fields. Thanks to heavy use of fertilizer, to careful cultivation, production rose and the quality of the soil was ameliorated.

At this stage each peasant maintains absolute control over his property. The next stage is the *semisocialist* co-operative. In it private ownership is respected, the usufruct pooled. Private lands are integrated into a joint fund: but each peasant receives a remuneration corresponding to the area of his lot and the value of its soil; similarly, he is paid a rental fee for the livestock and articles he lends to the co-operative. He may at any time withdraw and recover his property. As in the mutual-aid teams, there is a point evaluation of the labor contributed by each man, the factors being hours put in and results achieved. The net proceeds are thus shared among the group's members in accordance with property invested and points obtained, a part of the gross having been set aside for the common purchase of fertilizer, machines, draft animals, etc. Newcomers must pay a fee upon entering the group; thereby they buy the right to profit from the group's previously acquired stock in trade which also functions as an emergency insurance fund.

These co-operatives began to develop in 1951. By December of that year there was a great number of mutual-aid teams, but only 300 agricultural co-operatives. They totaled 4,000 in 1952 and

* The Government has always severely reprimanded cadres who have attempted to bully peasants into organizing.

14,000 by the autumn of 1953. If the figure is not considerable that is owing to the government's extremely cautious policy during those first two years. It was necessary to collectivize: but, precisely in order to achieve that aim, it was necessary not to incur the distrust or opposition of the peasants whose friendliness toward the regime was in great part due to the fact that it had turned them into proprietors in the first place. In addition, the apportioning of indemnities, of points for work accomplished, the sharing of profits gave rise to frequent contention. How was one to deal with the peasants who proved disinclined or unwilling to join a co-operative? The Party condemned two attitudes: that of certain rightists, who felt that the peasantry should be left to develop of its own accord, was qualified as "launching the rural areas along the road to capitalism";* and that of a left wing which, conversely, favored constraining the peasants to organize. "Characterized by hasty, thoughtless, and reckless progress, a deviation occurred between the fall of 1952 and spring of 1953 in the organizing of agricultural production co-operatives," the New China Agency reported in 1953. And the *Hopei Jih Pao* of March 14, 1953, specifies that in Hopei Province this deviation appears in three forms:

> First, certain cadres bundle the peasants into co-operatives in too much of a hurry, neglecting the local conditions of the various mutual-aid team foundations, and failing to take into account the peasants' degree of education, and even violating the principle of voluntary adherence. Second, the ways in which public property is accumulated for the co-operatives may be excessive and premature. Third, a rather large number of co-operatives encroach upon their members' private property and strive to eliminate it.

In February and March 1953 the Central Committee addressed directives to every Party organism:

> If the peasants are to strive wholeheartedly to increase agricultural production, there must be a thoroughgoing rectification of this irresponsible tendency toward precipitancy in the movement aiming at agrarian co-operation . . . The cadres must explain to the peasants that their individual holdings will be protected, bend every effort to renew their

* Kao Kang's *Report*, 1952.

ardor for work, and give undiscriminating aid to every peasant, even those who are not participating in either mutual-aid teams or production co-operatives.

However, at the close of 1953 the government concluded that it was necessary to accelerate agricultural socialization. "At the same time decreeing the planned purchase and distribution of foodstuffs, the State has decided to accelerate the mutual-aid team and co-operative movement," wrote *The People's Daily* on March 1, 1954. The wiser for experience, the cadres did all they could not to scare the peasants, helped them find the most satisfactory solutions to the questions of indemnities and work points; simultaneously, the increased yield resulting from co-operative organization furnished a persuasive argument: from 14,000 the number of co-operatives advanced, by spring 1954, to 95,000. By September 1955 it had risen to 650,000; the co-operatives then grouped 15,000,000 families: in other words, 13 per cent of the population belonged to these organizations. The figure of 670,000 had been attained that spring but a certain number of co-operatives had been established without adequate preparation and 20,000 were dissolved.

A concrete example of resistance encountered from the peasants is cited in an article in *China Reconstructs:** Hsieh Tuan, twenty-seven, is a middle-class peasant in the province of Hunan. The land reform did not affect the size of his property, bigger than the individual lots assigned to the peasants; as he too had been exploited by the local landowner, he took an active hand at the meeting where the latter was accused. He possessed six and one-half acres of land which he was just able to manage, his father being infirm; rains had often ruined his crops. He was therefore delighted to join the mutual-aid team; the division of labor would save the crop no matter what the weather. A year later it was proposed that the team be transformed into a semisocialist co-operative. Hsieh Tuan hesitated; he disliked the idea of pooling his land with the other peasants, for he believed it was more fertile than his neighbors': would they grant him a sufficient indemnity?

* If the reader is disposed to doubt the authenticity of the cited case, he is at liberty to do so. The fact remains that the text presents most of the real and material difficulties cadres frequently have to contend with.

He entered the co-operative because they promised him his profits would increase; but the indemnity he demanded was judged too high; he had to cede to the opinion of the majority. He consoled himself by the thought that eleven other families had taken the same decision he had and that, at worst, he could back out at the end of the year. Meanwhile he clung to his small proprietor's outlook; he wanted to have his field tilled first so that he would be the first to harvest grain. When his turn came to work the other peasants' fields he found that they were asking too much of him and thought of going off for a vacation; however, as nobody else seemed to wish to take a rest, he was loath to go alone, for that would mean falling behind in points. He also feared that when the time came to divide up the profits he would not be given his due share, and he learned arithmetic in order to verify the accounts; he was not sure either whether he would be sufficiently indemnified for the loan of his draft animals. He earned criticism for working more quickly and less carefully in his neighbors' fields than in his own. He had kept a little patch of ground aside for himself and was irritated at not having more spare time to devote to it. His bad humor notwithstanding, he plainly saw the advantages in organization: eight water wheels belonging to various peasants were all utilized for the benefit of each, and Hsieh Tuan's fields did not suffer from dryness. He was given 42 yuan in payment for the use of his ox and manure pile. At harvesttime he received 6,534 pounds of grain, that being 726 more than he had had the year before. Village industries earned everyone an additional 140 yuan.

He was again dissatisfied when the state monopoly system was inaugurated and he had to sell his surplus grain to the state. All the same, he put himself down for 770 pounds. The next year pumps were installed in the fields, making irrigation a great deal easier. So pleased was Hsieh that it was he who suggested that the entire soybean crop be sold to the state; the move was adopted. But he remained greedy; when some new members were enrolled in the co-operative he wished to demand 130 yuan in entrance dues; the sum was fixed at 50 yuan. He also demanded an excessive indemnity for the use of his buffalo. He still has a tendency to place his individual interests ahead of the group's; if he succeeds in overcoming this defect he will become a model worker.

To be sure, the story is edifying, and peasant resistance is not always so harmoniously surmounted. It does however shed light on just what sort of reasons lie behind that resistance. To start with, "the peasant's native tendency to capitalism" Li Fu-chuan speaks of in his "Report on the Five-Year Plan," then selfishness and the small proprietor's inbred suspiciousness. One also makes out one of the practical difficulties that has hampered the development of many a co-operative: if you award him too low an indemnity, the middle-class peasant balks at contributing his land and animals to the pool; if the amount is too high, the poor peasants consider themselves wronged. Nevertheless, as the quoted figures demonstrate, the incontestable increase in output that results from collectivizing is bringing enormous numbers of adherents. Yields jump from 10 to 20 per cent during the first two years, then tend to level out but remain higher than with the mutual-aid teams.

I visited two villages organized into semisocialist co-operatives. In each the number of families involved was very much above the average; these cases were, then, exceptional: my guides told me so beforehand. It was not to deceive me about the present situation that I was shown them, but in order that I get a picture of what tomorrow's society will be.

Not far from Peking, a tall peasant of some forty years, the head of the village, and another peasant who was the head of the co-operative received us in a shed furnished with a table and wooden benches; both men were former agricultural laborers, owning not a vestige of land in the past. While smoking long-stemmed pipes, their tiny bowls filled with a strongly aromatic tobacco they prepare and mix themselves, they explained to me in detail how and why farming is rationalized by means of collectivization.

Five brigades divide the work of cultivating the fields: everyone works, not necessarily in his own field, but in the one to which he has the easiest access. The village property actually being split into many very small parts, a peasant may own fields located a great way from his house; collectivization has greatly reduced the considerable fatigue and loss of time formerly occasioned by going back and forth. Formerly a wide variety of crops were grown on each holding: each family would raise its own cereals, vegetables, red peas, etc. At present, the over-all harvest being divided among everybody, crops can be concentrated in one place and on the terrain best suited to each. Plots used to be separated by boundary strips of untouchable ground; these have been brought under cultivation. But, above all, pooling their resources has enabled the peasants to buy fertilizers, disinfectants, new tools: for the old wooden plows which only scratched the surface of the soil they have substituted steel plowshares which cut a deep furrow.

As a result, production has risen considerably over the past two years. Why then, I ask, are some peasants keeping on in isolation? In this village, is the reply, the emphasis is on truck gardening; daily loads of vegetables are taken to Peking and sold in the markets there. The co-operative's members receive their shares of the proceeds at certain fixed dates; the farmers who are going it alone are those who prefer to earn less if they can get their money at once. Other general factors are probably operative also: attachment to private ownership, liking for independence, mistrust.

I made a tour of the village. Not one speck of garbage, not a pool of stagnant water left; the air smelled clean—I had not thought that a village could be so neat. Every inhabitant, old and young alike, is dressed in perfectly neat blue cotton clothes.* We go into one house, then into another; each is preceded by a courtyard surrounded by an earthen wall; ears of corn are drying on the impeccably swept ground. The dwellings, like all houses in the North, are made of mud-and-straw brick. To build a roof they lay cakes of molded mud upon a sort of mattress of kaoliang stalks lying on rafters held up by the main beams. It is always the same principle: vertical posts independent of the walls support the roof framework. Wood being rare, the framework was formerly considered a thing of such value as to warrant taking along when one moved to another place. Frames lined with paper serve as windows. Here at last with my own eyes I can see this k'ang mentioned in every novel of peasant life: a brick platform under which pipes run; in winter, the fire burning outside or in the kitchen heats the

* While in China, my journeys by rail took me past a great many villages: From the train I could not tell whether or not they were clean or determine their odor. But, looking out the window, the peasants I saw were all decently dressed.

water that circulates beneath the k'ang; the system is disconnected in summer. Meals are taken upon this dais, women sit there to sew or work; at night, wrapped in their blankets, the whole family stretches out upon it. During the daytime the blankets—all there is by way of bedding—are carefully folded and stacked at one corner of the k'ang. In bright cotton, they betoken great wealth: each costs about 20 yuan in materials if made by oneself. The government has distributed them to every peasant family. "*Before*, we had nothing but one old patched blanket; now we have four, all new," our hosts tell us. They also say that now at last they have ceased to know hunger: they eat sorghum or boiled millet, vegetables, vermicelli, good wheat bread, beans, and soy; rarely now and then a little meat and eggs. No electricity in the houses, but they get Peking on crystal sets. In a corner of the kitchen I notice a bicycle: many peasants have them now. Stone houses have been built to lodge co-operative stores, others for the peasants whose dwellings are the poorest. The co-operative has bought pumps, which make irrigation work much easier. The taxes are not high: 12 per cent on income. Prices are stable. In case of need the state grants loans without interest. A relief fund accords assistance to the sick and aged. Medical care is free. The peasants are not yet prosperous; but they at least possess one precious and altogether new asset: security.

The second village I saw lies between Mukden and Fushun on the bank of a river; its name is Kao Kan. We were greeted by the president of the local Women's Association and by the head of the co-operative, a man whose face bore traces of smallpox, once a very widespread disease. The agglomeration, we are told, includes 160 families—788 persons in all—cultivating 2,442 mus of ground. *Before*, eight landowners and peasants possessed 90 per cent of the fields: thus, the great majority of the villagers were day or part-time laborers. Redistribution led to almost all the land being divided up among the poor, the rich retaining title to a small portion of what had been previously theirs. In 1951 seven mutual-aid groups existed: they harvested 420 pounds of cereal per mu instead of the customary 370. They bought plows and five horses in common. In 1952 they associated themselves into a co-operative: over 29 mus were acquired by bringing the demarcation strips under cultivation; the fields were unified and modern plows bought. The mu yielded 445 pounds. In 1953, due to new fertilizers and the new plows, the figure reached 667 pounds. Part of the soil was flooded in 1954; nevertheless a new production record was set, due this time to the tractor furnished by the agricultural head office at Kao Kan which has several pieces of farming machinery and which when called on will, in return for a fee, send its equipment and drivers anywhere in the region.

The standard of living has improved. In 1953 each family was able to buy an average of three blankets. Rice has entered the diet, so has wheat flour, hitherto unheard-of luxuries. The co-operative has six wells and a pumping station which permits the growing of rice. Houses have been built: in all, 62 new rooms. The peasants are co-operatively raising 98 pigs, 600 chickens, 32 mules, 8 donkeys. They possess 16 rubber-tired carts and have bought new tools. Instead of a single cistern, 53 wells exist at the moment. The peasants, proceeding on their own, have increased housing by 65 new rooms. Each family privately owns an average of 1½ pigs and 15 to 16 chickens. One hundred and sixteen families belong to the co-operatives; the 44 "individuals" include the former "owners" and rich peasants, and also peasants who double as workers in Fushun or who are in business: their schedule prevents them from taking part in collective endeavor.

I visit the selling co-operative which stocks just about everything the peasants need. There are two primary schools at Kao Kan and few illiterates. All the children go to school, thirty-two of them to the secondary school which, *before*, used only to be open to two sons of rich peasants. No one practices religion here any more: not far from a city, familiar with farm machinery, the reign of the new spirit is uncontested at Kao Kan. Two inhabitants of the village are Communist Party members. Twenty young people belong to democratic youth organizations.

In the Hangchow area I saw one village where one of the co-operatives belong to the upper, that is, entirely socialist category. Of these there are still very few. It resembled a semisocialist co-operative except that here the property owner receives no indemnity for the land he cedes to the community; individual profits are calculated purely upon the basis of work contributed; for those peasants whose holdings are extensive and fertile the discontinuation of annual rental fees means a loss, but this loss is offset by the augmentation of the product. The semisocialist scheme has its drawbacks: I mentioned the numerous squabbles that arise in connection with the evaluation of the individual and instruments contributed; bookkeeping is complicated; and each peasant, looking for a higher indemnity, is tempted to demand that his own field be cultivated with particular care; in short, conflicts still exist between the interests of individuals and collective welfare, and that makes planning hard. In the socialist co-operative the land still belongs to the peasant; he can pull out and go back to farming his plot on his own. But so long as he remains a member of the co-operative, this piece of land is common property and he has no more private ownership of it than of any other plot. But such are its advantages that one hopes all the co-operatives will soon reach this stage.

The peasants of this village specialize in growing tea, for they have found it more profitable than anything else. Everyone earns about 250 yuan a year; owning his house, producing his food in his own garden, the peasant making such a sum is considered well-to-do. Those who grow rice and corn earn less; there are some who live on the other side of the river and who are hired to help pick the tea leaves. The co-operatives are not allowed to exploit the labor of outsiders, to take on hired hands for long periods, to speculate on land or produce. But when circumstances require it they can recruit a limited amount of help for brief spells; and that is what happens here. Many people must be enlisted in the tea picking, for the job must go quickly if it is to go well: the leaves all reach the right point of ripeness at the same time and must be collected in the space of three days: before then they are too green, afterward too dry. There are three harvests each year, and throughout the year meticulous care must be taken with the planting, with soil fertilization, with proper watering, etc.

Low in a valley green with tea bushes, this village is clearly a good deal richer than those I saw in the North. The houses here are bigger. Girls wear brightly colored jackets, they are dressed and groomed with a certain stylishness. The community is made up of 213 families, 1,103 inhabitants all told. Until 1952 it had gone only to the point of constituting mutual-aid groups; some of them have remained as originally formed. But in 1952 the poor peasants induced others to join them in creating co-operatives: 96 families founded two of the semisocialist type, another of the socialist. At present 425 persons are working 260 mus of tea, 160 mus of rice, 43 mus of cereal and vegetable crops. Family profits increased an annual 230 yuan per mu, as much as 400 yuan per mu for some families. Last year rain and floods caused severe damage; but production rose all the same because of scientific management.

I requested details on this last point and they were given to me by the head of the co-operative, a very alert and bright young man. To begin with, he said, production is subject to an over-all plan, its various aspects to secondary plans. Fertilizer is apportioned according to the specific needs of each particular lot. Instead of each person picking his own tea at harvesttime, everybody pitches in on that part of the grove which is readiest. Rice, tea, or cereals are grown on those plots best adapted to the particular crop. Every season a work program is drawn up; it is based upon previous experience; everyone offers his opinion and conclusions are reached after open discussion. The work-point system guides the distribution of the proceeds. At the end of each day every group evaluates the work accomplished by each of its members, the factors being quantity and quality. Each man is asked to rate his own performance; if the rest of the group agrees, his estimate stands, otherwise it is discussed and adjusted. The maximum rating is 10: to earn it, the amount stipulated in the plan must have been gathered and the leaves must be neither too broken, nor too green, nor too old, and so on. The amount of the salary is determined by final point tally.

Systematization was especially apparent in the drying room. Green tea is distinguished from black tea—much less widespread in China—in that it is not fermented. It is fired at a high temperature in order to destroy the enzymes, and the leaves retain their color; green tea has a greater vitamin content than black. Today, green tea is being processed in ten large Chinese plants where, for the first time, mechanical means are being employed. But ten factories are still not enough and this, like most other villages producing tea, treats it itself. The leaves are placed in large trays below which a fire is kept steadily burning, and the leaves are constantly stirred and sifted by hand all night long. The individual preparing his own tea needs at least one helper to keep the fire stoked while he himself stirs the leaves. Here, for eight trays a staff of nine rather than sixteen suffices, for one person tends all the fires; the trays occupying just one room, there is also a saving on space.

The village has a buying-and-selling co-operative store, an infirmary with a permanently resident nurse whose main work is as a midwife, to give vaccinations, to handle cases of mild sickness. A doctor pays regular visits to the village and if there is an emergency, someone gets on a bike and fetches him. Children are deposited in nurseries while their mothers are in the fields. Classes are held to teach illiterates to read and write, there are courses for the more advanced peasants. On holidays a theatrical group presents plays.

The hygiene campaign has transformed the sanitary conditions in every village. Harmful superstitions have been combatted; and those costly ceremonies the villagers used to have to put up with and pay for have been simplified where not suppressed. Gone are the wedding litter, the ruinously expensive wedding feast, the lavish costumes. A series of minute alterations in peasant life has helped make it much more worth living.

Anti-Communists shake their heads; they reproach the regime for having elected the "easier way" of an overnight land reform in preference to the harder but—they insist—more rewarding way of reconstruction: the government should not have divided up the land, it should have improved the seed, increased the output of chemical fertilizer, etc. The answer is that, taken within a capitalist framework, these measures would only have profited the propertied class, not the entire country; but neither has the reconstruction aspect of the problem been neglected by the government in whose view socialization and reconstruction go hand in hand. Between 1950 and 1955 it has made a considerable effort in behalf of agriculture; it has spent 4,600,000,000 yuan: loans, hydraulic projects, relief aid to disaster victims, etc. By the end of 1957, 1,800,000 ordinary steel plows, 500,000 others of the new model, 681,000 pumps furnishing 57,000 HP and 20,000,000 tons of chemical fertilizer will have been delivered to the peasants by state factories.

Moreover, agricultural experts are scientifically studying soil, climate, production methods. The Russian system of "close planting" has been introduced in several regions: a 20 per cent increase in yield has been obtained by sowing cereals in rows six inches apart instead of nine. Seed analysis and selection is being carried on; they are making experiments based on Michurin's theories. Numerous agricultural research institutes as well as thirty-two experimental stations and thirty-four colleges of agriculture have been created. The production and use of insecticides is being developed: grasshoppers, which are the greater part of the parasites, have been conquered by now. Small-scale land clearance is being encouraged.

A Program for Agricultural Development outlines the plan of tasks to be accomplished between 1956 and 1967: the production of modern plows, chemical fertilizers, and pumps, the fight against sicknesses and blights affecting animals and plants. But, unlike its adversaries, the regime considers that reconstruction can only bear fruit within the framework of socialization. That is why, even before the new plan was elaborated, a vast movement was launched in the beginning of autumn 1955: let us speed up the collectivization! In the second half of October 1955 Mao Tse-tung's July 31 speech was published together with the Central Committee's decision, neither of which had been made public until then. Every newspaper commented on them, they were discussed throughout the whole of China.

In order that everyone be fed and the country industrialized, grain is needed, said Mao: the population registers an annual 2 per cent growth; in exchange for the machines she must have, China can supply nothing but the fruits of her soil: harvests must increase a steady 3.3 per cent otherwise exports and consequently imports will be held in check. Socialization is the only means to a wholesale rise in production. Of the 650,000 existing co-operatives 80 per cent have pushed acre-for-acre production from 10 to 30 per cent higher; these co-operatives must be consolidated, those which have remained stagnant must be stimulated, those which have regressed must be improved; mutual-aid groups and semi-socialist co-operatives must be multiplied. The groundwork laid, it will then be possible to move ahead to the "entirely socialist and large-scale" stage of co-operatives. They are what the regime is striving after. China has only just begun her socialist revolution; it has a dual character: technological and social. Industry will replace handicraft, tractors the hoe. Correlatively, private capital will disappear and the land is to be collectivized.

Industrial and agricultural socialization are inseparable. So closely interdependent are the heavy-industry, light-industry, and farming sectors that no one of them can develop unaided by the others; and at the present time the key to the whole situation is held by the countryside: farming has got to be transformed.

> Socialist industrialization cannot be divorced from agricultural co-operativization nor undertaken separately. First of all, everyone knows that whereas in our country the production level of marketable grains and industrial raw materials is at the moment very low, the country's needs in this sphere are growing every year. This is a sharp contradiction . . . At the present moment, we are not only in the process of undertaking a revolution in the social system, replacing the system of private property by one of collective ownership; we are also in the process of undertaking a revolution in the technical domain, replacing handicraft production by mechanized and modernized mass production . . . In the domain of agriculture . . . there must first be organization into farming co-operatives, for it is only then that it will be possible to use heavy farm machinery . . .
>
> A relatively important share of the enormous capital necessary for accomplishing the industrialization and technical transformation of the country's agriculture must come from agriculture itself. That is to say, over and above direct taxation of agriculture, we must, if we are to satisfy the material requirements both of the peasants and of the state and at the same time accumulate capital for the state, develop light-industry production of consumer goods needed by the peasants and peasant production of commercial grains and raw materials . . . Now, large-scale development of light industry cannot be achieved upon the basis of a small peasant economy; it presupposes large-scale agriculture: in so far as China is concerned, that means co-operativized and socialized agriculture. Only after we have such agriculture will we be able to accord the peasants an infinitely higher buying power than the one they have now.

Necessary to the state, collectivization thus will also benefit the peasants. It is not a question of corralling their surpluses by means of supplementary taxation, but of increasing their buying power and hence of raising their standard of living. Their interest coincides with that of the entire nation; they are not being thrown into the maw of a heavy-industry Moloch; present-day prosperity is not being sacrificed to a future one: to the contrary, the first is indispensable to attaining the second.

The poor peasants' need to collectivize is especially keen; they still represent 60 to 70 per cent of the peasant class; their standard of living is far above that of the poor peasant in the old days, they are no longer threatened by indigence or insecurity, but even so their life is still difficult.

> The majority of the peasants will succeed in defeating poverty, in bettering their lives, in withstanding natural calamities only by falling into step along the broad path leading to socialism. This belief has already taken rapid hold among the poor peasants. Those who are well off or relatively so make up no more than 20 to 30 per cent of the peasant population; they are undecided . . .

The undertaking is guaranteed for success in the long run, for it has the support of the poor peasants. They were not theoretical considerations that induced Mao to launch the drive. In the spring he had made a long tour through the rural areas, had spoken with peasants, and made a thorough study of the situation. He became convinced that acceleration was not only necessary but possible. The cadres who had braked the co-operativizing had made a mistake. Too many co-operatives that could have made a go of it if consolidated had been dissolved. Above all, not enough encouragement had been given to the peasants who might have been very willing to create work teams. "The peasants are eager to work progressively, and under the Party's guidance, along the path to socialism. The Party is capable of leading the peasants toward socialism."

In the villages I visited I was struck by the fact that in every case the community and co-operative leaders were former poor peasants; it was always they who had taken the initiative in collectivizing. Those who are still poor today must continue to play a vanguard role; they are the men to count on and help, says Mao. In those places lacking co-operatives, the poor are all too often drifting into being exploited by the rich; a certain number of the rich are indeed steering back toward capitalism: they hire the poor peasant's labor and even, in return for the loan of draft animals, tools, fertilizer, oblige him to mortgage or eventually cede title to his fields. The poor have but one means of defense: form co-operatives, in order to raise draft animals, purchase equipment and fertilizers, and win better crops from their land.

In Mao's speech the twin objectives appear in the plainest light: the enriching of state and peasants, and the fight against capitalism; having shown that they are inextricably connected, that the poor need to produce more in order to escape the exploitation they are suffering from and which must be abolished, he stresses the class-struggle character of collectivization. It had been pointed out earlier when, in September 1954, Teng Tzu-hui declared that "the further the co-operatives advance, the closer we are coming to our goal: the definitive elimination of rich peasants qua class." And again:

> The accelerated growth of co-operatives is tied to the fight against rural capitalist elements and to the intensification of the struggle between capitalist evolution and socialist evolution in the rural areas. The struggle between these two tendencies is one in which the bourgeoisie and the proletariat are competing in an effort to win over the independent peasants.

Lia Liu-yen wrote in 1955: "Bourgeois class and counterrevolutionary elements are trying to lure the peasants away from the road to socialism. The peasants must reject these attempts just as through land reform they rejected feudal structures."

Mao Tse-tung speaks in the same vein in his July 1955 speech:

> In the rural areas at the present time there yet prevails a system wherein rich peasants exploit their holdings on a capitalist basis, and an ocean of individual peasants manage on a private basis. For several years now everyone has observed the daily development of rural capitalism, new rich peasants springing up everywhere, numerous middle-class peasants endeavoring to become rich peasants. Meanwhile, numerous poor peasants, owing to their lack of the equipment they need in order to produce, still live in wretched circumstances; some have run into debt, some have let their land for hire or sold it outright. If this situation is permitted to develop, the phenomenon of disjunction will only

become necessarily graver with every passing day . . . We must achieve the thorough socialist transformation of agriculture. That is to say, if we are to help the rural masses better their living conditions, we must effect collectivization and rid the countryside of the economic system of rich peasants and the system of individual economy.

The poor and middle-class peasants shall then be urged into partnership; the rich shall be kept outside the co-operatives, not to be admitted until these have at last established themselves as going concerns—when, that is, they have been in operation for several years and include more than three quarters of a given region's peasantry; the rich will then be accepted on an individual basis if explicitly approved by the group but shall not be eligible to occupy posts of authority until after a considerable period—several years—of membership. All this is to prevent rich individuals from using their economically advantageous position to twist the co-operative into a venture profiting themselves only, which is what not a few of them managed to do in 1952 and 1953.

The Five-Year Plan called for a third of the peasantry in co-operatives by 1957; Mao Tse-tung demanded 1,300,000 co-operatives by spring 1956 and half the peasants organized in semi-socialist co-operatives by spring 1958.

Results were swift: in December 1955 the cooperatives reached 1,400,000, with 40 per cent of the peasants included in them. In June 1956 90 per cent of the peasantry belonged to co-operatives. In 1957 all of agriculture will be collectivized. The estimate is the total number of co-operatives will only be 2,000,000, for they will all be of a larger size: each will group about 110 families cultivating about 275 acres.

The congressional Standing Committee in March 1956 drafted a body of "Model Rules for the Agricultural Producer Co-operative." The underlying principles to be followed are those of voluntary adherence and mutual benefit:

The co-operatives must not under any circumstances resort to coercion; members are to be enlisted through persuasion and example . . . The only means for inducing the peasants to voluntarily take the way to collectivization is by applying the principle of mutual benefit . . . The appeal must be particularly addressed to the poor peasants, these must be brought into alliance with the middle-class peasants . . . The co-operative must not conflict with the interests of any poor or middle-class peasant . . . When it reaches the upper stage—the pooling of the principal means of production—the distinction between poor and middle-class peasants will be abolished . . . Members wishing to withdraw may do so once the crops have been harvested.

The co-operative is to aid poor or middle-class outsiders. Semi-socialist co-operatives are being maintained as such: each family preserves private title to a piece of ground, poultry, domestic animals, and tools. As for rich peasants, they are not to be admitted except under the conditions outlined by Mao Tse-tung—which is to say that for the time being the co-operatives are not open to them. They are by and large considered an enemy class. "The co-operative must fight against rich peasants and other exploiters in such a way as to reduce and gradually abolish capitalist exploitation in the rural areas."

Some Western commentators have chosen to interpret this collectivization movement as a revolution ranking in importance with the land reform itself.* They have probably been misled by a false analogy with the turn in Soviet policy which in 1929 decided upon the liquidation of the kulaks as a class, a decision official Russian Communist Party historiographers qualify as "a revolutionary transformation, in its consequences equivalent to the October Revolution." This hasty comparison fired all sorts of hopes in anti-Communists; they predicted peasant uprisings, the massacre of kulaks which bloodied Russia in the 'thirties was, they calculated, about to occur in China too. It is a grave mistake to try to decipher the history of the Chinese Revolution in terms of the Russian Revolution: to be sure, the Chinese leaders have used the example of the latter, but as a source of instruction which has spared them from duplicating its faults. And the situation in Russia in 1929 was radically different from the Chinese situation in 1955. True, Mao Tse-tung said that "the socialist revolution is a new revolution." So saying, he underscored the importance of the objectives to be attained. But in 1949 he had distinguished the democratic from the socialist phase in the Chinese Revolution and affirmed that violence would not be employed in achieving the second. That socialist

* Isaac Deutscher, usually better informed, is one of those who holds this view; he has expressed it in *France-Observateur*.

phase was in fact started the day the Communists took power and Mao's speech rather than announcing an abrupt shift in policy, fits evenly into a continually adjusted but constantly maintained line of action. A leftist deviation was corrected in 1953, the brake was applied to collectivization; the foot pressed too hard; a rightist deviation resulted, and this time, sure of the masses' support, Mao Tse-tung has given the signal for full steam ahead. But the Standing Committee's recommended Model Rules clearly do no more than confirm procedures which have been previously observed. There are only two changes: the collectivizing process is to be speeded up, and collectivization is now frankly aimed at the rich as a class. These instructions in no way imply a reversal of past policy or a drastic revision of the country's economy.

The reconstruction of the USSR began with a communism forged during a war that had ruined the peasantry, roused an immense discontent in its ranks, and had driven Lenin to the New Economic Policy which gave the kulaks a considerable economic importance. The Revolution had been wrought by the working class; they were workers who were dispatched into the country to handle peasant problems with which neither the bureaucrats nor even the leaders had any previous concrete experience. The 1929 about-face, sudden and brutal, insufficiently prepared generally and vague in detail, had inevitably to provoke anger and hostility, lead to violence and temporary disaster.

The Chinese Republic was born not of defeat but of victory; it was not hounded by White armies from the outset, but backed by a powerful ally, the Soviet Union. In liberated zones the peasantry had for years collaborated with the Red Army, itself recruited among the peasants: actually, patently, peasants wanted the Revolution and produced it; it freed them from serfdom, gave them land outright and with no strings attached. The leaders had roots in the peasant class, they militated in it, fought at its side, had broad firsthand knowledge of its problems; Mao Tse-tung, for example, had participated in the great Honan peasant movements of 1927 and in them discerned all the enormous possibilities they held for the future. This intimate experience, the outstanding experiments carried out in the Red Zones during the Civil War permitted the elaboration of a policy geared intelligently to the situation and sensitive to its slightest fluctuations. At the start some cadres acted too energetically, but these excesses were promptly checked. In the main the Communists have proceeded slowly, with prudence and in close contact with the masses. As a result the regime has retained the allegiance of the peasants who are grateful to it for the lands it has distributed to them and for the moderate taxes it has imposed. Suspicion greeted one measure: the establishment of a state monopoly of commerce in grain. The peasants were accustomed to disposing of their surplus as they pleased and did not like the system of purchase and resale according to definite plan. In 1954, heavy floods having washed out the crops in many provinces, a dearth ensued: the Minister of Commerce acknowledged that faults had been committed in buying and redistributing grain. But while those mistakes created tension, it cannot be compared with the counterrevolutionary fury of the Russian peasants, ruined by requisitions and ready for anything if incited by the kulaks. And it was owing precisely to the grain monopoly that rich Chinese peasants were unable to become the Russian kulaks' counterparts. The latter produced, in 1927, 600 million poods* of wheat, 130 of them for the market. The Nep's policy had encourged monopolization: the kulaks were able to starve the cities by refusing to surrender their stocked grain, and that is what drove the urban proletariat to take terrible action against them. China has never resorted to any such dangerous expedient as the Nep. It has passed no laws authorizing the lease of land or hiring of salaried field hands; where these things have been done it has been on a restricted scale, and the existence of state purchasing and resale agencies plus the state monopoly have prevented them from having grave consequences. From the start the government barred the way to speculation, precluded all private stocking of wheat, rice, or kaoliang, and filled its own storehouses. This remarkable preventive caution is paying off today: the rich peasants do not constitute a major economic force. "At the present time," Liu Shao-ch'i declared in September 1954 in a report to Congress, "the average rich peasant's property is in fact no more than twice the size of the ordinary peasant's: that is why, and thanks to the development of agricultural production co-operatives, we are able

* A pood equals 36.113 lbs.

to proceed gradually in ridding the rural areas of capitalism." Liu adds that "a struggle is, of course, inevitable"—but this is lip service paid to the Stalinist thesis according to which the class struggle intensifies as socialism gains ground, a notion that has just been denounced in the USSR. Whereas, although they comprised a powerful class, the "painless" incorporation of the kulaks into Russian economy was probably an impossibility, that of the rich Chinese peasants is in all likelihood going to be accomplished smoothly. As a matter of fact they do not really constitute a class; scattered throughout the countryside, without reciprocal ties, with no grip upon the national economy, unable to do any damage, there is no official talk of expropriating them. Their privileges will vanish the day the rest of the peasantry is well on its feet: state aid accorded to the co-operatives—in the form of loans, fertilizer, equipment—and denied to wealthy individual farmers, plus the effective advantages of working in groups will lead to the disappearance of rich peasants. Once farming becomes mechanized they will indeed, in order to obtain the use of tractors and other machinery, have to apply to join the co-operatives; and, harmless by then, they will probably be admitted. Today they can still try their hand at sabotage; but they are incapable of doing much to hurt the collectivization movement. One of the unusual features about Chinese policy is that it is simultaneously patient and preventive; a procedure is struck off the list as soon as it reveals a disquieting aspect and long before it can constitute a serious peril. This is why in seven years the regime has never had to go through any one of the crises by which the youthful Soviet Republic was so profoundly shaken.

The while forbidding rich peasants present access to the co-operatives, the Government, in February 1956, indicated that the problem of their admission would soon have to be faced. One read in the review *Chan Wang*:

The socialist revolution has won a decisive victory in the villages. Since the land reform, moreover, a good many former landowners have already been re-educated through work. With the spread of the co-operative farm movement and the introduction of planned purchase and sale of grain, the danger of exploitation by rich peasants has greatly diminished.

In their great majority the co-operatives have made a business go of it; the understanding and the conscientiousness of the cadres and of the co-operative members have steadily improved. That is why the conditions are now ripe for resolving the problem of admitting rich peasants and proprietors into the co-operatives.

In May of the same year, the *Kuang Ming Jih Pao* and the *Jen Min Jih Pao* published editorials guaranteeing a comfortable future to former landowners and rich peasants who have been suitably re-educated. The marked slowdown during 1956 of the campaign against counterrevolutionaries is further evidence that collectivization has not produced the tragic convulsions the anti-Communists were counting on.

This success finds its explanation in the circumstances I have outlined and in the care the Government has taken to have the voluntary membership doctrine observed. Never basing its policy upon abstract theories, it is not through respect for individual freedom it has imposed this rule but because it knows that force does not pay. Every time overzealous cadres tried certain pressure methods they ran into a blank wall. Among the co-operatives that had to be disbanded were those created by coercion: sabotage or plain everyday foot dragging brought them to failure. The point is that the human factor is of vital importance at the level the Chinese economy occupies today. The system's elements interlock so closely that every least cause produces magnified effects: an extra sack of rice contains the promise of a tractor; but a sack too few can threaten to reverse the mechanism. In this nip-and-tuck situation, where the battle for prosperity is being waged barehanded, where the start is from nothing, every single mu counts: and whether that mu yields a bushel more or a bushel less depends on every man's individual effort. At certain economic stages it is technically possible to treat the individual as a pure machine; not now. When as a day laborer you carry a bucket of cement from one place to another or as an engineer press a button, it does not much matter what mood you happen to be in. But spading, sowing, reaping will not be done well if done grudgingly. For collectivization to succeed the peasant must believe in it; he must be an enthusiastic member of a group he joined of his own free will. The last Congress of the

Chinese Communist Party once again uttered the warning: no coercion. Instead, patient explanation, quiet persuasion through *ad hominem* argument.

It is interesting to contrast the triumph of the Chinese undertaking with the defeat collectivization met in the People's Democracies. Like China, the Eastern Europe of 1945 found itself lacking in the means of production, without fertilizer, livestock, mechanical equipment, but with a swiftly growing population; except for Czechoslovakia, it had almost no industry either. Hungary in particular, where no land reform had ever been put through, was living in a poverty not beyond comparison with China's. In Hungary and Poland from 42 to 45 per cent of the population was made up of an agrarian proletariat and only 36 per cent of the small holdings produced any margin of profit at all. In 1945 the reform was legislated by Communists; three years later collectivization was begun; it was a resounding failure. What accounts for this difference?

François Fejtö* writes,

> In Hungary the landless peasant masses had been subject to twenty-five years of terrific and uninterrupted ideological and police pressure from which they emerged in a state of intellectual paralysis, disorientation, and hopelessness. The poor peasants and agricultural laborers were entirely under the influence of the "rural bourgeoisie," of kulaks, and gendarmes whose nationalist ideas and rabid anti-Communism they shared. And finally—this is perhaps the most important point—Eastern European peasantry had been told about rural developments in the Soviet Union. Whence the general climate of surliness—of distrust, hesitation, doubt—in which, upon the instigation of the Red Army and the Communists, the land reform transpired in 1945.

The "climate" was more favorable in Poland and Yugoslavia. But the problems the reform engendered almost everywhere in Europe did not arise in China; there it ameliorated without upsetting the life of the peasants; by and large they went on cultivating the same fields as before, but were now exempt from the rent that had crushed them. In Europe there were major shifts of population. It was necessary in Hungary to create four hundred thousand new dwellings and they had to be improvised under lamentable conditions. Furthermore in Europe as in China the size of the

* In *La tragédie hongroise*, Paris, 1957.

apportioned lots was very small; this is not apt to cause grave disruption in a country where farming has always been akin to gardening; but in one where extensive farming has been the rule, the dismemberment of great estates can be disastrous.

It would hence seem that collectivization represented a more vital necessity in Europe than in China; the paradox is that it was met there by such stubborn resistance. This can be explained, however. The Chinese leaders, having won the confidence and good will of the peasants, were able to launch a campaign for hygiene, to combat superstitions, to put some elementary organization into human activity; they made a prodigious effort in behalf of peasant welfare: production rose immediately. Confidence in the regime increased. The snowball system began to work in favor of socialization. The earliest co-operatives, founded on a voluntary basis, functioned well: after wavering for a short while, other peasants leaped on the bandwagon. Care was taken to avoid single-crop specialization on the collectivized properties. The absence of mechanical equipment prevented any from-one-minute-to-the-next innovations in farming methods. The knotty problem of livestock hardly presented itself, since the raising of animals has always been just about nonexistent in China. The transformation of agriculture was slow in pace and modest in scope.

In Europe the peasants were hostile to the communism which did not eliminate their poverty and of which, knowing what had happened in Russia, they were mistrustful. Instead of waiting until the peasants had been won over, the leaders—forced to do so by orders from higher authority, orders dictated by purely doctrinal considerations—had to act prematurely. For lack of a solid hold on the rural areas, they artificially provoked a class conflict: the middle-class peasants—whose interests the Chinese have so skillfully safeguarded—were lumped with the kulaks and the latter were persecuted. The resulting disorders hampered production. The co-operatives created were too big; they went too fast in their desire to mechanize agriculture; the peasants could not adjust to these quick changes. Discontent, incompetence formed a vicious circle, the snowball system worked backward: the co-operatives produced less than free lances; these, out of hatred for the co-operatives they had been forced into, sabotaged them and they fell deeper and deeper into discredit. Little wonder that these methods, diametrically opposite those used by the Chinese, produced contrary results. In 1951 almost all the Yugoslav* co-operatives were dissolved; 1953 brought a vast disbanding movement in Hungary, Mátyás and Rákosi halted it by force.

In this comparison we see that from the start China was able to and did profit from a much healthier political situation than that of any European country; China also had the advantage, owing to Soviet aid—much less generously bestowed upon the satellites—of being able to make heavy cash investments in agriculture. But the crucial factor was the leadership: competent and intelligent, it succeeded in working with the masses, never against them.

The poor peasants swiftly realized that the co-operatives would improve their fate. The middle-class peasants were less readily convinced. One of the reasons why they held back lay in the existence of the family community, in itself an exclusive productive group and marked by asocial tendencies. To make collectivization succeed it was necessary to break the old social structure: it corresponded to the old division of private property; collectivization requires that agrarian manpower be assembled into operating jointly on a larger scale; the workers are grouped in inclusive, extensive organizations, exploiting land all hold in common and from which each extracts an individual profit—but before this new form of integration can come about the producer has first to be detached from the former production unit. Socialism and the emancipation of the individual advance *pari passu*. That is why the proclamation of the Marriage Act aimed against the traditional family set-up has been of such importance. The technological revolution having only begun, developments within the social sphere have a direct impact upon the economic sphere in present-day China, and reciprocally economic progress is being achieved via social transformations. The evolution of the family is closely connected to the co-operative movement.

* The Yugoslavs were deaf to the Cominform's orders; but, fearing lest they be outstripped by Bulgaria, they too tried to speed up measures designed to strengthen socialism.

# 3. THE FAMILY

New China's enemies take the regime very bitterly to task for the antifamilial policy they impute to it. The government, they charge, scoffs at, as good as denies the existence of blood ties, is riding roughshod over the most sacred values. In their appraisal of the situation the Gossets* enter "annihilation of the family" in the debit column of their ledger.

China is doing nothing of the sort. Or rather she is doing no more than was done in France between the sixteenth and nineteenth centuries when the patriarchal group was forced to give way and the conjugal group emerged. Land ownership is the basis of the former; in every country in the Occident its disappearance has coincided with the advent of industry, movable property, and a working-class proletariat. China only recently began to industrialize and that is why the archaic family form has lasted there this long; the surprising thing is not that the family is undergoing change today, but that the change has taken so long to occur.

The traditional Chinese family, we have seen, is to be explained by the country's agrarian economy. It assumed a more rigid form than in any other civilization because institutions strove to eliminate every conflicting principle which might possibly encourage its evolution. When the Roman wife was finally accepted as a member of two gentes—the father's and the husband's—conflicts

* *Chine Rouge. An VII* (Paris, 1956).

resulted and these led to her emancipation: this change had repercussions in the entire social structure; in China there was no such duality, for woman was denied the quality of a human being. Nor was there any wholesome debate between older and younger generations: unconditional obedience to the elders was required of their juniors. An edict of the first Sung emperor, dating between 966 and 977 A.D., prohibited the members of a given family from taking separate domicile until the fourth generation: this rule was perpetuated. Dwelling under the same roof, every member of the group was subject to the patriarch's authority. The father had the power of life and death over his children, and he often exercised his right to destroy at birth those daughters he considered unnecessary mouths to feed; or he could sell them as slaves and frequently did. The son had to obey his father, the younger son the elder, every woman every man in the house. Matches arranged by a go-between were imposed upon young people who ordinarily married without having previously met; they then remained subject to the young husband's elders.

Certain conservatives praise the wondrous equilibrium of a system which left room neither for any warring between the sexes nor for dispute between individuals; their classical liberalism revolts against the discipline instituted by the present regime but takes no exception to the mailed-fist oppression that characterized the old familial code.

When toward the beginning of the twentieth century an industrial and commercial bourgeoisie began to develop, the economic foundations of the ancient familial cell were undermined; they likewise collapsed in the working class. The traditional family structure persevered; but deprived of all material justification, the authority exerted over them by a group of which they were no longer in any concrete sense an integral part soon began to appear arbitrary and intolerable in the eyes of both the young bourgeois and the young proletarians. In despair they underwent forced marriages whose burdens were lightened by no joy; since earliest times untold numbers of Chinese wives have taken refuge in suicide, many young husbands have followed their example. Conjugal hatred was so intense and general that, according to the Ministry of Justice's statistics, half the criminals executed between May and September

1925 had been sentenced to death for murder of their marriage partner.

The "Fourth of May Movement" intellectuals, in hot revolt against the ancient order, vented their grievances in a quantity of ideological and literary works. Chinese literature had for centuries depicted the woes of the familial system's victims. Most of the operas I saw in China presented lovers reduced to the depths of despair by the tyranny of their elders. That is the theme of the famous *Liang Shan-po and Chou Ying-ti* from which a film was made and shown in Paris under the title of *Les Amoureux:* despotic father forbids his daughter to marry the boy she has been in love with for years, he weds her to a stranger; the boy dies of grief and on her wedding day she follows him into the grave. In *The Pavilion of the West,* another famous drama, it is the heroine's mother who thwarts her desires. At the end of the eighteenth century the novel entitled *The Dream of the Red Chamber* won an immense audience. It described the decadence of a traditional family, related the tragic affair between a young man and his cousin; the hero was forced into a marriage he loathed, the heroine died of a broken heart. Their story was not told with resigned sympathy: outrage shows between the lines, and this cry of revolt was what found an echo in so many readers. A hundred years later Chinese youth recognized its image in the sacrificed couple. From the Fourth of May onward novels aimed against the family increased. The greatest success was Pa-chin's *The Family.* It describes the family of a rich West China merchant; all its members live under the same roof, terrorized by a conservative and despotic grandfather. He has obliged his oldest grandson, in love with a cousin,* to enter into a marriage of money. Learning that one of his sons (over thirty years of age) has a mistress, his anger explodes against him; the culprit, his wife, his daughter are summoned; the rest of the household—children, concubines, and slaves—is gathered in an adjoining room; a little girl peeps through the keyhole. "Well," shouts the old man, "why don't you slap your face as I bade you to do?" and the child sees her uncle, crimson, slap

* The theme of cousins falling in love is frequent; in *The Red Chamber* the lovers are cousins too. Young men seldom had an opportunity to meet girls save within the confines of the family itself.

himself with his own hands. The tyrant's grandson, the young Kao Cheh-min, alone objects to this scene. Cheh-min—in whom the writer doubtless presents a self-portrait—and his brother Chu-hwei incarnate the cultivated and restless youth of the period. Chu-hwei edits a students' magazine and engages in political activities; his grandfather stops him but the boy resists. Cheh-min is in love with one of his cousins, a young girl of emancipated spirit who also defies the tyranny of her mother: she flees the house and despite the parents' opposition the young pair marries. However, the eldest of the three brothers, who yielded to an enforced match, can do no better than preach submission to established order: he is a passive spectator to the death of his wife, victim of the ignorant parents' superstitions; only in the final pages of the story does he at last stiffen in revolt. No Chinese novel had ever gone through more printings: it gave voice to the resentments and hopes of an entire generation.

The traditional family bullied every individual in it, denying freedom, love, and marital happiness to them all. But its chief victims were the women. The horror of their former situation has been many times described; in no other country, so far as I know, has it been so appalling. In every civilization the history of women's rights is directly linked to the history of inheritance* which has evolved as a dependent variable of the changing economic and social complex. In China, however, what with the monolithic permanence of family structure from the beginning of recorded history down to the twentieth century, the right of succession did not alter: it excluded the woman; she had no share in the paternal heritage; so long as her husband lived, she owned nothing; with her husband's death, whether she were his wife or concubine, she inherited from him only upon condition she had borne him a son —and that son was the real legatee; she merely exercised a wardship over his property. Because she did not attain economic autonomy, the Chinese woman was unable, down through the centuries, to achieve any kind of independence. Not only was she always held as inferior to the man, as the rites celebrated at her birth attest, but she was conceded no rights whatsoever; not even the right to live: it was for the clan to grant it to her or deny it.

* As I tried to show in *The Second Sex*.

Throughout her entire lifetime she was subject to "The Rule of Triple Obedience" as formulated in the *Li Chi:* "The woman always follows the man. In her childhood she follows her husband; after the death of her husband she follows her son." Declares Confucius: "Woman is a being subject to man." Eternally a minor, her very children do not properly belong to her. "She who was my wife was also the mother of my son. Upon ceasing (by reputation) to be my wife, she ceased to be the mother of my son," explains, a grandson of Confucius, according to the *Li Chi.* Traditional morality cloisters the woman in the house where she is to devote herself to domestic chores and to looking after her offspring. The virtues recommended to her—according to Pan Chao who, in 92 A.D. at the time of the Hans wrote a *Lessons for Women*—were four in number: "Be truly a woman; be of seemly speech; be of proper bearing; be earnest in endeavor." The Empress Jen-liao-wen, in the twenty chapters of her *Institutes for Women,* is, toward the end of the fourteenth century, inspired by the same principles. To these two works, Wang Siang added two more under the Mings; and this corpus, known as *The Four Books of Women,* up until the twentieth century defined the Chinese woman's ethic, the fundamental axiom of which is in fine, "Obey"; and to this the Ming period contributes, by way of an elucidating corollary: "In woman, foolishness is virtue."

Codes, moral treatises are one thing, common practice another: lax custom often attenuates the rigor of the law; in China exceptional circumstances made a certain independence available to certain women of the upper classes and to courtesans; imperial favorites and especially some dowagers—the most celebrated example being the Empress Tzu Hsi—succeeded in concentrating wide powers into their hands. But these are isolated cases, of only anecdotal interest. The oppression of the Chinese woman was no less practical than theoretical. In many countries women of the lower classes have achieved material emancipation through work; this opportunity was denied to Chinese women. Agriculture remaining at the gardening stage, nothing technically prevented women from participating in work in the fields; however—in the North at least—they were confined to the house and destined exclusively to indoor tasks. The reason, so it seems to me, is obvious.

In this overpopulated empire labor came cheap while every last millet seed had its price; by claiming for themselves a monopoly over production, the men kept a secure grip upon a vital privilege: too obsessed by hunger to care about the extent of the efforts it cost them to survive, they were less eager to yoke the energies of the women than to eliminate them altogether. Whence the curse that hung over the Chinese woman: her working potential being viewed as superfluous, she was considered simply as someone extra to feed. As a servant or female she represented a commodity with a certain market value, but it was far lower than the worth conferred upon a boy for his productive capacities; it was quite natural that a famished father with plentiful children regard one daughter more as a useless burden; his power of life or death over her was acknowledged, he would simply be exercising a right: millions of girl babies were drowned or given as fodder to swine; this kind of child murder became so much a part of custom that the new "Marriage Act" had to specify explicitly that it constitutes a crime. In his study *Peasant Life in China* (1938) Hsiu Tung-Fei reports:

The practice of infanticide is accepted; its more common victims are girls. They have little worth in the eyes of parents because, as women, they cannot perpetuate the hearth and worship and because, directly they come of age, they will leave them. Among children under five years old one finds very few girls. In this village the number of boys is one hundred and thirty-five, of girls one hundred. Girls under sixteen are found in only one hundred and thirty-one families—37 per cent of the total figure—and in only fourteen families is there more than one daughter.

Pearl Buck recalls:

Once in a small gathering of friends, and not all of them poor or farm folk, we fell to talking of killing girl babies. There were eleven women present and all except two confessed that at least one girl child had been killed in each home. They still wept when they spoke of it, and most of them had not done the deed themselves, and indeed they declared that they could not have done it, but that their husbands or mothers-in-law had ordered the midwife to do it because there were too many girls in the family already.*

* *My Several Worlds.*

Even if she escaped deliberate murder at the start of the journey, the odds were strong that a little girl would soon perish by the wayside. The wolf of famine stood everlastingly at the Chinese peasant's door; life or death, especially insofar as children were concerned, depended upon a handful of rice or millet granted or refused: the boys received the largest shares, and the girls, without any need for violence, died of undernourishment; they were the first victims in time of epidemic or famine.*

Those who survived were eagerly got rid of as quickly as possible. Wealthy or well-to-do families could afford to buy servile labor. Nor did it cost much. Poor families sold their little girls into veritable bondage. In a report published in 1925 the Shanghai Child Labor Commission found:

> Young female children are commonly purchased and employed as domestic servants. They probably begin to work as soon as it is possible for them physically to do so. This practice is general throughout the country. It obviously lends itself to great abuse . . . The Commission has reason to believe, from the evidence given before it, that many slave children are employed in native brothels and trained to prostitution. Such sale of female children, although undoubtedly contrary to Chinese law, does not appear to be interfered with in any way by those charged with the administration of justice.

From Kulp,† whose account dates from the same period, I borrow the following description:

> Poor families need money and have too many daughters. The daughters consume rice and need clothes; when they are grown up they leave the home and furnish additional service to the productivity of the economic family of the group into which the girl is married. The parents in poor families consider it better therefore to get rid of the girl at the first opportunity and thus free themselves of her expenses and at the same time get some cash.
>
> The treatment of the slaves or house-maids differs with the various families, depending upon the dispositions and ethical standards of the

* One of the consequences was that the number of males being greater than that of females, many poor Chinese men remained bachelors and even, like Ah Q, the figure in Lusin's story, never "knew" a woman in the course of their entire lives.

† *Op. cit.*

masters and mistresses. They are primarily under the control of the wife and ultimately under the authority of the head of the economic family. He has complete control of and may sell the slaves or marry them off whenever he wishes. Although they come close to chattel property, they are still human beings and this fact is not lost sight of by the community. Unfair or harsh treatment would be subjected to the criticism of gossip.

Under the circumstances the life of the slave is hard. They are brought in as workers or servants to do the difficult and toilsome tasks about the home. They must draw water, cut wood, pound rice, wash clothes, cook, clean, care for the children, and so on. They are the first up in the morning and the last to retire. When they attain maturity they are either sold off as concubines to rich persons or married to men of poor families.

It is one of these slaves who appears in the famous contemporary opera, *The White-haired Girl*, which has reduced so many Chinese women to tears. "Criticism" from the neighbors, the only curb upon the masters' caprices, was apt to be particularly ineffectual in cases where those masters were landowners: one of the "blood crimes" the latter have been most frequently convicted of was for causing the death of young slaves, either deliberately or by dint of blows and ill-treatment. The mistress of the "White-haired Girl" jabs an opium needle through her tongue. In the heavily realistic novel *Chin-ping-mei** the author describes, as though they were the most commonplace occurrences, the torture of young female slaves being lashed to ribbons by the master or his wives, or, by way of punishment, spending nights kneeling in the courtyard, a large stone balanced upon their heads. Suicides—and this novel provides an example of one—were frequent. In later times, many little girls were thus sold to Shanghai factory owners in whose service they led the existence of galley slaves.†

The fate of those who were destined for marriage was not a great deal more clement. The code of marriage laws, based upon ancient religious practices, remained in force, just about as drawn up under the Tangs, down to the time it was abrogated by the new regime; it was cruel to both boys and girls; but there was one

* Written in the sixteenth century, translated into English as *The Golden Lotus*.

† See the following chapter, "Industry."

custom which only victimized the little girl: often, while still very young, she was sold to her future husband's family for whose profit she was made to do whatever kind of work. Writes Kulp:

> Not all of the girls brought into the homes are slaves. . . . baby girls are bought into the poor families to be the future wives of their baby sons. This is known as adopting a baby daughter-in-law. The reasons for this practice are: (a) it is more economical; the baby costs less than an adult girl and the wedding ceremonies may be simplified or even omitted; (b) an additional worker is secured for the home; (c) the child is trained into the habits of the family. Sometimes instead of purchase there is an exchange of girl babies between families in which there are infant sons and daughters. . . .
>
> The practice does not always work out successfully, however, for the familiarity between the betrothed persons leads to disrespect. They do not love each other in many cases, murmur and quarrel, and even break out in open fights. Moreover, the treatment of the girl by the mother-in-law is sometimes of such a character as to create estrangement within the village groupings and with the girl's own family. It also encourages early marriage, which is bad when the persons have not attained biological maturity. It does, however, displace effectively infanticide.

Infanticide was avoided, but she who escaped death was not much better off alive. She was treated like a beast of burden and might well succumb to blows inflicted by her mother-in-law; when young, the latter had been similarly mistreated by her husband and in-laws; vindictive, thirsty for revenge, she would compensate for her own sufferings and impotence by tormenting her daughter-in-law. Very often if her son showed himself disinclined to beat his young wife, she would oblige him to. Generation after generation suffered the shackles of feminine resentments, and each newcomer fell victim to it. It was the mother-in-law who in the most everyday and implacable manner incarnated familial oppression; and the young wife had also to endure the father-in-law's tyranny. As for the husband, detesting a partner he had not chosen, he was often enough willing to beat her without being urged. There were concubines with whom, if he had the means, he could find consolation for the rigors of an imposed marriage; but no one raised a protest if a husband slew his adulterous wife. He could whenever he pleased repudiate his wife; in certain cases she had, in principle, the right to seek divorce: but as her family would not have agreed to have her back on its hands this exit from her plight was virtually blocked. It might happen that her husband sold her to a wealthy man who wanted a concubine either for his pleasure or in order to bear him a child. Widowhood would not free her: she remained the property of her husband's family. It was almost impossible for her to escape them through remarriage. Tai-tsu promulgated a decree in 1386: "That family shall be exempted from public service and the house shall be honored if in it there be a woman who widowed before the age of thirty observes widowhood until fifty."* Thenceforth families exerted upon widows all the pressure necessary to prevent them from taking new husbands. An inspector was specially charged to assemble reports on the moral character of widows. Until the Republic, no end of temples and pai lou were raised in honor of those widows who had remained chaste under particularly remarkable or trying circumstances. Needless to say, all this led to abundant fraud and chicanery. But tradition took root: remarriage was forbidden to widows. Were one of them to presume to violate the taboo, the men of her clan esteemed themselves authorized to kill her. Thus, having once entered a family with a wife's title, the woman could not leave it without relinquishing her life: which, over the course of the ages and down to our own times, was the solution elected by countless Chinese women; they would drown themselves in a near-by pond or hang themselves.

As for concubines, their status entirely depended upon their husband's good will; those who gave him sons were favored and often took precedence over a barren wife; in general they ranked below a legitimate wife; the husband could repudiate them if he so chose, they were guaranteed nothing.

It was not until she reached old age that a woman acquired a certain security; her children owed her that respect which is displayed to all aged persons in China. This was the reward held out to young wives: be patient, suffer in silence, you too will be a mother-in-law one of these days.

A striking symbol for the Chinese woman's servitude was provided by the custom of footbinding which was adopted during the eighth century A.D. Under the Tangs there was keen admiration for

* It was supposed that she stood slight chance of remarrying after fifty.

the tiny feet and arched slippers of certain dancers and courtesans. The sovereign of Nan-t'ang, a poetaster, conceived the delicate idea of artificially reducing the size of women's feet. Of this innovation Chinese eroticism made a law. Minstrels and bards sang untiringly of these miniature feet—designated lyrically as "golden lilies," "perfumed lilies"—and of the seductiveness of the tiny "night-slippers" they pattered in. In the novel I have mentioned, *Chin-ping-mei*, an erotic image par excellence is that of a naked young woman, her body whitened by lotions and creams, and her feet shod in crimson slippers. The heroine, Golden Lotus, drives a rival to suicide because she is so impudent as to step into Golden Lotus' slippers while wearing her own, thus demonstrating who has the smaller feet. The custom shocked the Manchu emperors who moved to abolish it; but they were to rescind their prohibition: infested by this Chinese refinement, the Manchus imposed it upon their own women. A man of letters, Fang Hsien, composed a whole book on the art of foot-binding. It was a rare city, he averred, that could boast ten perfect specimens. He arranged them in five main categories and eighteen different types: a well-bound foot, he felt, ought to be chubby, soft, and elegant. "Slender, a foot is cold; if muscled, hard and irredeemably vulgar . . . As for elegance, it is not to be judged save by the mind's eye." During the eighteenth and nineteenth centuries some writers did indeed attack this maiming practice; but it was not outlawed until 1911—and was continued a good while afterward, for old women with atrophied feet are not an uncommon sight in Peking itself.

The odd part is that this custom was not simply one of those erotic extravagances by which the so-called superior classes distinguish themselves; at least in the North, it was forced upon women of every rank and station.* The explanation is that it gave the appearance of a destiny to a fate that men had chosen to impose upon women: confinement. The lamed peasant woman was

* A Chinese of Nationalist sympathies, Lin Yutang, irritated—and justly so—by the white man's superiority complexes, notices a similarity between the "bound foot" and the "wasp waist" striven after by Western "waistbinding" techniques. But only bourgeois ladies had to put up with the inconveniences of the corset; Western peasant women knew nothing worse than the bodice. Likewise, it is the middle-class woman of today who goes to work in high heels; the peasant girl wears them only when going dancing.

definitively disqualified for work in the fields and permanently restricted to household activity. In the South, where she took a hand in tilling the fields, the fashion was not general. But the Northerners had the regrettable singularity of combining the ordinarily dissociated chores required of a woman: they viewed her both as a servant and an erotic object. This domestic animal who toiled from dawn to dark was subjected to the painful refinements applied to courtesans. The old habit so revolts Chinese today that it is against the law for a woman with bound feet to appear on the stage of a theater.

Now and then in the course of the centuries a lonely voice would speak out against the wretched fate reserved for women. It was decried in a poem written in the second century A.D. by Fu Hsuanam. In the twelfth century, Yuan Tsai deplored that woman was treated as an inferior creature. Lin Chien, in the sixteenth, pointed to the injustice of the laws governing divorce. Author of a book called *Feminine Models,* Lu Kouen demanded that women be given some education. At the end of the eighteenth century three writers with differing degrees of vigor attacked what Lin Yutang calls "the post-Confucianist sadico-puritan system." Yu Cheng-hsieh (1775-1840) contributed four essays: "On Chaste Widows," "On Chaste Maidens"—maidens, that is, who refused to marry after the death of a fiancé*—"Proving that feminine jealousy is not a vice," and a postcript to the book on Tang dynasty customs which is an essay on foot-binding. Yu denounced the abuses of "chastity," found that a wife had every reason to feel and show jealousy because of her husband's concubines, wished to have marriage based on sexual equality; and he castigated the custom of binding feet. He summarized his thought in these words: "Lower the status of women and that of men is lowered also."

Yüan Mei (1716-1797), a poet and thinker of revolutionary bent, held women in high esteem: he had some among his pupils, he encouraged them to write and published their work, he formed a veritable school of poetesses. Concubines he had in number, but he wanted women to be allowed equal sexual license. Feminist claims were included in his anarchistic revolt against the entirety

* In view of the age at which young people were betrothed, it was not rare for a young Chinese girl to become somewhat of a "widow" at sixteen; in which case she was very highly thought of if she abandoned all further ideas of marriage.

of the Confucian system; and the influence he had was considerable. Finally, Li Ju-Chen (1763-1830) in 1825 wrote a feminist novel, *Ching-hua yüan* which had a lively success. The author imagined that a hundred fairy folk had changed into women; endowed with manifold and wonderful powers, they grouped around a Tang dynasty empress, Wu Hou, who has a reputation—historically justified, it would seem—for nymphomania; they passed official examination, became mandarins, and instituted a "Kingdom of Women" in which it was the men who were oppressed: Lin, the hero of the story, recounts the terrible suffering he experienced as a result of having his ears pierced and his feet bound.

These protests had a moral character; men of letters in the eighteenth century professed a humanist ethic: they could not very well accept a tradition by which human beings, although of female sex, were treated as things and habitually tortured. Like all idealistic rebellions, this one came to nought. Woman's condition began to improve only when the economic structure of China started to evolve: when a Chinese capitalism and proletariat emerged. Women found jobs as workers in the cities: although this was a new form of servitude and one of frightful harshness, the fact of earning a little money by their own resources gave some of them a feeling of independence. At the close of the nineteenth century a curious movement of opposition to marriage was seen to take shape in Kwantung. In *The Dream of the Red Chamber* two of the heroines have so pronounced a disinclination for marriage that they decide to enter a convent and take the veil: girls sometimes resorted to that solution but it was accessible to only a few. The working girls of Kwangtung created communities of a sort; separated from their husbands or unmarried, they lived as wage earners. Originating above all in the silk mills, the movement attained such proportions that the government had to open asylums for these women who in their old age had neither family nor any other means of support. The organization was still alive in Canton in 1940.

But it was the bourgeoisie which, as it was a rising class, was winning control over society, manners, and laws. Parallel to the revolt against the feudal type of family ran a current in favor of the emancipation of women. Its beginnings were timid and in part stamped by Western influence. In 1860 missionaries opened the first primary education schools for girls. In 1898 the University of Tientsin created a branch for women and the first teaching program for women was established. The first woman's teachers college was opened in 1903. With the 1917 "Renaissance" and especially the Fourth of May Movement things began to move quickly. A class that was calling for a democratic constitution, that wanted to impose Western social structures upon China, that professed a humanism based upon respect for the human being and was demanding rights for the individual, could not allow woman to remain a domestic animal. Abase woman and you abase man, Yu Cheng-hsieh had said; the young Chinese bourgeoisie, passionately eager to rise economically and culturally, decided to elevate the status of the woman: upon her it bestowed a freedom comparable to that enjoyed by women in the West. Inspired by Ibsen, Hu Shih—one of the Fourth of May key figures—wrote *The Most Important Act in Life*, a play that concerned marriage and which had broad repercussions. In 1917 a feminist review appeared and was followed by many more. The first junior college for girls—theoretically founded in 1912—opened in 1919, and that same year women were allowed to take courses at the University of Peking. Most bourgeois girls made frivolous use of their new-found liberty: they put waves in their hair, removed the wrappings binding their feet and donned silk stockings and high-heeled shoes, went out, went dancing, had sexual flings. Others, the minority, took serious advantage of the new possibilities for study and work that were available to them.

The middle class demanded that the old feudal code be abolished and replaced by laws favorable to bourgeois supremacy. It had to wait until 1931: the Kuomintang then gave it satisfaction with a new "Code of the Family." The foremost innovation was that a woman could now inherit; she was presently considered a human being; movable property was no longer held to be indivisible, like real estate; able at last to be heir to the one, there was no longer any reason for excluding her from succession to the other. With regard to marriage, bourgeois individualism insisted that it be free. The code stipulated that it was not to be imposed by the parents, that it did not constitute a commercial transaction, and as a consequence it became illegal for go-betweens to take a broker's commission; engagements could not be contracted until the girl had reached the age of fifteen and the boy seventeen. The wife could sue for divorce in cases where the husband mistreated her or was unfaithful to her. The law did not officially allow concubinage.

In a woman the bourgeois man is looking for a counterpart, not an equal. The new code fell far short of according the same status to the two sexes; it was still imbued with ancient traditions. The family remained patronymic, agnatic, patriarchal: the paternal parents enjoyed preferential treatment. Were a child to become an orphan its guardians and the members of the family council looking after it were to be selected from among persons belonging to the father's side only. In the event of divorce it is still the father who keeps the children, and in all cases his authority is superior to the mother's.

In actual practice the new law went even less far; like a good many others Chiang Kai-shek proclaimed, its chief purpose was "to save face." Theoretically, it catered to individualistic and liberal tendencies in the bourgeoisie; but its more conservative aspects came to the fore in the manner it was applied. The regime was more interested in maintaining order than in furthering freedom; superficially modernizing the country, it was dedicated to preserving its ancient structures. As a result, most of the different articles of the code remained dead issues. Marriage was to be by free consent: but as the couple's signature was not required that freedom had no safeguard. Concubinage was widely tolerated; the father was given every facility to acknowledge his illegitimate issue; all the jurisprudence affirmed the concubine's right to alimony in the event that, repudiated, she became indigent. She was considered as a member of the family and thanks to this bias the clauses relating to the husband's adultery are nullified: for adultery exists only if the spouse enters into "extra-familial" sexual relations; but the concubine inhabits the conjugal house; thus the curious conclusion was arrived at, that the Chinese husband could lawfully betray his wife provided he did so at home. In any event, the only adultery for which the penal code prescribed punishment was that committed by women; the magistrate was not obliged to grant the request of a woman asking to file an affidavit. As for ill-treatment it was grounds for divorce only if it "rendered cohabitation impossible." Summarizing a certain number of court decisions, Wang Tse-sin, in his thesis on divorce, concludes: "Light or accidental injury or wounds inflicted in the course of dispute or reprimands are insufficient as grounds." From among many others I cite the following opinion delivered by the Nanking Tribunal (in 1933):

> Rendering cohabitation impossible signifies that the ill-treatment is habitual or has attained a degree that cannot be tolerated. If there have merely been blows given for an idle or momentary cause, since they are not habitual and have not attained a degree that cannot be tolerated, they do not fulfill the conditions requisite for the granting of divorce.

But at what point does habit begin? How many times a week may a husband beat his wife before these beatings qualify as habitual? And what amount of blows can the spouse tolerate? In effect, unless one of these scenes resulted in a broken limb or a community scandal, the wife remained without recourse against abusive treatment.

The code had been drafted because of bourgeois pressure and for the bourgeoisie's use. In China, as in France at the time of the Revolution, the bourgeoisie, the while thinking of itself as an all-inclusive class, was by no means anxious to share its privileges. Nobody bothered to overexercise laws that, had they become a concrete reality, would inevitably have precipitated profound social upheavals. The code was given no undue publicity; even in the cities it was ignored. Olga Lang* notes that as late as 1936 in Peking and Shanghai, wives and widows were still being sold by husbands or families for three hundred dollars. Certain working girls were marrying freely. Nevertheless, newspapers and hospital reports were filled every day with stories of young women being tortured, brutalized, driven to suicide. In the rural areas no one so much as heard mention of the new code: it would have implied an emancipation of the peasants, and that was the last thing the regime wanted. In 1936, Jean Escarra, a specialist in Chinese law, found that "the immense majority of the peasants know nothing and will continue to know nothing of these rules."

By this time, however, the Communists in the liberated regions had established new laws, new customs. The Marriage Act, passed

* Cf. *La Vie en Chine.*

and promulgated in 1950, confirmed and codified them. It asserts the individual's freedom within the context of the family; it affirms the complete equality of the sexes. It abolishes child marriage, forbids the adoption of child daughters-in-law, it requires the free consent of the partners who must register their marriage in writing, it outlaws infanticide, prohibits concubinage, authorizes the remarriage of widows, accords the right to seek divorce to the woman and to the man alike and in this procedure recognizes no pre-eminence of the father over the mother: neither the man's name nor his family are allowed any precedence as against those of the woman. In case of divorce, the child, if still in the cradle, is entrusted to the mother; later on, depending upon the child's interest, he is entrusted to either the one or the other of the two parents. Thus, in contrast to Chiang's 1931 code, the Marriage Act plainly and frankly establishes a conjugal family based upon the equality of man and wife and their equal right to self-determination.

This act has a concrete objective: to demolish the antique structure of rural society, and to replace it with another conforming to the requirements of the new economy. A campaign was launched the moment the Liberation was achieved. To topple the caste system, said Gandhi, one has but to focus one's efforts upon its nerve center: the condition of the untouchables. In similar fashion the Communists have concentrated upon the status of women. The preamble introducing the Marriage Act to the Chinese people emphasizes that its beneficiaries are "not only women, but the entire community." But in the interest of the community the accent is today being placed on a drive to emancipate the women. To achieve this end it is above all the women whose energies are being mobilized. Founded in 1949, the Federation of Women—presided over at the present time by Ts'ai Chang, wife of Li Fu-chuan—absorbed all the other women's organizations; subsidiary Women's Associations were formed in all cities and villages, their number one objective being the application of the Marriage Act. A Committee for the Implementation of the Marriage Act was also set up. Government authorities, the courts of justice, the trade unions, the youth organizations collaborated to this end. Literature, the theater especially, actively propagandized in behalf of free marriage and the emancipation of women.

Even in France common custom is, on this point, less enlightened than the law; matches are still arranged and some marriages are pure business deals. In China, the new legislation contradicts the several-thousand-year-old traditional practices of half a billion peasants; it was with joy they welcomed the land reform, but the abolition of the feudal family is, for many of them, a scandal. The members of the Women's Associations and the cadres encountered obstinate resistance. The following story was told to me in Peking: an old peasant, after the land reform an enthusiastic supporter of the regime but none the less as convinced as ever of his patriarchal rights, killed one of his daughters-in-law who, following several years of widowhood, had just remarried. Arrested, he was informed that this murder was a crime for which the Marriage Act prescribed capital punishment.

"Who made this law?" he asked.

"Chairman Mao."

The old man shook his head. "Ah, no," said he, "you'll never make me believe that a man as honest and wise as Chairman Mao could have made any such harebrained and unjust law."

I would not answer for the authenticity of the anecdote, but it is perfectly plausible. It seemed a flagrant injustice to the parents and clan chiefs that anyone presume to deny them their authority.

What worsened affairs was that the movement started off in high gear. Right away, many marriages concluded under parental pressure were dissolved: there were 396,000 divorces in the first half of 1952; in the countryside the Marriage Act was referred to as "The Divorce Law." This haste was justified by the urgency of individual domestic situations; it was necessary as well to liberate the child daughters-in-law immediately. Nevertheless, many a cadre's zeal carried him too far; their interpretations of the law were too strict, above all in questions concerning concubinage. The act forbade the perpetuation of the custom in the future; it did not require the abrupt dislocation of existing situations. Certain cadres compelled men to eject their concubines; rendered homeless, penniless, many of them took their lives. Peasants rose up; cadres were assassinated.

The government sharply condemned these clumsy tactics; it reiterated the principle of nonconstraint and assured the cadres that the peasants would not be won over save by tact, by patience, and in time. "Although feudalism has been rooted out of the political and economic life of the country, it still exists in customs," the cadres were reminded in 1953 by Liu Ching-fan, head of the Committee for the Implementation of the Marriage Act. He foresaw "a long and patient process of education." A report on the psychological climate in Shansi—liberated before 1949 and a relatively advanced region—discloses that between 10 and 15 per cent of the families have a thorough social consciousness; while from 5 to 10 per cent are distinctly backward in their attitudes. As for the bulk—some 75 per cent—"Abusive treatment of women has disappeared, but the idea of paternal authority remains to a varying extent." In the other provinces, "remnants of feudal attitudes survive to a greater or lesser degree."

As in the collectivization movement, a middle way must be found between two extremes: clashing head-on with the peasants or abandoning the work of winning acceptance for the new legislation. It is thumbs down on coercion; persuasion is the weapon to use. The act is patiently explained in the schools, evening courses, political education classes.

At the present moment, the transitional character of rural society is evident. Families are continuing to live under a common roof. However, the sale of children and pseudo-adoption has just about vanished; the wife is no longer beaten by her parents-in-law nor by her husband: the Women's Associations, the community at large would not put up with it. Murders and suicides have become rare. I asked how feudal vestiges could actually accommodate themselves to modern ways, how it was possible for new relationships to fit into the old structure. If a formerly brutal husband reforms, does not his wife continue to harbor some bitterness? In certain cases, yes, Madame Cheng told me; but she will not show it, for it has been explained to her that she should let bygones be bygones. By and large, though, wives are too readily inclined to forgiveness: behind them they have such a lengthy tradition of blind acceptance that they scarcely realize the extent to which they have been misused. And what about the husband? Has he become placid overnight? If his wife earns money, if she is reputed a good worker, he is proud of her. In other cases he may chafe under the bridle;

be that as it may, blows are at an end. Husband-wife relations are not, however, the major problem; for the young married woman, the real household tyrant is her mother-in-law. I noticed that education and propaganda lay particular stress on the relationship between mother-in-law and daughter-in-law. Numerous stories exhort older women to adjust to new customs; the young are urged to be understanding and polite. One propaganda poster that has been distributed almost everywhere shows a young wife and her mother-in-law going together to night school. It seems as though it is more difficult to bring about a reconciliation between different generations than between the sexes.

Madame Cheng spent two years in the village near Hangchow I spoke earlier of having visited, and she became closely acquainted with all its families. She told me that upon occasion the young wife abuses the new situation. There was one, the mother of three children, who lived with her husband and father-in-law; and it was she who beat the two men; they would use violent language with her but dared go no further because she threatened to drown herself: so many Chinese women used to do so that the threat means something; fearing lest they be accused of feudal brutality, the men would give verbal vent to their rage, and she would lay on all the more energetically. The village grew disturbed. The president of the co-operative, Madame Cheng, and some others entered into consultation. They betook themselves to the woman's house and reprimanded her. "I'm going to jump into the water!" she announced. "Do," was the reply. She did not jump; disarmed, she promised to turn over a new leaf, while the two men swore to each other that no matter what she did they would hold out.

Freedom of marriage, guaranteed by law, has yet to become concrete practice. A story, "The Registration," made into a very popular play, shows all the difficulties faced by two young people who wanted to get married just before the Marriage Act was passed; many of those difficulties still subsist. To begin with, the psychological pressure brought upon children by their parents—especially upon daughters by their mothers. One of the heroines of "The Registration," Yen-Yen, is in love; but her mother threatens to hang herself if the girl does not consent to an arranged marriage. Yen-Yen finally gives in, goes to the main town in the district to be married to the man selected for her and whom she has never set eyes on; a little boy trots up—her intended—he is charming, but only ten. The registrar of marriages refuses to wed Yen-Yen to a child; when later the Act is promulgated, Yen-Yen finds the courage to resist her mother and marry according to her own heart's desire. Madame Cheng told me of a similar blackmail case that had occurred in her village. A girl was in love with a young peasant, hard-working, engaging, and in love with her; a Hangchow worker, adorned with all the prestige conferred by life in the big city, was presented to the mother by a family cousin playing the role of an intermediary: he had a job, said she, in a silk-goods factory and earned a lot. This he proved by one day turning up in the village on a bicycle and with a bundle under his arm. Nobody knew its contents, but the word sped about: "He came with a bundle!" and his reputation grew. In imitation of Yen-Yen's mother, the mother of the girl in question employed the "Marry him or else I'll hang myself" threat. The girl did not dare resist. When he came to see his fiancée, the lucky suitor obtained leave to sleep in an attic. Meanwhile the rejected lover was meditating suicide too. One of his friends discovered that the alleged worker was in reality a Taoist priestling who lived grubbily in a partially ruined temple. Aghast, the mother wished to have no more to do with the impostor; but there he was, solidly installed in her attic. "They asked me to go and talk with him," said Madame Cheng. "He was sitting on his bed smoking a little pipe, and after I'd spoken to him, his reply was: 'What is said, is said.' In the end he was obliged to leave." It was explained to the weeping mother that she had acted very shabbily indeed. And in the meantime the young peasant had lost interest in the girl. "I want all of a heart," said he, "she only gave me half of hers." To help her forget her woes the victim in the story was sent to high school in Hangchow.

Peasant living conditions pose a further and serious obstacle to free marriage. In the past, the go-between, in return for a commission, used to arrange matches between young people living in separate villages; this practice has been abolished; but young countryfolk do not have much opportunity to meet. So it was that in 1955, on "Women's Day," the Government made an official announcement:

In many villages matters are still at the stage where marriage is arranged through the agency of a third party. This must be allowed to comprise a voluntary form of marriage, for a great number of villagers do not yet have a sufficient collective life.

The intermediary role is often adopted by the Women's Associations, by Party or Communist youth group members. It is of less importance in the cities: students, employers, workers, young Communists work together and become acquainted. But even in the city—and still more so in the village—the young are still hampered by the age-old tradition of passivity and shyness that has been inculcated in them. The heroines of "The Registration" are emancipated enough to go out for walks with their boy friends; and by doing so they have earned a bad reputation, which is the pretext advanced by the clerk for refusing to register the marriage of one of them, even though she has obtained her mother's consent. When the Act is issued, the cadres charged with seeing to its enforcement congratulate the two girls for having fought in behalf of free marriage. Notwithstanding, it takes a good deal of boldness before two young people can manage to see one another even today in the backward villages, which are numerous. The oldsters censure them. And they themselves are inhibited by ancient prejudices: they consider it unseemly to acknowledge their sentiments; still more so to declare them. Kang Chuo has written a story, "My Two Hosts," in which a young schoolteacher chats with a young peasant at whose house he has been lodging for several months; both are twenty-two and close friends. "Shuan-chou suddenly smiled; he gave me a dig with his elbow and, with an impish grin, asked: 'Lao-Kang, have you a girl friend?' 'Me? I . . . I—what do you want to know for?' I felt the color coming into my cheeks and hastened to add: 'If you ask me such a question it's because you've got one yourself.' 'No, I don't have one, not yet,' said Shuan-chou, turning scarlet. He looked the other way, a little smile on his lips." Boys that bashful are not liable to display much determination when in love. Propaganda, however, encourages them to: it is proof of good citizenship to dare court a girl and request her hand. I have read several stories where glowing praise is bestowed upon the heroic couple who agree to meet by moonlight, upon the dauntless peasant lad who at harvesttime had the grit to strike up a conversation with the girl working beside him.

The girls are still more reserved than the boys. In one of Madame Cheng's novels there figures a girl student who lives in Paris about 1930; she is bright, has advanced notions; several of her young compatriots are—silently—in love with her; she too is in love, but chooses to marry another: the first who ventures to propose to her. Such things are not exceptional. Tsai one day told me, "When several boys are interested in a girl, she usually marries not the one she is fondest of but whoever is the first to speak." Again many girls are blamed for still regarding marriage as a money matter. "They have always been viewed as merchandise," Madame Cheng said to me; "well, today, they're viewing themselves as merchandise." The *Kuang Ming* in May 1955 assailed the bourgeois spirit still presiding over a great many matches. Too many girls, rather than work, are on the lookout for a husband who will take care of them; working girls want a husband rich enough to enable them to leave the factory; village girls dream of setting up housekeeping in the city. "The women won't really be liberated until the day when they are earning their own livings," said Madame Cheng. When we were visiting her village she drew my attention to a girl who, for her, represented a typical example of a thoroughly emancipated peasant. Very intelligent, she took three months to learn two thousand characters by the new accelerated method. Unfortunately, she was poor in arithmetic and had failed the examination which would otherwise have allowed her to enter high school. Industrious, clever, she earns two hundred and fifty yuan a year picking tea and has a quantity of admirers. The year before, she was uncertain whether to marry or keep on with her studies. Madame Cheng recommended the latter alternative. She learned five hundred more characters and has so improved her mathematics that she is now the accountant in one of the co-operatives. However she is engaged to marry a clerk in the city. But as her work attaches her to the village she will continue—at least for the time being—to live there. She will see her husband on Sundays.

Clearly economic independence and freedom go hand in hand. One of the purposes behind the emancipation campaign is to make the working potential of women available to the country. Conversely, so long as the village woman confines herself to domestic chores, she will remain, in the family's eyes and in her own, a semiparasite even if she was not overlooked by the land reform. When, performing the work inside the framework of the family group, she helps at tasks in the fields, vagueness still clings to her economic contribution, and this being so, she cannot achieve a distinct individuality. But on the other hand the moment the co-operative pays a young woman a salary which she has earned entirely by herself and which belongs entirely to her, no one feels he has any prerogative over her; the autonomy she has won is meaningful. It is through extending the co-operatives that the Chinese peasant woman's emancipation will be brought about. In one propaganda text* a young wife and her mother-in-law are shown in conflict with each other. Chin-Kuei is an exemplary working girl, president of the village Women's Association; instead of spinning cotton, she prefers to sell charcoal in the winter and in the summer to work in the fields. The mother-in-law, receiving a visit from her own daughter, bitterly complains to her of Chin-Kuei's willfulness. Returning to the house with her brother-in-law, Chin-Kuei walks in upon their conversation; both reproach her, she argues in her own defense. "Figure it out for yourselves," says she. "It takes two days to spin a pound of cotton and earn five shengs of rice. I can easily sell enough charcoal in one day to earn five shengs of rice. So why not?" And she continues: "To make myself a suit would take two days, add seven to make a pair of shoes: all told, nine days. I earn five shengs of rice a day: forty-five in nine days. For twenty shengs I can get a better suit and shoes than I could make by myself; the advantage is self-evident." Convinced, the brother-in-law finally says to his own wife: "Do like Chin-Kuei. If you other women really want to emancipate yourselves you'll have to work harder and take on more responsibilities—that's the distaff that will stand you in better stead."

The majority of the city women are still housewives; but in many places they are organized. In 1950 some of the women of Fushun formed mutual-aid teams; there were misgivings at first but all the workers' wives belong to them today. Their children

* Chao Shu-li, "The Distaff."

are looked after in day nurseries; in case of illness or overwork "help services" send them assistance to take care of the cooking, the household, the youngsters; they attend evening classes on Mondays, Wednesdays, and Fridays; they read the press, listen to the radio, receive instruction in household management and a political education.

As for the workingwomen, their wages are the same as the men's; they deposit their children in nurseries where babies can be wet-nursed; they are granted pregnancy leave and a retirement pension at the age of forty-five. There are still few workingwomen. In the textile industry 60 per cent of the workers are women. Shanghai's mechanical industries employ 7 per cent women. In Kwangtung their number rose from 110,000 in 1952 to 170,000 in 1954. At Mukden there are 47,000 women workers, 14,000 at Anshan. Regarding the liberal professions, according to the 1955 report presented by Chang Yu, one of the Women's Federation vice-presidents, the proportion of women in universities and colleges is 17 per cent, 12 per cent in the magistracy, 16 per cent among bank employees.

In this sphere as in many others China offers instances of a backwardness on the one hand and on the other a progress that outdoes what can be found anywhere else in the world. Innumerable are the peasant women still under the yoke of tradition; meanwhile, there are women railway engineers and cabinet members.* The group which is the most radically delivered of the old mentality is that of the women students; they consider that they have the same responsibilities, the same independence as men, and they are readily and easily assuming both. I had a two-hour private conversation with a girl medical student whose French was faultless. She showed not a hint of an inferiority complex nor of its usual correlative, a militant self-assertiveness. Very pretty, her hair done in long braids, she was wearing a red sweater and a navy blue skirt. She spoke with a child's earnestness and the inimitable naturalness of the Chinese; she seemed quietly and completely at ease. She is in the second year of her studies and her chief interest is surgery,

* Twelve per cent of the members of the National People's Congress are women, i.e., 147 of a total 1,226. There are four Ministers and four Vice-Ministers who are women.

a career that is not closed to women in China; but she expects, and does not excessively regret, that she will be recommended to specialize in gynecology; she has directed several deliveries, emphasizing painless methods and, she told me with a degree of pride, in most of the cases she has handled, the patient has not suffered. At present she lives in Peking with her parents; she will, she knows, be sent to some faraway post and she does not entirely look forward to this exile, what with the infrequency of vacations and the great distances. "But when you're young you adjust to all that," she said confidently. "And I prefer to go where I'll be of most help" —this is not pious sentiment on her part: plainly what matters to her is getting an education and making herself useful. Never do Chinese women students, as is so often the case in France, envisage giving up their work when they are married;* the state has provided their education and maintenance, they want to repay the debt. I recall those American college girls at Smith and Vassar who used to tell me: "When we get out we'll take a job for a year or two. But it's not the job we're interested in. The point is to get married, that's all. A job's the best way to find a husband."

At school, I ask, is there any rivalry between the men and women students? The question surprises her. In China no intellectual need fear unemployment; cadres are lacking, there is room for everybody. Men do not view women as competitors. Moreover the woman's subservience having been institutional and extreme in the past, men were never called upon to reassure themselves of some innate supremacy by developing masculinity complexes. When young, they were, themselves, too beaten down by the authority of their elders to derive pride from their sexual prowesses. Neither the virility myth nor the battle between the sexes have ever existed among the Chinese.† And that is why their ancient love poems and stories are so touching; far from squaring off against one another in their dissimilarities, the partners feel themselves attached through a common plight: youth. Together, they would try to pit themselves against the persecuting older generation. It is disguised as a boy that the heroine of *Les Amoureux* inspires sentiments in

* The *Kuang Ming* has reprehended this tendency in a certain number of girls; but has not noticed it among girl students.

† For in China eroticism has always been a source of pleasure, not an exercise in self-affirmation.

her schoolmate, and for both love has the same countenance as friendship. Likewise, love-friendship unites the heroes of *The Red Chamber* in the same revolt. Freed of feudal notions, today's young Chinese have taken a double stride forward. Men and women are not sundered by myths, they do not enter their relationships as into trials of strength.

Nor, furthermore, do they grant them an extreme importance. Madame Lo Ta-Kang, professor at the University of Peking, tells me that between men and women students flirting does not exist. "They're very serious," she adds. "Perhaps even a bit too serious."

Numerous marriages are decided at the University, but they do not have emotional upsets as a prelude: study remains the major thing. When two students make up their minds to marry they advise the administration, which notes their decision: every effort will be made to give them adjacent posts when they leave the University. The state does in fact guarantee work to everyone who has taken a degree, but can send him wherever it pleases; every candidate's expressed wishes are taken into consideration but it is not always possible to satisfy them. It may happen that husband and wife are separated for a year or two, but seldom for longer; in its modern form the family is respected by the state. Nevertheless service to the country ranks ahead of marriage. As a rule it is based on esteem rather more than upon sentiments. At the registrar's bureau when young people are severally asked why they have chosen one another the standard reply is because he or she is a fine worker. "Students prefer the girls who are best at work," Tsai told me. One thing, at any rate, is certain: love does not appear to play a major role in the life of the young Chinese. Many Western observers, among them some of the most open-minded, lay the blame for this austerity at the regime's doorstep. Mistakenly, for it represents a carry-over from the past. For the Chinese woman the bed for so long signified a slavery so odious that her foremost preoccupation is to have no more of that constraint: it is not socialist enthusiasm that prevents her from dreaming of men, but she enthusiastically welcomes a socialism which frees her from men's clutches. In the West, even the woman with whom it is career first, last, and always still allots love a positive value. But for every Chinese woman, from the top to the bottom of the social scale, physical love has a negative coefficient. I was struck by a reaction on the part of Madame Cheng; we were seated together at the opera, on the stage a young heroine was desperately struggling in an emperor's lewd embrace. "That's why Chinese women wanted the Revolution," Madame Cheng said ardently, "in order to have the right to say no to that sort of thing—love." You often hear it: "Chinese women are cold." But coldness is not a physiological attribute; it is a complex reaction. In the Chinese woman it without doubt expresses a dread loathing for the traditional rape which, in her eyes, and for centuries, has been synonymous with love. She must be entirely delivered from the weight of the past before she will be able to adopt a positive attitude when, instead of feeling pleased with herself for having escaped love, she will be free to love as she pleases.

The regime does not by any means proscribe love as a manifestation of individualism; quite to the contrary, individualism is encouraged since every effort is being bent to free people from the groups they have been the traditional prisoners of hitherto; indeed, love is considered an altogether progressive sentiment. To fall in love, to act at love's behest is to repudiate the old conformism, to give evidence of autonomy: whoever demonstrates the capacity for being free is considered "an advanced element." Amazed at the forwardness of a suitor, a girl asked him in all seriousness: "Are you a member of the Party?"

It remains none the less that in China marriage is dictated more by reason than by passion; the couple's community of interests is ordinarily in agreement with that which binds each of them to the country. In case of conflicts, though, which is it to be: citizen or wife? In November 1954 the review *Women of New China* related a case which subsequently gave rise to heated discussion: the affair concerned a woman, Yang-Yun, a Communist militant, who had committed suicide.

At thirty-seven Yang-Yun was the secretary of the Central Labor Syndicate of Fushun and an important member of the Party. In 1933, then eighteen, she had married one Shih Pin who left for Yenan while she continued to work in Kuomintang territory. The Civil War separated them and in 1945 they no longer knew each other's whereabouts. When one had been three years without news of a spouse, the law, as it existed in 1948, allowed one the right to remarry; which is what Shih Pin did. He married another Communist. In 1949 he and Yang-Yun chanced to meet and she went to live with the new couple. But the husband wished to clarify the situation and requested a legal divorce from Yang-Yun; he was reproached for having remarried too hastily but the divorce was granted. Whereupon Yang-Yun poisoned herself. The review opened a kind of referendum: many of those who wrote in blamed the behavior of the husband; but the majority blamed Yang-Yun's. Prevailing opinion held that when the country is in the midst of building socialism one must not do away with oneself because of a marital problem. The life of a Party member belongs to the Party. One correspondent went so far as to declare that this suicide represented "an act of despicable individualism."

That is the official doctrine: the country comes first. Nevertheless Yang-Yun killed herself. The relationship between love, the desire to serve the country, the desire for self-fulfillment in each Chinese woman takes on an extraordinary pattern. To gain an idea of its complexity it would be necessary to have a long familiarity with a great many of them. One would like to see them someday produce a sincere and thorough account of the remarkable period they are now living through.

The restructuring of the family is being accomplished through the emancipation of the women; but this change is affecting all its members and the children most of all.

The Chinese have always been reputed for loving their children; but poverty often drove them to kill them at birth, to sell them, to exploit them: the father's right over them was supreme. The Kuomintang proclaimed a law forbidding the hiring out of little girls as servants or their sale as slaves; but in 1937 there were still two million girl slaves, not to mention the child daughters-in-law. In city and village one found little girls of eight reeling under the weight of crushing tasks. The boys labored too; they transported buckets of water, carried burdens, helped masons on building sites and artisans in their workshops. Parents let them out as workers.

In Shanghai this exploitation assumed colossal proportions; it also was current in every Chinese coal mine. Rewi Alley* writes:

Before the liberation the local coal miner belonged to a class that had no land. Its only production, apart from trying to dig coal in the upper seams where there was no water, was the production of children, many of whom were born dead. Those who survived would start doing heavy work in the mines at ten years of age, hauling up coal through long, winding galleries just big enough for them to crawl in . . . The children never washed. Their bodies were encrusted with coal dust and sweat, which would be rubbed off as they worked. Their teeth, set in red and bleeding gums, were yellow and loose. Their hearts were swollen. Across their skinny little backs were great thick callouses where the carrying pole had sat. They would be old men by their twenties.

Olga Lang,† who visited mines in the vicinity of Peking, also saw these child slaves:

They emerged almost naked from the dark tunnels, their ribs showing beneath a skin blackened by coal dust, gasping, carrying loads of over thirty-five pounds. They did not seem more than nine or ten although some were actually fourteen or fifteen years old. They received between ten and fifteen cents per day, lived at home, worked only one day out of two—otherwise they'd die too quickly, as the owner of the mine explained to me.

Even in the less underprivileged social categories childhood was not a gay experience. To begin with, infant mortality was high. Deliveries took place under such deplorable conditions—the umbilical cord would be cut with any dirty pair of scissors—that quantities of babies were seized by convulsions a few days after birth: this disease, called "the madness of the newborn," was in actual fact tetanus; it has disappeared. The new sanitary conditions, the abundance of dispensaries, hospitals, and medical supervision has enormously lowered the infant mortality rate. Children of under five—born, that is to say, under the regime—make up 15.6 per cent of the population, whereas those aged five to nine, born during the four years preceding it, only 11 per cent.

And, then, methods of upbringing have altered. "Spare the rod

* *Yo Banfa!*, p. 163.
† *La Vie en Chine.*

and spoil the child" was thought a very sage formula in the past. It was considered quite normal to beat children, now and then to death. They were less under the jurisdiction of the mother, perpetually a minor, than at the mercy of the father and especially of the grandparents; also, the old women in China, taking a long-postponed revenge for the sufferings of their own young years, would often turn out to be soured, tyrannical, and evil.* General P'êng Tên-huai recounted to Edgar Snow† how as a child he had bumped into and knocked over his grandmother's opium tray; she had summoned the family into council and demanded that the guilty one be drowned; after lengthy deliberation it was decided to expel him from the house: thus, at the age of ten, never again to return, he set forth with, as his only baggage, nothing but the clothes on his back. At school, children received the hickory stick; or else were obliged, when classes were over for the day, to kneel for long periods in a corner of the courtyard. Trained to the strictest obedience, to have unconditional respect for adults, they early lost all spontaneity. About 1936 Olga Lang wrote that "their timidity in the presence of grown-ups seemed excessive. One would have said that between the ages of three and seven their innate personality had undergone a paralyzing shock." This description contrasts strikingly with what I observed in the course of my own experiences. In the sunny Pei Hai Park nursery the children were aglow with health and gaiety in their brightly colored little outfits; but the most remarkable thing of all was the exuberant confidence they evinced in adults, their forwardness, their unconstraint. In no other country do youngsters of three to seven dare to throw their arms around strangers this way, to hug strangers to them with all this laughter and chattering. I had on red fingernail polish that day: all the children grabbed hold of my hands and displayed them as curiosities to the girl attendants; more than one little minx tried to peek under my skirt to see whether I was hiding some other

* Western grandparents usually play an intercessory, buffer role between the child and the authority of its mother and father: whence the "kindly grandmother" cliché, the "doting grandfather." But in China the grandparents were the ones who used to wield the authority in the house; and it was the mother who acted as a mediator between the child and the heads of the patriarchal family.

† *Red Star Over China.*

marvel. Laughing too, their teachers pulled them away; with their slender figures, their braids, their innocent faces, these young women themselves have the look of tall, well-behaved children, and the little ones plainly did not feel the difference of a generation between them. I often watched them guiding their flocks about or superintending their play in the parks: they are always cheerful, their voices are always mild, they never give imperative commands. They told me that not only are spankings forbidden but the idea of corporal punishment does not even exist any more; the wrongdoer is scolded, his misconduct explained to him; in really difficult cases expert advice is consulted. The result is that children are growing up in ignorance of fear and constraint.

Punishment has likewise ceased to be inflicted in the schools. And parents are being indoctrinated with these principles. Freed of the elders, the mother has re-entered into a direct relationship with her children. In the Peking streets I never once saw an adult strike a child or heard a child cry; everybody seemed to be getting along perfectly.

The older person's pre-eminence over the younger is a thing of the past; being a junior has ceased to equate with inferiority. Indeed, the young are beheld as the salt of the earth, they are tomorrow, progress. The greatest importance is attached to their education. At the close of 1954 there were 51,000,000 pupils in primary and 3,500,000 in secondary schools. School children have a newspaper—its circulation, 1,200,000, is China's largest. An abundant literature is provided for them: 2,800 new children's books totaling 60,000,000 copies have been printed since the Liberation. Wonder books and fairy tales, illustrated histories, all kinds of stories have been written for them. Eight hundred and fifty books have been translated; Pushkin, Mark Twain, Andersen, and so on—12,000,000 copies have been sold. But more are needed; there are now almost 120,000,000 children who know how to read, and there is a shortage of reading matter. Children recently invited writers to a tea and recited a little poem to them; it ran something like this: "Shame on you writers! How do you expect us to thrive on this skimpy literary fare?" The Writers' Association asked its members to make an effort to satisfy the youngsters' growing needs.

The youthful elite is grouped in the Young Pioneer organization, at present numbering 7,200,000 members aged nine to fourteen, and in the New Democratic Youth League—equivalent to the Soviet Comsomols—for those from fourteen to twenty-five years in age, and it has 600,000 branches.

The regime is hardly open to criticism on this score; nevertheless, its enemies have come up with this expedient: the state thus schemes to monopolize the feelings of the children and so destroy the family. Madame Rais declared—in *Paris-Presse,* December 1955—that concerted pressure is forcing every child to sign up as a Young Pioneer. Madame Berlioux confides to us that the sight of Young Pioneers walking about public parks made her think with alarm of Nazi *Jugend* formations. Those are daydreams. First of all, even if it wished to do so, the government is far from having the means to enroll all the children. The fifty-one million of them attending school represent but a fraction of the young people and according to the Five-Year Plan's provisions it will not be before 1957 that 70 per cent of the children will be in school on a regular basis: today, school attendance is not even compulsory. As for the Pioneers, 7,200,000 constitutes a minority; to join, one must pledge work and exemplary conduct, a program that does not tempt everybody: far from pressing youngsters into the ranks, their candidacy is refused unless they are outstanding students. I was told of a film: in it a little boy and a little girl wish to become Pioneers but owing to their faults—thoughtlessness, laziness, indiscipline, etc.—are turned down; it is only by dint of hard effort and by helping each other turn over a new leaf that they finally obtain the coveted red scarf. In order to be reminded of Hitlerian youth outfits upon seeing Girl Pioneers playing ring-around-a-rosy in the middle of Pei Hai Park or Boy Pioneers climbing the Coal Hill on the run, it is necessary to have decided in advance that New China is headed by a totalitarian regime.

As for the "indoctrination" of the children, they are, certainly, taught to love their country, to want to serve it, to respect the current ethic, and they are educated in the ideology that corresponds to the regime under which they live; and is it not the same in every other country? If Chinese educators are more convincing than their American colleagues, this, it would seem to me, ought rather to be set down to their credit than as villainy.

It is absolutely untrue that institutions, instructions, and propaganda have been welded into a combination whose purpose is to wrest the children away from the family; the family in China remains the cornerstone of society. The greater part of the nurseries—still too few, furthermore—watch the children during the daytime only. The Pei Hai nursery is intended for the youngsters of parents both of whom are employed in government services; it takes them at the age of three, they leave when they are seven. But while they are there the mother and father visit them as often as they like; every Saturday afternoon the child goes home and stays there till Monday morning: parent-child contact is never lost. Concerning the Pioneers, the three professors I visited had sons in the organization. When I asked if there was no conflict between "pioneer spirit" and "family spirit" the mother smiled. She answered that, to the contrary, one of the first things expected of Pioneers is that in good scout fashion they help about the house, do errands, wash the dishes, set the table, and comply when requests are made of them. They go off for holidays and trips together, but that does not prevent them from spending plenty of Sundays with their parents. Family feeling in China remains profound. Young city couples, even comparatively well off, are little able to gad about; but they see their parents frequently. And in the country the rule is still for several generations to live under the same roof.

This objection may be raised: that official morality and the propaganda tracts diffusing it proclaim that, where conflict arises between family and country allegiances, country must be chosen; but the same applies in the West when similar conflicts arise. While in the middle of preparing this chapter I happened upon a *Paris-Presse* article in which the writer remembers the auto race in which Louis Renault participated years ago. In the middle of the contest he was informed that his brother had just had a fatal accident; Renault clenched his teeth bravely and hit the track afresh; the higher interests of the Automobile were at stake. In France, it has always been deemed eminently moral to subordinate family sentiment to noble enterprises, especially war. To be admired are those parents who with buttoned lip and uptilted chin smilingly see their sons risk their lives in Indo-China, in Algeria. It must be that the patriarchal tradition has survived among us with a great deal of vigor; the sacrifice of the son by the father is justifiable and noble:* what galls the Westerner is to hear the Chinese preach the subordination of filial piety to love of country. Our bourgeoisie's scandalized reactions are all the more hypocritical inasmuch as, leaving heroism out of the picture, family solidarity is exceedingly slack in capitalist countries the moment cash interests become involved; blood ties are then forgotten in a flash. These ties are still a good deal firmer in China today, and the regime is in no wise attempting to destroy them: it is simply trying to replace their sacral character by a human one. Filial piety must cease to be based upon a principle of alienation.

There is a problem of which one is immediately reminded by a glance at the statistics: what is the official attitude toward the birth rate? In the past Westerners used to point admiringly to the divinely ordained scheme whereby floods, famines, cholera, and infant mortality kept the number of living Chinese in balance by shaving off quantities of "excess population." And at present there are some who sigh upon seeing the regime take vigorous steps to counteract nature's wisdom. The damage has been done: epidemics have been checked, disasters stemmed, and most newborn babies live. Every year there are 37 births and 17 deaths per 1,000 inhabitants: the population is increased annually by ten million persons. Every four years China is increased by the equivalent of an Italy or a France. Now, it is already difficult, as things are at present, to provide every Chinese with a decent standard of living; the leaders promise the masses a steady improvement in their situation—but what is to happen if the population keeps on soaring? For example, the Five-Year Plan anticipates that in 1957 70 per cent of the children will be installed in primary schools. If, between now and 1959, 40,000,000 more are born, will not the percentage of illiterates become once again enormous? It seems to me that a people who have taken their destiny into their own hands cannot allow this tumultuous proliferation. One of the guaranteeing factors behind prosperity in the United States is the

* The entire Right praised the conduct of the Francoist general who let his son be shot rather than surrender the Alcazar. If during the Civil War a young Chinese had sacrificed his father to the Communist cause, the "violation of his conscience" by the Party would have been spoken of with horror.

attitude adopted there toward birth control. India, on the other hand, is overwhelmed by a number of inhabitants far above what the country can sustain. What then is the view on birth control taken by the regime in China? I questioned a Women's Association vice-president; her reply, given with embarrassed reserve, was, "In the cities, couples are practicing planned parenthood. The system is less successful in the country. Abortion, in emergency cases, is legal; otherwise it is a crime punished by law." Fortunately, I received more definite and more detailed replies in the course of a discussion with Vice-Minister Chen Yi who granted us an interview about October 1.

He smiled at my question. "Others have asked the same thing," he said. "Some English Labourites wanted to know whether the growth in our population would not inevitably lead to imperialism. I told them," Chen Yi went on, recollecting his annoyance at the time, "that India is overpopulated, England isn't; it was England that conquered India." He then explained to us at length that the only question is to know whether a given nation's economy is or is not imperialistic. Well, China has no aims on the rest of the world. She possesses enormous, as yet undeveloped natural resources: the growing population will easily be absorbed within the limits of the country. He mentioned Sinkiang, still inhabited almost entirely by nomads, and other virgin territories awaiting settlement. Coal, iron, oil deposits are there in abundance; they must be extracted, that requires manpower. Great centers of industry are going to be created in the interior. True, there is some unemployment today; that does not mean however that the population must be reduced. Unemployment will end when a higher stage of development has been reached: and, as that will be soon, the nation's labor potential must, to the contrary, be increased—which means more workers. To satisfy her population's needs China must raise her production; but this will not go up unless the population does. The cities presently number 100,000,000 inhabitants; the figure for each city will not increase but new cities will be built.

And so China does not envisage limiting the birth rate? Yes, she does. Its excessive proportions have engendered too many evils, from infant mortality to child murder. The government considers that the prosperity of every single Chinese demands a rational approach to the problem. Malthusianism, incompatible with the spirit of Marxism, is strictly ruled out; the answer lies in planned parenthood. It is wished that young newlyweds wait two or three years before having their first child, that mothers already burdened with several children avoid having more for a while, that every couple be in a position to balance its budget and organize its existence. Thus, there is no hard and fast policy. On the one hand, China needs workers. "Which is why we have not launched a birth-control movement," says Chen Yi; "it might have overshot the mark." On the other hand, it must protect against the dangers of overpopulation. Without exerting imperious demands, contraceptive methods are being publicized.

I later learned that this birth-control trend had begun to take shape in 1954. At the National People's Congress, a sixty-three-year-old leader, Shao Li-tzu, had declared: "Giving birth to a new child every year is a great burden for mothers. We are not discussing the question of abortion; but a knowledge of birth-control techniques must be disseminated. Practical directives must be given in regard to both the method and the means of controlling childbirth." In December of that year, the Peking daily *Kuang Ming* made it known that birth-control practices had received state authorization. The monthly *Women of New China*, in January and March 1955, gave detailed instructions relating to contraceptive methods, and the Ministry of Health is supervising the manufacture of pessaries. The law is lenient with regard to abortion itself: "Abortion is permissible in any case where the continuation of pregnancy is not to be recommended or if the number of births is too frequent. Consent of the father and mother is required, as are a medical certificate and the approval of an authorized government official." In practice, authorization is granted after the fifth child. In all maternity wards and dispensaries while treatment is being administered to young women they are instructed in contraceptive methods; it even seems—I did not personally see them, but numerous friends assured me—that extremely down-to-earth propaganda posters are being used. Tsai also told me that the necessary supplies are sold in all pharmacies.

This line was confirmed again in September 1956 at the Eighth Communist Party Congress. Madame Ts'ai Chang, president of the

Federation of Democratic Women, declared that China must apply stern measures to curb the birth rate. Directives were formulated to this effect in March and the press gave them wide publicity.

The anti-Communists simultaneously accuse New China of demolishing the family and of annihilating the individual: both are lying allegations. Everything in the family that admits of free inter-individual relationships is being preserved, nay, strengthened; what has been done away with is the estrangement of the individual person wrought by an oppressive and imperiously sanctified institution. Reactionaries call this a Machiavellian policy and maintain that its unique purpose is to facilitate collectivizing the land. But it seems to me worth noting that, conversely, economic utilitarianism has an immediate humanistic result. Today in China substructure and superstructure so tightly interlock that in certain spheres they are one; the social factor possesses an economic dimension; but productivity depends on the human factor: the march toward socialism implies the emancipation of the individual, the affirmation of his right to self-determination. Marriage, motherhood have become free. Love is viewed as something "progressive." Far and away from being in contradiction, personal aspirations and duty to country jibe: for the commonweal everyone must strive after his own welfare. The road to collectivization is also that by which the woman is acceding to dignity, the youth to freedom. The bourgeoisie, which at one time used to take pride in having brought a condition of general well-being to Europe, ought to take pleasure in the fact that in China it has become the very foundation of good citizenship.

# 4.
# INDUSTRY

The entire economy of this great agricultural country is dominated by one imperative: industrialize. An examination of the national budget discloses some interesting particulars. In 1955,* China's revenue, including the balance carried over from 1954, had risen to 31,192,520,000 yuan, of which 28,490,180,000 had been realized during that year. The revenues were divided thus: taxes of all kinds, 49.13 per cent; profits deriving from state enterprises,† 39.63 per cent; insurance and credit, 11.24 per cent. The principal source of income, then, is from taxation. The state levies a 25 per cent profit tax upon manufacturers and businessmen, a tax of only 3 to 12 per cent upon farming proceeds; but as the peasantry comprises the immense majority of the population it is upon that sector the national treasury most heavily depends. Expenses were divided in this way: education, 12.95 per cent; administration, 7.54 per cent; national defense, 24.19 per cent; miscellaneous, 4.18 per cent; 47.72 per cent of the budget was devoted to economic construction which in 1956 was also to absorb the 3.12 per cent 1955 balance; the lion's share of these investments goes into heavy industry. These figures clearly sketch the general line of Chinese economy: China is using the wealth extracted from her soil to build the heavy industry necessary for the country's future prosperity and economic independence.

* The 1954 and 1956 budgets are similar to this one.

† The figure includes profits accruing to the state from joint (state and private) enterprises.

In the course of 1956 the theory that awards pre-eminence to heavy industry was challenged in socialist Europe; it is undoubtedly a mistake to suppose, a priori, that this doctrine is universally valid. But it was reaffirmed at the Chinese Communist Party's Eighth Congress, and for the soundest reasons. China's situation can in no wise be compared to that of Hungary or Poland. Far from sacrificing the Chinese masses in the name of an abstract principle and to a mythical future, as anti-Communists would have it, the regime, in emphasizing heavy industry, is serving the whole population's distant and immediate interests alike. This population is growing rapidly; in order that it subsist—better, in order that its standard of living be raised—the agricultural product must register a considerable and steady increase; this progress—and, in particular, the reclamation of virgin territories—requires machinery: trucks, tractors, cranes, bulldozers are needed for carrying out the major public works—roads, bridges, railways, dams, canals—indispensable to economic development. A nation of six hundred million must look to itself for finding ways and means to supply its tremendous needs: Soviet aid can only provide a beginning. By abandoning the idea of industrializing, China would condemn herself to remaining a poverty-stricken vassal of the USSR forever: she would slip back into the infernal cycle of overpopulation and famine. To elect such a destiny would be all the more insane in that China possesses vast untapped natural resources: coal, oil, mineral ores. The backwardness of her industry is not the effect of an unpromising subsoil but of historic conditions: the absence of an indigenous capitalism, the semicolonial status that was imposed upon her. China's chances for acquiring a heavy industry only began when she took charge of her own affairs and fate; conversely, China will not achieve a true autonomy until the level of her industrial output has risen to a sufficient point. If the meaning and shape of her present effort are to be rightly understood, one must first know something of the situation the new China has inherited and is having to grapple with.

Thinking to duplicate their feats in India by obtaining similar concessions in China, Western gentlemen ran into initial disappointments. "My Empire is overflowing with riches of every kind and is in need of nothing," Ch'ien Lung loftily notified King George III. The English merchantmen who rounded Cape Horn would make port in Mexico to fill up their chests with silver dollars before heading on to China to buy silk and tea: they had almost nothing to sell the Chinese. Then the English traders hit on opium; the Opium War ensued, the British won it, and from the Treaty of Nanking on the balance of trade was constantly unfavorable to China. Nevertheless foreign capitalists, not satisfied with what they were earning from the Chinese market, went after bigger things. At the end of the nineteenth century they found it more advantageous to invest funds in Chinese railways and shipping and to utilize Chinese labor to create industry in the territories they had annexed.

An imperialistic economy is distinguished by the seeking of immediate profits; it is not interested in equipping the country it exploits: no question obviously of developing heavy industry there. Capital is poured only into those enterprises guaranteeing a rate of return at least equal to what can be had from investment in developed regions. This consideration also eliminates the construction of any light industry. As a general rule colonists import manufactured articles from abroad and make the most profitable use possible of the productive forces locally available: labor, natural resources, native skills. China's case was special: she possessed a well-developed civilization based on crafts, and the standard of living of the inhabitants made her a likely market for certain foreign-produced consumer goods. The foreign capitalists were not content, then, to get firm control of raw-material industries; they considered it profitable to do some manufacturing on the spot: China furnished cotton and silk, so they built textile factories. Actually it requires a relatively small amount of capital to set up textile works; and cotton goods—plus, in the upper social classes, silkstuffs—are, for the Chinese consumer, products of prime necessity. It was on a similar basis that the manufacture of food products, matches, and other articles filling an immediate need was created. These factories were located not, as would have been logical, near sources of raw materials or near the market, but in some one or another of the coastal Treaty Ports that had been opened to Westerners, particularly Shanghai.

This foreign interference dealt a deathblow to the Chinese artisans. It gave rise to a new breed of merchants and compradors* who acted as middlemen between the Chinese people and its exploiters. Little by little a certain number of these businessmen began to use machines and to convert themselves into manufacturers. In 1861 the Foochow merchants bought equipment for pressing tea bricks; 1863 saw rice-hulling machines introduced in Shanghai. Landowners, major public officers, compradors invested capital in various enterprises. The Kiang-nan Shipyards had been founded in 1853; and from 1872 on The Chinese Steamship Company competed with foreign lines. In 1882 the Chinese government in co-operation with private capital installed a modern spinning mill in Shanghai; others were built at Wuchang and Hangchow; and silk was henceforth treated in steam filatures. Compradors became independent owners. However the rise of Chinese capitalism was hampered by the "unequal treaties" and the absence of protective tariffs.

The nascent bourgeoisie could not resign itself to the semi-imperialist regime the Manchu emperors had allowed foreign powers to install; it began to assert claims to political control of the country. When in 1898, beaten by the Japanese, the government found itself in a much weakened position, the bourgeoisie seized the opportunity and demanded reforms. It called for national independence, economic freedom, political rights. Its foremost leader, K'ang Yu-wei, wanted a Chinese system of government similar to the one Emperor Meiji had just inaugurated in Japan. The old Dowager Empress Tzu Hsi caused the downfall of his plans.

The bourgeoisie nevertheless did not feel that the game was up; there existed, above all in Overseas Chinese communities, the now flourishing descendents of poor emigrants who had gone to seek their fortune in America, the Hawaiian Islands, in the Asiatic colonies of England, France, and Holland. From contact with

* The word *comprador* (meaning "a buyer") was borrowed from the Portuguese, since it was only in Portuguese colonies that this brand of tradesman was encountered. Not knowing the language or customs of the Chinese, the Westerners were incapable of dealing directly with Chinese producers and workers. The compradors, profiting from the former and pressuring the latter, constituted a scorned and hated class.

modern ideas this prosperous bourgeoisie was progressive: it was the stimulating force behind the Revolution of 1911. The Manchus overthrown, China went through some years of anarchy. However World War I and the indignation caused by the Treaty of Versailles provoked a national reawakening expressed in 1919 by the Fourth of May Movement, at which time an alliance was sealed between the bourgeoisie and a proletariat which was beginning to organize and become a force.

Up until then the Chinese workers had possessed no weapon against foreign exploiters. The immunities conferred by extraterritoriality protected Western speculators and adventurers against any sanction whatsoever: their greed was restrained by nothing. Superabundant labor, peasant misery guaranteed the employers enormous manpower reserves. The situation was the same as in colonized countries: capitalists paid the cheapest possible price for labor which was there in practically unlimited quantity since, in a country numbering four hundred million perennially starving inhabitants, there were but two million openings in industry. The bosses allowed no rights to the natives they employed. Strikes were forbidden. Associations of any sort were permitted only by special authorization.

The workers none the less formed secret societies: The Three Points Association, The Red Guild, The Society of Heaven and Earth; they were founded sometimes on corporate bases, sometimes on local ones; their purpose was to give emergency aid to their members and to defend them against the employers; but there was little they could do to implement this second part of their program.

In 1897 there was a riot of the Shanghai wheelbarrow coolies—the earliest insurrection in the annals of the Chinese working-class movement. The Shanghai City Council—it had not one Chinese member—which levied a tax on wheelbarrows, had decided to raise it from four to six cents. Five thousand coolies stormed into the International Settlement and fought a pitched battle with the police. There were two dead. The strikers won their case. But the Westerners did not accept their defeat; they forced the City Council to resign and made the new Council reimpose the tax hike.

The labor movement did not really begin to take form until 1918, when the proletariat felt that it had the support of the entire country which had turned with hatred against the Westerners and the Japanese. One hundred and forty thousand laborers had been working in Europe during World War I; contact with the Western proletariat contributed toward a rebellion against their own conditions, and they exhorted their comrades to join them. In Shanghai in 1918 the workers in the Japanese spinning mills started a strike. As a result of a poor harvest in the Yangtze Valley the price of rice rose considerably; the workers demanded a raise of one dollar a month but the employers refused. On June 20 four thousand workers stopped work and smashed the machines. They were granted three tous—about thirty pounds—of rice per month, over and above their wages, until the normal price was re-established.

As of 1919 the laws banning associations and strikes were as good as abrogated. Students carried on street demonstrations and militated in support of the rebelling workers. In 1921 Sun Yat-sen, leader of the bourgeois revolution, was solidly installed in the South. His Kuomintang stood for the application of the San Min Chu I, or The Three People's Principles: "National Independence, Democracy, and the People's Livelihood." The Communist Party, founded at Shanghai in 1921, collaborated with the Kuomintang: for a few years bourgeoisie and proletariat formed a kind of national front. The Chinese CP organized the workers. Joffe, a secret USSR delegate, traveled about China in 1922 and effectively urged the workers' movement ahead. Trade unions developed swiftly. In 1922, 1925, and 1926 Labor Federation Congresses were held at Canton. That city in 1925 had a total of 125,573 unionized workers even though the working population had shrunk. There were 120,000 union members in Shanghai.

It was during this period that the workers' struggle was at its fiercest. In 1922 the Hong Kong sailors went on strike against the British who had sought to break the unions: after eight weeks of bloody fighting the British authorities capitulated, agreeing to an augmentation of wages, the re-establishment of the unions, the freeing of arrested strikers, and the payment of pensions to those who had been hurt and to the families of those who had been killed. Thereupon the Yangtze boatmen began to strike; three weeks later they emerged victorious. The Communist Party had organized the railway engineers particularly well: they struck repeatedly in 1922 and 1923. The most violent strike, begun February 4, 1923, occurred on the Peking-Hankow line; the railway men were demanding the right to unionize freely. On February 7, the British having exerted pressure on the military chiefs in North China, the latter repressed the strike by the use of arms. Strikes aimed at the British employers also took place in 1922 in the Kailan collieries and in the Tsiaotso mines on July 1 and August 9, 1925.

The episode that created the greatest stir was the series of strikes which union leaders, for the most part Communists, organized in Shanghai in 1925. The employers wanted to establish the piece-wages system in certain factories: the workers successfully opposed their attempts. Encouraged by this victory, thirty thousand workers demanded higher wages from their Japanese employers. While Chinese policemen stood idly by they took the Japanese factories by assault. Shortly afterward another strike broke out in the Japanese-owned Wai-Wai-mien textile mills. The employers decreed a lockout. Shop Number 7 refused to evacuate the premises. The Japanese guards fired, wounding seven workers and killing Chu Chen-hong, shop steward and Communist militant. Five thousand workers attended his burial. Students organized a sympathy demonstration; several of them were arrested by the Concession police. They began again on May 30: the marchers carried banners. Again some were jailed. The crowd wanted to free them, invaded police headquarters on Nanking Road. The British inspector gave the order to shoot: there were twelve dead and fifteen gravely injured.

The Nanking Road incident unleashed the entire country's fury: strikes and demonstrations exploded everywhere. The shops closed in Shanghai, there was a general strike. Martial law was proclaimed. Warships steamed into the port, marines were landed, and savage fighting ensued. Two hundred thousand workers and employees of foreign firms kept the strike going. Even the Chinese employers—all the way up to bankers, and generals—joined in the movement. They demanded revision of the treaties, abolition of extraterritoriality. The Westerners' reply was simple: they owned the power plants, they switched off the electricity in the Chinese factories. The employers gave up the struggle, and Western law and order was gradually restored. On June 19 a general strike hit Hong Kong; over 240,000 workers were involved. It lasted sixteen months and the whole of the Chinese people lent their support to it.

Meanwhile, however, the Chinese bourgeoisie was becoming alarmed at the proletariat's growing strength. It reached the conclusion that foreign capitalism was the less dangerous of the two allies and preferred coming to terms with it. When Sun Yat-sen died the Kuomintang leaders, all favorable to Communism, installed themselves in Hankow; the military chief, Chiang Kai-shek, was given the command of the Northern Expedition whose ostensible purpose was to unify all China. On March 21, 1927, while Chiang's army was heading for Shanghai, six hundred thousand workers under the leadership of Chou En-lai seized the key points of the city—the police stations, the arsenals, the garrison. Five thousand men were armed, six battalions created, and the government of the people was proclaimed. Arriving the next day, Chiang was greeted by a triumphant people's army; the International Settlement beheld the disquieting sight of the Kuomintang ensign, white sun on blue, flying from rooftops.

But the rich landowners, the big businessmen, the industrialists were seized by panic; the nation's interest gave way to class interests and the Chinese bourgeoisie negotiated with Chiang. The bankers advised him, through the intermediary of the French Consul, that they would not back him unless he broke with the Communists. Chiang thought a moment; then chose bourgeois order. He got in touch with Tu Yueh-sen, an underworld czar of the vice and opium rackets, and enrolled Tu's killers; on April 3, 1927 they "cleaned up" Shanghai with submachine guns and hand grenades. A quantity of Communists were massacred; those who were captured were tortured to death. Chiang seized Hankow and the White Terror reigned.

From now on the Communists' activity had to be entirely undercover. The Workers' movement was rigorously throttled. A law passed on October 21, 1929, fixed the unions' new status: reorganized on an employee-management co-operation basis, they subjugated the workers to the bosses. Severe restrictions were imposed upon the right to strike; it was almost totally abolished in 1930. The proletariat found itself reduced to helplessness.

By denouncing its alliance with the working class, the Chinese bourgeoisie was left stripped of all defense against foreign imperialism. It had been used by a few huge trusts that were out to monopolize Chinese industry; at their head were the "Four Families," Chiang, T. V. Soong, H. H. Kung, and Chen. They now contributed to the obliteration of small capital. The Chinese bourgeoisie was torn apart. As Mao Tse-tung wrote,

> The national bourgeoisie is a class possessed of a dual idiosyncrasy. It is opposed to imperialism and to the semifeudal elements, but as it has not entirely severed its ties with the latter, it lacks courage to participate wholeheartedly in the revolution. It is a fairly good ally for our cause, but it is of utmost importance that we keep a vigilant eye on this social stratum.

Incapable by itself of conquering an economic autonomy the bourgeoisie also failed to press home its nationalist claims: it was beaten by Japanese imperialism. North of Shanghai the Japanese had founded a community known as "Little Tokyo"; Chinese houses had been redone and furnished in the Japanese style; and in this settlement lived thirty thousand Japanese. When Japan occupied Manchuria, Shanghai retorted by boycotting Japanese products; an Anti-Japanese Committee of Public Safety saw to it that no merchandise of Japanese origin was either bought or sold: the Japanese businessmen were threatened with ruin. Anti-Japanese sentiment ran so high that (on January 18, 1932) five Japanese bonzes were roughed up in a suburb of the city. The Japanese consulate demanded that the boycott cease. The Mayor of Shanghai promised to take measures. But, on January 28 at eleven twenty-five p.m., the Japanese admiral suddenly landed his sailors; trucks full of soldiers rolled through the streets while aircraft bombed the North Station and the surrounding districts. The Chapei suburb was devastated. Six hundred thousand Chinese fled into the International Settlement. Commercial Press, China's largest printing works, was afire, the Chinese University, schools, shops burned. And then, after having seized the city, the Japanese just as suddenly withdrew, apologizing for what Tokyo called "an error."

But five years later, in 1937, the Japanese occupied Shanghai for good. An organized proletariat might have been able to fight them off or at least could have transported the factories into the interior of the country; but no force was there to face Japanese aggression and ravaged Shanghai became "a graveyard of Chinese industry."* Most of the machinery was carted off to Japan, 800,000 workers were thrown out of work; two million Chinese had taken shelter in the Settlement; over half a million had no shelter at all and slept in the streets. Three hundred thousand were jammed into a "neutral zone" which constituted a veritable concentration camp. People died like flies of hunger, cholera, typhus. The Japanese marched into Nanking and Peking despite the resistance waged faintheartedly by Chiang Kai-shek, furiously by Red guerrillas. A sizable slice of the bourgeoisie agreed to collaborate with the Japanese; but an important number refused to, pinning its hopes on revolution. "Half revolutionary in character, half moved by the spirit of compromise: a little of this, a little of that: there you have the two-faced Chinese bourgeoisie," wrote Mao Tse-tung† in 1940.

This brief history shows that the class struggle in China has not at all proceeded according to the pattern we are familiar with in the West. In France, in America, the employer depends on a worker who has the two capacities of a capitalist and a consumer; his countrymen insist that he exploit the men he hires not just to further his own personal interest, but also in a way that will further the country's interest: in the course of the nineteenth century the proletariat, producing the wealth of nations, quickly became a force to reckon with. Foreign industrialists had shot their way into China and founded their sway upon the use of violence; they unhesitatingly used violence to reassert their grip: the Chinese had no way to exert any control or pressure upon them. These foreigners cared not a fig for any Chinese general

* Edgar Snow, *Scorched Earth.*

† In *New Democracy.*

welfare. They were after fast profits; that was all. Exactly as in their full-fledged colonies their policy consisted of sucking the maximum out of the local labor potential and of paying a minimum wage. Manpower resources being inexhaustible, human life counted for nought with these men. Rather than a classical industrial town Shanghai more resembled a colossal forced-labor camp where the compradors played the role of *Kapos*,* where foreigners ruled like gods.

What aggravated the workers' plight even more was that they were victims not only of the Westerners' short-range rapacity but also of the greed of certain of their compatriots. The contracted labor system had been speedily abolished in Europe; but in China the foreign boss, unable to enter into direct contact with the Chinese worker, had to resort to an intermediary: he would give a certain sum to a contractor whose job was to furnish him a determined amount of labor; first, the boss, after listening to bids, selected the contractor who offered the lowest price; second, the contractor did his best to wring the biggest possible profit out of the skins of his workers who received only 70 per cent, nay 50 per cent, even a wretched 20 per cent of what the boss paid him. Working hours were fantastic. Never, anywhere, was the sweatshop system carried so far. Receiving starvation wages, dwelling in hovels, working under atrocious sanitary conditions for twelve and sometimes fifteen hours a day, forced by their misery to send their wives and children to the factory, the situation of the workers was worse than in any other country in the world; all investigators have concurred in finding that only in Egypt and India has the workers' standard of living ever been so low, and in those two countries they were less sordidly lodged than in Shanghai.

> Probably China has the worst working conditions, not only as compared with Europe and America, but even with India and Japan . . . In China there is as yet no effective law whatsoever for the protection of the workers.

* *Kapo* (no longer in polite use in Germany; still current elsewhere in Europe) comes from *Kaporal; Kapos,* recruited from among the prisoners, policed them in concentration camps and were responsible to the camp authorities. (Translator's note)

So wrote (in 1924) Mr. Thomas Chou, one of the directors of the Y.M.C.A.'s industrial bureau.*

Working-class families for the most part lived in huts covered over with straw matting. In his thesis on *Le mouvement ouvrier en Chine*† Tsing Chin-chun, commenting on an investigation conducted by Mr. Chou as presenting "every token of veracity and accuracy," concludes:

The workers lived packed in hovels whose number has steadily increased; these slums are more horrible than anything that has ever been seen in a Western country or in China itself except in an extraordinary period of famine, flood, or similar calamity.

Those without families slept in barracks, often infested with vermin, packed in like sardines on the k'angs; in many instances they slept right in the factories, on benches or the floor itself.

According to an inquiry begun in 1928‡ by a Shanghai municipal bureau:

One may say that the worker's standard of living is higher in Shanghai than in the other Chinese cities but lower than in the other countries of the world. And the worker's budget is insufficient to allow him to make ends meet. A quarter of his income is made up of money borrowed at an excessive rate of interest; or else the worker requests money from pawning establishments. The interest upon these loans gradually accrues and his budgetary deficit widens.

Numerous indeed were the Shanghai pawnshops with the sign over the door: "Loans at 18 per cent."

In a letter A. M. Anderson received while investigating the working conditions of the workers, one of them wrote to her:

"We work day in and day out with no rest days . . . We work twelve-hour shifts—day and night. But including the time coming to and going from the factory we spend fourteen hours a day for our work. When we change from day to night shift we have to work sixteen hours—four hours more than usual. We have no seats while we work. Should we human beings receive such treatment? . . . Among our

* Cited by Adelaide Mary Anderson, *Humanity and Labour in China. An Industrial Visit and Its Sequel (1923 to 1926)* (London, 1928), p. 117.

† Published in Lyon, 1929.

‡ Lu Ye-wen, in his thesis *Les Oeuvres sociales dans les chemins de fer chinois*, gave these findings as valid in 1937.

number the majority is illiterate . . . In fine we are treated as prisoners, animals, and machines . . . We may be called the factory animals of the world of darkness. When shall we see the daylight?"*

Tsing Chin-chun† gives the following figures:

In the industries where machine tools are used, the working day is frequently from fourteen to seventeen hours. In the Shanghai silk mills the working day is frequently fourteen and a half hours and the knitting machines often operate fourteen, sixteen, and even seventeen hours a day . . . In the steel mills the day runs from twelve to eighteen hours; it ranges between ten and fourteen hours in mechanical construction, sometimes, with overtime, reaching fifteen or sixteen hours.

Amid so many scandalous facts, one of those by which foreign observers were most struck was the total absence of any safety measures in the factories where the work was often dangerous:

Fire escapes, staircases, and other means of egress are frequently kept blocked with material, and doors are barred. Many old buildings are in a very unsafe condition. Officers of the Fire Brigade make tours of inspection, and attention is called to dangerous conditions, but very little notice is taken.

This was written in the Shanghai *Municipal Gazette* in 1924. Anderson reports:

Early in March 1924, at night, a small Chinese silk filature was burned to the ground in Chinese Shanghai. The workers were locked in at the time and it was reported in the daily Press that a hundred women were killed by burning or by jumping from windows. No apparent action was taken by Chinese authorities . . .‡

Rewi Alley, who was a health inspector at Shanghai ten years later, assures us that in 1935 the situation had hardly improved:

My chief concern was the number of workers who fell down chutes of the self-feeding boiler apparatus and went into the furnaces with the coal.

I would call on the American manager at Riverside. He would chew his cigar mediatatively while I explained how we needed a light chain

* *Op. cit.*, p. 169-70.
† *The Workers Movement in China,* Peking.
‡ *Op. cit.*, p. 90-1.

and belt which must be worn by workers who had to work naked on top of the stack of coal dust. Then when the coal caved in under them they would not go down with it. "Christ!" shouted this representative of a Christian nation, "if the silly bastards don't take more care, what can *I* do about it?" A mention of the American court and prosecution brought forth a smile. In those days of extraterritoriality foreigners were tried in their own courts and were thus exempt from Chinese law. The next time a worker died in this fashion the court was informed. They said they would "speak to the management."

. . . A Japanese who, in a secret part of his home, kept a line of workers making narcotics for sale, had some killed. He was fined one yen by the Japanese Court.

One day I went into a place where one of the apprentices had been beaten to death by the manager. "Very bad boy!" this gentleman shouted. The police arrested him, but when I passed the place a few months later he was back there again.

But there were many other ways of doing away with people. In the hot summertime, in badly ventilated workrooms, they died of fatigue or stumbled against unguarded machines and were caught by the old-fashioned clothing they wore. The dead body would be pulled away at night and tossed on the rubbish heaps at the back of Yangtsepoo for the dogs to eat, or taken out on the river and dropped in . . .

Stinking urinals in workrooms, no place to wash down and take away the sweat and grease, black bedding, bleeding gums, trachoma eyes, wretched food, industrial hazards, and lack of any creative opportunity—these were the wages of the worker of that day. Now recognized as the very basis of society, then he was regarded as something less than human.

The gangster-run factory to which I was called one Christmas morning, to see the floor covered with the dead bodies of workers who had been killed in an explosion of inflammable gas from an annealing furnace . . . The chromium-plating workshops in alleyways, the apprentices covered with grinding dust, sleeping with grinding dust, hands and feet bitten deep with chrome holes that bored right down to the bone and suppurated . . .

The Shen Shing Cotton Mill, in the western district of Shanghai, built latrines in the exit doors. A fire on straw matting outside caused a panic. Many girls were crushed to death trying to get out of the doors. The manager, who had been warned many times to keep the exits clear, was treated with tender consideration by the court. When some small fines, and various officials, had to be paid, Shanghai society cried,

"Poor fellow!" . . . So also when the handrails of the stairway at a silk filature broke and thirteen children were stamped to death; so when four hundred women were blasted to death in a rubber factory; so when some ninety women and children were burned to death in a celluloid factory explosion—and so on, and on . . .*

I quote from an English authority, E. R. Hughes, reader in Chinese religion and philosophy at Oxford, who wrote in 1937:†

> . . . There is the growth of slum areas in the new factory districts and the evils attending unregulated cheap labour . . . The factory-worker lives either in a one-roomed tenement or a mud hut, or in a dormitory where the beds are occupied for twenty-four hours on the Box and Cox principle. He eats machine-milled rice‡ and vegetables which have been exposed in the dusty market, or cheap tinned food. These conditions lower the standard not only of health but of morality. Disease, prostitution, and crime are more prevalent among the town labourers than among the villagers . . .
>
> . . . The greater number [of factories] have been erected with more thought of economy than of care for the workers, and very many small industries using rented electric power are carried on in ordinary dwelling-houses or outbuildings. The machinery imported into China has often lacked the safety-guards insisted on by modern western legislation, and so the locally manufactured machines, copied from imported models, are also without them. Little or no restriction has been enforced in the use of dangerous processes or materials. For instance, children are employed in match factories for putting the chemical material on the outside of the boxes . . . The working hours per day vary with different industries, some having . . . 12 hours for women and children as well as men . . . Female and child labour, being cheaper, is more in demand. Many of these women and children are brought in from the villages on contracts by which they are housed in dormitories run by the companies, and their board is deducted from their wages. The conditions are little better than slavery.

Under pressure from the League of Nations, China had committed herself to adopt the rules of the International Labour Office; but the Shanghai Municipal Council admitted in 1935:

* *Yo Banfa!*, Peking, 1952, p. 61 ff.

† *The Invasion of China by the Western World* (London, 1937), p. 275-277.

‡ In other words, deprived of its vitamin content.

A better system of safety and hygiene can be achieved only by a prolonged effort . . . The Council will have all it can do to reach an agreement with the factory owners and managers.

Besides the workers employed in the factories there was an entire proletariat that worked out-of-doors; a multitude sought to earn their livelihood as dock hands, carters; their work left them somewhat more respite but they paid for it by forever drifting within an ace of starvation; their health undermined by malnutrition, hosts of them would die of tuberculosis; twenty thousand corpses were scraped off the pavements of Shanghai every year.

The fate of women was particularly terrible: for doing the same grinding work they got half a man's wage:

The average monthly wage in a big shop was 20.65 dollars for a man, 13.92 for a woman, 9.80 for a child. Labor legislation intervened in 1929; Article 24 stipulated that . . . where the capacity of the two sexes is equal, the earnings must be equal . . . But in practice this law has so far remained a dead letter.*

Certain regulations also existed for the protection of pregnant women; these regulations were not applied either. Often, as soon as it was noticed that a woman was with child, she was dismissed. The parents and older children worked at the factory, the little children were entrusted to anyone at all or, as was common, brought along by the mother to the factory; the cradles were parked between the machines or in the latrines.

In numerous instances they followed their parents to the factory and waited for them next to the machines which sometimes meant hideous accidents. But worse yet was the state of health of those children.†

At the age of five the child stopped waiting: he would begin to work. Here is the darkest chapter in the story. The meager wages they paid represented a double saving for the bosses: it compelled the workers to sell their children's labor, and the bosses bought it for a ludicrous price. "The amount of its income thus indicates that it is of paramount necessity to the family that the children work," Lu Ye-wen remarks in conclusion. Apart from

* Written in 1937 by Lu Ye-wen, *op. cit.*
† *Ibid.*

those who, delivered to the factory by their parents, continued to live with their family, there were others, many others, whom procurers, moving from region to region on the heels of famine, would buy from peasants in exchange for a mouthful of bread. Under the pretext of recouping what their recruitment had cost, factory managers made them work four years without wages; they fed the children on spoiled foods, literal garbage, and had them sleep in guarded dormitories to prevent them from escaping: practically speaking they were slaves. It would also happen that the child would be paid a set figure by the contractor who was himself paid by the manufacturer according to the amount of work done; the contractor had every interest in squeezing the maximum out of the child and in reducing his expenses to a minimum; "the contractor is able to make a profit of about four dollars a month in respect of each child. The children are frequently most miserably housed and fed. They receive no money and their conditions are practically those of slavery."*

In 1923 child labor was the object of an extensive investigation; the Child Labor Commission named by the Municipal Council of Shanghai sat on thirty-three occasions, heard a long succession of witnesses, and its members went in person to look into the state of affairs in the factories. They submitted a report in 1924; its conclusions are terrifying:

There is no doubt that it is the general practice for the vast majority of Chinese children to be made . . . to commence to work at the earliest age possible. . . . This general practice obtains in the Shanghai district equally with the rest of China.†

From the age of five on they were employed at putting matches in boxes:

Young children certainly not more than five years of age were to be seen working with almost incredible rapidity . . . White phosphorus is used in some of these factories, and cases of phosphorus poisoning have been observed . . . While special risk of fire undoubtedly attaches to this industry no precautions . . . were observed.‡

Children of under nine were working in tobacco and cigarette

* Anderson, *op. cit.*, p. 151.
† Quoted by Anderson, *op. cit.*, p. 146.
‡ *Ibid.*, p. 149-50.

factories, in cotton and above all in silk mills where they did the job of unwinding the cocoons. Wrote Hauser, an American, in 1936:

> Children are installed in shops furnished with special machines scaled to their size; they stand from morning to night unwinding cocoons, their little hands doing the job more rapidly than an adult's. The unwinding is performed over basins of boiling water, and after a time the little hands have a lamentable appearance. The eyes also.

The windows of the workshops were never opened even in the height of summer when the temperature outside climbs to 105 degrees; a breath of air might have snapped the silk threads.

These were the conditions under which children were working twelve to fifteen hours a day, standing on their feet six hours at a stretch. Undernourished, anemic, tuberculosis killed them off like flies; trachoma blinded them; work accidents due to exhaustion were terribly frequent.

"It was agreed by all the medical witnesses that the existing industrial conditions in Shanghai are extremely adverse to the bodily and mental welfare of the Chinese child employee," the Commission observed. While Anderson writes:

> In the main they present a pitiable sight. Their physical condition is poor, and their faces are devoid of any expression of happiness or well-being. They appear to be miserable, both physically and mentally . . .†

From among her worst memories, the author describes,

> A drooping little girl of seven or eight years of age in the steaming atmosphere of a semi-industrialized silk filature, with swollen body and mask-like face of helpless suffering, whom I found standing during a long day, making the monotonous movements needed for stirring cocoons in nearly boiling water; a small boy of not more than eleven years discovered in a rambling old match factory boxing white phosphorus-tipped matches, face swollen with a suppurating wound on the cheekbone under the left eye and the expression of one who endures great suffering; a large ill-lighted cotton-spinning room, dusty and extremely hot, where numerous children, streaming with perspiration, work strenuously (on the night and day shift system) under Chinese foremen amid inadequately guarded machinery.‡

* *Ibid.*, p. 147.
† *Ibid.*, p. 154.
‡ *Ibid.*, p. 164-5.

One of these children, sinking from weariness, collapsed over the machine, was so gravely injured that her leg had to be amputated at the thigh. In the match factories children of five and six were eating with phosphorus-spattered fingers; their food was placed on benches, openly exposed to the chemicals. Far from looking after their safety, the foreman beat them upon the slightest pretext and sometimes to death. At night the children would slip away and, hiding, try to catch a moment's sleep; they were driven to their feet by blows.

Tsing Chin-chun reports:

In certain match factories, work goes on from four in the morning till eight at night. This schedule also applies to children. Extreme exhaustion is the result, and this in turn causes frequent accidents . . . It is usually not until evening that injured workers are taken to the hospital; the greater part are children with hand injuries.

The Commission's verdict was that the general situation was inexcusable; it demanded that no child under ten be employed, that their working day be limited to twelve hours; that they be given one day off every two weeks; that, in as much as possible, they be spared from working at night. But however modest these proposed reforms were, they were not carried out. Laws were passed by the Peking Government, later by the Kuomintang; they were ignored. When Rewi Alley inspected the Shanghai factories, he witnessed nightmarish scenes:*

The silk filatures of Shanghai had been amongst the more nightmarish of the places I had been inspecting, with their long lines of children, many not more than eight or nine years old, standing for 12 hours over boiling vats of cocoons, with swollen red fingers, eyes inflamed, eye muscles sagging, many crying from the beating of the foreman, who would walk up and down behind them with a piece of No. 8 gauge wire as a whip; with tiny arms often scalded in punishment if they passed a thread incorrectly; in rooms so full of steam that in the Shanghai heat just standing in them for a few minutes was unbearable for me . . .

A house built for one or two families to live in would be converted into a factory employing several hundred children making flashlight bulbs for the five and ten cent stores abroad . . . These children toiled

* *Yo Banfa!*

from dawn to dark in crowded lofts, their weary faces close to the Bunsen burners, their legs swollen with beri-beri, their sweating bodies covered with sores from bedbugs and lice. In the not too distant future their hearts would stop working, for they were already enlarged.

One of the worst dives was a place called Tien Kai Ziang, in an alleyway off what is now Peking Road West, in Shanghai. The management of this concern would subsidise orphanages to give him children. They had a battery of punch-presses, making parts for the sockets of electric light bulbs. The children would sleep beside the machines. They worked a 14-hour day . . . There was an armed guard at the door to prevent the escape of any child. Foremen could beat the children at will.

Of one batch of orphans sent in by the "Child Welfare Association," practically all received injuries from the fast-running, unguarded punch-presses. Of 29 children, 11 had suffered amputations. Out of some 64 children working at one time it was found that over 30 had fingers or portions of fingers missing. When a child had had more than two amputations, he was kicked into the street to fend for himself and fight with other waifs for scraps from the garbage cans in the alleyways, at the backs of the restaurants.

The situation of the workers was no less abominable in the rest of China. We have alluded to the fate of the children who worked in the mines. As for the adults, no security devices protected them against hazards, no hygiene measures existed to prevent occupational diseases. At Huchen 3,000 miners died in a single explosion; 800 were drowned when a Hunshan (Shantung) shaft flooded. From mining antimony at Hsi Kuangshan (Honan) there were, over the period 1898-1947, more than 90,000 workers who died of silicosis. Everywhere the standard of living was even lower than at Shanghai.

The Chinese proletariat was relatively so small, it had been reduced to such impotence that its role in the Revolution was to be of only secondary importance. In 1945, victory over the Japanese complete, the Kuomintang set itself up in Shanghai once again. The Westerners agreed to the abrogation of the unequal treaties and to forgo their extraterritoriality privilege. However, the Communists who demonstrated for peace and against the regime were executed. In 1927 the workers had taken over the city and created a people's army to control it; in 1949, broken, they did not budge: it was the Red Army, almost exclusively composed of peasants, who liberated Shanghai.

This great city, concentrating the virtual entirety of light industry—the only kind the country then possessed—represented for the Chinese the very incarnation of imperialist oppression: they did not like Shanghai. That all the factories should remain centered in coastal towns seemed patently irrational and in 1949 the government initiated a drive to relieve congestion, first of all in Shanghai. But the city's populace showed itself restive and, though pressure was exerted upon it, in the main stubbornly refused to move. A few textile mills were transported to Tientsin; some 400,000 refugees, desiring to return to the areas they had come from, were evacuated. But the government ceded to the feelings of the mass of the citizens and gave up the idea of partially emptying Shanghai. Certain factories—those for example that produced tobacco—have been closed down, others have however been opened. In Shanghai are lumped 29 per cent of the plants producing consumer goods, 31 per cent of the nation's industrial workers, 38 per cent of its invested capital; it boasts 800,000 workers, 500,000 salaried handicraftsmen. It is in this city that the problems concerning the reconstruction of light industry have been posed in a particularly acute form.

Mao Tse-tung foresaw as much years ago:

After the triumph of the revolution we may expect to see capitalist economy continue to develop to a certain extent inside Chinese society. This is why a new democratic revolution will be required in a country as economically backward as ours.

And in 1949:

The national bourgeoisie is, at the present stage, of primary importance . . . China must invite the nation's bourgeoisie to participate in the common struggle.

Accordingly, Western capitalists were more or less politely expelled after the Liberation; the holdings of "the bureaucrat capitalists" who had, as titled officials, served the Kuomintang's interests, were nationalized, starting with the banks, mines, industrial holdings, and commercial firms belonging to "the Four Families." But the national bourgeoisie's rights were respected.

Side by side with enterprises now run exclusively by the state, private enterprises continued in operation; the state invested capital in some of them, thus transformed them into joint corporations. Not every capitalist agreed to collaborate with the regime. Two hundred and forty big businessmen left Shanghai, 1,800 factories and firms of one size or another asked authorization to close up shop. But, on the other hand, many enterprises welcomed the state aid which enabled them to get back on their feet.

Pointing to the bourgeoisie's dualist mentality, Mao had reached the conclusion that this layer of society merited close watching. A policy of collaborating with capitalism presented obvious dangers. "We intend to liquidate capitalism, not capitalists," the Government declared. But a number of capitalists were too far gone in their love for capital to accept the distinction. They had not the faintest wish to help build socialism. On the other hand, they made the most of the "transitional period," actively pursuing whatever personal profits it could offer. With the Korean War, the hope of a defeat for socialism led them to throw all caution to the winds: chiseling and frauds—tax frauds especially—were rampant. To cope with them the Government launched the "Five Anti's" campaign, directed also against the corrupt civil servants who were accomplices to these thefts. Seven hundred million dollars is the sum estimated to have been embezzled by capitalists since the Liberation. Wherever possible, they were made to cough up what they had stolen; a considerable number were given jail sentences of varying lengths. A few preferred suicide to bankruptcy and financiers were seen hopping out of windows on the Bund. The anti-Communists present this campaign as a persecution of innocent victims. Severe perhaps it was; justified, certainly. No one denies the corruption which reigned in China in 1949. For want of trained functionaries the regime had to use Kuomintang personnel: no miracle had made it honest by 1952. As for the capitalists, their ethic has always allowed plenty of room for swindling and plunder. Indeed, the regime's denigrators hardly bother to hide that if they denounce the iniquity of this repression, it is in the name of "the right to injustice" they concede to capitalists. One Monsieur Dransard,* for example, recounts the touching story

* In a recent work entitled *Vu en Chine.*

of Chang Kuoleang, the Longuyen "Nut King," who was accused of frauds and exortions by seven of his employees. He "made haste to confess a few fraudulent operations and a little cheating on income tax." When charged with further offenses, he threw a fine banquet for his employees, their wives and children, poisoned them all, and perished with everyone else. M. Dransard interprets this gesture as "a supreme protest against the Communist regime: impossible for an honest man to live in this society. The only way out is suicide." Which is a superb way of demonstrating that *rich* is the a priori and infallibly exact synonym of *honest:* for, after all, Chang Kuoleang had, so his hagiographer admits, done ample swindling and with the clearest of consciences was able to poison women and children. Not all of Mao Tse-tung's enemies share M. Dransard's amiable naïveté; but their indictments are framed in the same spirit: dishonesty is the sacrosanct prerogative of the rich bourgeois, by definition an *honest man.* Swindling? Embezzling? Corruption? Nobody disputes their existence; the outrageous thing is that a regime could have decided to bring them to an end.

The leaders' confidence in the capitalists is not blind, even today: some 2 or 3 per cent of them, it is reckoned, go on trying to cheat. But so stringent are the regulations that they have no choice but to follow the prescribed path. Those who do so cheerfully will, as public officials, retain an important place in running the socialist economy. In 1955 a great number of private enterprises were fabricating machines, chemical and pharmaceutical products, rubber, paper, textiles. There were then 30,000 private manufacturers in Shanghai, 10,000 of them employing staffs of over sixteen workers. Shanghai's four great private textile mills had 20,784 more spindles than before the Liberation. The gross value of what was produced by private enterprise rose about 85 per cent between 1949 and 1954. Jointly owned factories were the ones that did the biggest business: they turned out 40 per cent of the total production. But a great share of their invested capital was private.

The Overseas Chinese have been encouraged to invest in the republic's enterprises. Chinese living abroad—in Indonesia, Viet-Nam, Burma—number about twelve million; China considers them as nationals and is trying to arrange to have them all granted a dual citizenship.* The bourgeois 1911 revolution had its seeds in the Overseas communities and they gave it active support. Many of their members favor the present regime. Joint companies have been founded to facilitate their investments: Canton now has the South China Company, Overseas China Industrial Construction, The Canton Investment Corporation—there is another at Foochow. The Hua Chien jute works, the South China sugar factory, and many others have been set up by means of Overseas capital. Even when the economy has become entirely socialized these capital funds will remain the personal property of those who have invested them; they will receive a dividend of at least 8 per cent a year.

Retaining capitalism and profit has not prevented the regime from simultaneously taking significant steps toward socialism; it has scrapped both free enterprise and competition. The private sector is itself subject to planning and severe control. Fifteen per cent of the firms supply their own raw-material requirements and sell a part of their production to individuals; they must however fill sizable orders made out by the state. In 85 per cent of the cases the state furnishes the raw materials and is the sole customer; often, it appoints government men to participaate in management; it is the state that determines production plans.

Profits are not inflexibly fixed. When state trading agencies contract with private industries their bids allow for a 10 to 30 per cent profit, sometimes more; these profits have greatly risen since 1953. The profit is divided four ways: (1) A part goes for taxes. These follow a progressive schedule: 5 to 30 per cent of net earnings; in certain branches of industry, those of greatest usefulness to the country, the percentage can be lower. (2) Another share goes into a reserve fund. (3) A third part is set aside for workers' bonuses and welfare. (4) The capitalist pockets as a dividend about 25 per cent, occasionally more. With it he can do as he likes: go out and spend his money or reinvest it. The same arrangement applies to private capital sums invested in joint enterprises.

Certain articles, upon leaving the factory, are subject to a "mutation tax." It is levied upon fifty-six products: cigarettes, wine, matches, etc. A sales tax is imposed upon some 176 other products.

* This is the subject of a treaty lately signed between China and Indonesia.

For certain enterprises there is also a tax on the volume of business done.

Planning is least easy in the private sector; and statistics have shown that production has mounted less quickly here than elsewhere. The regime hence decided at the end of 1955 to hasten its liquidation. Li Fu-chuan's "Report" anticipated its total disappearance in 1957 or thereabouts. The process has been swifter than expected. On January 15, 1956, over 200,000 people, massed before Tien An Men, celebrated Peking's entry into a "socialist society," that is, the abolition of the private sector of business. Branch companies had centralized the activity of the joint enterprises which had absorbed all the private enterprises. In Shanghai on January 21 fireworks and cannon salutes thundered a hearty farewell to the private enterprises. The movement has spread across the whole of China.

The private sector's disappearance represents a great stride forward along the road to socialization. Control and planning have been reinforced. But a joint enterprise can include up to 85 per cent privately invested funds. Capital has not yet vanished. The expectation is that it will require another fifteen years before the economy has been completely socialized.

It is whimsical to see the anti-Communists harry the regime both for continuing to tolerate profit-making and for liquidating capitalism; the regime, they cry, is topping off a very bourgeois injustice with a sacrilegious scorn for private property. The seeming contradiction vanishes and these complaints appear absurd once one views China in terms of its state of emergency. Here, as everywhere else, efficiency is what counts first. Had everything in the old society been scrapped at one fell swoop, production would inevitably have been dealt the gravest of blows; the shortage of qualified government personnel makes reliance upon former administrators and technicians necessary, but these men's services would have been lost had they been stripped of their holdings and instead of helping they would have sabotaged reconstruction; their rights were respected. However the Communists never concealed the fact that socialism was their primary goal and that they were keeping capitalism alive only in order to suppress it forever: all that was clear from the start, and still is.

As for those industrialists who are resigned to the inevitable, they are neither fools nor lambs heading for the slaughter as, among others, the Gossets fancy. If today they are unable to make yesterday's exorbitant profits, they still remain privileged individuals and those of them who get managerial posts from the state will continue as such for another fifteen years. What prompts their resigned attitude and will help enable socialism to evolve without violence is that the younger generations are not out to enrich themselves by looting their elders; permeated with socialist ideology, they disdain turning capitalism's heritage to their own personal accounts. Look at matters from a socialist viewpoint and one cannot but marvel at the Chinese government's prudence: it has obtained the bourgeoisie's vital collaboration—and at scant cost—and it has maneuvered with enough skill to expropriate the bourgeoisie gradually and without resorting to force.

It is owing to this wise discretion that the Shanghai industries are moving ahead at full tilt. When I visited the city an exposition on the ground floor of the Palace of Culture displayed evidence of this swift development, which is all the more remarkable in that the Japanese and the Westerners studiously prevented Chinese workers from becoming better than dime-a-dozen laborers. All the technicians were foreigners. In 1950 there was not a man in Shanghai who could fix a telephone. Factories manufacture them now. The exhibit booths also displayed bicycles, typewriters, an X-ray machine, farm machinery, phonographs, and brocaded or spun silks, cottons in handsome modern prints, quality woolens.

The textile mills, always Shanghai's main industrial asset, have been greatly expanded since the Liberation; new mills have been opened, the equipment in the old ones has been brought up to date. Prior to 1950 nearly all the machines were imported: but repair shops have been transformed into factories and a great weaving-machine plant has just been established in Shansi. Production has advanced considerably but is still short of what it ought to be, for cotton is subject to rationing: sixteen yards of material per person per year. The Five-Year Plan prescribes thirty-nine new factories totaling 1,800,000 spindles by 1957; in the meantime the watchword is to guard against all waste. A way has been found to reduce the amount of raw cotton needed to produce a bale of cotton thread: between 1954 and 1955 it was cut from 430.8 pounds to 427.

State Mill Number 17 groups four factories: two where cotton is worked into thread, two others where the cotton is both spun and woven; I visited one of the latter. It contains 140,000 single-thread spindles, 29,700 multiple spindles, 2,784 power looms. This one factory employs 7,216 workers and staff, whereof 4,724 are women.

A technician takes me on a tour of the plant. "There was a saying in the old days: it's the wind that sweeps the shop and the moon that lights it. We've changed that." And indeed they have. The workrooms are clean, well-ventilated, well-lit. The women work in blue cotton overalls, their hair tucked up under a cap; they all have a neat, healthy look, and seem attentive but unharassed; in a deft, competent way they check the bobbins, watch the thread, tie it when it breaks, reload a spindle. Every machine has safety guards. A nursery is located near the workrooms; seated on benches, workingwomen feed their infants; they suckle them for several twenty-minute sessions during the day. This time is not subtracted from their hours.

Since 1949 production has been boosted a good deal due to rationalizations suggested by workers whose photos are on display in the director's office. Ho Chien-hso, aged nineteen, parliamentary representative, invented a time-saving method: the machine is cleaned while it is running, and at the same time there is systematic inspection of the spindles so as to avoid breakdowns and waste. Li Feng-fan, twenty-two years old, she too a parliamentary representative, succeeded in handling 500 spindles instead of the customary 384 and even went as high as 960. Thanks to new, China-made machines, a single worker can now watch 1,400 spindles; and each machine now produces 30 per cent more than in the past. All in all the output of cotton thread has jumped 230 per cent over the 1949 level. But the desired mark has not yet been reached. The 1954 floods wiped out a large part of the year's crops and raw material is short. Nor, moreover, is the quality what it should be. "But all the same we've never slipped behind schedule," the director told me.

The First Five-Year Plan called for thirty-nine big textile mills to be constructed during the course of those five years. It also promised a rise in the manufacture of paper and raw sugar. The Second Plan stresses the necessity of further developing consumer-products industries. But this program cannot be carried through unless heavy industry first takes a leap forward. At the present moment 80 per cent of the consumer articles are still supplied by artisans. In order to move from handicraft to a vast light industry machines are needed: China must be able to manufacture those machines herself. Light industry also suffers from a shortage of basic raw materials: still, the cotton crops and silk output will not register a big increase until the day agriculture is mechanized. Therefore everything is so oriented as to award the top priority to heavy industry.

"If you really want to see what the new China is like you've got to go to Manchuria," the Chinese reiterated to me. China has begun to build enormous industrial complexes in the heart of the country, particularly in Sinkiang. But for the time being practically all of heavy industry is concentrated in the Northeast. And so one evening I got on a train for Shenyang—ancient Mukden—capital of that province which has had such an unusual destiny.

Manchuria is an immense plain formed by erosion and ringed by hills some thousand feet high. Until the thirteenth century only the Manchus and other tribes collectively forming the Tungus people dwelt there: they were nomads who lived as hunters and herdsmen. In the seventeenth century, Nurhachi, conquering the nomad clans of the northern forests, founded a border kingdom and called his followers Manchus; he declared war upon China, which held the southern part of the province. In 1622 he seized this southern region, made Mukden his capital, and strove in vain to force the Great Wall. His son Abakai succeeded, driving in 1629 to the gates of Peking and offering a sacrifice upon the tombs of the emperors of his race, the Chins.

After the fall of the last Ming, dethroned by Li the Bold, the Manchu kings became—in 1644—emperors of China. Most of their subjects went there to settle and Manchuria emptied: but down to 1878 the emperors forbade Chinese access to that promising country. Beginning in 1900, though, immigration was strongly encouraged, for at that time the density of population was only 70 inhabitants per square mile in Manchuria as against 650 on the great Chinese plain. This vast, half-virgin province possessed a very rich soil, a black humus especially favorable to growing cereals and soy. Although lying at the same latitude as France and Spain, Manchuria has severe winters, with the thermometer falling to 25 degrees below zero; but its summers are as warm as Canton's and cotton can be raised there. It has a bracing climate, like that of Lower Canada. One well understands why the peasants of Hopei and Shantung, coming from overcrowded provinces alternately wasted by drought and ravaged by flood, living on the brink of famine, leaped at the chance to go to Manchuria. The history of China is first of all that of the Chinese peasantry's outward expansion: little by little with the passing centuries it settled in the rich valleys south of the Yangtze. This time it spread north in a veritable land rush that bears comparison with the movement that settled Lower Canada and brought the American prairie under the plow. Immigration was at first seasonal, because the Chinese could not endure the harsh Manchurian winters; they would come to hire themselves out as field hands in the spring and would leave in the fall; later on, many stayed permanently in the Northeast. Between 1923 and 1929, 5,219,278 of them entered Manchuria, 54 per cent settling permanently. Two out of three went by ship to Dairen; the others traveled by land, many of them on foot. From 8,500,000 in 1905 the population had reached 38,000,000 in 1941, 95 per cent of it being Chinese. The area of land under cultivation doubled from 1915 to 1932 when it stood at 31,000,000 acres. The principal crops are kaoliang, representing 25 per cent of the total agricultural production, and soybeans, making up another 25 per cent. Wheat, millet, flax, and beets are grown, so is a little rice although the sandy soil complicates the matter of irrigating the paddies. The Manchurian peasant is rich enough to be able to keep draft animals; these are usually horses and mules.

At the start of the century Russia and Japan disputed possession of Manchuria; the Treaty of Portsmouth, ending the Russo-Japanese War in 1905, acknowledged the preponderance of Japanese interests in the South while Russia, having built the Trans-Manchurian railroad across the North, retained its influence there.

In 1931 the Japanese drove the Chinese garrisons out of Mukden and occupied the whole country, North and South. On March 1, 1932, they set it up as an independent state, called it Manchukuo, and proclaimed emperor, under the name of K'ang Tê, the last Manchu emperor whom the Revolution of 1912 had dethroned in China.* The Manchurian subsoil is rich in iron ore and coal: the Japanese decided to exploit it. They built railways and roads. Under their domination the regime was typically colonial: Manchuria shipped raw materials and semifinished products to Japan. The Chinese workers have preserved a terrible memory of those dark years. The Japanese treated them like beasts of burden. In the mines, in the factories accidents were the rule. Showing me the mines of Fushun, an engineer told me that "when the Japanese were here, workers died every day." Economic exploitation was coupled with political terror: a guerrilla had only to have set foot in a village for every last inhabitant to be butchered in reprisal.

Manchuria was liberated by the Russians in 1945. But the Soviet Union, allied with the United States, had agreed to pursue a policy of neutrality in China; it was only belatedly that she intervened in the struggle which brought the Nationalist and Communist armies into conflict. In 1948 however the Communists occupied Manchuria and put through the land reform. The retiring Japanese and Kuomintang had each sabotaged a certain number of factories, the Nationalists having done a particularly thorough job at Anshan. Nevertheless, the blast furnaces, the factories, the railroads constituted industrial assets of considerable value: they were all China had. It was essential to begin reconstruction without an instant's delay. Even before Mao Tse-tung was to proclaim the People's Republic at Peking, the Russians, in August 1949, had recognized the provisional government of Manchuria, later called the Northeast People's Government.

What with the importance of Manchuria's role in Chinese economy, the man who was put in charge of guiding the province's destinies found himself assuming enormous responsibilities. His

* K'ang Tê (born in 1906), whom the Japanese had made chief of state in 1932 and then puppet emperor of Manchukuo between the years 1934 and 1945, had from the age of two until six "ruled" in China as Hsüan T'ung. Dethroned, he became known to the West as Henry Pu-yi. (Translator's note)

name was Kao Kang. In 1937 he had been the CP's main representative in the Northwest and had conducted a brilliant war of resistance there. Recognized governor of the Northeast by the Russians prior to the proclamation of the Republic, in Manchuria he incarnated the government, the Party, and the army all at once. So effectively did he direct reconstruction that 40 per cent of the region's budget was already being invested in new industries by 1950. Kao occupied ninth place in the Central Committee and had such broad powers that he was sometimes referred to as "the Stalin of Manchuria." The Central Government seemed perfectly willing to have him keep his important position, for on January 15, 1952, he was named director of the Five-Year Plan; the choice was logical, as China's future primarily depended upon her heavy industry and this was almost entirely in Kao Kang's hands. It also seems that it was precisely in connection with the Plan that differences of opinion developed between him and the government. The details of the trouble are not known. In any case, on December 24, 1953, during a meeting of the Political Bureau, fierce speeches were made against factious personalities who were sowing dissension within the Party: Kao Kang was not openly named but he was plainly referred to. From January 20, 1954, on he made no more public appearances. He was once again attacked, but not named, by Liu Shao-ch'i at the Central Committee's Fourth Plenary Session in February 1954. The following year, in March and April, the National Conference of the Communist Party solemnly condemned Kao and Pao Shou-shih, accused of having conspired against the Party and the people. Both men were expelled from the Party. Kao was said to have done everything possible ever since 1949 "to seize power in the Party and in the State." He committed suicide; this act was accounted proof of his disloyalty and lack of patriotism. A further "revelation concerning the alliance of Kao Kang and Pao Shou-shih" declared: "In the Northeast and elsewhere he invented and spread calumnious rumors aimed against the Central Committee, rumors calculated to aggrandize his personal importance and to sow disunity. Many times over he violated Central Committee policy as it relates to work in the Northeast, he attempted to diminish the role of the Party . . . and to turn the Northeast into Kao Kang's independent kingdom."

In fine, he was reproached for having wished to reign in dictatorial style over the Party and over the country.

What is the precise meaning behind this accusation? The most plausible conjecture is that, his objective position conferring enormous power upon him, Kao Kang tried to push through a personal policy which ran counter to the Government's.* Rousset and his visionary brotherhood presented the affair as nothing short of a political revolution and the outcome of a crisis which was rocking the regime to its foundations. But their assertions were guesses based on fond hope and desire alone. After the disappearance of Kao Kang, Chinese economy continued to develop along the same lines as before, and the Communist Party showed no sign of faltering.

I woke one morning in a train that was rolling through a plain over which stretched endless fields of kaoliang. At nine a.m. I got off at Mukden. It is a city of two and a half million people; it measures nine and a half miles long by some six wide. At the entrance to the station there is a red colonnade surmounted by a lintel in blazing blue, raw green, indigo. On the esplanade there is a cylindrical brick structure commemorating something, I forget what. Two orange-red buildings flank the beginning of a broad avenue that goes in a straight line to the center of the town. In the middle of the station esplanade rises a kiosk: thirty feet high, circular but set on an octagonal base, and crowned by a pointed roof. That is where the officials are when there is a parade or a festival. A barren little square surrounds this building which with its red collar catches the eye. You go up a ramp to reach the hotel; from the outside it looks like a public bath house. The rooms are arranged according to Manchurian tradition; the bed, wide and low, resembles a k'ang; the mattress is bare; the blankets are folded in a pile at one corner. When you go to sleep you roll up in a quilt that is covered by a white slip buttoned all the way around. Upon a table they have put a huge thermos bottle decorated with flowers and doves. The thermos is full of tea.

*There is also the hypothesis that Kao Kang's administration of the Plan was putting the country completely into the hands of the USSR and that, in getting rid of him, the Government was manifesting a desire to preserve a maximum degree of independence for China.

A writer from Mukden, a young Women's Association secretary, a photographer accompany us about the city: that makes seven in the convoy, and there are two drivers besides. The rain has stopped, indeed the weather is fine; despite the difference in latitude this sunny morning is just as warm as a morning in Peking. For all that the city looks ugly to me; the streets are straight and bleak, the shops sad; there are a few large commercial arteries, colorful and lively, but most of the avenues slink between dark rows of brick wall behind which, amid buildings with blackened and sometimes broken windows where the offices are, factory chimneys belch smoke. Here and there a few trees are growing timidly. At the edge of the city there is a park: clumps of trees, ponds, lotuses, little bridges. Mukden's only monuments are the tombs of the early Manchu emperors. The architect who built them had visited Peking and imitated the style of Chinese sepulchers. A wide funerary walk bordered by yews and firs and stone elephants leads to pavilions raised on terraces and in architecture identical to that of the Peking Palace. In the last of the pavilions there is an imperial tomb; but, according to custom, the body was buried outside the sacred enclosure in a mound hidden somewhere in the mountains—all this to foil evil spirits and possible grave robbers.

I had come to Manchuria to see factories; factories I saw. At Shenyang I visited a machine-tool factory, another of compressed-air tools. In a two-car Diesel electric train specially chartered to transport a delegation of German women I went to Anshan, seventy-five miles south of Shenyang. Anshan has 730,000 inhabitants, all of them occupied in some connection with a gigantic industrial complex. Manchuria is the industrial core of China, and the heart of Manchuria is this city. It was almost entirely wrecked when in 1949 the Russian experts arrived to help the Chinese reorganize production. Rebuilding Anshan took two years. On December 26, 1953, three huge factories were opened: a rolling mill where steel plate is manufactured, a wholly automatized, seamless steel pipe factory, and the automatic blast furnaces designated as "Number 7." The inauguration was celebrated with all the ceremony of a national holiday. A film made about the Anshan industries was a great success in the Peking cinemas; a big exposition was also put on, showing what had been achieved in the "Steel City" renowned everywhere throughout the country.

The most interesting day was the one I spent in Fushun, forty miles away from Shenyang. The road there goes through gently rolling countryside watered by a wide river; kaoliang stalks, a deep, warm rust red, rise taller than our corn in France, but these coppery and waving fields, the low-lying hills on the horizon, the lazy drift of the river remind me of certain landscapes on the banks of the Loire. Fushun makes a gloomy contrast with this pleasing countryside. It is a smoke-ridden, somber place, like all great industrial cities. Since the Liberation some workers' housing developments have been built here, but for the most part the living areas resemble the miners' quarters in towns in the north of France. Fushun's population is 750,000; it was only 184,000 in 1949: industrial expansion has caused this growth. In the city are large oil refineries and factories of various sorts. But its greatest asset is the mines, the oldest in the country. Coal was discovered in China centuries earlier than in Europe and digging it began a good eight hundred years ago. Marco Polo alludes to those "manners of black stone which are drawn from the mountains as though from veins, which burn ruddily like torches and so well that in all Cathay nought else is burnt." The Fushun mine was one of the first to have been exploited. Modernized by the Japanese, in 1936 it furnished about one fifth of China's coal. The country's over-all production was in the neighborhood of thirty-five million tons, or 2.5 per cent of the world's output; anthracite made up 20 per cent, bituminous coal, 80 per cent of the total. This total sank to nineteen million tons in 1947. In 1952 it had risen to over sixty-three million; the Plan sets 113,000,000 as the target for 1957.

Fushun's major attraction is the open-pit mine: a huge fault 500 yards wide, 3 miles long, and 650 feet deep; it is not straight but winding and so cannot be seen all at once: from where we stand we have a view of a section a mile long. An amazing sight it is: a perfect example of geological stratification. Starting from the top there is a layer of yellow clay crowned by a reddish deposit of petroliferous stone residue; the next layer, a beautiful baleful green in color, is of stone which is not put to industrial use; below it is brownish stone from which oil is extracted; last, the world's thickest layer of bituminous coal, a slice 140 yards deep; there is no richer mine in the Far East. It will go on yielding another 180 years; and if accelerated operations reduce this figure there are seams underneath Fushun. "Sure, we'll move the city a couple of miles away," one guide says with a grin; he is an engineer and, like every other Chinese, handles the future with the-sky's-the-limit boldness. Between now and then it is not raw material that is lacking but, plainly, equipment. The great polychrome precipice descends in stages, like a tremendous colosseum. Tracks are laid on each level, trains are running on them. Steam shovels bite out coal and oil-rich stone, unload it into strings of dump trucks which move it along to where it automatically goes into huge gondola cars; these—automatically—haul it further on to a sorting and dispatch station. The whole process is thus mechanized from start to finish; but in the section I am watching only three excavators are in action, and they remain idle while the trains are busy taking their loads away. Everything is set up for a continuous operation: a circuit of trucks moving while the excavators keep going; but as things are now each convoy must move to the gondolas, then return; there is an obvious shortage of trucks and locomotives; digging is at a standstill until the train comes back. Lost time is held down as much as possible by the uninterrupted rotation of working teams; manpower abounds. Shifts relieve each other around the clock. The coal they extract all goes for the needs of heavy industry except for a tiny fraction that is sold as domestic fuel to the workers of the region.

For a better view of the mine we take a cograil car down to a terrace situated about midway; practically vertical, the descent makes something of an impression. Going down, I notice water conduits intended for extinguishing fires and indeed smoke is seeping out of crevices in the wall of coal. The fires are the fault of the Japanese: they dug at random, provoking air drafts and risks of cave-ins. The Chinese are proud of the superiority of their methods: they attack and destroy the upper layers while simultaneously working the coal beds below, thus keeping the cut vertical and preventing the dangerous overhangs which would result in a cave-in.

My tour of Manchuria was exceedingly incomplete. I did not

visit the famous push-button, seamless pipe factory or the cutting-tools factory at Harbin which is also a sample of almost 100 per cent automation. L——, my journalist friend, described to me the Chang Chun factory, started in 1953, and out of which the first Chinese automobile rolled in 1956. Enormous, equipped in an ultramodern fashion, Chang Chun is to furnish the tractors so urgently needed by agriculture. I should also have visited the underground factories of which I heard admiring reports from Isabelle Blume who, well-acquainted with the mines of Belgium, was able to make detailed comparisons. All the same my Northeast trip gave me a clear idea of Chinese industrial effort. A certain number of facts struck me.

First, the extent of Russian aid to the Chinese is apparent everywhere. Except for a few Czech machines and some very rare Chinese ones which were proudly pointed out to me, all the factory equipment is Russian. The USSR has lent China a considerable number of engineers and technicians—between fifteen and twenty thousand. In 1953 Li Fu-chuan's "Report" stated:

> The total extent of the technical and material assistance contributed by the Soviet Union comes to the construction or putting into working order of 141 major indusrial units concerned with metallurgy, hydraulics, mining, automobile and tractor construction, refineries, etc.

The USSR supplied another fifteen industrial units in 1954—which made 156 projects.* The USSR and China have common interests; their solidarity is an incontrovertible fact. Certain of the USSR's enemies caress optimistic dreams which feature a China about to break out of the traces and become a power capable of offsetting Russia's might. Pure poppycock. The industrialization of China will require another several decades during which she will depend upon Russian aid. Another sample of current nonsense is to claim that China must pay for this aid by huge exports which would ruin her. If one steady stream of trains ran for a year from Peking to Moscow it could not carry enough wheat to match the value of what the USSR has put into China; nor for that matter does

* In April 1956 Mikoyan signed an agreement raising the USSR's contribution to China's Five-Year Plan to 2,500,000,000 rubles: the Soviet Union is to supply aid in connection with fifty-six new industrial projects and to participate in the construction of several railroads.

Russia have any need of Chinese wheat. To maintain, in the elegant terms employed by Father Trivière, a specialist in the anti-Chinese science, that Mao Tse-tung must pay his "pound of flesh" in exchange for "a dish of Soviet porridge," is to fly in the face of everyday common sense as well as of the facts. This is not a "deal" as such things shape themselves in the capitalist brain; in so far as cash goes, Russian assistance—as the Chinese leaders make plain in every speech and report—is disinterested. That the USSR has its reasons for wanting a strong China at its side, no one doubts. But the result is that Russia's interests are identical with those of the Chinese and that the Chinese are deriving incomparable advantages from this concordance.

I said that certain factories are entirely equipped in the most modern manner, even totally automatized. But it will take years before the industrial system, considered as a whole, is completely rounded out. Today, at first glance, the inside of most of the factories looks downright queer. When one thinks of an industrially backward country one suppose that it possesses rickety, old-fashioned workshops where only uniformly outmoded techniques are in use. But China has skipped a stage: the past has bequeathed her next to nothing in the way of equipment and the USSR is supplying her with the very latest there is. Hence she finds herself in a position to make a flying start in certain departments but not in all. Whence the conspicuous unevenness. Tomorrow's factories, some of them already built, will place China on a par with the greatest industrial powers: that tomorrow is in evidence now, but most of it remains foreshadowed. The visitor is bewildered to find, cheek to jowl, some of the world's most highly developed techniques and some of the world's most obsolete.

Outside the factory buildings one is still moving in the world of the past: between the separate shops of the Shenyang machine-tool works the courtyards are full of scaffolding where, as everywhere else, the bricklayers are working without a single mechanical instrument: earth is being transported in baskets, the ground leveled by methods that have been in use for a thousand years. But inside the shops brand-new machines are milling steel under the supervision of a handful of workers: here, just about everything is done by pressing a button. We are shown thirty-nine-chuck drill presses, grinding machines, universal milling machines with four heads and forty-eight cutters—they can work two pieces of steel simultaneously and mill six surfaces at once. The foundry has an automatic furnace and the molten steel flows automatically from the crucible; the molds for pouring successive ingots are moved likewise automatically. But one link in the process is missing: there is as yet no mechanical provision for running the liquid metal over to the molds and for pouring it; this job is done by hand, which slows down the whole operation. Everything, however, is ready, the foundry will soon be functioning at its peak; and that future, impending, imminent, is more real than this present I see now and which, in a few months, maybe a few weeks, will have vanished. The quality I was so often aware of in China is manifest here: the reality is the future; here and now, one literally *sees what is going to be,* and the present, as a situation, is transitory, provisory, already superseded.

I have the same feeling in the open-pit mine at Fushun. I look around: everything is ready. Only the locomotives are lacking. In the Anshan complex where they make the seamless steel pipe all the equipment is there; but all the raw material is not. The factory runs at full production—but shuts down ten days every month. These temporary inadequacies give one the impression of a nearly boundless future: we are witness to a beginning that contains, not in the form of a hope but as a very concrete reality, the potentiality of stupendous developments.

But there is the manpower, it is unlimited. Just as in the yards, in the stores and offices, there is in the factories a swarm of people who are not doing much or even, at times, anything at all; some are busy at odd jobs: a few repair a heating apparatus, some are smoothing a concrete floor, some sweep; others hang around, waiting. They are taken on both in order to avoid unemployment and so that when the machines or materials arrive, as they shall any day now, all the necessary personnel will be on hand to put production instantly into high gear. I ask the machine-tool factory's director what the factory's annual output is. "Low," he replies, "this year. The new buildings aren't yet finished, we are short on materials. Next year we'll turn out a thousand machines." Then I ask how many workers the factory employs today. "Four thousand."

"And next year?" "The same number." And so between this almost inactive year and the moment when the factory really begins to function the number of workers will have remained constant.

In all the factories, whether they are ultramodern or still not completed, the workers are carefully protected against accidents and occupational illnesses. Every machine is fitted with safety devices. The blast furnaces are isolated, furnace openings screened, the temperature regulated automatically, ventilation provided for, especially in the mines. The most disagreeable work in the Anshan foundries is that done by the men who watch and govern the flow of the molten metal: armed with long steel rods, they control the fiery stream that issues from the furnace and spills with a hiss and a spray of sparks into an enormous tunnel. But they are well-masked, clad in a heat-resistant outfit, wear goggles, gloves, boots. The operation they are called upon to perform lasts thirty minutes and occurs once every four hours, or twice in the course of their working day. Their salaries, moreover, are high: 80 yuan a month.

The Chinese, I am told, are excellent workers; they are skillful, apt, they know how to work; they love their machines, enjoy taking them down and setting them up, are interested in how they operate and eager to master their use. This is why so many of them come up with good ideas for perfecting mechanisms and techniques. On the other hand, the trained cadres are a lot harder to find and their competence often leaves much to be desired—this is one of the bottlenecks holding back China's industrial progress today. The fifteen or twenty thousand Soviet experts constitute a tiny elite: hundreds of thousands of technicians are needed; to prepare them an army of teachers would be required. Now, concerning the sciences and technical studies, the intellectual level of China at the time of the Liberation was extremely low. There was a time, long ago, when scientific learning had flourished to a remarkable degree in China; the Chinese were forerunners in astronomy, algebra, solid geometry. But their evolution came to a premature halt. The contempt in which the merchant class was held resulted in a decline in the study of numbers. Nothing could have been further opposed to the analytical methods of science than the ideological tradition that prevailed under the Empire; it is only of late that the Chinese began to be exposed to scientific disciplines, and they had no easy time of it adapting themselves to a new way of thinking. Nor is it surprising if today they still approach these matters with a feeling of awkwardness. The solving of a problem in mathematics or physics requires an ability to analyze and make syntheses and also an inventive audacity; Chinese education stimulated none of these. The situation has changed; but the weight of the past always lies heavier than one is apt to imagine. For so long were the Chinese crushed by the West, and themselves convinced of Western superiority in the realms of science and technique, that they could not help but retain a feeling of inferiority: this modesty engenders a crippling timidity; for in science as in the arts, if you are to invent, be it on the humblest scale, at the simplest level, you must consider yourself your own master and the world yours, otherwise you will not dare to try to change it. Dread of being mistaken, an over-scrupulous conscience are brakes to inspiration. Chinese students have psychological blocks to surmount in order to become scientists or engineers of the first rank. Furthermore it was natural that steps were taken to accelerate the instruction of cadres, to reduce the training period to a minimum number of years: this hasty preparation led to hardly satisfactory results. Li Fu-chuan notes in his "Report":

> The insufficiency of scientific and technical personnel is clearly a serious obstacle. One of our foremost political duties is to train a great many engineers and technicans. The number of students has swelled too rapidly: their knowledge and skill are inadequate. The mines and factories have all besought us to send them technicians of a higher standing.

Li's remarks are echoed in any number of official texts: too few trained cadres, too many of them improperly trained. Old technicians who worked in the time of the Japanese, who became accustomed to Japanese (that is, American) methods, often turn up their noses at Russian innovations: and, for lack of competent new men, the old-timers must be relied upon. It is this that explains the importance given to improvements invented by the workers: their role would be much less vital if the technical personnel were fulfilling theirs more efficiently. In this connection let me cite two texts; I first read them with a certain incredulity. It disappeared when later on I came to understand the situation.

The first is a story, presented as authentic in the May 1955 issue of *China Pictorial,* and it is told by a Fushun worker. His job is in an old factory which in the past was a repair shop for coal-mining equipment and which has now undertaken to manufacture it. His factory one day received a big order for drilling machinery. "Liu Mao-yen who was operating a gear-cutting machine found that it was working too slowly . . ." He went to the library, took out some Soviet books, and discovered that "a reverse rotation is more efficient." But when he brought this to the attention of the foreman, the latter replied, "We've been running these machines this way for years now. What's all this about running them backward? Do you want to wreck them?" and the other factory hands chimed in with similar opinions. Ten days later, however, Mao-yen decided to give the Soviet method a try. He did, for thirty minutes. "At the end of which time he found he'd done what had formerly taken six hours to accomplish . . . The news spread like wildfire."

The moral of the anecdote is that employees, foremen, and technicians ought to cast a fresh glance at old routines and consider suggested Soviet techniques with an open mind. But the story would not be plausible were it not for the deficiency of the technical personnel: young engineers would of course have known about the "reverse rotation" and, without waiting for an ordinary worker to take the initiative, would have experimented with it themselves.

The second text—not presented as true, but as a piece of very likely fiction—implies that some technicians not only resist Russian methods but view all innovations with general disfavor. The title of the story is *Blast Furnace;* it was written in 1949 by one Lu-Chi. Here is the gist of it:

In July of 1948 Tsao is hired in a Northeast foundry. Wang, the foreman, asks him in a scornful tone: "Do you know anything about the job?" "A little," replies the young worker, irritated, "I hung around in a foundry for a couple of days once." Taking him at his word, Wang assigns him to carrying bricks. However Tsao begins to become interested in the way the furnace is being handled: on the surface of the molten steel he notices slag that theoretically ought to run off through an opening which is there for the purpose; in fact, to skim the dross away a worker is obliged to rake about with a long steel poker. Tsao asks Wang how much iron they are getting per kilo of coke. "Only four? Why so little?" "What do you mean, little? We never did better than that." And Tsao thinks to himself, "Something isn't running right in this furnace." He's convinced of it and carefully goes over the tuyères, the blast pipes; several days later the iron will not melt. Wang blames the new coke he has just received, says it is of low quality. But Tsao believes otherwise: actually, he has worked ten years in a foundry, he knows about furnaces. "The coke's fine," he declares. Wang turns a deaf ear, but Tsao's comrades, impressed by his self-confident manner, speak to the director who in turn asks Tsao's advice. The blast pipes should not be straight but elbowed, says Tsao, and their aperture is too large. "The air blast doesn't get all the way in to the coke, that's why the fire isn't hot enough. The clinkers harden, the iron melts too slowly." He and his mates get to work and fix the pipes. Production then climbs to eight kilos of iron for one of coke, even reaches 10.7 kilos. Wang admits that he was wrong and is reconciled with Tsao.

Literary documents are instructive in this country where literature is in the service of the regime; I will cite another that also demonstrates how technicians are lacking in qualification. *The Test*, a play which has had a wide success, brings a factory director to the stage; he has just been named to the post and is conscientiously readying himself to take over. He asks his fifteen-year-old daughter to teach him Ohm's law and he muses long over the relationship between current and resistance. True, a factory director in China is an administrator, not an engineer; but there would be an evident advantage in having one man able to act as both.

This generalized deficiency, needless to say, has its influence upon production quality. Li Fu-chuan alludes to the bad workmanship, the waste it causes:

> Many of our products are of low quality, and there are infinitely too many rejects . . . In 1954, regarding cast-iron products, there was a one-to-eight ratio of rejects and 20,000 tons of pig iron was spoiled.

Over the first quarter of 1954 30 per cent of the steel delivered by Anshan proved unusable due to incorrect chemical composition. The 380 drill presses furnished by Machine-Tool Factory Number 7 at Shenyang had to be remade because the prescribed testing procedures had not been followed; 40 per cent of the plowshares have been sent back to the factory because they were not correctly curved and because the metal was not sufficiently tempered.

I learned, as well, that whereas the tolerance allowed in gears is 0.2 per cent in Europe, it is 0.6 per cent in China.

And yet, with all these handicaps, 1939 Japanese production has been beaten all the way down the line. Li Fu-chuan announces these increases in production will occur over the period 1952-1957: steel, from 1,350,000 to 4,120,000 tons; coal, 63,530,000 to 113,-000,000 tons; electrical power, 7260 million to 15,900 million kwh.

These figures are far below what obtains in the United States, England, and Japan. But as Li Fu-chuan points out, China's first iron and steel mills were not built until 1907, at Hanyang, and turned out a bare 8,500 tons a year. In 1933 total production was 25,000 tons; 40,000 in 1936; and then the Japanese took over the Northeast. In 1943 China was producing 1,800,000 tons of pig iron and 900,000 of steel. Following the Kuomintang's sabotage operations the 1949 figures were 246,000 tons of pig iron, 158,000 tons of steel. These absurdly low figures indicate the point from which reconstruction began. Li Fu-chuan sums up:

> We have no recipes for accomplishing miracles, but this much can be said: we shall not need a century to match the industrial level of the capitalist countries and outstrip them. A few decades will be enough. In five years' time we shall do more than reactionary China achieved in scores of years.

Parallel to the development of heavy industry, China is in the midst of carrying out major projects necessary to protect agriculture, to develop subsoil resources, to insure the movement of raw materials and goods, and to create electrical power. Two roads—2,600 miles long—connecting Tibet with China have been built. On January 1, 1956, a new branch of the Trans-Siberian was inaugurated: crossing the Gobi, the line trims forty-eight hours off the Peking-Moscow rail journey. The Yangstze was once Szechwan's only outlet to the rest of China; with a new railroad, the country now benefits from that province's vast grain surpluses. Other lines are being laid down: by the end of 1957, China will have seven thousand miles of new track. A tremendous bridge is going up over the Yangtze at Hankow, spanning the river for the first time; this will greatly facilitate rail traffic between the North and South. But today the chief effort is being concentrated on flood control. A stop must be put to the permanent threat of inundation and drought that has always dominated the countryside; and water power must be converted into electrical energy.

I have referred to the age-old problems created by China's unbridled, silt-laden rivers. The legendary Yü, an emperor who is said to have reigned in the twenty-second century B.C., earned the gratitude of his people for having taught them to build dikes and canals. It is in fact true that, beginning thousands of years ago, the Chinese constructed levees made of bamboo fiber sacks full of pebbles. These primitive works can still be seen: in Honan and Shantung there are eleven hundred miles of old dikes; kept in meticulous and constant repair, they are still rendering a service. But as a whole the flood-control system that existed when the new regime arrived upon the scene could hardly have been more inadequate. There was above all the terrific summer flood of 1954: the rivers had still not subsided and resumed their normal paths in late 1955. Coming back to Peking from Canton we flew over them and it was impossible to tell where the Yangtze's banks began and ended: a band of the valley seventy miles or more wide was under water, tributary streams and lakes covered the earth, water extended as far as the eye could see. The Yellow River—the Hwang Ho—had also burst over an immense stretch of plain. I then realized of what gigantic proportions must be the undertakings untiringly featured in all the magazines I had leafed through since reaching Peking.

The Chinese are proud of the partial victory they won in 1954 against the rise of the Yangtze. More utilizable than the Yellow River, since it is navigable for a great length, the Blue River can be just as deadly. Its current is freighted with mud swept down from Tibet and the Szechwan highlands; deposits raise its bottom, choke its delta. Between 1868 and 1949 it overflowed its banks a number of times; the water rose ninety-two feet in 1931, the flood devastated everything up to the Wuhan tri-city industrial area above Nanking. Dikes were burst, Hankow, Hanyang, Wuchang were submerged, water stood seven feet deep in the streets for four months, industry was paralyzed. There were 800,000 disaster victims, 500,000 lost their homes and many lost their lives.

In June of 1954 the rains were torrential; both the Yangtze and the Han rivers, which join at Wuhan, began to rise; during the second half of the month the critical point was reached: people standing on the banks by the dikes saw boats sailing overhead. Alerted by radio, The Flood-Fighting Commission mobilized a veritable army of volunteers; 700,000 soldiers, peasants, workers, students strove night and day to reinforce the dikes. The great Chinghiang dam's fifty-four sluices were opened. The flood continued. More volunteers came to the rescue. Women took hot water and tea out to the men; loudspeakers broadcast songs, plays, and operas put on by actors and artists. The river rose, the dikes kept ahead of it: they reached the height of 98 feet 4 inches and then the river, at 97 feet 6 inches suddenly began to fall. Wuhan was saved after a battle that lasted over one hundred days. All of China had helped in the undertaking. More than a thousand trucks —an enormous number considering the very few China possesses— 300 barges, 500 boats, 30 locomotives, over 600 freight cars had been rushed in to transport 60,000,000 tons of earth and other material. The Government scraped up 300 Diesel pumps; Honan and near-by provinces sent 170,000 tree trunks for the dikes, Shanghai sent hundreds of anchors to moor the rafts. Each province sent vegetables to the people of Wuhan. From everywhere came experts, also doctors to fight against the epidemics which customarily threaten after floods.

Nanking and the other cities of the valley had battled against the flood with similar fury and similar success. Only a few small towns and country villages were overcome. Every effort was bent to make good their material losses. The countrypeople who were homeless were evacuated according to a pre-established plan which even included measures for saving pigs and poultry; children were vaccinated immediately. Refugees were housed in the Wuhan schools, in public buildings; the municipalities allocated considerable sums for their relief. Three fifths of the flooded ground was drained and dried right away, and the fall crops could be planted.

None the less, the grain and cotton yields were far below what they had been in previous years, and the trouble affected the entire country. The disaster only made the imperative need for flood control all the more evident.

One river has already been mastered: the Hwai, north of Nanking. In those parts the peasants had a grim saying: "Much rain, great flood; little rain, a little flood: no rain—drought." In 1950 Mao Tse-tung called for the regularizing of the Hwai; since, five reservoirs have been built, seventeen artificial lakes created, more than twenty-five hundred miles of canals dug. A principal canal irrigates the valley and drains water off toward the sea. The valley's ten million peasants dwell in security. The biggest project, to be spaced out over many years, is the one that involves the Yellow River. In connection with the Five-Year Plan, the governing and exploitation of the Yellow River were the subject of a special report heard and adopted by National People's Congress on July 30, 1955. The works under consideration will transform the living conditions of 80,000,000 peasants. The Yellow River basin is as large in size as France and Great Britain put together. More than 3,000 miles long, the river's silt content is higher than any other of the world's great rivers. "Go bathe once in the Yellow River," runs the proverb, "and you'll carry mud with you into the grave." Enough of that mud is borne down every year to make a wall a foot high and a foot thick and in length twenty-three times the earth's circumference. Accumulating at the lower end of the stream, these deposits have wreaked disasters: twenty-six times the river has changed its course and often swung as far as two hundred miles out of its former bed. As for floods, the valley lives in perpetual fear of them. Recorded history cites *fifteen hundred* major catastrophes caused by the Yellow River alone. When it is not excessive rainfall, it is blazing drought that spreads death through the basin.

The idea of taming the Yellow River dates back beyond yesterday. In 1931 a famous Chinese expert proposed a scheme for controlling the river midway along its course, arguing that there was no other way to make it manageable further down toward the sea. But the Kuomintang scoffed at the suggestion. Chiang Kai-shek consulted American specialists in 1946 and they advised dredging the lower reaches; "But regarding the middle Yellow River," they declared, "don't waste your time unless you've got centuries to spend."

The present Government's leaders do not share this pessimistic outlook; after an enormous amount of prospecting, observation, and tests conducted by Soviet conservation authorities in co-operation with Chinese engineers, the current guess is that the work can be achieved in several decades. This estimate is not of the sort to discourage men who have deliberately taken their stand in the future. They have just voted a "Multiple-Aim Plan for Control and Exploitation of the Hwang Ho." They will build forty-six dams scattered from one end of the river to the other. The loess highlands, arid and barren today, will be planted with forests and grasses to hold the soil. The upper Yellow River will deliver electrical power. The whole plain will be watered by means of canals tapping the river at mid-course which will be regulated to suit the needs of navigation. The third section appears to be the hardest to hold in check; but due to dams nearer the source, it will be possible to build hydroelectric plants here. Further downstream, the fourth section—the key to the lower reaches of the river—will contain dams to generate power and irrigate the countryside. Affluent streams will be interrupted by twenty-four reservoirs. The river bed, cleared of silt deposits, will become deeper and deeper and more and more stable.

These works will not be finished for a good long while; but the chief part of the whole project must be achieved by 1967. By then the dams in the Sanmen gorges, already under way, will be completed and the threat of floods removed. There will be in operation two enormous hydroelectric plants, each producing a million kilowatt-hours; a network of dams and reservoirs on the Hwang Ho tributaries will be supplying electricity to Kansu, Shensi, Shansi, Honan; the area of irrigated land will be four times greater than it is today; large ships will be able to go eleven hundred miles inland from the sea. These transformations will mean the submerging of certain regions. It is calculated that 600,000 people will have to be resettled; 215,000 to start with, the rest over the next fifteen years.

These grand plans are still just plans. But enough has already been brought about to dazzle foreign visitors; even the anti-Communists hardly doubt but that China is swiftly becoming a first-class industrial power. And it is precisely because the prospect terrifies them that they are stepping up their attacks. Their propaganda regularly turns upon one theme: the "toll in human happiness and lives" exacted by these "material successes" is appallingly high; the Chinese worker is being ruthlessly sacrificed for the sake of production. Some other commentators perceive it a little differently: for them, the workers constitute a new aristocracy in China, it is the peasant who is being sacrificed. What actually is the present situation of the Chinese workers?

Politically, it is paradoxical. Li Li-san remarked in November 1949, "The hallmark of the Chinese Revolution is that the cities were not liberated by working-class uprisings but thanks to the forces of the People's Army." That People's Liberation Army was mainly composed of peasants. Workers made up no more than a minute fraction of the population—a little over three million—as we have indicated, they often waged bitter and bloody struggles, but never with much enduring effect. Rural people made the Chinese Revolution. Be that as it may, the urban proletariat is considered the *avant-garde* today. Socialism's future is in its hands, for that future strictly depends upon industrialization. The large central star on the Chinese flag symbolizes the working class. In elections a worker's vote is worth ten peasant votes. Workers enjoy great prestige. Young village lads dream of working in factories; country girls hope to marry a worker; their parents wish to have one for a son-in-law. Do their concrete circumstances correspond to the dignity officially attributed to them? What do they earn? How do they live? What are their rights and privileges?

A Stalinist theory holds that the construction of socialism requires a more or less broad wage scale; that theory, operative in the People's Democracies, has also been taken over by the Chinese. Espousing this doctrine, Mao Tse-tung wrote in 1929:*

Both absolute egalitarianism and ultrademocratism in politics have the same source: in a crafts economy, in small-scale peasant enterprise. How to eliminate these tendencies? Show absolute egalitarianism for what it in truth is: the illusion of a small peasant proprietor. Explain that

* "Toward the Elimination of Erroneous Conceptions in the Party," December 1929.

there can be no absolute egalitarianism, not only so long as capitalism has not been destroyed, but even afterward, under socialism, when the distribution of wealth will be made pursuant to the principle of "from each according to his abilities, to each according to his working contribution," and in keeping with the relative importance of the work he performs.

The relative importance of the work he performs is the key to the situation of today's Chinese worker. The abstract notion of equality bows before considerations of efficiency. The skilled worker is better paid than the ordinary laborer. However the regime has scrapped the complicated system by which wages used to be determined: in the Tangshan steel mills, for example, the employees were divided into no fewer than 176 grades. The differentiated wage schedule presently in force was introduced in Manchuria in 1948 and in the rest in China two years later; it lists eight grades of qualification. A universal index—called the *Fen*—was introduced in 1951, fixed by the authorities in each individual region and based upon the prevailing cost of five groups of essential commodities: food, clothing, oil, salt, coal. In Peking the index was reviewed four times a month: on the fifth, tenth, twentieth, and twenty-fifth. Since the stabilization of currency these revisions are no longer necessary, wages are steady and in yuan. All workers belonging to a given work category receive the same salary. There is a special bonus, running up to 30 per cent of the basic wage, for specially qualified workers and employees; bonuses are also granted for outstanding performances. When in a given enterprise production mounts, wages do too. Because of the priority awarded to heavy industry those working in it are paid more than those working in light industry. At the Fushun mine the average monthly salary stood at 68 yuan in 1954, rose to 70 yuan in 1955. The Anshan foundry workers in charge of supervising the pouring of ingots—rated as exceedingly hard work—earn from 80 to 140 yuan. Wages in the Shanghai textile factory I visited averaged 61 yuan a month, skilled hands receiving 89, laborers (sweepers, etc.) about 40; 1 per cent of them got only 34 yuan.

And what do these figures represent in buying power? The working population is simply but decently dressed. Food, I am told, is cheap and abundant: I believe it is so, for nobody I saw, neither the workers nor their families, looked underfed. In Shanghai the food budget breaks down thus: 53 per cent of the money spent goes for cereals of which 90 per cent is rice; 18 per cent for vegetables, 16 per cent for meat, eggs, fish; 8 per cent for condiments; 3 per cent for fruit; 2 per cent for miscellaneous items. Rice being cheaper than anything else, it constitutes the basic food. It is rationed, but each adult is entitled to twenty-five pounds of it per month, which is ample; children receive slightly less.

On the other hand, the Chinese worker is badly housed. Certain unmarried men sleep in dormitories adjoining the factory and eat in factory canteens. Families live in cramped quarters. But one has to be quite unfair to attribute this shortage to the regime. I have endeavored to give some idea of the wretched slums the people of Shanghai used to live in; Japanese bombings razed vast workers' sections in 1932: those houses have been replaced by barracks. In the industrial cities, furthermore, population figures have soared: they tripled in Fushun in under six years. Despite its desire to provide decent shelter for everyone the government simply could not, during this tight period, make housing developments spring up overnight.

Constructing them has begun however. On the outskirts of Mukden I visited a workers' housing development that was finished in 1952. It lodges 7000 families, about 35,000 persons in all. Each unit includes two large, well-lit rooms, a kitchen, and a water closet. In each room, a huge bed suitable for four or five people sleeping side by side: brightly colored feather beds constitute the main furnishing. It is felt that a couple and four or five children can live here under acceptable conditions. Rent is 8 to 10 yuan a month. The walls are decorated with those color prints called "New Year Pictures" and which have displaced the old religious pictures; of these there is not a trace to be seen and nothing hints at the ancient ancestor worship: while it may survive in the rural areas, religion appears to be quite dead among the workers.

Several miles outside the center of Shanghai I saw a newly constructed workers' development, "The Village of the Sweetwater Spring." Four thousand families—approximately 20,000 persons—occupy it. The houses put up in 1952 and 1953 have three stories, those dating from 1954 have four. Lawns separate the rows of houses; each house has its own little garden, planted with flowers and often decorated by rockwork. Each dwelling unit contains one or two rather large rooms and a kitchen. Here there is one water closet per floor. Every unit has running water and electricity. The development includes three schools—two primary, one secondary—and a nursery; we are shown a children's playground where without a trace of shyness the youngsters reel off lots of songs for us, choruses first and then solos. The Village of the Sweetwater Spring also features a post office, three markets, co-operatives, a dispensary. It is served by two new bus lines. The factories have trucks that take the men to and from work; many of them have their own bicycles. The village is first of all for elite workers, also for those less distinguished workers whose previous housing was especially bad or who were living on boats. To gain admission to the development one usually needs a recommendation from the union and another from those in position of responsibility in the quarter where one was living before. Shanghai has ten such developments lodging a total of some 200,000 persons.

Ten is still very few. While waiting for the means to build many more, temporarily obliged to make do with the housing that already exists, the government is in the meantime remedying conditions in the old slum areas. I was taken to see a district called Pan Kia-wan in the northern zone of Shanghai. Contrary to what is commonly the case in other countries, the poor quarters in China look more sordid from a distance than from close by. Coming into this one, I am once again struck by the absence of any bad smells. Everywhere else in the world poverty breeds a stench; here, the narrow alleyways, the courtyards, and, insofar as can be seen, the interiors of houses are spotlessly clean. The gutters have been filled in, three public lavatories with running water have been built, numerous hydrants have been installed. The population sees to the daily collection and removal of garbage, sweeps the streets clean three times a month. In 1950 70 per cent of the houses were made of earth and roofed with matted straw; of this sort there is only 30 per cent now. Most are of brick heavily whitewashed; they rent at 4 to 6 yuan a month but many belong to the workers who, because of good wages, have been able to build for themselves.

Three thousand four hundred families—14,000 persons—live in this district, which is similar to hundreds of others: almost all the working-class sections of Shanghai have been put thus in order.

The house I enter is made of earth. Though extremely modest it is furnished with seats of bamboo polished so bright, so smooth that they have the appearance of pieces from an antique collection. Fastened to the far wall is a red picture showing three warrior gods; beneath it, a portrait of Mao; the main beam overhead is decorated with paper cutouts: the ceiling beams are visible, the walls are whitewashed. A ladder leads up to a loft fitted out as a room. Downstairs there are the living room, a bedroom, a kitchen. The floor is bare beaten earth; the seats are benches, two chairs, an armchair; I see a radio and, of course, a big thermos jug. Here dwell a couple, a grandmother, and seven children. The mother is a textile worker earning 60 yuan a month; the husband gets the same salary in a flour mill; the house is theirs; they save 20 yuan each month. Before, they were unable to make ends meet: today, they can buy four hundred-pound sacks of rice for every one they could afford then. The older children go to school; before, only 30 per cent of the youngsters ever learned how to read; today, there is room for everybody in the schools: half go in the morning, the other half in the afternoon. For adults there are four evening courses, each attended by three hundred people. Movies are shown once a month. I am told as well that ten thousand square yards of pavement have been completed: before, after a rain, everything was a quagmire for a week, going out meant putting on boots. The quarter has a fire brigade and fire-fighting equipment. Three public telephone booths have been installed. Whereas before one had to take a ferry to cross the river—4 cents per ride, thus 16 cents per day—a bridge now links the quarter with the city. An elected committee has charge of the quarter's administration. The head of the committee is appointed on a permanent basis. There are six subcommittees and six women's associations.

As in many countries undergoing rapid industrial growth, the worker's standard of living in China is markedly ahead of his housing conditions. An unmarried worker earning 50 to 60 yuan can put money in the bank. So can a couple if both husband and wife work; or else buy such articles as bicycles, radios. An employee

I talked to in Fushun is married to a mine worker and they have three children: their total monthly income is 110 yuan; she has bought herself a pedicab which she uses every morning to take her children to the nursery of the factory where she has a job. And they add to their savings every month.

The Chinese worker has a forty-eight-hour week; however when what is known as "shock work" comes up, he has to put in overtime. Everybody has one day off a week, but not the same day: the staggered arrangement keeps the factories going all the time. Each worker is also off on holidays—amounting to seven or eight days a year. Thus, he has not much by way of leisure. But he has a great deal of something else he never had before, something that concerns both his present and his future: security. The system of insurance established by the law passed on February 26, 1951, insures the worker against accidents, illness, old age. The money in the insurance fund is entirely supplied by the company. The management must turn over a sum equivalent to 3 per cent of the total salaries paid out—but which is not deducted from those salaries—to a fund that is administered by the union. In the event of accident incurred while on the job, the worker receives free medical care until he is able to return to work; and until he recovers, his regular salary goes on. If he is permanently disabled, he receives a pension which varies in amount according to his needs and obligations: it runs from 60 to 75 per cent of his salary. If he falls ill, all the expenses are paid by the company; for a six-month period he gets 100 to 60 per cent of his salary, from 60 to 40 per cent afterward. From the age of sixty on, a man who has worked for twenty-five years, of which at least five consecutive years must have been with the company concerned, receives a pension that varies between 50 and 70 per cent of his salary, depending upon his length of service. Women retire at fifty if they have worked for twenty years. In factories where the work is particularly taxing—mainly in the mines—the retirement age drops to fifty-five for men, forty-five for women. For each pregnancy a woman has the right to fifty-six days of leave with full pay. All the expenses during pregnancy and at childbirth are met by the company, and the mother receives a bonus when the baby is born. If a worker dies and leaves a family in need, it receives a pension of from 25 to 50 per cent of his salary.

There are many sanitariums where workers are treated; I visited several of them and a home for the aged too. All those places were remarkable for their neatness and comfort. Equally so were the nurseries connected with the factories; children are looked after free of charge.

The Chinese worker has another advantage: concrete facilities for acquiring added technical skills, hence real possibilities for bettering his material situation. Evening courses are given in every factory. The less advanced workers are in primary classes; there are just about no illiterates left among them, but there remains something like a bare 2 per cent who cannot write and who know fewer than five hundred characters. Technical courses enable those who want to do so to become specialists. If they do well they are given three years' paid leave to go to an accelerated school and take courses which prepare them for university training and cadre status. This specialization is keenly encouraged inasmuch as the shortage of cadres is, as we have seen, seriously holding up industrial progress. The factory is no dead end. It offers a future to the capable man, to the clever man, especially if he is young.

The leaders concede that the Chinese people's standard of living is, in the main, inadequate. "We do not deny that the standard of living in our country is relatively low," writes Li Fu-chuan in his "Report on the Five-Year Plan"; but in view of the point at which reconstruction had to begin and of the utter poverty of China in 1949 it would be absurd to compare the Chinese worker's standard of living with the Western proletarian's. But if one contrasts his situation with that of the preceding generation, the difference is immense; and in terms of conditions that prevail in other Asian countries, the Chinese worker is extraordinarily well off. Concerning the social-security legislation in China, the Gossets admit, "This is a downright wonder for whoever has done a little traveling between India and Indonesia, passing by way of Southeast Asia." To reproach the regime for not boosting salaries higher, for not increasing the quantity of consumer products is to take it to task for not cutting its own throat: if in a very short time China does not get a sufficient quantity of tractors, coal, electrical power, she and every last Chinese will be done for. Which is what Li Fu-chuan makes clear:

The satisfaction of the needs of the people is governed by the productive forces and the material resources that are at the society's disposition. An improvement of the standard of living must be based upon the expansion of production and the rise in output. Our industrial and agricultural production has grown year after year but yet remains very low; our over-all volume of production is small. If we are to develop production and maintain a high rate of increased development in order to lay the material foundations for a better life for the people, we must expand the construction of heavy industry and the other branches of our economy . . . Therefore, we cannot now turn all our profits into bettering the standard of living: we must invest a part of them in building up our country.

The final aim, he concludes, is to bring welfare to the country: but that cannot be achieved right away. This does not mean that the vital problems facing people today are to be neglected:

The correct thing is to integrate the people's immediate and long-term interests and all the while giving priority to the requirements of construction, to raise the people's standard of living in a suitable and steady manner.

Li Fu-chuan was led to feel that thrift measures must be redoubled; he wished to see a cut in the funds being invested in "unproductive construction," which is to say that he was calling for a slackening in the building of housing developments, hospitals, etc. However in September of 1956 at the close of the Eighth National Congress of the Communist Party of China, Chou En-lai stressed the importance of increasing the workers' welfare here and now. There had been no radical reversal of policy; the difference here is one of emphasis. In China, policy is subject to constant reappraisal and adjustment, the effort is to maintain the "correct" line. The underlying principle stands: the major share of capital investment is to go into heavy industry. Nevertheless one may legitimately expect that in the integration of the people's immediate and future interests a greater accent will henceforth be placed upon the former and that an intense effort will be made to better the workers' standard of living.

The problem of striking the proper balance between the individual's immediate interest and the remoter collective interest reappears in connection with workers' freedom, and here the problem is acute. The immense role assigned to the proletariat in the construction of socialism, the responsibility these three million men have toward a land of six hundred million, all this explains why their freedom is limited; but what is the worker's attitude in the face of these restrictions? What rights and liberties does he have? What means has he to prevent them from being infringed? These questions are not easy to settle.

The class struggle in China, say the leaders, is not yet over. But from now on the transition from capitalism to socialism is not to be prosecuted by revolutionary methods: rather capitalism will be liquidated through the positive edification of socialism. Private and joint enterprises obey directives emanating from the state: the latter has the effective upper hand over all production. In all sectors, whether or not they be entirely nationalized, the worker is therefore laboring in behalf of the whole country's welfare, that is, in his own behalf. It would be absurd to suppose that his individual will could enter into conflict with the needs of production.

Such is the official approach;* its consequence is that the

* It has been significantly modified since 1956. See Mao Tse-tung's speech, "On the Proper Manner for Dealing with the Contradictions Which Exist Within the Ranks of the People." This speech was delivered on February 27, 1957; its text was not published until June 18, but prior to that time Chinese press commentaries had divulged its essential points. Of these the foremost is surely the idea, probably never previously expressed by a major Communist leader (but not, as has been suggested, a "fundamentally un-Marxist" idea), that "contradictions" can very well exist within a socialist society. Mao gives numerous examples of them; "certain contradictions exist between the government and the masses. That includes contradictions between the interests of the state, collective interests, and individual interests; between democracy and centralization of authority; between the leaders and the led, and the contradictions due to the bureaucratic practices of certain civil servants in their relations with the masses." Mao hits out at those who, refusing to acknowledge the existence of these contradictions, allow them to worsen; and all the while maintaining that there is such a thing as socialist discipline and that the people understand that freedom is to be conceived within its limits, he insists that "in order to settle questions of an ideological nature as well as controversies in the ranks of the people, we can use only democratic methods, methods of discussion, criticism, persuasion, and education, and not coercive or authoritarian methods." (Translator's note)

workers do not possess the right to strike;* while disputes or dissensions may arise between workers and their overseers, these are not fundamental oppositions; they can be worked out through discussion; disagreements concerning questions of wages, working hours, hiring or dismissing personnel, insurance, discipline are taken before the local labor board. If its arbitration fails to establish an accord, the central bureau is notified, suit is filed, and the case is argued before the people's tribunal which has final jurisdiction. As for union organizations, their main business is in relation to matters of insurance, retirement, and organization. They are not there to back the workers' interest against those of production since these necessarily agree.

I suggested to a Shanghai labor-union president, a woman, that this harmony could perhaps be interrupted, at least temporarily; might not the plan expect too much by way of effort from the worker, should not the union's function then be to defend his immediate interests? Should it not safeguard the correct balance between today and tomorrow, between individuals and the community? She could not be made to take the problem into serious consideration. There's never any conflict, she declared; the plan is arrived at with the assent of the workers. True, they are not reduced to a situation in which only passive obedience is asked of them. Directives once received from the state, the management and the workers sit down to figure out the work norms necessary to fill the bill; if need be the norms are subsequently revised. Each shop takes steps to meet what the plan specifically requires of it. Workers hold discussions, formulate requests to be addressed to the administration: this amount of raw material, that amount and kind of equipment should be delivered to them at such and such a time. But these initiatives take place within the context of an over-all program, and the question is to find out what actual say the worker has in that program's contents. In 1953 Li Li-san, then president of the Federation of Labor, demanded that the lower echelons be allowed more control over management; Li was

* But strikes have recently occurred and, according to *The People's Daily* (as several times cited in the Paris *Monde* during May 1957), legitimate grievances may justify them. (Translator's note)

ousted. A contrary decision was reached, production discipline was tightened, the workers were asked to make an all-out effort. Competition at work has been fostered. As in the USSR, photographs of "work heroes" are hung up in the factories, red flags hang over their workbenches, and some of their exploits receive wide publicity.

By and large this competition has a collective character; on the walls are posted the work quota each team has assumed and, next to it, the results obtained; the rivalry is usually between shops rather than individuals; in this way the possible excesses of Stakhanovism are in some measure avoided. It appears that as a rule the effort expected of workers is not inordinate. The norms fixed by the plan are extremely moderate; Guillain even finds them somewhat silly. In the factories I visited, things were going along at what seemed to me an almost casual pace. Nevertheless management occasionally demands too much of the workers; at the end of the month it sometimes institutes "rush hours" which are nothing but compulsory overtime; or steps up the cadence to such a point that workers have been known to collapse from exhaustion.

The cadres I talked with gave me such little satisfactory information regarding these matters that I was surprised to find them frankly exposed in a play which has been widely staged and selected for translation: *The Test*. It focuses squarely upon the conflicts that sometimes divide management and employees, and no less clearly points up the difficulties the latter have to face in order to make their voices heard. Let me then give a detailed résumé of the play.

A certain Yang, who had been a hero of the war of liberation but who, being named director of a factory, has become infatuated with his own importance, treats the workers in highhanded fashion; he summons them to continual meetings but, instead of engaging them in discussions on how to tackle problems that have cropped up in connection with work, he delivers political diatribes. An early scene shows Yang confronted by a shop steward, Hsu, who has requested an interview.

YANG: What are the urgent matters you want to talk to me about?
HSU: Problems, the same ones as always. There's the scheme Com-

rade Ma Hsaio-pao has suggested for avoiding the short circuits in the electric cables. The men think it's a good idea; there's going to be some grumbling if someone doesn't listen to it soon. And they're already saying that the shock work at the end of the month isn't anything but another name for compulsory overtime. I don't mind putting off a discussion of the first item until next month. But the second one is urgent. If it isn't attended to right now we're not going to be able to meet the plan. And, what's worse, there'll be more accidents.

YANG: Who's been talking about overtime?

HSU: The workers have been talking about overtime. "Shock work" —that's the official word. But they don't always use the same vocabulary.

YANG: I know there are some malcontents around here. But they're just a handful—workers with retrograde mentalities. They've got to change their attitudes. All you can do is criticize them, explain to them where they're wrong, give them ideological briefings, and encourage them to think things over. For example, they might think about the difference between their life today and what it was before the Liberation. But if these people complain as soon as you ask them to make an effort, what else can you call them but retrograde. That's all there is to it. (*He is clearly listening to the sound of his own voice, appreciating his Leader-of-Men tone.*)

HSU: Sorry, I don't agree. "Machines can get along without sleep, but men can't"—that's what I heard Chang Ta-mei say during your last speech. And Chang Ta-mei is a first-rate worker—she's the best one in the whole of Ma's bunch. You can't call her retrograde.

YANG: Well, if even the activists are griping then all I can say is that you've been doing a pretty bad political job!

HSUEH: (*another shop steward, who tries to flatter Yang*) What if you were to call the team captains and the activists together this evening? The director and vice-director could speak to them—

HSU: (*bluntly*) No meetings. We've had more than enough of them already. Let the men go home and rest. They're dead tired. Look at things from their standpoint—

YANG: Sure, sure, their standpoint! Sure, you've got to see problems from the standpoint of the masses; but they've also got to be considered from the state's standpoint.

Whereupon report arrives of a new accident; there have already been five in the space of three days.

Fortunately, a new director, Ting, has just been appointed; Yang, with the grade of vice-director, had only been temporarily at the head of the factory. Ting is told of the situation by the Communist Party secretary who reproaches himself for not having known how to help Yang overcome his faults, of which one of the most glaring is the eternal speech-making that has wearied the men and left their problems unsolved. For his part, Hsu avows to Ting that he has written to the Party press in an attempt to draw attention to the sorry state production is in. Yang, furious, is all for firing Hsu for insubordination; Ting refuses to do so. The discussion is brought before the Party. Yang is severely reprimanded and relieved of his post. Ting puts a stop to all overtime, even voluntary overtime: the plan can and will be carried out by normal means. But when they proceed to certain rationalizations, when they discontinue the useless pep talks and order is restored to the factory, output rises and the workers of their own accord propose that the factory take on heavier production commitments.

So it all comes to a happy conclusion; be that as it may, *The Test* is a stern commentary upon the situation of the employees. For, after all, had Ting not entered the picture, Yang would have continued to stifle the workers' claims. Their sole recourse, according to the play, is to write to the Party newspapers: but if the general line is to leave the workers to grin and bear it such a letter is not apt to be published; and its author, moreover, risks being fired; it takes a good deal of courage to dare to do what Hsu did.

*The Test*'s official success indicates that by 1955 the government was prepared to check these abuses. At the stage China is, whether it be in the fields or in the factories, getting tough does not pay. You can prevent malcontents from giving vent to their gripes at meetings; but you cannot force them to behave like "work heroes." The human factor plays a crucial role: proof thereof is the disparity between the performances of the various shops. The worker's fatigue, his foot-dragging torpedo production. This the leaders have understood, and policy as it regards the workers has evolved in the course of the past year. Even stricter measures are being used to do away with the regular end-of-the-month and year's-end frenzy of activity, the *Sturmutchina* which it was earlier so hard to get rid of in Soviet enterprises; the wild last-minute attempt to meet production quotas leads mainly to accidents, overstraining men and machines and causing reject bins to overflow. Once started, irregular production cadences create a vicious circle whence escape is difficult; but a great effort is being made in this direction. Much emphasis is now being laid upon the necessity of subordinating the quantity of products to their quality; the latter was all too often sacrificed when workers, fearing lest they fall short of their norms, would slap things together, botch articles which factory managers would then try to foist off on the state: checkers are under instructions to forestall these malpractices and to demand ever better workmanship. Likewise, the dangers of a rampaging activism have been realized. At the end of September 1955 a big conference of young activists was held in Peking. From every corner of the country, 1,527 of them, including 368 women, assembled to compare their experiences, their undertakings, their accomplishments; there were peasants, miners, agronomists, architects. These are the "advanced elements" whose task it is to instruct their comrades, intellectually and politically, and to step up the production norms; they voted resolutions to raise them further. In May of the next year, however, Liu Shao-ch'i warned the activists to move more cautiously; bureaucratic abuses, the exaggerated number of lectures and political meetings were threatening to cut them off from the masses and to transform the *avant-garde* into retrograde elements instead. In June the Chinese press launched a broad campaign against "activist excesses," citing, for instance, the case of the foreman of a team of masons who had not done a lick of work for two hundred days because he was entirely taken up with social activities. Too many rallies and meetings were an added source of fatigue for the worker; far better that he be allowed to recover from weariness, it was argued, than belabored with incessant indoctrination periods.

A more important, more significant fact: Li Li-san, who had always been the spokesman for better working conditions, made a new appearance at the September 1956 Congress. Former president of the Federation of Labor, he had twice been ushered off the political stage: before the war and again in 1953. His return means that the workers are to take a bigger part in running the companies. It is to be hoped that under Li's influence the unions will assume their real function which is not to keep the workers in line but to defend their rights. In Poland the workers, while sending some elected delegates to the unions, send others to represent them at the board of directors, for they feel that even the members of a committee composed of workers are bound to be led into giving the collective interest a priority over that of their fellow workers.* And even more so, the state-designated cadre cannot but tend, sooner or later, to rate production above everything else: to maintain the equilibrium of interests, unions must incarnate and support workers' rights. Genuine teamwork between management and labor requires that the contradiction setting them at odds be constantly dealt with, surmounted, but never denied.

If there is no doubt but that an increase in the workers' welfare and liberties is necessary, one must also affirm that the regime has already wrought a wholesale transformation in the condition of the working class. The "animal-instruments" have become men. The road that will take them to a higher standard of living and to greater freedom is precisely the road China is following right now: toward wealth, toward production. Generally speaking the official thesis is true: the worker is working in his own behalf. It is simply a question of striking the right chord: both his immediate and his future interests must be considered. The failure to pay heed to those present interests is to jeopardize the whole of tomorrow.

* A Polish delegate told Claude Bourdet, "There's nothing more ridiculous than entrusting the one and the same man with the job of championing the workers and of looking out for the state's and the factory's interests." Cf. *France-Observateur*, November 15, 1956.

# 5.
# CULTURE

In 1942, with the revolutionary struggle at its peak, Mao Tse-tung declared at the Yenan Forum: "Our cultural tasks at once consist in the general diffusion and elevation of culture as well as in obtaining the correct relationship between the two. For the people the main thing is the spread of culture; but this question cannot be divorced from the other of raising its level." The horizontal diffusion of culture became the order of the day in 1949. Today intellectuals occupy a position in the forefront; one of the outstanding features of the new China is the importance granted to the intellectual development of the country.

Politics and culture have always been intimately associated in China; beginning with the reign of Wu Ti* the emperors came to rely upon men of letters, and knowledge of the classics was held a prerequisite for appointment to public office. One of the chief aims of bourgeois reformers and revolutionaries was to wrest control of culture away from the mandarins; intellectuals stood in the vanguard of the movement that kept the bourgeois revolution simmering until the advent of the People's Republic. However reference to the past will not provide the whole explanation for a new society which has taken its shape by breaking with the past; assuredly, it exerts an influence upon the leaders' projects; heirs to a rich civilization, they do not envision the land's future greatness simply in terms of China's coming material prosperity; they want her to match the West not only on the economic plane but to

* C. 157-87 B.C. (Translator's note)

make her its intellectual and artistic peer. But that, again, is a long-term ambition; it does not convey either the extent or the urgency of the altogether different cultural problems the regime is faced with now. Nor are these problems, or the steps being taken to solve them, to be understood save in light of the present situation: man is at once the end and the means of economic and social changes, while culture is man himself as he speaks of himself and of the world that is his; while expressing the state of humanity, culture must contribute to the bettering of man's fate; the technological revolution still being short of completion, culture is today, the instrument to a progress of which it will tomorrow be the consummation.

Today as in 1942 "the main thing is the spread of culture." A regime that deliberately fosters obscurantism, Franco's regime, Salazar's, thereby manifests its collusion with privilege: making the truth accessible to the people would be tantamount to inviting it to revolt. The Chinese government is aware of its duty to serve the entire nation; it considers truth its soundest ally. The effort being made to propagate it has a dual character, negative and positive. Superstition shall be combated; and education extended everywhere.

"Fight the superstitions"—the motto is officially inscribed in the government's program. However, an article in the Constitution declares that "all religions shall be tolerated." The ancient religion of the Chinese being superstitious, the problem posed to the leaders was complex. To understand precisely the facts in the case, to be able to judge the solution that has been reached, we must look into the content of Chinese religion.

China's people having been peasants since the beginning, her primitive religion was that of peasants the world over: the Chinese farmer's twin relationships, one to his fields and the other to his family, were expressed respectively by an animism and through worship of gods of the hearth. Sorcerers and soothsayers acted as intermediaries between man and a nature ruled over by invisible spirits; predicting the future was this priesthood's chief function. The most celebrated of the Confucian texts, the *Yi King*

(*The Book of Changes*), was a manual of divination.* Two principal sorts of oracles were consulted: the tortoise and the yarrow. The diviner touched a hot iron to the tortoise's shell, prefearably to the ventral plate; fissures were produced there, and their configuration was scrutinized; the procedure could likewise be accomplished using the scapula of a bull. As for the yarrow, its stalk was sliced into slender lengths, these were cast into a basin of water and their disposition considered. Interpretation was in either case based upon an elaborate mathematical lore, numbers being illustrated by various hexagrams.

The system of rites, taboos, magical and divinatory practices making up the religion was crowned by a cosmology. Living according to the rhythm of the seasons, utterly subject to the laws and whims of the heavens, Chinese peasants imagined the universe governed by the interplay of the five elements and especially by the alternation of two opposed and complementary principles: the *Yang*, corresponding to the sun-bathed side of mountains, the *Yin* to the other sunk in shadow; the indefinitely repeated turn of this wheel maintained a constant, unalterable order, the *Tao*, in which is condensed the world's profound and eternal unity.

When in the fifth century B.C. culture blossomed in China, religion was not enriched thereby. The single concern of the clerks, who were imperial administrators, was the well-being of the administration: they sought to insure social stability; they consolidated the structure of the family and put it under the authority of ancestors. Guised as worship of the household gods, submission to established order was the long and short of the people's religion. The masses had in olden days taken part in the ceremonies celebrated by the nobility; now they were excluded from sacrifices which the emperor alone was authorized to offer to the Lord on High.

The aggregate of social duties imposed upon them was not sufficient to satisfy the yearnings of the peasants. In Greece and Rome the city dwellers expected the mysteries to compensate for

* The *Yi King*, like the *Odes* invoked by Confucius (*c.* 551-479 B.C.) ought rather to be referred to as pre-Confucian, for it dates back to between the eighth and tenth centuries B.C. (Translator's note)

the impersonal coldness of the official cults; likewise the Chinese sought the hope of an individual salvation in heterodox doctrines: Taoism and Buddhism.

Upon the old foundations of Chinese thought the Taoist fathers had elaborated a wisdom that contrasted diametrically with the teachings of Confucius: they looked for salvation in a kind of quietist mysticism. It was not in this shape the peasants adopted it. What they were after in religion was some way of appealing successfully to nature and finding refuge from death; and so they incorporated certain Taoist themes into their ancient shamanism. For them salvation was not conceived of as renunciation of the self but as individual survival; not imagining that there could be any immaterial reality, they strove to find what would perpetuate the body's very own existence. Far and away from bending before nature's operations, popular Taoism claimed to be able to influence them. The Taoist mystique degenerated into magic: men hunted for the philosopher's stone, recipes for immortality were concocted, dietetic, alchemical, respiratory formulas were recommended. Taoism appropriated the local and domestic divinities of the old animism and hierarchized them, upon the administration of mortals superimposing deific functionaries; these exercised a regency over the existence of the living and looked after the souls of the dead; they were propitiated by means of sacrifices and various ritual practices. Influenced by Buddhism, under the Hans (about 175-179 A.D.) Taoism's adherents began to organize themselves into communities where ceremonies were held in public. The clergy split into two categories: the *tao shih* who led a monastic life and practiced an asceticism in the manner of Buddhist bonzes; and secular priests who married and who were in fact soothsayers and wizards: peculiarly gifted, they strode through fire and upon the cutting edges of sabers, pierced through their cheeks with needles, exorcised haunted houses, cured the sick, and at their bidding rain would fall. They acknowledged a kind of pope: he was descended from a family, the Changs, who had won renown through the accomplishment of extraordinary feats. A magician who claimed to be of their lineage was still living at the start of the present century in a great Kiangsi palace. He would receive visitors and proudly show them a long row of jars full of captive demons; he had a sword capable of exterminating any evil spirits that ventured within a range of ten thousand leagues. No other magician knew how to cope with cases of possession by the fox. A great opium smoker, he would, for a certain price, furnish soothsaying trainees with a diploma of initiation; but over the tao shih he had no authority: nothing resembling a Taoist church has ever existed. The majority of the sorcerers did without diplomas: anybody at all, women too, could set themselves up in business. Divination and magic often went along with other activities including clandestine ones: opium was smoked at the sorcerer's residence, he upon occasion doubled as a go-between for marriages and other less serious unions.

However owing to the fact it was born on the margin of an oppressive society and out of reaction against an enslaving morality, Taoism had a catalyzing effect upon the peasantry's revolutionary tendencies. The sorcerers did indeed exploit the rural masses; still, they were of those poor folk and there were some who made common cause with them: the great Chang family distributed grain to the needy, kept the roads and bridges in repair. In critical times the hopes and fears of the peasants were embodied in their religious chiefs. It was the Changs who assumed leadership of the great peasant "Revolt of the Yellow Turbans." Most of the peasant insurrections were organized by Taoist sects; they guided the Boxer uprising. Prior to the Liberation there were innumerable secret societies of a religious character that grouped *Lumpenproletariat* elements: ruined peasants, jobless artisans. These societies, with branches reaching into every segment of the population, were frequently armed. They battled against bureaucrats and landowners but were essentially anarchical. "These people are capable of putting up the bravest kind of fight," said Mao Tse-tung* in March 1946, "but their inclination is rather toward destructive deeds." In the Red Zones the reactionaries often manipulated them against the revolution.

Buddhism's evolution in China was similar to that of Taoism. Buddhism there has affinities with the doctrine attributed to Lao-tse. These two teachings behold the world as a tissue of illusions; the infinite, the completeness of which is the equivalent

* *On the Classes in Chinese Society.*

of absolute emptiness, is to be attained only through renunciation of the personal life; the ethic one finally achieves is an asocial quietism. But Taoist belief contradicted Lao-tse even though it claimed to have stemmed from him; it was self-seeking, materialistic, superstitious. Buddhism in its purity was thus the antithesis of Taoism; it preached the abandonment of all the worldly things the Chinese peasants coveted: family prosperity, personal immortality. The adventure of its infiltration into China turns upon a series of misunderstandings.

Historically the circumstances of how it came about are rather uncertain. A legend has it that in 64 A.D. the Emperor Ming Huang had a dream and in it perceived a man whose color was of gold: interpreters told him it was a Buddha, a divinity of the West. Upon his invitation two missionaries hied themselves to his capital, Loyang, three years later; they arrived upon a white horse whose name was given to the first Buddhist monastery established. This monastery may well have fathered the legend. What is more probable is that the earliest missionaries came in by the Silk Route in the wake of the merchants who fetched Persian and Kashmir rugs into China. One thing is certain: that by the year 65 A.D. a Buddhist community existed in the neighborhood of Loyang and that in the following hundred years a church developed in that city.

The Chinese were impressed by the superficial analogies that showed this worship to resemble theirs: neither involved sacrifices, to the faithful both recommended meditation, breathing exercises, a certain kind of diet. It was fancied that the men of the West were acquainted with hitherto undisclosed means for attaining immortality and everyone was eager to try out their system.

The misunderstanding was deepened due to the fact that they were Taoist translators who revealed the Buddhist texts to the Chinese. In 148 A.D. there came to China a missionary, one Anche Kao, reputedly the son of a Parthian king; a flock of others soon arrived; in order to make their sacred books known to the Chinese they had to solicit the aid of native editors; struck by the similarities I have mentioned, the Taoists lent them willing help; but in the choice of fragments, by the way they interpreted them, through the vocabulary they employed, they gave Buddhism a considerable twist and their rendering for a long time passed for a mere variant of their own faith. Legend has it that Lao-tse rode off to the West, mounted on a cow, to preach his doctrine there; it was thought that the doctrine had been brought back twisted. Later, Chinese pilgrims, desiring to get at the sources, went to India to bring back the books. A translation bureau was set up in the fifth century and work went on until the seventh at which time what was called Chinese Buddhism was born.

It was in its Mahayana version that Buddhism penetrated into China. This, the Great Vehicle sect, which has also spread through Central Asia, proposes a more readily accessible teaching than does the Hinayana sect. Whereas according to the latter one must pass through numerous trials and avatars in order to achieve salvation, that is to say, a oneness with nirvana wherein individuality is surrendered and finally lost, Mahayana Buddhism promises personal immortality to the believer. After death the soul descends into the underworld whence it is conveyed into the paradise over which the Buddha Amitabha (*O-mi-to*, in Chinese) reigns; this "pure land" situated to the west of the world enjoys perpetual springtime; there, bodies are resuscitated, rising afresh from the lotus flowers that cover marvelous ponds; bodies are now not material but ethereal; the mere desire thereof suffices to be fed and clad. Actually this afterlife is not in theory eternal, but in their practice the faithful thought of it as such. The gaining of paradise was facilitated for them by meditation upon the bodhisattvas (in Chinese, *P'ou-sa*), saints and sages who, having merited immortality, instead of entering that condition directly, chose to be reincarnated and to mingle with mankind so as to show it the way to salvation. The most celebrated of these divine saviors are Avalokiteshvara, the Providence Buddha, and Amitabha, the Metaphysical Buddha who is the father of Avalokiteshvara and who is often figured nestled in his son's hair. In the eighth century there arose in China the contemplative Dhyana sect (*Ch'an*, in Chinese) which occupied itself meditating in union with O-mi-to: it professed a kind of quietism based upon confidence in the goodness of Buddha and surrender to his will.

The Buddhist monks busied themselves spreading their creed through the countryside; they compiled versions of the holy writings, transcribing them in a mixture of simplified prose and verse, the *p'ien wen*. But insofar as it comprised a distinct church, possessing its own clergy, temples, dogmas, rites, Buddhism fell under severe persecution starting in the eighth century when 12,000 bonzes and nuns were driven from their convents. The ninth century brought another persecution that laicized 26,000 monks and nuns and closed 4,600 bonzeries and pagodas. Then, in the tenth century, Buddhism was outlawed and 3,000 temples were ordered shut. With the advent of the foreign dynasties its fortunes were restored. The Mongols' shamanism was eclectic: they dreaded all Powers and hence respected all religions. Kublai in 1267 invited a Tibetan monk, the Lama Phago-pa, to his court; and in the thirteenth century we see Buddhism reappear in the form of Tibetan Lamaism. Kublai's successors continued this policy and a veritable Lama clericalism developed in the Empire. Later the Manchus in their turn, and for political reasons, befriended the Lamas. And in the eighteenth century Emperor Ch'ien Lung offered them, in the heart of Peking, the temple that is sometimes called the "Lama Cathedral."

Lamaism is a synthesis of Mahayana Buddhism imported from India and of the old Tibetan religion, Bon-Po. The latter was a variety of shamanism, in numerous points similar to Taoism, which may perhaps have influenced its development. It is not surprising that Lamaism received a kindly welcome in minds imbued with Taoist traditions, for Lamaism was saturated with them too.

By and large it was only by degrading itself that persecuted Buddhism survived; like Taoism it became contaminated by rural spirit worship. Avalokiteshvara turned into the female Kuan Yin, the most popular goddess in all China: not only does she save souls but she is invoked by those who wish to have children. Thus, paradoxically, while Buddha had preached renunciation in this life, in China he assumed the figure of a deity safeguarding the family's perpetuity. The monastic and mystic religion of the Hindus was transformed into a religion calculated to assure men individual happiness in this world and in the next. Its priests—the overwhelming majority of them at least—had no interest in doctrinal speculation: they sought simply to earn their livelihood;

they differed little from the Taoist priests and the peasants simultaneously consulted both sorts. The Buddhist priest's main specialty was in funeral rites: he prayed for the deceased and presided at burial ceremonies. Divination, magic, spiritism were more the concern of the Taoists.

And so China's cultural development wrought no advancement in religion. The Confucian functionaries made culture a class privilege. It was only in a grotesquely warped form that Taoist and Buddhist ideologies ever reached the people. No organized church preserved the purity of the doctrines. The men to whom supernatural powers were attributed had ceased to be clerics. Religion boiled down to a mass of superstitions. It amalgamated ancestor worship, animism, Taoist themes, the Buddhist notions of paradise and the transmigration of souls. Demons and the dead became confounded; divinities, bodhisattvas, great ancestors and heroes composed a single multitudinous Pantheon. Believers frequented all sorts of shrines: some were Buddhist, others Taoist temples, still others dedicated to this god or that hero, and in a few all the cults were jumbled together. The essential characteristic of this religion is that it was utilitarian; it was addressed to personal gods but included neither dogma nor mystique, defining itself through a body of divinatory practices, rites, taboos, and magical formulas. Contact with spirits or with the deceased could ordinarily be made without the aid of intermediaries; worship was performed for the most part at home: the faithful did their own officiating, priests seldom intervening save in rare circumstances.

Varying with the region there existed a wide assortment of traditions and customs. Descriptions furnished by sociologists and divers researchers before the Liberation concur in a good many points, however. Their accounts show the Chinese peasant's life as governed from beginning to end by his belief in spirits: for him they are everywhere. To propitiate them one burns, in their honor and at the spot where their influence is active—at the foot of trees, by the side of brooks—holy paper; or else writes a prayer formula on a bit of red paper and pastes it on a boundary stone in the fields, on a spade, a pick, a boat. The house is protected by pasting holy pictures of the warrior gods on doors; these deities guard the entrance against evil spirits. Charms and rituals guard the individual from cradle to grave against evil spells. With the aid of necromancy it is possible to control the great impersonal forces of water and wind. Water conduits, irrigation trenches, furrows in the fields are laid out in the manner magic stipulates. Divines consult destiny, tell fortunes, weave spells. Magical principles determine dates for sowing and reaping, they are listed in almanacs. Spiritualism is the means for getting into touch with the souls of the dead.

In each house there is a little altar to the ancestors, before it stand an incense burner and candles which are lit on certain days. On the anniversary of the ancestor's birth and death, upon several other occasions too, the tablet that symbolically perpetuates his existence is brought out and exposed; offerings of flowers and incense are made to him, also food offerings which the members of the family consume. At least once each year a ceremony takes place upon the tombs; paper money is burned, firecrackers exploded, a little food is offered to the deceased. Rich people arrange grand picnics. The household gods are also worshiped on various days of the year. There are thirteen major festivals, the most important of which is that of the Kitchen God. On the twenty-fourth day of the twelfth month he ascends into heaven, in order to deliver an opinion to the superior deities upon the family he watches over and whose fate for the coming year will be determined upon the basis of his report; to win his good graces on the day of his departure people offer him a meal consisting of six dishes plus a cake made of red-bean flour, then his image is placed in a paper palanquin and everything is set on fire. The day he returns a new image of him is glued upon the sanctuary.

There was in every village one or more "Halls of the Ancestors" where complicated rites took place several times a year: the walls were decked with painted portraits of the ancestors, offerings were arranged on tables, music was played, and firecrackers were shot off; then the master of ceremonies called out the names of the members of the family in order of kinship: each poured wine into a goblet and prostrated himself thrice. The family had, in conformance with prescriptions detailed in the almanac, previously prepared cakes, fruits, sweets, which were now distributed among the different groups.

Apart from these halls there were temples that most of the time were restricted to no one particular faith. Ordinarily believers visit the temple on their own, not as part of the family group. Everyone lights joss sticks and places them in a receptacle; he bows to the ground before the god, gives a little money to the keeper of the shrine, and inquires into his fate. There are a good many ways of going about this. One of the commonest is by the use of pei, made by cutting the curved root of bamboo into two pieces: three times over they are cast upon the ground and depending upon the manner in which they lie one takes careful note of good omens or bad.

Religion assumed this or that form in accordance with the classes that practiced it. In the upper strata of society animism's role was of lesser importance, that of tradition greater; with them superstition became a system of symbols. But throughout these sublimations religion functioned in the same way: it bound society hand and foot and maintained it in the prison of the past.

At the beginning of the twentieth century one of the great items on the agenda of the young bourgeois revolutionaries was to throw traditional religion overboard: as this attitude was adopted upon purely theoretical grounds, their radicalism cost them nothing. The Kuomintang attempted to wage a struggle against the superstitions that were blocking the modernization of China: but these, if palpable, were lukewarm efforts. The problem the Chinese Communist Party has had to contend with has been how to get effective results from the campaign and at the same time avoid outraging the masses.

Sorcerers were forbidden to practice their art; those who owned no land were given their share of it with the proviso they till it like any other peasant. The Taoist sects have been dissolved. Mao, as we pointed out, had long since underscored their ambiguous character. Anarchists, the Taoists had always been hostile to both order and progress; the heirs of an old naturist tradition decayed into animism, they considered machines sacrilegious inventions: at the turn of the century Taoist brotherhoods persuaded the peasants that railroads were disturbing the repose of air and water spirits and that the tracks absolutely had to be torn up. Similar societies existed at the moment of the Liberation. When once it has ceased to be a question of destroying the old order and has become one of constructing a new world, then anarchism is no longer ambiguous: it shows up as a regressive force; these sects had to be wiped out. In Peking, that of the "Unified Wisdom"—Yi-Kwan-tao—which professed a syncretism blending Buddhist and Christian elements and which was a kind of Freemasonry whose members gave each other financial help, was dissolved in December of 1950. A certain number of its leaders were arrested, charged with counterrevolutionary activities, and the association proscribed. Its Shanghai branch was suppressed two years later. But it went underground and kept going; in the rural areas counter-revolutionary resistance—directed by former owners and certain wealthy peasants—usually concentrates around former Taoist sects. In 1955 a great number of Taoist brotherhood chiefs were rounded up in Shanghai, Hopei, Yünnan, and other provinces. Needless to say the regime's enemies qualify these as dictatorial measures; the Catholics—who never before manifested the faintest respect for Chinese religion, for whom the Taoists until now were never anything but the Devil's henchmen—suddenly work themselves into a lather of indignation. All these pious liberals found it normal that, at the start of the century, when the peasants were fanatically ripping up lengths of railroad track, they be butchered by the hundreds of thousands. It seems to me less scandalous to put a handful of ringleaders away where they cannot do any damage than to let them be, and then wipe out masses of people who have been taken in by their lies.

Taoism, as a religion, retains freedom of the city. There still exist Taoist temples kept up by celibate or married priests who can receive contributions, provided they are modest, from the faithful. The greater share of the population scorns them. In certain villages peasants still sometimes go at night to consult sorcerers; but their clients are becoming fewer and fewer.

With regard to the Buddhist bonzes the government's policy has been less simple. Those who were sorcerers in disguise have been pursued and barred from their calling. The women bonzes—who had generally been pushed into monastic life by their parents and against their own wishes—have been freed; they have returned to ordinary society and most have married. The Buddhist sects having a counterrevolutionary character have been dissolved; they were not so numerous as the Taoist sects. However Buddhism being the religion practiced by many national minority groups it has been respected for that reason.* Temples and monasteries, for the most part, were restored at the expense of the government which was eager to show the Tibetans and Mongolians that it held their beliefs in esteem. In and about Peking there exist some four hundred Buddhist temples. There, lectures on the sutra are given, the Seven venerated by Buddhism evoked; and the Vinaya rules recited twice a week. Ceremonies for the expiation of the sins of the dead take place in the great monasteries. The Buddhists, in exchange for the freedom of worship that has been granted them, have pledged their support to the regime.† In 1952 twenty eminent Buddhist dignitaries summoned their fellow believers to form a "Chinese Buddhist Association": to Peking came Living Buddhas, bonzes, and laity from Mongolia, Tibet, and Turkestan. On the nineteenth and twentieth of May 1953 the delegates gathered in Peking's famous Kwangtsi Temple to celebrate the memory of the birth of Buddha; the following days were devoted to discussions, the aforementioned association was officially founded on May 30: it promised to aid the government in ferreting out sorcerers hiding under the cover of religion. "We celebrate the victory whereby counterrevolutionary sects have been defeated and reactionary sects eliminated, for it has enabled the Buddhists to distinguish the wicked from the righteous and taught us to remain ever alert against secret conspiracies and how to safeguard the purity of our faith." The conference lasted until the third of June. Presided over by two Han Chinese, two Tibetans, a Mongol, and a Thai, the conference included Living Buddhas and lamas come from Lhasa and elsewhere; delegates of the Red and Yellow Sects, enemies hitherto, consorted peacefully. All the conference members wore golden yellow robes. The Dalai Lama sent a personal message. Among its honorary presidents the Association includes the Living Buddha of Inner

* The same holds true for Moslemism. Since neither the Moslem nor the Christian faiths have ever interested better than a minute fraction of the Chinese, I do not discuss either in this chapter.

† At least the majority of the Buddhists have; but a few have remained stubborn nonjurors.

Mongolia, the Dalai Lama, the Panchen Lama, the Reverend Hsu Yu who reached the age of one hundred and thirteen in 1952.

Buddhism as an organized and dogmatic religion was of little interest to the Chinese peasants. The equivocal rural clergy represented no hierarchy and that is why its virtual liquidation did not give rise to any major difficulty: no entrenched, consolidated power opposed the government's action. On the other side of the picture, what with the priests' subsidiary position, the measures taken against them have not significantly affected the population's ancient religious habits. Since the government does not want a head-on collision with the people, sacrifices and ceremonies continue in rural China. Joss sticks are still sold in the market places; in shops I saw the shining silvery paper that is burned in honor of the ancestors, pictures of gods and guardian spirits, and also those paper imitations of objects—houses, furniture, dolls representing servants—that are reduced to cinders over the graves of the dead. Many households still have an altar where on appointed days the ancestral tablets are revered; countless women continue to observe the sacrifice to the God of the Kitchen; he is less handsomely regaled than in olden times, the gift of a malted sugar cake in the shape of a melon seems to do the trick, but the elderly ladies of the house continue to court his favor. In a collection entitled *Scenes from Village Life** I found a story in which these practices are the theme. A little girl, Chen, lives with her mother, who is the local Woman's Association vice-president, and her grandmother. Teasing her mother, Chen asks:

"What's the use being the Vice-President of the Association if you can't persuade Granny not to sacrifice to the Kitchen God? She hasn't told you yet, but she's bought a sugar melon and I'm sure she's going to offer it to the God. Wouldn't it be simpler if she just bought herself a little piece of God instead of buying candy and things to give to him?"

"They aren't selling God any more these days, there aren't enough people in the market."

The grandmother has overheard the conversation. She settles herself on the k'ang, lights her pipe, and mutters:

* By Chin Chao-Yang, one of the editors of the magazine *Popular Literature*, published at Peking.

"You don't understand anything about the ways of your elders. I have sacrificed to the Kitchen God every year. I've done it all my life. 'Venerable God, rise swiftly into heaven and hasten back unto earth; take with thee all my sorrows, bring me joy and great fortune.' "

Wherewith she begins to chuckle to herself, for she knows perfectly well that these prayers have never accomplished a thing. Every year she has made a resolution not to repeat them again; but every year, when the time has come, she has lost courage and ceded to tradition. This year however she decides that she will give her sugar melon to the children; yes, that is what she will do, and her daughter and granddaughter hear the old lady declaim:

"O God of the Kitchen, if indeed thou dost exist, make great haste, get thee into heaven and thou wouldst do well to stay there. Nobody believes any more in thee, thy image is sold no longer, thou hast no further business here below and so I think thou hadst better remain above."

Chen and her mother burst out laughing and the grandmother ends up laughing too.

This innocent little tale indicates by what means the Chinese count on vanquishing the old prejudices. They are not being hammered. The idea is that the younger generations will help the oldsters to see through them. In school the teacher demonstrates the foolishness of these antiquated notions and advises the pupils in their turn to persuade their parents. The greater part of the battle has been won. The time for sowing and harvesting is no longer decided upon by consulting almanacs but by using common sense. There is no longer any hesitation about installing gates on the southern side of villages, about digging wells to the east when there are practical reasons that recommend doing so; the elders may protest, the young pay no attention. At present it is realized that to irrigate the soil or protect it against flood, work is more effective than the effigy of a dragon. Social and economic progress is expected to complete the change in peasant mentality. The occasional and vague resistance of a few old peasants, headstrong in their beliefs and customs, poses no very serious obstacle to the general advance; and so no great effort is made to suppress them. To bring youth round to a rational *Weltanschauung* is where the effort is being made, this is the great task of the moment: to disseminate knowledge, to educate.

There are no exact statistics on how many illiterates there were in 1949; the figure had reached something like 80 per cent of the population. The size of the figure can be explained first of all by the appallingly low standard of living then current among the Chinese peasants; next, by the fact that the written language is not easy to learn: instead of combining a small number of letters into words, as we do, Chinese has a single graphic character, an ideogram, for each separate word. Of the 40,000 characters listed in dictionaries, whereof authors use as many as 20,000, knowledge of 4,000 suffices to read newspapers and most simple books; with between 1,800 and 2,000, elementary texts can be deciphered, brief reports written: but mastering 4,000 and indeed only 2,000 is a considerable undertaking. Thanks to keys or radicals, once one has learned the first 2,000, the next 2,000 come more easily.* Nevertheless the apprenticeship is much longer than in the case of alphabetically written languages.

As the Communists moved ahead region by region they taught the peasants to read; with Liberation, a tremendous literacy campaign was unleashed at once. Various methods have been tried out. One of them was invented by a political instructor in the Army of the South, Chi Chien-hua, who devised an accelerated method by which a person is able to read and write after a very brief period of study. A phonetic alphabet is learned first, then, by two-word or three-word phrases, come the characters: in a month this scheme can raise one's vocabulary from 300 to 2,000 characters. Introduced into the army in 1951, accepted in 1952 by the Military Council at Peking, the accelerated method has been widely used; owing to this, two million illiterates learned how to read in 1952. Its greatest shortcoming is that the results obtained may not be lasting: the lesson learned too quickly is often quickly forgotten. Chi's method is less in favor now than it was three years

* Most often a character breaks down into two elements, one indicating the category to which the designated object belongs, the other, phonetic, specifying that object. The former of these elements—the key or radical—recurs in a plurality of words.

ago; its advantage is that the student can learn almost all by himself: the alphabet once grasped, he is given books where characters are printed opposite phonetic symbols: these convey the meaning of the characters, and he memorizes them, writes them out on paper without needing the help of a teacher. But today there is a general preference for the traditional method that has always been employed in the primary schools.

Reading and writing are taught to workers and peasants in courses which since 1949 have been set up in every factory, mine, workshop, and village. In the city the courses are scheduled in the evening; the custom in the countryside was at first to run adult-education schools during the winter only; but it was found that the peasants were forgetting one year what they had learned the year before and the study program now follows a more continuous schedule, stepping up in the winter, slacking off as work in the fields claims the peasants' attention. The over-all idea guiding adult education is that it ought to be oriented to each group's practical experience and to aim at giving everybody increased everyday skills and knowledge. The peasants are first taught the words for domestic animals, tools, plants, everything that makes up their surroundings. Renewing the scheme formerly used in the liberated zones, the appropriate character is written on familiar objects both around the house and in public places, indoors and out; the sign becomes etched in people's memories. The first texts offered to beginners treat work done on the farm. Meanwhile they are taught arithmetic so as to be able to keep their accounts with the aid of the traditional abacus. When further along they read newspapers edited in the basic vocabulary, political texts, works of general interest, popular stories.

It is estimated that since the Liberation ten million once-illiterate adults have learned to read, to write, and to calculate on the abacus. In the spring of 1956 the young and relatively young generations* included 200,000,000 illiterates and 45,000,000 with an elementary grounding. The elimination of illiteracy had not up until then been expected to be complete before the end of the third

* That is to say, all but children through the age of adolescence and elderly persons.

Five-Year Plan: 1967. But the pace of socializing the country and, particularly, of collectivizing agriculture having been quickened, the decision was taken to speed up cultural progress too. The development of co-operatives requires that illiteracy vanish not in the space of ten years, but in seven.

If he goes only by the statistics, anyone who has not been to China will pardonably consider such optimism sheer nonsense. There are fewer than 1,400,000 primary-school teachers in China, there are 70,000,000 youngsters in their classes; the number of adult pupils ranges from 200,000,000 to 220,000,000; each person must spend about three years at study if he is to acquire the indispensable rudiments—the figures advise that the job be given up in advance. Other figures also seemed to prove that it would be ages before China would be able to get rid of rats, flies, cholera; well, she managed without sanitation engineers, she mobilized the entire population. She is mobilizing it again. For lack of teaching personnel in sufficient numbers the answer is that "the people shall teach the people." The battle against illiteracy, like the one against unhygienic conditions, is a mass movement. Five million young people, their primary or secondary studies done, are tilling the soil at this moment; there will be more of them every year: they are teaching others. Forty-five million adults know how to read and write: they too are teaching. From the young activists' Congress held at Peking in October 1955 came the appeal: every peasant, every worker who knows how himself ought to communicate his knowledge of reading and writing to at least one comrade. That was not enough. Two hundred million as against forty-five million; no, each improvised teacher will take on four pupils. In towns or villages of some size the co-operatives arrange courses, make the best possible use of whatever skills there are at hand. Where the farms are scattered far apart volunteers assemble the peasants in small groups, the class is conducted now in one man's house, now in another's. School children share their attainments with their families. Knowledge thus spreads by chain reaction.

For the cadres—heads of co-operatives, rural civil servants—another system has been initiated: they take three-month leaves of absence and spend the time exclusively in study, usually at the chief locality in the hsien.* Tens of thousands of cadres have recently benefited from this system.

The Women's Associations and above all The New Democratic Youth League are playing a vital part in the movement. A chain of Anti-Illiteracy Associations has taken shape, its branches have multiplied. These associations recruit and prepare amateur, unpaid teachers, organize and help those needing instruction. The net result of this vast drive is that, as against 28,000,000 in 1954, some 62,000,000 peasants are now in regular attendance at the adult schools.

One of the big problems is of getting together the necessary material, especially the reading primers; this, too, is being solved by an appeal to everybody's co-operation. The government cannot hand down a standard program from the top: there are too many dissimilarities among the provinces; the texts need to be adapted to each particular area, and they are—which gives the lie to the anti-Communist catcall about People's China being uniformity incarnate. The department of education, the youth and cultural associations in each hsien work out the manuals to be used in the region's factories and co-operatives. Roving teams aid in compiling texts. For instance, in the hsien of Hung Chao, Shansi Province, eighteen hundred secondary-school students were divided into ninety-five squads; each visited a different locality and two days later had helped the local people put in shape 476 adaptations of texts dealing with work and profit.

The results achieved so far permit the prediction that five, six, or seven years from now 220,000,000 illiterates will each have learned some fifteen hundred characters and will be familiar with the use of the abacus. Within two years' time there will be no illiteracy left in the ranks of the civil service. Within five, industry will be rid of it. Primary schools for workers are to open in 1957; and the cultural level of the nation will gradually but steadily mount.

Above and beyond the fight against illiteracy, an effort is being made to establish a cultural structure that is primarily of a political nature. Upon the press has developed the larger share of the task of getting citizens to participate in the life of the country.

* A *hsien* is the equivalent of an American county.

Because of the shortage of material means the total number of newspapers printed each day is only four million; the number of readers is a great deal higher. Printed copies are multiplied by duplication process. In streets, factories, offices, villages you see newspapers tacked up on bulletin boards, and single copies are often read by groups.

There are seventeen national papers, six of them daily, seven weekly, four appearing three times a week; and there are 248 local or specialized papers. The most influential is Peking's *The People's Daily,* which has replaced the former *Yenan Daily* as the Communist Party's organ; it corresponds to the Russian *Pravda* and prints 730,000 copies. The weekly *Chinese Youth* runs off the biggest edition: 1,800,000. There are twenty newspapers published in national minority languages: Tibetan, Mongol, Uigur, etc. Certain publications are still in private hands: for example, the *Ta Kung Pao,* which has been in existence for over fifty years, and Shanghai's *Wen Houa Pao.* All are government-supervised. News reaches them over the wires of the official New China News Agency which also sends them suggestions and directives.

Since no opposition party exists in China,* one need never look in the press for negative criticism of policies being followed by the regime. The concept of a people's dictatorship is hardly compatible with freedom of the press such as it is conceived in the bourgeois democracies. The press in China is governmental. Be that as it may, it grants considerable space to positive criticism. On the one hand, the newspapers are, for the Party and for the Government, an instrument of self-criticism: they point out the deviations and mistakes that the leaders propose to correct. On the other, they solicit the active collaboration of their readers. If someone wishes to protest against an abuse or an error committed by a bureau of the state or a private organism, he writes to the newspapers; whenever it is of general interest the letter is printed and usually followed by a reply in which the incriminated party states his position and offers his apologies. The press thus

* But, it should be noted, China does not have a one-party system if one chooses—as the Chinese themselves do—to allow a meaningful existence to those other, smaller parties which, functioning side by side with the Chinese Communist Party, co-operate with rather than exist opposite it. (Translator's note)

enables the lower echelons to exert an authentic check upon persons holding posts of responsibility. Mail from readers amounts to a public-opinion poll; the government watches it closely.

As regards the reporting of news, newspapers are expected to be rigorously accurate. Twisted phrases and typographical errors are not viewed with any complacent eye. Facts and figures have got to be exact; anything short of that will incur a stern reprimand. The daily *Kuang Ming* in 1954 ran one of those false reports which are so frequent in the Western press: an imaginative reporter avowed that, visiting the little Orkura tribe, he was amazed at all the government had accomplished: it had built a town for them, with schools, dispensaries, and so on. The Chinese authorities energetically disclaimed having *done* any of these things: they were all only in the planning stage. The *Kuang Ming* was obliged to print an editorial in which it addressed an apology to its readers.

The anti-Communists will smile at this scrupulousness, for the government still retains the right to dispense the truth in its own way. Surely. But if we ourselves are so well-informed, why deliberately forget that up until yesterday virtually all the Chinese were maintained in strictest ignorance of the political world? They underwent their fate in passivity and darkness. "All the news that's fit to print" is our boast; it could be theirs; and a guided understanding of affairs, representing an immense improvement over absolutely none, is indeed the only one capable of dissipating that darkness. Set "the whole truth's" multitude of conflicting facts and opinions before the public while it still lacks the bases necessary for discriminating and judging for itself and you will succeed in doing little more than creating confusion.* Before any knowledge is possible there must be the initial phase in which chaos gives way to a rudimentary order: that which in the view of later ages constitutes the insufficiency of this knowledge is the very thing that has enabled it to develop further. Let us be honest instead of deploring the restrictions—imposed today out of necessity—upon the freedom of the press, we can rather admire the effort being

* I need hardly say that I am not partisan to an unfree press in any country. But China's case would seem to me a special one, what with the towering percentage of illiterates among the Chinese masses and their lack of political background or sophistication.

made by the regime to disseminate information. It does not demand blind obedience from the people. It is endeavoring to keep them abreast of events, to explain their causes, meanings, and implications. It is shaping the people politically, and thereby making them more fit to take on the leadership of the country with ever-broadening authority.

Before the Liberation almanacs and the picture albums called egg books provided all it ever had of culture to that part of the peasantry which was able to read. A hundred years ago a poor Hopei peasant, Liu, who knew a rich repertory of folk tales, got the idea of dictating them to a public scribe; a carpenter who knew how to do woodcuts illustrated and printed them. Cast in the language of popular speech interspersed with a few expressions borrowed from the idiom of the cultivated, these stories found their way throughout all of North China. At the gates of Peking Liu set up his Shop of the Treasures of Literature which grew under the management of his son and grandson. The egg books presented episodes excerpted from the great Chinese novels, adventures, fairy tales, sentimental narratives. With the Liberation, the leaders decided to use them as a medium for disseminating the new ideas in the back country. In 1950 three novelists offered their services to Liu Yu-Che; among others Lao-She and Kao Chou-li set to work. Nine hundred thousand copies of their stories were sold. Next, the ancient legends were rewritten in a new temper; and new stories were composed: stories of work heroes, Korean volunteers, the tracking down of Kuomintang spies, free marriage, love. In a year ten million copies of these picture books were sold. I read *The Special Delivery Letter* in a French translation. The adventure is of a little shepherd boy who goes through Japanese-controlled territory to carry a message from one group of partisans to another. The pictures are of an extreme simplicity, so is the story, but it is told well. Amateurs of pure literature will probably wince to hear that during evenings around the fireside it is no longer the old tales but propaganda common folk are reading; but those old tales were not so very pure either, nor so innocent. Foxes and dragons will doubtless again become entertaining subjects when nobody any longer dreads their powers. Nor, furthermore, are these picture books to continue to comprise the entirety of popular literature. A higher culture must be made available to everyone.

Once beyond the elementary stage constituted by the fight to overcome ignorance and superstitions, there arises the question, what sort of culture is it to be? Mao Tse-tung replied to it, two years before his *Addresses to the Yenan Forum,* in an editorial published in *Chinese Culture,* a Yenan review founded in 1940. He wrote,

We must achieve a suitable blending of the general truth of Marxism and the concrete realization of the Chinese Revolution: which is to say that Marxism will only be usefully practicable if given a national form. Chinese culture must have its own form. That is, a national form.

The allusion being to Sun Yat-sen's three principles which had been called "Tridemism," the platform laid down by Mao was referred to as "Neodemism." Commenting upon it, the Marxist Sung Yu declared:

The neodemist philosophy, the while criticizing it, makes welcome room for the entire spiritual heritage that runs from Confucius to Sun Wen,* molds it into a doctrine to guide the national revolution, forges it into the intellectual weapon for winning the confidence and support of the country.

And again:

Neodemism weds the universal reality of Marxism into a synthesis with the concrete practice of modern Chinese culture.

The new culture, then, is to have its roots in the old, to have a specifically Chinese form: the intimate tie between Chinese Communism and Chinese nationalism requires that it be so. The bourgeois—and many intellectuals of bourgeois origin—rallied to the Revolution out of hatred for foreign imperialism; the fight against capitalism was substantially the same as the fight against Japan and the Occident. And this still holds true: the Chinese's adherence to the regime is cemented by patriotism: they are grateful to the Communists for having made their country into a world

* Sun Yat-sen.

power. Nationalism cannot but affirm itself in the cultural domain: for all culture implies a continuity of tradition.

However when speaking of *the nation* the inference is that the sum total of the inhabitants of a country compose a unity; can this concept of *nation* square with that other of a society split up into enemy classes? National oneness is ordinarily affirmed by ruling classes when they find it useful to deny this cleavage: and thus the Kuomintang called itself nationalist. Its behavior during the anti-Japanese war proved that it had usurped the label; the Chinese Republic can easily claim it today since it is in the process of eliminating classes as such. But when it comes to endorsing the heritage of a divided past the question becomes delicate. Lately it has given rise to serious controversies between Chinese intellectuals. Culture is a superstructure: there can be nothing sound in the superstructure of a society that was rotten, some critics have maintained. Others have questioned the notion of a superstructure. The conclusion finally reached was that its cultural superstructure reflects the contradictions existing within a society, sometimes merely expressing them, but sometimes also exceeding them; there must be a clear distinction made between the two. This was the solution Mao proposed when he said at Yenan:

> One must distinguish between the rotten principles of the ancient feudal governing classes, and the excellent popular culture of antiquity which to varying extents contains democratic and revolutionary qualities.

He coined the famous slogans: "Let it be of the past we win the infant present"; "May our garden be wide, and all flowers grow there together." He wrote this as well:

> A brilliant culture arose during the long feudal period. We must purify what it produced, from it we must winnow out the national germ, this we shall keep, the feudal chaff we shall throw away.

According to these texts, *national* is to be identified with *popular*. But this solution appears to be something less than wholly justified if one glances back at China's history. And indeed it is the breach existing between these two concepts that explains the ambiguous attitude the Chinese today have toward their past.

It has often been said that the unity of China has been more that of a civilization than of a nation. True; and for a number of reasons. Unity was brought several times to the Empire; it did not always have the same frontiers or the same capital; its sovereigns did not come from the same line; actually the passing centuries saw a succession of various empires, with an interval of anarchy between the fall of one and the rise of the next. So vast was the territory they embraced that they constituted a federation rather than a country; the South, settled by people from the North, Szechwan, isolated from both North and South, have always remained fundamentally unalike. Emperor Shih Huang Ti standardized the span of axletrees, hence the width of roads, but these served first to ensure effective administration—the movement of mails, of officials—second, to bring provincial rice and corn to the imperial storehouses: their purpose was not to put separate regions into touch. Militarily, the Emperor's forces were inadequate for the size of his dominions. France did not become a real entity until the king's army gave his subjects effective protection against trouble brewed by contentious lordlings and against invasions from outside; from then on the people identified themselves with their sovereign and it is this alliance the story of Joan of Arc illustrates. In China, even after the great feudality had been defeated, war lords went on dominating provinces that often preferred to come out openly in favor of them and secede from the Empire. As for foreign threats, they had a very special character. Individual provinces suffered fearfully from barbarian raiders who, however, were not joined into powerful organized nations able to subdue and annex China. When annexations occur the interests of the vanquished are regularly sacrificed to those of the masters, their traditions, their customs, their languages are abolished; nothing of the sort ever happened in China; the barbarians were too backward and too few to be able to impose their yoke upon her: China absorbed them. Like domestic strife, the war would end with a mere change of dynasty; the new emperors quickly became Chinese and their administration was neither better nor worse than that of their native predecessors. All this accounts for the numerous "traitors" one meets with in Chinese annals;

the dynasties' prerogatives were founded on nothing but force, a situation that lay behind the idealistically styled observation that, when a dynasty weakened, it showed that it had lost the virtue which had anchored its right. The criminal general who went over to the enemy did not betray his country: he was bowing to the will of heaven; and those who in the twentieth century collaborated with the Japanese were acting within an age-old tradition. Fidelity to a dynasty was rather more feudal fealty than patriotism. In order to stand for something one must stand against something else; they were national wars waged against rival countries that sired the patriotic sentiment both in the Roman republic and in France. When the Roman Empire finally embraced the whole of the known world, then patriotism faded away: the title of Roman citizen betokened class superiority, not a national particularism. The Chinese had the keenest contempt for all barbarians—for, that is to say, whoever was not Chinese—this contempt which restricted the world to the Empire alone did away with the necessity for the Empire to assert that it was superior. For lack of a relationship with something other than itself, it never took a stand, never achieved the identity that is wrought of choice alone.

In France national consciousness and its attending sentiments came into being when, from below, the nation fused its elements into a concrete unity: this was the work of the bourgeoisie. Against feudal particularisms the bourgeois, leagued through community of interests, knit every part of the land into a whole; the close ties that bound trade, agriculture, and handicraft together made an organic unity of the country; the coexistence of a common national interest and a class struggle constituted a contradiction which governs the history of France; there were certain periods when that contradiction would be resolved into a balanced synthesis. The key fact in the history of China is that she had no middle class. The chief industries, iron and salt, became state monopolies twenty-two centuries ago. Whereas the kings of France in their struggle with the feudal magnates turned for help to the communes and the powerful townsmen, the Chinese emperors would demolish their opponents by dispatching an army of officials against them. What with the vastness of their territories and the character of Chinese civilization in which water—rivers, floods, seacoast, etc.—was a major factor, officials were indispensable; the major public works required to keep communications open and rivers from flooding meant deploying a considerable number of administrators. This class, that throughout the Empire embodied the central authority, would brook no rival power. The tradesmen were preyed upon: their speculations were designated as theft, their children were deprived of the right to take the examinations opening the way to a mandarin career; they were more or less deliberately crushed by massive taxation. In spite of intervals of prosperity—to which, among others, Marco Polo bears witness—the merchants never succeeded in forming a class; their greatest ambition was to become property holders and they bought real estate instead of amassing capital.* As a consequence, the volume of trade was always slender, the commercial centers of no great importance; handicraft remained on a family or village scale; and each social group—farm, hamlet, town, province—dwelled in self-sufficient isolation. The landowners, from whose ranks most of the mandarins were recruited, were not bound together by mutual interests, some even took a hand in regional secessions; their governorship consisted in executing orders received from above; they had no direct say in the development of the country, which moreover is why that development remained at a standstill: there was missing in China the leavening which in the West was provided by the bourgeois' enterprising spirit.

The emperors did not supply that lack. Save for Shih Huang Ti, who broke the feudality and built the Empire, none of them ever did anything that had a decisive influence on the course of subsequent history. The realm Shih Huang Ti assembled was too vast: his successors wore themselves out merely defending its borders and restoring unity with great difficulty. There being no economic solidarity among the separate regions, this unity was never actually realized. Wars were local affairs of no interest to the rest of the country; writers condemned them, very rightly, as

* One observes similar trends at the end of the Roman Empire. But that was a good fifteen hundred years ago, whereas this situation continued in China up until the close of the nineteenth century.

costly and pointless adventures. Because internal cohesion was not there, the Empire always seemed on the brink of collapse; nor did the sovereigns gamble much on the future; their administration was dominated by financial worries; their energies went not into developing China's resources, but into levying and collecting taxes. Peter the Great was an autocrat; but Russian nationalism can think very highly of him, for he set his country on the road to progress. The emperors of China did nothing but renew the same military contests and repeat the same administrative tasks; their reigns brought varying kinds of luck to their contemporaries, but all of them failed equally to forge a new future. Small wonder if today, in retrospect, the Chinese view them with a more hostile than friendly eye, for they exploited the people without creating a nation. When I visited the historical museum my guide pointed respectfully to the statue of Shih Huang Ti: he may be considered the founder of China. Concerning the Manchus, who practiced racial segregation, who bullied the country and sold it to Westerners, the attitude of the Chinese is one of out-and-out hate. The rest of the emperors, all of whom oppressed the people, fare little better in current opinion which however allows a certain esteem for some insofar as they incarnated a moment in Chinese civilization.

For, failing a national unity, there was a Chinese civilization and it was *one*; today's nationalism evokes it: "China has been the cradle of one of the world's greatest civilizations"—this leitmotiv recurs over and over again in official speeches. It is striking that to their history—which as a matter of fact has the appearance of an absence of history, not of the genesis of the present—the Chinese prefer the image of it that popular culture has perpetuated, that is to say, legend. Their past survives not as a succession of dated events but in the guise of tradition and symbols. For instance, the Chinese visualize the bloody and anarchic period called "The Epoch of the Three Kingdoms" through *The Romance of the Three Kingdoms* which was written several centuries after it; for the Chinese that time has become a golden and chivalric age. It is from *The Romance,* not from history, that the theater and literature have borrowed any number of heroes and episodes. One of its personages was even elevated to the rank of a god: Kuan Ti, the story's great general, entered the Chinese pantheon and was given the mission of preventing wars. Many historical happenings have undergone like transmutation. The Emperor Ming Huang and his lovely concubine Kuei-fei did nothing to promote the people's welfare; the senile and cowardly passion of the one, the calculated affections of the other are not in themselves particularly exalting; but the stories and especially the play which recount this lamentable love tragedy were such splendid and stirring works of literature and became so popular that in Chinese hearts the couple came to incarnate the whole grandeur and anguish of love.

Going through the most famous of the legendary themes and heroes one notices that the ethics they reflect are by no means coherent. One of Chinese history's greatest figures is Yo Fei who to his dying breath defended his beaten emperor; there is a temple dedicated to him at Hangchow; a walk guarded by stone warriors leads to the tomb where he is buried, a statue represents him holding a piece of jade before his lips: such was the posture every respectful mortal was to adopt before the Son of Heaven. Thus it is Yo Fei's submission and loyalty to his Lord which are celebrated here; and such was the Chinese's reverence for that general that in bygone days they customarily spat and urinated on the effigies of the two traitors who handed him over to the invading enemy. However, to the reader's admiration the famous *Shui-hu-chuan** holds up the example of eight hundred rebels who took to the hills to fight against the corrupt officialdom that represented the imperial administration in the flesh. The Chinese people have always had a keen affection for the Rebel; their fondness for his past exploits endures, and countless are the stories, the operas that celebrate him and his revolt.

This ambiguity is easily explained. First of all one must note that Yo Fei was deified when at the start of the twentieth century North China was trying to revive the official religion: a military government made Yo the patron of the armies. Chiang Kai-shek's Nationalist China made the most of this worship and it took such firm root that the Communists did not even try to dislodge it from men's minds; and indeed, as before, Yo Fei

* Translated as *All Men Are Brothers* by Pearl Buck.

can continue to symbolize public spirit today and to set an example of fidelity to the powers that be—who, at the present time, are the Communist leaders. But also considered as heroes are those men who combated the evil regime under which China groaned in the past. Chinese nationalistic communism harks back both to ancient patriotism and to the old struggle between classes: but no one ever ironed out the conflict between the territorial unity of China and the division of Chinese society, never before the twentieth century did the welfare of the country as a whole gain the ascendant over the clashing interests dividing the people from their rulers. The result is that the past has not bequeathed the example of any patriotic hero taking arms in behalf of the rights of the masses; the hero may have been of humble birth—indeed numerous emperors were—but he does not incarnate the people; thus, there is no comparing Yo Fei, who was only loyal to a dynasty, with Joan of Arc who, in fighting for the French king, fought also for the French peasants. "Our popular and national heritage"—a cursory examination of the figures remembered in the body of Chinese legend is enough to bring out the contradiction in terms. Earlier, I said that in Peking I remarked how the Chinese would hesitate before their great monuments: they admire without loving them. It is for the same reason. Palaces and temples are certainly a national heritage, but there is nothing popular in their character.

In what, then, does consist the culture which is authentically popular in China? One of the dominant facts in the history of Chinese culture is that the scholars who monopolized it were functionaries dedicated to the emperor's service: their relationship to the people was utterly different from that which the Western clerks maintained with them.

In ancient China, as in medieval France later, the clerks' essential role was to act as intermediaries between princes addicted to warlike activity and peasants who were nailed to their plots of ground. Knowing how to count and above all how to read and write, the clerks kept men in communication with one another. In both cases they assiduously monopolized its instruments. In France they employed Latin. In China, too, they used an esoteric language. The standardization of graphic signs Shih Huang Ti put through unified China spatially and temporarily; identical from one end of the land to the other, the written characters remained unaltered for centuries; but the literate gentry cut themselves off from the profane by doing their writing in *ku-wen*, a language they alone understood and the use of which they maintained until our own century. Despite some important similarities there was a considerable difference between the two clerical bodies: the Western clerks were clerics whose allegiance was primarily to the Church rather than to princes. Engrafting itself upon the Roman Empire, Christianity had assumed its universality and to a certain degree its humanism and rationalism. The church was catholic in the fullest sense of the word. Religion included not only practices but an ideology; it took over old spirit-worship cults, but in so doing attenuated their particularism and their magical character; it proposed universally applicable dogmas and precepts which represented considerable progress over the ancient superstitions: Christianity placed man in the center of a creation wrought expressly for him. The clerics affirmed the equality of all men in the eyes of God and to the extent that they preached peace and justice they served the people, opposing the excesses of feudal barons and kings. They moreover kept in close contact with the masses whose souls they desired to save. The sermons, the canticles, the bas-reliefs, and stained glass of churches availed the illiterate of a culture that the intellectual vigilance of a solidly organized clergy prevented from degenerating: the Church scholars watched over and strengthened the foundations whence the popular imagination took its departure. We know how fertile this collaboration proved. Canticles were born of ancient songs; mysteries evolved from the theater; the painters and sculptors were usually clerics who had risen from the humbler social strata. When in the thirteenth century the population grew and the conditions of social life improved a great popular art burst into flower.

In China, on the contrary, culture and religion were divorced; the clerks were lay administrators; young men who had specialized in religious sciences would speedily switch their vocations. Buddhism however, at the period it penetrated into China, had not yet lost its original richness; it influenced the plastic arts; in grottoes dedicated to the worship of Buddha painters represented the various figures belonging to the paradise of Amitabha. The great sculpture of the Wei epoch discloses the strait alliance between a religion and a people, just as Romanesque sculpture does in France. But as Buddhism proceeded to debase itself religious art sank apace. Lamaism elaborated an iconography which Taoism borrowed and which by dint of its abundance and ugliness evokes that of Saint Sulpice. Ideologically, from the standpoint of confessions claiming to universality, Buddhism and Taoism, like Confucianism, remained the appanage of a privileged class.

The counterpart of this cultural segregation was that it favored the emergence of a folklore while the universalization of culture deprived us of one in France. The Chinese people's plastic abilities manifested themselves in craftwork which took on various special characteristics from province to province. Beginning with the Mings, the making of porcelain, lacquerware, and cloisonné became officialized and workmanship degenerated, only worsening under the Manchus. But original and living traditions were perpetuated in the countryside where a literature developed also. Buddhism gave rise to stories of metamorphoses, of foxes turned into ladies, of fabulous animals. The tales inspired by Taoism take magical objects for themes, a favorite being the mirror endowed with extraordinary properties; these stories involve seers, sorcerers; they describe phenomena of disincarnation; they blend dream and reality. This mythology is monotonous and somewhat lackluster. Much more interesting are the legends through which the people conveyed their view of Chinese history; this epic treasure has been tapped and variously re-rendered in tales, spoken or sung, in dialogues, and especially in plays for the stage. About the time of the Mings there began to spring up an important literature that draws its sustenance from these sources.

The Chinese, then, possess a rich popular heritage—but to what extent can a folklore, stemming from a cultural segregation, be integrated into a culture aiming at universality? That which in China was national had no popular character—can that which was popular assume a national dimension today?

Another question comes to mind. At the start of the twentieth century the bourgeoisie managed to grab the culture monopoly away from the clerks. The Chinese bourgeoisie's "a little bit of this, a little bit of that" was reflected in its ideologies and in its literature. To what extent does Communist China acknowledge itself kin to the Fourth of May? The enjoinder to win the present from the past is less simple than it looks.

Of one thing we can be certain: China's eagerness to salvage, to recover her past. During the period of my stay in Peking numerous exhibits took place: of ancient musical instruments, porcelain since earliest times, and pottery. In the buildings flanking the Imperial Palace's outer courtyard there is a permanent historical museum where China's history is shown to unfold from remote Sinanthropus up until the Sung era. With tranquil innocence things very properly start at their beginning: tracing evolution, a genealogical tree emerges from the belly of a fish and, branch by branch, mounts to the worker in blue overalls. One thinks of Queneau's *Petite cosmogonie*—

*Le singe sans effort, le singe devient homme,*
*Lequel un peu plus tard désintégra l'atome.*

All the same, the exposition is very nicely done. One sees the tortoise shells once used for divination, the bamboo tablets upon which the first Chinese characters were engraved with a stylus, and bronzes, pottery, seals, prints. There are statues and portraits of Confucius, Shih Huang Ti, Kublai Khan, Mo Ti. Recent paintings show what the Chinese countryside probably looked like long ago: photographs show the statues in the Long Men grottoes. The success is all the more praiseworthy in that Peking has lost all but a handful of authentic relics from its past. Western countries have crammed their museums with Chinese art treasures; and before dashing to Formosa, Chiang Kai-shek laid hands on everything in sight: he packed off three hundred cases of archaeological finds, among them 25,000 "osteoglyphs" or "oracle bones," fragments of bulls' clavicles that were used in foretelling the future in remote times. The Peking Museum was looted: bronzes, porcelains, paintings, lacquer, silks, jades, rare books: off they went, 2,972 chests of them; 852 other chests were filled with the collections from the Central Museum; in addition, Chiang stole 120,000 ancient volumes belonging to the city's main public library. He shipped 4,000 trunkloads of this booty to America in October 1955.

The government took steps to prevent this pillage from continuing. Export of objects of cultural value was prohibited in May 1950 and Liu-li-chang Street, where most of the town's antique shops are, no longer sells anything but copies. Another law enacted the same year protects historical monuments and archaeological sites. But these negative measures are not the most interesting ones: China is rebuilding its collections by pushing ahead with archaeological studies. There have been Chinese archaeologists since the reign of the Sungs; until the present century they concentrated exclusively in epigraphy and typology. French scholars took a leading hand in opening up the era of the great excavations; major discoveries were made between 1920 and 1937. Then, because of the Anti-Japanese and Civil Wars, work was suspended. It was resumed again in 1950 and most of the bronzes and statues you see now in the Palace showcases have been unearthed since that date. The University of Peking added a department of archaeology in 1952; accelerated courses give students a quick introduction to the field, and 270 young archaeologists have been graduated so far. Circumstances have conspired to be helpful. Since during the last five years there has been a good deal of digging and shifting of soil with the construction of roads, the cutting of canals, the building of factories and railways, lots of treasures have come to light. When ground was broken for the Peking Hotel's new wing, a cache of Ming porcelains was uncovered. Extensive archaeological projects have also been systematically conducted. The Chinese, then, are actively going after traces of the old civilization they recognize as their own. The question is still of finding out in what measure and form it is being incorporated into the various intellectual and artistic domains.

### *Ideology*

The confusion of bureaucrat with clerk accounts for the monolithism that distinguished twenty centuries of Chinese ideology.

Outside the dominant class no intellectual existed, and there was no line to be drawn between the active members of that class and its conceptive ideologists. Functioning as clerks, the genteel scholars wove a doctrine; functioning as administrators, despite the resistance afforded by certain heterodox currents, they imposed it upon the whole of society.

When the feudal system's disintegration, military anarchy, social disorders had finished sapping the authority of the local princes, then the importance of the clerks grew; from servants they became advisers, and to secure their influence they contrived the weapons they were best able to wield: ideologies. The one that best accommodated itself to China's economic and social structure was of course sure to triumph: it was Confucianism. Created in order to restore feudalism, it had seemed inadequate when Shih Huang Ti transformed the regime by breaking the feudal power and unifying the Empire: the lettered class had joined the opposition, and the Books had been burned; but once the new order had been established, Emperor and clerks realized that their interests coincided; Wu Ti relied upon the scholars, who had no trouble adjusting their doctrine to the requirements of a centralized state. To attempt to pick out just what was Confucius' own contribution to the intricate system he fathered would be as idle as trying to discover which elements of Christianity can be traced back to Christ.* The entire class of scholars instituted and maintained the ideology which guaranteed its political supremacy and its moral justification.

The might of a military chief depends upon his armies; if after being a conqueror he turns administrator, functionaries take precedence over generals. The scholars set about persuading the sovereign that governing amounts to administering; "The art of governing simply consists in creating an order in things, that

* Confucius was primarily a teacher, not a systematic thinker; what we know of him and of his doctrine comes to us by way of his disciples (only some few of whom were his actual pupils) and through the tradition later generations molded according to hearsay, speculation, and their own exigencies and preferences. Only the *Lun Yü* (known to the English world as *The Analects,* also as *The Philosophical Dialogues,* and to a greater or lesser extent represented in the many *Sayings of Confucius* various translators have compiled) is nowadays allowed to be really authoritative as a source for the Master's life and teachings. (Translator's note)

is to say, in putting them in their rightful place." But what is the criterion of order and of right? If the government was to attune itself to "the reality of things in the present world," as the legalists would have it, politics would become something that every man endowed with a modicum of judgment could practice; it would fall into vulgar hands: that is exactly what was happening when Shih Huang Ti surrounded himself with legalists. The Confucians responded to the peril by shouldering past the legalists and unlimbering their unique erudition. The secret of order, they assured the suzerain, lay in the Books bequeathed to posterity by a distant golden age: to know how to govern one must first know how to read and then justly to appreciate the meaning of words. Like the clerics of the Middle Ages, and for similar reasons, the Chinese scholars stressed the crucial importance of the Word; they proposed that the order of things depended upon a system of "just denominations" which came down to making the Word the essence of reality; thus did they subordinate knowledge and experience to tradition, and judgment to logic; he who is master of words is alone capable of managing the affairs of society. Which in a trice dispels all doubt as to who is to run the whole show; enlisting the aid of the old cosmogony the scholars extracted all its advantages from a monism that strictly relates every element to the whole: from it they deduced that heaven befriends him who administers mankind. "Order in the world and the success of armies depend upon the same fortune, troubled times and unlucky years upon the same fate," wrote Tung Chung-shu, "whence it is seen, that the arrangements introduced into human affairs sort positively with the will of heaven." This megalomaniac bureaucrat's fantasy persevered until the twentieth century: in 1900 it was yet thought that administrational commotions were having their deleterious impact upon the celestial scheme. Inversely, if a dynasty lost power it was supposed that heaven had canceled its mandate and hence that it had lacked in virtue; good fortune or ill depended upon the mood and designs of heaven, which amounted to identifying success and privileges with merit. There are some who claim that Confucianism subordinates politics to morals; Mo Ti long ago denounced this lie. He was thoroughly aware that the privileged do not model their order after any pure idea of Good but that they call *good* the order they choose to institute. In every society the values extolled by the elite conceal a violence. The attitude of the scholars was analogous to that of the Puritans who handily mistook the good man for the man who owns goods, wealth in their eyes being a divinely accorded grace which attests to the virtue of the elect.

Within such a perspective, social activity, having cosmic implications and straightway setting itself up in relation with the supreme power, was the equivalent of a religious exercise. The Puritan arranged for his salvation in the next world by accumulating capital in this; he was his own priest. Neither did the Chinese functionary need a specialized clergy to put him in touch with heaven: he had simply to keep the taxes rolling in. Bureaucracy occupied the place of religion, which consolidated its authority: neither outside its ranks nor within them was there any officially existing group vested with any official powers capable of disputing its own.* Thus was it able to remain a homogeneous and virtually closed corporation. In Europe the democratic ferment contained in Christianity and the enterprising spirit inherent in burgeoning capitalism favored an upsurge during the eighteenth and nineteenth centuries which saw the lower strata thrust to the topmost ranks of the bourgeoisie. For their part, the Chinese scholars saw to it that the Books did not, like the Bible, become accessible to everybody, and that they were never transcribed into the vulgate. Beginning with the Tangs, they were, because of a system of examinations, recruited from their own midst, this co-optation enabling them to maintain a strict doctrinal orthodoxy and only parsimoniously to open their ranks to persons of modest means. Confucian society was no more moral than it was democratic. First of all, education, costly and requiring leisure, was reserved for the sons of the rich; and then recommendations were of greater usefulness than brains to the candidates who presented themselves for examination. There are many stories and plays in which a poor student is seen to become a mandarin: which means that these cases, like any rags-to-riches myth, appealed to the imagination, not that they were frequent. With rare exceptions

* If Taoists or Buddhists gained sway over certain emperors, the influence they exerted was only episodic and brief.

the bureaucratic class coincided with that of the great landowners, prosperous civil servants hastening to buy up land, big proprietors angling for official posts.

Laid down by the privileged, the Confucian order was obviously an order founded upon privilege. Confucius never dreamed of changing the hierarchized society he was born into. His great contribution belongs to the realm of individual ethics: his notion of virtue. In a time when China was divided into little seigniories the villeins were held in obedience by armed force, but the nobles, with soldiers at their heels, could rise against the suzerain or break their oath to him: the right functioning of everything depended upon their loyalty; it was a person-to-person relationship that was sound and meaningful so long as the seigniories remained small in size; if he failed in his duties, social pressure drove the miscreant to suicide. When kingdoms grew bigger this tie between the individual and the community relaxed. Group pressure was replaced by a universal and obscure order that could not be effective unless it became part of the individual.* That is why Confucius lays such emphasis upon the necessity of "observing oneself when alone." Only in solitude can one put one's heart to the test and determine whether one has translated received instructions into moral commandments; to do so is the mark of the sincerity Confucius expects in his "wise man." But if he invented the idea of moral conscience in China, the content he ascribes to it is by no means novel: Confucius' "right action" is infallibly conformance to established patterns of conduct. As in Kant, the individual will lay aside his unique sensibility and be ruled by the imperative dictates of his moral reason: he will take the ideal human being for his model. The difference is that Kant, expressing a bourgeois society, conceives of the human being in terms of a universal mode whereas Confucius defines him in those of feudal hierarchies. The righteous man is he who utterly identifies himself with his office: sovereign, administrator,

* American sociologists have shown that a similar process has occurred in every society; when traditional constraints relax they are replaced by a moralism which operates as a conditioning force upon the individual's psychology and attitudes. In this way, Puritanism arose to help nascent capitalism rid itself of encumbering traditional forms. Cf. *The Lonely Crowd* by Riesman, Glazer, and Denney.

father, subject, son. The caprices of princes, the appetites of officials, the discontent, the despair of the downtrodden, all these manifestations of subjectivity have no place in the social being that it is everybody's task to exemplify. Which is to say that the underlying truth of man qua man, the profound source of his individuality, is denied to the profit of a standardized consience, a superego which is imperiously imposed ready-made upon everyone: what certain reactionaries would have us take for a philosophy of freedom is in reality nothing but a functionary's moralism.

Not only does Confucianism accept society as it is; it introduces rites and institutions* designed to prevent its evolution into anything else: we have seen it operating in connection with the basic social unit, the family. Confucianism garbs the family in an aura of sanctity and, within it, reduces the individual to nothing. Filial piety here symbolizes the bond that in general subjects the weaker to the stronger. Justice is primarily acknowledgment of this relationship. "The sense of justice finds its highest expression in the honor rendered to those who are above me in dignity." Never is it a question of man altering his lot or station however wretched it may be; man accepts it: "Wise is he who regulates his conduct in accordance with the condition in which he finds himself . . . In poverty and abjection he behaves as befits a poor and despised man."

Meanwhile the superiors have duties which the sages are at pains to indicate to them, for in the eyes of the sage arbitrary conduct on the part of the prince is as much to be dreaded as indiscipline on the part of his subjects. Virtue is necessary to the highest dignitaries and to the emperor himself; it is not sufficient to found his right to rule, but it is inseparable from it. This relationship is clearly brought out in a passage in *The Invariable Mean*: "However he had the required dignity were someone not to have the necessary virtue he must not permit himself to introduce new rites and songs. Likewise, had he the necessary virtue but were he lacking in the required dignity, he must not think to work innovations in rites and music." Rites and music

* Cf. the *Li Chi* (the *Book of Rites and Ancient Ceremonies and of Institutions*), a work compiled toward the end of the first century B.C. (Translator's note)

standing for the entirety of institutions, the question here is of the exercise of the supreme power; we see that it implies the combination of virtue and dignity: the latter is founded upon birth and tradition. Traditional right must be confirmed by the merit of him who possesses it, but merit is not enough to engender the right to rule. Such a political regime is precisely an "enlightened despotism." All this applied as well to the ruling class as a whole. Officials have duties which are the counterparts of their privileges: this ethic in no wise differs from the paternalistic belief professed by "enlightened capitalists"; it is the one the Puritans preached; it has inspired many a Papal Encyclical. The recommended virtue is here called "benevolence" and its meaning is plain; the illusion fondly entertained by every ruling class is that it is an all-embracing class, the only class, and that its values are absolute, unrivaled: "the public welfare" is the name by which the elite are wont to call their own welfare. When you ask the rulers to think of their subjects' welfare, they reply, "But we always do!" and continue to promote the particular interests of their class. It is to the latter's interest, for example, that the people eat. For people work better when they eat, the harvests are bigger, there is more to tax. But benevolence has its limits; they are clearly indicated in this excerpt from *The Analects*:

> Tzu Kung asked about governing, and the Master said, "Adequate supplies of food, adequate stores of munitions, and the confidence of the people." Tzu Kung said, "Suppose you unavoidably had to dispense with one of these, which would you forgo?" The Master said, "Munitions." Thereat Tzu Kung asked if of the remaining two he had to dispense with one, which he would forgo. The Master said, "Food; for all down history death has come to all men, and yet society survives; but the people who have no confidence in their rulers are undone."

Which is to avow that the structure of society is of greater importance than men of flesh and bone; it is upon this point that there was disagreement between Mo Ti's "universal love" and the "humanism" of Confucius: the latter created the prototype of the elite's ethic: from top to bottom, every social category exists only in the name of the order which pretends to universality and which in fact serves the private interests of the privileged. The individual ethic, the political ethic aim at this ultimate objective:

maintaining order. It had to be restored in Confucius' day. Under Wu Ti, the job was to reshape it. Afterward, the one question was of perpetuating it. Rarely has conservatism been so extreme: in fact, it led to paralysis. Nothing advanced. The warrior wishes to add to his conquests, the capitalist to his profits, both are led to encourage innovations; the dream of the bureaucrat is to stay a bureaucrat and to get his son a bureaucrat's post; he is the figure of repetition; if he tries to make a little on the side, it is at odd hours, sneakily and by the most unproductive of all methods: squeezing, graft. The Chinese scholars were not out to make history, but to stop it in its tracks. That is why the one emperor who was to leave an indelible mark on Chinese history by replacing the feudal world with a centralized state turned to the realism of the legalists and away from Confucian moralism; if the latter opposed him, if its exponents remained faithful to the ancient ideal it was precisely because they abhorred any change and because their creed condemned all action as such; they and it adjusted themselves wonderfully to the Empire once the Empire had been established and once the only problem was how to preserve it from then on. Subsequently, the scholars were always against wars; in view of the economic and social conditions the scholars were anxious to maintain, they could only view wars as purposeless. But it was not humanitarianism that led them to discommend wars; no, it was they who instigated the bloodiest repressions whenever domestic order was threatened; they were pacifists because unrest interfered with the one thing that mattered to them: administration.

By and large they preferred hearty administering to fighting left and right. Where their ultraconservatism was disastrous to China was when it incited them to throttle the rise of trade and manufacture, thus prematurely halting the progress of scientific and technological thought. This however had got off to a remarkable start. The powerful class of manufacturers and businessmen who at the outset of the Han period, two hundred years before the Christian Era, were thriving from the mining of salt and the smelting of iron, had patronized inventors; numerous machines had been devised, the lever and paddle wheel, known since the fourth century B.C., were put to many new uses. In Szechwan where there were salt mines an ingenious system for deep drilling was found; a little later, drills were powered by water wheels and air pumps, delivering powerful blasts, were utilized too. Salt and iron came under state monopoly; but high officials went on encouraging technical discoveries. The loom appeared at the opening of this era. Starting in the seventh century waterways were spanned by the segmented-arch and iron-chain suspension bridges Europe was not to see yet for a long while. The emperors for their part patronized astronomy and medicine, the Chinese mind having always been interested in those two organisms, the world and the human body. Algebra was further advanced in thirteenth-century China than anywhere else at the time. However, beginning with the Mings, civilization petrified. The state stifled mercantilism, and this was the result. In the West commerce stimulated the development of mathematics, the growth and spread of the mechanistic learning which engendered modern science. Thus capitalism created the theoretical instrument which made possible the technological progress that aided in the increase of profit. But none of this in China, where the bureaucrats, whose single ambition was to become propertied, saw no need of forging new tools, whether theoretical or practical. Algebra remained frozen in a system of rigid notations. An organicist ideology continued to prevail in the sphere of mechanics. Although inventive, the Chinese, deprived of the theoretical groundwork which at this stage had become vital, ceased to invent. They fell behind the West; with every century the gap widened.

However the bureaucrats could not stop life from being lived nor, consequently, rule out all change. A certain evolution even occurred within orthodox Confucianism itself. Buddhist and Taoist infiltrations into Chinese thinking brought out the official system's metaphysical failings. Some scholars sought to palliate them under the Sungs. Chou Tun-i provided an ontological basis to the old Confucian ethic. Chu Hsi completed his work in the twelfth century, revising the *Four Books* and by means of glosses fixing the interpretation to which teaching conformed henceforth. More, he distinguished a rational principle in the universe, Li—a kind of cosmic reason, at once immanent and transcendent—and a material principle, Ki. Later on Wang Yang-ming, who lived from

1472 to 1529, influenced by Ch'an Buddhism, proposed an idealist interpretation of Confucianism: he identified consciousness and moral conscience and maintained that exterior objects, like ethical values, exist only inasmuch as they are present in the mind.

These speculations left the essential untouched. It has been often repeated that Confucius would have been scandalized by neo-Confucianism; but these are idle speculations that visualize a man conveyed from one age to another; coming a thousand years later, his ideological descendant would of course differ from the Master. What is striking is that Confucianism has undergone only those changes that could not be avoided in order to remain basically the same. Until the twentieth century it continued a matchless instrument of oppression in the hands of a managerial class composed of bureaucrat-landowners dedicated to sterile repetition and dead set against progress.

Subordinating a huge population to a handful of bureaucrats, immolating the living world to defunct ancestors, Confucian ideology undertook to annihilate the individual at the very moment when, fighting out of tradition's grip, the individual was becoming aware of himself; many literate persons revolted against this bondage and instead began to cultivate a concern which was then waking in them: that of their personal destiny. If Taoism and Buddhism were able to furnish an escape to the people it was because they had first proposed one, in a subtler form, to the intellectual elite.

Taoism also consulted the wellsprings of ancient Chinese thought but emerged with conclusions totally unlike those set forth by Confucius. Instead of making humanity the thrall of society it looked for men's salvation in his just relationship to the cosmos. Monism ultimately leaves the sage no alternative but mysticism, fatalism inevitably leading to quietism: those were the dominant theses of Taoist philosophy. It enjoins man to strive after the infinite point of view, to survey the world "from aloft in the Chariot of the Sun." Through contemplation he becomes one with the totality of things; through ecstasy he slips the tethers of his individuality, not however for society's benefit but for his own: renouncing everything, he becomes free to embrace everything. Taking up his stance in boundless eternity, he remarks the equivalence and then the futility of all worldly values and distinctions, even merging real with unreal, effacing the frontiers between perception and dream, and beholding death with indifference. Practically, he expounds a naturistic anarchism: one must live in accordance with nature, disallow the use of machines, refuse progress, and scorn the social order. Whatever comes of human contrivance merits derision only.

Upon Chinese culture Taoism has exerted a major influnece, especially in the realm of aesthetics. Its refusal of conformism spurred the artist toward originality; enemy of social existence, it bade the sage shun the city and go dwell amid the wild charms of nature: whence Chinese sensibility derived its liking for mountains, forests, lakes, wilderness prospects, a taste which was not to be found in the West until the eighteenth century. Contesting every recognized value, Taoism also invited the Chinese to break loose from his mortal confines, to transcend himself by plunging into dream; it urged, if not the disordering of all the senses, at least the extravagances of ecstasy and drunkenness. Imaginative deliriums, wondrous landscapes, the pleasures of wine nourished Chinese poetry which is in great part of Taoist inspiration. So in Chinese painting where the artist's brush describes so many jagged peaks, strange trees, and lonely streams. But owing to the fact that it entrenched itself in inaction, Taoism had no hold upon the social order; as a popular sect it stirred up numerous and terrible *jacqueries*; but in the main it left Confucianism a clear field. The schools periodically disputed the imperial favors and there would then be some sharp wrangling between them; but Taoist quietism accommodated itself to the victory of Confucianism. The two doctrines were conciliated in the life and mind of the Chinese. Socially, the "righteous" who was the well-bred man observed the precepts of Confucianism; as an artist or simply as an individual he leaned in the direction of Taoism. This compromising, sobering down Taoism, depleted it. For the gulfs and mountaintops dear to the ancient hermits the lettered squire substituted his gardens tricked out with ponds and stucco rockeries; in painted silk, the grandiose gave way to the decorative. Ecstasy was imbibed from a bowl of rice wine. Metaphysical dispute petered out into irony, quietism justified apathy; and yearning for the infinite satisfied itself with the comfortable morality of the mediocre Mean.

Buddhist teaching was, practically speaking, but little removed from the Taoist philosophy. The Ch'an sect,* which particularly influenced the Chinese scholars, preached refraining from action and even from speech. When a disciple would pose his Ch'an master a question regarding Buddha, the master would trounce the indiscreet novice or advise him as to the price of potatoes. Upon occasion he would assemble the people around him as though to deliver them a lecture; and would instead preserve an ostentatious silence. Buddhism was thus a quietism also, which abandoned the terrain to Confucianism. Actually, the metaphysics attributed to Lao-tse and to Buddha are perfectly meet ornaments to the Confucian system; and indeed neo-Confucianism borrowed heavily from them when it elaborated what it claimed was an autonomous ontology. These do-nothing doctrines which affirm the identicalness of yes and no without rising to the height of dialectical syntheses were in tune with a society that made history a perpetual rotation of the same cycle; they illustrated this outlook and history and had their roots in them. Perceiving no earthly change, no emergence, no goal, convinced that there was nothing to be done in this world, the Chinese philosophers took the stagnation their country was sunk in for an image of eternity. Spent after their bickering over details, they would all heave the same sigh of relief: "The Tao is everlastingly unalterable."

One of the chief aims of the Western bourgeoisie was to reduce that fortress which gave the clergy sole command of a key sector: that of linguistic communication between men. The bourgeoisie outflanked the clergy by creating its own clerks and devising instruments in answer to its own practical needs; it began to write in the vernacular it had codified and enriched; and the old scholastic thought was swept aside by an insurgent technological and scientific current. The Chinese bourgeoisie achieved the same revolution, but centuries later: it divested the clerks of their monopoly over culture and set about modernizing it.

* Its derivative in Japan is the Zen Buddhism with which the Western world is better acquainted. (Translator's note)

From its birth at the close of the nineteenth century it realized that, on the scientific and technical planes, China absolutely had to stand on an even footing with the West. The bourgeoisie sent its sons abroad with instructions to assimilate Occidental knowledge and methods. The first attempt was a failure. The students that entered an American university were greeted by Chinese professors who took them in charge, who obliged them to keep their pigtails and silken robes and to devote a great share of their time to the Chinese classics; they acquired precious little apart from a keen distaste for the old customs; when an official came from China to find out what progress they were making, they refused him the traditional kowtow obeisance; and were summoned home. In 1875 a French engineer took some young Chinese to France to serve their apprenticeship. Seven others accompanied a German officer to Germany the next year, thirty others set sail for England and France. Their 1894 defeat at the hands of the Japanese further convinced the Chinese of the necessity to modernize themselves. The government modified the school system in 1905 and from then on Chinese students flocked to Japan, America, France, and England. A mass of Western books was being translated in the meantime; the main thing was to get the secret of their military might away from foreigners, and the first works put in Chinese dealt with the art of warfare, strategy, ballistics. But the program soon broadened. A student, Yen Fu, came back from England with volumes of Spencer, Huxley, John Stuart Mill and acquainted the Chinese with Western philosophies. Of Huxley's *Evolution and Ethics* Hu Shih later said, "From the very moment it appeared, the book was read throughout the country and became the bedside text of students." Yen Fu also translated Spencer, Mill, Hume, Adam Smith while Ma Kiun-wu translated Charles Darwin whose evolutionist theories took the Chinese by storm. Western literary works became available too. An ingenious person named Lin Shu was responsible for translations of ninety-three English books, twenty-five French, nineteen American, and six Russian; he knew no foreign language; he enlisted the help of Occidentals who could speak a little Chinese, had them give approximations of the text while he sat, brush in hand, taking down what he heard and then putting it in classical Chinese; in this way Dickens, Scott,

Robert Louis Stevenson, Victor Hugo, Dumas, Balzac, Cervantes, Tolstoy, and others were made known to the Chinese. Lin Shu's method was widely copied; Japanese versions were the basis for many more translations into Chinese.

One of the key demands voiced by the reformers, who in 1898 attempted to replace autocracy with a constitutional monarchy, was that the Emperor gave the clerks' posts to members of the middle class; their leader, K'ang Yu-wei, was an intellectual, author of a vast body of works of political philosophy; he turned to the intellectuals for aid in spreading his ideas, organized the Strength Through Study Society which extended into several provinces. One of the Emperor's first decrees was K'ang's reward:

> The educational basis shall continue to be the Canon of the Sages but all branches of European learning appropriate to our present needs ought concurrently to be studied. Let the slavish parroting of obscure theories be avoided, let there be an end to scuffles over the meaning of words. That which we would do, is to clear deadwood out of our curricula and make ours a knowledge which, the while upholding our ancient principles, is in harmony with our time.

K'ang fled into exile after the checkmate of the "Hundred Days." Liang Ch'i-chao, another great intellectual, took refuge in Japan where his influence became considerable.* Hounded by Manchu censorship, many publishers installed their presses in Tokyo; seven reviews were founded and printed there between 1903 and 1907. Banned books and periodicals were shipped to firms located in Shanghai's foreign concessions whence they were smuggled into the interior of the country.

But the bourgeoisie had become too powerful, the Empress could hold out against it no longer and the ancient system of examinations was abolished in 1905; an ardent proponent of modern ideas, Tsai Yuan-pei, was named Minister of Public Education.

Immediately the Manchu dynasty was overthrown the young bourgeoisie launched a vigorous attack against the feudal culture. Hu Shih, a young Columbia University graduate and professor of philosophy at Peking, took the head of what at first was called

* Liang was later to make common cause with Sun Yat-sen; but K'ang always remained hostile to the Republic.

the "Renaissance." He was supported by a newly founded review, *New Youth*, edited by Ch'ên Tu-hsiu. The great nationalist awakening of May 4, 1919, reinforced this movement thereafter known as that of The Fourth of May.

At the moment the "Hundred Days' Reformation" opened, Confucianism still had its prestige and the attempt was made to conciliate it with Western culture. Created with an end to restore feudalism, Confucianism had been flexible enough to answer the needs of a centralized Empire; with a little adjusting it could now take its place in a constitutional monarchy. Confucian humanism has no bones to pick with any "democracy" provided it be solidly hierarchized and tempered by monolithic institutions. Cultivated bourgeois replaced the clerks but they too came round to a moralistic idealism; far be it from them to assail the principle or Order or the Rights of the Chosen. K'ang Yu-wei and T'an Ssu-t'ung preached the idea that reform ought to take its departure from a moral conversion and ethics should serve as the foundation of politics; and meanwhile Liang Ch'i-chao busied himself making a synthesis of Confucianism and Buddhism. He distinguished two sorts of Confucianism: one, inferior, which is expressed in the *Shih Ching*, the *Shu Ching*, and the *Li Chi*, is of conservative tendency and distorts the Master's true doctrine. Superior Confucianism, alone authentic, inspires the *Yi King* and the *Tso Chuan*:* it is democratic and progressive. Despite this theory nobody but conservatives continued to venerate Confucius after the turn of the century. He was deified by special decree in 1907.† Magistrates and school pupils were obliged to enact rites in his

* The *Shih Ching* (*The Book of Odes*) is a collection of three hundred or so old poems supposed to have been selected by Confucius; the *Shu Ching* is usually known in the West as *The Book of History*, or the *Scripture of Documents*, most of which was probably composed several hundred years after Confucius' death. The *Li Chi* (*The Book of Rites*) and the *Yi King* (*The Book of Changes*), as we have already noted, were written about the opening of the Christian Era and c. 700-900 B.C. respectively. Finally, the *Tso Chuan*, traditionally ascribed to Tso-ch'iu Ming, a personal disciple of Confucius, is now thought to have been written late in the fourth century B.C. (Translator's note)

† Confucianism, as we have seen, was never a religion however it may have encouraged ancestor worship. Confucian elements, in degraded form, were incorporated into the so-called "syncretic" religion; but, strictly speaking, there is no such thing as a "Confucianist religion."

honor; societies were founded to propagate his worship upon whose basis further efforts were made to construct a national religion. It was all in vain. The young middle class energetically repudiated Confucianism; it wanted to make changes in the world and turned a deaf ear to ideologies which professed immobilism. To all intents and purposes, Confucianism was indistinguishable from the old order: the second could not be destroyed without wiping out the first. The earliest story Lusin wrote, *The Diary of a Madman*, which created an enormous stir, was aimed at feudalism and Confucianism. "The doctrine of Confucius is incompatible with freedom, with a constitutional form of government," Ch'ên Tu-hsiu declared in his article on "Confucianism and Constitution"; in another, "The Way of Confucius and Modern Life," he demonstrated that Confucianism denied the most elementary human rights in requiring the subject's total submission to the emperor, the child's to his parents, the wife's to her husband. Hu Shih also lashed out at this obsolete creed; to assail the traditional family, to fight for the emancipation system, to extricate one's head from the sands of the classics, this was to gainsay the lot: "Chouism," every kind of neo-Confucianism, and Confucianism too.

Unanimous in what it said no to, the new intelligentsia was divided when it came to adopting a positive ideology: the split reflected the bourgeoisie's internal contradiction. Having become the leading class politically, it remained economically on the outside; it had not achieved concrete leadership in the country. The Manchu autocracy had been cleaned out, foreign imperialism was still there; except for a few powerful trusts which identified their interests with Japan's and the West's, Chinese capitalism lay strangled by the semicolonial regime China was saddled with; the active members of the bourgeoisie preferred this oppressive order to disruption they knuckled under, but they were not happy. Certain of its "conceptive ideologists" were satisfied with a partial victory and strove to give their class the kind of culture suitable to its new status. However, the Chinese bourgeoisie making its revolution the day it came into being and before having fashioned a cultural superstructure for itself, the majority of the intellectuals escaped that ideological alienation which in France explains the existence of numerous reactionary writers. Instead of defending fixed values most revived the fight whose issue had left them irritated, and now clamored for a radical social rearrangement: a new revolution. For lack of a tradition upon which they could have leaned, both wings, right and left, looked to the West. The apologists and theoreticians of the Occidental ruling classes became the guides of the former. The latter, anticipating history, leaped straight into adopting a proletarian point of view.

Huxley and Darwin were already famous. Nietzsche's influence grew. Kropotkin was vulgarized by several hands including the novelist Pa-chin. The ideas of Wundt, Hartmann, Schopenhauer, Bergson, Hegel, Kant were put in circulation. Bertrand Russell came to give a series of lectures in China and logic's stock went up. But it was above all John Dewey, who also visited China to spread his system, whom the right chose as master thinker. Hu Shih, trained in the United States, turned into his staunch disciple. This idealist pragmatism admirably suited a class in many respects similar to the American class for which Dewey was the spokesman: the Chinese bourgeoisie was also young, active, determined to develop techniques within the framework of capitalism that would increase its grip upon affairs and the world, and eager at the same time to refine its privileges. Hu Shih propagated a hodgepodge of the theses which best answer the purposes of a rising bourgeoisie: economic liberalism, individualism, scientism, anarchism, materialism, skepticism as regards established verities, an empirical criterion of knowledge; under relativistic form he posited the priority of consciousness over object, that is to say, posited an idealism. On the moral side, this philosophy strove above all to reject old traditions and in return proposed nothing but a free-for-all individualism. The skimpiness of this offering was not so noticeable to the Americans, for a solid Puritan core guaranteed the harmony between their capitalism and divine will. In a land where there was no such ready-made groundwork of optimism, pragmatism failed to furnish an ethic to the Chinese society which had always looked to morality as the source of a cohesive force. In 1923 this uneasiness was revealed in a hot debate that developed around the question of the relationship between morals and science. Ting Wen-kiang, pragmatist and scientist, maintained that science, unaided, can provide a master pattern for human behavior. He was answered by Chang Chun-wai, an idealist philosopher, who stoutly upheld the cause of human liberty. The quarrel interested a wide public.

When Chiang Kai-shek had established his dictatorship, Hu Shih's skeptical pragmatism struck him as altogether insufficient. He undertook to rally the Chinese to the ideal of "The New Life" which compounded national values with Confucian virtues. Fong Yeou-lan, later to adhere to Marxism, in 1939 elaborated "The New Norm," a system for which as the basis of individual morality and social organization he proposed the Confucian principle of the *Li*, which is simultaneously the right way and right reason. Drawing from Chu Hsi, Fong gave a positivist character to the ancient philosophy. And Ho Lin had recourse to Wang Yang-ming in his attempt to revive Confucianism and give it a pro-Kuomintang slant.

So much for the right; the left intelligentsia were meanwhile learning at the school of the Russian Revolution. Ch'ên Tu-hsiu had broken with Hu Shih and together with a comrade, Li Ta-chao, was performing Marxist studies in Peking. They had built a circle of young people around a review, *The Weekly Critic*. Ch'ên went to Shanghai upon the invitation of socialist and anarchist groups. The study sessions, behind the cloak of a foreign language school, took place in the French concession. A Comintern envoy, Voitinsky, helped the young Chinese Marxists start a review and form the "Association of Socialist Youth." In 1921 Ch'ên called a meeting which led to the creation of the Chinese Communist Party and the spread of Marxism began. It was in connection with the moralism *versus* scientism dispute that, for the first time, in 1923, Ch'ên brought Marxism into the open. However its initial importance was confined to the realm of the practical. Ch'ên clashed with Mao Tse-tung in 1927 over the subject of peasant revolts and lost the leading doctrinal role he had held up until then. Marxism's entry upon the intellectual scene came the following year. A polemic concerning the history of Chinese society opened between T'ao Hi Cheng, an erudite specialist in studies of antiquity, and Kuo Mo-jo. The latter employed Marxist schemata in an analysis of the Chinese past, descrying a Communist period, another of slavery, a third that was one of anarchy, a feudal period, and finally a capitalist period. T'ao acknowledged the existence of the first and last but disputed Kuo Mo-jo's classification of the intervening ages. The controversy gave a wide hearing to the theses of historical materialism. Another, from 1929 to 1934, brought into conflict Chang Tong-souen, a friend of the Chang chun-wai of whom I made previous mention and like the latter an anti-Marxist, and Yeh Ching, who was the advocate of dialectical materialism; the first published his articles in a review, *Renaissance*, and the second his essays in another review, *Twentieth Century*. Chang's articles were collected and reprinted as *Against Dialectical Materialism*, Yeh's in a volume entitled *Philosophical Polemics*, the one book appearing in 1934, the other in 1935. University professors, editors of reviews, many intellectuals took sides in the debate. But not Hu Shih; his *The Philosophical Critic*, a review in which he wrote regularly between 1927 and 1937, found the whole discussion of no interest.

Translation went ahead: the writings of Marx, many Marxist works and commentaries were issued in Chinese. A new dispute broke out in 1934, between Marxists this time. Yeh Ching, in a work entitled *Whither Philosophy?* predicted that it was heading for extinction. Ai Ssu-chi, a great exponent of dialectical materialism, took Yeh hotly to task, accusing him of having misread Engels' ideas and affirming that in its Marxist form philosophy could not disappear. In his *Philosophical Problems* of 1936 Yeh relapsed again: materialism and idealism would end up fusing into a synthesis in which science would shoulder out philosophy. Again his adversary retorted that in its dialectical figure philosophy will last as long as society does. Many other sideline discussions carried on during these years would illustrate the vitality of Marxist thinking in China. They were interrupted by her war with Japan; but the study of Marxism continued in Yenan under the direction of Mao Tse-tung and Ai Ssu-chi.

Marxism has won. And what is left of the ancient teachings? What, for example, has become of Confucianism?

Etiemble,* in an article as foolish as it is pedantic,† would have

* French novelist and critic, professor at the University of Montpellier, Etiemble, formerly a regular contributor to *Les Temps Modernes*, broke with Sartre at the time of the "Jewish Doctors Affair" and the wave of anti-Semitism it provoked in the USSR. (Translator's note)

† In the Paris monthly review *Diogène*.

us understand that "to honor Master K'ung"* and read the classics is currently rated a feudal crime in China. Noting that the Communist leaders, including Mao Tse-tung himself, make frequent references to Confucius, to Mencius, indeed to Chu Hsi, he is dismayed by the scene he discovers of intellectual confusion; and further alarmed to see that enemy of progress, Lao-tse, praised to the skies while Confucius' thought, revolutionary according to Etiemble, lies under a cloud. Etiemble maintains in passing that Kuo Mo-jo nurses a secret fondness for Confucianism withal, thereby suggesting that there are seeds of dissension in Party ranks. To be sure, it's Machiavellism that explains the attitude of the regime: by "persecuting" the Confucianists Mao has "the sole Chinese doctrine capable of resisting him" nicely by the throat.

All the allegations contained in this article are false. The "honoring of Master K'ung" is today a duty rather than a crime. Mao Tse-tung's cultural policy is, as we have seen, at odds with the one he reproaches Hu Shih for having originated: they were the revolutionaries of 1917-1919 who trampled upon the old sage. Eager to incorporate national tradition, Chinese Communism to the contrary beholds Confucius as a great man: to be sure, as when one approaches so many other productions of antiquity one must distinguish what is wholesome in Confucius' doctrine from what is feudal and noxious; but, seen in the context of his times, his teaching is eminently worthy of respect. Not only has his effigy been left standing in the temples†—which may not prove much—but in museums and cultural exhibits I often saw his portrait conspicuously placed and my guide would allude to him with reverence. The review *China Reconstructs,* where nothing but official opinion is expressed, designates Confucius "one of the most remarkable thinkers and teachers of the feudal era." The right and opportunity to read the classics is denied to no one and Etiemble himself reminds us that Marxist leaders cite them often.

* His disciples refer to Confucius as "the Master" or as "Master K'ung"; K'ung was Confucius' surname; and "Confucius" is the seventeenth-century Jesuit missionaries' Latinization of *K'ung Fu-tzŭ* (Master K'ung). (Translator's note)

† There exist temples dedicated to the worship of Confucius just as there are temples where other great men—Fei, for example—are worshiped. Owing to religious syncretism, some nonspecialized temples also contain statues of Confucius.

Their polite attitude is not enough for him, however. Confucius must be saluted as a great revolutionary philosopher whose authentic views were betrayed by neo-Confucianism. We have observed that, in actual fact, master and disciples were simply out to justify a society of oppression. Calling in the generals who had been selected to occupy China, the Japanese cabinet secretary, Akiru Kazami, knew just what he was about when he told them that "All you need in order to govern the Chinese is *The Analects* of Confucius." Certainly, there was something new in Confucius' doctrine; every thinker is an innovator; but it will not aid in the understanding of Thomas Aquinas to call him a revolutionary. Is it a professional handicap that incites Etiemble to exalt a moral system built for bureaucrats and college gatekeepers? When young, Etiemble knew what revolt meant; I am surprised to find that today he comfortably mates it with the resignation to misery and abjection preached by Master K'ung.

Indeed, it is startling to see the author of *L'Enfant de choeur* spit fire and smoke in favor of a doctrine which exalted discipline and familial values above everything else. Etiemble seems to be spellbound by his insights into Chinese culture; Yin, Yang, and Tao crop up in just about all his articles, regardless of their subject. It may well be intellectual snobbery that is at fault here: a teaching has only to bear a Chinese hallmark and be twenty-five centuries old in order for Etiemble to mistake the desire to maintain the world as it is for the desire to change it.

But on one point he is right: Lao-tse is no revolutionary either. And very false it is that the regime is acclaiming him to the detriment of Confucius. The Fourth of May intellectuals declared their sympathy for Lao-tse as well as for Mo Ti, and the present regime manifests a like regard; for the spirit animating Taoism is foremost of all a rebellious one: the Taoist masters mocked at institutions, rites, dignities, social virtues; they postulated the equality of all men. The revolutionary may for a time ally himself with anarchists against the old social order. Taoism is anarchist; its impulse is negative, it represents a negative moment; it repudiates ancient hierarchies and after a fashion constitutes the antithesis to Confucianism. But when the positive moment arrives, when the time for syntheses is at hand, when, instead of combating the past, the revolutionary buckles down to building the future, then the alliance dissolves; and the anarchist becomes an enemy.* In this perspective it is not hard to understand what in Lao-tse the Communists can accept and what in him they must reject.

Nothing could be plainer than that these ancient doctrines are incompatible with Marxism from the simple fact that they imply a classless world and deny history. Kuo Mo-Jo has been a systematic Marxist for a good long time; to insinuate that he inclines toward Confucianism is to propose an absurdity all his writings and speeches flatly contradict. As for the charge of Machiavellism brought against Mao, it indicates that Etiemble is unaware of what an idea is; to ideologies he attributes a merely bookish existence; very wrongly, for a doctrine has its roots and its verity in the society it expresses. New China is repudiating Confucianism for a reason that is crystal clear: it constituted the ideological sublimation of the social order Chinese Communism has shattered. It is not of itself "the sole Chinese doctrine capable of resisting" Mao. The people who are against the regime can just as easily use this archaic instrument as invent new ones. The truth of it is that—as Etiemble would realize were he better informed—Confucianism does not by any means represent the Marxist theoreticians' most redoubtable foe; they have no need to decree war against it for the excellent reason that it perished long ere this; it did not outlive The Fourth of May, and Chiang Kai-shek's efforts amounted to beating a dead horse. The ideology inherited by the intellectuals who are considered today to be nonprogressive is the one then dreamed up by the bourgeoisie: the amalgam of pragmatism and idealism Hu Shih borrowed from Dewey. Ai Ssu-chi, one of the Party's chief thinkers, mercilessly, incessantly attacks, not Confucius, but Hu on the grounds of his subjectivism and general agnosticism. The recasting of attitudes undertaken in 1951 was directed against Hu. Throughout the whole of China he was assailed in an avalanche of articles. In 1954, after the to-do concerning *The Dream of the Red Chamber*, the intellectuals opened up a campaign against surviving vestiges

* Every great peasant revolt up until and including the Boxer Rebellion was fomented by Taoist sects against Confucian society. But these secret organizations, pursuing their disruptive activities, were serving the interests of the counterrevolution until the regime dissolved them.

of Hu's idealism. The number-one objective was "to clean out the persisting poison of Hu Shih's reactionary philosophy," wrote Wang Jo-shui on November 5, 1954. Clearly, a modern conception of the world such as Marxism cannot seriously bother with any but other equally modern world views; the superstructures which capped the ancient world can be of no more than retrospective interest to it.

Nevertheless, the "Neodemism" defined at Yenan insists that Chinese culture renew its attachment to its traditions. Chinese Marxists conform to the program by quoting liberally from the old masters; upon certain articles they deliberately borrow from past doctrines; by and large these color their ideology in a more or less fortuitous manner. Thus the while rejecting the social ideas of Confucius they have retained certain themes from his individual morality: for instance, the notion of *cultivating the moral self** that relates to his idea of *sincerity*. The truly wise is not content to profess the love of wisdom: he seeks after it sincerely, puts it into practice even when by himself, his conduct unobserved. "The superior man," says Confucius, "is watchful of himself when alone." "The Master says: the odes of the *Shih Ching* are some three hundred in number; in one word here is their pith: be of right intentions."† Under the Mings a famous Confucian philosopher, Liu Chung-chou, made attention to oneself, that is, a certain inner vigilance, the basis of morality. I have indicated why: the desire was then to have the individual take unto himself as ethical laws the regulations decreed for the preservation of the social order. The problem is similar today. The Communist Party cannot everywhere and always exert direct pressure upon its militants; these are dispersed about a huge country of six hundred million people and are often performing their tasks alone: the Party has no sure hold over them unless their adherence is heartfelt and entire. That is why Mao Tse-tung in his ethical essays, Liu Shao-ch'i in his celebrated book on *How To Be a Good Communist*, revive the Confucian theme of inner vigilance also illustrated in countless contemporary novels and stories. A good Communist is he who is a militant through and

* Cf. *The Analects*.

† *Ibid*.

through: skin-deep conformism, a show of enthusiasm are not enough; he must be sincere, and his sincerity is measured by his deeds, especially by those he performs on his own and unwitnessed. As an example of genuine morality the Communists have often cited a hero of the Sung epoch, one Weng T'ien-hsiang, who refused to forswear allegiance to the dynasty even after the Mongols had annihilated it; jailed, nothing could induce him to abjure what was his faith. The true Communist is he who comes unscathed through the test of solitude.

Marxists as a rule are not prone to overconfidence in "human nature"; and yet amid the Chinese Marxists one comes across an optimism which is reminiscent of that found in Mencius.* No one is damned from the start; anyone may turn out a hero;

* Mencius believed that human nature was good; Hsün Tzŭ thought that it was evil—it would therefore seem to me a mistake to consider the two men as anything but fundamentally opposed. Only those who endow it with perversity postulate in a positive way the existence of a "nature," a reality charged with maleficent forces and a hard kernel that resists every attempt at organization by society. But to say, as Mencius says, that "Men's natural tendency toward goodness is like the water's tendency to find the lower level" and that evil comes "from outside events which lead the heart astray" is basically to consider man as conditioned by his environmental situation; divorced from it, man exists only in an abstract sense; if one views him as situated within a context of concrete circumstances, his inner self is wholly determined and hence to be defined by the outside pressure of his situation. "Were beans and millet as abundant as fire and water, among all the people you would not find a single one of those beings known as evil men," says Mencius. In his system, the notion of human nature operates a little like the unknown in an equation: it helps solve the equation, but does not appear in the answer. Likewise, when Mencius advises rulers, he speaks not of the human heart but of such matters as ownership and the tenure of land, taxation, aid to extend to the aged. "When they are deprived of the means of existence, men commonly forget all principles and, their hearts no longer being fixed, they let themselves go in vice and extravagance, there is nothing they will not do then. If after that they are betrayed into crimes and you follow this up with punishment, this is just catching the people in a trap . . . An enlightened prince who concerns himself with the welfare of his people will first of all see to it that they are sufficiently prosperous to be able to look after their parents and maintain their wives and children; that, during good years, they have at every meal as much as they desire to eat; and that during bad years they have not famine to fear. It is only when the prince has made these provisions that he may then think to hie himself unto goodness, and the people will not be loath to follow in his train. But in their sore distress, so lacking in wherewithal and constantly in danger of perishing of hunger, how can you expect them to be dutiful and thoughtful of the Way?" The Marxists have quite correctly noticed a list to materialism in Mencius' philosophy: he sees ethics as strictly dependent upon economics.

just give people an education, help them, show them the truth, they will recognize it and become good citizens; and developing this good citizenry is the primary task to which the Communist, this present-day sage, must devote himself. According to a commentary on *The Great Learning*,

> The character *ts'in*—to love—must be replaced by the character *sin*—to make new. *Sin*, make other men new, make the old faults disappear. By this is meant that the wise man, after having inwardly polished bright the gems of his virtues, must give generously of his wealth to mankind and act in such a way that others be aided to rid themselves of the impurities that have clung in them for so long.

The *cheng-fong* or "correction of bad tendencies" advocated by Mao Tse-tung can be compared to the Confucian *sin*. In today's China the watchword is everywhere in every sphere to remake, reform the old mentality, to renew oneself and renew others. And we know what stress has been laid there upon re-educating delinquents and counterrevolutionaries: the re-education sessions which take place in the re-education centers and in the prisons perpetuate a Confucian tradition.

Among the Chinese Communists one even discovers traces of that political optimism which associated *virtue* with *mandate* in the old China. Heaven willed that having lost its virtue a dyasty be divested of its mandate, hence of its power. So it was that its corruption dragged the Kuomintang to its ruin; and that through its honesty, its altruism, its "human-heartedness' the Red Army won the affection and the backing of the Chinese peasantry. A *Guide to Right-Thinking*, upon which Mao Tse-tung and Liu Shao-ch'i collaborated in 1949, evokes the famous story of Li the Bold: his virtues enabled him to overthrow the Ming dynasty, but victory went to his head and he made mistakes which led to his downfall: the Manchus defeated him. His success and failure are presented as symbolic of the dangers the Communist Party is also exposed to: it must continue to merit power, otherwise it will fail. One ought not deceive oneself as to the importance of these analogies, however; they are rather on the superficial side. The idea of social duty become an inner moral conviction is quite as Christian as it is Confucian, it recurs in every moral system and today it is circumstances which give Chinese Communism its ethical tinge: the psychological ties between individuals are yet slack, and social pressure still being insufficient as a means to tightening them, it is to the individual's conscience the appeal must be made. But the ultimate ends striven after and therefore the real content of the notions of good and evil are radically unlike those the ancient teachings proposed.

Let me repeat it: the true ideological problem in today's China is not of how Marxism is to square with beliefs of the past, but of Marxism's relationship to modern philosophies. Up until 1956 every doctrine other than historical materialism was condemned. The past year has witnessed a great change. In his January 1956 "Report on the Question of the Intellectuals," Chou En-lai fiercely criticized sectarian trends; he nevertheless made it plain that materialism and idealism are as much opposed as the socialism and capitalism of which they are the doctrinal superstructures, and that they are locked in the same implacable struggle. But the Address delivered on May 26, 1956, by Lu Ting-yi, head of the Propaganda Section of the Central Committee, has a very different ring. Under the evident influence of destalinization Lu declares that Chinese intellectual life must become much more liberal. Surely, the class struggle is reflected in philosophical quarrels: Hu Shih's bourgeois idealism has been rightly condemned as has the bourgeois sociology practiced by certain schools. However, a distinction needs to be drawn between politics and culture: the latter expresses the class struggle in a less direct manner, more sinuously; to ignore the difference is to fall prey to a "leftist" tendency to oversimplification. So long as classes exist the materialism-idealism conflict manifests itself in interclass tension: but this opposition extends beyond capitalist society into socialist and will continue even in communist society: for the very reason that Communists, being dialectical materialists, understand the necessity for this dualism, they will henceforth cease to block the propagation of idealism. Two attitudes, idealism and materialism, deserve an impartial airing and hearing, the two schools must break lances in fair fight. When ideological questions arise, attempting to settle them by administrative measures is wasted effort and must firmly be abandoned. If materialism is one day to overcome idealism the issue will be settled between two healthy adversaries; both must be left free to develop.

Never has a popular democracy carried liberalism so far. The line now being followed in China is in severest contradiction to the one it replaced and which, a short while ago, restricted philosophy to hidebound orthodoxy. Idealism was not just fought tooth and nail; the threat of finding himself charged with idealism paralyzed every independent thinker. The gag has been removed; at least in theory every curb on freedom of thought has been lifted. Original doctrines can be penned, printed, discussed; no philosopher need dread being tagged as this or that, no attitude is heretical any more. Having turned its back on monolithism, Marxism's own possibilities are enriched. The Chinese intellectuals are now in a position to invent anew an ideology that will give adequate expression to the new world.

### *Literature*

Admirers of Old China have maintained that literature used to be awarded a position of unexampled importance—it was made the keystone of society; the truth of the matter is that to the contrary literature was reduced to the level of a tool of the ruling class. A source of privileges, it was more tightly monopolized by the privileged than in any other civilization. Language, created for the purposes of communication, in the hands of the mandarins became an instrument to further separation: down to this century they preserved the use of the ku-wen which Hu Shih described this way: "It resembles the Low Latin of medieval Europe but it is even deader, since Latin can still be spoken and understood today whereas ku-wen has become unintelligible even to the scholars themselves." Reading was difficult; for the Chinese who was not a specialist, reading the classics was impossible. Moreover, owing to the subjects it treated, classical literature deliberately endeavored to be esoteric. The works composed by and for a bureaucratic elite pursued mainly educative ends; or else were ends in themselves and aimed at formal perfection. They fell into a small number of genres, each rigorously defined. The compilation Emperor Ch'ien Lung had executed in 1772 is corroborated by the list drawn up in 1776 by the critic Yao Nai: essays, political commentaries, epitaphs, epigrams, poetry, funeral orations, histories. No mention of plays, none of prose fiction. The scholar Yuan Cho-lang, toward the end of the seventeenth century, caused much commotion when he protested against this academism. Seconded by his two brothers, he declared that "the writer in any given epoch should write in the idiom of his times" and he wished each to write in his own style and about whatever he chose. Yuan cried in the wilderness. Cultural segregation went on. Rare were the mandarins who sprang from the people and once they had they cut off all connection with the people; in almost every more or less legendary tale of a parvenu functionary he forgets his humble family straightway he gets into his official robes; if he wrote, he was as conformist as his colleagues.

However, the writer's situation in society everywhere has always been ambiguous. Marx allowed the bourgeois intellectual the capacity to transcend his class's point of view and to adopt a universal one instead. In China, changes of dynasty, palace revolutions, social crises as well as circumstances in their own private lives led certain lettered persons to step back and take a more comprehensive view of the establishment. There were historians, there were essayists who criticized and even attacked the governors; more than one writer managed, within the imposed framework, to utter some original conceptions. The poets were most successful in eluding conformism; they probably came from amid the more individualistic of the scholars; not only did they expand upon anarchist themes, they also lent voice to the people's wretchedness, denounced wars and exploitation. Poetry without question represents the most living area in classical Chinese literature, the one in which form succeeded in taking on humane and even popular content.

On the margin of recognized literature there evolved another tradition which used another language than that of the clerks and assumed other than official forms. Mainly to amuse themselves, scribes wrote out folk tales at first in the Buddhists' *p'ien wen*, then in the spoken tongue, *pai-hua*. After the invention of printing in the tenth-century Sung period, collections of stories, narratives, and dramatic dialogues came forth in number; they served as memory aids to storytellers, as scripts to actors, and they entertained people who knew how to read. The genre developed when new printing techniques permitted the multiple reproduction of books. Beginning at the time of the Mings popular legends were strung into long novels; the work was performed in part by scholars, in part by candidates who had been turned down for the mandarinate and who were in possession of a cultural background but not of official posts; through their poverty sharing the lot of the people, they wrote for an audience they sympathized with and in its vernacular. Thus did the famous novels come into being: *The Romantic Tale of the Three Kingdoms, All Men Are Brothers, The Pilgrimage to the West*, the *Chin-ping-mei.*

Under the Manchus the decadence of the feudal world was mirrored in literature; it began to veer away from formal rules; new genres emerged. The novel became something else besides a diversion: many an author used it as a vehicle for expressing his outlook upon the world. *The Dream of the Red Chamber* is characteristic of the period: at once realistic, subjectivistic, pessimistic, it illustrates the Chinese writer's new-found individualism. Again and again one finds the author—like that of *The Dream*—projecting himself into his hero, mixing elements of autobiography with fiction. One of the age's best-known authors, P'u Sung-ling, composed stories, songs, popular ballads; in them he criticized corrupt officials, attacked the high and mighty; and at the same time he sought to raise the cultural level of the masses by turning out manuals on agriculture, medicinal herbs, folk traditions. At seventy-three he related the life of his family in a little autobiography. Self-portraits were then much in vogue: this outcropping of subjectivism was partially owing to the influence of Buddhism, which led its adepts to examine their conscience and from speculating upon it they came to be fond of the inner life.

The novel form had sunk by the start of the last century: a spate of cloak-and-dagger adventure stories smacked more of industry than of literature. But the novel had also achieved a blend of classical culture and popular inspiration. Poets expressed the masses' feelings in an erudite form; the novelists used the resources of their cultural background to master both the popular idiom and popular themes.

"I feel that literature should not be the exclusive property of a few individuals but a powerful current able to reach far out into the ocean of the masses. Literature must not be divorced from life," wrote Hu Shih in a diary entry dated July 1916. Like the French bourgeois of the Renaissance the new Chinese intellectuals demanded in the first place that writing be done in their language, that is, that the ku-wen be abandoned in favor of the pai-hua. They wanted to see writing break loose of the classical forms. Hu Shih outlined these points in the manifesto published by *New Youth* and to which he gave the title: "Suggestions for a Plan of Literary Reform." Ch'ên Tu-hsiu supported him in "The Literary Revolution," an article that was followed by a second manifesto from Hu Shih: "The Historic Conception of Literature."

"Do not imitate the ancients," Hu advised. "Write naturally in a language everyone may understand." The review *New Youth* set the example: it was cast in pai-hua from cover to cover. The campaign continued for several years. "Let's turn thumbs down on all noble, precious, obsequious writing, let's build a plain-spoken, straightforward literature, expressive and popular," Ch'ên wrote in *New Youth*. "Thumbs down on classical literature—decrepit, turgid—let's elaborate a realistic, a fresh, a sincere literature. Thumbs down on academic literature—obscure, devious, and unreadable—let's create a living literature, a lucid one, and let's anchor it in today." Four hundred periodicals edited in pai-hua, a profusion of novels, plays, stories were the enthusiastic response to that call; pai-hua was henceforth the medium used in translations; the most serious reviews adopted it and to prove that it lent itself to the expression of ideas howsoever abstract, it was in pai-hua that Hu Shih wrote—in 1919—his *History of Chinese Philosophy*; and many scientists and scholars imitated him from then on. These audacities excited the violent opposition of the conservatives. But the innovators won their case. "The popular tongue is to be employed in the first and second forms in all elementary schools," the Minister of Education announced in 1920. "All texts in the ancient style are to be suppressed in these forms. They may be used until 1923 in the third and fourth. They will not be used after then." There was an explosion of joy in the intellectual milieus. The day of feudal literature was done; a new one of bourgeois literature was about to dawn.

The middle class being uncertain which road to take now, the new intelligentsia's fold split on ideology; bourgeois hesitations also have their complicated echo in the literary history of the period. Around Hu Shih the Crescent School gathered, university teachers, writers, poets tending philosophically to idealism and aesthetically to symbolism. Considering theirs an all-embracing class and their values universally and eternally valid, they took both art and culture to be ends in themselves, and shunned politics. The posture is familiar. Only a small number of intellectuals assumed it, however; the great majority wanted a further revolution. But of what sort? Ought China to follow the trail the USSR had blazed and institute a dictatorship of the proletariat? Was there some other way? One thing counted very heavily with most of the writers: this very culture they had fought for. Did its interests accord with those of the revolution? So confused was the situation that for several years the intellectual left was most understandably divided.

Literature must be "engaged": upon this all leftist writers agreed. About the nature and extent of this commitment there was doubt. The "Literature" group that was created in January 1921 with Mao-tun and Lusin at its head issued a manifesto affirming the role of politics in literature: "We deny that literature is an entertainment, a pastime, or a joke. Its subject must be the blood and tears tyranny wrings from the oppressed." Mao-tun several times flayed the theories of art for art's sake. "Literature's mission," said he, "is not simply to hold up a mirror to the times, it must also affect them. Literature has more to do than revive the past; its mission is to open the way to the future." Mao-tun claimed Zola and Tolstoy for his masters; but neither he nor Lusin were Marxists then. The idea of subordinating literature to the class struggle displeased them. Of proletarian literature Mao-tun said: "It contradicts the very essence of literature in viewing it as nothing but a weapon of propaganda in the strictest sense of the word." Lusin shared this opinion and stood firm for the writer's unconditional freedom.

The same problem existed for the Creation Society that students returning from Japan founded in 1922. The outstanding one was Kuo Mo-jo: at the time he wavered between Tolstoy and Lenin;

he had been influenced by the German philosophers and poets; on the one side he had a hatred for feudalism, on the other he caressed a romantic ideal. He declared: "The object of poetry is to express the feelings with an almost unconscious spontaneity; it is the very vibration of life, the voice of the soul." The poems he later presented in a volume called *Goddess* were in line with those specifications. At his side Yü Ta-fu, who in Japan had gone in heavily for literature and alcohol—in four years' time he had read over a thousand novels and had come away a bit dizzy—figured dramas of adolescence in his stories and novels. Both fancied that art and literature could make up a tight little world in the core of a rotten society; they soon changed their minds. Eager to participate in events, Yü Ta-fu wrote:

> Our literature shall echo human despair. This cry of alarm shall be a relief to souls in distress. And at the same time it shall toll the hour of revolution against the unjust make-up of present society.

About 1923 Kuo Mo-jo adopted the proletarian point of view.

> We are against the capitalist hydra. We are against every religion that disavows life. We are against bootlicking literatures. Our movement intends to manifest the spirit of the proletarian class; this is new mankind, and we shall write of it, for it.

In 1925 he accounted for his evolution:

> Once upon a time I honored and I revered individualistic and free men. But of later years I have come into closer touch with the masses who lie drowning in misery. I have learned that the tremendous majority of men are denied independence and freedom and individuality.

The Nanking Road incident strengthened Creation in its revolutionary attitude. Yü and Kuo moved to Canton and gave themselves over to politics. Yü found the active life disappointing; he went up to Shanghai where he grumbled about as a misanthrope until 1939 when he left China to finish out his life obscurely in Sumatra in 1945.

In 1926 Kuo Mo-jo published a book, *Literature and Revolution*, in which he defended the thesis advanced two years earlier by Chen Cheng-to: "All literature which is not revolutionary is unworthy of the name. The travesty must be rejected." Another group, The Sun, at odds with Creation on personal rather than doctrinal grounds, also decided in favor of a literature of intense social and political consciousness.

Lusin, meanwhile, was maintaining his position: that literature must enjoy a certain autonomy. In 1925 he started the review *Yussu* on whose staff were satirist and humorist Lin Yutang, novelist Lao-She. Lusin flung darts to the left, against Creation and The Sun, and to the right, at The Crescent. His attitude had not altered since the Literature days; he wrote, for example:

> Literature must be the expression of the entirety of social life. It cannot then be exclusively revolutionary; but it will none the less bear the revolutionary imprint inasmuch as the present society it reflects is animated by a spirit of revolt.

The leftist writers finally decided that instead of persevering in their differences they would do better to seek an accord. In 1935 Creation, The Sun, Mao-tun, Lusin joined together in "The League of Writers of the Left" and chose Lusin for president. The platform adopted was firmly proletarian.

> Our art is antifeudal, anticapitalist, and opposed to the petty bourgoisie as well, for this last has disavowed its true condition. We propose to undertake the making of a proletarian literature.

Finding this program too radical, a few writers—Marxists, however—formed another group, The Contemporaries, in 1932; but preserved unity with members of The League; the front remained intact.

The leftist writers encountered no real adversaries on the cultural plane. In 1930 the nationalists formed Nationalist Literature, a society whose manifesto proclaimed, "The highest aim and ultimate end of a literature is to realize the ideas and spirit of the race whence it stems. Nationalism is its loftiest ideal." The Kuomintang's collusion with foreign imperialism reduced the Nationalist Ideal to sheer hogwash. The bourgeoisie double-talked itself into accepting a situation that called for continual compromise and plenty of bad faith; expressing itself in positive terms would have meant displaying its contradictions and thus serving the revolutionary cause. Right-wing writers therefore decided to say nothing: nothing came out in burbled nonsense very comparable to what we have today from a sizable fraction of the French literary right.* Lin Yutang, having parted company with Lusin, became the leader of a humorist school. I have read a certain number of his essays in English: he cultivates frivolity with the steadfast application of a Jacques Laurent. This fold-up of rightist literature, the mounting success of left-wing writers led the Kuomintang to experiment with violence. The "cultural bandits" were hunted down. A special police squad was given the job of ferreting out those hiding in the Shanghai concessions and instructions were to kidnap them bodily if need be. Several members of the League were arrested on February 1, 1931. Some were shot. Others were buried alive. In 1931 and 1932 forty writers were killed. In 1934 the Bureau of Propaganda black-listed 149 books by widely read authors, some of Lusin's works among them.

The surviving leftist writers did not however slacken their activities. Lusin translated Plekhanov and a number of the great Russian authors. The Chinese were made acquainted with Gorki, Tolstoy, Turgenev, and also with French writers: Hugo, Maupassant, Zola. It was in the field of the novel that throughout the whole of this period the achievements of literature were the most remarkable. Earlier, Liang Ch'i-chao had signaled its social importance; he attributed some share of China's misfortunes to her old novels and exhorted writers to compose new ones to disseminate their new political and social beliefs. At the University of Peking Lusin gave a course on the Chinese novel, his lectures were published in book form and were widely read: hitting out at the contempt in which the scholars had held them, he pointed to the value of the great novels that had been written since the Mings. The example of foreign literatures also encouraged the Chinese: starting in the mid-twenties they produced a quantity of novels which attacked familial traditions, taboos of sex, the old society's economic structure. Of them all, *The Family* by Pa-chin was the most celebrated. Mao-tun found a vast public when he described the new Chinese bourgeoisie in his *Twilight*. Centering his image of Pekingese social life around the story of the poor coolie "Light-

* In France the bourgeoisie is declining; in China it was oppressed. The two situations are not the same. But the task to which the bourgeois littérateurs of both countries apply themselves is: to mask failure with frivolity.

of-heart," Lao-She had a particularly keen following in Peking. He employed not only the vernacular but the slang peculiar to that city.

This period's greatest writer and the most famous was Lusin, today beheld by the Chinese as their own Gorki. His portrait hangs in the place of honor at all writers' meetings and congresses; his house in Shanghai is a place of pilgrimage crowded with visitors every day. Better than anyone else he incarnates the intelligentsia which during the years 1917-1936 forged modern language and literature, and harnessed them to the revolutionary cause.

His real name was Chou Shu-jen. He was born in Chekiang Province in 1881 and did his university studies at Nanking. A friend of his youth speaks of how during his adolescence Lusin was continually preoccupied with three questions: What is the ideal life? What is the underlying lack in the Chinese people? How can it be remedied? Like a good many other young men of his generation he believed that what China basically needed was scientists. At an early age he had lost his father, a victim of popular superstitions: instead of treating him scientifically, they had submitted him to witch doctoring. That death was clearly what induced the boy to go into medicine. He left to study in Japan; soon afterward he changed his vocation. He has himself related how it happened:

> Every now and then, after the bacteriology class, we'd be shown newsreels. Naturally, at that time, most of the shots were of victories the Japanese were winning against the Russians. And now here was one of a Chinese who had spied for the Russians, been caught by the Japanese, and who was being executed in front of other Chinese. I was watching too, I was there, in a classroom; I watched and they killed the man.
>
> "Bravo!" the students shouted.
>
> They'd been clapping at all the films; but that day their hurrahing was a mite too loud for my ears. Later on in China I saw loitering half-wits gawk while criminals were being shot and then applaud as if they were stinking drunk. Alas, And woe is me. What's to be done? Nothing. Maybe, I thought; but there, in that place, and then, on that day, what I saw made me decide to switch my field.

What had stunned Lusin was to see Chinese standing by and without a qualm observe their countrymen being killed. He therewith discovered the major defect in his compatriots: their apathy. He was often to blame them for it. "We become slaves at a moment's notice and once in slavery we get along fine," he wrote bitterly several years later.* And again: "If we are neither genuinely wise nor genuinely brave but just sulk and cringe, then verily our plight is grave." He decided that the essential task was to overcome this listlessness: he chose literature. He published articles and translations, but with no great success; he took up teaching in 1910 and went ahead preparing a study on the Chinese novel.

The defeat of the 1911 Revolution convinced him that his effort was vain: useless to talk if nobody responded or even listened. He drew into his shell and settled down to solitude. "I'd lost my young man's enthusiasm and passion," he confessed ten years later. He spent his time copying ancient texts, conversing only with the few friends who would come to visit him where he had holed up. Ching Hsing-yi, one of the *New Youth* editors, dropped in on him one evening. "You ought to write," said he. Lusin relates that he replied this way: "Imagine a cast-iron house, all iron, indestructible. It's full of people, all asleep and about to die of asphyxiation but painlessly, for death will take them off in their sleep. And now do you want me to shout, wake up a few? Awake, they'll suffer the tortures of the damned; is that doing them a favor?"

"If they wake up there's an outside chance—the bare hope—that they'll wreck the house," said Ching.

Lusin staked everything on that hope. Inspired by Gogol's *Diary of a Madman* he wrote a story in which he denounced the old Confucianism-based society. He wrote others, all violently revolutionary. They were collected in several volumes. *The Cry* contains fifteen dating from 1918 to 1922; *Quandary*, eleven from 1924 and 1925; *Old Tales*, eight more from the period 1922-1925. In addition to these short stories Lusin wrote several autobiographical narratives which he assembled under the title of *Flowers of the Morning Hour*. He translated many tales and fables and, charging them with symbolic overtones, retold ancient Chinese legends. In the form of thumbnail sketches and impressionistic notes he commented in *Wildweed* upon events that had transpired between 1924 and 1926 at Peking: he attacked the military regime that then held sway in

* *Tombstones.*

North China. Those eight years were the most fertile of his literary career. The short tale called "The Story of Ah Q" won him immense popularity. Soon after, for reasons that are apparent in those he wrote, he gave up imaginative works.

Stories, tales, narratives, they all reflect Lusin's discouragement after the events of 1911. For a bourgeoisie which let itself be cheated of victory and which then made a deal with oppression he feels nothing but disgust. "I detested my own class without feeling the least bit of pity for its wretchedness and its dejection," he wrote subsequently. All his compassion went to the poor folk, and particularly the peasants, whose fate remained the same after one ruling clique was replaced by another; he has described their disarray in *Tempest in a Teapot* and it serves as a backdrop to "The Story of Ah Q." In this pitiable figure Lusin dramatizes the destitution and faults he long decried in the Chinese: miserable, despised, deprived of women, deprived of everything, Ah Q of the pathetic bounce transforms each of his defeats into a moral victory; fiddle-faddling resignation and shrill bluster lead him straight to the worst: although he has committed no crime he ends up being executed, and dies without having understood one iota of what this last and his preceding misfortunes have been all about. Throughout the story Ah Q's woes are the object of a cruel derision; and yet Lusin's sympathy for him is evident and the blame is finally laid not on Ah Q but on the society that has made him such as he is. Almost all Lusin's characters—backward peasants, intellectual flops, idiots, drug addicts, beggars—are, like Ah Q, baffled, mystified souls; economic conditions and traditional morality bar all means of escape from them; some abandon all hope, others resign themselves, nearly all struggle and flutter in vain, seeking absurd consolations in fantasy or going for help to the very institutions and superstitions which are destroying them. The impotence of these victims, half conniving at, half in complicity with their own misfortune, gives a despairing accent to Lusin's short stories. The Chinese, as I have said, compare him to Gorki; I find him more closely related to Chekhov. By way of plots, which he seldom bothers to tack down neatly, he makes it plain that things set up as they are deny the individual even the slimmest chance of salvation. This conclusion is not stated didactically; it appears in the choking atmosphere Lusin creates and which takes the reader insidiously by the throat. Usually his heroes are done in a kind of chiaroscuro. Often, as in Chekhov, there is a narrator who is supposed to be the author himself and who is an outside witness to events: he is only partially in the know and this gives happenings their depth of uncertainty. This art which suggests much more than the bare details state is perfectly adapted to the intention: to express beings who are themselves obscure, utterly but dubiously defined by the queer circumstances they cannot grasp; by describing these circumstances Lusin brings out the inner stuff of his characters; never does he use psychology in the analytical sense of the word: but eliminates all the distance between what is inside a man and what is outside. Which does not mean that subjectivity is absent from his work, far from it; the situations become unbearable because one constantly senses the presence of the consciousness that is undergoing them; rather, one might say that in Lusin's writings subjectivity is everywhere. This is one of the fundamental aspects of his work which before 1930 separated him from the literature known as proletarian. The pretended objectivity of socialist realism was unable to satisfy him; for him, awareness of the world was something more than reporting its configuration. His reticences can be traced back to yet deeper-lying causes. Lusin was then an unshakable pessimist; he considered visions of cheerful tomorrows mirages, talk of them false; still, if he had begun to write it had been to summon his people to the good fight; he could not therefore believe that the future was irredeemably black; if he wrote it was because the iron house was not indestructible. These conflicting doubts and hopes are alluded to in the preface he wrote to his collection of stories, *The Cry*.

Whatever were my personal and deep-seated convictions, I could not say that no hope existed; for hope resides in the future . . . Since my cry is a call to arms, I must necessarily obey the orders of my general; that is why I do not always abide by the truth . . . Our leaders frowned on pessimism then. And for my part I was not overeager to communicate the feeling of solitude, which had gnawed so bitterly upon me, to young people who were in the midst of dreaming the golden dreams I too had dreamed when I was their age. Clearly, my stories are not works of art. But I am content if they are read.

Indeed, he had injected an all but imperceptible shade of optimism into two of his stories. But the idea of altering in the faintest way the truth as he perceived it seemed to him to betray what literature required: he thought of the work of art as an absolutely sincere attestation. He never retreated from this position; he wanted the revolution none the less; whence a conflict in the man. He carried it with him to the grave.

Howbeit, his pessimism was no cover for inaction. Appointed to a University of Peking professorship, his course on the Chinese novel was a resounding success: the lecture hall was regularly packed. He spoke slowly, never raising his tone, his face always impassive; he liked to make others laugh but never laughed himself. When at the zenith of his fame he used his influence to back the students against the government.

A half-alive half-lived life, there's total error; for, the while looking like life, it leads nowhere but to death. Our young people have got to break out of the ancient jail. Yesterday, though they did nothing else than sit in a meeting, many students were clubbed, some even killed . . .

The tenor of his protests, his teaching, the attacks in *Yu-ssu* aimed at rightist literature, Lusin's criticisms of the government ended in his being fired; his review was forbidden and his name inscribed on the black list. In 1926, some professors suspected of Communism having been executed, he left Peking and took refuge in the South. He taught a while at Amoy but did not like it and in 1927 installed himself in Canton where Sun Yat-sen University threw open its doors to him. After the 1927 riot he went to Shanghai where he remained for some time in hiding at the home of a Japanese friend.

South China and the Kuomintang represented the last, the only bastion of freedom, the one chance for social change. And then Chiang Kai-shek's treason undermined these remaining hopes. At that point Lusin seems to have sunk into utter discouragement. He wrote in 1927,

Revolution, counterrevolution, nonrevolution, the revolutionaries are killed by the counterrevolutionaries, counterrevolutionaries by revolutionaries. The nonrevolutionaries are now suspected of being revolutionaries and are being killed by the counterrevolutionaries, now thought to be counterrevolutionaries and killed by revolutionaries. Or again people who aren't anything at all are killed by both revolutionaries and counterrevolutionaries. Ah yes! revolution. Revolution.

He wrote the same year in *Wildweed:*

My heart was once full of impassioned song: blood and steel, fire and fervor, justice and vengeance! . . . Hope! Hope! So shielded you resist the dark night's ambushes and prowling emptiness—even though there is yet dark night and emptiness behind the shield. So did my youth pass gradually by. There where I went I did at least see certain springtimes flush at my side. But today how alone I feel! Have those springs faded too? has youth the world over become doddering age?

For Lusin, to doubt of youth was to reach the last depth of despair, for it was in youth he had put all his hope. "Save the children!"—that was the cry that closed his first short story. In another, "Homeland," he had written: "I hope that the lives of the young will not turn out as aimlessly unstable as ours have been. I want them to have a new life, one we never knew." And thus, thinking on youth, he rediscovers faith in the future. There is this in *Wildweed:*

The army of youth raises itself up before my eyes. The young have become violent or are going to become so. I love these bloodthirsty souls that are bred in pain: they are swearing proof that I belong to a world that lives.

A little further on he makes an impassioned apology for the revolutionary hero:

The heroic rebel looks with wide-open blazing eyes upon the world and stands straight. He sees the factories deserted, weeds overgrowing the graves. He remembers the old unending suffering. He contemplates the vestiges of what has been. All that which is dead he knows, he knows all that has just been born and all that has still to be born. He has understood the works and the days of the Creator. He is going to stand yet straighter, and revive the race of men or see perish all the sons of the Creator. In the eyes of the rebel the world is no longer what once it was.

First he will fight against the hosts of hypocrisy:

Above the enemy's head floats every kind of banner adorned with all sorts of splendid names: philanthropists, intellectuals, writers, prodigies, and the wise. They wear bright coats variously initialed with the emblems of science, virtue, national genius, logic, fair play, and Eastern Civilization. The rebel couches his lance, smiles, and runs the pack through with a single thrust. The whole host collapses, there's nothing left, only a pretty gown lying on the ground: it enveloped thin air only. And he remains alone, the vanquisher, the criminal who pricked the philanthropical bubbles.

Regarding politics then, Lusin does not abandon hope. But concerning the role literature can play in revolution he became highly skeptical. In *Warm Wind* we find: "The old idols must be felled if mankind is to progress"—but he no longer thinks the writer can aid in toppling them.

Politics is what shoves; literature simply follows in its train and eyes its deeds. To fancy that literature can modify the situation is sheer idealism; the facts have given that fond dream the lie.*

He also says:

The revolutionary doesn't open his mouth. He pulls triggers. The feeble chatters and is massacred. The cat that puts tooth and claw into the mouse does not scream. Its prey screams.†

However, while the writer had best relinquish the illusion that a book is a politically effective weapon, he will not disdain literature's authentic objective: which is to express the world in its truth. It is indeed only by dissociating action from the disclosure of action that he will fulfill his true mission. Lusin will contenance no escapism:

There are writers who retire from the scene of life, who putter in their gardens and talk about birds and flowers. For my part I consider that literature is the feeling one has of the life going on about one.‡

But to no less an extent than aesthetism, proletarian literature is also a flight:

Presently the so-called revolutionaries talk of fighting and of seeing beyond their times. But looking elsewhere than to one's times is to flee them. If one has not the courage to look reality squarely in the face, how can one claim the title of a revolutionary?§

* *San-hien-t'si.*
† *That's All.*
‡ *Miscellanies.*
§ *San-hien-t'si.*

And later:

Our revolutionary writers are afraid of ghosts at their backs and horrors beside them, they bid us look stoutly ahead and want to broad-jump over and past this hour: squeeze up your legs, squeeze shut your eyes and off with you, revolutionary champion, go break a record and win a medal. You'll win nothing else.

In short by endowing literature with an overdose of politics you lose on both counts. You write bad books and accomplish nothing useful.

Fine works aren't made to order and measure, they don't come of constraint, they spring from the depths of the heart. For making a revolution you need revolutionaries: but there's no urgent need for revolutionary literature.

Between literature and revolution Lusin finally chose revolution. "At that time," he explains, "I came to realize that the future lay utterly with the proletarian class."* To serve them both he agreed to be president of a League of Writers of the Left dedicated to revolutionary literature. But what is interesting is that from there on he confined himself to polemical writing and translation. He brought Plekhanov, Fadeev, Chekhov, Gogol, Pío Baroja to the Chinese; his translations fill two big volumes; he wrote no more narratives or short stories.

His attitude becomes clearer if compared to the one held by Mao-tun, of all the other writers the closest to Lusin. He had undergone Lusin's own disillusionment in 1927. Speaking of the years which preceded Chiang Kai-shek's sellout, he says, "It then seemed as if a golden age were on its way to dawning. Events dispelled those bright hopes and a profound grief lay heavy on our hearts." In his novel *Agitations* he describes what a chaos of mass butcheries and betrayal the 1927 Revolution was; and commenting upon another novel, *Searchings*, he writes:

I admit that the dark pall of sadness hangs over me; but the dissatisfaction of the young, their distress, their searchings for a way, the defeat of all their undertakings—these are irrefutable objective facts.

The while denouncing the blights on society, the while demonstra-

* *That's All.*

ting the imperative of changing it, Mao-tun struggles to wrench free of pessimism's grip:

I have experienced the difficulties of a China in turmoil. I was prey to all the conflicts and disillusions that can come of life, they fed upon me and ate me into pessimism. Yes: and now what I wish to do is introduce a ray of light into that confused and somber life.

This last step was the one Lusin could not take it upon himself to attempt. He was able to silence his misgivings, lay aside his doubts, and actively set store in a better future; he always refused to give positive expression to a hope which probably did not suffice to quell the grief he felt in the face of the present.

The year 1936 marks the close of an era. The Sino-Japanese War began. In December of 1935 Mao Tse-tung had induced the Communists to endorse the tactics of a common national front. Writers of every party decided to join forces. Certain Communists maintained that the proletariat was alone the real adversary of imperialism and that literature ought to continue to situate itself upon the terrain of class struggle; but the majority elected unity. Kuo Mo-jo, who had just completed six years of exile in Japan, Mao-tun, Lusin, these were the first to rally. "I subscribe unconditionally to this policy because I am not only a writer but a Chinese," wrote Lusin. Suffering from tuberculosis he died shortly after, leaving a son of seventeen to whom in his testament he spoke thus: "Shun them who recommend that you be tolerant of your enemies." Lusin's body lay in state; during the three days before his funeral, more than twenty thousand people paid homage to his remains. His death rang down the curtain upon "bourgeois culture" as such. His life and career reflect the drama of a class whose economic persecution had become only the more intolerable due to its political emancipation, a class which, thwarted of its victory, helpless, desperate, though scarcely in its infancy had no other choice than to bow out and watch the proletariat stride to the fore.

Now in 1938 came The Anti-Japanese Federation of Chinese Writers. Lin Yutang teamed with Kuo Mo-jo. Lao-She was named president and re-elected each succeeding year. This wedding of forces produced an almost exclusively propagandistic literature.

Patriotic novels were poured out, so were plays, far more effective than books in a country where 80 per cent of the population was unable to read. Among others, Kuo Mo-jo and Ts'ao-yü produced a great many dramas for the stage.

The writers dispersed. Some stayed in the Kuomintang Zone and were persecuted. In 1946, Wen I-to, a one-time Crescent symbolist turned revolutionary, was executed. Meanwhile Mao-tun worked for a while at Hong Kong with a group of Communist writers. Most of the intellectuals converged at Yenan. The *Addresses to the Forum* delivered in 1942 by Mao Tse-tung sealed the death of bourgeois literature. The question from there on became one of creating a people's culture. Socialist realism was the one aesthetic acknowledged, and the main task became that of extending culture horizontally rather than of raising its level.

Scarcely two decades had elapsed since The Fourth of May. Well may we understand that the interval was too brief to allow of one such great flowering as in the course of a century gave Russia its marvelous literature. The divorce of classical from popular culture denied Chinese civilization the possibility of engendering a Shakespeare or a Cervantes. Their reconciliation within the confines of bourgeois culture could not in so short a time supply the lack. As the new regime sets to its cultural labors it has, by way of background and guide, interesting works but no great tradition.

On July 19, 1949, The National Federation of Literature and Art was founded at Peking under the presidency of Kuo Mo-jo. For vice-president there was Chou Yang, a Communist from the old Yenan days. Its aim was "to unite all patriotic and democratic writers and artists together with the Chinese people in a joint effort to put a definitive end to surviving remnants of imperialism, feudalism, and bureaucratic capitalism." This larger organization gave rise to The Writers' Association, headed by Mao-tun. In the course of the meeting called in 1952 to celebrate the tenth anniversary of the Yenan Forum, Mao-tun reinvoked and forcefully drove home the theses Mao Tse-tung had proposed at Yenan: the writer is to serve the masses; in order to do so he must reshape his own mental habits. The role of the Association is to guide the writer along the lines of Marxism-Leninism and, as well, within a Marxist-Leninist perspective, to criticize former and Western literatures. First let us see how the New China is reappraising its own old literature; and after that we will glance at the problems that present-day literary creation is posing to the Chinese.

The "Neodemist" principles laid down at Yenan have been frequently voiced since the Liberation: China must assume her cultural heritage. That was repeated at the 1953 Writers' Congress by the poet Fong Chin: in particular, the old novels and popular tales, revised where necessary, must be diffused. Chou Yang declared the same year that "the recovery and systematic study of our national artistic heritage has become one of the crucial elements in our work as it relates to literature and to art." The *Literary Heritage,* supplement to the daily *Kuang Ming,* is dedicated to that task. The Ministry of Culture has set up a Bureau of Literary Research which exposes Western and ancient literatures to Marxist-Leninist analysis. To the great surprise of those of its adversaries who expected that Communism would mean return to barbarism, the regime ordered the reprinting in unexpurgated form first of the famous *Dream of the Red Chamber,** then of *All Men Are Brothers* and *The Romance of the Three Kingdoms.* A committee representing all the literary associations decided in 1954 to celebrate the 200th birthday of Wu Ching-tzŭ, author of the satirical novel *The Life of the Lettered;* and the 250th of Hong Cheng who wrote the story of the lovely imperial concubine Yang Kuei-fei. Today's most official critic, Feng Hsueh-feng, having declared that socialist realism does not remove romanticism to beyond the pale, the poetry of Chü Yüan and Tu Fu have been republished and presented as works displaying a deep affection for the people. Not only is the old literature being revived throughout China, it is being widely translated into English and distributed everywhere in Asia. I was thus able to read a good many of the critical notices that accompany outstanding reprints; here is their general drift.

The works of the past exhibit the deficiences and blind spots inherent in the period they were written in; but some of them rise above their own moment in time; either openly revolting against

* A number of the anti-Communist men of letters who had retreated to Hong Kong were quite taken aback by the reissuing of this old classic; it even induced some of them to change their minds about the regime.

oppression or at least criticizing the society of their day. Viewed within a dialectical framework they manifest a truth, incomplete perhaps, but positive. The circumstances of the artists who composed them reflected this ambiguity. Tu Fu, for example, came from a great aristocratic family, but his father, although a mandarin, was poor, and he himself lived in a poverty that enabled him to appreciate the depressed condition of the farmers and to sympathize with their revolt. Much the same applied to Yüan Chi, a poet who lived in the third century A.D. and a disciple of the realist school which was at odds with all the ruling classes: Yuan's anarchism reflects the people's revolt against their tyrants.

Three commentaries struck me as particularly significant. In the review *Chinese Literature* appeared translated excerpts from the great historian Ssŭ-ma Ch'ien* who composed *Historical Memoirs* covering three thousand years of Chinese history. Eminently commendable, says the critic, are the scientific value and importance of Ssŭ-ma's work and also his literary gifts; but yet more admirable is the fact that he lashed out at the tyrants and sided with the heroes who were combating them. He sympathized with the working masses and hated their exploiters; he does not apply the criteria of feudal morality in judging his central figures, he exalts them as defenders of the people. As a writer he is skillful at painting the typical within the context of the individual, which is what socialist realism calls for.

Another issue of the same review ran fragments from the famous *Palace of Eternal Youth*, the play that is based on the tragic love story involving Emperor Ming Huang and his lovely concubine. Here the critic reproaches the author for having been unduly sympathetic in his treatment of their attachment, but congratulates him for having assailed the feudal rulers' lust, their selfishness and their extravagance: the beauteous Yang, who has a fondness for a rare tropical fruit, mobilizes couriers and spends fortunes in order to have supplies of it fetched up from the South in every season. All told, while subjecting the vice-ridden high officials to a biting attack, the play eulogizes the integrity of the peasants and the common folk.

*The Life of the Lettered* was written in the middle of the

* 145-c. 86 B.C.

eighteenth century by Wu Ching-tzŭ. The author belonged to the ruling class, but his was an impoverished and declining family, and it was this that enabled Wu to portray the decadence of the mandarins and the rottenness of the political structure in his day. Lusin, in his *History of the Novel*, considers this the first Chinese novel of social satire and he considers that as such it has seldom been surpassed. Wu Ching-tzŭ passed his life in material want and was even obliged to sell his library in order to keep body and soul together; often completely penniless, he was able to get by only because of the charity of his friends; cruel personal experience was the source of his realism. At one point, having had a little success, he considered whether to try for an official post; but being an independent spirit, his disdain for the examination system then prevalent triumphed over ambition and he preferred to stay poor. He shows sympathy for the grand old families and esteem for Confucian virtues; these do not, however, translate a conservative bent: the old families dated from the Ming dynasty, which was Chinese, while the upstarts had made their fortunes under the Manchus. Hence, the author's attitude is nationalistic, not reactionary.

Personally, it would seem to me that regarding the last two works the critic's evaluations go somewhat astray. In *The Palace of Eternal Youth* the author's sympathies for the imperial lovers is patent while social criticism is incidental and marginal. *The Life of the Lettered* is a satire, to be sure, but less explicit and less precisely aimed than the commentator would have us believe: Wu Ching-tzŭ's irony is often ambiguous and in the episodes I read I noticed considerable nonchalance and gratuitousness.

Keen discussion has raged round the novel *All Men Are Brothers.* In it Hu Shih saw no more than a tale of thieves; whereas for the Communists these outlaws are in actuality popular heroes revolting against the social order. Likewise it is felt that *The Pilgrimage to the West* is more than a series of romantic adventures; the author shows us the downtrodden in revolt against the ruling class and this with especial clarity in the part dealing with the "King of the Monkeys" upon which the renowned opera, *Revolt in the Kingdom of Heaven,* was later based.

But the most spectacular chapter in this resurrection and reappraisal of the old literature has been the affair of *The Dream of the Red Chamber*. This lengthy novel of almost a million written characters dates from the end of the eighteenth century. Through the story of a given family it paints the decadence of the landowner-bureaucrat class and thereby foretells the downfall of the feudal order. The central figures are a pair of lovers who revolt against the old system and their love is founded, precisely, on their shared hope for a better world; but this hope is disappointed, the old system destroys them. The Manchu mandarins abominated the book, judging it seditious. For this reason it came into a tremendous vogue after 1911; so numerous were the commentaries written upon it that around it grew up what was referred to as the "Red Science." Hu Shih above all appreciated the fact that the novel had been written in the popular language; he praised its naturalism without seeing the work either one of social criticism or revolutionary. One of his disciples, Professor Yu Ping-po, published in 1923 a group of essays on *The Dream*. When the novel was reprinted in 1950, a publisher reissued Yu Ping-po's commentaries which were themselves prefaced by a notice advising the reader that the present study approached *The Dream* from a purely literary standpoint. Indeed, Yu did not ascribe any social implications to *The Dream*. As a novel of manners, said he, *The Dream*, through its naturalism, is related to the famous semipornographic Ming-period novel entitled *Chin-ping-mei*. In addition Yu detected Taoist overtones in *The Dream*, allowing its central point to be that "love is a hollow dream"; the related events would serve only to illustrate this theme which implies the Taoist outlook in which the distinction between dream and reality undulates, all human experiences floating in the mists of infinity.

Yu Ping-po's work was a success; it went into six printings totaling twenty-five thousand copies.* Several reviews, whereof the *Literary Gazette* which in this area is the most important of them all, gave it very favorable critical mention.

But in 1954 a monthly published at the University of Shantung carried an article by two students who sharply attacked Yu's book; the *Literary Gazette* reprinted their article but at its head ran a conspicuously cautious comment by the official CP critic, Feng

* The figure is small next to certain others I cite on a later page; but very creditable for a specialized work of literary criticism.

Hsueh-feng. The students sent a new paper to the *Kuang Ming's* literary supplement in which they demolished Yu Ping-po's interpretation, one, they said, that derived straight from Hu Shih's idealism. A certain tendency to nihilism notwithstanding and despite his lingering attachment to his own class, the author of *The Dream* had—such was their view—produced a profoundly realistic work; he had depicted the disintegration of the aristocracy; he had preached not flight into dream but the crusade against feudalism; and, they concluded, the two heroes' love has a genuine revolutionary substance.

This variety of debate is not unknown to us: in France both left and right have vehemently disputed the spoils of, for example, Stendhal. What is unusual about this affair is the social and political significance it took on, the breadth of the consequences it had.

A fortnight after the appearance of the second article, *The People's Daily* entered the fray; that was October 23, 1954, on the eve of the Congress of Literature scheduled by the Writers' Association. *The People's Daily* approved the two students and alluded to an article Yu had written in 1925 in which he declared that literature is simply a matter of personal taste. *The People's Daily* charged the professor with idealism and subjectivisim; and added that the debate was open to the public, all intellectuals being invited to take part in it. "We must," the editorialist concluded, "purge literary research of its subjective and bourgeois notions, teach the application of Marxist approach, view, ideas, and methods." The Congress which began the next day echoed these arguments. Kuo Mo-jo and the most important critics joined in condemning Yu's idealism. Wherewith *The People's Daily* hammered *The Literary Gazette* for having spoken praisingly of the professor and coolly of his opponents. It made use of the occasion to reproach the *Gazette* on other scores: for publishing too many articles by writers who were well known but who had retained their bourgeois attitudes, for snubbing the work of young writers whose essays were written from the Marxist viewpoint. The affair developed. Chou Ou-chang, who a good while before had treated *The Dream* in a book written under Lusin's influence, attacked the *Gazette*; others did too. Kuo Mo-jo declared in the course of an interview published November 8, 1954, "This is not just a question of a person or a book coming under criticism. The problem involved is that of the ideological conflict between Marxism and idealist thinking." Feng Hsueh-feng published a self-criticism in his review; he admitted that the two students were right. On November 23 the Association condemned Professor Yu's book afresh; and its author admitted his errors in the course of a meeting.

The students—Li Hsi-fan and Lan Ling—both University of Shantung graduates, were then working, one in the Literary Research office, the other as a teacher in an accelerated school. They were acclaimed; but they were also chided for having put *The Dream's* hero, Chia Pao-yo, on a pedestal; surely, the Congress agreed, Chia rebelled against the established order; but, sprung from a feudal family, his revolt had necessarily to be incomplete: it discloses a negative and nihilist inflection. Further and heated discussion arose therewith: does *The Dream* really announce the birth of a Chinese capitalism? Or does it merely betoken the decomposition of a class?

This affair had some far-reaching consequences which I will examine further on. One cannot but deplore the ex-cathedra character of the official pronouncements, their dictatorial dogmatism, and the public retraction required of Professor Yu. Whatever our distaste for the heavy-handedness demonstrated in this particular case we ought not to misunderstand the position the regime has taken toward the past. The regime values its treasures; as regards the future of Chinese culture, this is a fact of extreme importance. What must be remarked is that Chia Pao-yo is as much a subject of intense discussion in China as Julien Sorel is in France. This decision to salvage the past leads to strained interpretations, doubtless; critics yield to the temptation to tamper with the meaning of works which they raid for evidence justifying the present. One critic, Sa Fang, has lately protested against what he calls "the quoting-out-of-context mania": it is not enough, says he, to fish about for odd phrases if one is to prove that an author was hostile to feudalism; his work must be viewed as a whole. In his May 1956 speech Lu Ting-yi, discussing the relationship to the national heritage, points out two mistaken tendencies: first, that valuable works are often carelessly dismissed with a stroke of the pen, a practice which is all too prevalent. The other, less frequent but not uncommon, is that deficiencies in the cultural heritage are airily glossed over; and this is dishonesty. For my own part, I noticed one glaring abuse: inasmuch as marriage was not formerly free in China, it is easy to consider any love story a denunciation of the old feudal society. But that is a minor point; the major one is this: that the old masterpieces are being made accessible to everybody. I shall not blame their exegetes for simplifying them. Many readers totally lack in background, and these great books of the past are difficult and disconcerting if one comes to them unprovided with a key; it is absolutely necessary to place them and explain them. At a time when millions of men are only beginning to obtain an education, an excess of subtlety would be harmful: explanations must be simple and unequivocal. They can be contested later by minds that have acquired a culture founded upon the solid bases being laid down today.

The diffusion of ancient culture is obviously not the regime's sole or principal aim: it hopes to encourage the flowering of a living literature expressing the new society. To what extent has this ambition been achieved?

The Communist Party's policy toward the former society's intellectuals is to leave none of them adrift. They have all been given suitable employment, some have received responsible posts, the jobless have been given work or, failing that, aid. On the other hand, there is a considerable number of new intellectuals, and all are assured the means of earning their living. By and large Chinese writers have never enjoyed such material prosperity. Universal education has multiplied the number of their readers. Bookstores abound in Peking; there are kiosks full of books and magazines in the parks; people, especially young people, browse in shops and sometimes stand and read for hours on end, the way students do under the Odéon arcades in Paris. China has ninety publishing houses; editions of fifty thousand are common. Liu Shao-ch'i's *On the Party* has run to two and a half million. Four million copies have been sold of Hu Chiao-mo's *History of the Communist Party*. The novels of Ting-ling and Chou Li-po, both of whom have won the Stalin prize, have reached the half-million mark. It is the size of a volume that determines its price: from 1.00 to 1.20 yuan; author's royalties being 10 to 15 per cent, earnings may be very high; so high, indeed, that the government, while not professing egalitarianism, is now considering limiting them. If moreover a writer wishes to travel, to undertake research, if he needs spare time for study or creative work, if he needs medical care or rest, all sorts of facilities are at his disposal. This preferential treatment is paid for: in China whoever receives must give; the writer is expected to render *service*; accepting certain privileges, he takes on the commitment of responding to the demands that will be made upon him. Congresses and meetings claim his attendance; the youngsters, the peasants who are beginning to read need books which they can understand; young writers must be taught and advised, the task falls to their elders. Writers must be ready to participate in any one of a thousand ways in the huge enterprise of educating the Chinese people. Chou En-lai even indicated in his January 1956 speech that the social service required of writers is often excessive: he asked that it be reduced to one-sixth of their working time—that is, to eight hours out of the weekly forty-eight every kind of worker must put in.

On the other hand, conditions for their creative work are austere. In order to speak to the masses, in order to depict them in words, one must know them. Most Chinese intellectuals, like ours, are of bourgeois origin. Time spent in factories and villages is recommended; these stays are not obligatory, as certain journalists have falsely insinuated. In the first place, no one is ever forced to write; and each writer decides for himself what his next book is to be about. True, the Association, acting in accord with the Ministry of Culture, launches appeals: at the present time, for example, books dealing with the co-operatives and collectivization are in demand; no one is made to fill any bills but by dint of the implicit commitment I spoke of most writers do what they can to satisfy requests, and to meet these requests on-the-spot experience conferred by living in a village, working in a factory is necessary. Madame Cheng recently told me the history of her literary career since 1949: her example will show how much is left to the author's initiative, how much the choice of what he undertakes is oriented by outside pressure.

The first work she published after the Liberation had nothing to do with any program: she simply wanted to write a book, that is all. In fictionalized form she recounted her youth, her education, the development of her ideas during the war against Japan, and the moral crisis which resulted in her adherence to Communism. That book written, she spent a year teaching in a university, then wished to write another book. Like Ting-ling and Chou Li-po she had taken an active part in the land reform; writers were being asked to tell how this tremendous change had been effected and to explain its meaning; she related her experience both for her own pleasure and in order to perform a service. She then got the idea of describing the life of women cotton-mill workers and for several months held a job in the office of a cloth factory employees' union; afterward, feeling that she had not achieved a sufficiently intimate grasp upon what she had learned, feeling no inspiration, she abandoned her project. Having grown up near Hangchow, a region where tea is raised, she thought it might be easier to familiarize herself with peasant life: so she spent two years in a village, taking an active hand in the co-operatives, forming acquaintances with individual peasants; and eagerly wrote *The Tea of Spring*, proofs of which she was going over at the time I was in China.

Will it be said that these working conditions leave little room for the free play of inspiration? Our critics, however, have often gone to bat for the works composed for a specific occasion that were produced in the past; we have frequently heard them argue that necessity is the mother of invention, that a piece of writing, a painting, an oratorio done on commission need not be lacking in spontaneity. Indeeed, *Esther* and *Athalie*, Bach, Tintoretto are adequate proof that assignment need not rule out masterful results. To propose, even to dictate themes to a writer is not to condemn him automatically to mediocrity.

What is apt to be more harmful is to prescribe in advance the manner in which he is to treat these themes. But before entering into this question, it seems to me necessary to make one thing clear. M. Guillain travesties the truth when he avers that the Association exerts a tyrannical control over authors. Outraged, he cites the case of a *young* writer who is advised, after his manuscript has been read, to give less emphasis to agronomy and more to human problems—a recommendation which, a priori, strikes me as judicious. Writing being a craft that has to be learned, the idea of *helping* a novice does not seem ridiculous to me. There are in today's China countless young workers, soldiers, peasants who, eager to express themselves, have not the technical means to do so: writers' groups in the factories, in the army have the job of teaching and guiding them. Under the wing of the Writers' Association a Central Institute of Literature has been set up with the purpose of helping beginners acquire the cultural background and equipment they lack and develop their talent if talent they have: our own young bourgeois take similar courses in preparatory schools and at college. And is Guillain unaware that in France, in America, a young author is lucky indeed if his first book is printed as submitted? That he be obliged to cut, patch up, rewrite his text is less the exception than the rule; it is the publisher or a staff reader that calls the tune, or, in the United States, the literary agent. I do not find it scandalous that in China he receives his advice from professional writers rather than from merchants in the book game.

As for established writers, the Association does not interfere in their work. There is no preventive censorship. If, once it is published and out, constitutional or legal exception is taken to a book, a provisory judiciary committee is formed, writers sitting at the board, and it is decided whether or not the book warrants seizure; very seldom does it happen. Proof that in their selection of texts publishers and magazine editors are fettered by no official control is the hue and cry some of these texts provoke and the severity with which they are attacked by critics. So it was that in 1954 a film, purported to be the history of a famous nineteenth-century personage, Wu Hsin, was shown on Chinese screens; the movie represented Wu as a revolutionary hero, the critics gave rave notices to the script writer and the director. Then *The Literary Gazette* and a *People's Daily* editorial suddenly declared that in reality Wu Hsin had been a lackey of the feudal powers and that behind a front of selflessness he lent money to the peasants at exorbitant interest rates; he built schools, to be sure, but it was to promote reactionary ideas; they were the landowners' interests he served with zeal. The authors of the film were sharply rebuked for having falsified history; and intellectuals were scourged for having been accomplice to this mystification. Obviously had there been any preliminary censorship the film would not have reached the movie houses, the numerous articles praising it would not have been printed or even written. Nor, similarly, would the *Red Chamber* affair have occurred had Yu Ping-po's study been subject to a censor's scrutiny.

That much said it is fully evident that in today's China not anybody at all can publish whatever he likes. Censure emanating from the Party press, the Writers' Association, the Minister of Culture, the big reviews and magazines carries such weight that the publishers take care not to be the targets of their wrath. The author himself fears incurring it and, in his work, moves gingerly; he is careful to hew to the "line." Looking into the new Chinese literature, the first of its features the Western reader is likely to be struck by is its conformism.

To damn this conformism is not hard. It would be well, however, not to lose sight of the fact that the situation in China is entirely unlike what it is in France, and this for a reason we have slight cause to be proud of; we have two literatures: the one Jean Paulhan* reads, the other that millions of Frenchmen feed upon and which ranges from *True Confessions* to the comic strips in *France-Soir* via detective stories and *The Notebooks of Major Thompson*. One aims at quality, the other is content with quantitative smash hits; nothing more evident than that the writers laboring for "the big market" have kissed all freedom goodby: they cater to the editors who run the slicks and the pulps and apply the formulas and slants that cannot miss; as for the public that consumes these products, far from deriving the faintest intellectual benefit from them, it soaks up what is calculated only to stupefy. Two distinct audiences, two kinds of writings, two different jobs to be done. No such situation obtains in China. There, the problem is to create a literature that is both popular and of cultural worth. The undertaking, thus, has nothing in common with that assumed by bourgeois writers and cannot be properly judged by our Western criteria. Plainly, it does not favor the emergence of a Proust or a Kafka. But, on the other hand, Chou Li-po's *The Hurricane*, five hundred thousand copies of which have been printed, is, as writing,

* Contemporary French novelist, poet, critic; a "gray eminence" of French literature, once editor of the *Nouvelle Revue Française*, now editor of the *Nouvelle NRF*. (Translator's note)

far and away superior not only to Mickey Spillane but to our bourgeois monthly top ten headed by best-selling *Jalnas* and *Men in Whites.*

What I said apropos of the press prevails for literature too: since the question is that of instructing the illiterate masses, a degree of government control is imperative. Simone Weil, who is little suspected of sympathy for authoritarian regimes, wanted to see authors who lied to the public tried for a crime; she rightly considered that intellectual imposture is as grave a thing as poisoning a patient or building a bridge that is sure to fall. Even in a relatively cultivated society like ours people tend to believe as true whatever they read in print. The Chinese who is just now opening his eyes to culture, for whom the mere deciphering of a text is still something akin to performing a miracle, takes every written word as gospel truth: he is as incapable of ferreting out error as he is of spotting the cholera microbe in apparently clear water; it is for the regime to see to it that he is given a wholesome diet. When addressing an experienced public, the role of the writer is to show his reader the world in all its complexity and uncertainity, to probe that world and criticize it; but if his reader is not equipped to discern and to challenge, complexity gives rise to confusion only. People sunk in ignorance, beset still by superstitions and ridden with prejudice require first to be given the tools of understanding, that is to say, a clear image of the world; at this stage, clarity and simplicity go hand in hand; the seven kinds of ambiguity will have their day tomorrow.

Simplicity need not be the enemy of truth: to reconcile the two —that perhaps is the artist's great task. Unfortunately, the directives originally proposed by Mao Tse-tung have since had grafted onto them rules that are little conducive to literary sincerity. Chou Yang wisely suggests that "the writer needs to be free in his choice of subject and manner of treating it"; but then backtracks with "The writer must describe heroes and in them omit their unheroic aspects"—this amounts to instituting a new academism. I admit that in a society entirely oriented toward the future, in which a new type of man is in the process of being created, literature should manifest this march forward and represent "positive heroes"; but it is regrettable that, denying them their contingency and hence their truth, two-dimensional clichés are the result. Madame Cheng told me that her autobiographical novel had been coolly received by the critics, they had found the heroine's intellectual evolution too hesitant: one ought to become converted to Communism in a single clap of thunder; the book was not reprinted. Readers, however, wrote to the press and objected to this severity; a Writers' Congress in 1953 took the defense of the book which subsequently came out in a new edition. *The Literary Gazette,* in 1952, ran coverages on the famous Soviet discussions dealing with "the absence of conflict," and Mao-tun has reminded writers of the importance of basing their plots upon tensions and contrasts and of exploring these to their depths; many novelists have been content to skate over the surface and "as a result, these writers turn rich and complex social phenomena into drab and completely one-sided affairs, dry as dust and stereotyped." He avows that, above all, "the heroes have no personality," and "skeletons too shriveled to convey any ideological message," and, in the long run, "are mere idols, the very ones Marx criticized—'Deified and Raphaelesque portraits of this sort lose all descriptive truth.' The heroes in our books are neither vital nor yet even alive; they are limp puppets and they are boring." But Mao-tun follows these pertinent remarks with the disconcerting conclusion that the way to render these heroes more real is to render them still more heroic:

> We must demand that our writers concentrate every effort upon the problem of characters, especially upon that of creating positive characters . . . They must draw them more powerfully, giving us a more synthetic, more typical, more ideal, more dynamic image of men than real life affords us.

This seamless, idealized shape the "positive hero" assumes throughout contemporary Chinese literature is its worst feature. Mao-tun may unkindly announce that "the artistic and ideological level of our performances is not high enough." But it will not be raised unless—as he indicates in other texts—reality, even if it be that of a hero, is first squarely confronted and full due given its complexity and ambiguity. That is what he suggests as regards fictional situations—they ought not to be oversimplified—but he does not extend it to fictional characters and the result is that the books being turned out now are edifying tracts which fail to convince either artistically or indeed ideologically.

Many of the novels and stories I read informed me; their documentary value is indubitable; however superficial their conflicts, these are at least focused upon. Conflicts between generations over questions relating to free marriage, religion, woman's work, new agricultural methods; between the husband still steeped in feudal ideas and his progressive wife; the conflicts in a young peasant girl between her thirst for education and the chores which require her presence in the village; conflict at the factory between a manager obsessed by the Plan and the workers he is pushing too hard; between a shop foreman after nothing but quantity and the checker who, demanding quality, mercilessly rejects slipshod work —these themes are, on the whole, more interesting than those which bourgeois literature languidly handles. But excess of optimism mars these stories. I particularly noticed that in most of the novels the first half, critical and negative, is far superior to the second which winds up with a positive straightening out of affairs. In both *The Sun Shines Over the Sangkan River*, by Ting-ling, and *The Hurricane*, by Chou Li-po, there is first a description of a village where the land reform is about to be carried out; the inhabitants are presented such as they are, at once conditioned and free, stuck in the slough of the past, peering timidly toward the future: there are bad, there are good, there are others who are in between, wavering, confused, men of good will but halting, some who are lucid but fearful; they are struggling in a welter of contradictions that derive from circumstances and their own inner make-up. One believes in their existences and their personal dramas. All of a sudden a "positive hero" enters the picture. A Party man, he overcomes all the difficulties with startling ease. It is much the same thing in Tsao Ming's *Power Plant*. The scene is in the Northeast; the Japanese and the Kuomintang have sabotaged an electric power plant; some workers are trying to get it back into running order. They put their trust in smooth talkers who do not merit it, commit a great number of blunders, and come to the brink of disaster. The reader becomes interested in their mistakes. Then arrives the Communist fellow who fixes everything with a flick of the wrist. In *The Plains Afire* one is gripped by a fine tale of early guerrilla operations against the Japanese: the tentative, trial-and-error moves on the part of the leaders, the blunders of certain soldiers, their progress, their setbacks—these intrigue; and then, toward the end, it all founders in a sea of 100 per cent heroism.

I stated my criticisms to the writers I met, to Mao-tun himself; all agreed that my objections were justified. Modestly they said that their literature is still feeling its way along, that it will be a while yet before really satisfactory works would be coming out. However they were not considering any shift in principle. They perhaps believe that the public is not yet ripe for a subtler fare.

Or it may be that they realize that there is another difficulty, more serious still and not to be surmounted until a few years have gone by. The difference between naturalism and socialist realism is, in principle, that the first school presents the spectacle of a world that has ground to a halt, whereas the second reflects one that is on the move. But can an author portray the movement of life if he is not in its thick and moving too? Even if he passes several months amid workers and peasants he does not become one of them: it is not true that you can identify yourself with others and still stand apart from them; you are totally of their condition, or you are not of their condition at all. Writing is not registering what one found out in a factory. It is to extend an experience. Without entering into a discussion of the knotty problem of subjectivity one can affirm that the system of exposure to conditions in village or factory is, practically speaking, less than enough to span the gap separating the writer from the masses. Ting-ling has gone into the question in an interesting article, "Life and Literary Creation."* She starts by citing remarks certain writers have made to her.

Tolstoi, Chekhov, and Tsao Hsueh-chin,† they told me, produced masterpieces in part because they had genius, in part because they had the advantage of describing the people among whom they lived . . . "Of whom does the writer speak today?" my comrades asked me. "Of workers, peasants, soldiers, heroes, and heroines who are so remote from him that he must go live among them if he wishes to find out what they look like and what they say. He hunts for models the moment he

* Printed in *Chinese Literature*, No. 3, 1954.

† Author of *The Dream of the Red Chamber*.

begins to write. During a brief stay in their society he may indeed get to know their faces, but not much else. At home he is surrounded by intellectuals of petty bourgeois origin . . ."

Ting-ling owns that such working conditions are bad; in *The Plains Afire* the author, who as a partisan fought the Japanese for an entire decade, relates an experience that was in fact his own: and his novel is good. From Korea, where he spent only one year, he brought back stories that are less good. What one must do, Ting-ling finds, is plunge all the way into the socialist endeavor instead of taking quick research dips into special fields which cannot but remain alien territory. "To experience life means nothing short of total immersion in it and participation in its struggles." Taking an interest in a question simply because one wishes to write about it, gathering materials after having arbitrarily chosen a subject, this is a poor way to proceed: one must truly live amid the masses, to share their existence to the marrow, my future and thine must become one. Ting-ling is fully aware that until an experience be my own I cannot expect to be able to communicate it meaningfully to others. Herself long engaged in the revolutionary battle, her husband shot by the Kuomintang, she in jail, then as a Party member working in Yenan, after that participating actively in the land reform, she has indeed plunged into the life of the people. But she does not say just what a writer can do today in order to become other than he is. The times have changed. For the intellectual the only significant action possible now is writing. Settling down for longer periods of instruction in village or factory, working with his hands beside peasants or workers, these will always be manners of *finding out* about life, not of *living* it. Sound in theory, Ting-ling's suggestions become very vague when it comes to practice. Mao-tun had advanced the same ideas: "The writer must absolutely be in the thick of the fight personally; he should not *know* how to be a mere bystander." But the solution Mao-tun indicates—factory grime, countryside clay, training a solid Marxist-Leninist critical intelligence upon the experience and bringing it to life through a genuine revolutionary enthusiasm—is neither precise nor sufficient. One may legitimately suppose that so long as they limit themselves to "going to the masses" the writers will get nowhere in their effort to express them; what is necessary is that writers *come from the masses.* There are young writers emerging from the ranks of the people; the trouble is that save for rare exceptions they are not really writers yet; lacking a sense of tradition, lacking self-confidence, lacking mastery of the language, they stare at the blank sheet of paper and, suddenly alone, feel a helplessness whence, like all people of slight education, they escape only by clutching at platitudes and submitting to conventions. There is now evident, and for the time being probably unavoidable, a divorce between content and form: the elders possess the equipment but not the living experience they propose to convey; while the young who embody the movement of history lack technique and knowledge. Chinese literature will come into its own the day the breach is closed; the time will come when, for workers and peasants, culture is a familiar thing; language will no longer intimidate them; they will then be able to speak for themselves and frankly. In the meantime literature can hardly be more than preliterature; which is what Mao Tse-tung foresaw at Yenan when he said that the cultural level shall not begin to rise vertically until, horizontally, culture has first spread and taken root everywhere.

These reservations entered, it is no sign of honesty to condemn China's cultural effort by pointing to the Chinese artist and then observing that his Western counterpart is freer: our pseudo liberalism also implies contempt for the great mass of the people it puts at the mercy of a certain number of profiteers specializing in the printed page. It is noteworthy that the vast majority of the Chinese intellectuals have rallied to the regime and a good many of them in a very active sense. Some fled to Formosa, Hong Kong, or America; they were few. Those who stayed in China and whom the regime has taken on and put to work in many cases have what Chou En-lai calls "a complicated past" behind them; some were once openly anti-Communist. However, in his January 1956 report, Chou estimates that today four out of ten of them are progressives who energetically support socialism; another four are well disposed and are properly carrying out their tasks although their political attitude is lukewarm; something over 10 per cent are retrogrades; and a small number decidedly counterrevolutionary. Among the progressives one seems to find the finest writers of the period. According to the opinion of Shanghai missionaries themselves and that of other Sinologists devoid of any sympathy for Marxism, the most celebrated names in Chinese literature around 1940 were those of Kuo Mo-jo, Mao-tun, Pa-chin, Lao-She, Ts'ao-yü, Ting-ling: they all belong to the Writers' Association today. Neither Pa-chin nor Lao-She nor Ts'ao-yü were Communists then; the last two were visiting America in 1946 and could have stayed there; Pa-chin could have left China. The fact is that there was never any question of doing so; they adhered unhesitatingly to the regime and have put their pens into its service. Counterrevolutionaries whom this conduct bewilders and who with the editors of *Preuves** look for psychological clues to account for it simply demonstrate their fundamental misunderstanding of the situation. To begin with this "freedom of the writer" which the Western intellectual would take for an eternal value has never existed in China. Persecuted by the Manchus and by Chiang Kai-shek, jailed, exiled, shot, beheaded, buried alive, Chinese writers have long considered literature a form of combat, and perilous. During moments when they were not being hunted down they suffered from a feeling of being unable to achieve anything effective. "We were alone then, our voice would awaken no echo, or at any rate if it did it was inaudible to us," they all told me. "We now know who we are writing for. We receive letters, our work is liked, disliked, whatever, but between us and the public there is a dialogue. That is an immense encouragement." Contact with the public can invite to conformism; it is none the less stimulating. Today, the writer counts, he knows it, it is a good thing to know. We earlier saw that in 1936, when the issue was not one of socialism but of the nation's survival, every writer, even the most frivolous, had leaped into the fray. It is not Communism that persuaded them to surrender their independence, at least in part. The desire to act has always had a firm place in their hearts and they have never made the error of mistaking gratuitousness for liberty. They helped fight Japan before; they are helping build socialism now; in this case as in the other they believe they are doing no more than what the writer's true mission expects of him.

* Literary review published in Paris by a "Cultural Freedom" group. (Translator's note)

I do not say that they are not sometimes impatient of a conciliation between their social responsibility and their purely aesthetic concerns. Referring to one of his plays, Lao-She wrote in 1954 that he was delighted it had been well received and had contributed to propagating the idea of free marriage, but added that he did not regard it as a work of art. Pa-chin confesses to having trouble portraying heroes in the authorized style. Mao-tun would like spare time for writing, his functions as Minister of Culture leave him none at all. There is not the slightest doubt but that the writers are conscious of the weaknesses in present Chinese literature, but like every one of their countrymen they trust in what the future will bring.

Actually, they have grounds for hope, especially since the change in the line that occurred in the spring of 1956. Lu Ting-yi's speech was a turning point; it unpinioned literature and ideology too. Competition among a multiplicity of rival schools means that socialist realism is no longer the sole admissible aesthetic. "We judge it the best; but there are also other methods for creating. The writer is free to choose and employ whatever one he wishes so long as it is for the workers, the peasants, and the soldiers he writes." One may describe the new society and positive characters; one may also describe the old society and negative characters. Nothing prevents the writer from introducing unreal beings—spirits that crowd paradise, animals that speak. The subject matter ought to be as varied as possible. As for aesthetic theory, all opinions are allowable, men of letters should discuss them freely.

At the Third Session of the National People's Congress Mao-tun commented at length upon the injunction "May our garden be wide, and all flowers grow there together." He said,

> We must let the various schools enter freely into competition . . . The while encouraging socialist realism we consider that the writer must be at liberty to elect the creative method that suits him best . . . Concerning literary theories, there are today a good many points which remain moot . . . They must be discussed frankly and not simply in order to reach a fallacious unanimity or conclusions in a hurry.

Mao-tun calls for a less simplistic, a less sectarian mode of criticism: instead of peppering their commentaries with quotations out of Marx, instead of sticking arbitrary labels on writers, critics ought to subject the works they discuss to concrete analysis. As for authors, they are restricting themselves to too narrow a range of themes; all deal with the same subjects all viewed from the same angle, thus giving Chinese literature a regrettable monotony and conformity. In truth, "every aspect of life's realities can inspire art." Rather than copying one another writers must henceforth create a climate in which "everyone will sense the need to be an original person."

It would, I am afraid, be overly hopeful to suppose that these new instructions are all that is necessary to see a crop of literary masterpieces spring up overnight. The injunction of immediate efficacy remains in force, and it is, for certain, damaging to the richness and sincerity of a book. Paradoxically it is the very importance of its function that is impoverishing contemporary Chinese literature. I have already said as much: unable for the time being to transform techniques, superstructures are being resorted to as a means for modifying substructures. Literature hence finds itself signed with an economic coefficient. In 1955 the "Writers, to the fields!" slogan mobilized writers for the collectivizing campaign. Had agriculture been mechanized there would have been no need for verbal propaganda; but there was a dearth of tractors, literature was called upon to mitigate it. Literature's practical role is infinitely greater here than in any other country—with the result that it must frequently serve the most noncultural of ends.

Which exactly is why one may predict that it will see better days: Chinese economy is at present going through a stage of shortage and emergency; this stage once passed, literature will be in the realest sense released—in the sense one speaks of the release of atomic energy. Freed of the duty of ensuring the cohesion of society, it will then be able to express it and put it to the test of criticism; it will then have ceased to be a service, its scope will broaden, its objectives become less immediate. With enough elbowroom it may, for example, tackle the problem of finding out what in actual truth man is.

But as of now the intellectual climate in China has changed. The leaders are of the belief that the union of intellectuals must be founded not on mechanical obedience, but on the basis of free consent:

The Communist Party must protect freedom of thought in the domain of literature, the arts, and scientific research. It must guarantee free debate and allow everyone to preserve or reserve his opinion.

Lu Ting-yi specifies that unlike opinions must contend in an atmosphere of independence, no discussion must be shut off or decided by administrative order; the minority has the right to maintain its personal position, is not to be compelled to rectify it so as to concur with the majority. Criticism must no longer be what it too often has been hitherto, an attack mounted with the purpose of annihilating an adversary; but rather a commentary motivated by good will and striving to single out the positive elements which even error may contain. If he so chooses the intellectual under criticism will counter with a reply. But even when an error is manifest—which may occur above all in the realm of science—he who has committed it is in no wise forced to recant in a written or public self-criticism. The bulk of these principles look to be aimed expressly at doing away with the abuses of which we were furnished an example by the *Red Chamber* affair. To transform a mistake into a humiliating fault is to encourage cultural stagnation; the intellectual dares not risk an opinion, speaks guardedly, finally shuts up altogether. Lu Ting-yi's Address, in denying the Communist intellectual any superiority over his non-Party counterpart, aims at dissipating a climate of anxiety, at introducing a wholesome one in which the new intelligentsia's unity will be sealed by trust and friendship.

### *The Reform of Written Language*

The problem of language is the key problem in every literature; and nowhere is the fact more patent than in China. It was by freezing language in its rigid ku-wen form that the imperial bureaucrats obtained their monopoly over feudal culture. The rise of the bourgeoisie at once brought about a linguistic revolution; one wrote in pai-hua from then on. In its effort to become popular we see culture require a new reform; the proponents of a proletarian literature were demanding it as early as 1919; the present regime is determined to put it through.

Impossible to disseminate culture, declare the leaders, if reading and writing remain the complicated operations they are today. School children spend a dozen years simply in mastering the rudiments; that is too long even if they acquire other knowledge at the same time; because of this handicap their studies move more slowly than those of pupils in other countries. Illiterates need several years just to learn the most everyday vocabulary. Students are constantly encountering obstacles raised by the traditional writing: it is a serious impediment in the theoretical and applied sciences. Going through difficult works, readers are frequently brought up short by characters they are unable to pronounce and whose meaning they cannot decipher; or they will know a word by ear but not by its written equivalent. The transcription of foreign substantives poses insoluble problems: for example, Dostoevski's name may be written six ways. Graver still, it is often impossible to transcribe scientific terms borrowed from foreign languages and the forming of the new words required by technological advance is an equally awkward affair. There is no way of sending a telegram directly in Chinese; some Western language must be resorted to, or else it is composed in numerical code, each four-figure number representing a certain character; reading it is slow going and the two processes invite error. As for typewriters, they must be so complicated that writing can be done almost as quickly by hand. For all these reasons the government has taken the definitive decision to reform writing; concerning the means for proceeding with it, discussion is still open; but there is no further debate regarding the end: every newspaper, every official organ is backing the project.

Making Chinese phonetic is a tricky undertaking and big enough to take years. It has been started; meanwhile, a temporary measure has been decided upon: the simplification of the characters. This is one of the jobs that is being carried out by The Orthographical Reform Committee, first set up in 1952 and which publishes a monthly journal, *Language and Literature*.

The problem is not new. When the use of the brush succeeded that of the stylus, ideograms became more handsome and more complicated. Under the Sui and Tang dynasties the imperial bureaucrats and in particular the clerks in courts of law substituted less elaborate signs for them; the two systems existed side by side, one being employed by the printer, the other for cursive handwriting. The short cut which the regime is now introducing involves, first, the reduction of the number of strokes that compose the more complex ideograms and, second, a reduction in the number of characters themselves. In January 1955 the Committee released its detailed plan for going about this; it was discussed in March, newspapers and reviews started using, by way of an experiment, some 141 of the simplifications listed in the plan. A new program was soon established. Out of 7,000 basic characters, 1,093 which overlapped other simpler ones were discarded right away; 519 characters and 54 radicals were redrawn with fewer elements. The changing of the 54 radicals means that all the characters of which they are a part are simplified at the same time: the total number comes to more than 1,700. That much has been accomplished so far; the work is to be continued.

Another change, connected with the aforementioned, is that in a certain number of newspapers, among them the *Kuang Ming*, a horizontal typography has been adopted: the text no longer reads vertically but from left to right as in the West; in that the Chinese write numbers from left to right this is much the more rational arrangement where scientific works are concerned. It will be universalized.*

The Hong Kong reactionaries find these simplifications "slightly vulgar." No doubt about it, they make reading and writing a great deal easier. The real disadvantage of this reform is that learning the simplified characters entails a supplementary effort for those who already know how to read; while conversely those who learn characters only in their new form cannot decipher a text written a few years ago in the old. As a result one must have the two systems present in one's mind; and many are wondering whether the adoption of this intermediary measure has not rather contributed to making matters worse.

At any rate it is not in itself the answer. The objective now being aimed at is phoneticization. This aspect of the over-all reform is not new either. As early as the third century A.D. scholars came to recognize what could be gained by the phonetic transcription of language; in order to indicate the pronunciation of a character, they devised the means of breaking it up into two known charac-

* All Peking newspapers adopted it as of January 1, 1956.

ters one of which contained the consonant sound and the other corresponding to the vowel. This is the Fan-Chieh (cut-and-rejoin) system. For example, to render the sound of *Kan* it is designated by the characters K(uo) and (h)*an*. The system was perfected about 270 A.D., possibly under the influence of Sanskrit. A great dictionary published in the time of the Sui dynasty, in 601, utilized this method and it was subsequently employed in most classical dictionaries up until our era. The system underwent reforms necessitated by the changes that occurred in pronunciation between the Sui and the Sung periods; the pronunciation that was current in 1067 remained standard ever afterward. About a century and a half before then, at the close of the Tang period, a Buddhist monk had selected thirty-six letters from the so-called law-court writing and these were to serve as a phonetic alphabet. The veritable pioneers in phoneticization were the Jesuit Fathers Ricci and Trigault who had Bibles published in roman-lettered Chinese: but these Bibles were intended for foreigners who spoke but did not know how to read Chinese.

The Japanese having managed to phoneticize their writing by 1900, a Chinese linguist set about imitating them. He established an alphabet similar to theirs, basing it on the dialect spoken in North China; another corresponding to the Southern dialect was put together; but the attempt produced few results. Meanwhile Father Lamasse, another Jesuit, proposed an "interdialectical romanizing" scheme which would permit the phonetic transcription of several dialects, but which was extremely complicated. The government became interested in these studies. The great teacher at the University of Peking, Tsai Yuan-pei, in 1913 gave the impetus to the project which produced a national phonetic alphabet; in 1920 there was officially published the *Dictionary of National Phonology* where phonetic symbols are combined with the roman alphabet. Ten years later, the Nationalist government decided that, to facilitate reading, schoolbooks would henceforth be printed with the traditionally composed text on one page faced on the page opposite by national phonetic alphabet signs; but the type necessary for printing these signs was never cut.

The problem was one of especial interest to the revolutionary writers. Said Lusin:

There is nothing else to do but Romanize the characters, a matter which is inseparable from the question of a popular literature. I don't think the task will present insurmountable difficulties.

In his *Light on Literature* he wrote:

The continued use of Chinese characters means continued waste not only of mental effort but of time, ink, and paper . . . If we are to go on living, Chinese characters cannot; we have no choice left but to sacrifice them . . . The characters are a precious legacy handed down by our ancestors. I know. But we can sacrifice our inheritance or ourselves; which is it to be? I put the question to you; may idiots desist from replying . . . If the Chinese wish to survive they will not delay another instant getting rid of the characters that are a bane to their intelligence.

He reiterated in *Miscellanies*: "Are you eager to raise the level of Chinese culture? Then vote for popular language, elect a popular literature, install a romanized alphabet."

In 1919 Chinese intellectuals met with Soviet colleagues to investigate the question; their combined efforts produced, in 1927, a roman alphabet which was flexible enough to apply to several dialects. At Shanghai in 1934 a Society for the Study of Romanization was formed to explore the project; then in 1936 a press was started for printing books in "Latinxua" or "Soviet Romanization." This was the kind of writing which, with a degree of success, the Communists started to teach in the refugee camps in 1937; it was used above all in the composition of tracts and propaganda texts, but it is completely insufficient for the presentation of complicated works.

After the Liberation the Communists renewed the search for a romanizing method. They were confronted by a doctrinal problem: was the undertaking not in contradiction with the Stalinist theory that defines language not as a superstructure or product of class but as a direct expression of the people? Their conclusion was that spoken Chinese emanates from the people; but that the written language, formerly monopolized by the ruling class, became one of its privileges and was utilized as a weapon against the people whom it maintained in ignorance. Thus Mao Tse-tung could declare in 1951: "Writing must be reformed, it must become phonetic as all written languages are the world over." It was in the same spirit that two years before in Peking The Association for the Reform of Written Chinese had been organized under the chairmanship of Wu Yu-chang who is also president of the People's University.

The objection that has been frequently raised to the whole idea is that Chinese is a monosyllabic language which does not employ the entire gamut of consonants, vowels, and diphthongs, the *r*, for example, being nonexistent; out of the total number of possible combinations only 58 per cent occur; this reduces the number of phonemes to only 412; they can be modified, though, by pitching them in any of four tones, which gives about 1,280 separate sounds; the necessary result being that a given sound has a quantity of meanings and corresponds to several characters. Perfectly clear as written, a text may, when read aloud, become equivocal because of the multiplicty of homonyms.

But a Chinese philologist has recently written an article in which it is advanced that spoken Chinese is not monosyllabic, and French Sinologists specializing in linguistics have confirmed this to me. The original phonemes only rarely appear alone; it is by combining them that words are formed. Thus the term *chih* means upward of forty different things and hence corresponds to that many different characters; it may be pronounced in four different ways; the first intonation may designate nine meanings: but among these homonyms there are but two that are used in isolation; the rest enter into combinations which enable them to be understood unambiguously; of the sixteen phonemes which the fourth intonation embraces, only one is employed independently. Whence did the idea originate that Chinese is monosyllabic? With the pedantry of the mandarins: sole possessors of the ability to write, they wished to have it thought that the truth of language lay in monosyllables and thus to make the character the real substance of a word; spoken discourse, they said, was a kind of clumsy translation of written language. But it is on the lips of the people who speak it that you discover the truth of a language and what language truly is; if there be inappropriateness it lies in the way the spoken language is transcribed onto paper; Chinese was spoken first, written later; nothing authorizes the belief that it was originally monosyllabic. When the characters were invented each of them was made to correspond to a monosyllabic phoneme and with these signs were built words in which the character was now represented by only one sound; but these words already existed synthetically before an analysis, at once ideological and phonetic, fixed them graphically as a compound of elements. Phoneticization begins obviously not with characters, but with speech and therefore it is not at all impossible.

A much more real difficulty is that, while writing is the same everywhere in China, spoken idiom varies from North to South. In Father Ricci's day the Cantonese understood the Northern language; but with the Manchu emperors, and by way of protest against these foreign usurpers, the use of Mandarin—the Peking dialect—declined in the South. It came back again under the Republic; however there are still schools in the South where Mandarin is neither taught nor yet spoken and the popular tongue there is completely different from the one that is current in the North. One word, designated by the same character in both places, is pronounced *woo* in Peking and *ng* in Canton: the two dialects are more unlike than French and Italian. Our interpreter's name is pronounced *Tsah* in Peking, *Tsay* in Shanghai. Just from Peking to Mukden things become very different: Tsai and Madame Cheng had great trouble understanding the North Chinese and getting through to them. The interdialect attempts at phoneticization tried to skirt this difficulty but led to such complications that it was not possible to give the system a serious try. Specialists are now agreed that there is only one solution left open: to abolish this troublesome diversity, to standardize spoken language. It is Mandarin that has been chosen to be the national tongue, for it is the most widespread; ever since the Sungs and the Yüans Mandarin has been the language of popular literature, the language whose generalized use the Fourth of May intellectuals had stood for. During recent decades it has always been to Mandarin that reference was made in dictionaries when phonetic equivalents were indicated for written signs. Lately, the radio, the cinema, the theater have favored its expansion throughout the country. From now on active and systematic efforts are to be made to spread it in such a way as to unify vocabulary and pronunciation. The idea of national oneness, so important in China today, will be much strengthened thereby. Fifteen years is the estimate for the time it will take to achieve this standardization; thereafter, phoneticization will be feasible. Its vital importance was again stressed by Wu Yu-chang in his official report of March 15, 1955. As an instrument Old Chinese is no longer adequate to the country's needs.

The alphabet which will serve as the basis for romanization was established in the winter of 1956. It contains our own twenty-six letters plus a few extra vowels. For a while they will be printed opposite the old characters, then the latter will be gradually eliminated. The study of "ancient" writing will appear only in the curriculum of the most cultivated strata of the population. Linguists tell me that it is desirable that this higher culture be very widely disseminated for the ancient texts will be undecipherable for those who know phonetic writing only, and since they were cast in ku-wen, alphabetical transcription of them will be impossible: they will have to be translated quite as Latin books are put into English. This is by way of comment, not of objection. In France prior to this century all young people heading for the liberal professions were required to know Latin: why should not a large part of China's intellectual elite learn an ancient language? That elite's growth will be stimulated by the dissemination of culture for which phoneticization will be responsible; one has every right to suppose that a good many more Chinese will know the characters twenty years from now than do today.

The Hong Kong mandarins are disturbed. Calligraphy took a long time to learn, the Nationalist press explains, but in itself it constituted an entire artistic initiation; if once gone, noble values shall be no more. Etiemble, who fancies himself a mandarin too, chimes right in: "Robbed of her characters, China will lose her character."* By means of this skimpy pun he proves that, in his eyes, China is confined to a couple of old books. The truth is that if the reform is exciting stout resistance in anti-Communist circles, it is because the material aim of the reform is to democratize culture and to increase the ranks of the cultivated elite: in defending the cause of the characters the happy few of yesterday were pleading in behalf of their privileges.

One would be wrong to assume that, today, the Chinese are dis-

* Behind the quip sits the axiom to which every "civilized Westerner" wholeheartedly adheres: that, in order to be anyone at all, you must be *different*.

avowing or misappreciating the aesthetic value of their writing. Like the Emperor Ch'ien Lung, Kuo Mo-jo and Mao Tse-tung enjoy tracing inscriptions in their own hands. But, speaking in the name of the people, their attitude is Lusin's: either we ourselves or the characters have to go. The choice has been made.

### *Theater*

The theater has a very special history in China. It was the medium which provided its main means of expression to an illiterate population, and it was the main nucleus about which a rich peasant folklore crystallized. The scholars meanwhile gave it esoteric forms more to their taste. These two theaters were in the time of the Manchus squared off in a veritable cultural "class war"; but it is nevertheless in the sphere of drama that the collaboration between classical literature and popular tradition bore the finest fruits.

The origins of Chinese theater are at once sacred, aristocratic, and plebeian. Dances and pantomime accompanied religious ceremonies in the olden days. The *Shu Ching* cites liturgical ballets in which mythical or historical heroes are evoked. In addition, according to the *Lieh Tzu*, shadow plays and puppet shows have diverted the great and the humble since the earliest times. Shantung bas-reliefs, mural paintings dating from the Han age represent buffoons, jugglers, acrobats, and masked actors as well. Court fools amused princes and emperors; bards sang long stories during feasts. In the time of the Five Dynasties history mentions actors staging comedies and farces; there are allusions, about 550-577 A.D. among the Ts'i in the North, to ballets and military pantomimes, probably influenced by the costumes and music of Central Asia; dances and pantomimes imported from those regions were very much in fashion under the Tangs, an age which saw the first music and dance conservatories established. The actors wore masks or stage paint: for example, drunkards daubed their faces with vermilion. They enacted comedies in dialogue, without music, more or less improvised, and ordinarily satirical in temper. These as yet rudimentary entertainments developed and became more complicated in South China under the Sungs. It was then that the theater, strictly speaking, was born. It grew along two lines. First, the emperors and wealthy mandarins maintained companies in their households; one of the most famous was the Indoors Troupe composed of eunuchs who put on plays within the Imperial Palace's enclosure; they were still in existence in the reign of the late Empress Tzu Hsi. Second, in the countryside, strolling players went about from village to village. Over the centuries each region came to have its own tradition: the style and gesture and costume of the actors, the type of musical accompaniment would vary from one area to the next.

According to official catalogues the literary theater included 280 plays at the time of the Sungs; the Chin repertory listed 680. But none of them has survived. The earliest plays we have date from the Yüan dynasty. They are rigorously ordered works in four acts, sometimes with a prologue; there are nine characters: each, in a brief monologue, would announce to the audience which of the traditional parts he was taking; the influence of the earlier period's sung narrations is still evident: in each act some one of the characters would sing, the others declaiming only; he would sing various airs, but they all had to have the same rhyme scheme. Most of the actors lived in the Peking vicinity, the theater in this area being known as the Northern Theater; when the Mongols conquered China nearly all the actors emigrated to Hangchow and Southern writers came up and took over in their stead: theatrical style changed, so did the musical accompaniment. It was then the custom set in of summarizing the play in a prologue; acts were no longer separated by pauses; dialogue became more literary and now several characters were allowed to sing. With a few variants these rules were observed under the succeeding Ming dynasty. Soon, however, the number of acts ceased to be limited and within each given act rhyme no longer had to be constant. The theater became steadily more refined: by the time it had reached the form known as *K'uen-k'iu* it was meaningful to and attended by hardly anyone but scholars. The Ming tradition continued under the Manchus; plays by now had become works of literature bearing their author's signatures. *The Guitar, The Pavilion of Peonies, The Pavilion of the West, The Palace of Eternal Youth* were among the most celebrated.

Around the year 1600, while the private and the itinerant village troupes kept on, there arose a public theater intended for city dwellers. In order to please a wide audience authors adopted the habit of injecting everyday pai-hua into the classical language; the theater, having become popular in Manchu days, was considered a low medium and scorned by the polite: as we have remarked, it was not included in the lists the clerks drew up of officially recognized literary forms. At this point the plays were composed by the leaders of the troupes or by outstanding actors; they would sometimes consult the help of a scribe, but he would insist upon secrecy: a great share of the repertory is anonymous. In general the authors had stopped composing original works and were borrowing their subjects from the great popular novels, among them *The Romance of the Three Kingdoms* and *All Men Are Brothers*. The wars that ended in the advent of the Manchus brought military dramas into fashion. The librettos of these operas were never considered definitively fixed; each epoch and even each company presented different versions of them to the public. The actors who, not belonging to the lettered class, performed no productive labor, were victims of discrimination; like the sons of butchers, barbers, merchants, their sons were barred from taking the examinations and hence from acceding to the mandarinate.

In the nineteenth century emerged the genre which is called "Peking Opera" or Classical Opera; it absorbed both the *K'uen-k'iu*, inaccessible to the general public, and assorted local operas; and it is primarily in this form that the traditional Chinese theater has come to be known abroad. France became acquainted with it through the performances given in 1955 by the most renowned of the Peking companies, and through the books and articles those performances occasioned.* Peking Opera's characteristics are a certain sort of music, of singing and of delivery, a few props but no scenery, exaggerated and ritualistic make-up, and an entire system of conventions and symbols: a central role is played by movements, especially of the hands, gesture taking its meaning from Buddhist sources. The costumes are usually those the Chinese wore during the Ming period, but stylized, most noticeably so in the white cuffs, sometimes twelve inches long, that are sewn

* See Claude Roy, "*L'Opéra chinois*" and Mayoux, "*Le Théâtre chinois*" in the special issue of *Europe*, August-September 1955.

inside sleeves and used in connection with a great deal of dumb show. Apart from this Peking Opera, there are also local operas in the provinces where style and convention to a greater or less degree diverge from classical patterns.

The bourgeoisie could not be satisfied with these feudal and popular theaters; it had to have *its* theater. The latter came into being in the most modern of the Chinese cities, Shanghai, in 1906 when plays divided into acts and scenes and utilizing scenery were staged for the first time. Wang Chong-cheng, an actor, wrote the first and, as it happened, revolutionary modern drama, *A Cry of Indignation From Black Slaves,* which was played in Western dress and accompanied by Chinese music. Wang next organized a company and put on a play all in dialogue, *The Story of Kia-Yin.* Following some unlucky speculations the owner of the theater had to shut it down; Wang was hired by another director. He adapted *La Dame aux camélias** which was a triumph first in Shanghai, then in Tientsin and Peking. Marguerite Gauthier reminded the Chinese of the "singsong girls" in so many of their own novels and stories, and such was their sympathy for her that Wang, instead of allowing her to die, married her off in happiness to the man she loved. *Uncle Tom's Cabin* and Wilde's *Salomé* also met with success. Wang wrote further revolutionary plays, among them *Human Life Is Cheap Out Here* in which he lashed the regime and corruption of the Manchu mandarins. He was arrested and shot to death in Tientsin in 1910.

Built that same year in Shanghai was China's first European-style theater—one, that is to say, with wings and a stage which instead of projecting into the audience lay in front of it. Classical opera in realistic settings was played there, so also were plays cast in popular idiom; but many conventions of traditional theater were retained, including the soliloquy by which each character introduces himself. Thus it was that *Napoleon,* a play first staged in 1912, opened with these words: "I, Napoleon, Emperor of France, a hero who in all the world has not his match . . ." etc. One of the greatest successes of this period was a drama in twenty-three scenes, *The Captives of Smoke,* which showed the evils of opium and the viciousness of the gangs trafficking in the drug.

* Of Dumas fils.

About that same time the movie industry tried to get its start in China, failed, and its promoter, Cheng Chen-ts'ieou, grouped his artists in The New People's Company which staged love and revolutionary dramas in modern style. This "new theater," dropping a great many of classical opera's conventions, adapted its structure to contemporary subjects.

Peking got its first European theater in 1916. *New Youth* in 1918 devoted a special issue to Ibsen whose influence became preponderant at once. Hu Shih's *The Great Affair* and *Insomnia* by Ngo-Ying Yu-ts'ien derive from *The Doll's House.*

The ideas of the Soviet director Stanislavsky spread in China in 1930. They exerted an influence upon plays that arose in connection with the fight against the Japanese. Theater, the most effective as a vehicle for propaganda, then supplanted other literary forms. Ts'ao-yü, called "the giant of Chinese theater," and Kuo Mo-jo, who had already composed political dramas on historical themes, wrote most of their works in the thirties. Kuo would produce a play in ten days. He spent longer over his tragedy, *Chü Yüan,* whose hero is the old poet of that name. Mao-tun in 1945 presented a comedy of manners, *Sidelights on the Feast of the Dead,* which showed the misery of small artisans being obliterated by capitalism. Amateur groups and the soldiers themselves gave shows in the guerrilla zones. Foreign observers—Jack Belden, Edgar Snow—were amazed by this crude but incisive and convincing art. Ts'ao-yü wrote in 1946,

> The revolution was the cradle of the new theater, and, having to fight for its existence from the very first, it has never forgotten its responsibilities toward its audience. It has continually striven to mirror our living hopes and fears and honestly to reflect the numerous changes, political, social, cultural, which have resulted from Western civilization's contacts with the Old China. Our new theater began propagandistic, avowedly and unashamedly.

Theater remains much attended by the public whose free evenings are as yet little disputed by a cinema still in its infancy. Not counting those in the villages, China now has some 2,000 theatrical companies grouping some 200,000 players; daily theater attendance figures stand at a million. Shanghai has 168 theaters, a total of

8,000 actors; at the end of 1953 one found 20 theaters, 46 troupes —37 of them private—in Peking. The financial situation of the actors is standardized; they all receive a fixed monthly salary, varying according to the category they belong to. Their apprenticeship has been changed and regulated; not very long ago, it was rough on the young actors because mastery of the acrobatic feats of classical opera meant hard work. While there is no official agency whose censorship books must pass, there is one for plays: every six months directors of private or state companies must submit their program and scripts for the Minister of Culture's seal of approval.

Arriving in China, I was particularly eager to find out more about modern Chinese theater; shortly before leaving France I had seen Bertolt Brecht's *Caucasian Chalk Circle* in which the hero is a figure from Chinese folklore, and which is set in Asia: that play may have been what had led me to think that the Chinese, utilizing the resources of classical opera, had, like Brecht, succeeded in inventing an art that stunningly and strangely exceeds realism's ordinary confines. I very quickly became aware, as I talked with Ts'ao-yü and Lao-She, that the Chinese are striving for something altogether different.

To begin with they are not sure just what place traditional opera ought to be allowed; its character is equivocal, a blend of the feudal and the popular. Some argued in 1950 that it should be rejected wholesale. But Chou Yang, faithful to the Yenan precepts, felt "We must hold on to that which is national in it and get rid of the feudal." He reasoned that opera at once reflected the mentality of the ruling class and the people's struggle against their oppressors; he defended the position Soviet artists have taken: religious superstitions must go, popular legend must be kept. In 1951 the decision was reached to ban all pornographic episodes from the stage—the old operas were exceedingly licentious—to rule out scenes of torture, to bar the appearance of women with bound feet; and, having thus sifted it, to encourage the opera.

Soon, however, a more thoroughgoing revision of the repertory became necessary and was executed. There was nothing unethical about doing so—the majority of the plays have no one fixed version —nor anything new: the Manchus eliminated the plays' nationalistic and revolutionary contents and accentuated their feudal character; the new regime is, as it were, carrying on the tradition when it does the same thing but in reverse. Today the fault commonly found with the old theater is that it shows the contradiction in former society but without settling the issues it raises; the altered versions propose positive solutions to the public. For example, the opera entitled *The Butterfly Goblet* relates the following story: an old fisherman sells his daughter to the son of a general; but when he demands payment he is beaten to death. A young man, Tien Yu-chuan, furious at the crime, kills the general's son; thanks to the young woman's complicity he manages to escape, they flee together, fall in love, and he makes her a present of the butterfly goblet. Later, going under a false name, Tien saves the life of the general who gives him his daughter in marriage. His true identity is one day discovered: but such is the general's gratitude to Tien that, far from doing him any harm, he authorizes him to marry the fisherman's daughter. Chinese critics consider that this play, while exposing oppression, comes to terms with it. To set matters straight, the new version has been given a different ending: The fisherman's daughter refuses to marry Tien because he has made peace with the enemy. *Revolt in the Kingdom of Heaven,** which we saw in Paris, has likewise been given a new slant. In Manchu days the play was called *Disturbances in the Kingdom of Heaven* and the Monkey, who incarnated rebellion, was punished, the gods coming off with the victory. The Monkey wins today. Other revisions were much more questionable, and have been condemned: there was for instance the troupe which, playing *The Weaver and the Herdsman,* substituted a tractor for a cow, doves for magpies, and trundled Truman's tanks and planes onto the stage.

The question of reforming the opera returned to the fore again in 1954. The magazine *Theater* published an article, "Further Reforms Necessary in the Art of Peking Opera," by Ma Shao-po, Deputy Director of The Chinese Opera Institute. In November and December of that year The Union of Actors and Dramatists organized four round tables among known authors, actors, and stage directors. There was some sharp quarreling, oral at first, then in a spate of articles. Everybody agreed that some changes were neces-

* Taken from the classical novel, *The Pilgrimage to the West.*

sary: staging ought to be planned, the librettos revised, the acting and musical accompaniment improved. But how? Opinion split into two factions. Lao-She maintained that the art of the opera is a whole certain elements of which cannot be modified analytically. For example, as he told me, realistic scenery clashes with traditional costume: you cannot walk through a real door if you are wearing the great plumed headgear which characterizes generals. Opera then must be considered a special art, unique through its symbolism, and must be represented according to the established rules; next to it one may perfectly well create another and tradition-free theater that answers others of the public's needs. The second faction demanded, to the contrary, that classical opera itself be altered; the introductory soliloquies are outmoded, the minimal scenery is boring, it should be added to, enlivened, varied; the heavy layers of grease paint, turning faces into masks, prohibit any subtle mimicry. Were these drawbacks countered, were décor, lighting, make-up more skillfully handled and the actors given something more realistic to do on stage, the Peking Opera would be in a position to represent not simply hoary old legends but what goes on in people's lives today.

For the time being it is in its classical form the opera is continuing. I did not see many examples of genuine Peking Opera because the major troupes were then off on world tours. However, the first performance I went to was in this style.

I already knew a little about Chinese theater. In San Francisco, the theater resembled what appalled Westerners had always described: a confused situation lasting for hours during which the spectators—all Chinese—came in, went out, got up, sat down; some men munched sandwiches, some women suckled babies. At Peking there used to be plentiful spitting of sunflower and melon seeds; the atmosphere at present in a big Peking theater is quite different. First of all, since the disappearance of a leisure class, the performances have been limited: they start at seven-thirty in the evening and finish before eleven. It became customary in the nineteenth century to present a varied program: usually a farce plus several other plays. The endlessly long dramas once in favor—such as *The White Snake*—are given piecemeal. The public pays attention, is silent, sits still, and manifests its reactions measuredly. That evening there were a good many foreign delegates sitting in the front rows of the orchestra: Spaniards and Portuguese from the Irkutsk settlement, Danes, Russians, Hindus. As soon as the curtain went up the interpreters all lowered their voices to a whisper; but the whispering went on and I admire the Chinese for their graciousness in putting up with this disturbance.

We began with a scene from *The White Snake.* Next came a Hupeh opera: a short comedy of manners which made me think of faraway Molière farces. Here we have old Ma To: since betrothing his daughter to a poor student he has struck it rich and wishes to break the engagement. A valet, Ko Ma, who happens to be the young man's cousin, employs assorted stratagems to rescue his relative; Ko Ma is a kind of Scapin, but the psychological lever he counts on to make his schemes work is specifically Chinese: the wealthier a man is, the greater the care he must take to "keep face." For fear of losing it, Ma To is maneuvered into inviting the student to supper, lending him elegant clothes, and, one thing leading to another, he ends up obliged to consent to the match. The public around me laughs heartily; but, unable to understand what is being said—and the play leans on verbal dexterities—my feelings are lukewarm.

The second part of the program is a mock-heroic drama and I like it better. The play is drawn from a novel, an ancient one but with an appeal to present-day taste. The hero of this adventure is a kind of Falstaff, a guzzler and vociferous but loyal and brave, who belongs to an army of partisans entrenched in the mountains and running out of provisions. He offers to go down to the plain in search of food; the captain agrees but makes the doughty fellow swear not to drink a drop of wine; while he is gaily making his way down the slope a drama is taking place in the village below: the feudal overlord covets the innkeeper's ravishing daughter; aided by his myrmidons, he, posing as the partisans' chieftain in order to divert suspicion, carries the girl off by main force while the hapless father looks on. It is then that, tears in his eyes and curses in his mouth, the innkeeper greets his friend the soldier; the latter at first refuses to believe that his commander is the author of the villainy; then, convinced, by way of reprisal he drinks a few bowls of wine and sets off for headquarters, determined to kill the miscreant and brandishing his hunting knife. Of this he is relieved by his comrades upon his arrival in their midst. He bares his grievances. To exonerate himself the captain accompanies him back to the village. The innkeeper realizes that he has been deceived: it is the owner who has done the thing. Several of his comrades at his side, the soldier goes off to kill the tyrant. Proof is once again given that the partisans are sincere friends of the people and never commit either pillage or rape. Conscience-stricken to have doubted thereof, the hero falls at the captain's feet and begs to die; the captain scolds him mildly, exhorts him to mend his ways and faults: a too quick temper, thoughtlessness, and overfondness for drink; this comprehensive criticism once delivered, he forgives him.

Despite numerous allusions this play at no moment founders into preaching; comic, poetic, dramatic, it holds together well and held me breathless from beginning to end. The role of the captain was taken by a woman. The old classical opera tradition required all the actors to be men; that convention has been abolished but characters are often enacted by persons of a different sex. It seemed to me that the play could have been better cast: next to his robust soldiers, to his powerfully built lieutenants, this lady captain was too small, too slender, he lacked the martial bearing one would have preferred. "Why did they pick a woman for the part?" I asked Tsai. "Because it's harder to play a man's role when you're a woman," he replied. Some Italian delegates having confessed a similar surprise, they were provided with another explanation: the partisan leader is a political leader, he overshadows his companions by dint of intelligence, not of physical strength. There is a distinction; it is stressed by giving the role to a woman. At any rate, what is striking here is the deliberate unrealism. There is indeed an analogy between the Peking Opera and the art of Brecht: the Chinese seek to obtain a similar effect of "distance."*

* Bertolt Brecht expressed the idea in a series of essays and observed it in directing his Berliner Ensemble. Conceiving of a play, not as *the thing*, but as a *play*, distinguishing between what happens on stage and what happens in life, between the ideal and the real, he wished, not to have his actors "lose themselves" *in* their parts, but to enact them critically, at a "distance" from them and as it were *to incarnate a criticism of the situation being dramatized*. Thereby —and through extreme simplicity of accessories, scenery, props, costume, through popular ballads and popular speech—he wished to present a naked situation, and to encourage his audience, not to watch the spectacle passively

They perhaps also have a liking for virtuosity. I notice that when the play ends there is little applause from the audience; but during the performance, a sigh, a bit of mimicry, a clever gesture on stage will cause a stir of admiration in the audience. The real theater-lovers know almost all the repertory by heart; their chief interest is in the subtleties of interpretation, they wait for certain passages as connoisseurs of Italian opera used to wait for the top note of a famous tenor. "You have to know all about it," said Tsai, "otherwise it's not very interesting. That's why we younger people prefer the cinema." Only rarely do his friends go to the theater, he adds, and admits that he finds it on the tedious side.

This avowal perplexed me. In the debate over classical opera I incline to think Lao-She is right. There is a scene where the White Snake plucks the magical herb which will save her husband's life; I have seen it interpreted in two manners. In the classical style it was exceedingly fine. The modern version utilized built and painted scenery, the guardians of the herb had almost no make-up on; the music, showing a strong Western influence, leaned toward melody to the detriment of rhythm—one had the feeling of being at a pops concert. By letting classical conventions—which are aesthetically motivated—go by the board, the acting had gained nothing in verisimilitude or persuasiveness—rather, it drooped into academism.

However, I think of what Tsai said: "You have to know what it's all about." Jealously preserving its purity, is not opera in danger of becoming an archaic curiosity of interest to no one except an initiated few? Its fate is far from having been decided, and depends less upon the initiative of producers than upon the public's cultural evolution.

It is a certainty, however, that, alongside classical opera, the very greatest effort is being made to develop local operas of a more openly popular character, because they were never taken over by the ruling class, which indeed upon numerous occasions forbade their public showing in Peking, Shanghai, and the other great urban centers. Over one hundred varieties of them have been

---

or to become "absorbed" *in* it, but actively and from a distance to look *at* and hence to criticize the drama in order to see the situation: the situation of workers, peasants, and soldiers. (Translator's note)

enumerated. A national festival took place at Peking in 1952, the Szechwan and Shanghai operas (called Shao-ching) having a particular success. During a second festival (in 1954) classical operas were presented but so also were chin chiang operas from Shensi Province, ping chou and chou chou plays; the latter genre is only four years old, but ping chou derives from *The Lotus Tales* which, in Manchu days, Shantung peasants used to sing to the accompaniment of bamboo castanets, and which spread through all of northern China. These duets developed into plays involving numerous actors. When they made their first appearance in Peking some fifty years ago the old theater-lovers were horrified, considering ping chou provincial and vulgar. As it was only too willing to treat contemporary problems, it was outlawed by the Kuomintang; today it has become one of the Chinese theater's most living and vigorous forms.

I saw a good many "local" operas. The first I went to was played in a little theater in Peking's Chinese City; the audience that evening was made up of members of national minorities probably belonging to some delegation groups, for buses were parked waiting for them on a near-by avenue. It was there that I made an acquaintance with the long, belted robes of bright silk the Mongols wear, the big fur hats of the Tibetans, the Uzbeks' squarish tuques. Their faces were of an astonishing diversity: broad, powerful Tartar faces with high cheekbones, Semitic faces adorned with long wispy beards, fine, delicately featured Southeast Asian faces where the yellow race's characteristic traits are only faintly evident. The play we were watching had been taken from a very popular legend in North China; the style of the performance differed considerably from the classical manner. There were very attractive settings, new ones for each scene; make-up was no heavier than in the West; the style of acting was relatively realistic; the music stronger on melody, its pathos less emphatic than in classical opera: the over-all impression given was much more that of opera such as we have it; speeches alternated with singing. The heroes wore Korean costumes; the story was a melodramatic one of love, the acting and the beauty of the songs succeeded in rendering it moving.

In another, rather poor Chinese City theater I saw a local version of a play that is frequently interpreted in the classical manner:

*The Weaver and the Herdsman.* These two stars, brought together in the firmament only once each year, on the seventh night of the seventh month, symbolize for the Chinese the two sexes which traditional taboos once kept apart: the woman who spins and weaves indoors, the man who toils out in the fields. During the night when the astral couple conjoins woman were wont to float figurines of infants upon the surface of ponds so as to obtain many and felicitous pregnancies of the Weaver. Flower and fruit offerings were made to her; it is common to find her image painted on the walls of funerary vaults. In her an ideal of feminine purity and industrious life was venerated. Legend has it that the two lovers were once servants to the celestial queen; mindful only of their love for each other they dropped a precious cup of jade which broke —it was during a feast the queen was giving for the gods. The irate goddess exiled the Weaver into a region midway between Heaven and Earth and condemned her to weave clouds perpetually; the young swain became a poor herdsman on Earth, a single cow was all he had. But it turned out that this cow was a reincarnated god, he too undergoing punishment inflicted by the Queen of Heaven, for he had incurred her wrath by siding with the two lovers. He led the Herdsman to the edge of the Celestial River one evening when the Weaver was bathing there with her companions, and counseled the Herdsman to steal his beloved's clothing: thus was she obliged to wed the Herdsman whom she fell in love with straightway. They had two children and were very happy: the Weaver earned much money from the wonderful stuffs she wove. Her companions safeguarded her happiness by fashioning Heaven's clouds in her stead. A year passed by and then the fraud came to the notice of the queen: she dispatched warriors and had the Weaver fetched back into Heaven. The despairing Herdsman set out in search of his wife, bearing his two children lying in each of two baskets at the ends of a bamboo shoulder pole. But he was unable to cross the river; and the two would have remained separated forever had not magpies taken pity on them: those birds fought the sentinels of Heaven and managed to build a bridge over the river; and the queen consented to allow the Weaver and the Herdsman to meet together once each year.

The Shao-ching is the most interesting of the local operas. Forty years ago it was a purely rural form of opera found in the Chekiang countryside only. Its songs were based on peasant ballads and tunes; the orchestra was often reduced to a single musician in charge of a drum and bamboo castanets. For actors it had the peasants themselves and men assumed all the roles. From the back country this popular entertainment reached into the cities, even took hold in Shanghai; in 1923 a company of actresses began to specialize in Shao-ching theater and now it is performed exclusively by women. During the war against Japan it spread into all the free zones and with success. It has further flourished since the Liberation. In 1953 a team of musicians went to Chenghsien, the Chekiang region whence the form originates, in search of old melodies. Shao-ching's style lies halfway between the conventions of classical opera and realism. It involves a liberal but natural use of make-up, actors thus being able to vary their facial expressions; and scenery and lighting are used. *Les Amoureux*, the filmed opera which was shown in Paris, belongs to the Shao-ching variety.

What interested me most, as I say, is the way—the several ways—in which Chinese theater has been adapted to modern themes. During the Sino-Japanese War original plays were staged and their musical accompaniments arranged in a Western style; as, for example, the most widely renowned of the contemporary Chinese operas, *The White-Haired Girl*. These new works were extremely successful and composers and librettists have done a great many more of them since the Liberation. During my second stay in Peking I saw *The Song of the Steppes*, much influenced by the great Russian operas; the scenery and costumes had the splendor of *Boris Godunov* and *Prince Igor*; while the music was reminiscent of *Madame Butterfly*, although certain very engaging arias had been derived from Tibetan folk songs.

The story does, as a matter of fact, take place in Tibet, on the eve of the Kuomintang's collapse. To keep their grip on the country the reactionaries try to stir two powerful tribes into mutual strife; a young man belonging to one of them and a girl who belongs to the other, both in love, vainly attempt to forestall war. Chinese theater often sets up an immediate relationship between two people's desire to have one another and the revolution necessary if that desire is to be fulfilled; so it is that here their love reveals the absurdity of fratricidal struggles. I add parenthetically that in contradistinction to the classical tradition—which keeps classical lovers, in the throes of passion, at arm's length—the amorous pair in the *Song of the Steppes* clasp each other with the fervor Western operas ascribe to Romeo and Juliet. Comes the Red Army; one of its officers is none other than the heroine's brother—a coincidence not so unlikely since preferably native-born officers would be sent to liberate a national minority region—his clever management of the situation re-establishes harmony between the tribes. The traitorous troublemaker is felled, everybody toasts peace, and the lovers marry. This happy ending symbolized the one that brought an end to the wranglings between the Dalai Lama and the Panchen Lama, reconciled by the new importance that is attached to the question of national minorities, especially to that of Tibet.

An operatic spectacle on the grand scale like *The Song of the Steppes* is a rare thing in Chinese theaters. Much more common and well adapted to the treatment of current topics is the ping chou. One of its great successes is *The Little Son-in-Law* where the story is that of child betrothal. A girl is sold as a daughter-in-law to a family whose son is barely eleven years old. On the wedding night the youthful husband does no better than wet his bed. Thanks to the Marriage Act the heroine obtains a divorce and marries the man she loves. Over 300,000 people have seen this play.

A recent development, chou chou is related to operetta and to stage comedy; played in this style was *The Lady Delegate* which won the 1953 prize for one-act plays and which has to do with the problem of the emancipation of women. The contest had been started in order to encourage the composition of short comedies; 667 entries were submitted: 40 per cent of them dealt with life in the country, 19 per cent with city life, 17 per cent with the situation of workers, 6 per cent with that of soldiers, 0.5 per cent concerned minority groups, the rest treated various other subjects. And only one out of thirty plays came from a professional writer.

Long or short, many plays are enacted without music. They belong properly to "spoken theater" in which as in most Western dramas the dialogue is most important. Here, everything—scenery, staging, acting—aims at one quality only: realism. I saw several such plays. The most interesting one was the epic *Across Plains and Over Mountains*. Numerous tableaux retrace the famous Long March which in 1934 took the Red Army from Kiangsi to Shensi. The play's intention was of course didactic and improving, but it was so well done that even the "positive hero" made one willingly suspend disbelief. The mere evocation of that tremendous adventure contributed to the richness of the play: it fired the imagination, which is something in itself. On the other hand, the actual story of Liu Lu-han, the peasant girl who helped the guerrillas and paid for it with her life, struck me as the most unfortunate of melodramas.

The Chinese are the first to admit that despite the aid contributed by seasoned writers, despite the new playwrights who have appeared, the repertory is, in view of the demands of the public, quantitatively insufficient and in quality far short of what it ought to be. When, beforehand, I imagined a theater which, applying the ancient opera's aesthetics to contemporary themes, would move beyond realism, I was much mistaken. For the moment old and modern forms are being juxtaposed; there is also a mingling of different styles; but as yet no one has anywhere hit upon the right creative synthesis a truly new art would require. I was perhaps disappointed; but, after all, that dream of mine was somewhat wishful thinking. Spoken theater is, in China, a recent conquest; it has grown too fast and will find itself in due time. The Chinese directors have not yet mastered the realist aesthetics such as that which triumphs upon certain stages in the USSR—which is precisely what enables the Russians to depart from realism now and then. Chinese directors will go on exploring in this direction for a while yet. It is not until you have reached a point that you can move beyond it: one ought to bear this much in mind if one is to come to sane conclusions in judging China's cultural achievements. When once the Chinese have overtaken the West they will then be able to try to go further. A great tradition, excellent actors, a devoted public* warrant the guess that the coexistence of classical opera and spoken theater will in time prove fertile.

* It was only in connection with classical opera that Tsai's feelings were lukewarm. When a new play is put on in Peking one must reserve seats days in advance. And sometimes each family is allowed only a limited number of seats.

### *The Plastic Arts*

I saw more than one delegate come back downcast after a visit to the Institute of Fine Arts. What with the magnificent pictorial tradition China has behind her, must she fall in line behind Gerasimov* today? But traditions are sometimes more burdensome than helpful. The beauty of her classical opera has not enabled China to go straight into the invention of a modern theater. The situation is similar concerning painting.

In this area too the Chinese are exceedingly eager to make the public acquainted with the splendors of the past. One of the greatest and most ancient treasures of Chinese civilization is the Tunhwang frescoes. In large format and small, every bookshop—even the one downstairs in my hotel—sells reproductions of them in series of post cards, scrolls, or individual prints. Tunhwang, a western frontier outpost on the way to the Tarim country and Turkestan, was the point where the Silk Route's northern and southern branches forked and through which Central Asian influences and Greco-Buddhist traditions seeped eastward into China. Numerous eroded cliffs in Central Asia were turned into Buddhist grottoes, all modeled after those that one finds in Afghanistan's Bamian escarpment. In the year 366 A.D. similar grottoes were hollowed out nine miles away from Tunhwang; destroyed, then remade about 453 A.D., they were filled with statues and their walls and ceilings covered with paintings. The artistic value of these works is not extraordinary but they accumulate marks of every succeeding epoch of civilization. In the most ancient grottoes the pure Indian style prevails; then the paintings become progressively more Chinese: under the Tangs the tendency of Chinese art and literature was toward the epic and Buddhist tradition was modified in that direction. It is then one sees the legendary figures emerge, figures which, having been perpetuated over the centuries, yet animate the temples, inspire the "New Year pictures" the peasants paste upon the doors of their houses, and come to life in the operas: bearded, helmeted, sword in hand, and wild of mien, the gods be-

* Alexander Gerasimov: contemporary Soviet painter and the most notorious exponent of the Stalinist school of socialist realism. (Translator's note)

come redoubtable warriors. Hindu themes persist, however. On the grotto ceilings amid billowing draperies there swarm those apsaras which decorated the lanterns and the beds at the Peking Hotel. On the cave walls broad landscapes unfurl; knights ride in fairyland hills where wild animals dwell. Many frescoes show the Amitabha or "Paradise of the West," bowers of bliss which in part acknowledge Indian conventions; but other, episodic scenes evoke everyday life in ancient China: men hunt, plow, here are houses, carts, horses. For historians these paintings constitute a remarkable documentation.

At the end of my stay there was a big exhibit of Tunhwang sculpture and paintings at the Imperial Palace; I went to it, and was not pleased. My irritation stemmed from a regret that instead of copies of doubtful value they had not shown large-scale and accurate photographic reproductions. But my reaction was that of someone from a wealthy country, and highly unfair. The Chinese do not have photographic materiel; the general dearth of equipment is manifest also in the cultural sphere and here too ingenuity must supply the lack poverty creates. A team of draftsmen was sent out to make the most exact copies possible of the Tunhwang frescoes, and here on public display are the results. Looking at them one cannot rightly tell the dimensions of the originals, nor whether the drawings or colors are true; but one pauses a moment when one realizes that notwithstanding the absence of appropriate means the regime is still sparing no efforts to familiarize the people with their national heritage.

The Imperial Museum's collections of paintings are not often displayed: fragile silk ill withstands sunlight, the pictures are up for only a few weeks each year. Great emphasis is however being given to the art of reproduction. Copies of paintings by Chi Pai-shih, by Jupeon, and of old masterpieces appeared in every well-to-do household I visited. Brocaded silk-bound albums contain series of reproductions of a given painter's work or of a period; the Chinese buy a great many of them. The printing process used is chromoxylography which derives originally from the black-and-white woodcut that dates back over a thousand years. The Chinese had invented it by 868 A.D., i.e., four hundred and fifty years before the earliest engraving on wood appeared in Europe. The technique developed under the Yüans and the Mings and by the end of the sixteenth century color prints were common throughout much of China. It was used especially for decorating letter paper and also the sheets upon which poets drew their verses. At the close of the Manchu dynasty Peking had at least fifteen shops specializing in the sale of these prints. The most famous one was the Studio of the Pine and the Bamboo established some two hundred years ago; after a brief eclipse about 1900 the Studio revived again and in 1952 became a state enterprise under the name of the Studio of Abounding Prosperity.

With Lusin as its adviser the Studio began, twenty years ago, to reproduce many works by contemporary artists. The prints appear either in rolls or in bound folios. Those being manufactured at present, the director of the Studio told me the day I visited it, are larger than in the past and far more perfect. Neither photo-engraving nor any other mechanical process gives such exact results. It is possible to use the same paper, the same ink, the same coloring materials the artist employed; the technique has been refined to the point where only an expert can distinguish the copy from the original.

In the first workroom men and women seated behind desks are closely scanning pictures laid out before them. These are the copyists, and the success of the operation depends largely upon them. They must break down the original picture into various color zones; working with tracing paper they outline the green leaves, stems, grass; on another sheet they pick up details that show in pink; and so on. Each tracing sheet is glued on a wooden block which is then chiseled as indicated in the design. Thus a dozen or even fifteen blocks are sometimes used for certain flower pictures. This analytic copying may be done so the picture is the original size, or it may be made larger or smaller by use of a blown-up or reduced photograph of the original.

The second operation is the printing. The Chinese aquarellist's own paints are used: mineral pigments mixed with a certain proportion of a water-solvent peach-tree resin; paper is also carefully selected to match the exact sort the artist used. Each wooden block—the green block, the pink block, etc.—is "inked" with brushed-on water color. The paper is then applied to the block and squeegeed with a cloth roller; successive applications to each of the blocks are made in such manner that the colors left on the paper reconstitute the original picture. The work is clearly very tricky, requiring the most precise gauging if blots and blurred edges are to be avoided. The order in which the colors are applied is, it seems, of key importance: some must be allowed to dry before proceeding to the next, others must still be wet. Depending upon whether the original was painted with this or that sort of brush, the printing pigment is thinned with more or less water and the pressure used in rubbing is firmer or lighter. The finer gradations of color can be laid in by brush, and the sheet and blocks so handled as to get the original's faintest nuances.

The Museum of Peking showed its paintings on about the first of October. Combining considerations of economy with respect for their past, the Chinese have not constructed exhibition halls, they use the Imperial Palace pavilions. The light in them was poor, lattices stretched with rice paper partially masking the windows. There were no very ancient paintings. Tang era writers were already deploring the loss of high period works destroyed in the course of fires or wars; even of Tang paintings there is not much left. The oldest I saw dated from the Sung dynasty. They were long horizontal rolls of silk presented flat under glass: one of them measured a good twelve yards in length. They represented panoramas to be viewed from right to left; looking at them is truly to take a trip: the eye voyages. It stops in a village, lingers by the banks of a stream, contemplates personages as tiny as those in Breughel's *Tower of Babel* and painted with no less vitality and truth. The realism of these old works often reminds one of Holland and Flanders. Here is a road, upon it are carts, people afoot, mules, porters; outside the walls of a town men are drinking around tables in taverns; we enter the gate, cross a bridge; this is a world very much one of men. I was particularly taken by a landscape in stinging blues and greens done by a young painter who died at twenty. The lyricism of its tones was specifically Chinese; it did not prevent the drawing from being realistic: those were true skiffs, true houses, true men dwelling in that countryside of enchanted color. Horses appear in many paintings: the lands of Central Asia sent entire herds of them as tribute to the Emperor;

and Ming Huang is said to have had more than forty thousand horses some of which were trained to perform circus stunts. Many were the painters who specialized in horses; there was, for example, Ts'ao Pa of whom the poet Tu Fu sang, and Ts'ao's pupil Han Kan to whom the majority of horse portraits are erroneously attributed.

Realism faded out swiftly. The picture continued to follow panoramic lines; but instead of worldly goings-on, the painter sought to express the metaphysical bias of his times. One no longer enters into a landscape, one glides above it; this is the Taoist's cosmological revery, the game of void simulacra into which the Buddhist universe melts. The men, the water, the mountains older painters strove to render as they are now acquire symbolic meaning and contour. Mist declares the unreality of being; hills and streams stand for the bone structure and arteries of this great universal organism. Whence the odd result that China, this country of plains, this continental land unaware of the sea, becomes, in the prints, a China ribbed with mountains and laced with rivers. Men cease to be presented for what they are, but as lost in the womb of nature that transcends mankind; here is a figure dreaming at the foot of a tree, there another straying small by a river: little, lonely men, insignificant and expiring. With the passing ages the pictures become ever more literary. One of the curious things about Chinese art is that the same instrument—the brush—served for both writing and painting; calligraphy was as much appreciated as drawing; it penetrated into the picture, and long poems often comment the landscape whose features are no more than mere signs. The greater share of the exhibit was taken up by Ming and Ch'ing period works by now divested of all trace of originality: the same imitations recur in showcase after showcase.

I confess that save for the foremost works, this art, while often pleasant to look at, strikes me as without any depth. It suffers from the leanness of Chinese religion and mythology. Christianity, with its incarnated and murdered God, with its Virgin Mother, its men and women saints, beckons the artist to exalt, by guising them as sacred, the human figure and every human drama; the world of Christian art pivots around the crucial themes of birth and pain, death and joy; and for a long period its adepts were men sprung from the people and who spoke to the people. Afterward technical innovations made possible by painting in oils led to a great outpouring of richly meaningful achievements. In China, however, the art of the brush—whether it were a question of painting or of calligraphy—was confined to literate and genteel practitioners and as a consequence art was, barring rare exceptions, nothing but a mandarin pastime; very often, art was made to imperial order and the emperors themselves did not disdain to dabble in it. That is why art turned academic so rapidly, endlessly chewing over the same subject matter, and concerning itself solely with formal perfection. Compared to Western painting the meaning-content of Chinese pictures appears slender, their plastic quality monotonous. And after a brief early rush of creativity stretch out long centuries of boredom which spawned craftsmen who were nothing more than imitators.

If one takes Chinese painting's long period of stagnation into account one will be less harsh in one's judgment of its present efforts. The Chinese lavish an at once official and sincere admiration upon the old painter Chi Pai-shih whom they call, improperly in my view, the Chinese Matisse; they rate highly the painter Jupeon who died a few years ago and who had specialized in paintings of horses. But it is self-evident that the young painters cannot limit themselves to imitating these heirs of an ancient tradition who, talented though they were, themselves often did no more than imitate other several-centuries-old imitations. At the Imperial Palace showing I do not know how many times I saw Chi Pai-shih's shrimps and crabs, quite unchanged today after centuries of identical repetition. Things have very definitely got to take an-another tack. Painters are now moving in two directions. Some are studying oil techniques and are being guided by Soviet socialist realism. Others are trying simultaneously to keep within Chinese tradition and to achieve new expression. "We're still painting with the traditional brush on absorbent paper, using line to render form and contour to suggest depth," one of them explained. "But we are also introducing elements of modern technique: light and shadow, perspective, a greater range of color. Color, though, is very hard to get by this approach."

The search for a conciliation wedding the allusive art of Old

China with realism sometimes nets happy results: certain new landscapes have the freshness of a Dufy. Oil painting, on the other hand, has so far—to my knowledge—produced nothing but large-scale ugliness. But, again, I must repeat: there is no getting past realism until realism is safely tucked away under one's belt. Once the Chinese have mastered oil techniques, once they have acquired the craftsmanship necessary to realize their new ambitions, then properly aesthetic problems can be posed and tackled. Until then one has no cause to compare past splendors to present fumblings. The past was rich—for a brief moment only. Then, overly fascinated by antique wonders, artists ended up unable to do other than repeat them in an ever more minor key. The newness of the world at hand requires a renovation of art; charming pictures of flowers and birds such as certain Chinese are still painting is to mark time in a blind alley: there must be a clean break with the past even if that means having to undergo a period of disarray and failure.

### *The Handicrafts*

The government is actively encouraging the crafts. Lacquerwork, cloisonné objects, carved jades, brocaded silks are exposed under official auspices; big counters are given over to them in the state stores and numerous private shops deal in them; reviews and brochures advertise their qualities to foreign buyers. Technically most of these articles are remarkable; many can be praised for their beauty; that of the silk goods, for example, is manifest. But insofar as they attempt to preserve folk art, they fail. Save for the silhouettes used in shadow theaters, bits of cutout parchment painted after ancient models, nearly everything I saw in this general category was dreadful. Clay figurines have lost all their charm in becoming realistic; silk tapestries, instead of suggesting landscapes, all too often feature the visage of Karl Marx or allegorize the friendship uniting Peking to Moscow. Paper cutouts and woodcarvings treat edifying themes. The lovely New Year pictures splashed with helmeted demons in bold colors have yielded to chromotypes in which frolic unduly pink children.

Is Communism to be made responsible for this decline? Certainly not. I remarked the same degeneration in the handicraft schools opened in Africa by colonists who styled themselves friends of native art. Whether the regime be capitalistic, colonialist, or socialist, it is the notion of a "guided folk art" which is self-contradictory. What confers its interest and value upon a work of popular art is that the group which is represents therein of its own volition and as it were unconsciously expresses its particularity; in China cultural segregation gave rise to a rich folklore which, necessarily, the universalization of culture is destroying; attempts are being made to keep its vestiges alive; but a directed artisan class no longer expresses the masses, it simply manifests the abstract idea of it that exists in the directors' heads; nothing is more academic than the artificial imitation of naive spontaneity. If the Chinese refuse to admit that the decadence of their popular art is inevitable, the real reason for this is economic: 80 per cent of the objects purchased by the peasants are made by hand: you ascribe a value to what you are obliged to use. But when light industry has been developed industrial art will have to replace handicraft, it alone being capable of producing furnishings and utensils suitable to an industrialized society. Lenin said that one must not disdain borrowing whatever of worth capitalism possesses and in June 1956 the Chinese intellectuals reaffirmed that axiom; it applies here: industrial art, geared to a socialist society, will become socialist. Devotees of the past will not be pleased to see handmade objects relegated to museums; however, expressing a moment in the people's history, those objects are meaningful only as commentaries upon it. Mass-produced, denying the real thrust of history, they balk the present and lie about the past. The fact that pre-Colombian art is not perpetuated in New York City ateliers never wrung a tear from me; nor will I shed one when Peking has forgotten Sung cloisonné and Ming brocade.

### *Chinese Medicine*

One can hardly expect, of course, as one turns to consider the sciences, to come upon any national tradition. And yet however there is such a thing in one domain: that of medicine. Walking about Peking you quickly notice that there are two sorts of pharmacies: in one they sell Western drugs, in the other traditional remedies. In the big children's hospital that had just been inaugurated these two pharmaceutical schools were represented, very curiously, by adjoining dispensaries: one looked exactly like one of our own modern laboratories, in the other there were huge cupboards with drawers full of plants and, as I entered, a doctor was in the midst of grinding up a mixture of dessicated herbs intended for a youngster who had been vomiting blood. Chiang Kai-shek had sought to impose the exclusive use of Western medicine, imported into Canton and then into Shanghai after the Opium War; the Chinese had begun to take an interest in it back in 1867 when the use of ether as an anesthetic had opened up new possibilities in surgery; however, in that it came from the West, people in general had viewed it with suspicion. At the turn of the century the bourgeois revolution advocated its dissemination. Chiang even went so far as to declare traditional medicine illegal; following a protest from three hundred Nanking doctors he had to rescind his proclamation, but he did so with reluctance. Taking the opposite approach, the present regime is patronizing this science qualified as "Chinese" to distinguish it from the modern world-wide form of medicine.

The importance the Chinese accorded to the study of the human body, their idea of the interdependence of the organism and the world, their quest for a material immortality account for the remarkable advances that Chinese medicine registered a good thousand years ago. Its two fundamentals were *chien* (acupuncture) and *chiu* (cautery). Cauterization was done with a hot iron and also by burning an amount of moxa (a soft woolly mass prepared from the leaf of *Artemisia moxa*, or Chinese wormwood) over the ailing part of the body in such a way that the combustion, without affecting the skin, would stimulate the nerves. In the course of the centuries several kinds of combustibles were employed: the leaves of another plant—ai—were dried, rolled into a little cone roughly half the size of a prune pit; the base of the cone was set upon the body, the tip was ignited; today ai is used in sticks of the thickness of a cigarette.

One finds these medications described in a compilation that was made around 200 B.C. In 1023 A.D. under the Sungs, a treatise was drawn up, explaining, through references to a bronze dummy of the human body, in just what places chien chiu could be put to rewarding use: seven hundred individual points are cited, as are the effects the treatment will produce when applied to each of them. In the thirteenth century similar bronze models were fashioned, riddled with little perforations corresponding to the spots where acupuncture was to be performed; these figures were given a thin coating of opaque wax and students practiced finding the exact place where the pin was to be inserted. There were five kinds of pins listed under three categories according to their several uses: to scratch the skin, to pierce it, to strike through to the nerve. Needles of a silver-steel alloy are now manufactured, they are made in a wide variety of shapes and run in length from three-eighths of an inch to about three inches and a half.

Among the outstanding discoveries of ancient Chinese medicine we must mention the one, made in the fifth century B.C., whereby the pulse came to be used as an element in diagnosis; also, under the Hans, the use of anesthetic permitting major abdominal operations; the concept of preventive medicine; of the body's automatic adjustment to its environmental conditions; hydrotherapy; the gymnastics used in "Chinese boxing"; the cure of skin infections by means of mercury and sulfur. Between the years 600 and 1000 A.D. China possessed the world's most advanced medical center. The Imperial Institute of Medicine was created in 700 A.D., or two hundred years before the Italian Salerno School. The first hospitals were in existence by 501 A.D. Buddhists and Taoists vied in the art of healing the sick.

The most extraordinary aspect of this medicine was its pharmacopoeias. Catalogues of remedies, prescriptions, and treatments succeeded one another for two thousand years. From among the medications current under the Hans—whose dynasty straddled the beginning of the Christian Era—there are some eighty in use today. The sixteenth century brought the publication of *The Compendium of Medicine* which lists 1,892 remedies upon which its approximately 10,000 prescriptions are based. Smallpox vaccination was discovered in that period. And then with the coming of the Manchus progress halted. But the knowledge that had already been amassed over the centuries was considerable.

Directly after the Liberation, in 1950, the First National Conference on Public Health studied the problems connected with putting that knowledge to the best advantage. The value of traditional medicine was officially recognized. The Medical Association was opened to "Chinese" doctors; their private practice was authorized, the qualification "Doctor of Chinese Medicine" being inscribed on their name plate; certain hospitals have been placed under their exclusive supervision, as have, of course, the acupuncture clinics! in other establishments they collaborate with the "Westerners."* There is a national academy where research is undertaken along the "traditional" line and in the Ministry of Public Health a Chinese division has been created. An experimental institute for the study of acupuncture and moxibustion (moxa cautery) has been founded also, one of its purposes being to arrive at theoretical bases for these systems. Up until now the institute has built its conclusions around Pavlov's theories: by stimulating the nerves one may, in certain parts of the human body, provoke reactions triggering reflexes which act upon the central nervous system; which is why the point where the pin or the burning is applied can sometimes be a good distance away from the regions affected by the illness: certain headaches are treated by inducing nervous excitation in the big toe, etc.

Acupuncture yields good results in the correction of the motor and digestive disorders. But it is above all the value of traditional pharmacology that recent tests have confirmed. Over the period 1951-1954, 9,513 patients—suffering from a total of more than two hundred ailments—were treated according to traditional method: 90 per cent of the cases improved, 40 per cent of the patients were cured. Particularly good results were obtained with cases involving nervous, locomotive, and digestive troubles; but also with cases of rheumatism, neuralgia, malaria, chorea, hypertension, and certain forms of eczema and tuberculosis.

In June 1957 Chinese medicine registered a veritable triumph; the press announced that out of thirty-seven dysentery cases treated by a two-thousand-year-old formula (followed exactly, save for a slight variation of the doses prescribed) there had been thirty-seven complete recoveries. Chinese remedies often cure gastro-

* I.e., Chinese practitioners of Western medicine.

intestinal ailments which Western medicine is unable to overcome. They have also managed to cure encephalitis. Western medicine is particularly helpess before type B encephalitis, a grave illness provoked by a virus carried by a certain mosquito. However, the *Treatise on Epidemics* by Wu Yu-sing published in 1642 during the Ming dynasty and A *Clinical Analysis of Febrile Maladies* published in 1813 by Wu Tang, summarizing the age-old experience of Chinese doctors, contain effective remedies against encephalitis. Fifty-four cases of it were treated in 1954-1955, there were fifty-one cures. The principal ingredients employed are gypsum, rhinoceros horn and buckhorn, scorpion, centipede, cinnamon bark, ginseng, and medicinal asphodel. Many Occidental remedies, moreover, are derived from plants utilized in Chinese medicine. The *Sarpagan* sold in France to combat hypertension is compounded from herbs gathered in the Tibetan uplands. Our santonine is an alkaloid used in pharmacy and extracted from moxa. The chief difference is that in their Chinese form remedies are administered in copious doses: the patient swallows bowls of broth instead of gulping down a pill. As a consequence the Western doctor practicing in a back-country region where the inhabitants are accustomed to traditional medicine only will have great trouble persuading his patients to employ with moderation the remedies he prescribes: in the belief that a single aspirin tablet cannot produce any effect whatever, the ailing individual will consume the whole bottle all at once. The Society of Pharmacology proposes to standardize hundreds of traditional remedies over the coming five years.

Chinese doctors are also encouraged to acquire Western learning; but in June 1956, during the meeting of intellectuals at which it was decided to "liberalize" thinking, Lu Ting-yi once again defended traditional medicine against those who esteem it anti-Marxist and nonscientific; he castigated the "sectarians" who snub Chinese medicine as feudal and brand Western medicine capitalist, the while reserving the epithet "socialist" for Pavlov and Michurin's theories. There are no grounds or cause for repudiating Mendel on heredity. In a general sense, "we ought to borrow everything worthwhile the capitalists have devised in the domain of science and technology."

Hitherto the main outside influence upon Western medicine in China had, since the Liberation, come from the USSR. Western-type medicine, when all is said and done, is accorded the greater importance. Western doctors are for the most part grouped in "unified dispensaries," some still remaining unorganized.

For operations of minor or average seriousness the Soviet procedure of local anesthesia is preferred. Women are taught methods of painless childbirth. By and large Chinese doctors and surgeons are following the lead of their Russian colleagues.

*The Sciences*

Apart from medicine the natural sciences in China have no peculiarly Chinese character and none of them wears any class label. In this sphere, then, China has no doctrinal problems to face, only this one practical question: how to increase the ranks of her scientific personnel and raise its standard. The visitor who comes to find out about China trains most of his attentions upon the unsual and unique aspects of her culture; but the Chinese themselves are infinitely more interested in developing the general knowledge they must have if they are to stand on a par with all other nations.

Chinese students are taken care of by the state which houses, feeds, and maintains them at its own expense;* university-level studies usually last four years and end with examinations—which are not competitive—a major part of which are oral; polytechnical school students must submit an original thesis for the appproval of experts, but in China, as in Russia, it is felt that, in the main, oral tests are better than written ones for bringing out the qualifications of candidates for degrees. The curriculums are modeled after those in Soviet universities. Professors have come on loan from the USSR to help the Chinese reorganize their institutions of higher learning and to train teaching staffs. I visited the University of Peking,† a normal school, the Polytechnical Institute: there

* This arrangement was under discussion in September 1955. The majority of the students felt that those who have well-to-do parents ought to pay for their own food, which would allow an improvement in the welfare of all.

† Western newspapers told their readers that Sartre had been received as "a mandarin" (!) at the University of Peking; and Rousset, with an inside wire on everything, wrote that Sartre "had accepted its honors." Is it thought that

are few domains where one can establish so little from "seeing with one's own eyes." I can simply say that a great deal of building is going on in the parks surrounding the college buildings: dormitories, classrooms, laboratories are being constructed as fast as possible. Existing space is inadequate everywhere, for student registration is leaping every year.

Between 1950 and 1956, 217,000 university-level students took degrees; the figure is low in terms of the country's needs, which are gigantic; the development of industry, the vast public works require armies of engineers, chemists, geologists, and also teachers capable of training new specialists. The January 1956 estimate of the total number of intellectuals was 3,840,000; but only 100,000 of them can be considered first-class intellectuals, that is to say persons who are thoroughly equipped in their particular fields.

This deficiency means that fledglings straight out of college must be assigned to major posts. Thus of the 42,000 teachers in the higher institutions only 17.8 per cent are of some professorial rank; 24 per cent are lecturers, assistants, teaching fellows; and 58.2 per cent of the classes are conducted by teachers without any official faculty rank. Likewise, there are but 31,000 certified engineers in the country, and another 63,000 technical assistants who have been given a regular engineer's responsibilities. The hasty employing of inadequately trained technical personnel, as we have pointed out, has led to grave difficulties. "In our country science and technology are still lagging far behind," Chou En-lai said in his January 1956 report. He insists upon the imperative need to catch up: China cannot go on relying forever upon Russian experts. But he does not belittle the obstacles that must be surmounted, "Nor must we forget that while we are struggling to get started, others are continuing to make great strides ahead." The method Chou suggests is that instead of turning out second-rate intellectuals on an assembly line it would be wiser to raise the level of a small elite able to perform first-rate work. To this end, Chinese scientists will be sent to the USSR, Soviet scientists will be invited to China in order to lay the foundations for scientific research at the

---

the mandarinate lives on in China? or that traditional masquerades go on there as at Oxford or at Cambridge? The University of Peking is a place for work. It does not dole out "honors."

level that has been attained in the USSR. The National Planning Commission has been charged to draw up a long-range schedule for the development of science between 1956 and 1967. The hope is that in the most essential branches of science the level will, by the end of the third Five-Year Plan, at least be keeping pace with the advancing international standard. Just when Chinese science will overtake it it is impossible to say. In his May 1956 Address Lu Ting-yi specified that Chinese science must not look alone to Russia and to the other People's Democracies, but must profit as well from everything capitalist societies have to offer.

### *Conclusion*

Presently, in China, the matter of *extending* culture still has a priority over raising it. And rightly so. The value of a writer, an artist, a scientist narrowly depends upon the quality of the common mass he emerges from and which constitutes his audience. Only on that day when knowledge and the critical faculty have become widespread will China, as Mao Tse-tung promised she would, become "a land of great culture."

What will that culture be like? China refuses to become "Westernized to the core." Substantially, however, notwithstanding the survival of a few archaic forms—particularly in the realms of theater and painting—the so-called "national and popular tradition" is having slight influence upon the ways in which modern art, thought, and literature are evolving. This does not signify that the Chinese have become too "barbaric" to be able to carry on or take with them their old civilization: if despite the official urgings they are failing in their attempts to do so, this, I for my part believe, is because that old civilization has been dead many a long day. The great moment in Chinese art and thought coincides with what we in the West call Antiquity and the Early Middle Ages. The heritage of those remote periods was kept alive in France and Italy only due to the meditation of the Renaissance and subsequent ages. Rome and Athens engendered ways of thinking not so very dissimilar to ours today: an entire complex of feelings and of notions which one may qualify as modern make Homer and the Acropolis meaningful to us. One will not fail to notice that for want of a continuing tradition present-day Greece derives precious little profit from her glorious heritage. Different historical circumstances have caused a comparable rupture in China; the reigns of the Mings and the Manchus were artistically and ideologically stagnant; the recent past did not carry on but let die the distant past which broad bleak swamps now separate from the present. Literature flowered later; but we have indicated that having failed to fuse classical and popular currents it did not produce the great works that remain lastingly fresh and live despite the passing ages; the Chinese can admire and love their old novels, but only in retrospect. As for the folk-art side of their culture, it cannot but perish once the country's unity has been profoundly achieved.

Is then China doomed willy-nilly to ape the West? The truth is that she is drawing from it heavily. She has transformed herself socially and economically thanks to Western science and technique: in order to express her newness she is obliged to borrow from countries which are ahead of her. Many civilized Western souls bemoan this; convinced of their definitive superiority, the idea of China remaining "different" tickles their fancy. She is, they wail, going "to become banal." They are very vague indeed about her thought and art, their ignorance of her language and literature is total; but it's this mysteriousness that appeals to them, it looks something like infinity; they love to dream that in this otherwise banal world there is still a special somewhere yet full of unfathomable marvels. The Chinese, though, do not dream their culture, they live it; they sense its limitations; they also know those limitations may be surmounted; they are refusing to stay put in that supposed wonderland to which the perhaps innocent but none the less essentially contemptuous admiration of certain Westerners would assign them. The day—it will come—when they are the equal of the world's most advanced nations, there will not be any more drawing distinctions between China and the West: everyone will share in a universal culture. This assumes its particular figure in each particular country: no question but that China shall put her impress upon it; but her originality lies ahead of her, not behind; she shall forge it out of a living future. She is not to be defined or checked by a dead past.

# 6. THE DEFENSIVE EFFORT

Unity within the continental frontiers had still not been entirely achieved, and the enemy, driven out of the land, was still in arms at the moment the regime fell to the task of rebuilding the country. The leaders dedicated their efforts to welding the nation into a coherent whole; this positive undertaking was necessarily accompanied by a parallel defensive action.

Consolidating China meant firmly, thoroughly incorporating what are referred to as the national minorities. Of the six hundred million people inhabiting the territory the immense majority belong to the Han race; 35,000,000 others are the descendants of natives whom, as they expanded, the Hans pushed back into the most arid and least accessible hinterland regions. For centuries these hordes have been living in the highlands, most of them as tent-dwelling shepherds. Formerly they were beheld with contempt, the Hans considering indeed that existing creatures sort themselves into three varieties: Hans, barbarians, and animals. In their view, Mongols, Uigurs, Miaos, Tibetans were barbarians. Reacting against the discrimination and ill-use they were the victims of, these minorities, no matter what the regime in the East, were always hotbeds of restlessness and revolt. Today there are forty-four such minority groups speaking thirteen tongues of which only four are written; eighteen groups inhabit the Northwest, Sinkiang by itself containing twelve; twenty others in the Northeast embrace a total of 21,000,000 people; the rest are scattered about China. Altogether they occupy over half the area of Greater China; some still live in their original homelands, others have emigrated out of them and are sprinkled amid the Han populations. The dialects spoken by those of the North have Altaic features, those of the South are related to Sino-Tibetan. Most of these peoples are yet living in feudal or semifeudal circumstances; certain ones are divided into primitive clans and tribes; among them slavery is still not unknown.

Whereas Chiang Kai-shek kept them well outside the Chinese community the new regime considers their inclusion within it of paramount importance. Their territories have been peacefully annexed. A campaign to extinguish racist sentiments in the Hans was launched and is being pursued. The Lolo people, whose name, when written, is designated by a character also meaning *dog*, have been renamed the Yi. Two plays I attended revolved, one of them entirely and the other in part, around the problem of the minority groups; this was the theme of numerous short stories I read in English translation. Concurrently, the government is, by deed as well as by word, proving to the minorities that it respects their customs, languages, creeds, and that it intends to guarantee them a measure of autonomy. Above all it hopes to win their trust and enlist them into the community by raising their social level and by aiding them economically.

One of the principal regions inhabited by minority groups is the northwest province of Sinkiang where the population is mainly Uigur and Mongol. Having risen against Chiang Kai-shek, Sinkiang in 1944 set itself up as an independent "Republic of Eastern Turkestan" governed until 1950 by Sai Fadin. He made Communist China's cause his own end, Sinkiang having been peacefully occupied by the Red Army, he was put at the head of this region of 4,780,000 inhabitants with an area three times the size of France. A tremendous effort has been made to develop Sinkiang's agricultural economy; it has for example been furnished a relatively large number of tractors; major industrial centers are being created there and Uigur Sinkiang has just been granted the autonomy earlier accorded to the 600,000 Tibetans dwelling in the province.

New China has also endeavored to strengthen its authority over Tibet. This land of high plateaus is inhabited in part by settled farmers, in part by sheep-raising nomads and seminomads. Its relations with China proper date from the seventh century when a Tibetan king wedded a Tang dynasty princess. The Mongol emperors made contact with the lamas. Political authority was effectively in the hands of priests associated in large and wealthy monasteries. The Lamaist religion—a mixture of indigenous *Bon Po* and Buddhism—was in the fifteenth century reformed by the Yellow Sect whose founder bade his two main disciples, the Dalai Lama and the Panchen Lama, carry on his work. They were to govern jointly, the elder of the pair remaining the younger's tutor throughout their successive reincarnations: both were Living Buddhas, in actual practice chosen by the clergy. They reigned over a select and intensely hierarchized brotherhood made up of literates versed in sutra learning, and over a nomadic population that lived in a kind of permanent anarchy. The Manchu emperor's idea was to annex Tibet. K'ang-hsi dispatched an army to Lhasa and in 1720 maneuvered a pro-Chinese Dalai Lama onto the throne and put a brace of Chinese officials at his elbow. Following an anti-Chinese riot, Ch'ien Lung in his turn sent the military to occupy Lhasa in 1751. The two Chinese high commissioners disposed of all the political power and themselves appointed Dalai Lamas; these, by way of compensation, were given the title of King of Tibet. But the Panchen Lama, meanwhile, was named King of Shigatse and the rivalry between the two pontiffs was scrupulously turned into an enmity that endured from then on. In 1904 the British, of a mind to secure a foothold in this land lying at the doorway to India, entered Lhasa. The then Dalai Lama, the thirteenth of the line, fled, later came back to the holy city where he put up with British influence until 1934. At that date the Nanking Government tried, unsuccessfully, to set up a branch office in Lhasa. The Panchen Lama had quit Tibet in 1924, and he died in 1937; the Panchen's successors being minors, priests reigned in their stead. An American military mission reached Lhasa in

1945. The Panchen Lama, a refugee in Chinghai, a Chinese province, went over to the Communist regime at once and returned to Tibet with the Red Army when it quietly moved into that area. The Dalai Lama was more loath to yield but finally did. The two Living Buddhas, reconciled, came to Peking in 1954 for the October 1 National Independence Day celebrations. They were sumptuously received in apartments decked with yellow silk and they preached sermons at the Lamaist cathedral—Yung-ho-kung Temple—which Emperor Ch'ien Lung had given as a gift to the Tibetan Lamas and which the present regime has lately restored. On either side of Mao Tse-tung the two Lamas witnessed the parade. At the present moment the 2,800,000 inhabitants of Tibet are represented on the Standing Committee of the First National Assembly by the Dalai Lama who is indeed one of the Committee's vice-presidents. Elementary schools have been set up in Tibet, a people's bank which grants interest-free loans to farmers, loans at interest to merchants and artisans; the state purchasing agency buys Tibetan wool. But the greatest enterprise, the one that materially links Tibet to China, is the construction of two new roads: Sining-Lhasa and Yenan-Lhasa, respectively 1,300 and 1,725 miles long. The latter was opened on Christmas Day 1954 and the Chinese are justifiably proud of their achievement; I saw photos of it in all the illustrated magazines, I read I do not know how many stories, statistics, or anecdotes concerning its construction, and it has also inspired paintings. It follows the old caravan road and goes over fourteen passes at altitudes of from 9,800 to 16,400 feet; it borders precipices, crosses rivers; the Tibetans call it "The Miraculous Rainbow" or "The Golden Bridge" because it enables them at last to get tea, salt, cloth, machines, medicines in sufficient quantity and to ship out their local products: wool, hides, leather, medicinal plants.

Just as Buddhism is respected out of consideration for Tibet, the Moslems have the right to practice their religion, for it is that of a good number of national minorities, among them the Sinkiang Uigurs and the Hwei peoples one encounters in several regions; there are in all approximately ten million Chinese Moslems. They were frequently persecuted in the past, especially in Manchu and Kuomintang days: their mosques were sacked, even massacres were not unknown. Since 1952 they have come together to form a Chinese Islamic Association. Many mosques have been restored, including an old one at Canton that dates from the Tang period and another very venerable one at Hangchow. Religious schools are attached to them, although, of course, all schools are open to Moslems. In Peking itself there are 2,800 Hwei Moslem families living in the Nicoukai Street neighborhood; they have a Sung dynasty mosque while other, less ancient mosques are to be found here and there in the city. On their religious holidays Moslem employees are granted leave from the factories; where large numbers of Moslem workers are concentrated they have special canteens, otherwise they receive extra pay so that they can take their meals outside. Groups of Chinese pilgrims go to Mecca every year.

All national minorities elect parliamentary representatives, representation being proportional to population: but any group of 70,000 members or more is entitled to at least one representative. They hold 177 of 1,226 seats, or 14 per cent, though coming to less than 7 per cent of China's total population. Owing to the economic and geographical conditions they live in, their level of civilization is low, too low to permit them self-administration in every instance; but as soon as a group reaches the stage where it is ready for it, autonomy* is accorded to it—Tibet's will be recognized shortly, if all goes according to plan. When is a region considered "ready"? When, first of all, it has emerged from backwardness to the extent of possessing the qualified personnel administration demands. Where is this personnel to come from? An institute for the purposes of training it has been created at Peking. To it go members of the different minorities to complete their secondary schooling and to undertake advanced work. Chinese is taught to those who do not know it; but far from trying to wean them away from their own languages, specialists are engaged upon the project of devising written languages for those minorities which have none. The job is difficult but in two or three cases a phonetic alphabet has finally been worked out. Courses are conducted in Chinese but with translators on hand. I sat in on a geography class where the students were Tibetans: an inter-

* This autonomy is administrative. Needless to say, all the national minorities remain politically dependent upon Peking.

preter gave a running Tibetan translation of what the teacher was saying. I was struck by the look of keenest attention in all those faces, for the most part already marked by age.

The institute in question was conceived down to its finest detail so as to minimize the students' feeling of being out of their element; provisions allow for their group customs and various religious beliefs. There are several refectories, one for Moslems, another for the Tibetans; in the main dining hall allowance is also made for everyone's peculiarities of habit and taste. The names of the students enrolled are listed in several columns on a big blackboard, each column corresponding to a certain kind of diet. The first column is for those without diet restrictions; the next category is headed "No Chicken or Fish"; above another one reads "No Pork"; there is another for vegetarians. Tibetan cooks have been brought in to serve up home-style meals for Tibetan students. I also saw the places set aside for various forms of worship: a Lamaist chapel with the usual images of Buddha, the incense-burners and the incense, and the usual offerings; while a large unfurnished room serves as a mosque.

This policy has paid off. There were in 1956 some disturbances in Tibet where certain nomad tribes tried to revive their anarchic traditions. But by and large the national minorities are solidly lined up with the rest of the country.

The leaders have had to cope with another domestic problem: the corruption and disorder which, when they took over, they found rampant throughout society in China proper. Even their enemies concede that they have accomplished a miracle in putting a stop to this situation; once infested by bandits and thieves, China is today a land where honesty holds sway. On the positive side of their "scorecard" the Gossets noted, "No more beggars. No more prostitution. Infinitely fewer opium 'junkies' and gamblers. Disappearance of pickpockets. Guillain too remarks how society has become "moralized." Such however is his partiality that he goes so far as to rebuke the regime for these achievements; it is trampling on people's rights when you deprive them of opportunities for wrongdoing. In this connection it is worthwhile comparing the attitude adopted in Indonesia—newly delivered from the Dutch—

with the one observed in China. Robbery is tacitly, implicitly accepted at Jakarta; organized bands stage holdups in broad daylight, especially of foreigners, under the placid gaze of the police. "It's such a new thing here, freedom," an official said in substance to Tibor Mende,* "one really must let the people take advantage of it." For in Indonesia foreign capitalism yet subsists and the government views stealing as something on the order of profit sharing. Its attitude is consistent: doing nothing to prevent theft, it never punishes it either. But the Chinese no longer have foreigners on their hands, but just themselves to contend with. The government cannot tolerate robbery: and so the one reasonable policy is to make it impossible. That is why everyone from the big businessman to the pedicab operator is subject to close surveillance. Nor is it sure that outside pressure is still as necessary as when the regime came to power; most people in China now seem to have an inner preference for probity.

The elements of China's situation as regards foreign relations include being barred from the United Nations, being diplomatically unrecognized by most Western powers, being the object of a blockade, and being still at war with the Kuomintang. Kept alive by a sympathy Eisenhower and Nixon have just reiterated† and by the brawn of the American Armed Forces, Chiang Kai-shek, dug in on the island of Taiwan‡ off the Chinese coast, bullheadedly prolongs his losing battle. He had in 1950 announced that 1955 would see him the winner; in summer 1955 he confessed he had been just five years off in his calculation but promised he would be master of the mainland by 1960. No one takes this blustering seriously in China; all in all, Nationalist aviation regularly bombs factories and strategic points along the coast and Formosa's belligerent presence is a constant irritant to the Chinese. When you go for a walk in one of Peking's parks no sooner are you within the gates than you see a large map of Formosa below which "Let's Liberate Formosa" is spelled out in Chinese characters. Billboards carry cartoons of Chiang. For example one sees an

* See his *L'Asie du Sud-Est.*

† The allusion is to the 1956 United States presidential election campaign speeches. (Translator's note)

‡ The Chinese name for Formosa is Taiwan.

American general standing on a wee little isle—Formosa—with a huge sack of silver dollars beside him; he is tossing coins out into the sea; while, endeavoring to retrieve them, a dog-headed Chiang paddles energetically in the direction of the mainland. "Training the dog" reads the caption. Another drawing shows a sea monster, Chiang-headed this time, rearing halfway out of the water; its arms grotesquely stretched, with one hand it clutches the edge of Formosa, with the other an American warship; on both ship and island guns are trained toward the Chinese coast while between his teeth Chiang grips a very small cutlass. Under the picture, the word "Piracy."

There are, in addition, Nationalist troops, in fairly sizable numbers and in part American-equipped, who in defiance of the Rangoon government are raiding along the Sino-Burmese border. Hong Kong,* a few miles from Canton, is the hang-out of a large number of Kuomintang partisans and the kettle in which all anti-Communist propaganda is brewed. The Chinese Republic thus finds itself faced along an extended front by an enemy which has not yet consented to acknowledge defeat; in itself puny, it need never say die, for a sudden shift in unpredictable American foreign policy could at any minute augment its strength. Little wonder that China considers this situation unacceptable. On April 11, 1954, returning from New Delhi, Chou En-lai declared that Formosa, being Chinese soil, must be restored to China; since then the walls of Peking have been covered with the slogan calling for the liberation of Formosa, the Chinese radio broadcasts it. It is in no contradiction with that other slogan calling for peace; China assuredly does not intend to play the aggressor; it is to put an end to war that she demands this territorial restitution. "The struggle for peace and the struggle for the liberation of Formosa are indissolubly linked," Chou affirmed. Chiang Kai-shek's presence off China's shores weighs as a constant threat upon the country; the war will not be really over until all of China has been unified, that is, not until Formosa has been recovered.

During 1956 Chou En-lai made numerous overtures designed

* The October 1956 riots in Cholon—the Chinese section of Hong Kong—illustrated how tense the situation between Chinese Nationalists and Communists had become.

to bring Formosa peacefully to terms; but even if she would prefer to settle the question by arbitration, China intends also to be in a position to employ intimidation. She attaches great importance to her army. Its status became that of a regular army in 1955. On July 16 of that year P'êng Têh-huai presented a bill to substitute compulsory for voluntary military service. The volunteer army was exceedingly large and too loosely organized; the regular, conscripted army is to be smaller but will supply China with a powerful trained reserve corps; and a reduction in the number of men on active duty will save the state money.*

Between the Liberation and 1954, 4,520,000 soldiers were demobilized. In November 1954, at which time the bill had still not been enacted and the entire country was discussing it, conscription was given a try in twenty-five provinces plus Inner Mongolia: 10,032,000 young men registered, only 930,000 were called up. Since then 1,570,000 more soldiers have been discharged. Compulsory military service will not be a hardship: for the number of those eligible for the draft is far above the total the government can or wishes to put in uniform. After those exempted on grounds of health, family obligations, etc., many more fit lads in each village will remain behind than will be taken for duty. Those who do not want to go will not go; indeed a great many of those who may wish to will not be able to.

In *China Reconstructs* I read something called "From the Diary of a Young Recruit." The author, nineteen years old, describes how glad he was when on February 21, 1955, he was "taken" and how dejected his brother was at having been turned down. The edifying character of the text was so apparent that I doubted its authenticity. But Madame Cheng assured me that while she was not able to answer for the details she could vouch for the truth of the rest. The mistake made by many of these propaganda journals is to present as caused by "enthusiasm for the building of socialism" behavior which springs from much more worldly motives; as for the leaders, they not only realize but do nothing but repeat that it is only when given concrete motivation that any enthusiasm

* In 1954 the outlay for national defense was 23.6 per cent of the total budget (i.e., 24,632,444,000 yuan); in 1955 it came to 24.19 per cent (31,192,520,000 yuan). Soviet troops having left Dairen, they were replaced by Chinese garrisons: 1955 military expenses were consequently higher.

is apt to be aroused.* The fact of the matter is that the young peasant is exceedingly eager to be a soldier, not because his head is crammed with slogans, but because being a soldier strikes him as desirable for several sound reasons. Now that he is reading newspapers, frequenting cultural centers, now that he has some political education, the peasant boy has a broader mental horizon than his elders; he feels cramped in his village, the simple work he is given seems tedious; things will change when agriculture has been mechanized, but at the moment he comes running for nothing more than the chance to drive a truck or, more modestly, to get his hands on something mechanical, even if it is a submachine gun; and his second greatest wish is to see something of the world. He will return home knowing more about it than his friends who have remained stuck in the village; maybe they will recommend him to be a cadre. And then the soldier's standard of living is higher than the average peasant's; he is better clothed, better fed. From one of the most venomous of anti-Communist bulletins, *The China News Analysis* published in Hong Kong, I cite the following:

> Five years ago, the Kuomintang troops, poorly paid, poorly fed, and poorly clad, constituted a more or less scorned segment of the population. Today, the army is the pride of the government. The soldiers are well nourished, well dressed; the military academies are filled with the cream of the up-and-coming generation.

One has but to look at the young recruits walking in the parks, in the temples to see that the Chinese soldier is well-off and kindly viewed by the population at large. "I used to be antimilitarist," Madame Lo Ta-Kang said to me, "the Kuomintang soldiers were wretched scoundrels and generally detested. These boys now behave so well, are so polite and likable that they've won everybody's heart." They are today, as before, the same young peasants; it is the institution that is different. Its meaning has changed too: formerly, the army served a hated order; today, its job is to defend

* From repeated checking I was able to substantiate the accuracy of the *facts* reported in these publications which indeed comprise a mine of valuable information. But the propaganda element comes out in the far too virtuous and greatly oversimplified *explanation* and *interpretation* that accompanies the facts. This sugariness stands in strong contrast with the tough-minded lucidity of the official texts which are also translated for foreign consumption.

the country. Nobody is antimilitarist any more, for everybody is nationalistic and the nation needs soldiers.

The army having become regular, the government decided in September 1955 that henceforth there would be a sharper distinction between officers and enlisted men. A solemn ceremony was held on September 27 and Mao Tse-tung conferred marshal's rank on a certain number of generals, among them Vice-President Chu Teh, Vice-Minister Chen Yi; other officers were raised to general and colonel general, and decorations and medals were distributed in quantity.

•

What the leaders are particularly anxious about is the collusion between outside adversaries and internal opposition elements; the war that is going on is a civil war pitting countrymen against one another, which makes it easy for spies, saboteurs, agitators to infiltrate the country and lose themselves in the Chinese crowd. A good many spots afford them favorable terrain, for the situation is confusion inside the country. The previously privileged classes have not rallied to the regime en bloc; a certain number of capitalists, intellectuals, and, above all, landowners are indomitable: the intransigent squires, relying especially upon former Taoist priests and wizards, play upon the discontent of the rural population's most retrograde members. It appears that in the spring and summer of 1955 their activities assumed a particularly intense form. This recrudescence of opposition, I am told, has two main causes. A great number of counterrevolutionaries who were originally locked up were given only a few years in jail; now, out again, embittered and vindictive, they are starting in afresh. But, more than anything else, the country's swift socialization means that time is playing against the anti-Communists; their plight is desperate and they are flinging in their last firecracker before the door slams with the completion of agricultural collectivization and the liquidation of private enterprise. The leaders had anticipated this and warned against it repeatedly. In April 1955, during its Fifth Plenary Session, the Central Committee had declared:

Concurrently with the progress registered by the socialist cause in our country, the remnants of counterrevolutionary elements and reactionary elements of the bourgeoisie that are determined in their opposition to our socialist transformation are presently reactivating their conspiracy which aims at restoring the counterrevolutionaries to power.

Chien Ying, the Controls Minister, re-emphasized the same thing on July 25:

The class struggle in our country has not waned but has become sharper and more complex. Acts of resistance and of sabotage perpetrated by counterrevolutionaries of every sort against the socialist conversion have become steadily more numerous and more violent.

From Lo Jui-ching, Minister of Public Security, this on July 29:

We must bear in mind that we are still in the transitional phase of the class struggle. Among the counterrevolutionary elements exist landed proprietors and other criminals many of whom, released after serving prison terms, are out to take their revenge.

In its present stage, what distinguishes the struggle "is that the enemy's acts of sabotage are more cunningly concealed and more vicious than ever before," Lo Jui-ching stressed. This is why the government advised keenest vigilance. The *Jen Min Jih Pao* wrote on the 27th:

If the counterrevolutionaries are able to disguise themselves in our governmental organisms, in the Army, in the Party, in democratic groups and people's organizations, that is in large measure due to our faint degree of alertness and circumspection . . . We all, including cadres and Communist Party members, have developed an extremely dangerous and mistaken lethargy and carelessness.

"Let all of us sharpen our eyes and our wits," Lo Jui-ching had asked. Even a foreigner could sense, in that month of September 1955, that the defensive battle was going through a critical period. Vigilance was the subject Lao-She was planning to treat in his next play. Madame Cheng and Tsai complained that so far the regime had been much too lax; they told me of spies ferried in from Taiwan by boat or parachuted in or slipped in through Hong Kong; they related instances of the sabotage and arson the newspapers were full of. The atmosphere, especially at Canton, was noticeably strained.

Depending upon whichever theory they aim to prove on whichever day, David Rousset* and his fellows maintain either that (a) these acts do indeed authentically exist on a vast scale and portend the imminent collapse of the regime; or that (b) these acts do not exist, but are dreamed up by the leaders and serve as an excuse for a reign of terror. I would suggest that in order to appreciate the situation in China one ought to compare it with the situation in other Asian nations. Whatever its political hue, no government can ever transform a backward country into a relatively advanced country without stepping on toes. Asiatic populations being at once extremely poor and extremely numerous the backlash created by change must be particularly formidable: the struggle for independence and to modernize has brought furious upheavals in Burma, Indonesia, Pakistan. Despite a far superior centralization and discipline China had also to expect troubles. Nevertheless, the while accomplishing the most radical metamorphosis, she has managed to avoid the convulsions which have rocked her neighbors. I have described her cautious rural policy; it spared her the tragedy of the great peasant uprisings that bloodied Russia. Religious fanaticism, military banditry were handcuffed in 1949; never for a single instant has the regime been rattled.

This does not however warrant the supposition that the "vigilance campaign" has been orchestrated for the fun of it. A country that is forced to cut corners in the customarily gradual developmental process cannot smile upon those who throw obstacles in its path; sabotage, peculation, waste, all these slow its advance, and that is reason enough for it to combat them vigorously. Moreover one of the constants in Chinese policy is its preventive slant: just as it thwarted a return to landowning capitalism before it could turn into an actual danger the regime is nipping the counterrevolution in the bud. This is not to resort to the Terror; but, to the contrary, to take the only steps by which its drastic consequences can be avoided.

Efforts to be made against counterrevolutionary activity have been prescribed by two provisional rulings: the "Directives for the Suppression of Counterrevolutionary Activities" issued July 23, 1950, and the "Procedures Concerning the Repression of Counter-

* Vice-President of "La Commission internationale contre le régime concentrationnaire." (Translator's note)

revolutionary Activities" of February 21, 1951. Legal action is based upon two laws, both passed in September 1954, one for use by the Ministry, the other to be enforced in the people's courts. The Minister of Public Security in July 1956 again specified in what spirit the law was to be applied:

Under no circumstances are interrogations to be accompanied by tortures or confessions to be extracted by force; investigation and questioning is to be carried out in a proper and lawful manner, statements must be substantiated by proof, idle speculation, hearsay disallowed; a clear and conscientious distinction must be drawn between what is true and what is not of importance, depositions must be sifted, arrests strictly confined to immediate suspects, no one arrested save those parties whom the law expressly forbids from being left at large, and no one arrested at all if arrest is not necessary.

In short, the "redouble vigilance, root out the secret agents" program must be implemented by the means another slogan proposes: "Let's each be firm, but let's be fair to all."*

Theoretically justified, prudent and moderate in practice, the repression of counterrevolutionary activities is the fact to which the counterrevolutionaries point with the warmest and readiest indignation. They bellow about the extent of this repression and against the methods employed in it. With reference to the first point, their statements are fantastically gratuitous. Poring over an official speech, they will, for example, fasten upon the statement that 90 per cent of China's capitalists and peasants have shown themselves loyal to the regime. Which they translate thus: the regime views the remaining 10 per cent as dangerous counterrevolutionaries. Another step gives them what they are after: leaving aside the children in a total population of 600,000,000 there can be no fewer than 20,000,000 individuals languishing in forced-labor camps. The figure is patently absurd. For its part, the Chinese government declares that some 600,000 political prisoners are under sentence, most of them to terms of less than ten years. There is no way of verifying the assertion. As Rousset admits, the quantitative aspect of the problem cannot be profitably discussed. The

* The very institution of police necessarily and universally leads to abuses; China has not been exempt from them. But one ought not to dismiss the fact that these abuses have been found out, publicized, castigated; and that an effort is now being made to eliminate them.

anti-Communists attack the very principle of repression, and the question is one of finding out whether the latter has or has not any legitimate *raison d'être*.

To deny that it has, the anti-Communists resort to an extraordinary clumsy piece of sophistry. In France, the citizens' political activity, in the immense majority of cases, goes no further than expressing opinions; opinion ought to be free; if, as in China, you repress political opposition, then you violate that freedom. And so Gérard Rosenthal winds up his Brussels "indictment" with this:

> In the People's Republic of China there exists a system of forced labor intended *to rectify the political opinions of individuals who do not accept the ideology of the Government.*

He neglects to say that these individuals are arrested only when and if they have manifested their nonacceptance through patent acts of sabotage, of setting fire to forests or granaries, of murder—in fine, through crimes no government on earth would or could leave unpunished—or, at the very least, through agitations and propagandizing in such a way as to endanger the security of the state—acts which are in every country on earth characterized as unlawful.* No citizen in China is bothered on account of his opinions; the anti-Communists acknowledge as much when they allude contentedly to official texts indicating the existence of restive citizens—disaffected intellectuals, peasants—who have not accepted "the ideology of the government."

Another fallacy maintained by Rousset is that the counter-revolutionaries aim their gestures at the government, not at the country. The Chinese leaders have often gone to the trouble to demonstrate the contrary, and rightly: flood control being vital, it is the peasants who are ruined or drowned when someone wrecks the dikes. Rosenthal is upset because "political intention" worsens instead of attenuates a crime while under bourgeois regimes it is violation of common law that is the more severely chastised. But

* Above all in France, statutes relating to "demoralization of the army" and to "demoralization of the nation" leave the way open for the most arbitrary arrests and imprisonments. We saw these laws invoked in connection with the Henri Martin affair, in the case of Claude Bourdet and, more recently, in that of Marrou who was indicted for "demoralization of the army" because of an article he contributed to *Le Monde*.

why, I wonder, why insist upon making an absolute standard out of the kind of upper-class-made justice which obtains in our democracies? The indulgence of the Chinese toward common-law criminals is a feature for which I unhesitatingly give them credit. And circumstances are sufficient explanation for why, on the other hand, they deal sternly with the activities in which their political enemies are engaged.

Rousset, Rosenthal, and the hardly nonpartisan Commission they collected around them in Brussels claim that irregularities characterized the trials at which the accused were found guilty. This is a flagrant lie; the entire organization of the Chinese judiciary denies it.

The Chinese Revolution abolished the old legal code, disqualified the former judges and lawyers; the new legislation it is establishing is not as yet complete. Even Rousset's Commission refrained from blaming the regime on this score; for, as everyone realized, a new legal code was necessary and elaborating one requires several years of work. However, apart from the Constitution, which is a prime legal reference, a certain number of laws have been promulgated since 1950. In particular, the act of September 21, 1954, pertaining to Judiciary Organization and the other concerning arrest and detention of December 20, 1954, protect the citizen against all arbitrary arrest. Reproducing Article 89 of the Constitution, the latter piece of legislation reads:

> The individual liberty of the citizens of the People's Republic of China is inviolable. No one may be arrested without due order from the People's Tribunal or without due warrant emanating from an officer of the Public Ministry.

Police may perform arrest only in cases of *flagrante delicto,* and must submit justification for arrest within a time limit of twenty-four hours. In China there exists no equivalent of the "administrative internment" which made arbitrary imprisonment possible in the USSR:* only the tribunals are empowered to decide an internment.

* At the Brussels "hearings" Rosenthal attempted to raise doubts on this score. He refers to Article 36 of the "Ruling Concerning Reform Through Work": "In order that a criminal may be imprisoned, one of the following is required: an act of court, an administrative act (a letter of execution of

These tribunals are people's courts. They are echeloned into three categories: lower, intermediary, and upper courts. Final appeal rests with the People's Supreme Court. Each is constituted corporately, includes specialized magistrates and popular assessors. Presiding judges are elected by the local legislatures; the Chief Justice of the Supreme Court is elected by the National Assembly. The other judges are appointed by governmental organisms. The assessors to the magistrates are elected by the people: they are persons from every walk of life—workers, peasants, artisans, also intellectuals, manufacturers, businessmen.

> The assessors come from the masses, are fully acquainted with their will and desires, and are capable of reflecting and expressing the opinion of the masses before the people's courts. The judges are assisted and supervised by people's assessors so that subjective findings and unfair sentences may be avoided.

This was noted in a *Kuang Ming Jih Pao* editorial of January 28, 1956.

Article 78 of the Constitution stipulates:

> In the exercise of their judiciary functions, the people's courts are independent and are to observe no obedience save to the law of the land.

True, judges are responsible for their decisions and are not irremovable; the government holds them accountable for their actions, as it does every other public officer. The Supreme Court is answerable to the National Assembly. The Judiciary is, then, not absolutely independent; rather, it is co-ordinated with the Executive and Legislative. But this does not mean that the courts are mere tools in the hands of the regime. Verdicts delivered by the courts can in no wise be suspended by any political branch or bureau; the Assembly cannot alter Supreme Court decisions. Judges are removed only if guilty of specified misconduct, and such

---

sentence), or a writ of detention. Imprisonment of a criminal is not allowable without one of the aforementioned documents." A letter of execution of sentence is an administrative warrant demanding that an already pronounced judgment be executed, and Article 36 signifies that imprisonment can only follow upon an earlier court decision. But Rosenthal harps on the word "administrative," forgets the rest and declares: "The fact that this article is based on the article in the Russian ruling is *disquieting*." (My italics.) He does however admit, "It is not possible to come to any categorical conclusions."

cases just about never arise. In actual fact the courts enjoy an extreme independence; and indeed Shih Leang has sometimes complained of their excessive leniency.

A certain people's court, dealing with a counterrevolutionary who was arrested in the act of writing reactionary slogans upon a wall and who had done the same thing on six previous occasions, recognized that the inculpated had no reactionary antecedents or background, and acquitted him.

By and large, however, the impartiality and independence of their courts are facts the Chinese are proud of and which foreign observers admire. Wrote the eminent Italian jurist Calamandrei:*

The personal contacts I had with Peking and Shanghai magistrates, the care with which the hearings I witnessed were conducted, the concurring testimony of European observers who had spent some time in China and who were in a position to compare the present administration of justice with what went before, everything led me to conclude that the law is enforced with the highest degree of impartiality in China today.

The principle of "the defendant's right to legal counsel" appears in the 1950 "General Ruling" and is reiterated in the law enacted in 1954. Rosenthal, in his "indictment," alludes to the scarcity of trained attorneys in order to go on to affirm that the aforementioned right is not respected in China. Nothing authorizes the statement. The number of lawyers practicing under the former regime—some of whom have been expelled from the bar—and that of law students has been insufficient in view of the new China's needs; although young lawyers are being trained as rapidly as possible, there are still very few of them. But the regime endeavors to skirt this difficulty. Rarely do parties to a suit act as their own counsel: that happens only in such civil actions as divorce cases. The accused always has the right to choose counsel; if he is unable to find any, the court supplies it to him. Usually there is recourse to members of people's associations, including the Women's Association. An attempt is being made also to establish a "people's bar" system. The prosecuting attorney, moreover, is obliged to stress every point which may be in the defendant's favor. An

* Shortly before his death, in the review *Il Ponte*, April 1956.

English barrister has made a thorough study of the question. "No country," he observes, "can pull an entire body of professional lawyers out of a hat. For the time being China is doing its best to create a bar and to minimize present difficulties." It is sheer dishonesty to willfully confuse the current—and unavoidable—shortage of trained lawyers in China with the denial of the right to legal counsel.

Confession, it is important to note, is not accepted as proof in China. The trial is conducted publicly; serious cases are tried before a vast popular audience. The verdict, pronounced orally and put in writing within three days after the case has been decided, must be motivated. If condemned, a man may appeal; there are two higher instances to which death sentences may be appealed.

Death sentences are exceedingly uncommon. On this point, Rosenthal's "indictment" contains a curious contradiction. He affirms that where it relates to counterrevolutionary activities the 1951 law "in almost every case prescribes the death penalty." However, his whole argument is that slave labor plays a vital role in China's national economy; and the implication seems to be that Rosenthal's "slaves" are corpses.

The truth is that prison terms are what the laws generally stipulate:

> Those who participate in a conspiracy or in an insurrection will be sentenced to a maximum of ten years in prison. ("Rulings," Article 4*)

The death sentence is seldom pronounced, still less often carried out. Even when upheld by the court of appeals and the Supreme Court, execution is immediate only in exceptional instances. Generally the criminal is allowed a stay of two years and if by the end of that period he has mended his ways, his sentence is commuted.†

The punishment ordinarily inflicted upon those found guilty of civil or political offenses is detention, in prison or in labor camps. The fundamental idea behind the entire penitentiary system is

* Article 4 goes on to say, "Punishment will be more severe in cases that are judged to be of a graver nature." But this does not mean that the court is invited to pronounce death sentences.

† Rosenthal's prejudice is so strong that even this measure is included in his sweeping condemnation.

rehabilitation, re-education through work. It was officially set forth in the "Common Program" which urges that delinquent elements be "reformed through work," in the "Regulations Concerning Re-education Camps" and "Measures Concerning the Liberation of Criminals from Confinement" both promulgated April 26, 1954. We read:

Criminals must be taught to recognize their errors and to respect the law; they must be kept abreast of current political happenings, taught to labor in behalf of production, given a cultural education whereby they may themselves discover the sources of crime, weed out and destroy their criminal attitudes and replace them with a new concept of good behavior.

"The production and re-education through work," it is added, "must usefully coincide with the national effort at economic reconstruction."

These are the lines Rousset manipulates into a pretext for denouncing what he calls "concentration camp terror in China." The expression "forced labor" is his springboard for some fancy conjectural diving. Prisoners do *useful, productive* work: this is his cue for affirming that Stalinism's greatest villainies have been repeated in China. Rousset cannot be unaware that prisoners also work in France; the difference is that we saddle them with stupid and stupefying chores: they are made to fabricate paper bags or to paint lead soldiers or to sew felt bedroom slippers together. China dislikes waste: all work must be *useful, productive.* She also reckons that a man is less degraded by being taught a trade or a craft than by forcing him to smash rocks with a sledge hammer or dig ditches for the sole purpose of filling them in again. By the time he is freed the Chinese convict goes out a craftsman, a skilled or at the very least a specialized worker; the French convict goes out empty-handed, empty-headed. Which of the two is the better off?

The principle of useful, productive labor is, it may be argued, dangerous; for might it not encourage arbitrary jailings as a means to procuring cheap labor? But labor is just exactly what lacks least in China. When the government undertakes major public works—roads, dams, railway construction—it signs up volunteers from adjoining country districts; nearly every peasant has the ambition to become a worker; by putting in a season as bricklayer or stonecutter he hopes to become one for good; he is delighted by the opportunity to earn some extra cash; and the peasants rush to the government's call. When it announces openings on wilderness reclamation projects, any number of jobless men present themselves as candidates. And the very point of a good many of these enterprises is first of all to absorb unemployed labor; at a time when China is making a prodigious effort in this direction nothing would be less to her advantage than deliberately to concentrate menial labor in prison camps. For menial it is; furthermore, everybody knows that forced labor is much less efficient, yields much less than free labor, this being one of the essential reasons for the disappearance of slavery toward the close of ancient times. The apparent saving realized by employing a large percentage of nonpaid labor would be offset by the most baneful consequences. It is a fact that the work potential of Chinese prisoners is utilized; everything argues against the allegation that it is in order to exploit this work potential that the authorities imprison men in China.*

As for prison conditions, it is obvious, I believe, that jails and penitentiaries are not playgrounds in any country; and it is graceless on the part of the visitor to declare that he tasted the soup and found it first-rate. Good soup or no, the prisoner's situation is universally frightful. The one question is to determine whether or not it is worse in China than elsewhere.

I did not personally see any labor camps. But from a French friend I received an eye-witness account of the building of a railroad line upon which 70,000 workers and 40,000 prisoners were engaged. Everyone lived in the same kind of barracks, ate identical fare, worked under identical conditions. The prisoners were not paid. The jobs requiring the highest degree of skill—and they often were the most arduous and dangerous—were all done by free workers.

However, I did personally see one prison. And several years back I visited a model prison in Chicago. This one in Peking was not a model prison; it was simply the only one in the city area and, for that matter, in the province; and all central prisons are the same

* Now that light has been shed on the forced-labor camps in Russia it is recognized that they did not play the important economic role Rousset and Rosenthal ascribed to them. They did not constitute the necessary basis of socialist reconstruction in the USSR; repression there had a political character.

in China. What a difference between this and the American system! At Chicago the authorities took custody of my handbag so that I would not be able to pass cigarettes or my lipstick out to the prisoners; corridors and cells were sealed by stoutly locked steel doors, between bars I caught a glimpse of the shop where the inmates were working. Here, the prison is in the depths of a kind of park; two soldiers are on duty at the outer gate; but once you are inside it you see no wardens, no guards, no guides, only un-uniformed and—a fact of some importance—unarmed overseers. They exercise the functions of foremen and political and cultural instructors. The inmates wear no special costume, they are dressed like everybody else, and nothing distinguishes them from the employees who supervise their work. The shops are located in the middle of a big garden planted with sunflowers; were it not for the watchtower—unoccupied, furthermore—which rises above the group of buildings, one would take this for an ordinary factory. Cotton clothing and headgear is made here, the working day being on a nine-hour-shift basis; every man has one day off each week. Eight of the daily twenty-four hours are allotted for sleeping, three for classwork: two hours of ideological instruction, one of general culture. After subtracting the time taken up by meals and the details of personal hygiene, the prisoners are still left with a considerable amount of leisure. They have a field for sports at their disposal, a big courtyard with a theater where a movie is shown or a play presented once every week; the day I was there they were rehearsing a play of their own. There is also a reading room stocked with books and periodicals where they can sit and relax. We visit this library first, then the kitchens, then the laundry. We file down a long hallway, its walls covered with charts indicating production figures in each shop, also with copies of the latest newspapers and educational texts. A door stands ajar, we peer through it, there are men asleep on cots; they belong to the night shift. The prison was built by the Kuomintang; each cell was then an individual kennel, bars over its little window; since, the in-between partitions have been knocked out, and eight or nine inmates now share relatively spacious, well-lit rooms which on one side give out on the garden and on the other open upon this hallway that is closed by a grill but only at night.

The director gives me the following particulars. Four kinds of prisons exist: "confinement jails" where persons under accusation await trial and others under death sentence execution; prisons like the present one where inmates are serving their terms; re-education-through-work camps which include, for example, state farms; and re-education centers for juvenile delinquents aged thirteen to eighteen. Peking has a confinement jail; and certain Peking prisoners are sent to a re-education farm at Ching-ho which now has 4,000. The prison we are visiting—the only one in the city—contains 1,800 inmates, of whom 120 are women. Of the eighteen hundred, two thirds are political criminals, one third common-law criminals (for women the proportion is the reverse). Most of the prisoners are under sentences ranging from three to ten years; a few are under life sentence. The supervising staff numbers one hundred and fifty employees. Blows, threats, insulting language, humiliation of whatever sort, all this is categorically ruled out.* Punishments go from a verbal rebuke to solitary confinement, depending upon what the culprit has done. Conversely, prisoners whose general attitude and performance at work prove satisfactory receive public praise and bonuses that may run as high as 150 yuan; their sentences may sometimes be shortened. During scheduled hours they can buy various articles in a little store adjacent to the workshops; the employees make purchases there too. Prisoners cannot be sold matches or cigarettes. The director asserts that the re-educating idea works well with common-law criminals—these are beheld as the victims of the old vicious society; poverty, a lack of good education, unemployment drove them into crime; they are taught a trade and society acquires decent citizens—but as for the counter-revolutionaries, changing their mental habits is no easy task.

I dare say it must be horribly dull to have to undergo two hours of political indoctrination at the end of a day's work. But what is outstanding in all this is not the cruelty of the procedure but its naïveté. Rosenthal talks about "technically refined physical and

* The ill-treatment sustained by certain missionaries smacks of the methods customarily employed by every police force in the world. It is obviously regrettable that in China there still exist procedures which are utilized day in and day out in France. But these abuses are one thing; the system applied by the penitentiary administration in the prisons and in the labor camps is something else again.

moral means utilized to recondition the individual and administered under circumstances ranging up to torture." He deliberately fails to distinguish between the abuses the Chinese police have sometimes been guilty of and the system in force in the internment centers, where no "physical" pressure whatever is exerted upon the inmate, where two hours in the classroom, boring as they may be, do not constitute torture. The re-education process—and this can be scored both for and against it—fails. Not indoctrination, but teaching him a trade is what restores the common-law criminal to society; while the political criminal's psyche is so little tampered with that he marches out of prison in the same state he was marched into it. The re-education method, as I see it, looks like an illusion, not like "soul murder"; and I believe similar ones are practiced in Western reformatories.

Free, the ex-prisoner may look for work on his own; or he may go to an employment bureau; or again stay on in the prison shops as a free worker, in which case he will live in town or in one of the administration buildings. At the moment there are two hundred such free workers here; outwardly, they resemble everyone else, but work only eight hours a day and, of course, earn a normal salary. Land is sometimes distributed to ex-prisoners in the re-education farms. Over the last four years out of 5,380 individuals released from Ching-ho 1,455 have remained there as free laborers. This last is one of the facts which excites Rousset's indignation.

It was only a few weeks ago that, traveling in Brittany, I came across a woebegone fellow, a carter then three months out of the Le Puy prison where they had locked him up for vagrancy. Uneducated, unskilled, he had been searching for a job for those three months: every hiring interview would end as soon as his prison record came up. "Lady," he said, "what would you do? Me, one of these days I'm going to shin up a pole and grab onto the high-tension wires. Then," he added, "they'll figure out something to do with me. I told them I'm not a vagrant just for the hell of it. Give me a job, I said. But they don't give me a job and because I haven't got a job they give me six months." He is probably up for another six months right now; or perhaps he shinnied up a telephone pole; newspapers carry lots of these items in small print down at the bottom of the page. All Rousset's double talk fails to convince me that it is better to founder somewhere along a highway than to work at whatever proximity to a prison.

Closely inspecting Rosenthal's "indictment," which served as a basis for *The White Paper* on China, one is impressed by the flimsiness of his allegations; they repose upon a postulate requiring to be proved: that the Chinese penitentiary system is an exact duplication to the one in the USSR. I have already pointed out that one must avoid flatly interpreting the Chinese Revolution in terms of the Russian Revolution: the Chinese have carefully studied that precedent in order not to repeat its mistakes. They are keenly aware of their country's specific needs and concrete possibilities. They draw their inspiration from Russia but do not copy her. Nothing warrants the blank assumption that the two systems are identical. Rosenthal studiously distorts the meaning of Chinese law by sifting it through a Soviet filter. By means of a conjectured analogy with the USSR he feels himself free to conclude that in China "forced labor avers itself susceptible to wearing the characteristics of a concentration camp system." The phrasing is as awkward as it is slippery: does forced labor wear the said characteristics, or does it not? Certainly, declared the "Commission"; for it convened in Brussels with its certitudes ready-made. Be that as it may, the dissimilarity to the Stalinist system is patent, since no administrative internment exists in China. "Forced labor" is to be met with the world over and if in China it is productive that redounds wholly to China's credit. No society today seems able to do without its police and its prisons; that these institutions include much that is odious I acknowledge; that they are more odious in China than elsewhere I deny.

To China her detractors impute what they apparently consider a peculiar characteristic: she incites her citizens to be informers. If this is a seriously meant criticism it contains a liberal dose of pharisaism. Urging the people to vigilance, the government does indeed exhort them to report the counterrevolutionary activities whereof they may have cognizance; but we must not forget that these activities consist in arson, the sabotage of bridges and dikes, in assassinations: in France no less, whosoever were knowingly to allow such crimes to be prepared and perpetrated would be held accomplice to them; and go see whether the French crowd does not raise the hue and cry when a ragamuffin is seen filching a jar of marmalade.* This co-operation with the police seems more shocking to me here in our country where the law is determined by the interests of a class than there where justice is made to correspond to the welfare of the people. China moreover considers herself still at war: I recall a good many edifying counterespionage stories dating from 1914-1918, and I can think of more than one land where hunting down spies is still looked upon as a patriotic duty.

It must also be remembered that the Chinese do not have an inherent sense of civism. They formerly lived not as members of a nation but as those belonging to a *Kia*. As family solidarity extended to embrace the entire village every individual who was at odds with the state could count on the connivance of the community: a government attempting to rebuild the nation has perforce to fight against this mentality; it must also combat the shoulder-shrugging attitude whereby for centuries the Chinese responded to the utterly hopeless situation they lived in. Statesmen and thinkers who believed there was some possible way out of the mess have always militated against this passivity. The *Mo Tzŭ*, which in answer to Confucianism teaches the logic of "All-embracing Love," dethrones the family, ranks it second to mankind; it declares that good and evil affect all alike, that each individual is responsible to the many: "Whosoever learns that another has done ill to his country is bound to point out the wrongdoer; failing which, he will be punished as though he were himself the author of the crime." A little later, the "Legalists" or "Realists," trying to further the right functioning of the state, proposed that citizens, organized into groups, be held "mutually responsible each for the other and for the reciprocal divulgence of their crimes." The fact that these ideas were endlessly reiterated, that they are echoed over and over again today, indicates not that they were scrupulously observed but

* I was walking along the Boulevard Montparnasse yesterday. Two policemen begin to chase a man. "Stop him!" shrieks a concierge. "What's he done?" I ask her. "I don't know," she says. A shopkeeper suddenly emerges from nowhere, tears after the fugitive, brings him down with a crunching tackle, then strides proudly back toward his shop. I ask the shopkeeper: "What did he do?" "Haven't any idea," he says, "I just saw the guy running." This glowing "civism" in the French isn't outdone by anything one can blame the Chinese for.

that, to the contrary, the tendency to disregard them yet prevails.*

That said, there is no question but that the principle of intervention can turn into excessive interference and that suspicion is the other side of the vigilance coin. Every revolutionary society has been plagued by distrust. Much self-confidence and determination are needed ere a man will renounce the past, and change always appears laden with dark uncertainty and peril; fear becomes transformed into guilt: the peasants who continue to pay rent to expropriated landowners dread both the old regime's return and the wrath of heaven. Every man, we know, is susceptible of a Manichean temptation: you project your own uneasiness and qualms into the Others. So long as the Revolution remains short of its definitive triumph, my neighbor will keep on looking like a potential counterrevolutionary and I shall feel suspected too, which adds to my fears and feeds my own suspicions. That China had to undergo this malaise was inevitable. It reached its climax during the Korean War. But with increasing internal and external national security, distrust will progressively subside and human relations will become steadily healthier. Things have already, during 1956, vastly improved. In their speeches at the Eighth Congress, the Communist leaders repeatedly stressed that the reaction is as of now crippled and they called for a letting up in every domain. Of particular importance is the speech Lo Jui-ching, the Minister of Public Security, delivered before the National Assembly's Third Session in June 1956.

The victory achieved in the battle to repress counterrevolutionaries has weakened the counterrevolution's power. Since the second half of 1955, a divided and hesitant tendency has become constantly more noticeable among the subsisting counterrevolutionary forces. This phenomenon is not accidental: it is closely connected with the fact that our country's political and economic situation has undergone great change.

Only the total victory of socialism will bring the battle to an end; but while, the year before, Lo Jui-ching spoke of their virulence, he could in 1956 point to the isolation of counterrevolutionary elements and to their impotence. As a consequence of the progress in

* There is a French law—and one can hardly disapprove of it—which requires that neighbors who know of a child being tormented by its parents report the fact to the authorities.

socialization accomplished in the course of the winter, he was able to say,

> The social foundation upon which the counterrevolutionaries based their hopes has been considerably weakened, the arguments and excuses the counterrevolutionaries were able to evoke have in large measure ceased to exist. The counterrevolutionaries' devices and their own illusions have been demolished . . . As for those who "pinned their hope" on Chiang Kai-shek, they cannot but be filled with despair today. They are indeed; and that is why many counterrevolutionaries are anxiously reappraising their future prospects and altering their hostile attitude toward the people.

Those who are changing their minds as a result of the success of the regime are being treated indulgently by it. Guilty persons who are eager to bury the hatchet and who sincerely avow their errors will not be prosecuted save for grave offenses, and in that case may expect clement treatment; even major criminals need not consider their plight hopeless if they are willing to earn forgiveness through meritorious conduct. In the countryside, apart from a handful who continue to perpetrate acts of sabotage, all other counterrevolutionary elements will be placed as regular or candidate members in co-operatives or given responsible posts in production. In Honan Province and in Kwangtung statistics demonstrate that the virtual totality of former counterrevolutionaries have entered co-operatives. A "fine and prosperous future" is likewise promised to city-dwelling counterrevolutionaries who rally to the regime.

Lo Jui-ching concludes,

> If we act in this manner, it is because we are able to, thanks to a radical change in our country's concrete situation . . . We need a greater number of persons participating in the socialist rebuilding of our homeland, we are also perfectly able to re-educate and win over most subsisting counterrevolutionary elements by means of honest work and a political education. Our hope is that those who are still holding apart from our socialist endeavor, who in the past have had a negative attitude, or who have committed sabotages will decide to walk upright along a righteous path and to adopt a positive and decent attitude toward their own country and people.

In China the counterrevolutionary campaign has produced no sensational trials of the Moscow or Prague variety. Certain leaders have been edged out of the political scene as a result of some change in the line: that was how Li Li-san entered an eclipse in 1953; a change in the other direction has just brought him back on the stage again. One major political figure has been publicly attacked and excluded from the Party: Kao Kang. He might perhaps have been sent to jail had he not chosen suicide; but here one is reduced to conjecture. Conjecturing, Rousset finds nothing that is not sinister behind the regime's moderation. "With the exception of Kao Kang," he writes, "few* big heads have rolled as yet: but the ax is ready and waiting!" I think one may rightfully retain one's doubts in the face of this lame dialectic that jiggles a minus into signifying a plus.

While there has been no great political trial, there has however been an "affair"—the only major one in six years, that involving Hu Feng. It still has not ended, which makes it all the more disconcerting. It began as a literary controversy, then warmed up with the unveiling of a counterrevolutionary plot which served as the excuse for a vast campaign against deviationist intellectuals; the timeliness of the discovery leads one to doubt its authenticity. But the "one-two punch" hypothesis does not provide a very satisfactory explanation of what happened either.

The affair hitched onto the *Dream of the Red Chamber* polemic. After Kuo Mo-jo emphasized the importance of a debate which was pitting idealism against Marxism, Hu Feng entered the picture. He was a well-known writer, above all reputed for his work in criticism; at the start of the Sino-Japanese War he had been one of the leaders of the "July Society" made up of resistance writers; he had taken a hand in numerous cultural reviews. A Communist Party member since 1937, Hu was now a representative to the National Assembly, a member of The Writers' Association, and for a while had been on the editorial staff of *The Literary Gazette*. Because of the high opinion generally held of him, he was both closely listened to and widely heard. He made two speeches; in

* Rousset's stylistic device "With the exception of . . . few . . ." is simply his clever way of telling us that Kao Kang's is the *only* "big head" to have "rolled" in the course of a political quarrel. And Kao Kang was his own executioner.

them he too attacked Hu Shih and Yu Ping-po. But he also lashed out at "those who are turning Marxism into a dueling pistol." He unsparingly assailed the *Gazette;* it had, he said, built up a kind of secret coterie whose members alone saw their articles printed; it was catering to old, safe writers with outworn ideas and ignoring young and authentically progressive talents. And Hu Feng also charged the *Gazette* with having plastered the counterrevolutionary label on his friend, the poet Ah Lung.

Chou Yang—who had not shown undue affection for the *Gazette* circle—nevertheless refuted these accusations and reproached Hu Feng on several scores. He reminded his listeners that in 1944, two years after the "cheng-fong" movement launched by Mao Tse-tung at Yenan "to correct bad tendencies," Hu had published, in his review *Hope*, a book by Su Wu entitled *On the Subjective* which extols subjectivism and idealism. As for Ah Lung, he had disfigured Marxism in his *Poetry and Reality*. Chou Yang also blamed another of Hu's friends, one Liu Sing, author of an excellent story, "First Snow," published in *Literature of the People*, for having afterward under the influence of Hu written an execrable story, "Swamp War," published in the same magazine in March 1954 and amounting to an insult to the heroism of Korean War volunteers.

Following these discussions, the Central Committee received a 300,000-word memorandum from Hu Feng; in it, he protested against "the five daggers plunged into the skulls of the writers," to wit: forcing writers to adopt a Marxist world view; to lump themselves with workers and peasants; to remold their thought; to employ a national style in arts and letters; and to make literature a political instrument. He demanded the abolition of The Writers' Association and that cultural affairs be taken out of the hands of the state. This two-hundred-page libel was not only published, it was distributed free as a supplement to the fortnightly *Wen Yi Pao* (*Literature and Art*).

To do so was to manifest nothing if not liberalism; but this part of the story only makes its sequel seem the stranger. Since these theses were considered noxious, why were they broadcast far and wide? At any rate, on February 5, 1955, at the opening of the Writers' Union Congress. Chou Yang severely criticized this document. The Congress damned Hu Feng for a "bourgeois idealist" preferring "spontaneity"—that is, "the subjective spirit"—to objective reality: Hu contradicted the Yenan precepts. More, he was accused of having created a group opposed to the Party's cultural principles and the Union voted a campaign against bourgeois idealism as exemplified by Hu Shih and Hu Feng. The Propaganda Division of the CP's Central Committee decided to organize lectures, meetings at which the two writers' theses would be exposed and taken apart. The movement reached nation-wide proportions.

On May 13, 1955, *The People's Daily* printed the self-criticism Hu Feng had sketched toward the end of January and completed in February and March. He admitted that he had been wrong "to minimize the role of the Marxist world view." He did not however abandon all his positions—and his confession, although published, was prefaced by an editorial comment qualifying it as hypocritical and incomplete.

It was at this point that the affair began to take on a new complexion. Su Wu, Hu Feng's former friend, in the same issue of *The People's Daily* made public some letters Hu had written to him and tending to prove Hu was a counterrevolutionary. On May 24, under the heading "A Second Series of Facts Concerning the Hu Feng Clique," other, more compromising letters appeared, these written by Hu to counterrevolutionaries between 1949 and 1955. Letters his wife had written were published also. He ceased to be considered merely as an ideological adversary, he became a public enemy. He was charged with conspiracy and arrested. The authenticity of certain of these letters looks doubtful; and the excerpts from them I found in *People's China*—where some fragments had been translated into English—showed indeed that Hu Feng had been violently opposed to Mao Tse-tung's cultural policy but not that he was tangled up in any counterrevolutionary plot.

What kind of reasoning lay behind this? To explode his literary theses was it necessary utterly to discredit Hu Feng? Or has he simply been the pure and simple victim of a police frame-up? Or again was he really so closely tied up with some counterrevolutionary groups that one is justified in attributing a political significance to his opposition? No matter what the answer, one cannot but feel extremely disturbed by the manner in which the entire business has been handled, by the publication of personal letters, by the fact that they were turned over by the very people to whom they had been addressed.

In his February 1956 speech before the Writers' Congress, Chou Yang took up the matter again:

> The battle against Hu Feng's counterrevolutionary clique has been the fiercest and the most complex in the annals of our literary history. Our entire intellectual world has been involved in the debates to which it has given rise. It has reflected the class struggle being waged in our country. It was a fight between the principle that literature must serve the people and the reactionary line which is opposed to the people, to socialism, to realism. It was a conflict between Marxist aesthetic and bourgeois idealism. Politically, it was a battle between revolution and counterrevolution . . .
>
> The theories of Hu Feng were reactionary, not because they were based upon a bourgeois conception of the world, but because they served to disguise his counterrevolutionary activities.

The line of reasoning which carries Chou Yang from the counterrevolutionary *tendency* to the counterrevolutionary *act* takes one's breath away. Chou's speech attacks the concepts of sincerity, of subjectivity, the "negative" side in the heroes described in the writing of Hu Feng's associates. And yet the selfsame Propaganda Division which one year before had set the anti-Hu Feng campaign in motion now, in June 1956, adopted his theses as its own: socialist realism is not the sole literary method authorized, everybody has a right to invent his personal method, the writer may therefore cultivate "spontaneity" and "sincerity"; a broad new freedom is accorded him. None the less, Lu Ting-yi reasserts Hu Feng's guilt; it is precisely, says he, because Hu's clique has been checkmated that we can today envisage a cultural liberalization. To give the lie outright to the charges leveled against Hu would have cost too many people too much "loss of face"; we cannot hence conclude anything from Lu Ting-yi's reiteration. The fact that Hu still has not been brought to trial would suggest that the affair is going to be hushed up; a number of people will tell you that he was quietly released from jail a long time ago.* One

* In May 1957 it was announced in the French press (and in June 1957 in *Time*) that Hu Feng had been released, not from jail, but from house arrest. (Translator's note)

trusts that after having made such welcome changes in its cultural policy the Party will see fit to clarify opinion upon one of the most tumultuous episodes in its ideological history.*

In connection with "the extension of culture" I spoke of the government's contest with the reactionary forces that exploit Taoist and Buddhist religious beliefs. Likewise, Christian ideology's collusion with Western imperialism had inevitably to create difficult problems both for the leaders and for Chinese Christians. If one wishes to get a clear grasp of these problems, one must go back to where the story begins.

Christianity filtered into China a good long while ago. The Church of Mesopotamia, having under the influence of Nestorius broken away from Rome, planted itself in Bagdad and fanned out into Central Asia. At Changan, capital of the Tang Empire, in 635 A.D. arrived a monk whom the Chinese called Olopan;† he built a church which under the patronage of Tai Tsung the Great rallied round it tributaries come from Central Asia: they were then numerous in China.

A Changan stone inscription cut in 781 outlines, in Syriac and Chinese, "The Luminous Teaching of Ta-T'sin"‡ and recounts the history of the Nestorian community to which the Tang em-

* Mao Tse-tung's February 27, 1957, speech, again insisting upon the importance of a healthy debate between unlike minds and different points of view and ideologies, reminds intellectuals that, just as does everyone else, they have their responsibilities to society and that society needs their honest and positive contribution. "We believe that, generally speaking, words and acts may be judged good: (1) If they serve to unite the people and our various national elements, and not to divide them; (2) If they are favorable and not harmful to socialist transformation and construction; (3) If they serve to consolidate and not to undermine or weaken the democratic dictatorship of the people; (4) If they serve to consolidate and not to undermine or weaken democratic centralization; (5) If they tend to reinforce and not to reject or weaken the leadership of the Communist Party; (6) If they are favorable and not harmful to international socialist solidarity and to the solidarity of the peoples in the world who are friendly to peace. . . . These are political criteria. In order to judge the validity of scientific theories or to determine the esthetic worth of works of art, other pertinent criteria are of course necessary. But these six political criteria are also applicable to all activities in the arts and sciences." (Translator's note)

† The Chinese transcription of the Syriac *Rabban*.

‡ By Ta-T'sin (meaning "Great China") the Chinese designated the Roman Empire.

perors granted copious favors. In 845, however, Nestorianism vanished, bracketed in the persecution then unleashed against Buddhism. It lingered on only among the federated Turks in the frontier regions; the thirteenth century reveals evidence of it among the Onguts, the Kereits, and other Gobi clans. Kublai's mother was a practicing Nestorian and her son dealt kindly with that religion. A Mongol prince, one Hayan, a Nestorian and in revolt against Kublai Khan, adorned his battle standards with the Cross; having vanquished him, Kublai considered that the Christian god had manifested wisdom in declining to protect the upstart; Marco Polo relates that at the following Easter Kublai kissed and made public obeisances before the Holy Writ. A Nestorian archdiocese was founded in Peking; Nestorian churches were raised at Yangchow and at Hangchow. In 1289 the Emperor created a special bureau to handle Christian affairs and at its head put a Syrian Nestorian who acted also as one of his ministers.

Hearing of the existence of these Christendoms, Pope Nicholas IV dispatched the Franciscan John of Montecorvino to China where John constructed two churches and baptized forty slaves bought for that purpose. Next, he converted "ten thousand and more Tartars." Three other Franciscan friars were sent out, then came Oderic of Pordenone who gave a long account of his Chinese travels. The mission flourished for three-quarters of a century, but when the dynasty was overthrown the Christians found no more friends in the Chinese emperors who indeed proscribed "foreign doctrines."

Three centuries later it was the Jesuits who resumed the offensive; Francis Xavier died on an island off Canton, having converted but one Chinese, his valet Antonio. But in 1582 Valignani and Ruggieri disembarked at Canton, disguised as Buddhist monks and laden down with timepieces and divers gifts; they contrived to build a church; later, their sphere of activity was confined to the little town of Shiuchow. Matteo Ricci joined them there and decided to forge on to Peking where he did indeed arrive in 1598, bearing a wide assortment of watches and scientific apparatus; in 1600 he was given permission to reside in Peking where he lived another ten years. German and Spanish Jesuits relieved them. Their strategy was to propagate Christianity without frontally attacking Confucianism; the two creeds were not, in their expressed view, irreconcilable; for, they reasoned, one could consider ancestor worship a lay rather than a religious rite. This attitude and their scientific knowledge gained them the friendship of the Chinese. Johann Schall von Bell, appointed astrologer to the Emperor, was invited to reform the calendar and Jesuits remained in command of the astrological bureau for two hundred years. Schall von Bell consented also to manufacture cannons, and baptized them with the names of Christian saints. He was named Vice-President of the Office of Imperial Sacrifices, Superintendent of the Imperial Stud Farm, and First Cupbearer at the Banquets. Attacked by a Chinese scholar, Yang Kuang-hsien, the Jesuits spent time in jail during the regency of K'ang-hsi, and Schall von Bell died in 1666. When he mounted the throne K'ang-hsi had the persecutions cease but forbade the Christians from making conversions; thereafter the Jesuit Verbiest also busied himself mainly with constructing and baptizing guns. When he died France sent two priests, Gerbillon and Bouvet, who persuaded the Emperor to sign an edict of tolerance in 1692: it gave the Jesuits the right to move freely about the country; they became court physicians and built a church next to the Imperial Palace. But then things began to go badly. The Dominicans, installed in Fukien Province, notably Moralès, the Order's Superior in China, had long been complaining to Rome of the Jesuits' policies, accusing them of favoring the observance of heathen rites; this "Controversy of the Rites" had already raged a long time to the tune of unending pamphleteering warfare, the Pope now siding with this camp, now with that. An Apostolic Vicar, Charles Maigrot, appeared at Peking in 1693 to advise the Jesuits that Rome had condemned them. The Jesuits then addressed themselves to the Emperor, submitting to him an interpretation of the Chinese rites; he endorsed it. From the Pope came another Legate, Monsignor de Tournon. He was cordially received in 1706; but after having openly opposed the Emperor, he was thrown out and from headquarters at Canton trumpeted against the Jesuits. K'ang-hsi swore he would brook no interference from any foreign authority, spiritual or otherwise, and Tournon was turned over to the Portuguese. The quarrel did not abate and the Jesuits incurred unpopularity. K'ang-hsi's son persecuted them.

"What would you say," he demanded, "if I sent bonzes and lamas to preach in your country?" In 1724 all the foreign missionaries save those who were rendering important services to the court were packed off to Canton. A few Jesuits stayed on at Peking and worked as painters and architects for Ch'ien Lung, but the missions disappeared. In 1742 a bull issued by Benedict XIV confirmed the hostility Innocent XIII had earlier expressed: excommunication was to be their penalty if the Jesuits did not abandon their policy.

Henceforth Christianity was considered a pernicious doctrine in China and its practice was forbidden by law. No very high opinion of this faith could be had if one were to judge it from the behavior of the missionaries in the Portuguese enclave. Regarding them, Monsignor Lambert de la Motte had written in 1667:

> All are nought but self-seeking and greedy of mind. All are governed by maxims that sort so very ill with the spirit of Christ's message that it is not possible that they ever could succeed to convert souls unto the Faith. All are acquainted with none but human means to make O.L.J.C. known and beloved. Is it not passing strange that the Jesuit Fathers hereabouts have magazines in their Macao dwellings filled with merchandises of all kinds, and possess vessels, and in all their private houses are engaged in commerces?

When at the start of the nineteenth century trading companies installed themselves in certain Chinese ports, they offered the missionaries profitable opportunities. Robert Morrison, a Protestant, sailed into Canton in 1807; he acquired a translator's post with the East India Company and during the twenty-seven years he toiled in that city, if he found time to translate many Christian books into Chinese, he accomplished only ten baptisms. An English divine, Gutzlaff, had a following of Chinese whose purported aim was to spread the Word through the countryside but who never emerged from the Hong Kong opium dens.

The Nanking Treaties opened the big Chinese ports to Western businessmen and speculators and to missionaries also. Although they were forbidden access to the rest of the country they drifted about the rural areas on the sly, which made them come to be looked upon as a breed of smugglers. They were suspected of working hand in glove with those kidnapers who stole children and sold them to factories or to brothels. It was further imagined that the foreign-operated orphanages dealt commercially in the eyes of Chinese children which, so it was said, were useful to alchemists for transforming lead into silver.

Absurd as these inventions were they reflected a truth of which the Chinese have always been profoundly conscious. That the Westerners simultaneously imported the Bible and drugs is more than one of those unfathomable and sad quirks of history; however wide the variety of means they employed, they pursued a single end: profit. In their hands Christianity was an instrument of oppression; its purpose was to give spiritual sanction to an order naked force imposed. When in 1858 treaties enabled missionaries to go wherever they wished in China and to solicit their consuls' intervention in behalf of the religious interests of Chinese converts, the British Resident Minister gruffly remarked "the absurdity in tacking a proselytizing concession onto a commercial agreement"; but this "absurdity" contained its kernel of crystal-clear logic. Western imperialism's structures and superstructures were knit in a compact, indivisible whole. The question was of ramming both an economic system and its ideological sublimation down the throats of the Chinese. No misplaced scruples therefore: political treaties could perfectly well open up China to Christianity and the Word of God could steam in on gunboats. The population of Yangchow burned the mission buildings to the ground in 1867; the British Consul, escorted by four warships, went to Nanking, demanded and obtained the resignation of the magistrates responsible for the riot. Similarly, after two missions had been pillaged, the French Chargé d'Affaires plus two gunboats arrived at Nanking to extract damages from the city's viceroy. A quantity of other such episodes occurred. They were inevitable; the missions once established, they had to be protected: but they proved that their very existence was a provocation and their continuance a violence. This is shown with utmost clarity in Chanoine Leclerq's *La Vie du père Lebbe.** Leclerq demonstrates how by the end of the last century "the confusion between the Christian religion and European politics had become inextricable. The missionaries profit

* Those Catholics who wish to arrive at a balanced understanding of the question would be well advised to read this book, written by a priest who cannot be suspected of having had any sympathy whatever for Communism, and which amounts to a crushing exposé of the missions.

from Europe's armed might and suffer from the hatred it arouses." A substantial share of the missions' funds came from the war indemnities wrung from China. In a pamphlet, *La France au Chékiang,* Monsignor Reynaud, Bishop of Ningpo, defends the rights of French missionaries against the encroachments of foreign rivals, proudly recalling the feats of French soldiery in that province. Leclerq comments,

> Small wonder then that from the Chinese viewpoint the missionaries are Western invaders in different uniform and Christians not only the henchmen of foreigners, but of barbaric, brutal, invading foreigners.

The missionaries at first viewed the Taiping Rebellion with a certain favor. Hung Hsiu-chüan, converted by a Baptist and persuaded he was a new Messiah, planned to govern the world in the name of God. The missionaries fancied their hour had come: they were at last going to be able to carry the Bible's message into every hut in China. They were swiftly disenchanted. The Messiah, Jesus' younger brother, intended to do his own preaching of the Word; that meant gettting rid of foreign priests. His design was to bring about, here and now, the Kingdom of God on earth: he wished to abolish classes and to distribute land to the poor and humble in spirit. His partisans exhibited images of the crucified Christ to the people: this man, naked and bleeding, He is yourselves, they told the peasants and coolies; the rich are they who are putting you to death. Against these Christians who had the criminal folly to wish to take the Gospel seriously was sent the eminent English Christian Charles "Chinese" Gordon who smashed them by force. The breadth, the ferocity of the repression further augmented the hatreds inspired by the Westerners and their priests.

It none the less enabled the missions to proliferate like weeds. England sent out a great number of preachers whose avowed aim was to Westernize the country. Between 1860 and 1900, 498 Protestant missions were founded. The Catholics, under the wing of France, after having set themselves up in Siccawei—later to become a Shanghai suburb—headed into the interior of China. Catholics and Protestants bought properties, founded orphanages, built hospitals, started colleges. At Tientsin in 1869 the French, without bothering to request authorization, raised a cathedral on the site of a temple. "The French nation and the Catholic missionaries were the object of the same indomitable hatred at Tientsin," writes the American historian Morse. This hatred was focused especially upon the orphan asylums. The nuns did not kidnap children as public report had it; but they purchased them, which encouraged kidnaping. They also gave a small gratuity to whoever brought them a dying child to baptize. Then an epidemic broke out, the children died like flies. The French consul refused to allow a Chinese commission to inspect the orphanage. On June 21, 1870, the Tientsin crowd lynched several French Catholics, also the consul—who had fired on them—and ten nuns. There were of course severe reprisals.

Riots occurred almost every year. The missionaries, abhorred by the people, were also detested by the functionaries upon whose prerogatives they infringed. "Making abusive use of their strength, the Christians oppress the non-Christians," ran a memorandum sent in 1871 by the Chinese government to the representatives of France in Peking. "Whence rancors, brawls between Christians and non-Christians, a ferment of discord that produces suits and contentions beyond number." When a convert was cited by a tribunal the missionaries would automatically rush to his defense; they would claim that he had been molested because of his religion and that, therefore, he was entitled to an indemnity; many people, "individuals, families and sometimes even entire villages"* would become converts to the Faith in order to benefit from this immunity. Converts had yet another motive: when a Chinese agreed to be baptized the mission gave him an initial allotment of rice, later on, a sum of cash. The converts refused to pay the Chinese community the oboles the latter expected of its members to defray the costs of religious festivals; meanwhile, forever alleging some service or other they had rendered to the state, the missionaries constantly barked after indemnities. Daily friction exacerbated a hatred whose underlying cause was the teamwork between Christianity and the forces of oppression. Speaking of this period, Chanoine Leclerq concludes: "The missions are always

* K. S. Latourette, *A History of Christian Missions in China* (New York, 1929).

and everywhere intimately connected with international brigandage." When the Boxer Rebellion exploded, the missionaries and the "underling devils" (i.e., the converts) were slaughtered—it could not have been otherwise—among the victims were 186 foreign Protestants and 50 foreign Catholics, but far higher was the toll in Chinese Christians whom their countrymen considered sellouts and traitors.

After the Boxers were put down, says Leclerq, "the missions become yet more firmly attached to armies and to legations." They had another spell of growth; Christianity did not for all that become one whit more popular. The Conference of Missionaries held at Edinburgh in 1910 allowed that the existence of the "unequal treaties" and political conditions in general had introduced lamentable habits into Christian missionary circles. A Catholic canon's book on Christianity in the Far East created a scandal by explaining that the evangelization of China had been a failure due to the total absence of Christian spirit in the missionaries. One of them affirmed,*

> We are not here to develop the resources of the country, not for the advancement of commerce, not for the mere promotion of civilization; but to do battle with the powers of darkness.

In their vocabulary the Chinese were *pagans,* in their view the Devil's creatures. They were anxious to save souls for the greater glory of God; but they cared precious little for the men to whom those souls belonged. Samuel Wells Williams, an American Protestant, wrote in a letter in 1850,

> It is much easier loving the souls of the heathen in the abstract, when one is in America, than it is in the concrete, encompassed as they are with such dirty bodies, speaking forth their foul language and vile natures.†

Another declared this people composed "of ignorant men, drug addicts and hardened sinners." Extremely few were the missionaries who, like Timothy Richard, won a place in the hearts of the Chinese by speaking their tongue, by adopting their customs,

* Quoted by E. R. Hughes, *The Invasion of China by the Western World,* p. 77.

† Quoted in *ibid.,* p. 64.

by laboring in behalf of their welfare; in the main they exhibited nothing but contempt for the population. "Themselves Europeans, they were stoutly convinced of the superiority of all that is European," says Leclerq apropos of the French, English, and German priests. When Father Lebbe reached Peking he was astounded to discover that a veritable segregation reigned in the mission: white priests and Chinese priests dined at separate tables, only whites were admitted to high table; European food was served to everyone. One of the young missionary's friends, a priest, was in the habit of beating his domestic. "You too?" demanded Father Lebbe. "What do you expect?" was the rejoinder; "I'm told that it's the only language they'll listen to." Father Lebbe's superiors forbade him to have anything to do with his Chinese colleagues; the native seminarists received only a very elementary education, for they were to be "kept in their place" and from holding important positions. The Bishop of Peking took him sternly to task for treating the Chinese as equals. Father Lebbe was no less distressed to discover that there was a "baptism bonus" and that the population at large loathed those converts who came into the fold not for Jesus' sake but for that of "the dole."

When, following the Fourth of May, a great wind of nationalism swept across China it occurred to the missionaries that reforms were perhaps in order. They were advised to show somewhat more respect to the natives. On October 24, 1926, the first six Chinese-born bishops were consecrated under the dome of St. Peter's and the decision was taken to promote the development of a national clergy. That did not prevent the outbreak of a furious wave of anti-Christian ideology. The Young China Association demanded atheism of its members. At Shanghai in 1922 there was founded an Anti-Christian Federation which identified Christianity as the ally of capitalism and imperialism. At Peking appeared an antireligious students' federation, with Christianity for its number one foe.

A hundred different pamphlets alluded to the indemnities the missionaries had squeezed out of the country, the manner in which they would interfere in judiciary and political affairs and, in short, denounced them as capitalist exploitation's right-hand men.*

* K. M. Panikkar, *L'Asie et la domination occidentale.*

The younger generation was particularly enraged by the Christian schools. Young China declared in 1924:

We are adamantly opposed to this Christian education which is destroying the spirit of the nation and propagating a culture intended to undermine Chinese civilization from within.

In November 1925 the Peking Government instituted an agency for the supervision of foreign schools and the Canton authorities decreed stringent regulations.

Materially, however, the expansion of Western capitalism carried the missionary enterprises right along with it. The missions bought real estate, did some big farming. The Catholic Church became a major landowner; in Shanghai it was the proprietor of buildings and even controlled—through middlemen—gambling houses and brothels. The schools and hospitals were run on a hard-headed business basis and fetched in handsome revenues. In 1922 China had 6,000 Protestant male missionaries and 1,110 female; also 1,745 Chinese pastors, 402,599 baptized and 400,000 catechized Christians. Three years later the number of missionaries was 8,158. For its part, the Catholic Church included 2,650 foreign priests, 1,100 Chinese priests, and 2,000,000 converts. Chiang Kai-shek dealt benevolently with the Christians; he did not enforce the regulations which prescribed a neutral attitude toward religion in their schools, and students coming out of them bitterly complained of having been forced to practice their teachers' religion and to undergo a theological indoctrination. One stunt which aroused an indelible hostility in every progressive Chinese was that pleasant one which priests used then to perform upon political prisoners under death sentence: for a small fee they bought the right to administer a last-minute baptism as the victims were about to be led out to die—victims who were paying with their lives for their revolt against an imperialism whose temporal and spiritual agents they hated.

The missionaries' attitude during the war with Japan incurred further anger. Chanoine Leclerq admits,

In Japanese-occupied territories several bishops collaborated, with an innocence which borders on ignorance, others forbade Chinese priests from intervening in the conflict.

And the Chinese took this as further evidence that, for them, Catholicism was incompatible with patriotism.

It is this body of facts which explains why, although the West managed to reduce China to a semicolonial status, Western religions fared so poorly there. In 1949, despite the development of a national clergy, despite the forty Chinese bishops, there were only 700,000 Protestants and three million Catholics in a country containing nigh on to six hundred million inhabitants.

Albert Béguin, in his preface to K. M. Panikkar's book, defends the missions. His most serious argument is that they helped the Occidentals discover the Orient. Doubtless; and one may forgive the ingratitude of the Chinese. Béguin goes on to speak, more vaguely, of the positive aspects of the missionaries' activity; well, no record can be entirely black, Japanese and Western violence also produced one or two positive results; they are unjustifiable none the less. If the Protestants and their Y.M.C.A. timidly tried to dab a little Mercurochrome here and there on the gaping wounds created by the regime they were by and large solidly for—capitalism, semicolonialism—the Catholics seem to have been worried about nothing but sprinkling the purifying water on as many heads as possible. Unless one believes—as few Christians believe any more—that every unbaptized soul is due to groan in Limbo or roast everlastingly in the Fire, one is hard put to see what service they rendered the "natives." Béguin reminds us that "they gave unstintingly of their lives and energies"; but no one prevailed upon their generosity: the Chinese would have been better pleased had they been less lavish in their gifts. Pearl Buck was well acquainted with the Chinese and, being a minister's daughter, with the missionaries; her remarks on this question have the ring of common sense.

> . . . I knew intuitively that they were not in China primarily because they loved the people . . . No, they were there, these missionaries, to fulfill some spiritual need of their own. It was a noble need . . . But somewhere I had learned from Thoreau, who doubtless learned it from Confucius, that if a man comes to do his own good for you, then must you flee that man and save yourself.*

* *My Several Worlds.*

When as a child she would remind her father of all the good things the missions had done, he himself would reply: "We must never forget that missionaries went to China without invitation and solely from our own sense of duty. The Chinese therefore owe us nothing."* She sums up the situation in these sober words: "I could not bear preaching from any white man, knowing what white men had done in Asia . . ."†

These facts, I repeat, ought to be borne in mind if one wishes to understand the Chinese government's attitude toward Catholicism. From the very first the regime announced its decision—expressed in an article in the Constitution—to tolerate all religious creeds. Three million Catholics—that is not many in a country of China's size; and in the eyes of a Chinese Marxist the cult of the Virgin is neither more nor less "retrograde" than worship of the goddess Kuan Yin. If, concerning Christianity, tolerance was made dependent upon certain conditions, that is because the government had excellent reasons for mistrusting it politically. First, this religion, Western imperialism's confederate, had for eighty years offended the feelings of the Chinese nation; ever since 1920 it had been under violent attack as anti-Chinese. Second, Catholicism is radically anti-Communist. Father Lebbe—who, for a missionary, was remarkably open-minded—could understand that a man might be a Chinese; but a Communist, no. Shortly before his death he repeated:

> The Chinese Communists are not Chinese. The Chinese Communists are not men. The Communists are devils incarnate.

It is generally known that since the moment Communism was born the Catholic Church has manifested the most determined hostility toward it. Pius IX, in a text of November 9, 1846, which reappeared in the *Syllabus*, condemned "this baneful doctrine which is called communism, utterly contrary to the very law of nature; once admitted, any such belief would be the complete ruination of all rights, of all institutions, and of human society itself." Later, Leo XIII, in the Encyclical *Quod apostolici numeris*, designates it "a mortal pestilence which attacks the marrow of

* *Ibid.*
† *Ibid.*

human society and would annihilate it." Pius XI assailed it in an allocution addressed in 1924 to the whole world; and then in a series of five Encyclicals dating between May 8, 1928, and June 3, 1933. Again, in 1939, in the Encyclical *Divini redemptoris,* he summoned all Catholics to fight Communism energetically: the anti-Communist crusade mobilizes above all the priests and the auxiliary forces of Catholic action groups, among others the Marian Congregations. The July 1, 1949, decree promulgated by Pius XII contains "The favoring of communism is prohibited under pain of denial of the Sacraments" and "The profession of communism is prohibited under pain of excommunication." The *Osservatore Romano* officially commented: "Any adherence, any aid furnished to the Communists is, whether one likes it or not, co-operation with and furtherance of their antireligious activity."

The meaning of all this is plain; when the government under Mao Tse-tung's presidency took power, the Church automatically declared war on the regime it embodied. Naturally enough, before authorizing the Chinese clergy to maintain its influence over a segment of the population, the new regime felt itself obliged to impose certain precautionary restrictions. Its attitude is clearly set forth in a *People's Daily* article of November 24, 1950:

> The problem of Catholicism and of Protestantism in China presents itself to us in a twofold manner: the question of faith, and the question of these two beliefs as tools manipulated by the imperialists to further their aggressive aims against China . . . In his work *New Democracy,* Chairman Mao emphasized that the Communists may enter into an anti-imperialist common front with certain spiritualists, indeed, with devout believers, without however adhering to their spiritualism or condoning their sects. Consequently, Chinese patriots should and shall enjoy freedom of religion, provided that the imperialist grip upon Catholicism and Protestantism be broken.

It was in this spirit that the Chinese Government asked the various Churches to subscribe to the "Triple Autonomy" principle: administrative, financial, and apostolic independence. The Chinese Church, Catholic or Protestant, must be administered and financed by Chinese, it must propagate the Gospel in accordance with instructions proceeding from Chinese clergymen. The Protestants agreed to these conditions. Dr. Chao Tso-jen, Dean of the

Theological School at Yenching University in Peking, in 1949 called for "co-operation with the Communists in order to build a new world and to merit a new heaven"; if Christianity is to maintain its presence in Communist society, it has no choice, said he, but to work with the new regime. Assembled under the chairmanship of Wu Yao-chung, thirty years a member of the Y.M.C.A., the Protestants began in 1951 and finished in 1954 the Reform which delivered their Churches and associations out of Western influence. "To achieve a veritable apostolical autonomy, Chinese Christians must by themselves discover the treasures of the Gospel of Christ," Wu Yao-chung declared in behalf of the Chinese Protestants.

As for the Catholics, the problem was not quite the same. The Chinese leaders undertook to distinguish the temporal from the spiritual spheres; they agreed that Catholics might go on recognizing the Pope's doctrinal authority; but in political matters they denied His Holiness any say whatever. Chou En-lai made this position abundantly clear in the course of a discussion with a Chinese Catholic. He said,

> The Vatican is the heart of Catholicism. One may have relations with it. But if it indulges in political activities and aids American imperialism in harming the People's Republic of China, why then we shall oppose the Vatican also . . . When the Pope defines the dogma of the Immaculate Conception, you Catholics are duty-bound to believe him. But if he sides with America against China, you, as Chinese citizens, have the duty to choose your country.

A certain number of Catholics accepted this distinction. Led by Abbot Li Wei-kuang, Vicar-General of Nanking, Hu Wen-yao, Rector of the Catholic Aurora University, and the Bishop of Peking, they constituted the so-called Reformed Church whose members now carry on the Catholic worship in China. Their point of view has been expressed by, among others, a Shanghai doctor named Yang Shih-ta, a graduate of Aurora University (run by Jesuits), who in September of 1955 wrote:

> It was decided that the Chinese people should enjoy religious freedom, and this decision is now framed in law, and that law is enforced. For example, there are over fifty thousand Shanghai Catholics who attend more than twenty churches. We go to mass, evening services, and con-

fession just as we always used to do. All the ceremonies of the liturgical year are strictly observed. On holidays it is a common thing to see three or four thousand people attending High Mass in Siccawei Cathedral. The seminaries continue to train young priests: those who have the vocation are admitted every year to the priesthood. Representatives of the Catholic Church participated last year in the drafting of the Constitution . . . Many bishops and priests have been elected to Congress: I am a member of Congress myself . . . At our college there are twenty-seven Catholic students who are aided in such a way as to be able to live by the lights of their belief: on Friday no meat is served in their dining room . . . We have Catholic newspapers. As a Christian, I give my entire support to the government because it is dedicated to the betterment of my countrymen's lives. As a Chinese, I support it because it has at last given my country its independence. We find no contradiction between our personal faith and our public duty.

Other Catholics, however, consider their Chinese "patriot" brethren schismatics; according to them, recognition of the Pope's doctrinal and spiritual supremacy is not enough: the ecclesiastical hierarchy must be subordinated to the Holy See in an administrative and temporal sense as well. So argued the Papal Nuncio, Monsignor Ribieri, who in 1951 expressed himself to the Chinese clergy thus:

You must not compose with the Devil. You must fight. You must employ every means to destroy the demon.

The Government deported him. Thereupon the Pope excommunicated (1) the Catholics who adhere to the Communist Party and to all its immediately related organizations; (2) those who endeavor to replace the orthodox hierarchy with some other directorial power; and a personal excommunication was pronounced against (3) the leader of the Catholic patriots, Abbot Li Wei-kuang, Vicar-General of Nanking.

The Pope's attitude is tantamount to a frank declaration of war. From their standpoint, the nonreformed Catholics are perfectly within their rights to fight against the Chinese government; but when you decide to "employ every means to destroy the demon" and when the demon happens to be the present regime, then you must not be startled or vexed to find yourself classified as a counterrevolutionary. One sees no reason why in the course of the various campaigns directed against counterrevolutionaries the Catholics should have enjoyed any special immunity. They have vehemently protested against, among other things, the dissolution of the Legion of Mary—which was one of those Marian Congregations uniquely dedicated, said Pius XI, to defeating Communism. Father Lefeuvre* admits that this organism "ensured a co-ordination between influential and active Catholics," which is simply to declare that it was a nucleus of resistance to the regime. In particular, it militated in the countryside against the land reform and the Marriage Act. At a time when the Korean War put their country in danger the nonreformed Catholics flatly refused to participate in the anti-imperialist campaign. One had no cause to be taken aback by the expulsion of most of the foreign missionaries and by the arrest of certain Chinese priests on charges of counterrevolutionary intriguing. Once again the Government explained its views, this time through the agency of Chen Yi:

> The Government's policy is clear and precise: the people's religious freedom is guaranteed an absolute protection within the limits specified by law . . . But the imperialists who utilize religion as a means to sabotage may expect categorical repression.

However the leaders renewed their attempts to reach an accord. The Conference of Patriotic Catholics held at Nanking in August 1953 drew up a series of Ten Articles in which even the triple autonomy went by the board; the document recognized the Pope's authority in matters of dogma. All the priests present signed it; later, several of them retracted; but after that retracted their reretraction. Local reformist committees convened all over China and rallied the majority of the Catholics to this proposition: that the spiritual and dogmatic power belongs to Rome, the temporal power to Peking.

The center of the stiffest resistance was the Shanghai church. During the night of September 8-9, 1955, Bishop Kiung P'in-mei was apprehended, so were priests, Jesuits, and nuns. The *Hsinwen Pao* editorialized the next morning that the object of these

* *Les Enfants dans la ville.*

arrests was "once and for all to destroy the Kiung P'in-mei counterrevolutionary band and to eliminate all the subversive elements concealed in the Catholic Church." At the time I write, the nonreformed Catholic Church in China is finished.

There is not the slightest doubt but that the Pope, instead of choosing this annihilation, could have preferred the alternative of conciliation. The subordination of the hierarchy to the Holy See is an affair pertaining to dogma; between the act of naming bishops and that of consecrating them exists leeway enough to permit the rendering unto Caesar of that which is Caesar's, and upon which many a concordat has been established in the course of the centuries. It is certainly not the ingenuity of casuists that has been wanting here; but rather the good will of the Roman Church. The Pope was bent on forestalling any collusion between Church and Communism, on proscribing it definitively; if Christianity will live on in the bosom of Marxist society, it will do so unlawfully, schismatically. This is a strictly political attitude, affirming little but the indissoluble alliance of the Church with capitalism. Never do the Catholics more patently attest the firmness of this attachment than when they cry their indignation to hear the Communists denounce it. The Catholics' strongest argument is that, had they agreed to the compromise proposed by the regime, they would have left Catholicism open to "destruction from within." In other words they acknowledged as a foregone conclusion that Marxist ideology would defeat Christian ideology: to a slow death they preferred a flashy martyrdom,* a good deal more edifying, doubtless, in the eyes of the Christian world. They had the right to choose. And they chose; but their insincerity shows up at the point where, themselves capitalizing on this wholly voluntary martyrdom, they shower outraged accusations upon their persecutors. Indeed, nothing better corroborates the charges leveled against these aggressive victims than the books in which they display their blind hate for the Communist regime. Can such impassioned conviction avoid being translated into words and

* Father Lefeuvre admits that if the authorities waited so long to arrest Monsignor Kiung it is because the regime would rather persuade its adversaries than clamp down; and indeed, patient until the last, it sought for years to reach a *modus vivendi* with Catholics who, stubbornly refusing to accept any compromise, finally left the Government no other choice than repression.

deeds? These would justify the measures the Government has taken.*

The gravest of the accusations brought against the missions are those relating to the orphanages. Nuns having always been more thoughtful of saving souls than of feeding bodies, their charity was, as we have noticed, largely and constantly suspect in the eyes of the Chinese population. Statistics, whose objectivity the parties concerned vainly strive to refute, indicate that this mistrust was not groundless. According to the right-minded and well-intentioned the very enormity of the adduced facts would deprive them of all likelihood: they must be reminded that in France the fate of orphans sheltered in pious institutions is usually abominable. I have personally known orphans who have spoken to me of their childhood as of a nightmare. Up at five thirty a.m. in dormitories so cold in winter that to wash one had first to crack the ice in the ewer; ten hours each day bent over needlework sold to a genteel clientele for money no part of which the embroiderers ever saw; by way of recreation, mass, vespers, evening services; virtually no formal instruction; for food, watery soups often thickened by cockroaches, milk and meat on inspection days only; whoever dared complain was locked away in a cellar, the undernourished children were withered by corporal punishments; no sanitation. As a result, half the little girls would perish of tuberculosis. These are old stories; the hygienic conditions in these places are probably more closely supervised today. But if such things were common in France thirty years ago one may well imagine how the little Chinese may have been treated. The nuns are wont to behold unkemptness and filth about the body as testifying to the Christian virtues of disdain for the carnal and submissiveness to the will of God: what with the attendant circumstances in China this pious neglect must have bred the most appalling consequences. It was reinforced by the little account in which the whites, missionary or other, held the life of a Chinese: very praiseworthy it was to rescue their souls, but as regarded their terrestrial existence, it was commonly felt that they were only too numerous.

* By these measures I mean the arrests and expulsions. As for brutal police methods, let me say once again how much I regret that the Revolution has not abolished this old tradition too.

The good sisters did not deliberately assassinate their wards, certainly not, that would have been a sin; but they considered their death with philosophical calm at best: one little angel the more in heaven, one little mouth the less to feed here on earth. This state of mind explains the scandal of the orphanages, to which thorough investigations—conducted by the Women's Associations and other organisms—and a host of individual depositions bear witness. I will cite from only a few of them.*

In connection with Nanking's Tze-Ai Home (the Home of Motherly Love), the Secretary of General Affairs, Tsui Tien-pei, gives us the following picture:

The registry for the period July 1-December 31, 1949, records that 54 of the 60 children entered that semester died. The following year the mortality rate rose each month. In January it was 61%, in May 83%. Three, four or five children would sometimes die in one day. The nuns claimed they were afflicted by prenatal diseases and congenital syphilis. But when the authorities closed the orphanage the 58 children then in it were examined: one had syphilis. The nuns, moreover, had themselves written the cause of death down in the registers; in 98% of the cases they had noted the child's death as due to "wasting away" . . . Of the 58 children examined, 97% were suffering from malnutrition and a third of them to such a degree that attempts to save their lives failed; 98% had skin diseases and 81% trachoma. Nearly all were tubercular . . . they had been given a little rice and gruel and only one half pint of milk per day—skim-milk. The sisters used the cream to make butter for their own use. The elder children had no milk at all: only a bouillon of rice and some cabbage leaves . . . The same wash-basins and pitchers were used by all the children, their skin ailments thus spreading from one to the other.

However, the children were not maintained at the orphanage free of charge. Their relatives had to pay, as fees, three to five *tous*† of rice every month. If they did not discharge their debts, the child was disposed of: sold, for 133 pounds of rice.

The same reproaches recur in every indictment: the children were not fed. Their clothing was almost never changed, their bodies were covered with open sores. Liu Tsui-ying, who was a

* Collected by the Hygiene Committee and presented in a brochure, *Children's Tears*, published (in English) at Shanghai.

† A *tou* equals 13.3 lbs.

nurse at the Sisters of Saint Joseph orphanage from 1949 to 1951, says:

> The children were deliberately starved. They were given mildewed powdered milk twice a day. They lived jammed in two little rooms stinking of urine and excrements. Almost never were they washed, almost never given a change of clothing . . . Mosquitoes devoured them in summer. UNRRA gave the orphanage some 4,000 yards of mosquito netting: Bishop Kowaski sold it . . . Most of the children were fit and happy when they arrived, but they would drop off in a few weeks.

Figuring from 1923, 57,817 little ones were deposited in the above institution and only 126 lived more than a few months: these statistics have been established by the Women's Association of China. They are not belied by Bishop Schneider, who with Bishop Kowaski directed the home, and who in a letter to the Pope owned that the mortality rate for 1946-1950 averaged 94 per cent.

More eloquent than eye-witness accounts are the registers themselves. In that kept by the Sacred Heart Children's Home in Nanking one finds, for a thirteen-month period, 192 admissions and 118 deaths. Next to the child's name one sees the word *baptized* and a date. Then, further to the right, the word *deceased* and a date. The dates are close. The cause of death is not even indicated. Older children, some however of only five, were forced to work; the work was harsh. The standard regime was undernourishment, chastisement, and mistreatment which sometimes led to death. Those youngsters who survived have come away with hair-raising stories. I need not cite them here, for the most extreme cases were obviously exceptional. But what was not exceptional but the rule was the practice of selling the girl orphans when they were seventeen or eighteen to husbands, most often degenerates. A report on the *Senmouyeu* that appeared in a Shanghai newspaper, *Liberation*, relates: "I do not know how many girls were thus forced into marriage with mental defectives, vagabonds, misfits, unbalanced individuals. Many went insane after marriage." Lin Wu-tsui, an orphan, writes: "We were married to all kinds of husbands: blind, aged, and mine was an idiot."

Here is the record of the Penn Tse T'ang home in Peking: 25,680 children admitted over an eighty-eight-year period, 23,403 premature deaths. At the age of six, or of five, they were put to work; from fourteen on, they worked fourteen hours a day. They lived on millet, in inadequate quantity. They received no education. When the Chinese government took charge of the orphanage, 95 to 98 per cent of the children were suffering from dietary deficiencies, 80 per cent had to be sent straight to sanitariums.

Rewi Alley confirmed these facts for me. He saw the little children in the Shanghai sweatshops. He saw the registers bearing the long dismal tales of babies *baptized* and *deceased*. He told me that at Sandan he took in a great many abandoned waifs, that in ten years only two of them died; while in the hands of nuns they expired by the hundred. Those sisters who have been expelled from China do not indeed deny the death figures thrown in their faces, but by way of defense argue that the children entrusted to them were half dead upon arrival. Medical examinations show that the deficiencies of the survivors resulted not from hereditary flaws but from a lack of food and of care; and when the government took over the orphanages the mortality rate plummeted instantly. The nuns' protestations are doubtless sincere, in part: they simply acted within the framework of their own system of values which makes no great case of miserable flesh. What mattered to them was saving souls and baptizing the greatest possible number of small pagans.* They do not comprehend why this attitude should be judged criminal in a country which, unlike themselves, holds human life to be the measure of good and evil. Their expulsion was simply a necessary episode in the hygiene campaign conducted by the Government.

* In a very moving little poem deploring the ingratitude of the Chinese who expelled her, a Canadian nun especially emphasizes the pleasures of the paradise which her ministrations made accessible to Chinese infants.

# 7. THE FIRST OF OCTOBER

Scattered over the length and breadth of the country, visitors usually head back for Peking in time for the First of October celebrations. I too return there at the end of September after my trip up to Manchuria. Peking looks changed. They have completed the new wing of the Peking Hotel. Downstairs in the lobby of the old building they have put in a shop selling umbrellas, silk brocades, lacquer ware, porcelains, all sorts of knicknacks. The hotel's façade, the fronts of the public buildings are festooned with red-and-gold streamers and pennants, hung with big red lanterns bellying out like pumpkins; red flags fly on rooftops. Ever since anyone can remember, Chinese towns have always brightened their predominant grays with scarlet trimmings. Red is today the color of the regime, but it has always been that of holiday and merrymaking. The streets—with which I had gradually become so familiar as just about to stop noticing them—surprise me all over again; they have become exotic—exotic even for the Chinese who also pause to watch Tibetans go by in their trailing yellow robes, a copper ring hung in one ear, and Mongols, whose tunics are gathered at the waist by bright-colored belts, and white-capped Moslems and Sinkiang mountaineers in their great fur-trimmed peaked hats. There are about seventeen hundred of us foreign delegates. During the days before and after the First travelers come to the city and leave it in a steady stream. Out of an issue of *The New Day Release* I pick these headlines at random: "Chou En-lai Greets Japanese Delegates . . . Party Given for the Kabuki Troupe . . . Interview with the Indian Minister of Health . . . Nenni Welcomed by the Press . . . Burmese Buddhist Delegation Homage to Buddha Relic . . . Italian Women's Delegation Leaves China . . . Arrival of Yugoslav Deaf-Mute Delegation."

This is no run-of-the-mill cosmopolitan atmosphere. Led by the accidental twists and turns in their individual histories, you will see people from everywhere rubbing elbows in the lounges of big New York hotels; but the only thing they have in common is the thick wall-to-wall carpet they are walking on. Here, when I run into a Spaniard, a Portuguese, a Czech, a South African, I immediately sense a nearness, a complicity with him; he and I know that different as our languages may be, words have the same meaning for us. There is no need for ceremony here; it even seems out of place. Already feeling like an old-timer, I am delighted to give tips to newcomers. As I had, they are having a bit of a time of it getting their bearings. Before you step out of the plane at the Peking airport your fancy roves. Flying in, I imagined climbing about the Tibetan plateaus; in another plane the German historian had been musing in anticipation of exploring the Tunhwang grottoes, the Italian painter had seen himself settled down in a southern village for a month of sketching, others had camped under Mongol tents. Then all of a sudden you smell the Chinese soil, and its tart odor penetrates you like truth; you look about you, you feel the heartbeat of six hundred million men, and thundering China spreads out for thousands of miles in every direction. Just where, you wonder with a twinge of anxiety, just where is the borderline drawn between the possible and the impossible? I have not been to Lhasa, I am not going there. The journalists who left two months ago for Tibet by the new road, traveling by truck and on muleback, won't return before mid-November. To get to the painted caves of Tunhwang, you must, from Lanchow on, cross the desert for a couple of days with a camel caravan—

the historian will have to be content with looking at reproductions. But, on the other hand, Canton is easy to get to . . .

The while we trade information, I pay close attention to the visitors' reactions. I have understood that, more so in China than anywhere else, there is one mistake you have to avoid: judging things as though they were *final, fixed as such.* In this country which is ceaselessly on the move, the present derives its meaning from the past it has left in its wake, from the future it is ushering in. To denigrate the regime because the standard of living here is still low or because capitalism yet subsists is to be unmindful of China's situation: you need a place to stand if you are going to move the world, to transform China you must use the past as fulcrum and lever. But what aggravates me most is this shiny ready-made benevolence which permits certain travelers to extol as absolute those achievements which only make sense as stepping-stones to something else. It is not true that a Chinese village is more comfortable and richer than a village in France; what is extraordinary about it is the progress it represents over the villages of the past. It is likewise untrue that the Chinese woman is generally the most emancipated in the world. It is naive to be overawed by the fact the Archbishop of Peking openly approves of the regime; if he didn't he'd lose his miter tomorrow. This rapturous enthusiasm offends me not only through the errors it leads to but because China deserves to be seen for what she is; you will sell her efforts short if you do not recognize the difficulties they involve. I very much fear that these perfervid bearers of good tidings with their travel diaries all but written up in advance will have trouble convincing the folks back home. It is a pity. This moment in China's history is stirring precisely because of the as yet incomplete character of the victories she has won, because of the immensity of the obstacles she has still to subdue and the toughness of the struggle she is engaged in.

*September 29.* Chou En-lai's banquet given this evening in honor of the diplomatic corps and the foreign delegates; 2,200 guests. Half of them seated in the huge banquet hall in the new wing just added to the Peking Hotel; the others in the adjoining rooms; the whole ground floor full of people.

Between the main entrance to the banquet hall and the little theater at the far end is a long table set for a hundred; to right and left, a hundred other circular tables with places at each for nine. I had plenty of time to study the surroundings, the *décor*: fifty columns—twenty-five full columns, twenty-five half-niched in the wall, all about eighteen or twenty inches in diameter and painted red—carry overhead beams done in green, blue, gold, red; lighting by means of three chandeliers, each with twenty-five electric bulbs, and by separate suspended globes: three hundred lights all told. The ceiling is about fifty feet high; a balcony draped with gray materials runs along three walls. The little theater's red curtain is lowered.

The table is covered with food. This is a cold meal. There are two orchestras, one on either side of the entrance; they play alternately, one of them Chinese music, the other Western. At seven they strike up the national anthem: Chou sits down at the head of the table near the stage; at the other end one of the marshals takes his place, he is in a glittering new uniform, bright blue and gold. The waiters begin to fill our glasses with rice wine, with wild-grape wine, with lemonade, beer, sparkling wine, whichever we want, while Chou, spotlights focused on him, makes a speech thanking us for having come to China: he ends with a toast: raises his glass to friendship and peace among nations. He sits down, rises again; proposes toast after toast to each group of guests, finally to all of them together; each time he gets up it is into a brilliant pool of light from the projectors. Then the Burmese Ambassador makes a speech in behalf of the diplomatic corps. Then the musicians break out with "Toreadoro" and Chou moves from table to table, clinks glasses with every last guest, exchanges smiles, a few cheery words with some of them, in particular bows before the mother of Zoya, the famous Soviet heroine whose story is known to every youngster in China.

"Who's this Chou En-lai fellow?" Mr. Dulles demanded one day. No further possibility of feigning ignorance any more; the name is known the world over. Twenty years ago, Edgar Snow* described Chou's trim, willowy figure; he has not lost it; and the charm of his George Raft smile is legendary. There is something

* *Red Star Over China.*

in his face you do not often encounter in China: it is not cynicism, it is not irony either, but a keen, challenging look of ready intellect. He gives one the impression of a man who, though engaged to the hilt in what he is doing, still stands far enough away from it to be able to appraise it critically. At the moment he is walking around from one table to the next with Bizet playing; his movements, his gestures are relaxed, but that sharp gaze seems in the exactest sense to recognize all these people he has never seen before; and you would call this a succession of happy discoveries and say that he is drinking with others who are not strangers any more. When he goes on into the neighboring rooms full of youth delegates and actors and dancers and sportsmen, cheers break loose: he is surrounded, embraced, deluged with gifts; and the applause and acclamations last until the banquet is over.

It is not a drawn-out affair: the Chinese have a sense of proportion and, as I said, are not much for growing old around tables. The meal over, the young people dance next door; there are Albanian and Polish soldiers in uniform and national minority delegates in their traditional attire. We step out-of-doors, and my heart beats a stroke faster: Peking is lit, everywhere. Lanterns etch the crests and cornices of roofs, bring out façades; the outlines of the public monuments and the fortified gates stand, sparkling and flat, against the night sky; this absence of relief, this sharply defined drawing gives one a stage-set feeling—it does not look like a real city, but like the light-swept pavilions of some world's fair. But all the same Peking is very real indeed; its ephemeral fineries seem to reassert what, behind them, is no mirage at all.

The avenue is ordinarily deserted at this hour; it is thronged tonight. Saunterers idle about, merchants have set up stalls against the Palace's red wall or on the edge of the sidewalk; they are vending piping hot tea, frankfurters, fruits, and there are a few who have even rigged up veritable restaurants out of a table, a bench, and a charcoal stove on wheels. Some people are eating; others watch, they are waiting. Loudspeakers attached to the lampposts along the avenue give out band music, popular tune, speeches, slogans. Mongols, Miaos, Tibetans, Uigurs in full array, red-scarfed, white-shirted Young Pioneers are drawn up in motionless groups on the curb or mark time; musicians are sitting cross-legged on the ground, little drums on their laps: tonight's dress rehearsal for the parade. Tomorrow is to be a holiday for everybody. We pass abreast Tien An Men whose famous outline glows: big red lanterns are strung across its façade.

The little adjoining streets are alive with people; children and adults are carrying bouquets of artificial flowers, they have been passed out in the factories, the offices, the schools. For the first time since coming to China I catch sight of men being taken in tow by policemen; there is no sign of handcuffs and no one is so impolite as to turn and stare as they go by. There are three of them, perhaps pickpockets or drunks. Eating, drinking going on everywhere. In secluded streets I see carnival floats, sometimes they are simply cube-shaped pedestals covered with draperies, sometimes statues, scenes, or *tableaux vivants* are set upon these pedestals. Back again in the hotel, I go out on the balcony: in the moonlight the entire city shines, falsely false. Suddenly a great raw white statue on a red pedestal comes into view: the float seems to be moving all by itself. Men pass by carrying great panels, portraits of Marx and of Mao; now a dragon at least a hundred yards long borne by a line of boys who are half hidden underneath its shell. These detached, stray fragments of festival are odd and quite wonderful to look at. But I get into bed and fall asleep. Then at about a quarter past two I awake, as much out of curiosity as because of the noise: the loudspeakers are still roaring songs. It is almost chilly now; the avenue is covered with white shirts and red flags: young men in phalanxes carry the flags high and in a mass; other youths are sprawled out on the terrace in front of the hotel, their flags lying beside them. The rehearsal will last late into the night; but tomorrow everyone can sleep to his heart's content to be ready and fresh for the big day which is approaching.

*September 30.* Morning, and Peking is sound asleep. Everybody is off. No program. Breakfast; then, under a not very promising sky, we go for a stroll, alone, in a spot in Peking we are especially fond of, behind the Imperial Palace: the wall is black at this point, flanked by two golden-roofed watchtowers, and the foot of the wall slips down into the waters of the canal; tall sunflowers push their black-and-gold heads far up the side of the rampart. It cuts at a right angle, so does the canal which on its further bank is bordered by little, low-lying houses, blank walls turned to the water, walls sheathed in dark, peeling plaster. That long strip of water reflecting the somber battlements and on the other side a humble little street . . . it has a desolate charm.

The Peking Hotel is just about upside-down. The lobby is full of tiny Burmese dancers, Hindus, Mongols. The Asiatic delegates far outnumber the Westerners. Athletic teams, religious associations, and above all cultural groups, ensembles of artists. During my stay in Peking there have been an exhibit of Hindu art, a Hindu film festival; I have seen Indonesian and Burmese dancing, ballets given by the Viet Minh, and the Kabuki troupe is about to give a series of representations. It was first and foremost to the peoples of Asia that Chou En-lai extended his "Come and see" invitation; for China considers herself the pacemaker in Asia and to have a mission there.

This evening Chou is giving a banquet in honor of the People's Liberation Army and the national minority delegates: three thousand guests are coming. There will not be an inch of space left here, so we go over to the Hotel Sin Kiao which, before the new wing of ours was added, used to be the biggest hotel in town. The Chinese were so proud of it that they put it on the visitors' itinerary; it was built with funds contributed by Overseas Chinese. The dining room is packed. We walk about the streets with some friends then go up to the roof terrace of our hotel to look at an illuminated Peking. A clear night. And we say to one another what everybody else is saying this evening: "Let's hope it's fine weather tomorrow!"

*October 1*. It is not very fine. The temperature fell twenty degrees during the night, and the sky is overcast. I get into my coat and pin the badge Tsai gave me upon my lapel—a red ribbon with black Chinese lettering on it and a red medallion showing the seal of the Chinese Republic; this is to get me admitted to the stands backed up against Tien An Men.

We start off from the hotel early, at nine, and by car, even though Tien An Men is close by: we go there by a roundabout way, the main avenue being roped off. We circle the Imperial Palace; floats carrying dummies of machines, statues, signboards, posters are parked in little side streets, knots of people are waiting by them: we are in the wings of this huge theater central Peking constitutes today. We take the northern gate into the Forbidden City, cross the park from one end to the other. Ushers direct us toward the left-hand grandstand. Underneath are little stands selling tea, lemonade, sandwiches; one can take time out during the parade to go down for a cigarette or something to drink or just to rest. The government has seen to everything required for the comfort of its guests; along the whole length of the parade route there are water pipes and taps, for the spectators are in for a long show.

We settle down in the front row—we have come early, the grandstand is still half empty. Behind us and a little to the right the pavilion rises from the terrace; Mao's picture is hung just over the entranceway. All over the red walls enormous Chinese characters spell out "Long Live the Republic of China . . . Long Live the Brotherhood of All United Peoples . . . Long Live Marxism-Leninism . . . Peace!" The avenue at our feet is bare: but further away upon the huge Red Square is a deployment of soldiers buttoned up in their beige uniforms, sailors, Pioneers in white shirts holding sprays of red and rose artificial flowers and greenery. Red flags, others of sharp bright colors or in softer pastels fly above this plaza. Military bands occupy the front ranks drawn up along the avenue. And it is really cold; to keep warm, the soldiers are doing calisthenics in rhythm. From this distance they look like a parade of little wooden soldiers. Fine showmanship in the way the colors are arranged: white shirts to offset brown uniforms, as accessory the rich hues of banners and bouquets.

The grandstand is filling up; there are places for twelve thousand people on the tiers ringing the square. Friends arrive, we make new acquaintances: here is Pietro Nenni who reached Peking three days ago, and the Polish physicist Leopold Infeld who worked with Einstein, and the German historian Matthias who came in yesterday with a planeload of French women delegates. "Well, how does it all strike you?"—we exchange impressions. "The

Chinese, I tell you," says Infeld, who is in the habit of proffering frank personal observations that are pungent and pithy, "the Chinese are the one people on earth who know absolutely nothing about cynicism."

It is ten o'clock and the orchestras strike up the national anthem; a roar of applause explodes as Mao Tse-tung accompanied by Chu Teh, Liu Shao-ch'i, Chou En-lai, Soong Ch'ing-ling—the widow of Sun Yat-sen—by other ministers and marshals, appears under the colonnade running along the terrace; Mao's place is just beneath his portrait. He is wearing the customary greenish-gray woolen suit and a cap which he will doff during the parade and wave to the cheering crowd. From afar he cannot be distinguished from the other officials; nothing draws particular attention to him. The Peking ceremonies last year were a national affair, with delegates from the whole of China flocking to the city and Mao sitting between the Dalai Lama and the Panchen Lama. This year, all the cities are celebrating their own First of Octobers and the spectacle we are witnessing is exclusively Pekingese. Peking's inhabitants are to be the marchers; it is the Mayor of the city who now speaks several words into the microphone to declare the festival open . . .

Cannons roar, prodigious salvos, again and again, the noise is shattering, the world seems to be coming apart; smoke hangs thick over the square. Then a dense silence. Two big open automobiles drive out, one from each side of the avenue, and come slowly together in front of Tien An Men. In each car stands a man in blue-and-gold uniform: Marshal P'êng Têh-huai, Minister of National Defense, and the Commander in Chief of the Army salute one another. P'êng Têh-huai quickly reviews the troops then mounts to the Tien An Men terrace and reads out the order of the day. Then the Commander in Chief's car moves slowly away, followed by soldiers, tanks, artillery: the parade has begun.

I understand that the Quaker delegates presently visiting China have refused to watch these ceremonies by way of protest against the military parade which, however, is over with very soon. Some jet aircraft zoom noisily by and that is that; the civilians arrive. First comes a formation of color guards belonging to the various minorities: they carry enormous red streamers aloft, against the red stand out gilt inscriptions: "Long Live the First Five-Year Plan . . . Let's Free Formosa . . . Long Live Peace." Next come great pictures like those one sees in Moscow parades: portraits of Mao, Chou En-lai, Sun Yat-sen, Marx, Engels, Lenin, Stalin, portraits also of Molotov, Malenkov, Bulganin, Khrushchev rise above black-haired heads. Slogans and pictures are due to reappear many times during the next four hours. Suddenly it is a huge garden that is marching our way: thousands of youngsters are waving bouquets in the air, the color of hawthorns in bloom; they arrive opposite Tien An Men and then, all at once, release a cloud of doves as though out of a magician's hat; the birds soar upward; above the crowd rise multicolored clusters of balloons pulling bouquets, flags, red standards written over with "Five-Year Plan, Formosa, Peace"; the sky turns into a vast fairground.

The children are succeeded by fifteen hundred activists who have just finished having their congress; coming eighty abreast and ranked six or seven deep, spanning the entire width of the avenue, for three solid hours a steady tide of men in dark blue cotton flows past: the workers, employees, students, artisans, shopkeepers of Peking and the peasants from Peking's environs. They carry flowers, banners, flags, olive branches, white paper or jigsawed plywood doves; they surround those floats I saw waiting in the side streets and which are now in full regalia; each float symbolizes the work done by each group: model locomotives, gearboxes, generators, reaper-and-binder combines, blast furnaces, a 6,000-kilowatt turbine, a sheaf of wheat, a basket of fruits, a bolt of blue material. On panels are drawn production charts and graphs showing how it has risen. All these paraders look gay—they are smiling and laughing. When they get to in front of the officials' platform, they stop, jump, spring about, wave and toss their flowers, and laugh aloud. "Can you possibly tell me that all this is faked?" Rewi Alley asks me. No. This cannot be faked. These people are making this holiday because they want to; they are happy and five hundred thousand radiant faces are overwhelming proof of it. I am struck by the unusually personal, direct character of their relation to Mao. Nothing here of what is called "collective hysteria," "mass hypnosis," the "mystic leader." None of these men is in any "trance," none "absorbed body and soul into the mob"; these are half a million individuals, each asserting his own self, having his own good time; it is not browbeaten servility you see in these faces, nor the glassy stare of fascination you see in these eyes; but rather downright affection. This worker, that artisan greets Mao as one man shakes hands with another; waving a bunch of flowers, looking up with a broad grin, he says thanks, just as you would to a friend who had done you a good turn.

Let me pause here a moment. In the spring of 1956 the bourgeois press gave us to understand that "destalinization" had "Mao up a tree," that he had been practicing some "cult of the personality" on his own. This same press, suddenly unveiling a "Chinese Stalin," had, a few months earlier, broadcast mysterious rumors concerning Mao's failing health, his frequent absences, his eclipse. According to this low-down, Liu Shao-ch'i, Communist Party Secretary, was "the real boss of China"—which, needless to say, led to some clever speculation. Eyebrows were raised when Mao emerged from nowhere in July to make his major speech on the co-operatives: plainly, China was in a desperate fix. Back in Paris after my trip, friends were much surprised to hear that I had several times seen an altogether hale and hearty Mao; they had thought him bedridden and done for. How does this retiring—and suspicious—behavior jibe with "the cult of the personality"? Which then is it going to be: Mao as a moribund puppet, or Mao the ubiquitous despot? The journalists must make up their minds, for Rousset's following cannot be expected to swallow both absurdities at the same time.

The truth is that Mao Tse-tung's official position, that of President of the Republic, involves a rather light burden of duties. His personal prestige, his qualities, his competence assure him a preponderant role however; since 1927 he has been above all the unchallenged specialist on peasant questions. But the power he exercises is no more dictatorial than, for example, Roosevelt's was. New China's Constitution renders impossible the concentration of authority in one man's hands; the country is governed by a team whose members have been united through a long common struggle and by a close friendship. Moreover, Mao's extreme simplicity of habits, the quiet confidence with which he moves here and there without squads of motorcycle police, indeed without any bodyguard at all, would rather liken him to Lenin than to Stalin. There are a good many pictures of him in China and there are one or two songs that are sung about him; no doubt at all, the man is popular, he is loved. Is that the lot of tyrants only?

The parade continues. All the while watching it, we cast sidelong glances at each other: Poles, Frenchmen, Italians, we were all bred on irony, taught to keep our emotions on a leash, and our sophistication includes the keenest unwillingness to be made a fool of; each of us wonders to himself whether he is all alone in feeling moved by the earnest joyousness of this crowd on the march. It is a relief to hear Infeld murmur: "When you see that, you don't much want to be a cynic any more." And we even feel a little bit ashamed: what is all this false modesty of ours about? these categorical imperatives of skepticism? Now it is Nenni who expresses our common remorse as, shaking his head, he murmurs: "Impossible to imagine anything like this in Rome or Paris. I don't know. One has to have a certain freshness in the soul; and we've gone stale somehow." Yes; it is perhaps this that is most moving about China: this freshness which now and then gives human life here the luster of a well-washed sky.

Students from the aeronautical school release gliders and little gas-powered model planes which rise like a shot, level out, descend in spirals toward the gilt roof of Tien An Men or into the crowd; some keep climbing right out of sight. These people coming now are the cultural workers. Eight thousand actors and dancers. It is the big moment in the parade: there is the "theater in the street" the Surrealists dreamed of. First, borne along on floats whose wheels and drivers are invisible, *tableaux vivants* evoke the plays now being staged in Peking: *The Song of the Steppes, Across Plains and Over Mountains.* Then dozens of artists disguised as lions, monkeys, and warriors of opera leap, prance, dance, battle according to classical tradition; tremendous dragons swim through blue billows: canvas rippled by unseen stagehands simulates the undulation of the sea; the dragons' sinuous bodies are a hundred yards long and more—a gigantic and wonderfully co-ordinated ballet. Jugglers performing their feats come by, human pyramids advance balanced on bicycles or on unicycles, acrobats do cartwheels, handsprings, great leaps. Gymnasts and sports associations bring up the rear of the parade: young women spring in unison through rolling hoops, male weight-lifters press bar bells all together; each group does something different. Four hours have passed by, we all have stood the whole time. And we have not noticed the hours or felt tired watching this incredible pageant which started with a military parade and ended up with a circus.

Now the soldiers and Pioneers massed on the Red Square race toward Tien An Men, waving flags and flowers—the avenue is covered with them. Mao walks slowly to one end of the terrace, then to the other, greeting the foreign guests and waving his cap to the people.

It is two in the afternoon and the crowd begins to disperse.

The sky has cleared during the day; it is a cool but bright evening as at seven thirty we climb the stairway leading to the Tien An Men terrace: a hundred delegates have been invited to come and watch the fireworks from there. We go over to the balustrade. There are four hundred thousand people gathered on the square and on the avenue: "Caviar," says Sartre, peering at all those dark heads pressed close together. Still other people are scattered through the parks. Innumerable flags sprout from the throng, around them circles form, people are dancing; most remain grouped by schools, by factories, by workshops, but some pass from one circle to another. They dance rounds, farandoles, there is another dance to music something like blues, and also the national *yang-koo* which somewhat resembles our old three-quarter-time *bourrée*; others play blindman's buff; actors have donned their theater costumes and are giving pantomimes. Every light in Peking is ablaze: thousands of lampions sparkle, candelabra illuminate the avenue. We sit about little tables on which there are teacups, cigarettes, fruit, candies; while I chat with Mao-tun and his wife, Chou En-lai moves amid the guests, exchanging words, shaking hands; then, similarly at ease, Mao Tse-tung, by himself, with quiet unostentation makes the rounds of the tables. What is so winning about all the Chinese leaders is that not a one of them plays a part; they are dressed like anybody else, anybody at all, and their faces are not deformed either by class mannerisms or by those who, occupying high office or having the need to maintain a front, so often foster; these are just faces, plainly and wholly human. Never before have I seen official dignitaries whom their positions did not hold some distance apart from the rest of the crowd. This thoroughgoing simplicity is not demagogy; the Americans—Truman, Eisenhower, for example—are demagogues:* with more or less success they mimic the guileless good guy and smile the million-dollar smile. Mao, Chou are not comedians. They have this inimitable naturalness you scarcely find anywhere save among the Chinese—a naturalness which perhaps comes from their profound ties with the peasantry and with the soil—and the serene modesty of men too involved in the world to worry about their television appearance. But let there be no mistake here: powerful or subtle, their visage manifests an uncommon personality. Not only do they seduce, they inspire a sentiment that has become rare these days: respect.

Fireworks start. If I am not mistaken, the Chinese were the ones who invented them; for centuries firecrackers have been shot off in China on any and all occasions, especially before altars or over ancestral graves. This nighttime festival far outdoes all our own Fourteenth of Julys: countless suns glitter everywhere across the dark heavens, cataracts of sparks, whirlpools of fire spin out fast-dying galaxies; eyes open wide with wonder. Rockets soar, burst parachutes which stray slowly through starry space; bubbles, networks, streaks of fabulously colored lights; searchlights sweep the sky with blue, yellow, violet beams: a ballet of pure color.

When we are tired of watching we go and sit down inside the pavilion. It is decorated entirely with flowers. A resting place. Here too are tables, teapots and cups, and delegates from all the countries of the world are talking together. We go down to the street, slip our way through the press. I have never seen such a well-mannered, such a decent crowd. To begin with, no one is drinking; in France or Italy a public ball is unthinkable without a bistro near by; here, when people are weary from dancing, they move to the edge of the circle, squat, and watch the others. And then you would say that as far as these young people are concerned sex does not exist. Partners dance a good foot and a half

* I believe Roosevelt and one or two others have been exceptions—the rare exceptions—to the rule.

away from each other; and boys and girls dance with boys or girls, it does not seem to matter which; but in no case is the behavior of the couples questionable. No yelling, no riotous laughter, no quarreling or pushing, no disorderliness at all. Simply gentle gaiety everywhere, and smiling faces. They are going to dance all night.

During the week following the First of October the foreign delegates are invited out to parties nearly every evening. I heard *The Song of the Volga Boatmen* sung by a boy who took first prize at the Chinese conservatory, *Rigoletto* by an Albanian soldier in uniform, and the great *Carmen* aria by a Soviet singer. I saw the celebrated Mei Li-fan in a young girl's role: I was reminded of those somewhat special exhibitions we have at the Carrousel. I took in the Japanese theater's "first night"; all of Peking was there: women had put jacket and trousers aside and had come out in Western-style gowns; men wore woolen suits like ours.

I am beginning to get accustomed to the ways and manners of the Chinese. They disconcerted me at first, for they then struck me as both much more natural and much more stilted than Westerners. Little by little I came to understand; in their own company they conduct themselves with a remarkable artlessness; the relationship between bodies, between needs shows no affectation; and in all that pertains to communication with outsiders they are greatly restrained. Madame Cheng's naturalness won me instantly. "I'm sleepy," she once said at Anshan after an official luncheon. And leaving us to drink our tea with those who were our hosts that day, she went off, lay down, and took a fifteen-minute nap. Tsai confided to me that in the West he didn't feel comfortable. "In Czechoslovakia and France it was—excuse me for having to say so—dreadful. I felt hemmed in all the time. For instance, there's nothing wrong with making noise when you eat soup or drink tea in China. At Prague or Paris it's very impolite. When we're on a trip my friends and I are always looking at each other to see if maybe we haven't made some awful blunder." The Chinese have had the habit of expectorating for thousands of years and they find spitting in public perfectly normal, even during a rather ceremonious conversation—quite as normal as we find blowing our nose. If I had wanted to bring home samples of the most typical objects I saw in Peking I would have bought a spittoon and a thermos bottle. You enter a shop and that is what you will see first: shelf after shelf of these two articles, both covered with painted flowers and birds. Spittoons everywhere: in family living rooms, in offices, trains, public parks. As for thermos bottles, they turn up in every house, on the clerk's desk, the shopkeeper's counter; no Chinese lets an hour go by without having a drink of tea. "Tea fountains" are installed in station waiting rooms, in theater lobbies: there is a big tank concealed somewhere, all you do is turn a spigot. Eliminating what you have drunk appears no more shameful to the Chinese than drinking; in Peking you will not see women simpering and mumbling their way off in search of the door to the toilet. Hereabouts, the body is tranquilly accepted for what it is; but there are hard and fast taboos for its sexual functions. Once again it is probably to their deep-rooted peasant origins that the Chinese owe a simplicity unsullied by any vulgarity.

Artifice appears, on the other hand, in their relations with the outside world. The kindness of the Chinese, their thoughtfulness and gentility are profound, their consideration of others delicate; and today they gladly express cordiality to their visitors by means of applause; and women embrace women. But intimate acquaintance is difficult to attain. Mine with Madame Cheng seems entirely exceptional. A long tradition has taught the Chinese to contain their feelings and not to express their views, to avoid personal questions and confidences. Our South African friend having inquired of the delegate who welcomed him at Nanking, "Are you a married man? Do you have children?" the interpreter smiled and declined to translate the questions. "It's not discreet," he explained. A Frenchman in his fifties asked his young interpreter whether she was married. "Indeed!" she replied with a frown, "what would you say if anyone were to put such a question to you?" "Why," said he, laughing, "I'd say that I was married and had two youngsters." The young lady hesitated, unbent. "I have a fiancé in the South." After two or three weeks had gone by Tsai began to talk to me with complete openness; but at the start he had been a perfect clam. When I lunched with Ting-ling I noticed paintbrushes on her worktable; I asked if she painted; she simply smiled and said nothing. The Northerners are even harder to get at; when we were in Mukden the contrast was striking between, on the one hand, Madame Cheng and Tsai who are both from the South, and the tall, wooden-faced Manchurians. Dinner was ending; as he raised a final toast, the writer who had silently escorted us here and there during the whole day said, smiling: "I've a dreadful fault. It's not knowing how to show the feelings I feel in my heart." Tsai, having translated that succinct self-reproach, nodded his head. "Yes," said he, "they often say we Chinese are like our thermos bottles: a cold exterior but warm inside." The fact is that, failing outgoingness, certain Chinese are so sensitive and have a graciousness so exquisite that it succeeded in creating a strong and living human contact between us, strangers that we were one to the other.

# 8.

# CITIES OF CHINA

I remember an old Soviet film, *The Mongolian Train*. Some Westerners and a few compradors strut around in their Pullman cars while a wretched herd of people stifle in the heat and dirt of the overcrowded third-class coaches. I was curious to see something of today's Chinese trains. It is twenty hours by rail from Peking to Mukden; thirty from Peking to Nanking; three days from Nanking to Canton. I saw something of them.

There are several classes; the seats, arranged in two rows on either side of a central aisle,* are sometimes bare wood, sometimes upholstered. In the night trains there are several categories of sleepers. I slept in a compartment of two double-decker bunks; each passenger makes his own bed with the bedding the railroad supplies: a spread which takes the place of a mattress and a woolen blanket protected by a changeable white slip. Other sleeping cars are not divided into compartments but consist of long dormitories in which the bunks are stacked three high; a green canvas curtain isolates each person: he brings his own blankets along with him; down the middle of the corridor runs a little bench where you can sit and read or drink tea. In either case, the collective toilets are installed midway in the coach. Each passenger has his own place, whether

* That is, the way they are in American railroad coaches. Seating by compartments containing six or eight persons is traditional in Europe. (Translator's note)

for sitting or for sleeping. Notebooks for writing down complaints or suggestions are hung in each dormitory. I leafed through one: one traveler had suggested that train schedules be posted in the cars; another complained over every square inch of an entire page: "I got aboard at midnight. There wasn't anyone there to give me a blanket. I shivered for hours and caught cold." The dining cars are decorated with potted plants and pictures; as a good many Russian technicians ride the Chinese railways, international meals can be had; I even notice that the tea here is served in the Russian way: sweetened and in glasses.

It is not easy to read in a Chinese train. The radio—built in—goes all the time: opera airs or folk music come over the air, so do announcements of the next stop, so does advice on hygiene. Employees armed with brooms and dusters scour the corridors without letup; one of them pops into our compartment once every hour, carries zeal to the point of picking up the pile of books I have laid on a pull-out table and tidying underneath them. Another attendant carries an enormous watering pot swathed in rags, from it he pours boiling water alternately into the spittoons ranged the length of the corridor, and into the tea mugs. As we boarded the train, we were given faience receptacles furnished with a lid and a handle, the shape and size of certain alepots; we are sold packets of green tea; you open the packet, dump its contents into the mug, and the man with the sprinkler fills it up whenever it is empty. By about the fifth refill the tea gets pretty weak; so you buy another packet.

I leave for Nanking around six p.m. and cross the Yellow River after nightfall. I wake up early, look out to see that we are in the middle of a plain framed to left and right by low-lying mountains. All day long the train rolls on, the horizon keeps retreating and the same landscape keeps unfurling: it seems at the same time familiar and very odd. Neither moors nor forests nor rocks: not an inch of raw nature; practically no trees; the ground, flat as a Dutch polder, is cut into a multitude of fields growing vegetables, soy, beans, peanuts; each plot is about the size of a tennis court and is as variegated as a backyard kitchen garden. These features—small holding and general farming—are what one finds in much of the French countryside: but only in scattered spots, on a reduced scale; our great plains tend to be covered with uniform stretches of beet here, wheat there, or else vineyard; so, in Manchuria, there seemed nothing amiss about the kaoliang waving as far as the eye could see. What I find hard to get used to here is that from dawn to dark, over hundreds of miles, I see nothing but the monotonous diversity of the truck farms that surround Paris. Nor again, in any country, have I ever seen so many peasants busy tilling the soil; they care for it as assiduously as if they were tending a garden, and employ gardening tools: pronged weeding hoes, mattocks, knives shovels, spades, trowels. Now and then someone is plowing: the plow being drawn by a squat ox is identical to the plows figured in the Tunhwang frescoes. When the plowman, as we saw two or three times during the journey, wears a long black gown with an ancient look, then the old stereotypes become startlingly true to life and one feels as if one had slid back forty centuries into the past. Most of the men in the fields, however, are dressed in the usual blue cotton outfit; all are neat, none in rags.* Between the fields I note upright gray stones: boundary markers, the land is studded with them; they catch the eye all the more in that save for human silhouettes no vertical line breaks the horizon. This region is as treeless as the one I flew over. For a couple of hours we do see rows of young poplars planted since the Liberation; then no more trees, not one. For heating purposes the peasants burn the brush they gather in the mountains; or burn kaoliang stalks.

The mountains surging on the left and right are as monotonous as the plain. But one of the peaks is famous; Madame Cheng points to Mount Tai Shan which, in the middle of Shantung, is the Mountain of the East, the most renowned of China's four sacred mountains. Its summit, 5,060 feet high, is crowned by temples to which pilgrims by the hundreds of thousands come to pray. Since the beginning of recorded history only five emperors have dared go there to perform the *Fong* sacrifice, the most solemn of all and one which demands absolutely pure hands. Innumerable legends revolve around Tai Shan.

As day fades, spots of vivid color break out against the gray-green background of the fields; little trees bear orange fruits: per-

* This, M. Guillain is forced to concede, is a radical and truly extraordinary change.

simmons; the purplish-red bushes are a species of gorse from which brooms are made.

Night darkens the windows. It is eleven o'clock before we reach the bank of the Yangtze; no bridge crosses it. When the one under construction at Hankow is finished, north-south rail traffic will be transformed. For the time being it must be a ferryboat. This entails lengthy maneuvering.

### *Nanking*

Nanking lies on the farther, the right, bank of the Yangtze; for three centuries—from 318 to 589 A.D.—it was the seat of that kind of Eastern Roman Empire that South China became when the Chin dynasty abandoned the North to Turko-Mongol hordes. Reconquered by the first Sui emperor, it enjoyed a new period of glory when Chu Yüan-chang, later the Ming dynasty's founder, fixed upon it for his capital in 1368. He enclosed it within a wall ninety-six li long, and resided there for the remainder of his life. Destroyed by the Taiping rebels, shoddily rebuilt by Chiang Kai-shek who made it his headquarters, Nanking lacks character. In 1937 the Japanese sacked it: they butchered no fewer than forty-two thousand people. Children were massacred and all women from ten to seventy raped.* Edgar Snow recounts† that, afterward, the girls of Nanking habitually walked with their heads lowered, avoiding every gaze, unable to bear the sight of a man. Countless houses had been put to the torch; orgy and looting had gone on and on, day and night. The international zone to which 250,000 people had fled for their lives became a full-blown concentration camp: thousands of men and women were plucked out of it and killed by the Japanese.

Nanking numbers 1,400,000 inhabitants; it has little industry. The houses here do not resemble those in Peking. Instead of being hidden behind walls they stand at the edge of the street, have windows looking out upon it, are three or four stories high. On the outskirts of town are many large wooden sheds built in the form of a hollow square: inside is a vacant lot serving as a court-

* The facts and figures were established by the Nanking International Rescue Committee.

† See his *Scorched Earth*.

yard, behind it the part of the building where people live, and in the rest artisans are engaged in metalwork or carpentry.

Round about Nanking there are numerous monuments which for the most part I find only mildly interesting; there is, leading to the tomb of the Mings, an admirable funerary walk bordered by stone statues of men and animals twice life-size. I was also taken by the lake which, encompassed by a black wall, is a vast expanse of lotus. The lotus plant, whose roots are submerged in mud, below, whose flower, wonderfully white and pure, opens in the sunshine, is not only rich in symbol, and sacred, it is nourishing too. Its fruit is eaten, so is its root; meat and other foods are enfolded in its leaves which, impermeable to oily substances, give things a delicate aroma and taste which Southerners are fond of. The season for flowers and fruits is now over; the lotus' stem ends in a pin-cushion whence all the pins are gone. But the leaves are green and lush, and now is just the right time for picking them. Women in high boots, wading knee-deep in the muck at the bottom of the lake, are gathering them today; they load them into skiffs which take them to artificial hills rising in the middle of the park; there the leaves are laid out to dry in the sun. The aquatic gardens have thus spread out over land, lotus is everywhere. Other women collect the dried leaves and thread them on strings.

As we are drinking tea on a lawn a delegation of Japanese comes round a bend in the path. They all have mustaches, horn-rimmed glasses, wear snappy Western business suits, and each carries a leather briefcase. I think of the sack of Nanking and wonder whether the Chinese, before their Japanese guests, must not have much the same feelings Europeans had when the first German tourists began to reappear after the war. I ask Madame Cheng. "We must learn to forget," she says with a quick faint smile. A smile which shows that she has not forgotten.

We take the train at midnight. From Nanking to Shanghai, I am told, the line traverses 164 bridges. I am not aware of going over them, though, for I fall asleep. But when I gaze out of the window early in the morning I see that we are indeed crossing many streams and canals. There are cotton fields on both sides of the tracks. The peasants here look better dressed than in the North: the women wear bright-colored cotton print vests. We are getting near; the barge-filled canals become ever more numerous. The suburbs are poor, they seem overcrowded: there is an endless throng in these streets whose surfaces are paved with small stones and upon either side of which stand mud huts with thatched roofs. Further away smokestacks rise and, further still, skyscrapers: a queer sight for one arriving from Peking.

The train slows; we enter Shanghai.

*Shanghai*

Then called Houating, Shanghai was originally nothing but a little fishing village in the middle of the Yangtze delta; when silt had choked the port of Soochow, at the mouth of Soochow Creek, boats began to cast anchor at Houating. A commissioner of trade empowered to collect taxes was assigned to the town in the eleventh century; a customhouse was established by and by; the year 1279 saw Houating become independent of Soochow and thereafter pay taxes directly to Peking. The town ranked only as the seat of a hsien and was of such little account that Marco Polo does not even mention it. Japanese pirates raided it frequently; they ravaged it in the beginning of the sixteenth century; therewith the Ming emperors raised a wall three miles long around it. The treeless swampland it lay upon was so flat, so desolate that a French traveler wrote in the mid-nineteenth century, "Compared with such a landscape, La Camargue and the edges of the Charente are quaint." Economically speaking however its location was choice. It stood at the juncture of Soochow Creek and a canal that connected the creek with a branch of the Yangtze; widened in 1403 by the Mings, this canal made an important stream of the lower part of the creek whose upper part henceforth was simply a branch of the large, semiartificial Hwang Pu River which flows from Shanghai down to the sea. By means of a great network of canals and watercourses the city is in touch with regions that are among the richest in the world: the Yangtze Valley, the fertile plateaus of Szechwan, the Great Plain in the North. Shanghai is swept by the cool dry winds which blow down from Central Asia and also by the mild trade winds of the Pacific: its climate is semitropical during a third of the year, temperate during the rest. Sheltered from typhoons and high tides, the waters of the Hwang

Pu offer ships a safe haven. Shanghai gradually grew into the center of traffic between North and South China. Dissatisfied with the situation imposed upon them in Canton, the British were delighted with the advantages Shanghai afforded. Lindsay, sent by the East India Company to negotiate with the Chinese government, in 1832 obtained an audience with the supervisor of the port and learned that shipping activity at Shanghai was heavier than at Canton; in a week he himself counted four hundred junks carrying cargoes of from one hundred to four hundred tons tie up at the Hwang Pu docks. He related as much in his report and listed the various factors which rendered Shanghai a singularly propitious town for commercial undertakings. American missionaries corroborated Lindsay's observations. And so, on June 11, 1842, the British cruiser *Nemesis* steamed up to the city while two thousand British infantrymen attacked its flank. Shanghai fell after nineteen days of fighting and General Hugh Gough set up his headquarters in the temple of the city's guardian deity. The aggressor's reward was the Treaty of Nanking, signed in August 1842. Shanghai became an open port; a five-mile-wide strip of territory by the river was not sold but—which comes to the same—leased indefinitely to the British who also received the privilege of extraterritoriality. They created a Municipal Committee which in 1869 promulgated "The Land Regulations": by means of this allegedly "freely consented charter" the Committee arrogated the right to raise taxes, to collect duties, to provide the city's police force and health department. The East India Company's monopoly having been abolished in 1836, in rushed a mob of English and American businessmen who got together to form the "International Settlement" while the French set themselves up near the Chinese part of the city. Thus, at the same moment the first alleys of Chicago were making their appearance on the shore of Lake Michigan, and as adventurers were throwing up the first shacks of San Francisco on the edge of the Pacific, the Chinese saw the first hongs rise along the left bank of the Hwang Pu.

By the river ran a towpath. Straining on ropes, half-naked coolies would haul the heavy grain-laden junks upstream; on the spongy ground running parallel to and just behind that narrow strip of earth along which the gasping Chinese toiled, Chinese contractors built, with bricks imported from England and in conformance to

British blueprints, two-story homes with a big veranda downstairs and a big balcony upstairs: from one end to the other of the great boulevard dubbed "The Bund" ran brick arcades; the four ground-floor rooms served as offices; the occupants lived in the second story. These were the hongs; the building style was nicknamed "the comprador style" because, like the comprador himself, it was a bastard compromise between the Chinese and the Occidental. Around the houses stretched private gardens and public parks which then gave the city an aristocratic air: the *taipans** were said to dwell in palaces.

They were less well off than the Canton traders in one respect: communications were poor between Shanghai and the outside world. The mailboats called at Woosung on the coast and a good distance from the city: pony-express riders would come galloping down the Bund, tossing mail pouches onto the doorsteps of the firms. A telegraph wire crossing Siberia put Shanghai in touch with London in 1871; in 1908 the first train rolled into the city. That rail line connected Shanghai with Nanking; and the next year a spur was brought up from Hangchow. But the corresponding highways were not opened until 1932. Holed up in their concessions, the Westerners thus lived in virtually total isolation. In addition, although well sheltered, the port had its drawbacks. The Hwang Pu channel had been fifteen feet deep at the start but by 1905 alluvial deposits raised the river bed five feet. Much labor and expense were necessary before, in 1928, one could count on a twenty-two-foot depth and then only for a few hours during the day; and dredging operations had to be carried on continually. At the entrance to the estuary there was a particularly large bar of silt—the English called it "Fairy Flats"—which compelled large ships to wait for high tide; the biggest vessels were not able to pass at all. In 1936 Shanghai was the shallowest, the narrowest, and the most encumbered of the major Far Eastern harbors.

Nevertheless, Shanghai grew in population more rapidly than Chicago or San Francisco or Sydney. Its expansion was owing to a fact that has left a lasting mark on the city's character: it filled up with refugees. Some three hundred thousand Chinese, driven from their towns and villages by the bloody Taiping Rebellion, sought sanctuary in Shanghai. The old Chinese sections, hemmed

* As Western businessmen were called.

in by a wall and already too densely settled, could afford them no space; they asked the Westerners to cede them some of the land they had leased for next to nothing. Frenchmen, Americans, Britishers stepped right up in answer to the call: they broke their gardens and lawns into tiny lots, and sold them at astronomical prices to homeless and threadbare Chinese; or else they slapped up houses in a hurry and rented them for fancy prices; so profitable was this real-estate game that the British Consul even went to the point of parting with half his magnolia park. The city lost its aristocratic charm; it became strewn with ramshackle houses and there was no way of avoiding the crowd of natives if you stepped out into the street. These natives, however, possessed no rights save those of paying rent and taxes. They were tried for minor offenses before a mixed court, graver cases were referred to the Chinese tribunals. The Taiping uprising once quelled, many of them trickled home; but others poured in when, at the turn of the century, Shanghai developed into an industrial town.

At first it had been devoted exclusively to commerce; the Westerners bought and sold tea, silk and, above all, the opium they imported from India and which they had also taught the Chinese how to grow. Officially abolished in 1917, this business became clandestine but thrived none the less. The first factories were built by the Japanese north of the city; the English followed their example, putting up a textile works, the Ewo Mill. Soon, without turning away from its profitable trade, the city went in strongly for manufacturing: there were factories everywhere, most of them textile works belonging to the Japanese. All the poverty-stricken peasants whom floods, famine, and war were driving from their huts went to the city in search of work; men, women, children were taken on at laughable wages; thus a proletariat was born, and it grew swiftly. In 1925 there was a further influx of 250,000 Chinese; they brought Shanghai's total population to three million. Immense and appalling slums budded on the rim of the city, especially to the north.

While the native proletariat increased by leaps and bounds the white population also grew, capital accumulated, the city expanded and beautified itself. The Boxer Rebellion precipitated a sharp but brief recession. Nanking Avenue, a main thoroughfare running off at right angles from the Bund, was laid out and lined with fancy shops; buildings shortly rose to four and five stories. Beyond the quarter where the Chinese lived they built, on either side of the road leading to a place called "Bubbling Well," a residential section of large villas surrounded by spacious gardens swarming with mosquitoes. The original hongs were supplanted by tall modern office buildings. In attractive parks—"No Chinese, No Dogs"—good society would stroll for a breath of fresh air. Tramways appeared at the start of the century—the company was a British monopoly—and then the first autos, a pair of Oldsmobiles, were unloaded on the Hwang Pu wharf; more cars soon arrived and people also went about in rickshaws which in 1874 a Frenchman had the idea of introducing from Japan. The Westerners were not pleased by the arrival, in 1923, of three hundred White Russians, more of whom later came to Shanghai from Manchuria. Penniless, they worked as laborers or entered into the service of wealthy Chinese; all of which the English, the French, the Americans considered very damaging to white prestige.

Together with its splendors Shanghai had more than one sordid side; it boasted elegant villas, lovely gardens, but its water supply was meager. At first drinking water, which had to be filtered and boiled, came straight from the Hwang Pu. A company set out in 1883 to tap the river further up and to pipe water down to Shanghai, there to filter and purify it with chlorine and alum: it tasted bad and remained dubious. One French and two Chinese companies also went into the water business; but the purification was still insufficient: and polluted water was in 1926 responsible for a cholera epidemic which ravaged the Chapei workers' districts north of the city. As regards quantity, in 1936 it was estimated that Shanghai consumed a daily hundred million gallons of water,* or less than enough to supply New York City—with scarcely twice Shanghai's population—for two and a half hours. The water shortage had the most disagreeable consequences. The current in the sewers—open ditches, rather—was too weak to budge the waste that piled up in them and rotted. Until 1923 there was no running water in Shanghai latrines. Household garbage and human excre-

* The figure does not include water that was drawn from private wells. But of these there were exceedingly few.

ment was bought by collectors who carted it off in barrels, loaded it upon scows, then resold it as fertilizer to the peasants in the outlying areas. This business continued to flourish notwithstanding the sewage system and two incinerators installed about 1934.

Meanwhile Shanghai was turning into a modern city. In 1925 the wealthy Sassoon family had the first skyscraper erected; in view of the nature of the soil, the undertaking seemed impossible; but the difficulties were surmounted and the result was Sassoon House, a fifteen-story edifice, white, bulky, topped by a sort of black belfry; a whole row of skyscrapers soon stood along the Bund, their overall effect reminding one of Chicago's Michigan Avenue for ugliness; they sit on veritable rafts of reinforced concrete, floating on the mud of the ancient swamp. Toward 1933 the price of silver shot up: Washington was in the market. The bankers sold every ounce of it they could find: entire shiploads of dollars left for the United States. A catastrophic inflation ensued; but before it was fully under way Shanghai knew a moment of unparalleled prosperity: more big buildings, hotels, department stores, new banks mushroomed out of the mud.

Fashionable society's favorite amusement was horse racing and dog racing. During three days in the first week of May, during three others in the first week of November, all the offices would close and off all the Westerners went to the English-owned race track in the center of town. Each taipan had his stables: the most famous were those of the wealthy and celebrated Jardine. No jockeys, though; most of these gentlemen did their own riding. The greyhounds in the dog races were so plentifully doped that it was no uncommon sight to behold one of them fall dead in the middle of the contest.

The rich adventurers and the poor sailors who drifted about the streets expected other pleasures: "a sink of iniquity" was the phrase an English preacher used to qualify Shanghai at the turn of the century. Next to the lush Shanghai Club—with its "longest bar in the world"—flourished a swarm of cafés, dance halls, cabarets, gaming houses of every description, opium dens, and brothels. Ostensibly illicit, the sale of opium was openly carried on in the French concession: the drug came in packages bearing a label upon which the purveyor's name and address were printed. As for the brothels, Shanghai had, in proportion to its population, more prostitutes than any other city in the world: in 1934 the ratio stood at one whore to every 130 inhabitants (while Paris made a relatively poor showing with one to 481); a few Western women plied the trade in Shanghai but the great majority were Chinese girls whom procurers bought at a tender age from needy families for two or three dollars a head, or who were kidnaped with impunity and put into action at the age of thirteen.

The city was infested with beggars, underlings of a powerful crime czar; they robbed people in broad daylight and especially preyed upon travelers just off the boat. Quantities of gangs terrorized the population; the racketeers paid protection money to the police. Press gangs were active: after they had loaded a man up on alcohol he would be given a paper to sign and would wake up at sea and the member of a crew; this goes on in all port towns but the practice was so widespread here that it entered the American language as a verb: *to shanghai.*

Bombed in 1932 by the Japanese, occupied by them as of 1937, Shanghai was in Chiang Kai-shek's hands again in 1945. For four years it was the scene of indescribable corruption and lawlessness. The Nationalist officers had sworn to turn Shanghai into "another Verdun"; when the Red Army drew near, they scampered out of town and the enlisted men went over to the Communists en masse. They entered Shanghai on May 25, 1949, almost without firing a shot.

I mentioned earlier that, after first wishing to siphon off some of Shanghai's unnaturally swollen population, the government gave up the idea. The city now contains six million inhabitants, nearly all members of working-class families.

Where Soochow Creek and the Hwang Pu meet there is a hotel of over ten stories: between 1945 and 1949 it served as a brothel for American soldiers; today, its occupants are Soviet technicians and their families. From its roof one can see the entire city: huge, sprawling, with its jutting skyscrapers, it is as depressing a sight as some city in the Middle West. You make out the sharp spires of a Catholic Church, the royal blue domes of an Orthodox Church, phony palaces that look like Pennsylvania Station and something large topped with vanilla ice cream that turns out to be the Russian exposition and information center.

The Bund skyscrapers propped up on underground beds of cement are now taken up with people's banks, offices; trolley cars and lanes of automobiles cover the avenue—this aspect of Shanghai is altogether Western. But the river belongs to another world. Barges, junks, sampans slip noiselessly along: not one is powered by a motor; the breeze fills matted sails stiffened with full-width battens; men row; sometimes an entire family will wield sculls or poles to bring a heavy vessel in. Traffic on the river is intense; a dispatcher posted where the two streams join calls out instructions through a megaphone: sails are lowered to decrease their speed and avoid collisions. Few boats move seaward; there is a little coastwise trade, but most of it is upstream and with the interior: something like thirty thousand miles of canal link Shanghai with an area of inland China where two hundred million people dwell. All transport is by water in the delta. Boats are not only used for moving goods, many are stationary; a fraction of the population lives aboard them in regular villages strung out on the banks of rivers and canals. Owing to the embargo, things are very quiet nowadays in the port bordering the Hwang Pu. I saw only one large foreign ship: it was flying the Union Jack, Asiatics made up its crew. Men were unloading bales of cotton and sacks of rice brought down in junks; they were singing a kind of plaintive, incisively rhythmic chantey while they worked.

Behind the Bund lies the former International Settlement, a museum concentrating every variety of Western tastelessness. It is not easy to decide which merits the prize for ugliness: the American-style tall buildings, the English cottages, or the villas reminiscent of Deauville's most deplorable crazes in gimcrackery. Many of these nests hide in gardens fenced round by weather-stained palisades of close-spaced, graying bamboo stakes. Here now is the onetime hippodrome; the Japanese made it into a military camp; the Americans turned it into a recreation center for their troops; and today it is a sort of stadium in which parades take place. As for the dog track over there, it was used for a while as a people's court where a good many criminals were put on public trial; and now it has become a great open-air theater.

The heart of the old foreign concession is now occupied by a vast commercial district, its biggest building being a state department store. Nearly 150 feet high, a light muddy yellow in color, it is as unhandsome as the rest of the monstrosities with which Western capitalism endowed Shanghai. But the interior has been admirably refitted: good ventilation, no excessive heat, lots of elevators and escalators. The store contains a banking department, telephone booths, machines where you get free tea, restrooms and lounges one of which is reserved for women accompanied by children. Some one hundred thousand customers are handled every day, twice that many on Sundays. The afternoon I went there the place was crowded indeed; it less resembled a store than an amusement park: youngsters were playing tag, dashing around counters and sliding on the waxed floor; grown-ups were just having a look at things. There were plenty of them to see: here a terrific array of thermos jugs covered with painted flowers and birds and big enough to hold a day's supply of tea for the whole family; here silk coverlets, bright yellow, pink, soft green; silk material, either plain or tastefully, delightfully embroidered with trees, pagodas, simple geometrical patterns; and here some magnificent dressing gowns of silk brocade, quilted lounging jackets in black and gold silk, kimonos, brightly colored negligees. At the fur counter they were selling some mink coats but mainly sheepskins to be sewn inside winter clothing. Many counters were given over to craftwork: porcelains, cloisonné, plaited bamboo, basketry. The people come and go, appraise the articles, and smile. Until recent years, most of these modestly dressed men and women had never set foot in a place as luxurious as this: entry into the expensive shops used to be reserved for the rich only; these people are not at all rich but they are welcome all the same; the elegance of the displays, the lights, the colors, the smell of new things, it is all for them that these exist. Most of the goods are priced within the range of their pocketbooks. They do considerable buying, especially of woolen cloth and even of silk, something whereof, in the past, no worker would ever have dreamed of owning the tiniest rag. There are plenty of customers at the toy counters and over there where they sell musical instruments. And still more at the shoe department where they have nine hundred models in stock.

The houses along the commercial streets are of wood and two or three stories high; on the second floor there is usually a balcony which juts out over the ground-floor shop: a doorless and windowless stall closed at night by a sliding grille. A signboard, red or white, is set at an angle between the overhang of the balcony and the front of the building, which is flat and ends at the invisible roof. In these shops you find all sorts of manufactured articles, handmade ones too: furniture, coffins, household utensils, clothing, cloth; many furs, silk and woolen dresses, fur-lined capes. One street specializes in birds: hung up on the façades, framing the doorway are cages containing canaries and every species of small bird. Off in another area they sell opera costumes and accessories: embroidered silk robes with dragon's heads on their sashes, tunics, buskins, swords, wigs and false beards, diadems, helmets, and tiaras. Elsewhere, there are shops that trade in musical instruments: Chinese violins, drums, and tambourines. The outdoor restaurants are as numerous as in Peking, they push out over the narrow sidewalks, but the Shanghai chefs are not busy twisting skeins of spaghetti: the people here mainly eat rice.

On the whole the shops have a greater and more luxurious variety of merchandise than in Peking; the embroidered silks are particularly lavish: each slight difference in shading is the result of a difference in the thickness of the thread. Nanking Avenue is lined with expensive shops that have window displays and interiors like their counterparts in the West.

The common folk of Shanghai and the peasants from the outlying areas do their buying in a very different quarter, the one which today occupies the site of ancient Houating. The walls were torn down in 1911 but the old "Chinese City" still comprises a special little town: cement posts and signs in the street keep automobiles, pedicabs, and even bicycles from entering; everybody goes about on foot, which is one of the reasons why one is reminded here of Venice; and the other is the existence everywhere of canals, and a maze of bridges, quays, islands. There is any number of things to see in these busy little streets. Everything is cheaper here than elsewhere: toiletries, hosiery, haberdashery, household equipment, looking glasses. This is the place to buy the glittering tinfoil burned in connection with ancestor worship, and sticks of incense, New

Year pictures in the old and modern styles; and big mirrors upon which are painted gods, demigods, and heroes from the opera. On the quays itinerant tradesmen hawk shrimps, crabs, octopus, fowl, turtles, crickets in tiny cages. Vivid posters announce to passers-by that strange and wonderful sights await them inside this or that doorway; monkeys and reptiles are on display. There are many teahouses. The largest is a three-story pavilion perched on an island surrounded by canals. The interior is dark; the walls are of wood, the windows half-masked by lattices; wooden chairs and tables shine softly in the greenish dusk. On the top floor they play cards, Chinese billiards, Chinese chess, a game much in favor now that mah-jongg is outlawed; all the clients are men. It seems as though the women stay at home in all Chinese cities.

The narrow streets are tidy, odorless. Shanghai too was set to rights in the course of a thoroughgoing sanitation drive. The open drains and sewers were filled; the level of those streets which a rise in the river used to flood has been raised. I have already spoken of what was done to improve the workers' districts. But still the Shanghai populace looks less trim than the Pekingese. The city is much more densely settled; the children are not as clean and are thinner here, the people look poorer; vendors sell shoelaces, bits of lace, cakes of soap—they nearly beg. The writer escorting us tells me that one still finds out-and-out begging in Shanghai, while Madame Cheng suggests that I keep a firm grip on my purse: "There used to be so many thieves in this town that they can't all have disappeared."

All told, however, the Communists have done a major job of cleaning up the "sink of iniquity" Shanghai used to be. When they liberated the city they found eight hundred brothels going; seventy-one were left in 1950; and none by 1951. The prostitutes had to be taken in hand; they were re-educated in centers established for this purpose; some—and most of these are among the oldest—defy every effort to reform them, but most have learned another trade, many have been resettled in the countryside. Clandestine prostitution still goes on, says our guide; but the police are steadily clamping down on it. The gangs and the gangsters have all gone; they used to owe their impunity solely to the corruption of the police authorities and of the regime in general. The opium dens have been closed and traffic in the drug effectively banned; it is against the law not only to import opium but to grow poppy. There may perhaps be some fields of it left in remote corners of China; but the great cities, and above all Shanghai, have the most vigilant narcotics bureaus; the Opium War has finally been won.

Those who knew Shanghai in the old days will be able to gauge the transformation that has occurred by what has happened to the erstwhile "Big World," a kind of sinister Luna Park. The building remains: a hideous reinforced concrete structure surmounted by something like a five-story-high minaret. "*Before*, I'd never have been found dead in this place," said Madame Cheng. Tsai, who is from Shanghai, admitted to having been inside once: but his parents had forbidden him to go above the first floor. Opened in 1916 right in the middle of the French concession, this "Shanghai in Miniature" was a concentration of all the city's blemishes and vices; in 1949, before the Liberation, swarms of prostitutes would scrap for those clients whom pickpockets and thieves, also there in strength, had not got to first; obscene dramas were staged there, cabaret shows of vile or at least questionable taste were presented. A French journalist told, in 1936, of having seen there a little girl of six to whose distended belly a manager complacently drew his audience's attention: a pregnant child, no less.

Today the place is called "The People's Recreation Center." It is as heavily frequented as ever before but the whores, pimps, and adventurers are missing; the crowd is now composed of families out for a Sunday afternoon. In the entrance lobby eight enormous characters spell out Mao Tse-tung's "May our garden be wide, and all flowers grow there together: pluck out those that are fading, and let the new buds bloom." Visitors are amused by trick mirrors that line the lobby. It opens on to a court containing an open-air theater; four galleries rise above it. On the mezzanine there is a restaurant-tea-salon where you eat and drink out-of-doors; off the gallery lead many large rooms. In one of them are Ping-pong and Chinese billiard tables, a shooting gallery. Most of these rooms are theaters; it is the same on the floors above. All told there are no fewer than eleven theaters where seventeen companies stage old operas and modern plays; within this one building you can take in samples of everything, or nearly everything, the theater in China has to offer today. We watched a classical opera, a Shao-ching opera, another played in the old K'uen-k'iu style, and two contemporary plays. One of them presented the story of a Kuomintang spy; he was born and raised in a little port on the coast opposite Formosa, it is to his home town he now returns and with dark designs. His wife and father are first overjoyed to have him back, then discover why he has come: to engineer a sabotage. The father strikes his son and ties him up; then his wife joins the father to explain to the criminal the seriousness of his offense; convinced, the son recants and begs their forgiveness.

There are storytellers in other rooms; their style is unlike the Peking raconteur's. Here, two women and a man are ensconced on high, straight-backed, overstuffed chairs; their feet rest on round stools. On the right, the storyteller is a pretty girl who is wearing a green jacket; in the middle, a woman who is not so young nor so pretty; and to the left, a man, his long weary face stirred by twitches. In their hands each holds a kind of zither, picking it while narrating, intoning, or singing: dialogues alternate with couplets. Before the elder woman is a microphone which she passes to the one whose turn it is to speak. The text, Tsai tells me, is half comic, half didactic; a mother is giving advice to her daughter who is about to go on a journey. The public at large seems to have a great liking for this kind of entertainment: there is as big an audience here as in the rooms where operas and plays are staged.

Shanghai is not a particularly agreeable place for a foreigner to walk about in. The people are a great deal less courteous than in Peking: they turn and stare, trail along behind us, halt squarely in front of us, and gape. For five minutes or so a little girl, facing me, her toes touching mine, walked backward as I walked ahead. "But they ought to be accustomed enough by now to seeing Westerners," I said to Madame Cheng. "Oh indeed they are," said she. "Shanghai has always been a great town for idlers. When I used to walk with my friends we'd have only to stop at a street corner to discuss something and there'd be a circle of listeners all around us in an instant."

This tactless crowd is not homogeneous, as Peking's is. Inequalities of means and condition are conspicuous here. The working-class sections are very poor, whereas the luxurious dwellings in the former concessions belong to a wealthy upper class. One senses that the dregs and downtrodden of the old society have still to attain their place in the sun, that not all the unemployed have found situations. Although many have been sent back to their native villages, the pedicab men are numerous, and seeing the long lines of waiting vehicles, I have the impression they have a hard time making a go of it. Many jobs look like drudgery. The bridges over the canals arch steeply; stripped to the waist, men haul and push rubber-wheeled carts loaded with sacks of cement, metal pipe, and reinforcing rods up those sharp inclines; the absence of trucks and draft animals makes itself sorely felt. And meanwhile in the elegant sections of town the women cut their hair short, go to beauty parlors for permanents, wear rouge on their lips, dress in fashionable suits or in tweed or ratteen jackets with nicely tailored slacks or trousers; their sweaters, their silk jumpers, their skirts are stylish. Men go in for comfortable Western suits. The furs, the silks, the handsome clothing and accessories sold on Nanking Avenue point to the existence of a moneyed class.

Little wonder then that the class struggle remains a living actuality in Shanghai. While I was there an exhibit was on at the Palace of Culture; the theme was the history of the workers' movement: on display were yellowed photographs, newspaper clippings, personal letters alluding to the riots, to the blood-bath repressions. A picture of the place where, back in 1921, the first Communist Party meetings were held; portraits of labor-union leaders murdered by the Kuomintang; shots of demonstrating workers; of the mutilated corpses of workers; of a young lad wearing a quiet smile as he is being marched toward the scene of execution; of another demonstration; and of more dead bodies. These memories, and a great many more, blaze in the Shanghai worker's mind. It is they who represent Chinese Communism's most extreme left wing: they are impatient of the lingering vestiges of capitalism, are urging the government to shorten the transitional period. There is nothing more farfetched than to suggest, as does Guillain, that Shanghai is a city full of counterrevolutionaries; the mysterious Communist friend who obligingly whispered in his ear that "we've got the backing of only 20 per cent of the population here" sounds like a first cousin of those Western fallen angels several specimens of whom I had the privilege to meet, and whose wishful thinking I was able to judge. No: Shanghai is rather the city where the workers' demands are the most adamantly revolutionary and the most pressing; less well paid than heavy-industry workers, discontent surely does exist among the Shanghai proletariat; but it is just as sure that they have no eagerness to return to the old regime: to the contrary, their complaint is that socialization is not moving ahead fast enough. Contemplate the propaganda posters plastered on walls and decide whether the class struggle is not a heated issue; in Peking, these are fairly mild cartoons: of, for example, a profiteer, green about the gills, staggering under the weight of the sack of money on his back. In Shanghai the pictures are realistic and violent. A soldier has his rifle trained on a counterrevolutionary who, surrounded by an angry crowd, slithers up out of his hiding place in a sewer.

Shanghai's working population takes an intense interest in what pertains to the progress of industry. The unsightly pavilion built by the USSR was, during my Shanghai stay, given over to an exhibit of Czechoslovakian manufactured articles: tractors, long-playing records, and the rest. On Sunday morning there was a huge queue, not of organized parties but of husbands and wives and their families who were there out of curiosity—a bigger crowd than the one that lined up to buy tickets for a basketball game that afternoon; two hundred thousand visitors had gone through the turnstiles during the first week the show was on. It is a lie to declare that the Chinese are indifferent to what is happening in other parts of the world. They are, to start with, passionately interested in developments in the USSR and the People's Democracies; and in a general sense avid to find out, eager to learn everything. Attendance was high at all the economic and artistic exhibits in Peking.

In Shanghai there still hangs on a tiny colony of foreign capitalists: some are staying of their own accord, the government is detaining others until such time as they shall have properly wound up their affairs. Whenever they espy a Western visitor they catch at his sleeve and recount their woes. It was thus I encountered, shortly before he was due to leave, the Monsieur

Fano who, several months later, made the readers of *Le Figaro* privy to all he had undergone; while acknowledging his and Madame Fano's hospitality, I nevertheless feel obliged to rectify the impression certain details in M. Fano's published account may have created.*

The hotel I stayed at in Shanghai was an unlovely skyscraper on the edge of what was once the French concession. In the door to each room is a small optical device which enables you to see a caller outside without being seen by him: the existence of this gadget eloquently testifies to the feeling of insecurity which must have dominated the Westerners in the palmy days. At any rate, Tsai knocks one afternoon and informs me that some French people have come to visit us; he discreetly disappears after having ushered in Madame Fano and a nervous French Southerner whose name I did not quite get. They are dumfounded at having been allowed to enter the hotel and meet us without witnesses being present; which rather detracts from a theory they have entertained, and depriving it of punch, lessens their pleasure in telling their hard-luck story. They outline it all the same, but guardedly, tersely, meanwhile scrutinizing the walls, looking into corners for the hidden microphone. "Come to the house," says Madame Fano, "we'll be able to have a good heart-to-heart talk." Making ready to leave, she proposes showing us something of gay Shanghai. Gay Shanghai?—a couple of bars where a few White Russians still get soused and two or three women engage in a little soliciting. I beg off. But lunch tomorrow at her home? It is agreed.

*Figaro* depicts M. Fano as a hunted man who had "to flee," leaving all his worldly possessions behind him. The day he had us to lunch he was still inhabiting—and was never subsequently evicted from—a vast colonial-style house set in the middle of a large garden. Most of his furniture, all his treasures and personal effects

* It was illustrated by photographs which Cartier Bresson made *before* the Liberation and which *Figaro* presented as pictures of today's China. The shot of famished Chinese children lining up for a bowl of rice was taken in 1949. All these photographs, plainly dated, appeared in the volume entitled *D'une Chine à l'autre*. Thus, there was no possibility of making an editorial mistake; and none was made: *Figaro* deliberately tried to dupe its readers. But it would be most unfair to hold M. Fano in any way accountable for this fraud.

had already been crated off to France; as a private individual, his rights had not been meddled with, only his "capitalist's rights" were contested. Madame Fano, being simply a private individual, could leave China whenever she chose; she chose to stay with her husband who was being prevented from leaving the country until, as I said, he had concluded his business. Why this? Because the government denies the head of a firm the right to heave his sometimes very numerous employees out onto the street; what with the shortage of managerial personnel, he cannot just move out and be replaced the next morning by a competent Chinese administrator; and so the foreign boss is required to stay put and exercise his functions for a while. Obviously, this is all very irritating to the boss; but it is also obvious—and, I think, quite normal—that the government should subordinate his convenience to the country's welfare.

"Oh, just wait till we get back, we'll tell them a thing or two about this place!" said Fano and his friends, with feeling. They seemed strangely ill-informed, however, of the general situation in "this place." In *Figaro* Fano tells how some of his Hong Kong cronies split their sides listening to a delegate, who did not know the language, report on his visit to China. But as my host expatiated on the common folks' discontent, and remarked on how they were wont to weep on his shoulder, I asked him whether he knew Chinese. He said he didn't.

The truth is that save for his pedicab driver* and his cook he had had no contact at all with the Chinese for the past five years; he never stirred out of his house except to go to his office. The same seemed to apply to the Southerner, also there at lunch; he and Fano came out with statements so full of contradictions that even *Figaro* had to discard some and tidy up others. "The standard of living of the workers of Shanghai," Fano declared, "used to be very high." "Nothing has been done for the welfare of the workers,"

* As a vital source of inside information, the Shanghai pedicab driver figures even more prominently in the report written by New China's adversaries than does the Moscow taxi driver whose observations are a mainstay of the anti-Soviet press. Not only M. Guillain, but Mesdames Rais and Gosset appear to have had the luck to fall upon pedicab men of the broadest acquaintances and with a creditable command of English.

cried the Southerner. "Aren't public health conditions improved?" I inquired. "Cholera, for example: hasn't it been stamped out?" "Cholera! Ah yes," the Southerner rejoined; "but they *made* the people be vaccinated! Those are fascist methods." Wherewith I was deluged with trivial facts which I later found out to be false. This one, for instance: you are not allowed to take Chinese newspapers out of the country. The customs officials waved me aboard my plane with a bundle of them. That day at lunch, its accusers inveighed with particular vehemence against the regime's authoritarian handling of two burning questions: that of prostitution and that of religion; for our hosts, these two words seemed to sum up all that is essential in a precious Western freedom. Their mental confusion was such that Fano could explain to us that the "Five Anti's" drive—a campaign aimed at the malpractices of which capitalists and dishonest civil servants had been guilty—had cost the regime the support of . . . the working class. He was specific: 80 per cent* of the population of Shanghai is against the government. How does he know? He knows, do not worry. And what does the proletariat want instead? "A third world war that will change the situation." I gasped when I heard that reply. Later, thinking about it, I found it encouraging: for it indicates that, as an alternative to the regime, its worst enemies are incapable of advancing the least shred of a constructive program and dream only in terms of devastation.

In all fairness I should add that foreign capitalists have without doubt had a few trying moments in Shanghai; what I cannot understand is why, instead of getting out in time, and they had plenty of it, they preferred to suppose that the new regime would "honor their rights." Illegal is how the Communist leaders have always and openly described the profits Westerners have wrung from the China upon which they imposed a semicolonial status; they have from the start made it equally plain that one of their foremost objectives is to eliminate foreign capital. Did M. Fano and his associates expect to be able to "make a deal" the way deals had always been made in China before? If so, they have

* This figure admirably accords with the one quoted by Guillain. A coincidence? Or was Guillain's "Communist" informant a man of quite a different color?

no one but themselves to blame for a calculated risk that just did not work out.

*Hangchow*

From the moment I reached China everybody told me how delighted I would be with Hangchow. It was the capital of the Sungs whose rule coincided with the apogee of Chinese civilization, and the city is considered the Athens of China. Its lake, "The Sea of the West," has inspired countless paintings and poems. Upon its banks the Chinese place the most famous of their legends, that of the White Snake; and out on "The Solitary Isle" anchorites meditated upon and lived the "Way of the Mean" whereof Taoist and Latin traditions alike were so endeared. This lake? Truth to tell, I prefer the one in the Bois de Boulogne; while as for the monuments and sculpture I saw in the neighboring countryside, they struck me as singularly lacking in any artistic value.

I visited several Buddhist sanctuaries. The barbarousness of their statuary astonished me. In the hall preceding the prayer room would loom up an outsized P'ou-sa, potbellied and sneering. Everybody has seen small-scale reproductions of it. Through nationalistic sentiment, tenth-century bronzes substituted this P'ou-sa, specifically Chinese, for the traditional but not indigenous Buddha figure. At once cynical, gluttonous, and detached from all worldly things, the image of this mendicant preacher exhales a kinship to Diogenes of the Barrel and Till Eulenspiegel. He is surrounded by four crowned and paint-splashed giants, terrible of mien and the guardians of the temple. In the central hall one usually finds a statue of the goddess Kuan Yin; she is shown standing upon a mammoth fish whose thrashings would have rent the universe asunder had she not, St. George-like, subdued it. Carved wooden panels recount extraordinary adventures; one is reminded of Spanish retables, also of those vast eighteenth-century nativities containing a foreshortened image of the whole world. The panels retrace the life of Sakyamuni and the travels of the celebrated pilgrim Hsüan Tsang who in 629 A.D. traversed the Gobi Desert, crossed the Tarim Basin, Turkestan, and Afghanistan before entering India whence he fetched back the Buddhist books; sculptures show him contending with elephants, monkeys, serpents, and devils; he passes through forests, on his journey meets monks and hermits, fords streams.

The bonzes do not seem to take their religion too seriously. We bestowed alms and were thereupon authorized to consult the oracle. It is a vessel shaped like a big pickle jar but filled with wooden sticks; the vessel is shaken, then you draw out a stick: upon it is written a number. A bonze then delivers you a little scrap of paper corresponding to your number. Your fortune may fall into one of several categories: very good, good, middling, bad, very bad. All our papers, when unfolded, allowed us the very best of prospects. Madame Cheng translated the prediction concerning me: "In autumn the carp leap forth from the water. The five grains will be gathered. Unto the emperor will the harvest be borne, and he will be glad. The family is happy and will remain united, for the granary is replete."

At Hangchow I visited a Taoist temple also. In the entranceway were enthroned Lao-tse, the Jade Emperor, and the future Savior of the World; Buddhism's influence helped invent this trinity; statues, offerings, incense are disposed in roughly the same manner as in Buddhist shrines. But right away one feels that this religion is a more superstitious, less refined affair. The garden abounds in rockeries, grottoes, nooks. Suddenly, stepping over a bridge, I find myself face to face with a dragon: glaring colors, bulging eyes, gaping maw—altogether the sort of scary apparition you bang up against in amusement-park fun houses. The temple is in bedraggled shape: the oriflammes are threadbare, the heads of the drums cracked and half gone. I saw no priest. Visitors drink tea out in the garden, throw food to the fish, picnic amid the rockeries. It is my impression that these temples are hardly much more now than recreational spots and places to make excursions to.

The city of Hangchow itself struck me as provincial and rather dreary. It is a middle-sized town of 600,000. Sitting in the shade of little trees merchants sell candy, nuts, sugared peanuts, combs, soap, dimestore jewelry. There are still some rickshaws in the streets; I find it painful to see barefoot men pulling these carriages on the run.* The city's one extravagant feature is the silks piled high in the shops.

Madame Cheng invited me to her home for tea. Her house—once occupied by a Kuomintang functionary who fled—belongs to the state which rents it to her. It is located, at quite some distance from town, on the edge of a small village; near by are a disused temple, some tumbledown pai lou, and a few peasant houses surrounded by cabbage patches. A "rich peasant" has just returned to the village after two years of re-education. With a smile he declares: "I'm a progressive now." The peasants find him arrogant, he is not liked. This seems to indicate that re-education is not a very sure-fire thing, and that people view the re-educated with a degree of wariness.

Of the memories I preserve of China the most ineffaceable is of that countryside I crossed during the forty hours by rail from Hangchow to Canton.

It is four in the afternoon when I board the train; the sun sets at six. Before the light fails, it is an unaltering scene that slips by: distant mountains are the landscape's backdrop; the plain between is one tremendous golden rice field laced by narrow, slow-flowing streams upon which boats and single-masted sampans advance. The villages nestle under clumps of trees, to each village there is a pond; their houses are tile-roofed, walls are of whitewashed brick: this white, which is raw and mat rather than shiny, together with the stony blackness of the tiles makes me think of a mourning card. The water in the pond also looks black in the light of the day's end; a man squatting in a little dinghy reaches out and picks the water chestnuts; or else a woman seated on a flat rock bathes her feet and looks far away, dreamy and still. These mountains on the horizon, this sparse foliage over rooftops, the water, the flat light compose a China—at last—similar to the one prints show: many Sung era painters treated these landscapes. But I am most of all struck by this great extent to which every living person seems sealed up within himself, self-

* At the time of the Liberation there were 5,000 rickshaws and 7,000 rickshaw men in Shanghai. A few of the vehicles were still left in 1955 when I was there. In February 1956 only two remained: they were presented to a museum in the city.

contained, and none the less like everybody else. It is always the same village, the same woman washing the same work clothes in the same pond; and each is unknown to every other; I pass by and for a moment knit them all into a single view; the truth about them, though, is their separateness; and there is something heartbreaking about the everlasting repetition of the identical solitudes.

Night falls. I draw away from the window. Opposite me Tsai is reading a French translation of a Russian novel. Earlier, having just bought himself a new camera, he had been busy studying manuals on photography. But he had said, "from listening to you people talk about literature I've begun to get interested in it too." Madame Cheng is leafing through some children's magazines. She is looking at them carefully because she thinks that writing for children is very difficult.

The scene outside has changed when I wake up the next morning. The rice fields alternate with fields of grain among which peasants are working; in this region of intensive farming, oats, legumes, beans are sometimes put in the ground once the rice has been harvested. It has already been harvested in many places and there the fields are studded with little dry yellow sheaves. Grain is being flailed on threshing floors in the villages. Now the houses have turned red, made of earth, with thatched roofs. Between the fields, nearly all of them tiny, run little ridges of yellow earth. Many men at work; and very few animals. For the first time I see some water buffalo: gray, long-haired, with graceful horns—a cross, you'd say, between a bull and a gazelle. They draw ancient plows. But there are not many of them; and though I watch the whole day, I see not one donkey, not one mule. Unaided men carry on their backs all that must be carried. Today is Sunday and the peasants are taking the grain they owe the state into town. Long caravans stretch out upon the narrow dirt roads cutting through fields; most of the men are pushing wheelbarrows consisting simply of a plank with a wheel fitted in its notched lower end; no carts; the sacks hang down on both sides of the wheel. In the middle of the fields I notice a great many grass-covered tumuluses: these are graves and they are so numerous that they give the landscape a very distinctive look: the plain seems afflicted by knobby outgrowths. University of Nanking students have reckoned that they cut the arable land area by 6 per cent and sometimes as much as 9 per cent.

There are rather frequent stops. On the platform are men selling rolls, pancakes, fruits, local products. They sold apples in Manchuria. At one station we are offered chickens—the cheapest chickens to be had anywhere in China. Bananas and oranges appear toward the end of the day. Evening's approach is less melancholy than it was yesterday: we are really in the South. As night draws on the peasants gather under the porch just before their front doors; they dine alfresco and wave to the passing train.

Night again. And another awakening, the landscape is truly beautiful. Mist steams up from the Pearl River, shrouds the mountains as in the paintings. The reddish earth is covered with a dense, intense green growth of grass sparkling with spider webs pearly with dew. But a clear blue sky promises a hot day. Rafts laden with timber descend the river. Here once again the rice fields open out; now not a village, not a house, not a tree; the rice sweeps back into the valleys, flows between hills, fills the narrowest vales, spreading like wildfire, growing with force: it is as green as meadow grass. Whereas it was just coming ripe up at Hangchow, down here they have three rice harvests a year and this is the final one that is springing up from the soil. When the green shoots stab up round the feet of cloud-girt mountains one thinks of Alpine pasture lands in Switzerland.

The fields are no longer irrigated by streams. Water comes in by way of low-lying canals; to get it up into the irrigation ditches which furrow the fields they use an ancient apparatus: the peasants work a kind of treadmill that makes a driving shaft rotate and it drives a belt system of buckets which dip water from the canal and spill it into the troughs higher up. This work is done mainly by women and boys, in teams of four or five, often shaded by a broad umbrella. You see many men wading about in the mud of the canals, looking for no telling what. All are wearing huge flat hats of gleaming black straw; those I saw in Peking seemed big to me but these are more parasols than hats. The people hereabouts are better dressed than in the North, their cotton outfits fresher, newer, and the women are often in bright jackets. However, the further south we move, the more numerous are those going barefoot. It is because, down here, they work in the mud of the rice paddies; and the weather is warm.

The mountains have vanished, the river has angled away; rice has submerged everything. The land in these parts must be collectivized for there are no more idle strips between fields. And here is a new sort of well; it is the government that has had them sunk and, as against the old wells, they represent a vast improvement: a very tall post is planted vertically in the ground; at its top is a swinging boom with a heavy counterweight at the short end and at the other a long rope to which a wooden bucket is attached. The peasant pulls down on the rope, the bucket descends into the well; and, when filled, comes back up automatically; its content is then dumped into the trough next to the well. Instead of a group of people operating the treadmill device, one woman can easily handle the job which, with the lifting arrangement, is not strenuous. Moreover, whereas the relatively shallow canals dry up in time of drought, these wells, ten or twelve feet deep, are fed by underground springs that never give out. It is a strange landscape: the level stretches of green rice and these high spear-like poles with their booms tilted at odd angles—they seem like old semaphores wigwagging messages from one end of the plain to the other. A straw sunshade or one of faded cloth protects the woman stationed by the well. Women are much more in evidence than up North; Southern women were by and large spared foot-binding and have always participated in work in the fields. Here too the same undeviating scenery and activities repeat themselves ad infinitum; but instead of an unending sequence of solitudes, a collectivity unfurls; these folk have common interests, they have put their heads together, planned their work, they will share the profits: and I finally find myself gazing not at a simple spectacle of coexistence but at one of organized co-operation—which, in China, is still rare.

The South declares itself in the growing brilliance of the sky, in palm trees, in banana trees, and in thick groves of soaring bamboo. The hills are bare; peasants go up into them in search of brush, dried grass, and while trees may once have grown there, they have all long since been felled. Countrymen are being taught the importance of standing timber and to conserve it, but this particular region has not yet been reforested. Only the lowlands are farmed; the red earth of the mountain slopes is poor whereas the soil of the alluvial plain is rich. It is manured with human waste. Owing to its fertility this region has almost never known famine, even though the population here is dense: in 1939 there were some 3,445 people per square mile and in certain spots the figure climbs to nearly 4,000 at present. Apart from rice they cultivate vegetables, tobacco, sugar cane, tea, citrus fruits, bananas, and that litchi of which the beauteous imperial concubine Yang Kuei-fei was once so fond.

We are approaching Canton. The funerary barrows multiply. Hills are covered with steles and tombs some of which are very imposing; every now and then one sees a collective altar where sacrifices are performed.

And then we are at Canton. But it will be a long time before I forget that plain where millions of men, without mechanical instruments, without beasts of burden, tear from the soil, with their bare hands, the treasures that make it possible for China to build the future.

### *Canton*

Contrary to the malicious propaganda that attributes a bleak uniformity to the new China, I found it otherwise. Peking, Nanking, Shanghai, Mukden, Hangchow—these cities are as unalike as the cities of France or Italy. But upon getting to Canton my feeling was almost of having entered a different land; there is nothing else in China quite like this big tropical port.

Lying on a parallel twenty miles below the Tropic of Cancer and on the Pearl River forty miles up from the sea, Canton did not until a relatively late date become a part of China. Jealous of its sovereignty, the city held off all the conquerors and resisted the Manchus with particular stubbornness. When it was opened by imperial edict in 1685 to Western trade, Europeans were given the very coolest greeting and relegated to the Shameen quarter, a sand bar about one thousand feet by seven hundred, where new houses were put up, and to which women were denied access. "Again in 1830 the Viceroy threatened to shut down the trading posts if the English ladies from Macao continued to come to visit them," reported Sir John Pratt. Foreigners had to comply with a good many other stiff conditions: they were not to introduce warships, weapons, wives, or families into the port, and the number of servants they could employ was limited. They were not permitted to own sedan chairs or pleasure boats; their movements were restricted; three times a month, in parties of no more than ten and always under supervision, they were allowed to go to the island of Honam—and they had to be back again by nightfall. They could sojourn at Shameen only during the period from September to April: they would ordinarily spend the remaining months in the Portuguese colony of Macao, seventy miles due south of Canton. What they were least able to resign themselves to was being obliged, in all their transactions, to work through the Co-hong Merchants Guild, an agency set up for the express purpose of keeping an eye on their business activities.

The Opium War started at Canton. Although beaten, the city never digested defeat. The international port into which traders flocked from everywhere under the sun was also the door by which a flood of emigrants left: many Cantonese removed temporarily to Indo-China, Thailand, and Malaya; other settled down there for good but kept in close touch with their homeland. Near to Macao and to Hong Kong, Canton was in shorter range of Westtern civilization and its gifts than were the other Chinese cities; Canton flung down her ancient walls; the Cantonese adopted modern architectural styles and themselves built a Bund flanking the Pearl River. In the meantime new ideas filtered in. The "advanced" character of the city and its solid tradition of independence explain why it was destined to play a leading revolutionary role. It was in the vicinity of Canton that the Taiping Rebellion's instigator, Hung Hsiu-chüan, was born; the "Hundred Days" reformist K'ang Yu-wei also came from Canton. The bourgeois revolution was fomented, in large part, by Overseas Chinese of Cantonese extraction. At the end of the nineteenth century the young Sun Yat-sen and his comrade in arms Luke Ho-tong installed themselves at Canton and held secret meetings there; it was there that the first attempt at an uprising occurred in 1895, and there it was quashed; Sun Yat-sen escaped, but four of his lieutenants, including Luke, were executed, and a fifth died in prison. There was another attempt in 1904: the secret societies rose in the expectation of reinforcements: three thousand armed men failed to come to the appointed rendezvous and no one was at the port to guide the seven hundred coolies who landed and then wandered at random through the streets. A packing case addressed to the rebels having smashed while being unloaded, its contents—revolvers—coming to light, the authorities, putting two and two together, rounded up, tortured, and killed most of the coolies and, as well, decapitated sixteen persons, innocent for the most part, who were picked up in the streets of the district, where government headquarters were. Canton was yet thrice again the center of revolt; the effort to seize the government district failed each time.

When in 1911 the revolution had triumphed Sun Yat-sen ceded the presidency of the Republic to Yüan Shih-k'ai; and in 1916 Yüan had himself crowned emperor. Wherewith Canton joined a separatist confederation of southern provinces. Sun arrived there and organized an opposition government. He left the city in 1918 but in 1921 the parliament of the southern confederacy elected him president of the Republic. Driven out by Chen Chiung-ming, Commander in Chief of the Army of the South, he recovered power again in 1923 and made Canton his capital. There he received a visit from Mikhail Borodin and his help plus that of thirty-four Soviet experts, thirty of them military advisers. He founded the Whampoa Military Academy. The city holds Sun's memory in reverence. Upon a hill overlooking a brand-new stadium seating 50,000 persons there stands a monument in his honor; a little further down is a memorial designed by the same architect who did his tomb in Nanking. The memorial is an auditorium; when I went up to see it, Soviet dancers were rehearsing a ballet on the stage.

During the years when the Kuomintang and the CP were working together Canton was the heart of the proletarian movement and the scene of the Federation of Labor conventions. In July 1924 the English decided that any Chinese wishing to enter the concession would henceforth have to show a special pass; the Shameen workers struck; the new police regulation was rescinded.

In the center of town existed a school where Mao Tse-tung, Chou En-lai, and other famous Communists trained young cadres; the place has been transformed into a museum, and it was on my itinerary. The classes were held in an abandoned temple. Beds, tables, desks, sleeping quarters were all of an extreme modesty; in a gallery are displayed the portraits of the men who taught there: most of those men stood beside Mao on the Tien An Men platform on the First of October.

Canton did not smile indulgently upon Chiang Kai-shek's betrayal. A Kuomintang general, Chang Fa-kwei, having occupied the city on November 17, 1927, the CP drew up the scheme for an insurrection. Yeh Ting assumed the head of a revolutionary military committee of five and the Party designated a general staff for the Red Guard. They mobilized a thousand Communists and formed armed commandos. On December 7 the Kwangtung central committee passed out the orders and on the eleventh, at three in the morning, the uprising started. The partisans forced the barracks of the regiment of trainees all of whom, with most of their officers, joined the Reds; Nationalist Army trucks were seized and with a handful of partisans the president of Canton's Revolutionary Committee, Chang Tai-lai, drove through the city. The Red Guard disarmed other units: thirty fieldpieces, fifteen hundred rifles and machine guns were collected and distributed to the men. By three in the afternoon the insurgents held all the police stations and the government buildings: the entire city, except for the foreign concessions, Tong Shan and Shameen. But the Cantonese merchant middle class was frightened by this revolt, the maritime union wouldn't support it, and the rebels were inadequately armed. On December 13 Nationalist troops retook the city: the Canton Commune hadn't lived three days. The Communists never tried an insurrection again.

A little outside the city is a mausoleum that commemorates the victims of the repression; most of them are buried there. Among the Overseas Chinese who had lent their support to the 1911 revolution six million were of Cantonese origin; they gave generously out of their pockets to help build this monument and upon each stone a name is engraved: San Francisco, Chicago, Malacca . . . to signify that it was contributed by the Chinese communities in each of those cities.

Between 1911 and 1927 Canton spearheaded the revolutionary movement. Today, however, the "march toward socialism" is much less apparent here than in the rest of China. Late to be liberated, possessing almost no industry, virtually no proletariat, twelve hundred miles by air from Peking, this city of small shopkeepers and small artisans had yet to feel the transforming impact of the regime. The traveler landing there from Hong Kong doubtless has the feeling he has left the capitalist world; but for me, coming from Peking and Shanghai, it is like sliding back into the old semifeudal world.

My hotel is fourteen stories high, the main skyscraper in the city. It is grayish, squat, quite awful, but it dominates "The Long Quay" and from my window I look out upon a considerable strip of river. During this whole trip I have not hitherto been confronted by all that the words "Far East," "South," "great southern port" promise and which a single glance discovers now. The river is literally surfaced by boats beating upstream and coasting down with the current; enormous rafts freighted with logs edge softly in the direction of the sea while junks sail for inland destinations. There are sampans whose deckhouses seem roofed with some sort of raffia—woven bamboo perhaps, grayish at any rate, and sloping down toward the bow. I love the great paddle-wheel boats,* some of which transport passengers and goods seaward, still more of which head for the hinterlands. They are wooden, painted in fine green and gold tints; they have two decks astern, one deck amidships; the stern, boxlike, perpendicular, and with windows, resembles a house front; a kind of ledge, painted yellow, is sandwiched between the two decks and above it runs an inscription in Chinese; the over-all effect recalls Columbus' caravels. On the wharf crates and bales are being loaded and unloaded. An entire system of streams and canals connects the river

* When Europeans first beheld these boats in China they took them to be an imitation of their own. But Chinese paddle-wheel boats existed in the seventh century A.D. and were probably invented even earlier.

with the inland country. Thousands of boats arrive and depart every day; they transport 300,000 tons of cargo and 200,000 passengers each month. Traffic slackens little if at all at night. The river then becomes alive with little red lamps: candles, lanterns are lit on the small craft where as many as 60,000 Cantonese have their permanent dwellings. From my vantage point I saw, at dawn, a herd of gray buffalo going downstream on a boat; and even at that early hour the wharves were bustling with activity. All day long it is an endless flow of pedestrians, bicycles, pedicabs, pushcarts.

One's impression of intense movement is further confirmed by a walk through the streets; the population is not so numerous but it is denser than at Peking and even than at Shanghai. There are broad commercial streets bordered by houses of two or three stories: the second juts out over the sidewalk and is supported by white pillars—or yellow or blue or red ones—on either side of the roadway you thus have a covered arcade. The columns are decorated with red and black lettering to indicate the names of shops, which are also announced on red silk banners; most of the shops have no doors but are grottoes which you step straight into or which you reach by way of an obscure corridor, lit sometimes by fluorescent lamps.

I wend my way through a side alley, narrow, barred to vehicles, and where there is no arcade. But overhead are awnings similar to the *toldos* in Seville: triangular in shape and faintly convex as you glance up at them, these bits of tarpaulin are held by strings fastened to the second stories of the houses on both sides of the street: every now and then a gap in this roofing lets through a bright patch of striated sunlight, and shadows dance underfoot—and now I am reminded of the *souks* of Marrakech or Tunis. The four-story façades are surmounted by fancifully cut fretwork. This street is a market frequented chiefly by the peasants from the outer districts; the usual goods are on sale, but I also notice certain peculiarly Cantonese articles: heaps of wooden clogs, varnished and painted and similar to what Japanese women wear; in the South people do not care much for shoes and down here women go about barefoot in these clogs. Once again as in Japan, young mothers carry their infants on their backs; the baby sits in a kind of sling held on, like a knapsack, by canvas straps which go over the shoulders and fasten in front; the little one's head emerges, so do his feet which he braces against the mother's back. All sorts and varieties of these slings in bright cotton material are sold in the shops I pass; they also offer children's garments: coats of silk and multicolored cotton, visored caps. There is a profusion of fabrics, some of them luxurious. One of Canton's specialties is a washable black silk which neither creases nor rumples, which needs no ironing—and which from wear, unfortunately, takes on a reddish sheen and loses all its freshness; new, it gleams like anthracite; only women of ill-repute used to wear it in the past, today one sees it on a great many women and men.

"I'm going to show you a reactionary street," says Madame Cheng, meaning by that one where expensive shops used to cater to foreign buyers. Arcades flank it on either side. Jutting out from the columns and a little overhead, and catching one's eye as one walks along, are somewhat faded advertising shingles which naively evoke another era: an elegant blonde in high heels gets off a "blue-ribbon" train, a superb leather suitcase in her hand.

I walked—alone most of the time—in a good many other streets. There was one where shop after shop sold nothing but articles made of bamboo: chairs, tables, fishing rods, screens, baskets, cages. Another was given over to pictures: pictures painted on mirrors, New Year pictures representing dancers, scenes from the opera, scenes of home life, portraits of warriors, genii, heroes, all done in the ancient style. Wanting to buy one of these rich-colored paintings, I stepped into a shop where a young man was engaged in recopying the effigy of one of the figures decorating the wall at the rear; he did not so much as look up and, discouraged, I walked out. Ten yards further on I saw another shop grinning with the same genii; there too a man was carefully copying an ancient image, but a second seemed willing to receive clients: I enter, take money from my purse, point to the pictures: the merchant laughs, shakes his head; I insist; he scribbles something on a slip of paper; the pictures are apparently not for sale. That evening Madame Cheng told me that I had been in the market for sacred effigies which are posted on doors of houses or burned over the graves of the dead; they are made to order for religious families; it would be an impiety to sell one to a foreigner.

These paintings are in abundance enough to suggest that the old superstitions yet cling on in Canton; this is substantiated by something else: the prevalence of chiromancers' shops. They are tiny little booths; on the door leading in are drawings of hands and faces divided up into sections, marked with reference codes, all according to the laws of a magical lore. Here and there I see vendors selling the old-fashioned kind of "egg books." And little theaters of acrobats with the entrance right on the street; inside, a few benches, a tiny stage; there is probably little by way of up-to-date political content in the stories the minstrels are telling.

I especially remark the number of the teahouses and their lavishness; plenty of tea is drunk in the South, not only because the heat breeds thirst but because the people like to get together in public places. These salons are so big that one will often take up what would be an entire block of houses; the tables are of dark wood, in the middle a stairway leads up to the second floor, and on the farther side a window gives out upon another street. There are also ice-cream parlors where seated at a marble-top table you are served all sorts of flavors: vanilla, pineapple, banana, red pea. I lunched in one Canton restaurant. Instead of the booths which isolate each table in Peking, they have here big open dining rooms where a crowd of diners sit elbow to elbow; these rooms occupy the ground floor and the next two as well; seated at little round tables, modestly dressed and in certain cases seemingly rather poor people are eating what is known as a Cantonese tea: actually a pretty substantial meal but one composed only of cakes, pastry, and fritters. On the fourth floor is another big room, more elegant than the ones below, and several little private dining rooms in addition. The windows overlook the river; the dark mahogany furniture is upholstered in a kind of rose-colored rubber material. I was brought fried shrimp, duck *pâtés*, breast of chicken, *vol-au-vents*, puffs, little stuffed rolls, rissoles, little thumb-sized bits of bread accompanying morsels of pickled pork, a dessert made of cookies and ample whipped cream.

Canton cakes are well known, the pastry shops are numerous. One sees too a great many taverns with stone and brick counters where they serve tea and sweets. In the evening they are full of people who smoke and drink and eat together. Instead of facing the street, as in Peking, the company sits out in gardens under the sky; groups are up till late at night chatting in the neon-lit taverns.

The residential streets, paved with flat stones, are so narrow that one can go through them only on foot. Itinerant peddlers seated against the walls sell vegetables, fruits, fish. A few steps lead down to front doors, the ground floors being below street level; looking in through an open window one sees that interiors are less Spartan than in Peking; pictures hang on walls, upon buffets sit vases and trinkets.

Generally speaking, the streets of Canton are far more animated and colorful than in Peking or Shanghai. The women here are very different and infinitely more coquettish. They wear tight-fitting black silk trousers and cotton blouses gathered in at the waist; no jackets; sleeveless or short-sleeved jumpers, rather, with a small stand-up collar. Which is something one is not prepared for in China; everywhere in the North the tradition is that women are not to show a square inch of bare skin; hot though the day may be, every woman in Peking or Shanghai has socks as well as shoes on her feet; while the Cantonese women go stockingless in their clogs and partly, or even entirely, display charming arms. Petite, prettily made, they are extremely graceful; their femininity does not seem to hinder them from performing the most arduous chores. In the north I never saw a woman *carry* a heavy burden. Here, on the other hand—also by universal tradition—women pull carts, carry shoulder poles supporting weighty buckets; and it is mainly women who, on the river, on the canals, perform the rude task of poling and sculling the heavy-laden boats.

At once more nonchalant and more lively than the Pekingese, the people of Canton are also more sociable and nevertheless, greater individualists. The racial type is less purely Chinese than in the other cities I saw. The mixture of races, the fact that one finds many customs in Canton which are identical to those of

Japan, give the visitor a cosmopolitan impression: this is the Far East but scarcely China. Likewise, after first making contact with France, through Paris, a foreigner is apt to feel that Marseilles is less French than Mediterranean.

In Canton there used to be two kinds of racial discrimination and segregation. The Hakka, an indigenous minority residing in the surrounding mountains, were denied the right to enter the city. And the inhabitants of the "floating quarters" were not allowed to mingle with the urban population.

These floating villages have existed since the time of the Yüans. Famine-hounded peasants who forsook their fields, destitute fishermen, vagabonds, fugitives from justice, and old offenders, every sort of uprooted person came by boat to seek his fortune in the city. Its populace reacted by prohibiting these poor souls from gaining a foothold on land and by treating them as pariahs. Their descendants suffered the same fate; they constituted a caste of untouchables, were scorned, given insulting nicknames. Among them were bargemen, boatmen, dockers, but also a vast underworld. Nineteenth-century travelers often described "the pleasure boats" anchored between Canton and Whampoa, and which were simply water-borne brothels. From the rail of high, brightly painted barges, silk-clad and bejeweled sirens would smile down. Westerners steered clear of them ever after the day one European gentleman climbed aboard and was not heard from again. The inhabitants of the floating quarters had no liking for foreigners whom, when they came near by, they were wont to pelt with rocks and rotten oranges.

Chiang Kai-shek did nothing in behalf of these outcasts. They had to go on living on their boats, were barred from trade, from taking examinations for official posts, and even from attending school; they had to marry within their group and when they came ashore in the city had to walk barefoot to show that they were not members of the community.

The new regime has done away with this segregation, explained to the Cantonese that the river folk are Chinese citizens on a par with everybody else, and ruled it a slander to address them by their former sobriquets. It has built some houses for them. I walked along a canal full of small boats in which, on Sundays, Cantonese go for outings; so numerous are these boats that they lie with their sides touching. Each seems to be a little room: the superstructure is wooden, usually painted a light blue, overlaid with painted flowers; inside are lateral seats, and a stern seat strewn with cushions, behind which, for a back, is a big fan-shaped mirror decorated with painted flowers again, and with painted birds. The muscular, black-clad boatmen, often young, handsome, and aware of it, squat up by the bow and call to passers-by. There are several rows of houses on the bank: they are modest, of frail bamboo and clay, but they sit on indubitably solid ground. They comprise a real little village.

Plans call for building more of them. But for the moment sixty thousand people are still living on the water. I got into a motorboat and went to see one of these floating towns. There are rows of moored sampans separated by high wooden jetties, veritable streets from which ladders lead down to the boats alongside. Each jetty has a name, each boat its number. These floating houses are often ornamented with weathervanes which turn with the shifting breeze. Others have sprouted an outrigger where some flowers grow. I climb onto a jetty, I climb down into a boat. Forward in the bow is a first compartment half closed by a wooden panel and by some shelves upon which lie cooking utensils; in the middle is a symmetrical compartment; and aft of it a narrow space is divided into a kitchen on one side and a water closet on the other. The seats are little wooden benches only four or five inches high. Clothing and tools are stowed under the waxed floor, whose slats lift up. The boat is encircled by wooden panels; they are taken down in daytime; at night, when they are up, the boat is safe and snug. On my way up the ladder again I glance at the neighboring boats: they are just the same as this one. In one I detect a young boy wearing nothing but shorts, stretched out on the floor and absorbed in a book.

Today, the floating quarters form an administrative district exactly like any other. It has its own municipal council and it is represented at the People's Assembly. Eight primary schools have been organized for it; in 1949 only twenty-seven youngsters were attending school, two thousand are now, and seventy started secondary school this year. Classes were at first held out on the water, later moved into regular school buildings on land. There is a cultural club, evening adult-education courses, political lectures. A hygiene department inspects conditions aboard the boats, infirmaries have been set up. There are consumers' co-operatives and the fishermen have been grouped into production co-operatives. Efforts have been made to weed out doubtful elements and reduce prostitution. It has not altogether disappeared. Girls saunter about The Long Quay in the evening, proposing, by means of word and gesture, an enjoyable ride on the river. A Frenchman recounted to me that urged on by curiosity he and two friends one evening stepped aboard one of these boat-women's skiffs. For half an hour she sculled at the stern, and they had nothing but an enjoyable ride; disappointed, they were about to tell her to scull them home when they saw a cluster of lights ahead: women were seated in the bows of gaily illuminated junks, men were circulating on jetties as though in the little streets of a secluded part of town. The boatwoman invited them to disembark; ever spurred on by the love of knowledge, the three Frenchmen each entered one of those aquatic boudoirs. Their experiences were identical. Each of their hostesses had them lie down—fully dressed—on the floor boards, and subjected their backs, torsos, and legs to a series of massages and pummelings which, all three later agreed, had not been at all to their taste. Those who had wished to go on had, by dint of a supplementary fee, obtained caresses more in line with an international brand of eroticism. The story confirmed my own impression: that the progressive outlook has not yet definitely triumphed in Canton.

Revolutionary, superstitious, cosmopolitan, and southern, Canton has yet another characteristic: located on the coast and barely a hundred miles from Hong Kong, it is a frontier town. As we were nearing it in the train a conductor requested me to roll up my window: "We're about to go under a bridge." I looked inquiringly at Tsai. "It's probably to make sure nobody flings a bomb into one of the compartments," he suggested. All bridges in China are patrolled by soldiers but I had not before seen this precaution taken on a train. At Canton Tsai was in the middle of snapping a picture of a public square when a man in a black silk suit sidled up and spoke a few words to him. They talked for a moment, then the man went away. "Oh, he's just eager," Tsai muttered. The stranger had advised him that we were not far away from a bridge and that photographing it was illegal. The bridge in question was the Haichou Bridge, wrecked in 1949, since rebuilt and the longest—two hundred yards—in South China; it connects the two banks of the Pearl River. Tsai took his picture anyhow—the bridge did not figure in it, as a matter of fact. I also noticed that soldiers were stationed by the Sun Yat-sen Memorial and most of the other public monuments.

The third evening after my arrival, as I was gazing out of my window at the dim little lights scattered over the river, and at the neon signs glowing on the Bund, I suddenly heard sirens—a totally unexpected and weird whine. And, yes, indeed, the neon winks out, invisible mouths blow out all the candles, there is a scurrying in the streets. It looks like a real alert. And that's just what it is. Madame Cheng knocks at my door. We are to go downstairs, she explains, not necessarily into the cellar, but at least to the ground-floor corridors. All the hotel guests are gathered there in the darkness. There is a delegation of Hindu trackmen guided by an interpreter who turns out to be a friend of Tsai, who brightens up at the chance encounter, and they have a fine chat together. Formosa is not far, Madame Cheng reminds me; factories and industrial centers on the coast are frequently attacked; and whenever an enemy plane is detected in the vicinity the alarm is sounded at Canton. There is no danger: interception and antiaircraft defenses are capable of stopping any marauding planes. Nor, as I think about it, is Chiang apt to be fool enough to bomb an open city. The alert, I suppose, constitutes a kind of practice in case matters take a more serious turn; and this is a forceful reminder to the Chinese that the Formosa question remains unsettled and that some final solution has got to be found soon.

These incidents and the general tension are due to the proximity of the counterrevolutionary stronghold. The "watchfulness" rule is enforced with greater strictness here than anywhere else. The Canton daily *Hang Fang* in March 1954 announced the arrest of forty ringleaders of a secret organization, "The Green Lance," according to the press, made up of United States and Kuomintang hirelings who had entered China through Hong Kong and whose mission included sabotage of trains and bridges along the Hankow-Canton rail line; their main headquarters was a barbershop in Canton. Some of them were state civil servants, one was an officer's housemaid. The tribunal, invoking the law of January 29, 1951, on counterrevolutionary activities, pronounced thirteen death sentences; the other members of the band were sent to prison. Another similar conspiracy, it is said, was uncovered in October. Whence, in Canton, a tense atmosphere which has not even a remote parallel in Peking or, for that matter, in Shanghai.

Twelve hours of flying over broad wet plains; and Peking once again. Autumn has come. The leaves on the trees are the color of the imperial roofs. Chestnuts are being roasted at street corners, their aroma mixes with an odor of fine coal dust. I rediscover Cézanne blues laid down the length of peaceful avenues. Seeing Peking again I realize how much I love this city. It is less lively than Shanghai, less colorful than Canton. But in all China nothing can compare with the beauty of a gray hutung under a moon as cold as an iceberg and stars as sharp as icicles. The voice of a vendor crying his wares reverberates between blind walls; far off, a door knocker bangs on a wooden door; not another sound. The acid smell of earth pervades the night. Peking is one of those rare places in the world where certain moments are perfect.

# CONCLUSIONS

According to some Sinologists, China ceased being China in 1949: the date of "the deluge." Similarly, anti-Communists feel that socialist "barbarism" has doomed one of the oldest and most splendid of the world's civilizations; a new regime has feigned respect for it only in order to assassinate it the more conveniently. The Chinese past, declares Etiemble, is to be taken or left alone; if you break with it, then you ought not to pretend to carry on with it. Superb uncompromise! and have we preserved entire all of our own Judaeo-Christian heritage, is all of the French past yet with us? Why, no; and the most meaningful and worthwhile aspects of Old China subsist where they rightly belong: in libraries and in museums;* a great educational effort has been made to divulge these treasures to the nation. As for the climate in which the Chinese lived during these later centuries, I do not in the least regret that it has been superseded by another; and I am quite of Pearl Buck's opinion:

> If I really have any fault to find with the beauty of China . . . it is that it is too secluded, too reserved. It does not permeate enough to the uttermost parts of the people to whom it belongs . . . The opportunity to pursue beauty has been too much the prerogative of the wealthy and leisured.†

Not only was the sense and cultivation of the beautiful restricted to a handful of privileged persons, what the arts in China essentially illustrated was man's oppression and mutilation of man.

Until the last few years, the Chinese lived naked in the face of brute nature. For tilling his fields, for fertilizing them, the peasant

* Mainly in Western museums, but this is not the regime's fault.
† *My Several Worlds.*

had no animals; nothing stood between his bare hand and the earth; he was his own beast of burden. And he eyed his progeny as an animal brood: some of the farrow he drowned, upon occasion he sold a part of it, and what was kept and fed by the producing group belonged to it body and soul. Little distinguished the family from the very fields it cultivated and the individual did not isolate himself from the family; a man of the laboring class was not reckoned a human person. Leisure and wealth enabled the mandarins to put a booted foot upon the neck of the masses, and a gloved hand to nature. But also bound to the soil, since their fortune was in land, and prisoners of a society which at its base saw human fade into wild beast, they, the rich, were incapable of extricating themselves from the pit or of seeing beyond the fact: they did no more than tease with it recklessly. They piled up small rocks; they nursed stunted bushes; they raised grotesque little fish; they had a passion for thwarted and warped "things"; oddity, jittery eccentricity characterize the sculpture, the curios, the architecture of the later period; nor was even the human body spared from the effects of an imperious taste for distortion: the atrophied feet of women, the castrated men, the puerile and misshapen eroticism in the old fictions, the vogue of homosexuality, the art of torture derived from a dread of nature, a dread which, in the barren Chinese elite, came out in the hatred of nature which perversion expresses. These sophisticated refinements ill conceal the monotony of a civilization mired down in immanence. The rigidity of institutions, the stopping of technological progress fixed the Empire in an eternal present and barred man from his transcendence: art, instead of forcing the gates of a tomorrow of infinite possibilities, remained a pale and idle pastime. The full-blooded creations China produced at those moments of her history when she lived were forgotten or else endlessly imitated to hollowness and death. The gardens, the paintings, the monuments—countless variations upon the same theme; variations which rather than breaking new ground simply reaffirm the ancient rut. The passage from Greek column and lintel to the arch, from basilica to the Romanesque church and thence to the Gothic—there is no equivalent evolution in China. How is one to demand that the new civilization prolong the movement of a culture which ceased to budge ages ago? If anything is to blame for the hiatus separating the present from the past it is that past itself. Communism is not responsible for this situation; nor is this situation new: every regime which ever made any attempt to modernize China was, on the artistic and intellectual planes, compelled to make a fresh departure and to start from scratch. And indeed, what with their nationalist propensities, the present leaders are far more thoughtful of safeguarding the old patrimony than were, for example, the bourgeois of the Fourth of May. Those leaders have actually been reproached for not having created a new civilization overnight. A society in the process of building itself does not simply pluck its means of expression out of thin air. The respectively quantitative and qualitative undertakings of extending and raising culture interrelate in a complex manner; at certain instants they clash, at others they attune. It is beyond all doubt that the cultural level of the people as a whole has risen considerably; while as for the development of painting and writing in their higher forms, there are no grounds, as yet, for either optimism or pessimism. The question remains open—it could not be otherwise—and in my summing up it is under this one heading, of art and letters, that I would leave a question mark. There have been—and I have alluded to—hesitancies, excesses, mistakes; be all that as it may, China's effort and achievements strike me as admirable.

But since the winter of 1955 the attacks against China have been redoubled; a number of bourgeois democracies, sorely tempted to recognize China diplomatically and vote her into the United Nations, must be convinced that she does not yet merit either. This well-orchestrated campaign perturbs some minds: as sane and honorable a man as Ricoeur ends up not being sure his own eyes do not deceive him. So, comparing them with the results of my own investigation, let me examine the kind and gravity of the charges out of which these indictments are formulated.

The traveler who makes a superficial tour of China is impressed by clean streets, trains that run on time, the scrupulous honesty of officials, the energy and thoroughness with which the country is administered: in a word, by the existence of a discipline no one would have even dreamed possible in China five years ago.

Before the advent of the present regime, the dominant attitude was one of "laissez faire" and rugged individualism. The Confucian code of the family still exerted a wide influence, but in the modern cities on the coast there was an undisguised display of wealth while in the rural areas the age-old routine of work continued unchanged. The country at the time was rent by political factions and military strife, and by the intellectual chaos resulting from the intrusion of conflicting Western ways of thought and behavior.

All that has changed. The country is united; being ruled by a single central government, its power and prestige have been enormously enhanced. Not only is it politically unified; it is also unified in an economic and cultural sense.

Whose words are these? Those of one of the regime's propagandists? No; the passage comes from the most venomous of the periodicals whose purpose is to vilify People's China: *The China News Analysis*, published at Hong Kong, written by deep-dyed conservatives.

Whatever their prejudices and antipathies, those people who lived in the China of yesterday, those who have some acquaintance with Asia as a whole, are unfailingly impressed by what today's China has accomplished and, with Guillain, forced to concede that "materially speaking, the over-all picture is remarkable"; or with Pierre and Renée Gosset, to write down to New China's credit,

The battle won through health and hygiene . . . The drive to eliminate social cancers . . . The disappearance of thieves . . . Tremendous reforestation effort, the birth of an industry, land reform, flood control . . . China is in a fair way to becoming a major industrial power . . . Elimination of famine . . . The people are properly dressed, apparently well fed. Law and order reign everywhere. The emergence of a sense of patriotism, the birth of a national army. Stable currency, sound finance. Completely honest government. The immense campaign to overcome illiteracy.

But, of course, things do not end here. Driven by the evidence to make these confessions, the anti-Communists hasten to fill in the other, the darker side of the picture. What is this other, this darker side of the picture?

The Western capitalists still residing in Shanghai, the expelled missionaries, Chiang Kai-shek's buddies, the counterrevolutionaries barricaded in Formosa or Hong Kong, those who are still waging the good fight on the Chinese borders, and certain Americans affiliated with the China Lobby constitute the most fanatical wing of the opposition. They vent their fury in cataclysmic prophecies: Chiang will reassume power, or a third World War is around the corner. It is a trifling matter, how this revolution ends; what must be borne in mind is that it is just a flash in the pan, a passing episode. Nothing new about it either; and they make freewheeling comparisons between the present state control and the old empire's centralism; furthermore, there is the Tao: it is immutable, it is invincible. The pendulum has swung to Ying today. It will swing to Yang tomorrow. And in the seeming victory of Chinese Communism the Old Hands discern proof positive of its forthcoming downfall.

Very true it is that far from being at odds with the pattern of the Chinese past the Communist Revolution culminates the series of abrupt severances which describe it. Upon the ruins of feudality Shih Huang Ti shattered in the third century B.C. dynasty after dynasty rose and sank into decay; the collapse of each would bring anarchy in its wake, and out of anarchy a new authority would emerge to reconstruct the country. Likewise, the disintegration of the Kuomintang precipitated the civil war whence the Communist Party came out the winner. Some of the problems the leaders then found themselves faced with had long before been the concern of the empire's unifiers who moreover had attempted to solve them in similar manners. When, the first to do so, Shih Huang Ti forged the political and administrative unity Mao Tse-tung has just achieved anew, he too set about the task of developing the land and water communications systems; and he standardized the written language as the spoken language is being standardized today. Flood-control projects date back to the legendary Yao and were promoted by many of his imperial successors. The vastness of China, this civilization's water-based character have always necessitated economic planning; only a heavily centralized political authority can undertake the major public works, build the roads and dikes, palliate the crises produced by natural disasters, pierce the geographical and other barriers which divide up China into countless small local markets. Again and again in the course of Chinese history we see officials entrusted with the job of fixing prices, of stocking and reapportioning supplies of millet and rice. The grains monopoly established in 1953 has its antecedents in Sung era "ever-normal granaries." Once having seized the throne, China's newest master would often institute a land reform, carving up the great estates for the benefit of the small holders. And there are many other meaningful analogies: the same refusal to brook foreign interference led K'ang-hsi to throw out that legate whom the Pope had sent to arrange the question of the rites, and incited the People's Government to expel Riberi the other day; and it was in both instances to consolidate their hold on Tibet that Ch'ien Lung, befriending the Lamaic creed, gave Yung-ho-kung Temple to the bonzes, and Mao Tse-tung had that same sanctuary renovated.

From these parallels the conservatives deduce that the fatal cycle is bound to recur and that the Communists will go the foreordained way of the Hans, the Tangs, the Mings, and the Ch'ings. They shut their eyes to one crucial fact. If until now the history of China has been scarcely more than a series of repetitions, that has been owing to her economic stagnation. In the age when the iron industry developed, Shih Huang Ti, dismantling the feudal principalities, enduringly reshaped China: he transformed it into a centralized empire. But the ensuing rise of commerce and industry was throttled, technical progress frustrated by the imperial bureaucrats, and China went back to marking time. New statesmen succeeded old: confronted by an identical situation, they had ready to hand only those same instruments their predecessors had disposed of. This rotation of managerial elites to which Burnham is inclined to reduce revolutions is not, however, sufficient to originate revolutions. And that is the point; for there was any amount of rotating in China, teams were forever fading out and coming to the fore, barbarians replacing Chinese on the throne, a man of mean birth wresting the scepter from an aristocrat and acceding to his supreme dignities; and history wobbled in a circle withal. But the upheaval effected by the Communist Party is something of a different sort: this new order is founded upon economic and technological innovations. A working class exists today in China, industry on a nation-wide scale has been got under way; the latifundia need not be broken up, for tractors will soon consolidate co-operation and the great estates will be collectivized. This time it is a profound and authentic revolution China is undergoing: the ancient structures have not been repainted, they have been irrevocably shattered; hitherto it was always a sterile impetus that was given to the wheel revolving around a stationary hub; today, the entire machine is in motion, and China is going forward. She has ceased living from day to day, from hand to mouth, dreaming of a mythical Golden Age; she is oriented toward the future and is driving toward it.

This in itself is a tremendous change. Before, the future existed solely in the shape of menace; it depended upon an unpredictable nature's kindliness or wrath, upon the flukes of war, of brigandage, upon political imponderables: no one was master of his destiny. A steely law, forged by the great and lesser beneficiaries of the old regime, so made it that tomorrow might well bring misery but prosperity never: were the harvest bad, peasants and laborers suffered; if good, then profitable, but to speculators only. Inflation ruined artisans, merchants, even the small capitalists; once down, nobody ever recovered his feet. The Tao was unalterable; but the ideal alternation of Yin and Yang did not manifest itself in the facts: it was constant nighttime in China, never any sun. To a hopeless situation the Chinese reacted with a mournful apathy which broke the hearts of such revolutionary intellectuals as Lusin, and which, with a knowing chuckle, Westerners jotted down as another trait in "Oriental character." The teachings of the wise men reflected this bleak quietism. Confucianism urged obedience and resignation; Taoism and Buddhism recommended inertia. What is a man to do today when he can count on no tomorrow? "Before, it was utter despair," Robert Guillain admits; but this did not prevent him from assuring the Gossets, "The Chinese used to be famished and in rags. But they were gay and carefree."* Certain platitudes, alas, seem destined to outlive the ages: the one concerning the starving but jolly native has held its own against the Chinese Revolution, the war in Indo-China and the one in Algeria. The prince of these lightsome beggars is the quaint old

* *Chine Rouge: An VII.*

Neapolitan lazzarone; but the dying Hindu exhales his incomparable serenity; and until not long ago the ingenious North African laborer cheerfully got along on nothing: he just did not have any needs. I will agree that, viewed from a sufficient altitude, despair resembles insouciance: but whoever confuses one for the other, in so doing proves his extraordinary ignorance of the world of men and discretion would advise him against venturing opinions upon it.

A life confined to a bitter today without some toehold in tomorrow does not deserve to be called human. Pre-eminent among the blessings bestowed by the regime—as its fiercest denigrators concede—are the stability and security it has infused into Chinese society; and it has thereby supplied to life in China that which the Chinese never had before: a solid grip upon the future. No longer are they the toys of fate; there is something that can be done. The rising suburbs of new Peking, the Manchurian factories, the still unfinished bridge that will span the Yangtze, the dam that holds the Hwai in check—it is here that the present is storming into the citadel of the future. No dream, no Utopia, China's future is exactly outlined, exact figures measure it, and the date of its embodiment is fixed. If the estimate is sometimes in error, it is because calculations are made on the conservative side and results outstrip expectations. To gain their view of the world the Taoist sages used to clamber into "The Chariot of the Sun"; the First, the Third Five-Year Plans furnish the Chinese their vantage points today. The living reality present in China is her future.

"That's right," says the anti-Communist, "the country is going ahead, but its inhabitants aren't getting anything out of it." Here is the point upon which most of the regime's less panicky adversaries focus the brunt of their attack. Too sensible to predict its imminent fall, they labor at discrediting it; the results it has achieved are undeniable, but what are they worth if they are not profitable to anybody? Thus can M. Guillain warn that the system is "fine for China but bad for the Chinese"; and M. Fano earnestly puzzle over the question, For whom are six hundred million people sacrificing themselves and why? An impenetrable mystery; and all the more so because, in the eyes of the anti-Communists, each Chinese appears worse off than every other. The peasants are the prey of the regime; but so also are the workers, their case is desperate, while the plight of the businessmen and the capitalist artisans is not one whit better. What whale is devouring these small fry? Racketeering officialdom? No, the anti-Communists will tell through gritted teeth, no, "the officials are scrupulously honest." Nor does anyone accuse the leaders of wallowing in a luxury bought by the sweat and tears of the people. How can you both claim that one part of the community is being sacrificed to the whole and that all its parts are? One is reminded of the story of the courtier who was lame in both legs—and who walked without a limp. "To be sure; but," I hear an anti-Communist scold, "the present generation is being sacrificed to the future." But before brandishing that trusty old formula ought one not to remember that *sacrifice* implies that the *sacrificed* surrender or are deprived of something? And what have the Chinese lost? Workers, peasants, artisans lived in an abominable state, small shopkeepers in a well-nigh intolerable one. "Before," Guillain writes, "it was appalling—that truth predominated over every other. Poverty, corruption, inefficiency, misery, contempt for the people and for the commonweal, those were the elements which made up the most wretched nation on earth. And I knew China then." Any regime at all, he adds, could not help but be better than the old one. Neither Guillain nor anyone else dares maintain that the Chinese people have traded a good horse for a bad. The Gossets' opinion is that "the Chinese people . . . are probably happier now than they have ever been." Sacrifice? What? where? The Chinese are still leading an austere life if one compares their standard of living with those common in wealthier nations and with the one their children will enjoy—oh, yes, to all this I heartily agree, and the government itself has never pretended the contrary; but to resent this present situation amounts to deploring that any man is willing to be and stay a Chinese. One could not forget that China formerly ranked with Indonesia as the poorest nation in the world, that her working population's living standard was lower than that of workers in Egypt and in India. Is it going to be asserted that in the space of a day the Communists ought to have provided six hundred million poverty-stricken mortals with a situation matching that of a Western factory worker? Talk is cheap; like Anouilh's Antigone, but more complacently than she, the specialists in anti-Communism demand "everything, and at once"; absolutes roll off their wrists as smoothly as the ink flows out of this pen. But when you reconstruct a country elsewhere than on paper the dividing line between possible and impossible becomes sharp and time becomes a factor.

But: "The degree to which this or that person is sacrificed varies. The system is unfair," say some, and with them the liberal Gossets whose ire is excited by the surviving remnants of capitalism and by "the flagrant inequality of this future system with its Communist cadres and bureaucracy at the top, then its privileged working class, and its peasants at the very bottom of the ladder." The Right prefers to brand communism as Utopian and to expound its own "hard-headed realism"; but just let communism materialize and demonstrate that it is more than a fuzzy idea, then the same Right thunders against its "Machiavellian realism." In China inequality is justified by the needs of production. Best paid are the most difficult jobs and those requiring the greatest degree of skill. But differences in economic status are not great, for the wage scale is not broad; and every additional advantage is paid for in the coin of effort. Those in positions of authority have hardly a moment's respite from work, and if such things as automobiles are put at their disposal it's to aid them in their work: their every minute counts. The workers are "privileged" to the extent that they have, man for man, a greater electoral power and earn more cash than the peasant; generally speaking the latter is better housed, he himself produces what he consumes and, above all, he is not obliged to put as much hard work in as the worker. I was much less impressed by inequalities in China than by the justness of the balance struck between the advantages and the disadvantages of a given man's situation.

The chief contention of those who condemn the Government's economic policy is that the capital funds which are being invested in heavy industry ought rather to go into furthering the people's immediate welfare. I can only suppose that they recommend this program because they know that by putting it into practice the Chinese Republic would be cutting its own throat. China has not, in these last five years, eliminated poverty. In 1954 the rivers flooded; want, epidemics threatened the country; these dangers could recur; and in good years as in bad, the population increases annually by 2 per cent. It is impossible to find a balancing point in such a precarious situation; if it is prolonged, China will inevitably fall back into the vicious circle of overpopulation, undernourishment, lethargy; consuming their scant resources immediately instead of using them wisely is a policy which would not only toll the knell of future generations but would cast the present one into the depths of misery. The sacrifice of these people to heavy industry is but sacrifice to themselves. The allegedly "humane" objections proffered by the counterrevolutionaries are all the more misplaced inasmuch as China's gamble is almost dead certain to pay off; in view of her immense potential in natural resources, the development of production will bring virtually limitless possibilities to within her grasp and will permit an extraordinary improvement in the Chinese standard of living.

There are those who doggedly insist that this increased wealth is going to profit China but not the Chinese. The assertion betrays a total failure to understand the way in which the system is ordered; the great good fortune of the Chinese today is that the private interest of each individual very precisely coincides with the general interest of the country. Among the rich peasants and the capitalists there is a handful of profiteers who are making hay from the opportunities afforded by this economic transitional period; but nearly six hundred million men know that their personal prosperity is indissolubly linked to that of the state and its to theirs: it is this last point which is especially to be noted, and it was stressed in Mao-tung's July 1955 speech. When, because of collectivization, agricultural production rises, the last thing the government plans to do is grab the surpluses by way of taxes and cheat the peasant of his gain; the state's revenues in large part come through the sale of light-industry products: in order that the state become richer the market must expand: which is to say that the peasants must become consumers; and they will not become consumers until a better livelihood gives them greater purchasing power. Their present welfare is not being neglected in the name of a remote Utopian prosperity. Hardly; for their prosperity is ruled out unless, today, the living conditions of the masses improve.

Nation-wide productivity therefore is synonymous with the improvement of every individual's material fortunes. Far from being "inhumane" the imperative of "Production First" signifies that man's well-being is, in China, the ultimate measure of values. Neither some impersonal entity nor a faraway future in which the individual is not now immediately involved takes precedence over him; nor again are his interests sacrificed to those of doctrine or principle. One could hardly go further astray than to imagine that the Chinese are the victims of fanatically upheld and mercilessly enforced theories. Chinese policy is never molded by inflexible abstract concepts, but always in accordance with the concrete situation, which is fluid: utility has a priority over every other consideration. The socialist ideal is inimical to capitalism and private property—but these were not scrapped in its name; rather, where they were found to be of use, room was left for both in the new economy. There has been no waving of banners bearing the slogan, "Equality." Land has been redistributed, the wage scale so established as best to conform to the interests of productivity. Jobs are never grandly done away with in the name of human dignity if by doing away with them there is the danger of throwing men into unemployment or of depriving the country of an asset. It is with every imaginable handicap that this nation has set forth in the pursuit of prosperity; to achieve it, every little bit helps, the least detail counts. Separate fields were formerly demarcated by strips of unused land; recuperating this additional soil can make all the difference to a struggling co-operative. The country is genuinely indebted to the mill which finds a way to reduce the amount of raw cotton needed to fabricate a bolt of cloth.

Now, for the time being, the principal source of energy in China is human labor; and just as there must be no waste or misuse of materials, so must men be carefully looked after. If a maximum effort is to be obtained from them their living conditions must be satisfactory: every person counts. Every visitor is impressed by the extent and detail of the government's solicitude for the workers; sanitary improvements in the poor districts, efforts to provide better housing, nurseries, pregnancy leave, infirmaries and dispensaries, the distribution of blankets: despite an exceedingly slender budget the regime has provided everyone with public health conditions and a standard of living which, ten years ago, seemed inconceivable. These measures are not designed to "save face"; their object is to produce concrete results. The infant mortality rate must be lowered, epidemics and diseases must be checked, decent food and enough of it must be guaranteed to everybody; for otherwise the country will necessarily lack what it must absolutely have: strong arms and backs. They who judge deeds by the intentions behind them will find the Government's policy crammed with ulterior motives; so indeed it is; and the Chinese workers have cause to rejoice therefor. There is nothing more suspect than the "benevolence" which maintains the discrepancy between its position and yours, with you at its mercy: for a "benevolent" spirit may also be agitated by qualms, scruples, and whims.

The anti-Communists will reply that the Chinese worker pays dearly for these advantages: they cost him his freedom. The cliché has made a big hit: the Chinese have turned into a colony of ants. Ants—the simile isn't new. For self-evident reasons eager to affirm the community of interests uniting exploiters with the exploited, conservative philosophy has always been organicist; oddly enough though, while the beehive is held up as an example of the good society, comparison with the ant hill has a pejorative connotation. Grousset earlier employed it in connection with Asia. Guillain, proud of his originality, has been talking about ant hills for years. The Gossets say that, as they were taking down their notes, the words *ant hill* seemed to recur in their notebooks quite of its own accord. There are few countries, however, for which the ant-hill description is less fitting. It implies a rigorously planned and rationalized society where undertakings are with utmost precision subdivided into specialized tasks. But China is the very epitome of repetition. Her countryside reminds one of the truck-gardening outskirts ringing Paris; instead of scurrying hither and thither along prescribed trajectories composing a complex scheme, the peasants, employing identical gestures, cultivate the isolated patches of ground they are riveted to; family units, villages adjoin and duplicate one another: their economies are self-sufficient. As for the cities, they have no organic oneness as European cities have but rather seem to be ruled off into a maze of little isolated enclaves: merchants' shops and artisans' shops are there by the thousand, each is alike, each is self-sustaining. Speaking of farming and of handicraft, admirers of the past have often eulogized the "humane," the "satisfying," the "rewarding" qualities of activities which encompass the entirety of an individual and insure that all the fruit of his endeavor bears the impress of his hand; why then should a country numbering over five hundred million peasants, one where seventy-five million people live as artisans and a mere three million as workers, why then should this country be likened to a colony of insects? Man is human everywhere; but if one wishes to play with startling figures of speech one may perhaps turn up a horde of giant ants in Pittsburgh or Detroit. But not in Peking.

"Just wait a while," say its opponents, who explain that the regime has not yet attained its ends. But the grim process, they assure us, has been begun: wherever factories have been built or land collectivized, men have started to turn into robots. The Chinese economy is a ruthless machine: in it, every worker occupies a rigidly defined position and, under the pressure of ineluctable forces, produces a mathematically prescribed amount of work: the peasants, the workers have become the slaves of the system.

The regime's critics cannot be unaware of what at any rate every economist knows: that it is never by means of coercion one extracts the best effort, quantitatively or qualitatively, from a worker. To suppose that terror is the surest method of government is to manifest that contempt for men which has become habitual with our humanists. Realists, the Chinese consider that the accomplishments they are banking on can only be had from men who, because they want to and because it pays, put their heart into doing a good job. These considerations are idle in certain economic stages —those where techniques are either in an extremely retarded or in an extremely advanced state, and where the human factor is virtually nil. But this human factor happens to play a crucial role in present-day China. Techniques have reached that mid-point of development at which output depends in the strictest fashion upon the worker's free initiative. Proof thereof is that certain cooperatives progress, others stand still, and some peter out into failures. A latheworker who does not care about his work, who takes no pride in a job well done, will not do it well; while if he is wide-awake and interested he will figure out a way to do it faster, easier, better. Some shops turn out first-rate products at a rapid tempo, others trail behind schedules and produce slipshod work. How is all this to be explained? By the varying degrees of competence and enthusiasm of the men in this or that factory. Propaganda doubtless tends to magnify the importance of the short cuts ordinary workers have proposed; but it is equally certain that their role is far from negligible in a country that is still suffering from an acute shortage of qualified technical personnel. Engineers being scarce, outstanding workers are at a premium, and we need not smile at the term "work heroes." This "heroism" in a worker does not consist in passive obedience; rather, it presupposes the most active, wholehearted participation. A very queer picture, this, of impotent human beings steam-rollered by the juggernaut of Chinese economy. To the contrary, the machine's operation depends entirely upon the men. It is true that the workers have not enough independence yet; they are not in a position to defend their interests, but these the leaders must perforce take into account. Discontent among the workers would slow down production. A sulking and inert peasantry would completely undermine the system.

Which is why the government has always avoided tough measures. It does not condemn them out of abstract respect for an abstract freedom; it realizes that if it is to be meaningful and fruitful the collaboration of the population must be willingly consented. Whence the great emphasis laid upon education, upon explanation, upon persuasion.

The best way to obtain results in a hurry is to launch a "movement." The chain letter or chain anything else is one of the nostalgic dreams of isolated individuals lost in the lonely crowd of capitalist society; all you need is for each person to get in touch with four others and everybody hits a jackpot; or you can stop cruelty to animals; or you can revamp the universe. The scheme never quite pans out; for the word somehow doesn't get around; the cleavage in society limits its spread to a tiny group, and the chain completes its own small circle.

In China there are no social cleavages; the community of interests, the economic solidarity of all individuals make the collectivity into a homogenous and concrete reality: a slogan launched in Peking will go through cities, towns, and country villages, will carry as much weight, make as much sense in frontier outposts as in the capital where it originated. The movement does not stop snowballing until the whole nation is involved: thus the stunning success of, above all, the hygiene campaign. Toward 1940, one observer—Robert Payne—wrote:

> In a country where dead rats lie rotting in every street, where the sewers are clogged up, where in the best homes the toilets empty into a gutter no more than ten yards from the well for drinking water, the wonder is that there are any people alive at all. When the war ends China will first of all need railroad engineers, but then, and for a long time to come, some good public health engineers.

Viewed in terms of experience in capitalist societies, the situation seemed to call for an army of experts and a gigantic financial outlay: no one could have foreseen that every adult, every aged person, and every child would be summoned to the job of killing flies and burying garbage.* The Hong Kong Cassandras are predicting today that it will take years to stamp out illiteracy—where are the teachers going to be found? and the money to pay them? The answer is that, free of charge, each peasant who knows how to read will teach four other persons: in seven years' time every Chinese will have learned. More, the standardization of the spoken language is due to be completed before very long. As for the collectivizing movement, its speed has exceeded every estimate: individual example, emulation at the grass-roots level are getting results no authoritarianism could ever have achieved. When the cadres have tried to hustle the masses into anything—into, for example, complying with the Marriage Act—these tactics have met with failure. The leaders have learned from experience; earlier errors are not being repeated today.

The success of these movements, drives, campaigns, the Chinese's voluntary and eager support of them—all these, in the eyes of bourgeois liberals, are downright alarming symptoms: for no-

* The stinginess, the pettiness of the regime's adversaries are invincible. What can one possibly reply to a person who like M. Fano seeks to belittle this titanic victory by invoking the fact that certain rascals made a business of raising rats in order to collect the money for their dead bodies? The law of averages indicates that such small dishonesties may be expected to occur. Well, the state was cheated to the tune of a few yuan. Do these outweigh the results obtained? Does Fano wish to say that the campaign was a mistake?

body is more enthralled than the slave who fancies himself free. And the luckless blue-clad ants have transformed the outside pressure weighing on them into an inner moral imperative. The regime has them in the palm of its hand; how did it get them there? By shrewd and diabolic maneuvers: it has reduced the ants to not being able to want anything other than . . . what they want, Guillain explains. Only wicked witchcraft preserves the accord between people and government: and its very popularity is made out to be the most conclusive proof of the government's tyranny. Behold to what subtleties a resolute denial of the evidence may lead! In fact, these strange subjective mysteries could hardly have been concocted had not objectivity been flung into the dustbin by way of a start; but pluck it back out again and the clouds lift. And now go ask the starving man: "My good chap, would you like a bite to eat?" Count on it: his entirely unprompted reply will be in the affirmative. But that unambiguous yes is not apt to sound well in M. Guillain's delicate ear; for what distresses him is that this option is not based upon the freedom to not choose, the freedom which was the undoing of Buridan's ass. Indeed, if the young peasant is eager to do his military service or get a job as a bricklayer it's because he has his reasons. But, precisely, while the Chinese used to have no reason to be eager to do anything and trembled all day long in terror of tomorrow, they are now being offered goals and ways and means to attain them. The range of possibilities may not be limited; but is it fancied that in the West a worker or a peasant's son has only glittering and unnumbered prospects? The Yellow River will probably float a great deal of silt down to the sea before the lad toiling on its bank has a wide choice of vocations to pick from. But the essential thing is that he has been rescued from his animal existence and is being given a chance to become a man. It is not surprising that he snatches at it.

It bears repeating that the Chinese have not by any means responded to appeals with a docile and sure alacrity. Collectivization remained bogged down for quite a while. In 1950 the government sought to relieve the congestion in Shanghai; the populace was asked to return to the country villages; most of it refused to budge; and the government abandoned the project.

It does not in such cases move from urgings to blows; when its policy does not work, it changes it. And that is the critical item bewildered reactionaries overlook: the people say yes to what the regime asks so long as the regime wants what the people want. A general increase in everybody's wealth, for instance. Sartre's remarks about the Communist Party* are wonderfully apposite here: the leaders lead the masses only upon condition they lead them where they have a mind to go. If, in China, their campaigns are usually crowned with success, it is because they are extremely careful to establish their programs, not according to the dictates of theories, but squarely in line with down-to-earth daily experience. During a lengthy tour through the rural areas Mao Tse-tung became convinced that the peasants were ready for collectivization and that the cadres were pushing it too timidly; he came home, delivered his July 1955 speech and in October launched the drive to quicken the co-operative movement's pace. A proposed bill, before it is enacted, is immediately discussed throughout the country, and a measure, such as for example the compulsory military service act, will sometimes be tested in practice before being made into law. This amounts to sounding out public opinion and to a kind of experimentation. And if in spite of these precautions a measure turns out to have been a mistake, the mistake is corrected. It is hard to imagine leadership more strictly controlled by the led. The government's tactics, these past seven years, have been exceedingly pliant; its agrarian policy looks like a series of tightenings and loosenings, of speed-ups and slowdowns. Thanks to incessant self-criticism and readjustment the over-all line has preserved a remarkable continuity: lots of little shifts, no abrupt swerves. There has been one personal drama: the denunciation of Kao Kang, "the Stalin of Manchuria"; but it did not affect policy as a whole. There are periods when a tendency becomes stronger: thus the fight against corrupt practices, which had been going on before and which continued in a milder form afterward, was intensified at the time the "Five Anti's" campaign was launched. China has been rocked by not a single one of those "crises" America and Formosa have been anxiously expecting to break out at any moment.

Rather than having anything in common with Machiavellism,

* In *Les Communistes et la paix.*

this intelligent policy, enjoined by the force of circumstances, is a humanism. Machiavellism, as the term is currently used, implies the deceitful substitution of an apparent goal for a concealed one. The Communist Party's enterprise, as expressed in such projects as the one designed to control the Yellow River, aims at "multiple objectives" all of which are equally visible and equally genuine. The leaders urge collectivization because—as they candidly declare—heavy industry requires that agricultural production increase. But the cadres are reciting no lies when they tell the peasants that this boosted output will raise their standard of living. In present-day China the benefits accorded to each man are profitable to all, and conversely.

The fact may appear startling but it is true none the less: production depending upon the capacities and the good will of each person, the country will not prosper unless every aspect of the individual's standard of living goes up. There is no cause to estimate the "price" of China's achievements in terms of their "human cost": they profit the Chinese themselves and if they have been possible it is because the situation of the Chinese has already registered an improvement.

If this much is accepted, then some observers' attempts to show that the positive material picture is offset by a negative spiritual picture must necessarily repose on sophistries. But let's examine them.

New China, Guillain asserts, manifests an odious "contempt for the human person"; among the faults which disfigured the old regime, faults which Guillain congratulates the new for having eliminated, he notes "contempt for the people." The contradiction here can probably be got around if one adopts the standpoint of the elite and makes a sharp distinction between "human persons" and the plebeian elements that compose the crowd. But Guillain still ought to specify that when he says "spiritual goods" he means the advantages which profit the happy few, and that "material goods" are of interest only to the wretched many. Whoever rejects this standpoint may legitimately suppose that in treating the people with respect rather than with contempt, the new regime has restored their human dignity to six hundred million men, and that what they have thereby gained is other than merely "material."

This respect for the people is feigned, the anti-Communists say: the regime has stolen their freedom and doomed them to conformity. I have already disproved the famous robot theory. Perhaps not convincingly; but who is to convince me that the Chinese masses have ever been free? The peasants were the helpless victims not only of economic exploitation, but of a chance spell of mean weather: this total powerlessness need not be mistaken for freedom. The peasants are being aided today; organization need not be mistaken for slavery; or if such it be, then the West is also a world of slaves. I very much like this dialogue the Gossets report having had with a Communist worker. They asked him:

"But tell us, Sin, what does that mean for you, being free?"

Sin thought for a moment. "I am free to play basketball."

"Why, you aren't going to say that you weren't free to play basketball before?"

"You don't understand," he replied patiently. "I've always played basketball. And then one day the soles came off my shoes. I was always poor and I was never able to buy myself a new pair. Today I have two pairs. Now do you see what I mean? I'm free to play basketball."

Sin clearly defines the point of view of six hundred million Chinese: to be free to eat meat is to have the money to buy some. One is not free to enjoy the sunshine today if one is gnawed by anxiety about tomorrow. In the past every door was locked. To be sure, every door does not stand wide open today; there is not room enough in the factories for every young peasant who wants to become a worker; leisure hours are limited. But a quantity of new possibilities are already accessible to everyone; the individual is no longer on the family's leash, boys and girls marry whom they wish, young couples run their own lives; the country standing in great need of cadres, whoever aims to work his way up is given every sort of helping hand. Above all for the younger generation, this new freedom is a very concrete reality.

But Guillain is not taken in by it: for, he declares, this freedom has no spiritual worth. With a keen nose for moral implications he scents hell-fire and brimstone behind the remark made to him by the novelist Pa-chin: "But one can only take the good way: the path to evil has been barred." China is delivered from her ancient social ills, integrity and fair dealing reign there. All very well; but, according to Guillain, this virtue is not authentic for it does not imply an inner conversion from wickedness; his good deeds confer no merit upon the man who is not subject to the temptation of evil-doing: hence, he must be left the possibility to steal—and the robbed the possibility to jail him. When a nobleman, Wen of T'ang, consulted Mencius for advice on how to rule his territory, the philosopher told him, "Neglect of what concerns your people's welfare will not do . . . The people constitute the Way. If . . . they are betrayed into crimes and you follow this up with punishment, this is catching the people in a trap. Surely, if a human-hearted man be at the head, there can be no entrapping of the people . . ." The Bible teaches that the blackest of sins is to lead others into temptation. What, I wonder, is the ethical principle that prompts Guillain to blame the regime for blocking the citizens' access to the path to evil?

Guillain's attitude is worth pondering in that it illustrates what a good many French mean by *freedom.* A recent poll conducted by *France-Soir* reveals that the quality rated highest by the French, after the cleverness of the go-getter, is the roughneck's ability to raise a stink. The big thing, as Alain's example illustrates, is to say *no*. That is freedom; bourgeois individualism confounds negativeness with ordinary negation. The *no* said for the sake of saying *no* is destructive. The Chinese shopkeeper does not feel that, as a free man, he is freely entitled to cheat his customers; and why is that? Because he places his freedom elsewhere.

The view taken by bourgeois reporters is that the Chinese, being deprived of freedom, possess no individuality since—according to the civilized Westerner's credo—being free is above all else to be different. Today, Guillain proclaims, all the Chinese are alike. The Gossets go him one better; they record the "ferocious, shrewd, merciless annihilation of the individual. China's unity has been established. It's that of the spuds in a pot of mashed potatoes." How is that again? Why certainly: everybody wears the same clothes, they explain. Now, "freedom begins in the clothes closet," affirmed some *Figaro* staff writer reviewing Guillain's book. The critic went on to add, glibly, that "True enough, freedom often gets no further," which gave the reader a moment's pause, wondering whether human freedom can after all be boiled down to what may happen to be hanging in a man's wardrobe. For my part I find something powerfully monotonous in the French upper crust, with its language, vocabulary, mannerisms, and tone of voice uniformly shaped by its good breeding and fancy schooling; the universally shared eagerness to affirm their individual personalities only accentuates the resemblance among the members of this elite. The Chinese, however, escapes this conformism: he does not care a fig whether he is or is not the same as others; his behavior is natural, hence as varied as life itself is various. Anyone who comes home swearing that all the Chinese are identical had better see an eye specialist.

"No matter whom you talk to in China, it's like listening to the same old record," Guillain and the Gossets maintain. They came into contact with almost nobody apart from the cadres whose job is to show foreign visitors around; the function of these cadres is to supply information, not to air their personal opinions. I see no reason why they should step out of their role and open up their hearts to strangers whose good will is by no means a sure thing. And I might add that in the course of my own experience abroad I always heard French or foreign officials recite their lessons with the same tiresome unctuousness. But France is something more than her embassy attachés, and it would be a considerable error to presume that the State Department is America. To conclude that "all the Chinese are conformists" is on a par with repeating the nonsense about all Frenchwomen having red hair. The people I encountered on the streets, the peasants I talked to in villages seemed to me to have the most clear-cut individual personalities. As for the intellectuals, it is very safe to say that in this article Lao-She, Tsao-yü, Cheng Shan-tsau, Lo Ta-kang, and the others stand up very well in comparison with M. Guillain. In connection with "the socialization of brains," a catchy little phrase of Guillain's coining, Locquin* has already pointed out how precious few were the Chinese who used to be able to indulge in the luxury of thinking for themselves. Strange it is to see these same Western journalists, who set such mighty store by the critical spirit and the liberal intelligence, make such sparing use of either. Ignorant of or ignoring the elementary facts—the past situation, present con-

* *Les Temps Modernes*, May 1956.

ditions—which would enable them to reach a comprehensive understanding of the Chinese scene and of whither a China on the go is going, they measure everything and judge all by the absolute yardstick of the manners, values, and prejudices of the French bourgeoisie; and thus reveal themselves more naive than even Montesquieu's Parisians, since it is standing smack on Chinese soil that they scratch their heads and wonder how in heaven's name anyone could ever be Chinese. Never for an instant do they question their superiority. Fano cannot even imagine anybody glancing at China from other than a Western capitalist's point of view. Guillain considers that any civilization unable to procure a Guillain is of an inferior type. The Gossets, more frank, more open, wind up their report with the admission that they have "the uncomfortable feeling of not being absolutely certain of how closely it corresponds to the truth"; but this quaver of doubt seems gratuitous in light of the cocksure tone that runs through the bulk of their account.

One thing, however, ought to have made them all stop and think for a moment: not one of the regime's detractors has been capable of devising a single positive criticism. They titter, they sneer, they fume, they deplore, they rage; but when I asked M. Fano what he supposed the workers really want he simply ascribed his own desires to them and boomed back: "A third world war." That is just what the Formosa and Hong Kong lunatics are waiting for, through their negative attitude exposing a bankrupt imagination. Some, to be sure, seek to camouflage it. Their argument is that instead of redistributing the land, agriculture should have been "built up," that, within the framework of a bourgeois democracy, American aid would have straightened out the Chinese economy in no time at all. These suppositions are roundly contradicted by what has happened elsewhere in Asia. After having studied the case of the Philippines, Tibor Mende, although hostile to Communism, found:

> With an economy founded strictly upon free enterprise and in the absence of all state planning, dollar aid, however generous it has been, has only intensified the existing crisis in society . . . First to liberate colonial peoples,* leaving power in the hands of a small minority of

* The same holds true for semicolonial peoples.

businessmen and landowners, then to pump dollars in to support these regimes most often characterized by the reign of corruption and incompetence, is also to fan the fires of social strife and to promote violence and rebellion.*

Which is exactly what occurred when the United States tried to keep Chiang Kai-shek going on a dollar-diet. The current experience in Indonesia is equally conclusive: discouraged to find that nothing has been accomplished anywhere except in the Communist zones of the country, America is thinking of cutting off aid to Jakarta. If meanwhile Soviet aid to China has brought about such stunning results it is because that aid is utilized in the interests of the entire country and in accordance with the most thorough planning. The old Chinese emperors realized it too: planning is of vital necessity in the underdeveloped countries of Asia: they do not have that margin of prosperity that will enable them to muddle through with an unplanned economy. Well, only Communism is capable of proposing and implementing planning; it therefore appears to be the one possible hope for the peoples of Asia.

The connection between Communism and planning is not accidental: the latter requires that free enterprise and profit making be done away with, hence that capitalism be ruled out, and capitalism can be counted upon to put up a fight. To expect otherwise, or to suppose that planning will not require drastic change, is sheer wishful thinking of the sort some starry-eyed American idealists—including Pearl Buck—seem to go in for. The land reform yesterday, the people's dictatorship today are strictly necessary phases in this long march which is going to bring China into the company of great powers.

The evidence of this necessity gives the Chinese Revolution a very particular hue; at no moment has this revolution appeared to develop in obedience to the letter of orthodox Marxism; many observers are struck by the fact that the program being applied by the regime is the very one that would have been adopted by any modern and enlightened government desiring to improve its country: the nationalistic character of the enterprise is, in a sense, more emphatic than its communistic character. One reason for this is that from 1927 on Mao Tse-tung worked at elaborating a

* *La Révolte de l'Asie.*

"Chinese Communism" which has proved admirably suited to the specific concrete needs of the nation; the other reason is that his Communist program was the only possible way out for China. Every other sane regime, had it been in the Communists' place, would have done what they are doing; but there was not and there is nobody else who could have or who can occupy that place. China is not a paradise. Obviously. She must become richer. She must become more liberal. But if one sets partiality aside and considers where she has come from and where she is going, then one will perhaps join me in feeling that this new China embodies a particularly exciting moment in history: that in which man, so long reduced to dreaming of what humanity might be, is setting out to become it. Toiling in order to eat, eating in order to toil, using his excrements to fertilize the little field where he grew the little millet he fed on, the Chinese peasant turned within the agonizingly hopeless circle of an animal existence. The Revolution split that circle apart; it liberated a spark of energy, still tiny, but which has begun its own chain reaction. Life in China is still hard, its roots show: if they do not take hold, if they wither, then all will die. But in this morning's early light the prospect ahead is already visible; and it is limitless.

# INDEX